Making Law in Papua New Guinea

Making Law in Papua New Guinea

The Colonial Origins of a Postcolonial Legal System

BRUCE L. OTTLEY
Professor of Law
DePaul University College of Law

DAVID WEISBROT
Emeritus Professor of Law
University of Sydney

JEAN G. ZORN
Professor of Law Emerita
City University of New York School of Law

CAROLINA ACADEMIC PRESS
Durham, North Carolina

Library of Congress Cataloging-in-Publication Data

Names: Ottley, Bruce L., author. | Weisbrot, David, author. |
Zorn, Jean G., author.
Title: Making law in Papua New Guinea : the colonial
origins of a postcolonial legal system / by Bruce L. Ottley,
David Weisbrot, Jean G. Zorn.
Description: Durham, North Carolina : Carolina Academic
Press, LLC, [2020]
Identifiers: LCCN 2020038495 (print) | LCCN 2020038496
(ebook) | ISBN 9781531005504 (paperback) |
ISBN 9781531005511 (ebook)
Subjects: LCSH: Law—Papua New Guinea—History. |
Legislation—Papua New Guinea—History. |
Papua New Guinea—Politics and government—History.
Classification: LCC KWH12 .O88 2020 (print) |
LCC KWH12 (ebook) | DDC 349.953—dc23
LC record available at https://lccn.loc.gov/2020038495
LC ebook record available at https://lccn.loc.gov/2020038496

Carolina Academic Press
700 Kent Street
Durham, North Carolina 27701
Telephone (919) 489-7486
Fax (919) 493-5668
www.cap-press.com

Making Law in Papua New Guinea

The Colonial Origins of a Postcolonial Legal System

BRUCE L. OTTLEY
Professor of Law
DePaul University College of Law

DAVID WEISBROT
Emeritus Professor of Law
University of Sydney

JEAN G. ZORN
Professor of Law Emerita
City University of New York School of Law

CAROLINA ACADEMIC PRESS
Durham, North Carolina

Library of Congress Cataloging-in-Publication Data

Names: Ottley, Bruce L., author. | Weisbrot, David, author. | Zorn, Jean G., author.
Title: Making law in Papua New Guinea : the colonial origins of a postcolonial legal system / by Bruce L. Ottley, David Weisbrot, Jean G. Zorn.
Description: Durham, North Carolina : Carolina Academic Press, LLC, [2020]
Identifiers: LCCN 2020038495 (print) | LCCN 2020038496 (ebook) | ISBN 9781531005504 (paperback) | ISBN 9781531005511 (ebook)
Subjects: LCSH: Law—Papua New Guinea—History. | Legislation—Papua New Guinea—History. | Papua New Guinea—Politics and government—History.
Classification: LCC KWH12 .O88 2020 (print) | LCC KWH12 (ebook) | DDC 349.953—dc23
LC record available at https://lccn.loc.gov/2020038495
LC ebook record available at https://lccn.loc.gov/2020038496

Carolina Academic Press
700 Kent Street
Durham, North Carolina 27701
Telephone (919) 489-7486
Fax (919) 493-5668
www.cap-press.com

This book is dedicated to the memories of Bernard Narokobi and Josepha Namsu Kiris, who served as leaders of the PNG Law Reform Commission at the height of its influence and productivity. Through their writing, their work on the Law Reform Commission and in other areas of government, and by the examples they set in their own lives, they kept alive the generous principles that underlie the PNG Constitution, and the notion that PNG could move successfully into the twenty-first century while remaining true to custom, tradition and the Melanesian Way. They were two of the smartest, most talented, most generous, most gracious, and most visionary people that we have ever had the extraordinary luck to meet and work for—in PNG or anywhere else.

Contents

Preface

This book has been a true labor of love—although, mercifully, few labors last anywhere near as long.

It began informally as a project by its three authors, who were fortunate to have been part of a diverse group of young faculty members teaching law at the University of Papua New Guinea (UPNG) in the years immediately before and after independence was achieved in September 1975.

Those were very special years in Papua New Guinea's intellectual development, and we were lucky enough to be part of them. Australia's strangle hold on PNG's sources of knowledge was loosening. The newly founded University of Papua New Gunea attracted scholars in all academic disciplines from across the world, many with experience in the breakup of colonial structures, and all of them excited to be part of PNG's movement toward independence, and to contribute their ideas and analysis to the process. They were joined by public servants, some Australian, some not, but all the highly educated products of a new focus on recruiting from universities and the professions. In the mix, also, were the members of a new generation of Papua New Guineans, among the first to attain tertiary educations. They, too, had much to contribute to the excited discussions about PNG's future that were taking place in faculty clubs, government offices, and at the Zaharas' famous Sunday afternoon get-togethers.

Closer to home, in the UPNG Law Faculty itself, we were blessed with extraordinary colleagues, some of whom had previously taught in Africa, Asia and the West Indies and had experience of the interaction between colonialism, nationalism and self-determination. They were the perfect people to learn from, share insights and experiences with, and bounce ideas off. And we had the very good fortune to share our classrooms—and often our living rooms and gardens—with a remarkable crop of students, arguably the golden generation of UPNG, a very high proportion of whom went on to become leading judges, academics, legal practitioners, politicians and government ministers, business leaders and ambassadors.

Bruce Ottley also served as a Magistrate for the National Capital District Court in Port Moresby in 1976–1977 (and experienced the rare pleasure of a litigant referring to him as "Your Majesty"). In deciding civil and criminal cases, Bruce applied laws adopted or enacted during the colonial period and retained after independence.

While at UPNG, Jean Zorn created the Law Faculty's first Customary Law course, something she could not have done without the generous help and advice of her students. Jean also created a Land Law course which, while teaching students all the arcane rules of real property law that British law students have been forced to learn for generations, also devoted a significant portion of the semester to a study of customary land law rules and processes. Jean's third major contribution to the Law Faculty curriculum was a seminar in Law and Development, during which the students took on the task of helping a village near Port Moresby to incorporate their business of making and selling traditional handcrafts. She was lured away from UPNG by Bernard Narokobi, who made her chief researcher for the Papua New Guinea Law Reform Commission, which had just been established to help transform PNG's westernized legal system into something more closely resembling customary law. Jean's reports for the Law Reform Commission included ground breaking work bringing customary law rules and practices into contracts law, as well as the law of wills and succession. Her partner Steve Zorn, senior adviser to Pangu Pati leader Michael Somare, who was the Chief Minister and then the first Prime Minister, was a co-author of the Eight-Point Plan and one of the lead developers of the excess profits tax and other measures aimed to curb the greed of foreign mining and other corporations. Jean and Steve's relationship with Papua New Guinea continued, even after they returned to teaching positions in the United States; both of them spent several northern hemisphere summers working for the Law Reform Commission when it was chaired by Josepha Namsu Kiris.

David Weisbrot was assigned to teach the compulsory course on Customary Law straight off the airplane, and had to make every effort to

swim rather than sink, by turning it into an interactive program requiring students to consider and record their own experiences of custom, law and dispute resolution in their home areas. David then also served as a consultant to the Law Reform Commission, which in those early years was engaged in reviewing and recommending changes to a number of laws introduced during the colonial period in order to better meet the needs and conditions of an independent country, as well as restoring local customs, concepts (such as the extended family, and group ownership) and modes of dispute resolution as the basis for a new, just and more relevant legal system. Much to his own surprise, David was elected Dean of the UPNG Law Faculty in 1978, at age 26. Two decades later, as President of the Australia Law Reform Commission (1999–2009) he was directly involved—at the request of former student and colleague, and then PNG Attorney-General, Alan Marat—in the training of PNG Law Reform Commission staff in both Port Moresby and Sydney.

As we each left PNG in the late 1970s for law schools and other careers in the United States and Australia, we were confident that the structural legal reforms created by the Constitution and operationalized by the Law Reform Commission would soon be achieved. By the mid-1980s, however, it was already becoming apparent that the transformation project had been abandoned, and we thought it would be worthwhile to chronicle this as it was happening. In the event, however, our contemporary report has become a work of history.

Initially, we hoped to have this book completed by the early 1990s—and, once that deadline was passed, we aimed for the 25th anniversary of PNG independence in 2000. At least we nearly made it in time for the 45th! We hope that all of that additional time spent on reflection, reading, talking, comparing and arguing has made it an indisputably better book that it would have been 20 years ago.

This book relies heavily on original contemporaneous sources: newspaper accounts, journal articles, and government reports, as well as extracts from speeches and books written by those who participated in the events being discussed. Beginning with 1972, we have also been able to draw on our own experiences, observations, and contacts with those involved in governmental, educational, and legal affairs.

Each of the three authors was primarily responsible for the initial drafts of a few chapters, but we then workshopped them relentlessly, so that in the best tradition of a genuine collaboration it is now hard to remember who supplied which insight (although our individual writing styles do try hard to shine through!). The final manuscript then, is the product of a healthy mixture of compromise, consensus and resignation.

It is our fondest hope that this book is viewed in PNG—and elsewhere—as a contribution to knowledge and an accurate record of a crucial time in PNG's history. Although we are very critical of some actions and decisions (or the absence of actions and decisions), our intention is not to point fingers or apportion blame, but to detail the history, offer explanations for these phenomena, and perhaps suggest the way forward for a just and effective legal system that serves the interests of those governed. We hope this book will be of interest and value not only to judges, political leaders, scholars, lawyers, historians, policy-makers and others in Papua New Guinea and the Pacific Islands, but also internationally to those with an interest in colonialism, neo-colonialism, self-determination, the recognition and integration of customary law, law and society, law reform, legal development, legal pluralism and comparative law.

Special credit should be given to Bruce Ottley for keeping this book on life support at times, when the exigencies of life, love, work, family and lockdowns might so easily have derailed it. And to David Weisbrot for always knowing when humor was the medicine we needed. Special credit also to Jean Zorn for taking charge of the pre-publication editing work to ensure accuracy, consistency and purpose. As with all books, it is precisely at the moment that the authors think it is "finished" that much of the hard work really begins.

Thanks to our editors at Carolina Academic Press for their unwavering support and remarkable patience, and for believing in the intellectual merit and commercial viability of this rather unique project.

Last, but certainly not least, we would like to acknowledge the immense love, support, patience and editing skills of our families, so thank you very much, Younghee Ottley, Faith Wieland, Steve Zorn, Charlotte Bendayan, Joshua Weisbrot, Ella Weisbrot, Sora Hwang, Chase Zorn, his parents and aunt.

BRUCE OTTLEY
DAVID WEISBROT
JEAN G. ZORN
2 January 2021

Making Law in Papua New Guinea

1 Introduction

Imagining Papua New Guinea

Papua New Guinea in the Western Imagination

If Papua New Guinea (PNG) did not exist, someone would have had to invent it. The fact that it does exist, however, has not stopped repeated inventions and reinventions.

With its spectacular scenery of tropical islands and rugged mountains; exotically decorated "wigmen" and "mudmen"; tribal wars conducted with spears and bows and arrows; belief systems incorporating ancestor worship, sorcery, and witchcraft; and, in some areas, in earlier times, traditional practices involving cannibalism, PNG was distinctly well placed to embody "the Other" in the "Boy's Own" adventure sagas of the late nineteenth and early twentieth centuries.

Western audiences could not get enough of the dark-skinned "primitive tribesmen," with their exotic (and generally minimal) dress, lavish ceremonies, occult beliefs, and occasionally ferocious ways, providing the perfect mixture of danger, titillation, and reflection upon the diversity of the human experience. This, in turn, meshed with the self-serving received wisdom of the time that it was incumbent upon the supposedly moral and sophisticated West to shoulder the "white man's burden" and "bring civilization to the natives." At the same time, there was a fascination with and attraction to people, like Papua New Guineans, who had maintained their genuine selves in the state of nature, as Westerners increasingly recognized and lamented their own alienation. What is more surprising is that, at the end of the twentieth century and the start of the twenty-first, PNG still features in this role in the Western imagination.

In the 1998 film *Krippendorf's Tribe*, produced by Disney's Touchstone Films, actor Richard Dreyfus plays an anthropologist at a major American university (resembling the University of California) who has failed to do any work on his grant-funded research on PNG, using his time instead to raise his three young children following the death of his wife. Instead of admitting the truth, and facing the professional consequences, he concocts the discovery of a "missing tribe," which he documents on film by dressing up his children and himself in traditional dress (*bilas*) and building a PNG-style thatched house in his backyard.

The film is essentially a throwback to the "ooga-booga" school of 1930–50s Tarzan-style jungle films, with little excuse for this still occurring seventy years after Edgar Rice Burrows and forty years after the international decolonization movement and the U.S. civil rights movement. It is far less likely that Hollywood would now make a film with a similarly gauche depiction of Africans, Asians, or Native Americans. However, there is residual confidence that Pacific Islanders (or at least Melanesians—black, "primitive," rural, nontechnological) can be treated in this stereotypically pejorative way and played for laughs, with their culture being appropriated and "bluffed" with blackface makeup, baby-talk language, and lots of spear-shaking.

In 1999, the normally arch-sophisticated *New Yorker* magazine published an oddly uncritical piece about the Italian anthropologist Giancarlo Scoditti, who had been working on and off in the Trobriand Islands for thirty years, recording oral history but specializing in the art of the carved canoe prow. Among other things, there was a breathless description of Scoditti as "the sole repository of an entire civilization,"[1] as well as the obligatory brush with cannibalism.

According to the story, Scoditti first turned up unannounced on Kitawa Island (near Kiriwina) in 1973, by which time PNG was a self-governing territory under the leadership of Chief Minister Sir Michael Somare, and only two years away from independence. Traditional Trobriand culture was rich and complex, and, it is worth noting that by 1973, the Trobrianders had a long history of contact by missionaries, traders, and others. There was a mission school in which English was taught in

Kiriwina until World War II, and others opened after the war. Thanks to the missions and to their own drive and acumen, Trobrianders had become a very well educated people. Anthropologists had a significant presence, starting with Bronislaw Malinowski in 1914. By World War II, and increasingly in the years immediately after, many Trobrianders got jobs with the colonial administration because they could not only speak English, but also read and write it. Among the public servants reporting directly to Chief Minister Somare was Charles Lepani, a Trobriander, an economist with degrees from both the University of Papua New Guinea and the University of New South Wales, and, by 1973, Deputy Director of the PNG Central Planning Office.

Scoditti had not sought the permission of the local people, nor given them any notice, and he could not explain his intentions when he arrived because he did not speak a word of the local language. Nevertheless,

> the Kitawans helped unload numerous heavy trunks containing Scoditti's food supplies, cameras, batteries, and other equipment. In total silence, since they had no language in common, Scoditti and this caravan of Kitawans trudged slowly up through the forest toward the village. . . .
>
> As an intellectual and rather impractical young man, Scoditti had asked his advisers everything possible about research methodology but not a single question about the problems he would encounter living on a remote Pacific island, such as how he would eat, drink, wash, shave, or go to the bathroom without any means of communicating with his hosts. The villagers kindly brought him baked yams and fresh water. "They never let me lack for anything," Scoditti said. It was a courtesy that Scoditti grew to appreciate greatly, since food can be scarce, and women and children had to cart heavy vessels of water up from the wells near the beach every morning.[2]

Incredibly, no adverse comment is made about the sheer stupidity and gross discourtesy of this conduct, much less the questionable ethics of imposing in this way upon his hosts, who themselves eke out a subsistence existence. Scoditti apparently did not pay for any of this routine "courtesy," nor apparently was he inclined to help cart any water. A large collection of local artwork was inveigled from the islanders and sent to a museum in Italy, which was willing to pay for these striking works, "but Scoditti explained that the people had no use for money."[3] Charles Lepani would have been among the many Trobrianders to disagree. Scoditti was disappointed to learn that "an attractive young woman" he "took" as a wife had repartnered when he returned from Italy after an absence of several years. Although Scoditti "understands" the woman's action, given he had chosen to live his life in Italy, he determined "not to get involved with any other women on Kitawa, not wanting to fall into the typical Western habit of using the Pacific Islands for sexual tourism."[4] Completely mistaking the difference between form and substance, marriage is described in the article as a "relatively low-key affair in Melanesia,"[5] an astonishing statement about a culture in which marriage is an integral part of the social order, and reciprocity among kinship relations is the key to communal cooperation, and thus to survival.

It would be difficult intentionally to construct a more offensive picture of modern Melanesians: childlike, passive, subservient, unaware of the value of their labor and their own culture. And, yet, it would be difficult intentionally to construct a more devastatingly accurate portrait of Western ignorance of Melanesian culture and society and the effects of this paternalistic Western attitude toward Melanesians. The Western view can be summed up as: Papua New Guineans are here to serve; their hospitality and forbearance are eminently exploitable; they do not deserve equal rights, nor should they be accorded equal dignity; their quaint culture and traditions are "dying," which is a bit of a pity; the interventions of the West are well motivated, if sometimes naïve, but in any event are ultimately benign; and such aspects of Melanesian culture that are worth preserving should be done so in European museums. This view also shaped the attitudes and actions of almost every Australian colonial administrative officer, from the higher level officials to the patrol officers, as evidenced by their own reports and memoirs.

Background: A Primer on Papua New Guinea

PNG is Australia's northern neighbor, comprising the eastern half of the world's second largest island (after Greenland), some large offshore islands including Manus, New Britain, New Ireland, and Bougainville, and many hundreds of smaller islands and coral atolls. The western half of the mainland currently forms the contested Indonesian province of Irian Jaya, claimed by Indonesia after Dutch colonialism ended in the region, although it is populated by Melanesians.

In geological terms, the PNG mainland initially was part of the Australian continental development, before rising sea levels divided the two land masses between about 8,000 and 6,500 BC. The area, especially the northern fringe islands, forms part of the "Pacific Ring of Fire," which features active volcanoes and, from time to time, severe earthquakes and devastating tsunamis.

Although close to Southeast Asia, the plant and animal life in Papua New Guinea more closely resembles that of northern Australia. For example, there are wallabies and cassowaries as in Australia, but none of the elephants, tigers, or water buffalo that are found in Southeast Asia. Horticulture has been practiced for at least nine thousand years, with the major crops including sugar cane, taro, yam, and winged beans—and locals understood the importance of crop rotation and other good farming practices. For example, families tended to plant in the same garden for only three or four years, and then allowed that garden to lie fallow for a dozen years or more, while making a new garden somewhere else.

PNG has been populated for at least fifty thousand years, probably via Asia, by land bridges or boat, before the seas rose. Research by Flinders University archaeologist Tim Denham has demonstrated "conclusively that Papua New Guinea was indeed one of the world's cradles of agriculture."[6] People in the Wahgi Valley were intensively growing taro and bananas seven thousand years ago, and perhaps as long as ten thousand years ago. This compares favorably with agricultural practices in China and the Fertile Crescent in the Middle East (9,500 years ago), central Mexico (9,000 years ago), southern China (8,500 years ago), and the Andes (7,000 years ago).

The current population of about 8.25 million (substantially more than New Zealand's five million) is divided into roughly one thousand different ethnic communities speaking nearly as many distinct languages, posing an enormous problem for nation building and administration. This is compounded by a high annual population growth rate of about 2.4 percent (compared to New Zealand's 1.1 percent), with nearly 40 percent of PNG's population under fourteen years of age.

The fragmentation of the population is as much a consequence of geography as culture. The extremely rugged terrain of the mainland, with steep mountain ranges and rapid rivers, produced a population largely housed in scattered settlements in isolated valleys. The neighboring valley likely would contain traditional rivals, rather than trading partners, with different languages and customs, and simmering hostilities.

The fraught nature of the physical environment, the threat from neighbors, and the absence of pack animals meant that, traditionally, trade and communication with the outside world, to the extent they existed, were more likely to occur by sea than within the interior. For example, the Kula ring trade of shells in the Trobriand Islands (what is now the Milne Bay Province) was famously documented by the anthropologist Bronislaw Malinowski in 1922, and thereafter seen as emblematic of Melanesian ceremonial exchanges, wealth creation, and entrepreneurialism. There was also a similar trading ring along the coast west of what is now the Central Province, and considerable trade between coastal and inland Papuans, giving fishing communities access to fresh vegetables and inland villages fresh and smoked fish. There was also trade among Highlands communities, because things grown at one elevation might not be able to be grown at another, and between Highlanders and coastal communities directly or indirectly. As a consequence, Highlanders used *kina* and *toia* shells as valuables, even though sea shells naturally exist only in the ocean, a body of water most Highlanders had never seen and possibly did not believe existed. Even today, there are limited road connections in PNG, especially from the southern capital, Port Moresby. It is notable that, in the PNG Highlands, the airplane was known long before the truck or car—and the Tok Pisin word for motor vehicle initially was *balus igo long graun* (airplane that goes along the ground). As a consequence, PNG Defence Force officer Yauka Liria, who has written about his experiences during the military response to the Bougainville secessionist crisis (see below), made the following reflection upon the typical understanding of "nationalism":

> The Papua New Guinean's loyalty is firstly to his parents, then his immediate relatives, then in order, the clan, the village, the tribe, the district, the region, the occupational identity such as the defence force, and the nation state of PNG comes last.[7]

Papua New Guinea in the Pacific

For most Westerners, including government officials, policymakers, journalists, and business leaders, the "Pacific Basin" appears to be rather empty. The "Pacific Rim" is a better understood concept, connoting the developed and emerging economies that serve as a counterweight to the growing power and influence of Europe, bounded by the west coast of North America and South America on one side, and China, Japan, Korea, and Southeast Asian countries like the Philippines, Indonesia, and Malaysia on the other. Australia is usually included, and New Zealand sometimes is. However, the countries of the Pacific Islands rarely warrant a thought, except perhaps when a major natural disaster strikes or there is the threat or reality of a coup or other internecine warfare or civil unrest, or there is a perceived threat to Western military and strategic dominance in the region.

Although little known elsewhere in the world, PNG dominates the Pacific Islands region, accounting for roughly two-thirds of the population, 84 percent of the total land area, and nearly half of the combined economic activity, as measured by gross domestic product (GDP).

In reality, the Pacific Basin is far from empty, and not merely because it is full of water. The South Pacific Commission currently has twenty-six members, of which there are only four Western, developed countries—Australia, New Zealand, the United States, and France—which have had, or still have, territories or associated states in the Pacific Islands.[8] The remaining Pacific Islands contain a great deal of diversity of political status, including:

- an independent state with a constitutional monarchy: the Kingdom of Tonga;
- "associated free states," which, as a general matter, are internally self-governing and may have independent status and United Nations membership, but formally relinquished aspects of defense and international affairs in favor of the metropolitan power, owing to the continuing concern for strategic (military, defense) denial: the Federated States of Micronesia, the Republic of the Marshall Islands, and Palau have this relationship with the United States; the Cook Islands and Niue have this relationship with

New Zealand;[9] and Tokelau is a self-administering but dependent territory of New Zealand;[10]

- the Commonwealth of the Northern Mariana Islands, which is said to be in a "political union" with the United States;[11]
- one "organized, unincorporated territory of the United States": Guam;[12]
- an "unincorporated and unorganized territory of the United States": American Samoa;[13]
- an overseas territory of the United Kingdom since 1790: the Pitcairn Islands; and
- several overseas territories of France: French Polynesia, New Caledonia, and the Wallis and Futuna Islands.

By and large, the political and legal systems of the Pacific Islands closely follow the pattern established during the colonial period. All of the states previously under the administration of Australia, New Zealand, or the United Kingdom have adopted Westminster-style parliamentary systems and common law legal systems.[14] Almost all of the former (and, of course, all of the current) American territories have adopted Washington-style, presidential political arrangements, with an elected house of representatives, plus a separate and directly elected executive. The sole exception is the Marshall Islands, which decided upon a mixture of American- and British-style arrangements that, among other things, were thought to reflect more sensitively the important role of traditional chiefs. The legislative power of the Marshall Islands is vested in a popularly elected legislature, the Nitijela, which also elects a president from among its numbers. The president is also the head of state. However, the Marshall Islands Constitution also provides for an advisory Council of Iroij, comprised of twelve high chiefs, charged with advising the cabinet and reviewing legislation affecting customary law or traditional practices, including land tenure.

For most of the twentieth century, the Pacific Islands even contained a rare international "condominium," when responsibility for the New Hebrides island group, now the independent state of Vanuatu, was formally shared between the United Kingdom and France from 1906 until independence in 1980. The resulting separate-but-equal policy of colonial governance led to the establishment of separate French- and English-speaking courts and legal systems,[15] schools, police forces, and medical services, as well as two national anthems, two currencies, and three official languages (including the local pidgin, Bislama), producing a rule "so inefficient and cumbersome that it was popularly known as the Pandemonium. The Vanuatu people were neither consulted in its establishment, nor involved in its operation."[16] The eminent international lawyer, the late D. P. O'Connell, once speculated that the manner of British and French involvement in the New Hebrides was "so bizarre as to suggest that history took a cynical revenge on European expansionism."[17]

In all cases, the adoption of Western-style political systems meant the formal importation of adversarial winner-takes-all politics, something new and alien to Pacific Island cultures, which place a premium on family and clan allegiances, rather than ideological groupings. The traditional forms of politics also demonstrated a decided preference for negotiation and consensus, rather than the automatic opposition and zero-sum outcomes featured in Western systems. As a consequence, the reality of modern Pacific politics often belies the form.

It may be said that representative democracy has "thrived" in PNG, but in a very Melanesian way, operating in a climate that favors consensus and is comfortable with dynamic change and accepting of a touch of chaos. Political parties tend to be numerous and non-ideological. Allegiances and alliances are fluid. For example, it is common in PNG politics for some elected members of a political party to be in the cabinet, while others (not offered ministries) sit on the opposition benches. Many parties have primarily regional (or clan) bases, and personalities are usually far more important than policies, especially since the latter are rarely distinguishable, with a universal emphasis on more and faster development. In the English-speaking Pacific, the political parties rarely have any significant link with parties in the metropolitan countries, even where the name (i.e., "Labor" or "Democrats") might suggest otherwise.

Whatever the difficulties with putting meaning into party politics and enforcing party discipline, it would be wrong to suggest that representative democracy has not firmly taken root in PNG, and in the Pacific generally. Indeed, PNG is one of the world's most vibrant democracies. There has never been anything other than a peaceful, constitutionally mandated change of government since independence in 1975. PNG must be one of the few countries in the world where the head of the military (in this case Brigadier-General Ted Diro, the first commander of the PNG Defence Force) would resign his command in order to stand in a free election in 1979, in a highly contested seat that he had no certainty of winning.

PNG has held free and contested elections, on schedule, for nearly fifty years (including the period of self-government), with very large numbers of candidates and very high voter turnouts. Despite the obvious advantages of incumbency, roughly half the members of Parliament lose their seats at each election. Unfortunately, some of the national elections have contained incidents of violence, intimidation, bribery, and fraud. However, these matters were dealt with through the judicial and political processes, rather than through further violence or, as in many other parts of the world, military intervention.

The explanation for the vitality of electoral politics in PNG may lie in the fact that, of all the transplanted Western institutions, its features best match traditional Melanesian culture: it is colorful, chaotic, and territorial; the mastery of fiery and flowery rhetoric (*tok bokis*) is important; and consistent ideology is less important than family, clan, and strategic alliances. In the absence of hereditary leadership in most of Melanesia (unlike Polynesia and parts of Micronesia), traditional "big men" gain power through the ability to marshal access to wealth and resources, a strong command of rhetoric, carefully cultivated strategic alliances, and a knack for cooperation and reciprocity.

In other words, Melanesian big men do not assume that they are entitled to unchallenged and enduring authority; they have to work assiduously to gain and maintain it. PNG historian John Waiko has described the system:

> In most societies . . . authority resided with a leader known as a "big man" who had achieved his position through personal ability and not through inheritance. A man who rose to the position of "big man" usually earned his status as a result of his physical strength and endurance, industriousness, organising ability, skills as an orator, and material wealth. He was a man regarded by his peers as performing most capably in social, political, economic and ceremonial activities.

> A "big man" did not exercise authority by command but by setting an example with his personal guidance and influence. His role was to initiate and facilitate activities seen to be beneficial to the group and lead members of the group to resolve issues by discussion and compromise.[18]

It is ironic that, although the Melanesian big man system aligns well with Western ideas about the importance of meritocracy, personal achievement, and entrepreneurialism, Western colonial authorities much preferred dealing with hereditary chiefs, who could then enforce authority down the line, and viewed the much more hierarchical Polynesian societies as more "advanced."

By way of contrast, the cultural fit between Melanesian culture and the Western legal system is much more problematic. Since no individual in traditional Melanesian society has the personal authority to command or enforce the resolution of disputes, negotiated and conciliated processes are required, as are more consensual outcomes. The zero-sum outcome of formal adjudication is poorly suited to small-scale societies, in which the disputants (and their relatives) invariably will have ongoing relationships and a continuing need for cooperation (and not grudging dislike or enmity) in the future. The aim of traditional Melanesian justice is not to vindicate individual rights, but to "restore the balance" in the community.[19]

The Western legal system, at least as imported into most of the Pacific Islands, contains fewer opportunities for community participation or the incorporation of local perspectives and sensibilities. For example, the jury system is rare in the Pacific (and does not exist at all in PNG), and Pacific courts and constitutions generally leave matters of justice to the "experts": judges, lawyers, and court personnel.

First Western Contact with the Pacific Islands

The first Western contact with the Pacific Islands is thought to have begun with Ferdinand Magellan's voyage in 1521, which reached Pukapuka in the Tuamotu Archipelago in French Polynesia, and Guam and Rota in the Mariana Islands. Even the earliest explorers were impressed by the enormity of the Pacific, spanning thirteen time zones plus the International Date Line. From an early stage, Europeans divided and discussed the Pacific Islands in terms of three loose groupings: the Polynesian ("many") islands; Micronesian ("small") islands; and the Melanesian ("black") islands.

Broadly speaking, the vast Polynesian triangle extends from the Hawaiian Islands in the north to New Zealand in the south, and French Polynesia, the Pitcairn Islands, and Easter Island to the east. The Polynesian group includes Niue, Samoa (formerly Western Samoa) and American Samoa, Tonga, Tuvalu, Tokelau, and Wallis and Futuna. Polynesia contains a number of sizable high islands, such as those in New Zealand, Hawaii, and the Samoas, but a much larger number of coral atolls and fringing reefs.

Micronesia encompasses the Palau group, the Caroline Islands (now part of the Federated States of Micronesia), the Mariana Islands, the Marshall Islands, Kiribati, and Nauru. There are a few substantial high islands in Micronesia (such as Guam and Saipan in the Marianas, Kosrae in the Carolines, and Babelthuap in Palau), but Micronesia is primarily comprised of coral atolls. Any significant rise in ocean levels due to global warming would engulf most of these islands, including whole states, which lie barely above sea level.

Melanesia contains the biggest islands in the Pacific, apart from the two main islands of New Zealand. It encompasses the PNG mainland and associated large islands (Manus, New Britain, New Ireland, and Bougainville), as well as the Solomon Islands, Fiji, Vanuatu, and New Caledonia. Melanesian cultural influences also are found in western Micronesia, especially in Palau and to a lesser extent in Yap, echoing traditional trade routes.

Polynesia is probably the best-known group in the West, and references to the "South Pacific," the "South Seas," or the "Pacific Islands" lead to an automatic association in most minds with the languages, culture, and stories of Polynesia. Polynesian cultural influences (including social organization, such as hereditary chieftaincy) also are pronounced in other parts of the Pacific, in some cases a natural product of proximity, but in others spread to remote areas by remarkable ocean voyagers. For example, Polynesian social and linguistic influences are apparent in the eastern parts of the Fiji Islands, such as the Lau group (near Tonga), but also in

Kiribati and such far-flung outliers as Kapingamarangi and Nukuoru Atolls, Pohnpei and Kosrae in Micronesia, and Tikopia in Melanesia.

As is the case elsewhere in the world, the colonial concepts of cultural groupings and the arbitrary delineation of boundaries may have had little or no validity prior to the colonial period but have come to impose a logic of their own in modern times. Writing in 1945, the anthropologist Felix Keesing noted that, in relation to the three major groupings: "The names given here are obviously scientific labels. They have as yet little if any meaning to the peoples concerned. Most of the islanders, still living within very local horizons, speak of themselves by their district, tribal, or village." However, as Robert C. Kiste has pointed out:

> Keesing was correct for his time but, ironically, in the last four decades Pacific Islanders have taken notions that were once the purview of anthropologists and given them meanings of their own. The distinctions between Polynesians, Micronesians, and Melanesians now have significance with regard to cultural and national identities, political agendas, and regional affairs. They are no longer categories of use only to outsiders. Further, and again for the indigenous people themselves, the very notion of a "Pacific region" and the identity of "Pacific Islander" have only become meaningful since World War Two.[20]

First Contact with Melanesia: Colonialism and Economic Exploitation

Western contact with the peoples of the Melanesian region began in the mid-sixteenth century with visits from Spanish and Portuguese explorers. More significant and enduring Western contact with the islands of the South Pacific began in the early 1800s, starting with Hawaii and Tahiti, and then moving on to (what are now) New Zealand, the Cook Islands, Tonga, and Samoa in the period between 1815 and 1830; Fiji, New Caledonia, and Vanuatu between the 1830s and 1850s; the Micronesian Islands in the 1850s; and the Solomon Islands and Papua New Guinea in the 1870s and 1880s. For example, after the sandalwood supply was depleted in the Hawaiian Islands, traders turned to the New Hebrides in the 1830s, and traders and missionaries began to arrive in force in the 1840s. By the 1860s, sandalwood was exhausted throughout the New Hebrides. In the

1860s, "blackbirding" labor recruiters kidnapped large numbers of young Melanesian men to work on the sugar and cotton plantations in Queensland and Fiji. It is thought that as many as forty thousand men from the New Hebrides, out of a total population at that time of about 100,000, worked as plantation laborers, that is, as slaves, between the 1860s and the beginning of the twentieth century.

There was relatively less colonial contact with the PNG mainland, with its rugged geography, malaria, and inhospitable climate (at least for Westerners) serving as the main defenses against the outside world. Apart from the plantations on the offshore islands, PNG was not seen as a good prospect for economic exploitation, with relatively little accessible arable land and no apparent mineral wealth (until the gold rush of the 1930s). The Germans established some plantations on the North Coast and in the islands, but relatively little land was alienated in PNG during the colonial period—only about 3 percent overall—compared with much greater proportions in New Caledonia and Fiji, and the almost total dispossession of the Indigenous populations in Hawaii and Australia.

The primary reason for British, and later Australian, interest in PNG was less economic than strategic, especially what has been termed "strategic denial:" keeping the territory out of the hands of rivals and antagonists. Australia tried from time to time to make PNG economically viable as a settler colony, especially by giving away plantation land to returning servicemen. However, those attempts never succeeded, not only because of the adverse geographical and climate factors, but also because, unlike overpopulated and densely settled European countries facing land pressures, Australia hardly needed a colonial outpost to provide anything to its economy. Imperial partition came relatively late to Melanesia, but gathered momentum reflecting European rivalries half a world away. In 1828, the Dutch annexed the western half of the PNG mainland. In 1853, the French annexed New Caledonia. Fiji came under British rule by 1874, with the increased importance of its sugar and cotton plantations, the latter becoming critical as the American Civil War dried up the cotton supply to Europe.

In November 1884, Germany declared a protectorate over the northeast quadrant of New Guinea to check growing Dutch influence in the region, and to establish copra plantations, particularly in the fertile volcanic offshore islands. Under pressure from its Australian colonies fearful of German expansionism, and eager to preserve the Torres Strait as a strategic British waterway, Britain declared a protectorate over the southeast quadrant in November 1884. Commodore James E. Erskine read a proclamation that stated (in part):

> Whereas it has become essential, for the protection of the lives and properties of the native inhabitants of New Guinea, and for the purpose of preventing the occupation of portions of that country by persons whose proceedings, unsanctioned by any lawful authority, might tend to injustice, strife and bloodshed, and who, under the pretence of legitimate trade and intercourse, might endanger the liberties and possess themselves of the lands of such native inhabitants, that a British Protectorate should be established over a certain portion of such country and the islands adjacent thereto.[21]

In sharp contrast to his position with respect to the land rights of the Indigenous people of the Australian colonies, where the legal fiction of *terra nullius* was applied, Erskine further assured the native inhabitants that:

> Your lands will be secured to you; your wives and children will be protected. Should any injury be done to you, you will immediately inform Her Majesty's officers, who will reside amongst you, and they will hear your complaints and do you justice. You will look upon all white persons whom the Queen permits to reside amongst you as your friends. . . . You will under no circumstances inflict punishment upon any white person. . . .[22]

In 1886, an Anglo-German treaty created an east–west divide between the two powers, allowing colonial acquisition to proceed in a more orderly fashion, and a German protectorate was established over the northern Solomon Islands (Bougainville and Buka). In 1893, the British declared a protectorate over the remainder of the Solomon Islands. German interests were subsequently transferred to Britain under the Samoa Tripartite Convention of 1899, in exchange for recognition of the German claim to Western Samoa. Germany also purchased the Micronesian islands from Spain, with the latter requiring funds following its defeat in the 1898 Spanish–American War.

By the turn of the twentieth century, virtually all of the Pacific Islands were under Western control. These various moves have been described aptly as: "Incidental means of regulating the disorderly process of investment, land confiscation, and labor recruiting though the clientage networks already established in the islands."[23]

The Protectorate of British New Guinea was transferred to Australian control and renamed the Territory of Papua in 1906, only five years after Australia's own independence. The German colony of New Guinea (Kaiser Wilhelm's Land) also came under Australian control in 1914, initially through military conquest during World War I. New Guinea was designated a League of Nations Class "C" Mandate in 1921, after Germany was divested of its overseas colonies by the 1919 Treaty of Versailles. The two territories were governed separately until they became a major battleground in World War II, and a military Australian New Guinea Administrative Unit (ANGAU) replaced the civil administration in the face of the Japanese invasion. With the end of the war in 1945, the Territory of Papua and the new United Nations Trusteeship of New Guinea were amalgamated under a single Australian civil administration, the charter for government eventually being set out in the *Papua and New Guinea Act 1949*.

It was fashionable in the early 1970s for Papua New Guinean nationalists to bemoan the indignity of being merely "a colony of a colony," referring to Australia's own deferential relationships with Great Britain and the United States. However, it can be argued that this situation ultimately worked in PNG's favor.

Australia's vast land mass, natural resources, and low population meant that there was no pressure to expand its territories compared, for example, to Indonesia. In addition, PNG was not seen as a strategic area, except in so far as there was a continuing need for "strategic denial" to ensure the absence of any Soviet or Chinese influence.

Australia's self-image and national uncertainty, together with the prevailing political philosophy of decolonization, meant that it was far less likely than France or the United States to seek to maintain, and justify as natural or beneficent, enduring control over its Pacific Islands territories.

In an earlier era, or in slightly different circumstances, it would not have been surprising to find much more internal political pressure to annex the islands (and more international acceptance of this), and to apply

Australian laws and policies similar to those applied to Aboriginal and Torres Strait Islander peoples during that time. That would have included policies that refused to recognize customary ownership and native title, with the consequent mass alienation of land; assimilationist social policies, producing the *stolen generations* of Indigenous children taken from their parents; and other educational and social policies that led to the loss of most of the estimated five hundred languages spoken in Australia prior to contact.

The Decolonization Movement

The Pacific was both the last region in the world to be colonized and the last to be decolonized, well after most of the former colonies of Asia and Africa. Following the end of World War II, Indonesia declared its independence from the Netherlands in 1945 (formalized in 1949); the Philippines gained independence from the United States in 1946; India in 1947 and Sri Lanka in 1948 (from the United Kingdom); Libya in 1951 (from Italy); Cambodia in 1953 (from France); Ghana and Malaysia in 1957 (from the United Kingdom); Cameroon (former French Trust Territory), the French and Belgian parts of Congo, and Nigeria (from the United Kingdom) in 1960; Tanganyika (a former UK Trust Territory) in 1961; Zanzibar (from the United Kingdom) in 1963; and Zambia (from the United Kingdom) in 1964.

By 1960, the weight of numbers had shifted sufficiently for the United Nations no longer to be seen as a "European club." The General Assembly passed a declaration granting independence to colonial countries and peoples. Paragraph 5 of the declaration provided that:

> Immediate steps shall be taken, in Trust and Non–Self-Governing Territories or all other territories which have not yet attained independence, to transfer all powers to the peoples of those territories, without any conditions or reservations, in accordance with their freely expressed will and desire, without any distinction as to race, creed or colour, in order to enable them to enjoy complete independence and freedom.

The following year, the United Nations reaffirmed its strong commitment to the decolonization process, while:

> *Noting with regret* that, with a few exceptions, the provisions contained in the aforementioned paragraph of the Declaration have not been carried out,
>
> *Noting* that, contrary to the provisions of paragraph 4 of the Declaration, armed action and repressive measures continue to be taken in certain areas with increasing ruthlessness against dependent peoples, depriving them of their prerogative to exercise peacefully and freely their right to complete independence,
>
> *Deeply concerned* that, contrary to the provisions of paragraph 6 of the Declaration, acts aimed at the partial or total disruption of national unity and territorial integrity are still being carried out in certain countries in the process of decolonization,
>
> *Convinced* that further delay in the application of the Declaration is a continuing source of international conflict and disharmony, seriously impedes international co-operation, and is creating an increasingly dangerous situation in many parts of the world which may threaten international peace and security,
>
> *Emphasizing* that inadequacy of political, economic, social or educational preparedness should never serve as a pretext for delaying independence. . . .[24]

In order to promote the implementation of the 1960 resolution and monitor progress, the United Nations established a Special Committee on Decolonization with seventeen members (subsequently increased to twenty-four).[25]

It was also in 1960, at a meeting of the British Commonwealth of Nations Prime Ministers' Conference, that conservative Australian Prime Minister Robert Menzies (the founder of the modern Liberal Party) was reportedly struck by the fact that, for the first time, black leaders outnumbered white leaders. At a press conference held upon his return from London, Menzies discussed issues of decolonization and the future of the Commonwealth in light of contemporary developments in Africa. Menzies noted his agreement with English Prime Minister Harold Macmillan that, "if in doubt about the granting of independence to a dependent territory, it was better to go sooner than later."[26] Pressed about the specific fate of PNG, Menzies replied that:

> Australia would go on doing a faithful job in New Guinea. Either he or his successor might reach the point when, although self-determination might seem premature, it would be better to take the risk than delay so long that the demand for self-determination became explosive and produced hostility.[27]

The first Pacific Island nations to gain independence were Polynesian, reflecting Western perceptions about the more "advanced" (and hierarchical) nature of their societies. Western Samoa (now known as Samoa) became independent of New Zealand in 1962. In 1965, the Cook Islands entered into a (freely severable) "Free Association Agreement" with New Zealand, pointedly expressed as a compact "between two sovereign governments." Under the agreement, New Zealand is "responsible" for defense and external affairs, in consultation with Cook Islands authorities, and may legislate with respect to the islands only with the consent of the Cook Islands Assembly.

In 1968, the UN Trusteeship jointly administered by the United Kingdom, Australia, and New Zealand was wound up, and Nauru was granted independence. In 1970, the Fiji Islands gained independence from the United Kingdom. That same year, the Kingdom of Tonga gained—or perhaps more accurately, regained—formal independence, having been a British "protected state" since 1900. In 1974, Niue entered into a Free Association Agreement with New Zealand, along the lines of the Cook Islands.

However, the decolonization of PNG seemed to be a long way off even in the 1960s, with most Australian politicians and administrators of that time suggesting that independence would not come "in our lifetime," or would be "a century off," or at best would not eventuate for perhaps "the next 30 years."[28] The election of the Whitlam Labor Government in December 1972 created more impetus in Australia for status change. As early as 1960, Gough Whitlam had called for independence to be granted by 1970. By that time, Michael Somare's Pangu Party and other Papua New Guinean voices for independence were very articulate and active in creating pressure for self-determination.

Shortly after the Australian Labor Party's election victory in 1972, Whitlam reaffirmed his commitment to the decolonization process, "not just because it is Australia's obligation to the United Nations but because we believe it wrong and unnatural that a nation like Australia should continue to run a colony."[29] By December 1973, PNG achieved a measure of self-government through an elected House of Assembly, and full independence came less than two years after that, on September 16, 1975.

Although only the seventh Pacific Island state to achieve independence, the decolonization of PNG represented something of a watershed in the legal and political development of the region. As mentioned, PNG is by far the geographically largest, most populous, and resource-rich of the Pacific Island states and territories, and its independence created real momentum and pressure, felt most keenly by Great Britain, for further decolonization in the region. As a result, in the space of just a few years, from 1978 to 1980, four more independent states emerged in the Pacific: Tuvalu (formerly the British colony of the Ellice Islands), the Solomon Islands (a British protectorate), Kiribati (formerly the British colony of the Gilbert Islands), and Vanuatu (formerly the Anglo-French condominium of the New Hebrides).

Notwithstanding growing scrutiny and pressure from the United Nations Committee on Decolonization, the United States was slower to devolve self-government and independence to the various components of the United Nations Trust Territory of the Pacific Islands in Micronesia, over which the United States gained authority in the aftermath of World War II. The Federated States of Micronesia and Marshall Islands finally entered into agreements with the United States in 1986, establishing their status as associated free states, and the Republic of Palau did likewise in 1994.

The economic vulnerability and desperation of many Pacific Island states and territories pushed them to explore dubious methods of securing additional revenues, such as through establishing tax havens and selling citizenship and passports. Some of the Pacific Island states, including PNG, have been the gullible victims of conmen and fly-by-night entrepreneurs hawking all manner of get-rich-quick schemes, losing scarce funds in the process. Even in areas of more orthodox economic development, poor management, limited controls, and corruption have led to severe pollution and other environmental problems, caused primarily by overmining, overfishing and deforestation.

Ol i Kam: Colonialism and Culture Shock

The cultural and physical shock of Pacific Islander contact with Europeans, and the nature and assumptions of Western colonialism, were brilliantly captured in the 1984 award-winning documentary film *First Contact*. The film covers the expeditions into the PNG Highlands in the early 1930s by the Leahy brothers, Australian explorers and gold prospectors, one of whom carried a movie camera and recorded the striking images of "first contact" for posterity. The film also contains contemporary interviews with a number of the Melanesian people who remembered these encounters from their childhood, including the general awe, the specific terror (after several men were killed by rifle shots), and the intense speculation about whether these interlopers were ancestors returned from the afterlife with new technology, wealth, tight-fitting clothing, and white skins—or perhaps were aliens, or perhaps "just men."

In his 1979 novel *Visitants*, the Australian writer Randolph Stow explicitly used the metaphor of aliens, or "visitants" or "star-people" in their "star machines," to reflect upon the surreal nature of the contact experience for both the colonizers and the colonized. The novel is set in the PNG islands in the late 1960s, where strange things were happening, including reports of sightings of spacecraft, the suicide of an administrative patrol officer, and the mysterious disappearance of three men guarding the chief's yam gardens on a remote island. The disturbances, and other dissatisfactions with life under colonial rule, fostered the emergence of a cargo cult that urged local people to stop working and cooperating with the colonial authorities and missionaries and, literally, place their hopes in the heavens.

A number of exchanges in the novel offer striking insights into local attitudes, suggesting that if the traditional world of the islanders can be so suddenly, completely, and unexpectedly turned upside down by the arrival of the *dimdims* (white men), whose ways and sources of power still cannot be understood, then the arrival of star people may not be so farfetched, or unwelcome, since this might lead to the removal of the whites, "who bring nothing but disappointment and shame."[30]

In the late 1970s, the broadcaster and playwright Jonbili Tokome wrote and produced a remarkable work entitled, in Melanesian Tok Pisin, "*Ol i*

Kam Nau Pulim Yumi," or, loosely translated in English, "They come and pull us in all directions." Tokome had a sharp eye for the funny and bittersweet nature of the successive waves of Western "magic" to hit PNG. The basic conundrum for the local people was: How can it be that Europeans have all the goods and technology that we desire when they are clearly no smarter than we are and most certainly do not work harder than we do? Indeed, they hire or coerce us into doing all the hard work for them. So, what is their secret? What is the script we locals must follow if we, too, are to have "development," with access to the wealth and easy lifestyle of Europeans?

In the play, the villagers' first contact is with the Australian patrol officers, or *kiaps*, whose message is: live in orderly villages, submit to the census and pay your taxes, and do not engage in tribal warfare or other troublemaking. Then, Christian missionaries arrive, and their message is: pray to Jesus, study the Bible, burn the traditional longhouses, wear clothes, avoid sex outside of marriage, abandon bigamy, and so on. Then come the bureaucrats, the cargo cult leaders, and Western liberal academics. They are followed by Melanesian radical firebrands, preaching independence and anti-colonialism. Finally, independence comes, bringing local politicians and their promises and prescriptions. Yet, despite the fact that the people have scrambled to embrace each new set of rules *guaranteed* to lead to the promised land of "development," nothing has actually changed for the better for ordinary villagers.

The Resilient Paradigm of Colonial Superiority

Despite the later arrival of Western colonialism in the Pacific, the ideological underpinnings were much the same as applied a century earlier in Africa and Asia. Colonial policy and practice proceeded from the basic assumptions that European civilization (incorporating Western culture and religion, as well as legal, political, and social institutions) was superior and more advanced, and that people from other cultures, especially non-white, traditional, or "native" peoples, were backward, superstitious, and childlike. In this worldview, such "primitive" peoples were vulnerable and incapable of self-management, and would almost certainly "die out" in a matter of generations, particularly if they were not rescued by some form of benevolent despotism, hence the establishment in the Pacific of trusts and protectorates.

Western governments and colonial authorities told themselves that colonialism conferred substantial benefits upon the local populations: better education, better health care, law and order, and, not least, spiritual enlightenment through Christianity. They also told themselves that Western legal, social, and political institutions—developed in and for the radically different conditions of England and Australia—were as worthy and capable of universal application as penicillin (Western medicine), a view shared equally by conservative colonialists and the liberal Law and Development school of the 1970s. They believed that there was no fatal contradiction in promoting the primacy of equality and the rule of law as the basis for social organization, while operating colonial administrative regimes that were almost always unequal, undemocratic, and in breach of the fundamental principles of human rights and natural justice.

According to this ideology, all societies inexorably proceed in a linear fashion from primitive beginnings toward a modern state, and if the process is done correctly, this arc will lead not merely to any state structure and any legal system, but to one exactly like those existing in Western societies today. The role of the colonizer then is merely to guide Papua New Guineans more quickly toward that inevitable goal, even if the colonizers did not see colonial rule ending for at least a century.

In sum, the Australian colonial administration was able to embrace three semi-conflicting ideas simultaneously: (1) all cultures, including those in PNG, will automatically move from primitive to modern, both in their politics and in their economies; (2) PNG is made up of hopelessly savage, childlike, and backward people who may never be capable of that much sophistication or, if they ever are, it will not be for hundreds of years; and (3) it is only through the adoption of modern Western law that cultures can move from traditional backward modes into a modern economy.

Particularly in comparison to the heyday of the British Raj, colonial regimes in the Pacific Islands tended to be small and modestly resourced; at the same time, however, they were able to sustain formal control for many years in the face of overwhelming numbers at the local level. Some of the reasons for this were the consciously maintained European monopolies on dealing with the outside world, capital accumulation, access to Western technology and expertise, and modern weaponry.

This book may appear to be critical of the Australian administration and personnel in PNG, and there is much truth in that, both in terms of the legal systems and the individuals who established and operated them. For example, it was assumed that "advanced" Western law and institutions should be reserved for whites, while local people should make do with their own customs or the special administrative fiat of patrol officers (*kiaps*) and their "police boys." While the lack of resources meant that the local population was largely left to be ruled by their own customs, there was little or no formal recognition that those customs and processes constituted anything like a "real" (that is, Western) legal system. Certainly by the 1960s, there was little excuse for white men to continue to take for granted their inherent superiority. Not only was there evidence of brown and black people being highly educated and sophisticated and successfully assuming power all over the world, but there was also such evidence in PNG itself, where there were more and more educated Papua New Guineans despite indifference and antipathy from the administration.

In considering the same dynamic in Australian colonial history, the brilliant Indigenous historian Bruce Pascoe noted that:

> The first colonists had their minds wrought by ideas of race and destiny; by the rumours heard as children of the great British Empire. They were immersed in these stories as infants, and later while marching in to school to "Men of Harlech" standing to attention for "God Save the King", and poring breathlessly over the stories of Horatio Nelson, the Christian Crusaders, King Arthur, Oliver Cromwell, and, of course, Captain James Cook. Europe was convinced that its superiority in science, economy, and religion directed its destiny. In particular, the British believed that their successes in industry accorded their colonial ambition natural authority, and that it was their duty to spread their version of civilization and the word of God to heathens. In return, they would capture the wealth of the colonized lands. . . .
>
> The first British visitors sailed to Australia contemplating what they were about to find, and innate superiority was the prism through which their new world was seen.[31]

Under the influence of those powerful cultural assumptions, coupled with Darwin's persuasive new theories, "how would it have been possible for the colonists not to believe that Englishmen were on the steepest ascent of human endeavor?"[32]

As a consequence, the colonists were so deeply inculcated in their own culture and belief in their own superiority that they were incapable of seeing the richness, complexity, and successful adaptations of Melanesian culture. Pascoe concluded that:

> the economy and culture of Aboriginal and Torres Strait Islander people has been grossly undervalued. . . . I would have to begin from the sources upon which Australia's idea of history is based: the journals and diaries of explorers and colonists. These journals revealed a much more complicated Aboriginal economy than the primitive hunter-gatherer lifestyle we had been told was the simple lot of Australia's First People. Hunter-gatherer societies forage and hunt for food, and do not employ agricultural methods or build permanent dwellings; they are nomadic. But as I read these journals, I came across repeated references to people building dams and wells; planting, irrigating, and harvesting seed; preserving the surplus and storing it in houses, sheds, or secure vessels; and creating elaborate cemeteries and manipulating the landscape—none of which fitted the definition of a hunter-gatherer. Could it be that the accepted view of Indigenous Australians simply wandering from plant to plant, kangaroo to kangaroo, in hapless opportunism, was incorrect? It is exciting to revisit the words of the first Europeans to "witness" the pre-colonial Aboriginal economy. . . by adjusting our perspective by only a few degrees, we see a vastly different world through the same window.[33]

Early Australian explorers, settlers, and administrators created a fairly accurate historical record of what they observed and were told, but then "selectively filtered the information brought to them"[34] because it did not fit their assumptions and they had little incentive to recognize the industry and ingenuity of Indigenous culture:

> It is clear from the journals of the explorers that few were in Australia to marvel at a new civilisation; they were there to replace it. Most were simply describing a landscape from which the settlers could profit.

Few bothered with the evidence of the existing economy, because they knew it was about to be subsumed.[35]

Colonial rule also depended on the formation of alliances between colonizers and locals, which itself involved a mix of divide-and-rule tactics and strategic recognition and co-optation of figures and institutions possessing traditional authority. Although such indirect rule was less pronounced in colonial-era PNG than in Africa or other parts of the Pacific (such as in Fiji and parts of Polynesia, in which chiefly authority was recognized), the administration in New Guinea did appoint some traditional leaders as *luluais* and *tultuls*, with some administrative and quasi-judicial powers that could be exercised in their local areas. However, Edward Wolfers has pointed out that while British colonial administrators appointed or recognized local leaders and afforded them a good measure of autonomy, Australian colonial administrators saw their appointees as slotting into a hierarchal system and taking orders from above.[36]

Another critical factor, which is of particular importance to the issues considered in this book, was the powerful degree of "ideological transference" conveyed through the colonial experience. Everything about the colonial experience was set up, whether purposefully or incidentally, to convey the message of Western/white superiority and the inferiority of local people, beliefs, and institutions. For example, the colonial administrators in both Papua and New Guinea promulgated *Native Regulations* that were not repealed until the mid-1960s, which applied only to the local population and which were very detailed and intrusive, regulating virtually every aspect of life and aimed at maintaining Papua New Guinean inferiority. Among other things, the "Native Regs," as they were known, dictated dress codes (men could not wear shirts in the townships); language (locals were forbidden from speaking English to Europeans); health and hygiene (compulsory submission to testing for venereal disease, as well as less offensive provisions regarding disposal of waste); relations with Europeans (locals must be out of the white town areas by 9 p.m.); village life (linear placement of housing, sweeping village squares); agriculture (promoting cash cropping); and marriage (interracial couples needed administrative approval) and sexual relations (prohibitions on adultery and interracial sex).

As Tokome's play vividly depicted, the broad colonial message was that Western education, culture, law, religion, government, and economic organization were all far superior to their traditional counterparts, and success (moral and material) rested upon the efforts of Melanesian people to accept their fate, work hard to learn these new technologies, and "catch up" with the West sometime down the road. Of course, between the infantilizing Native Regulations and the lack of government schools, Papua New Guineans would have had a nearly impossible time trying even to find that road, let alone walk on it.

With the emergence of Melanesian nationalism in the late 1960s, Papua New Guineans began to question these assumptions, to resent the assignment of their culture to an inferior status, and to chafe under external rule. Nevertheless, from the 1960s up to the present, most Melanesian leaders, who had been educated in Western-style schools (often still run by missionaries) and socialized into Western professions (law, medicine, academia), who embraced Christianity, and who owed their current authority and success to their mastery of Western institutions (including education, Parliament, law and the courts, business, and religion), internalized to some degree the ideology of colonialism, and consciously or subconsciously rejected the residual influence of traditional culture as "backward" and "primitive." Thus, the new true god of "development" had to be pursued through a warm embrace of "modernism."

It would be wrong, however, to suggest that the nature of Western contact and later colonialism in the Pacific Islands involved the unrelenting imposition of Western ways on an entirely passive and put-upon population—some sort of assembly line in which Pacific Islanders came out the other end as Westerners. This stark view of the effects of Western contact was implicit in most of the writing about the Pacific Islands over the years, and the polemic suits both those who seek to justify colonialism as necessary to "save" and then modernize Islanders (who are thus characterized as simple, childlike folk) as well as those who decry colonialism, assigning guilt for the cynical exploitation of the Islanders (who are thus, likewise, characterized as naïve, simple, childlike folk).

The best historical works reject the Eurocentric view of Pacific history in which Westerners initiated all change (positive and negative) while infantilized Pacific Islanders remained passive and used. Arguing in favor of a "new historiography," leading Pacific historians such as Kerry Howe have made a powerful case that the history of contact and colonialism in the region was more dynamic and interactive:

> The new approach, bringing Islanders into focus and studying their activities, reveals a whole range of hitherto-ignored considerations. The imperial historians simply did not question the dominance and cultural superiority of their European subjects whose initiative, they believed, determined every course of events. Their assumptions still exist in popular views of Pacific history. . . for example, that explorers left behind a trail of dead Islanders whose surviving companions stared in mute amazement at the power and superiority of the strangely coloured newcomers; that missionaries imposed their will on hapless Islanders and converted them to Christianity, so instilling in island culture the missionaries' own guilts and obsessions (or, alternatively, saving the Islanders from their own brutish lifestyles); or that traders indulged their evil ways with women and rum and were exploiters and destroyers wherever they made landfall.
>
> Recent historical research suggests that the processes of culture contact were not always so one-sided, that Islanders were quite capable of taking their own initiative and, rather than passively accepting Europeans and their ways, either rejected or deliberately exploited the newcomers for their own reasons. Individual Islanders or whole communities made use of explorers and missionaries and traders, using, adopting, adapting, applying new ideas and customs and technologies and institutions within the context of the priorities and expectations of their respective indigenous cultures. In some situations, Europeans held the advantage; in others, Islanders did. But usually. . . there were many subtle and complex levels of mutual exploitation and accommodation.[37]

Howe concludes that:

> Later generations of anthropologists . . . showed that social changes in the Pacific and elsewhere were not necessarily imposed by Europeans, and that change in itself was not necessarily destructive. Changes could come as much from within island communities as from direct outside stimulus. Change could be creative. Many societies were shown to be highly adaptable. . . . Finally, modern Pacific historians . . . try to do away with more blatant, European centred value judgments, and they deny the cultural inferiority of Island peoples and

their inability to think and act for themselves. They believe in the justness of these people controlling their own destinies. . . .

There is no suggestion that Western influences were always of benefit to Pacific peoples; most modern historians make no claims that Islanders were better or worse off as a result of European contact. But their research strongly suggests that the blanket interpretation of a fatal impact cannot be sustained. To see Islanders as passive, helpless, and always persecuted and suffering at the hands of Europeans not only excludes modern research findings but, it is now argued, denies the Islanders their humanity. . . . Once the Europeans did come, island societies proved adaptable, resourceful, and resilient. A history of culture contact can no longer be interpreted in terms of European initiatives; the course of events was very much influenced by the nature of the Islanders' own social and political arrangements. . . . Islanders had long been masters of their own environment. . . . Although at various points in the nineteenth century a political and economic control was finally assumed by European interests, this did not necessarily mean the destruction of island values, perceptions, and social organisations; to suggest that it did is to ignore the lifestyles that still flourish in many parts of the Pacific today. Injustice, intolerance, and interference can easily be documented, especially in the colonial period, but these must not be permitted to overshadow the other dimensions of the more intimate workings of island societies.[38]

The Cultural Force of Christianity

Christianity has been by far the most important Western cultural force in the Pacific over the past two centuries, arguably to a far greater extent than in any other region in the world. Missionaries were very effective in promoting religion as a moral and spiritual good in itself, but they coupled this with the provision of other services that were highly prized, such as education and health. In turn, Pacific Islanders saw religion as a powerful technology for obtaining virtue, wealth, power, and sophistication. In part because Australia built no schools in PNG until the 1960s, most Papua New Guinean leaders (in politics, business, the professions, and, of course, religion) were educated in mission schools, and those islands and areas with strong mission schools developed more rapidly than those without.

The strong cultural connection to Christianity is expressly recognized in the preambles to many Pacific Island constitutions. The Preamble to the PNG Constitution pledges that people will "guard and pass on to those who come after us our noble traditions and the Christian principles that are ours now," and provides that: "WE, THE PEOPLE, do now establish this sovereign nation and declare ourselves, under the guiding hand of God, to be the Independent State of Papua New Guinea."

Similarly, many other Pacific Islands constitutions expressly "acknowledge God as the almighty and everlasting Lord and the giver of all good things" (Nauru); note that the political system operates "under the guiding hand of God" (Solomon Islands); express trust in "God, the Giver of our life, liberty, identity and our inherent rights" (Marshall Islands); acknowledge "God as the Almighty Father in whom we put our trust, and with faith in the enduring value of our traditions and heritage" (Kiribati); and recognize that the modern state is "founded on traditional Melanesian values, faith in God, and Christian principles" (Vanuatu), or is "based on Christian principles and Samoan custom and tradition" (Samoa) or "based on Christian principles, the Rule of Law, and Tuvaluan custom and tradition" (Tuvalu).

In Fiji, the leader of the 1987 military coup, Major-General Sitiveni Rabuka, regularly made claims along the lines of "If this land is run by Christians, or Fijians who are Christians, everything will be in place."[39] It has been noted that a "rhetorical political strategy of divine intervention" works well in Fiji, along with appeals to the importance of Fijian chiefs, warnings about betrayal of customary land rights,[40] and fears that the Indigenous population would be swamped by Hindus and Muslims brought from the Indian subcontinent by the British to work in the sugar cane fields. Rabuka tied these all together in a novel fashion, suggesting that the legitimacy of both chiefs and traditional land rights is sourced in Christianity.[41] Rabuka subsequently resigned from the military and successfully contested the next election, becoming prime minister.

The 1997 Fiji Constitution, drafted after a second set of military coups by a government with close ties to the Methodist church (as almost all Fijian governments have had), commences by "seeking the blessing of

God who has always watched over these islands." The Preamble to that constitution notes the successive waves of settlement in the Fiji Islands and the consequent ethnic diversity, and then expressly refers to:

> The conversion of the indigenous inhabitants of these islands from heathenism to Christianity through the power of the name of Jesus Christ; the enduring influence of Christianity in these islands and its contribution, along with that of other faiths, to the spiritual life of Fiji.

The late historian Sione Latukefu pointed out that the blurring of the church–state distinction in Polynesia has its cultural roots in precontact times, when there was a:

> close alliance between the priests and the chiefs in pre-missionary Tongan society. It was therefore not surprising to find the converted chiefs, who wished to pursue their politics according to Christian principles, as early as 1827, consulting the missionaries on political matters.[42]

Latukefu also noted that the absence of a substantial Western settler community in Tonga, as in PNG and many other parts of the Pacific Islands, also contributed to the special relationship between Indigenous people and Christian missionaries:

> Unlike Hawaii, Fiji, Samoa and many other Pacific islands, which had quite large numbers of white settlers, Tonga, in the first half of the nineteenth century, had only a small number of Europeans and, apart from the missionaries, they were mostly escaped convicts and runaway sailors. . . . The absence of a settler class to whom to turn made the chiefs . . . rely almost entirely upon the Wesleyan missionaries for advice. . . . The missionaries, for their part, were not only willing to give their advice, but they expected to be consulted in almost every important matter, so much so that when their advice was not sought by the chiefs, they were deeply disappointed.[43]

As was the case with other Western influences, Pacific Islanders steadily refashioned Christianity to incorporate a more Pacific flavor, merging the central religious dogmas with traditional cultural beliefs, symbols, mythologies, and sensibilities. Vilisoni Hereniko has noted that following European contact

> came the *ao taf ta* (time of light) when missionisation transformed cultural identities of Pacific Islanders by converting them to a new religious order while suppressing certain cultural practices. However, as Islanders embraced Christianity, they infused it with their own cultural symbols and ways of worshipping that reflect their cultural heritage. Then came World War Two, decolonisation, and independence movements. In their quest for a cultural identity at the personal, national, and regional levels, islanders sought ways to reconcile indigenous culture, Christianity, and Euro-American values of materialism and progress. A wide range of possible fusions ensued, creating different identities from which to choose and multiple ways of symbolising each particular one.[44]

Different missionary groups have been more or less accommodating of efforts by Pacific Islanders to "customize" Christian symbols and practices. Early contact often involved mass conversions, mass destruction of symbols of the old "heathen" ways, such as the spirit houses, or *haus tambaran*, found across many parts of PNG, and other artwork, such as carvings, thought to be associated with "idolatry," and the general suppression of traditional beliefs and ceremonies. Today, however, most mainstream churches accept, and many even promote, the use of local languages and the incorporation of traditional dress, body decoration, song, dance, and symbols, both as part of Christian worship and in (newly tolerated) traditional ceremonies, such as those marking birth, death, and initiation.

The leading thinker in PNG about matters of culture and pluralism, Bernard Narokobi, described himself as "a baptised Melanesian Christian, and a nationalist, deeply committed to promote Melanesian culture and values, within a Christian context."[45] Narokobi noted that while Christianity has the potential to be a major force for national unity in PNG, the large number of contesting churches has created significant division in practice:

> It is well known that many villages of Papua New Guinea and their families are divided between one brand of Christian faith and another.... In the early days of missionary activity, open hostility between foreign missionaries was common. Hostility was so great that Australian administrators found it necessary to divide the country into districts to avoid "sheep grabbing." Even today, that hostility still continues.... What proudly can be said for Papua New Guinea is that in spite of foreign missionary conflict, antagonisms and sometimes

> hatred our people are still united in their villages, families and cultural values. . . . Christ came to Melanesia not to ignore, neglect or destroy the noble Melanesian culture and values, but to fulfil these.[46]

Similar concerns have been expressed elsewhere in the Pacific Islands, particularly where new churches, often associated with American evangelical movements, have set up in areas with already established churches, creating rivalries and straining allegiances. In 2000, the Supreme Court of Samoa outlawed religious banishments, citing the constitutional guarantee of freedom of religion. However, concern about the continuing growth of the new religious groups has led Samoa's National Council of Churches to pressure the government to amend the constitution to restrict the protection to established mainstream Christian denominations. In 2003, the Samoan government asked its Law Reform Commission to consider "the conflict between traditional customs and Christianity," after several cases in which "village chiefs have used traditional custom to exile people who professed belief in new denominations."[47]

The small Muslim presence in the Pacific Islands also has excited some controversy. In November 2002, the deputy prime minister of PNG publicly canvassed the possibility of amending the constitutional guarantee of religious freedom in order to ban "religious groups that seem to condone violence in their teachings," a proposition that was soon rejected by the Catholic Bishops Conference of Papua New Guinea and the Solomon Islands.[48] Narokobi consistently called for local people to develop and assert their own brand of Christianity, incorporating a large measure of Melanesian customs and traditional ways:

> Melanesians have very little to learn from the Western version of Christianity because for many of us, Westerners are identified with colonialism and Christianity is seen as part of the colonial process of subordination, subjugation and dominance of the Western peoples over the native races.[49]

The Vision of a Uniquely Melanesian Jurisprudence

While substantial energy and creativity has gone into customizing Western religion to adapt it to the current needs, beliefs, and aspirations of local people, the same level of vigor has not been evident in relation to matters of secular law and justice.

In the 1960s and 1970s, nationalist sentiment grew powerfully for self-government and self-determination, but there was also a strong view that independence should not mean simply a change of rulers and a continuation of the status quo. Given that colonial law played such a critical role in entrenching and implementing colonial rule, many Papua New Guinean leaders urged the replacement of the imposed system of Western law and courts with a more appropriate and culturally sensitive system of "Melanesian jurisprudence," springing from the new constitution and developed over time by the courts, the government, and the legislature. The Constitutional Planning Committee (CPC) recommended a way forward, involving constitutional recognition of customary law as the primary source of a new "underlying law" for the country, steadily replacing the imposed common law.

Now, after five decades, the euphoria, residual good will, and optimism of the immediate pre- and post-independence period have dissipated. The earliest days saw the development and proclamation of PNG's home-grown constitution; the inclusion of constitutional provisions aimed at promoting the development of the "underlying law" of PNG; the establishment of a Law Reform Commission with special constitutional responsibility for nurturing the development of that underlying law; the enactment of a number of statutes recognizing customary beliefs and usages; and other innovations. There is a sad irony here, in that the constitution, which was supposed to take the country back to custom, ultimately was put together not by the CPC members themselves but by Australian legislative drafters who, although they included some of the CPC's ideals in the (nonjusticiable) Preamble, produced a highly legalistic document more closely resembling a typical Australian regulatory statute than a transformational constitution embodying the CPC's heartfelt call for a return to custom.

Unfortunately, whatever willingness to reform existed at independence soon was lost in the mundane responsibilities of governance. Instead, the prevailing attitude was that, so long as there is sufficient law and order to allow for private sector investment and economic development, there is no pressing need to tackle the larger and more difficult questions of law reform and jurisprudence.

This perception of the divisibility of law and economics, and the primacy of economic imperatives, was reflected in the annoyance of two senior government ministers in 1980 that parliamentary time was being used to debate an alleged serious breach of ethics by an expatriate Supreme Court judge:

> Because of this matter of public importance, we have wasted our time, and now we cannot debate about roads and other necessary things which the country badly needs. I do not regard this as a matter of public importance, and it should be thrown out to make way for something important. . . .[50]
>
> We should be concerned about the development of our people. What is the importance of . . . the Judiciary? We should be more concerned about development and not waste our time discussing matters of less significance. I do not think the public is concerned about small things such as this. We are playing round too much with small matters which do not really affect our people.[51]

Since independence, there has been an almost total preoccupation in PNG with economic development, to the near exclusion of nation building through the careful, customized development of appropriate political, legal, and social institutions. What never seems to be said in PNG is that the leadership probably has attacked the problem from the wrong end. Political and legal systems that promoted greater social equity and cohesion would help provide the order, stability, and other conditions required for sound and sustainable economic development. Neglecting this has led to major problems with law and order, social dislocation and corruption, as well as economic stagnation, despite the immense, unrealized potential of PNG in terms of human resources, natural resources, ecotourism, and more.

Further, postcolonial PNG also inherited a "strong State" model from Australia, a system that was heavily promoted to PNG's local leaders in the 1970s and 1980s by both Western capitalist nations and influential, progressive, developing countries, such as Tanzania. This generated another fundamental tension, between customary norms and the authority of the state. Any move to build upon the former was likely to produce a dramatically decentralized polity, greatly reducing the potential for central action. That may well have been beneficial in the long run, but it represented a very different model of development from that being pursued by local leaders. Finally, greater decentralization also would have had dramatic distributional consequences, because centrally directed development generally produces centrally directed riches, a phenomenon which played out so tragically in the Bougainville separatist conflict.

Beyond any rational cost–benefit considerations, however, lay a deeper and more troubling malaise: Papua New Guinean elites feared that, despite their passionate rhetoric, custom simply was not up to the task of development and modernization—and they were not alone in that reasoning, since it accorded with the Law and Development and Law and Modernization schools of "progressive" legal thinking, as well as advice from the World Bank, the Commonwealth Secretariat, leading consultants, and others. These crippling doubts stemmed in part from the colonial past, with its ideological opposition so deeply engrained against custom that even Papua New Guineans came to believe it. But in significant part, there was also the fear that fundamentally reorganizing the whole legal system—business law, land law, family law, criminal law, civil dispute resolution and so on—would be a massive, complex, and frightening undertaking, with no established road map.

On top of all of that, potential reformers were likely to face entrenched opposition from judges (all expatriates at that time), Australian and even Papua New Guinean traders, miners, and plantation owners, the Australian government (which, after December 1975, was no longer Labor), as well as from many top Papua New Guinean politicians, including Prime Minister Michael Somare himself, who were listening to the concerns of a nervous business community, which, by that time, was coming to be dominated by the large-scale foreign corporations promising to make sizable investments in Papua New Guinea's natural resources. Taking all of this into account, consciously or not, Papua New Guinean leaders came to believe that it would be significantly easier, and far less risky, to do nothing much at all, which meant retaining the westernized legal system that colonizers had imposed.

Law, Colonialism, and Postcolonial Papua New Guinea

We did not write this book solely, or even primarily, because colonial law is an interesting topic of study in its own right—although it is. The colonial legal systems continue to be the primary sources of law for the courts of the Independent State of Papua New Guinea, to the detriment of customary law. At independence, that did not seem inevitable. Many of us were hopeful that the end of colonialism would also spell the end of colonial law and the beginnings of a new legal system based upon custom and fashioned in ways that mirrored and supported Papua New Guinean culture and conditions. That did not happen, and, since then, we have been persuaded by the law and dependency theorists, especially Andre Gunder Frank, that Papua New Guinea's acceptance at independence of a capitalist economy in general and of large-scale investment by giant corporations in particular meant that the continued dominance of a legal system supportive of the global market economy was all but inevitable. The form that legal system would take has been best described by postcolonial theorists such as Edward Said, Gayatri Spivak, and Homi Bhabha.

They have discussed the "othering" process used to create and define other cultures and societies through an ethnocentric Western framework, which constructed a demonized or fantasized "Other" against which legitimating images of the Metropolitan Self were defined. Beginning in 1978, Said wrote about the Western scholarly construction of the "East" and "the Orient" through a "fantasy Orient" projected onto, and then inscribed upon, the lands and peoples of the region. Said argued that:

> [T]he Orient has helped to define Europe (or the West) as its contrasting image, idea, personality, experience, making it an integral part of European material civilization and culture.
>
> Yet none of this Orient is merely imaginative. The Orient is an integral part of European material civilization and culture. Orientalism expresses and represents that part culturally and even ideologically as a mode of discourse with supporting institutions, vocabulary, scholarship, imagery, doctrines, even colonial bureaucracies and colonial styles.[52]

The colonizing authorities in PNG similarly developed a fantasy New Guinea of tropical jungles, head-hunters, and "savage races," owing much to British conceptions of Africa, which was then projected back upon the lands and people of what is now PNG. Indeed, the late medieval European figure of the Wild Man who lived on the outer edges of civilizations and was "hairy, nude, violent, lacking in moral sense and excessively sensual"[53] had its counterpart in the popular "Boy's Own" type of literature about white people's adventures among the so-called savages of the South

Sea Islands, themselves highly influenced by the Tarzan genre transplanted from Africa. These same fantasies pervaded representations of the Pacific Islands in the popular Australian literature of the 1920s including the books of Beatrice Grimshaw and Jack McLaren, early twentieth-century travel writers who popularized the romanticized view of a wild and savage PNG.

A belief in the libidinal excesses and uncivilized nature of Indigenous peoples was held at the highest levels of colonial administration in New Guinea, as evidenced in the laws themselves. As Amirah Inglis has pointed out, the passing of the *White Women's Protection Ordinance* in January 1926 occurred despite the admission in 1925 of its promulgator, Sir Hubert Murray, the Administrator of the Territory of Papua, that attacks on white women were rare and that there had never been one in which the circumstances suggested an intention to commit rape. Given such a deviant-free context with respect to the subject matter of the ordinance, its only valid justification may be found in the West's historical equating of blackness with uncontrollable lust.

This belief in an Indigenous lack of sexual restraint was reflected in the writings of PNG colonials such as the missionary William G. Lawes, who described Motu dancing as "a carnival of licentiousness and sensuality . . . [in which] the people gave themselves up to lust and immorality."[54] Such colonial representations of the "Other," and a widespread belief shared by Sir Hubert Murray, even after thirty years as lieutenant-governor, that "Europeans as a whole have an innate superiority over Papuans,"[55] inevitably had consequences for the way in which a colonial legal system was constructed and applied in PNG. Further, as Albert Memmi has suggested:

> Whenever, the colonizer adds, in order not to fall prey to anxiety, that the colonized is a wicked, backward person with evil, thievish, somewhat sadistic instincts, he thus justifies his police and his legitimate severity. After all, he must defend himself against the dangerous foolish acts of the irresponsible, and at the same time—what meritorious concern!—protect him against himself![56]

At the time of colonization of PNG, Australia was itself an uncertain frontier society, heavily dependent upon British culture and traditions for its identity. Australia's sense of itself as a provincial outpost of the British Empire was reflected in the primacy given to British history and literature in education; the maintenance of the British flag and head of state; the awarding of British honors; the adoption of British laws, courts, and legal traditions; and even British citizenship (or, more accurately, "British subjecthood"). That Australia historically viewed itself as an integral part of the white British Empire was reflected in its "white Australia" immigration policy.

Arguably, then, Australian colonization of PNG was a mutually constitutive process, whereby Australia, which was deeply uncertain about its own national identity, culture, and standing in relation to the United Kingdom and the United States, sought to take the opportunity provided by colonization to define itself as advanced, sophisticated, modern, progressive, and white by constituting PNG as (in Said's words) "its contrasting image, idea, personality, experience."[57]

This process of othering, the attaching of images of savagery and lack of civilization to Melanesian society, had significant consequences for the legal system that the colonizers introduced. As Memmi has argued in the context of Africa, the mythical portrait of the colonized is "supported by a very solid organization, a government and a judicial system fed and renewed by the colonizer's historic, economic and cultural needs."[58] Memmi notes that:

> Not being master of its destiny, not being its own legislator, not controlling its organization, colonized society can no longer adapt its institutions to its grievous needs. But it is those needs which practically shape the organizational face of every normal society.[59]

Despite the obvious importance of colonialism to the legal system of an independent PNG, postcolonial studies theorists have drawn primarily on culture, literature, and language, and have paid surprisingly little attention to the role of law and legal institutions as a tool of colonialism. In fact, neither Said's *Orientalism* nor *Culture and Imperialism*, considered the classic works in postcolonial studies, contains a single reference to law, legal systems, legal culture, judges, or courts. This is remarkable, given the central role of law and legal institutions in establishing and maintaining the colonial apparatus in the Pacific, and as a constructor of identity. In PNG and other Pacific Island territories, colonial military and police power, and even economic power, were limited. By default, laws and courts became important regulators of social and economic relations, most notably in the towns, but also in rural areas. The absence of law from postcolonial studies probably owes more to the fact that legal academics have been slower to move into this field than their counterparts in the arts and humanities than it does to the correlations between the subject matter of these disciplines.

In the remainder of this book, we consider the potential for Melanesian custom to serve as a transformational agent for political, legal, and social institutions in postcolonial PNG, which would require a sensitive and well-targeted integration of customary laws, processes, and understandings with the transplanted Western systems. The ultimate goal must be to infuse national institutions with real meaning and legitimacy in Melanesian eyes, while pragmatically retaining those features of the inherited ways that have proven value, and permit PNG to operate effectively in the international arena.

The Study of Papua New Guinea's Colonial Legal System

This book focuses on the colonial legal systems created by the British, and later by the Australians, for their territories of Papua and New Guinea between 1884 and 1975. Like many former European colonies, PNG's colonial history generally has been the subject of numerous books and articles. However, there are only two studies that deal specifically with aspects of PNG's colonial legal history. The first is an unpublished 1978 LL.M thesis by Donald R. C. Chalmers, which is a history of the colonial courts. The second is a study by Peter Sack of the colonial legal system in German New Guinea between 1884 and 1914. In the years since those works were completed, much more material about the colonial era in Papua and New Guinea has become available through books and documents, as well as newspapers, diaries, and other resources available on the internet. This makes it possible to come to a much better understanding of the rationales used by colonial officers to support their application of an imported legal system to Papua and New Guinea, as well as their experiences at applying and enforcing colonial laws.

The authors are indebted for many of our insights and conclusions about the origins and impact of colonial legal systems to a number of different but complementary theories about the legal process and the imposition of law. Chief among them is critical race theory, which underlies our entire narrative. Critical race theory begins from the premise that so long as society is unequal, and so long as law is enacted and enforced by those in power, one of the major purposes of the legal system will be the continued subordination by the dominant class of the other groups and classes that make up the polity. In developing and demonstrating this critique, critical race theorists like Richard Delgado, Kimberlé Crenshaw, and Mari Matsuda look at both the laws themselves and at their impact. The theory was initially developed in the United States, and most of the studies based on it to date have been in that context, but its applicability to the colonial situation is so stark as to be obvious. The history of the colonial legal systems of Papua and New Guinea provide textbook examples of the use of law as a lever not only to continue the subordination of subject peoples but to convince them that they are being subordinated in a good cause.

We have also been influenced by intersectionality theory, which was developed by Kimberlé Crenshaw, herself one of the founders of critical race theory. It is particularly useful at explicating the workings of the PNG colonial legal system, because it teaches that people who belong to more than one subordinated group are the subjects not only of the prejudice visited upon members of each of the groups to which they belong, but also of a special bias reserved just for people belonging simultaneously to more than one minority group. Papuans and New Guineans, for example, who were both brown and, in the eyes of their colonial masters, "primitive," were discriminated against in the ways that whites at the time discriminated against brown and black people; they were also subordinated as colonial subjects; and, finally, they were the subjects of a special bias in that they were a colony of people who were both brown and "primitive."

For all three authors of this book, theory illuminates our own experience of Papua New Guinea and its legal system. We each were fortunate to have been part of a diverse group of faculty members who taught law at the University of Papua New Guinea in the years immediately before and after independence in September 1975. In addition to teaching, one of the authors (Bruce Ottley) served as a magistrate for the National Capital District Court in Port Moresby from 1976 to 1977. In deciding civil and criminal cases, he applied laws adopted or enacted during the colonial period and retained after independence. The other two authors (Jean Zorn and David Weisbrot) also served as chief researcher and consultant, respectively, for the PNG Law Reform Commission, which itself had been established in accordance with the provisions of the Independence Constitution in order to create a legal system that would be influenced more by custom than by the Western laws and legal processes that had been a predominant feature of colonial law. During those years, under the dynamic leadership of Bernard Narokobi (chairman) and Josepha Namsu Kanawi (secretary), the commission reviewed and recommended changes to a number of laws introduced during the colonial period, in order to meet the needs and conditions of their newly independent country, as well as to reestablish custom as the basis of the legal system.

The focus of this book is on the colonial legal systems in Papua and New Guinea. Although the legal systems created by Britain and Australia played an important role during the colonial period, they were not the only, or even the primary, rules and procedures that governed the lives of the Indigenous peoples of Papua and New Guinea. Thus, Chapter 2 examines the customary legal systems that local people used to regulate themselves and to resolve their disputes. Because customary law often came into contact and conflict with the colonial legal systems, European understanding (or, more often, misunderstanding) of it and the societies in which it operated was an important factor in how the colonial legal systems functioned.

Chapters 3 and 4 begin the discussion of the colonial legal systems; chapter 3 focuses on the four years (1884–1888) that British New Guinea (later named the Territory of Papua) was a British protectorate. Although British rule was brief and there was no formal legal system in place during that period, the policies and practices established by the protectorate administrators laid the foundation for the colonial legal systems.

With the establishment of British New Guinea as a colony in September 1888, Britain began the process of creating a formal colonial legal system for the territory; British colonial law consisted of English common law and equity and locally enacted ordinances, some of which applied only to New Guineans. Chapter 4 focuses on the development and application of the colonial legal system during that period of British rule, as well as the changes that occurred after the territory became an Australian colony in 1905 and was renamed the Territory of Papua.

The German presence in New Guinea lasted for thirty years, from 1884 until the outbreak of World War I in 1914. However, this book does not discuss in any detail the colonial legal system in German New Guinea. Australia took over German New Guinea at the outbreak of the war, and administered it under military rule until 1921, when New Guinea's relationship to Australia was formalized, first, from 1921 until 1942, as a League of Nations Mandate, and then, after 1949, as a United Nations Trust Territory. In 1921, Australia replaced the colonial legal system established by Germany with one similar to that in the Territory of Papua. As a result, except for some remnants of land law, German law played little or no part in New Guinea's colonial legal system after that date.

With the colonial legal systems in place in Papua and New Guinea, Chapters 6 and 7 examine their operation and evolution during the twenty years between 1921 and the suspension of civilian rule in the two territories in 1942, with Chapter 6 focusing on the role of the legal system in administration and economic development and Chapter 7 highlighting the role of the legal system in making contact with and then establishing colonial control over the local population. During this period Australia expanded and strengthened its rule, particularly with the expansion of Australian contact into the Highlands, which brought hundreds of thousands of New Guineans under nominal Australian hegemony.

With the outbreak of World War II, civilian rule was again suspended in Papua and New Guinea; once again, the two territories were placed under military rule. The end of the war led to the resumption of Australia colonial rule and in 1949 the merger of the two territories into a single administrative unit in 1949. Chapters 8 (1942–1949) and 9 (the 1950s) focus on Australia's attempts after the upheavals of the war to reestablish civilian control over PNG and to extend it into areas of the Highlands that had not been pacified prior to the war. British colonies in Asia and Africa were achieving independence, but the Australians remained firm in their belief that it would be at least another hundred years before PNG would be ready for a step like that.

However, the times were leaving the colonial authorities behind. Chapter 10 details the manifold changes in the dozen years from 1960 to 1972 that culminated in self-government and, three years later, in independence. In the end, Papua New Guineans and Australians both sought early independence, although there were dissenting voices in both camps, and, although the era saw Papuans and New Guineans, their ideas, and customs and processes playing a greater role in governance and law, it also laid the groundwork for the postcolonial situation that exists today.

Chapter 11 looks at the brief but highly dynamic period between December 1972 and September 1975, during which impending independence made it imperative to dismantle many of the more discriminatory elements of the colonial legal system. Papua New Guineans and their supporters attempted, in those three years, to decide what the content of the independence legal system would be. Though there was considerable debate over the roles that custom and the imposed western law should play, the period also saw a real movement towards giving customary law a more prominent role through legislation, through a new system of village courts, and, most importantly, through a constitution that envisaged the development of a homegrown legal system based on customary law. We conclude with an Epilogue that briefly describes the post-independence legal system and the continuing powerful influence that the colonial legal systems have had on it.

This book relies heavily on original contemporaneous sources: newspaper accounts, journal articles, and government reports, as well as extracts from speeches and books written by people who participated in the events being discussed. Through the 1960s, almost all accounts of PNG were produced by British and Australian administrative officers, missionaries, journalists, historians, and anthropologists, and reflected the perspectives, agendas, and biases of the white colonial class. There was no description of the colonial or earlier periods written by a Papua New Guinean until 1968, when Albert Maori Kiki, who was born in the present-day Gulf Province in 1931, became the first Papua New Guinean to publish an autobiography.[60]

Beginning with 1972, the authors are able to draw on our own direct experiences, observations, and contacts with those involved in government, education, and legal affairs in PNG, both nationals and expatriates. For us, this book represents a longtime professional preoccupation—but it is also very personal.

Sources

Books and Articles

ABC Radio News, "Arsonists Target PNG Mosque," *ABC Radio News*, November 8, 2002, http://abc.net.au/news/2002/11/item20021107175713_1.htm.

Don Aitkin and Edward P. Wolfers, "Australian Attitudes towards the Papua New Guinea Area since World War II," *Australian Outlook* 27(2) (1973) 202–214.

Robert Aldrich and John Connell, *The Last Colonies* (Cambridge: Cambridge University Press, 1998).

H. A. Amankwah, J. T. Mugambwa, and G. Muroa (eds.), *Land Law in Papua New Guinea* (Port Moresby: University of Papua New Guinea Press, 2009).

Peter J. Bayne, "Legal Policy-Making," in J. A. Ballard (ed.), *Policy-Making in a New State: Papua New Guinea 1972–1977* (Brisbane: University of Queensland Press, 1981) 139–156.

Homi K. Bhabha, *The Location of Culture* (London: Psychology Press, 2004).

Peter Biskup (ed.), *The New Guinea Memoirs of Jean Baptiste Octave Mouton* (Canberra: Australian National University Press, 1974).

Peter Biskup, Brian Jinks, and Hank Nelson, *A Short History of Papua New Guinea* (Sydney: Angus and Robertson, 1968).

Peter Biskup, Brian Jinks, and Hank Nelson (eds.), *Readings in New Guinea History* (Sydney: Angus and Robertson, 1973).

J. I. Brookes, *International Rivalry in the Pacific Islands 1800–1875* (New York: Russell & Russell, 1941).

B. J. Brown (ed.), *Fashion of Law in New Guinea* (Sydney: Butterworths, 1969).

Donald R. C. Chalmers, *Full Circle: A History of the Courts of Papua New Guinea* (master's thesis, Faculty of Law, University of Papua New Guinea, 1978).

Donald R. C. Chalmers, "A History of the Role of Traditional Dispute Settlement Procedures in the Courts of Papua New Guinea," in David Weisbrot, Abdul Paliwala, and Aki Sawyerr (eds.), *Law and Social Change in Papua New Guinea* (Oxford: Butterworths, 1982) 169–189.

Donald R. C. Chalmers, David Weisbrot, Salamo Injia, and Warwick Andrew, *Criminal Law and Practice of Papua New Guinea*, 3rd ed. (Sydney: Law Book Company, 1985).

Percy Chatterton, *Day That I Have Loved* (Sydney: Pacific Publications, 1974).

Amy Chua, "Markets, Democracy, and Ethnicity: Toward a New Paradigm for Law and Development," *Yale Law Journal* 108(1) (1998) 4–107.

Bob Connolly and Robin Anderson, *First Contact: New Guinea's Highlanders Encounter the Outside World* (New York: Viking Penguin, 1987).

Peter Corris, "Blackbirding in New Guinea Waters 1883–84: An Episode in the Queensland Labor Trade," *Journal of Pacific History* 3(1) (1968) 85–105.

Kimberlé Crenshaw, "Mapping the Margins: Intersectionality, Identity Politics, and Violence against Women," *Stanford Law Review* 43(6) (1991) 1241–1299.

Kimberlé Crenshaw, Neil Gotanda, Gary Peller and Kendall Thomas (eds.), *Critical Race Theory: The Key Writings that Formed the Movement* (New York: The New Press, 1996).

Ron Crocombe and Ahmed Ali (eds.), *Politics in Melanesia* (Suva: Institute of Pacific Studies, University of the South Pacific, 1982).

Ron Crocombe and Ahmed Ali (eds.), *Politics in Polynesia* (Suva: Institute of Pacific Studies, University of the South Pacific, 1983).

Ron Crocombe and Ahmed Ali (eds.), *Politics in Micronesia* (Suva: Institute of Pacific Studies, University of the South Pacific, 1983).

Eddie Dean and Stan Ritova, *Rabuka: No Other Way* (Sydney: Doubleday, 1988).

Richard Delgado and Jean Stefancic, *Critical Race Theory: An Introduction* (New York: New York University Press, 3rd ed., 2017).

Sean Dorney, *Papua New Guinea: People, Politics and History since 1975* (New York: Random House, 1990).

Ron Duncan, "An Overview of Decentralisation and Local Governance Structures in the Pacific Region," paper presented to the Pacific Regional Symposium "Making Local Governance Work," the Commonwealth Local Government Forum Pacific Project, Suva, December 4–8, 2004, http://www.shareefweb.com/documents/LocalGovReforms/References/Duncan%20Pacific.pdf.

A. E. Epstein, *Matupit: Land, Politics, and Change Among the Tolai of New Britain* (Canberra: Australian National University Press, 1969).

"Fiji PM: Climate Change Threatens Our Survival," *BBC News*, April 3, 2018, https://www.bbc.com/news/world-asia-43625608.

Ben Finney, *Big-Men and Business: Entrepreneurship and Economic Growth in the New Guinea Highlands* (Honolulu: University of Hawaii Press, 1973).

First Contact, a film by Bob Connolly and Robin Anderson (New York: Filmakers Library, 1983)

Stewart Firth, *New Guinea under the Germans* (Melbourne: Melbourne Univ. Press, 1983).

Peter Fitzpatrick, *Law and State in Papua New Guinea* (New York: Academic Press, 1980).

Tim Flannery, *Throwim Way Leg: An Adventure* (Melbourne: Melbourne Text Publishing, 1998).

Andre Gunder Frank, "The development of underdevelopment." *Monthly Review*, 18(4) (1966) 17–31

Graham Freudenberg, *A Certain Grandeur: Gough Whitlam in Politics* (New York: Penguin Books, 1987).

Yash Ghai (ed.), *Law, Politics and Government in the Pacific Island States* (Suva: Institute of Pacific Studies, University of the South Pacific, 1988).

James Griffin, Hank Nelson, and Stewart Firth, *Papua Guinea: A Political History* (Richmond: Heinemann Educational Australia, 1979).

Bonnie Glass-Coffin, "Anthropology, Shamanism, and the 'New Age,'" *The Chronicle of Higher Education* (June 15, 1994) A48.

Beatrice Grimshaw, *The New New Guinea* (London: Hutchinson & Co, 1911).

Beatrice Grimshaw, *White Savage Simon* (Sydney: John Sands, 1919).

Beatrice Grimshaw, *The Valley of Never-Come-Back, and Other Stories* (London: Hurst & Blackett Ltd, 1923).

Beatrice Grimshaw, *Isles of Adventure* (London: Herbert Jenkins Ltd, 1930).

Beatrice Grimshaw, *Mystery of Tumbling Reef* (Boston: Houghton Miflin, 1932).

Murray Groves, "Dancing in Poreporena," *The Journal of the Royal Anthropological Institute of Great Britain and Ireland* 84(1) (1954) 75–90.

Paul Hasluck, *A Time for Building: Australian Administration in Papua New Guinea 1951–1963* (Melbourne: Melbourne University Press, 1976).

Ihab Hassan, "Queries for Postcolonial Studies," *Philosophy and Literature* 22(2) (1998) 328–342.

Peter Hempenstall, "The Neglected Empire: the Superstructure of the Colonial State in German Melanesia," in Sione Latukefu (ed.), *Papua New Guinea: A Century of Colonial Impact* (Port Moresby: National Research Institute and the University of Papua New Guinea, 1989) 133–162.

Vilsoni Hereniko, "Representations of Cultural Identities," in K. R. Howe, Robert C. Kiste, and Brij V. Lal (eds.), *Tides of History: The Pacific Islands in the Twentieth Century* (Honolulu: University of Hawaii Press, 1994) 406–434.

Will Higginbotham, "Blackbirding: Australia's History of Luring, Tricking and Kidnapping Pacific Islanders," *ABC News*, September 17, 2017, https://www.abc.net.au/news/2017-09-17/blackbirding-australias-history-of-kidnapping-pacific-islanders/8860754>.

Alan Howard, "Cultural Paradigms, History and the Search for Identity in Oceania," in Jocelyn Linnekin and Lin Poyer (eds.), *Cultural Identity and Ethnicity in the Pacific Islands* (Honolulu: University of Hawaii Press, 1990) 259–279.

K. R. Howe, *Where the Waves Fall: A New South Seas History from First Settlement to Colonial Rule* (Sydney: George Allen & Unwin, 1984).

K. R. Howe, Robert C. Kiste, and Brij V. Lal (eds.), *Tides of History: The Pacific Islands in the Twentieth Century* (Honolulu: University of Hawaii Press, 1994).

Amirah Inglis, *The White Women's Protection Ordinance: Sexual Anxiety and Politics in Papua* (London: University of Sussex Press, 1975).

R. W. James, *Land Law and Policy of Papua New Guinea* (Port Moresby: Papua New Guinea Law Reform Commission, 1985).

Owen Jessep and John Luluaki, *Principles of Family Law in Papua New Guinea* (Port Moresby: University of Papua New Guinea Press, 1985, 2nd ed., 1994).

Brian Jinks, Peter Biskup, and Hank Nelson (eds.), *Readings in New Guinea History* (Sydney: Angus & Robertson, 1973).

John Kaputin, "Ministerial Policy Statement," *Memo* (1973).

John Kaputin, "The Law—A Colonial Fraud?" *New Guinea* 10(1) (1975) 4–15.

Felix M. Keesing, *Native Peoples of the Pacific World* (New York: Macmillan, 1945).

Robert C. Kiste, "Pre-Colonial Times," in K. R. Howe, Robert C. Kiste, and Brij V. Lal, *Tides of History: The Pacific Islands in the Twentieth Century* (Honolulu: University of Hawaii Press, 1994) 3–28.

Eric L. Kwa, *Development of Administrative Law in Papua New Guinea* (Port Moresby: University of Papua New Guinea, 2000).

Eric L. Kwa, *Constitutional Law of Papua New Guinea* (Sydney: Law Book Co., 2001).

Brij V. Lal, *Broken Waves: A History of the Fiji Islands in the Twentieth Century* (Honolulu: University of Hawaii Press, 1992).

Brij V. Lal and Kate Fortune (eds.), *The Pacific Islands: An Encyclopedia* (Honolulu: University of Hawaii Press, 2000).

Sione Latukefu, *Church and State in Tonga* (Canberra: Australian National University Press, 1974).

Sione Latukefu (ed.), *Papua New Guinea: A Century of Colonial Impact* (Port Moresby: National Research Institute and the University of Papua New Guinea, 1989).

Lewis Lett, *The Papuan Achievement* (Melbourne: Melbourne University Press, 1942).

D. C. Lewis, *The Plantation Dream: Developing British New Guinea and Papua 1884–1942* (Canberra: Journal of Pacific History, 1996).

Yauka Liria, *Bougainville Campaign Diary* (Melbourne: Indra Publishing, 1993).

Ania Loomba, *Colonialism/Postcolonialism*, 3rd ed. (London: Routledge, 2015).

Bronislaw Malinowski, *Argonauts of the Western Pacific* (London: Routledge & Kegan Paul, 1922).

Jack McLaren, *Spear-Eye* (Sydney: States Publishing Co, 1925).

Jack McLaren, *Isle of Escape: A Story of the South Seas* (London: T. Fisher Unwin, 1926).

Jack McLaren, *Sun Man* (London: Ernest Benn, 1928).

Albert Memmi, *The Colonizer and the Colonized* (Boston: Beacon Press, 1957).

Grace Molisa, Nikenike Vurobaravu, and Howard Van Trease, "Vanuatu—Overcoming Pandemonium," *Politics in Melanesia* (Suva: Institute of Pacific Studies, University of the South Pacific, 1982) 83–115.

John Moses, "Imperial German Priorities in New Guinea 1885–1914," in Sione Latukefu (ed.), *Papua New Guinea: A Century of Colonial Impact*

(Port Moresby: National Research Institute and the University of Papua New Guinea, 1989) 163–177.

V. Y. Mudimbe, *The Invention of Africa: Gnosis, Philosophy, and the Order of Knowledge* (Bloomington: Indiana University Press, 1988).

J. H. P. Murray, *The Machinery of Indirect Rule* (Port Moresby: Edward George Baker, Government Printer, 1935).

Bernard Narokobi, *The Melanesian Way* (Port Moresby: Institute of Papua New Guinea Studies, 1980).

Bernard Narokobi, *Life and Leadership in Melanesia* (Port Moresby: Institute of Papua New Guinea Studies, 1983).

The National, "Archbishop Says Generalising All Muslims as Violent Is Wrong and Evil," *The National*, November 6, 2002, http://www.thenational.com.pg/1106/nation4.htm

R. R. Nayacakalou, *Leadership in Fiji* (Oxford: Oxford University Press, 1975).

Hank Nelson, *Papua New Guinea: Black Unity or Black Chaos?* (Melbourne: Penguin Books Australia, 1974).

Hank Nelson, *Taim Bilong Masta: The Australian Involvement with Papua New Guinea* (Sydney: ABC Books, 1982).

Colin Newbury, "The Melanesian Labor Reserve: Some Reflections on Pacific Labor Markets in the Nineteenth Century," *Pacific Studies* 4(1) (1980) 1–25.

Robert Norton, *Race and Politics in Fiji* (Brisbane: University of Queensland Press, 1977).

Michael A. Ntumy (ed.), *South Pacific Islands Legal Systems* (Honolulu: University of Hawaii Press, 1993).

D. P. O'Connell, "The Condominium of the New Hebrides," *British Year Book of International Law* 43 (1968–1969) 71–145.

Douglas Oliver, *The Pacific Islands* (Honolulu: University of Hawaii Press, 3rd ed., 1989).

Douglas Oliver, *Black Islanders: A Personal Perspective of Bougainville 1937–1991* (Melbourne: Hyland House, 1991).

Nigel Oram, *Colonial Town to Melanesian City: Port Moresby 1884–1974* (Canberra: Australian National University Press, 1976).

Lillian Overell, *A Woman's Impression of German New Guinea* (London: The Bodley Head Ltd., 1923).

Abdul Paliwala, Jean Zorn, and Peter Bayne, "Economic Development and the Changing Legal System of Papua New Guinea," *African Law Studies* 16 (1978) 3–79.

Bruce Pascoe, *Dark Emu: Aboriginal Australia and the Birth of Agriculture* (Broome: Magabala Books, 2018).

Fred Phillips, *Freedom in the Caribbean: A Study in Constitutional Change* (New York: Oceana Publications, Inc., 1977).

Fred Phillips, *West Indian Constitutions: Post-Independence Reform* (New York: Oceana Publications, 1985).

Fred Phillips, *Commonwealth Caribbean Constitutional Law* (London: Cavendish, 2002).

Wilfred Powell, *Wandering in a Wild Country: Three Years Amongst the Cannibals of New Britain* (London: S. Low, Marston, Searle & Rivington, 1884).

Guy Powles and Mere Pulea, *Pacific Courts and Legal Systems* (Suva: University of the South Pacific, 1988).

Satendra Prasad (ed.), *Coup and Crisis: Fiji—A Year Later* (North Carlton: Arena Publications, 1988).

Alison Quentin-Baxter, "Sustained Autonomy—An Alternative Political Status for Small Islands?" *Victoria University of Wellington Law Review* 24(1) (1994) 1–18.

Radio Australia, "Religious Freedom Put to the Test," *Pacific Islands Report* (Pacific Islands Development Program, East/West Center), January 30, 2003, http://pidp.eastwestcenter.org/pireport/2003/January/01-30-18.htm.

P. de Renzio and David Kavanamur, "Tradition, Society and Development: Social Capital in Papua New Guinea," *Pacific Economic Bulletin* 14(2) (1999) 37–47.

Jan Roberts, *Voices from a Lost World: Australian Women and Children in Papua New Guinea before the Japanese Invasion* (Sydney: Millennium Books, 1996).

Robert T. Robertson and Akosita Tamanisau, *Fiji: Shattered Coups* (London: Pluto Press, 1988).

Derek Roebuck, D. K. Srivastava, and John Nonggorr, *The Context of Contract in Papua New Guinea* (Port Moresby: University of Papua New Guinea, 1984).

Henry J. Rutz, "Occupying the Headwaters of Tradition: Rhetorical Strategies of Nation Making in Fiji," in Robert J Foster (ed.), *Nation Making: Emergent Identities in Postcolonial Melanesia* (Ann Arbor: University of Michigan Press, 1995) 71–94.

Peter G. Sack (ed.), *Problem of Choice: Land in Papua New Guinea's Future* (Canberra: Australian National University Press, 1974).

Peter G. Sack, *Phantom History: The Rule of Law and the Colonial State, the Case of German New Guinea* (Canberra: Australian National University Press, 2001).

Edward W. Said, *Orientalism* (New York: Vintage Books, 1978).

Christophe Sand, "Melanesian Tribes vs. Polynesian Chiefdoms: Recent Archaeological Assessment of a Classic Model of Sociopolitical Types in Oceania," *Asian Perspectives* 41(2) (2002) 284–296.

Edward L. Schieffelin and Robert Crittenden, *Like People You See in a Dream: First Contact in Six Papuan Societies* (Stanford: Stanford University Press, 1991).

John Sharpham, *Rabuka of Fiji* (Norman Gardens: Central Queensland University Press, 2000).

James Sinclair, *Kiap: Australia's Patrol Officers in Papua New Guinea* (Bathurst: Robert Brown & Associates, 1984).

Deborah Smith, "Eden in the Pacific," *Sydney Morning Herald* (June 21, 2003) 39.

Michael Somare, "Law and the Needs of Papua New Guinea's People," in Jean Zorn and Peter Bayne (eds.), *Lo Bilong Ol Manmeri* (Port Moresby: University of Papua New Guinea, 1974) 14–18.

Gayatri Chakravorty Spivak, "Can the Subaltern Speak?" in Rosalind C. Morris (ed.), *Can the Subaltern Speak? Reflections on the History of an Idea* (New York: Columbia University Press, 2010) 21–78.

Alexander Stille, "The Man Who Remembers," *The New Yorker* (February 15, 1999) 56–69.

Randolph Stow, *Visitants* (London: Secker & Warburg, 1979; Picador edition, 1981).

Ian Stuart, *Port Moresby: Yesterday and Today* (Sydney: Pacific Publications, 1970).

Graham Taylor, *A Kiap's Story* (Hervey Bay: Pukpuk Publishing, 2014).

D. Trubek and M. Galanter, "Scholars in Self-Estrangement: Some Reflections on the Crisis in Law and Development Studies in the United States," *Wisconsin Law Review* 1974(4) (1974) 1062–1102.

John Dademo Waiko, *A Short History of Papua New Guinea* (Oxford: Oxford University Press, 1993).

Elizabeth Webby, "Why Australian Literature?" *Arts: The Journal of the Sydney University Arts Association* 16 (1993): 42–53.

David Weisbrot, "Law and Native Custom in Vanuatu," *Law and Anthropology (Internationales Jahrbuch fur Rechtsanthropologie)* 3 (1988) 103–134.

David Weisbrot, "Integration of Laws in Papua New Guinea: Custom and the Criminal Law in Conflict," in David Weisbrot, Abdul Paliwala, and Aki Sawyerr (eds.), *Law and Social Change in Papua New Guinea* (Oxford: Butterworths, 1982) 59–103.

David Weisbrot, "Custom, Pluralism and Realism in Vanuatu: Legal Development and the Role of Customary Law," *Pacific Studies* 13(1) (1989) 65–97.

E. Gough Whitlam, *The Whitlam Government 1972–1975* (New York: Penguin Books, 1985).

J. L. Whittaker, N. G. Nash, J. R. Hookey, and R. J. Lacey (eds.), *Documents and Readings in New Guinea History: Prehistory to 1889* (Milton: Jacaranda Press, 1975).

John Noble Wilford, "An Early Heartland of Agriculture is Found in New Guinea," *New York Times*, June 24, 2003, A2, https://www.nytimes.com/2003/06/24/science/an-early-heartland-of-agriculture-is-found-in-new-guinea.html.

Trevelyan Wing, "Submerging Paradise: Climate Change in the Pacific Islands," December 28, 2017, http://climate.org/submerging-paradise-climate-change-in-the-pacific-islands/.

Edward P. Wolfers, *Race Relations and Colonial Rule in Papua New Guinea* (Sydney: Australia and New Zealand Book Company, 1975).

Edward P. Wolfers, "Decentralisation: Meaning, Forms, Objectives and Methods," in Peter Larmour and Ropate Qalo (eds.), *Decentralisation in the South Pacific: Local, Provincial and State Government in Twenty Countries* (Suva: University of the South Pacific, 1985) 1–23.

Don Woolford, *Papua New Guinea: Initiation and Independence* (Brisbane: University of Queensland Press, 1976).

World Religion News Service, "Samoan Village Exiling Dozens of Followers of New Religions," *World Religion News Service*, June 19, 2002, http://www.hrwf.net/newhrwf/html/samoa2002.html.

Government Documents

Constitutional Planning Committee, *Final Report Part I* (Port Moresby: Government Printing Office, 1974).

Financial Action Task Force, *Report on Non-Cooperative Countries and Territories* (Paris: Organization for Economic Co-operation and Development, 22 June 2000).

Papua New Guinea Parliamentary Debates, *Hansard*, June 19, 1980, p. 28/2/3.

Territory of Papua, *Annual Report 1937–38* (Melbourne: Government Printer, 1939)

The World Bank, *Papua New Guinea: Improving Governance and Performance* (Washington, DC: The World Bank, 1999).

United Nations Resolution 1654 (XVI), November 27, 1961.

Statutes

Papua and New Guinea Act 1949 (Australia)

White Women's Protection Ordinance 1926 (Papua)

Notes

1. Alexander Stille, "The Man Who Remembers," *New Yorker*, February 15, 1999, 50.
2. *Id.* at 54–55.
3. *Id.* at 61.
4. *Id.* at 60.
5. *Id.*
6. Deborah Smith, "Eden in the Pacific," *Sydney Morning Herald*, June 21, 2003, 39; John Noble Wilford, "An Early Heartland of Agriculture is Found in New Guinea," *New York Times*, June 24, 2003, A2, https://www.nytimes.com/2003/06/24/science/an-early-heartland-of-agriculture-is-found-in-new-guinea.html.
7. Yauka Liria, *Bougainville Campaign Diary* (Melbourne: Indra Publishing, 1993) 41.
8. The South Pacific Forum comprises the independent or associated free states in the Pacific Islands: Cook Islands, Federated States of Micronesia, Fiji, Kiribati, Nauru, Niue, Palau, Papua New Guinea, Marshall Islands,

Samoa, Solomon Islands, Tonga, Tuvalu, and Vanuatu, as well as Australia and New Zealand, the two metropolitan states in the region.

9. Cook Islanders and Niueans also have New Zealand citizenship, and there are about twice as many Cook Islanders resident in New Zealand as in the Cook Islands.
10. Tokelau has triennial elections and has elected its own government and head of state since 1973. However, it is still listed as one of the United Nations General Assembly's seventeen non–self-governing territories. Tokelauans have voted against further self-determination twice, apparently on the basis that the small population limits the possibilities of viable independence.
11. Citizens of the Commonwealth of the Northern Mariana Islands are also U.S. citizens. The Commonwealth relies heavily on its semi-internal status for economic purposes, since it can ship goods to the United States without tariffs or customs duties.
12. Guamanians are U.S. citizens. Guam is still a major military strategic asset, increasing in significance in recent years with China's growing presence in the region and the United States' somewhat fraught relationship with the Philippines.
13. American Samoans are classified as "United States nationals," rather than as full citizens.
14. Tonga remains a Kingdom, with a limited parliamentary process.
15. There was also a Joint Court for high-level criminal offenses, with one French judge, one English judge, and a third supposedly neutral judge. If convicted, the defendant could choose which law to be sentenced under. The local population (ni-Vanuatu) could choose whether they wanted French or English law to apply to them.
16. David Weisbrot, "Law and Native Custom in Vanuatu," *Law and Anthropology (Internationales Jahrbuch fur Rechtsanthropologie)* 3 (1988) 103.
17. D. P. O'Connell, "The Condominium of the New Hebrides," *British Year Book of International Law* 43 (1969) 72.
18. John Dademo Waiko, *A Short History of Papua New Guinea* (Oxford: Oxford University Press, 1993) 9.
19. In Melanesian Pisin, *ol i sindaun level*—or "everyone is at the same level."
20. Robert C. Kiste, "Pre-Colonial Times," in K. R. Howe, Robert C. Kiste, and Brij V. Lal, *Tides of History: The Pacific Islands in the Twentieth Century* (Honolulu: University of Hawaii Press, 1994) 6.
21. Reprinted in Brian Jinks, Peter Biskup, and Hank Nelson (eds.), *Readings in New Guinea History* (Sydney: Angus & Robertson, 1973) 39.
22. *Id.* at 38.

23. Colin Newbury, "The Melanesian Labor Reserve: Some Reflections on Pacific Labor Markets in the Nineteenth Century," *Pacific Studies* 4 (1980) 23.
24. *United Nations Resolution 1654* (XVI), November 27, 1961.
25. *Id.*
26. Paul Hasluck, *A Time for Building: Australian Administration in Papua New Guinea 1951–1963* (Melbourne: Melbourne University Press, 1976) 254.
27. *Id.*
28. Don Aitkin and Edward P. Wolfers, "Australian Attitudes towards the Papua New Guinea Area since World War II," *Australian Outlook* 27 (1973) 206.
29. E. Gough Whitlam, *The Whitlam Government 1972–1975* (New York: Penguin Books, 1985) 93.
30. Randolph Stow, *Visitants* (London: Secker & Warburg, 1979; Picador edition, 1981) 120.
31. Bruce Pascoe, *Dark Emu: Aboriginal Australia and the Birth of Agriculture* (Broome: Magabala Books, 2018) 3–4.
32. *Id.* at 4.
33. *Id.* at 1–3.
34. *Id.* at 4.
35. *Id.* at 5.
36. Edward P. Wolfers, "Decentralisation: Meaning, Forms, Objectives and Methods," in Peter Larmour and Ropate Qalo (eds.), *Decentralisation in the South Pacific: Local, Provincial and State Government in Twenty Countries* (Suva: University of the South Pacific, 1985).
37. K. R. Howe, *Where the Waves Fall: A New South Seas History from First Settlement to Colonial Rule* (Sydney: George Allen & Unwin, 1984) 347–348.
38. *Id.* at 351–352.
39. Eddie Dean and Stan Ritova, *Rabuka: No Other Way* (Sydney: Doubleday, 1988) 36.
40. Henry J. Rutz, "Occupying the Headwaters of Tradition: Rhetorical Strategies of Nation Making in Fiji," in Robert J Foster (ed.), *Nation Making: Emergent Identities in Postcolonial Melanesia* (Ann Arbor: University of Michigan Press, 1995) 78.
41. *Id.* at 85.
42. Sione Latukefu, *Church and State in Tonga* (Canberra: Australian National University Press, 1974) 119.
43. *Id.* at 120–121.
44. Vilsoni Hereniko, "Representations of Cultural Identities," in K. R. Howe,

Robert C. Kiste, and Brij V. Lal (eds.), *Tides of History: The Pacific Islands in the Twentieth Century* (Honolulu: University of Hawaii Press, 1994) 429.

45. Bernard Narokobi, *The Melanesian Way* (Port Moresby: Institute of Papua New Guinea Studies, 1980) 153.
46. *Id.* at 153–154..
47. Radio Australia, "Religious Freedom Put to the Test," *Pacific Islands Report* (Pacific Islands Development Program, East/West Center), January 30, 2003, http://pidp.eastwestcenter.org/pireport/2003/January/01-30-18.htm.
48. The National, "Archbishop Says Generalising All Muslims as Violent Is Wrong and Evil," *The National*, November 6, 2002, http://www.thenational.com.pg/1106/nation4.htm.
49. Bernard Narokobi, *The Melanesian Way* (Port Moresby: Institute of Papua New Guinea Studies, 1980) 154–155.
50. Papua New Guinea Parliamentary Debates, *Hansard*, June 19, 1980, p. 28/2/3.
51. *Id.* at p. 29/2/1.
52. Edward W. Said, *Orientalism* (New York: Vintage Books Edition, 1978) 1–3.
53. Ania Loomba, *Colonialism/Postcolonialism*, 3rd ed. (London: Routledge, 2015) 57.
54. Murray Groves, "Dancing in Poreporena," *The Journal of the Royal Anthropological Institute of Great Britain and Ireland* 84 (1954) 75–90.
55. Territory of Papua, *Annual Report 1937–38.*
56. Albert Memmi, *The Colonizer and the Colonized* (Boston: Beacon Press, 1991) 82.
57. Edward W. Said, *Orientalism* (London: Routledge & Kegan Paul, 1978) 10.
58. Albert Memmi, *The Colonizer and the Colonized* (Boston: Beacon Press, 1991) 91.
59. *Id.* at 98.
60. Albert Maori Kiki, *Kiki: Ten Thousand Years in a Lifetime* (Melbourne: F. W. Cheshire Publishing Pty Ltd, 1968)

2 Custom and Customary Law

Reciprocity, Revenge, and Resolution

In precolonial times, Melanesia was a patchwork of small, homogenous village societies, each consisting of no more than a few hundred people. Membership and status in village society depended primarily on kinship—on having been born or married into a resident clan or lineage—and for the most part, the social order was maintained and expressed through these kinship and quasi-kinship obligations and relations.[1] Apart from chiefs or big men, and excepting the men's house, there were no separate political or legal institutions in Melanesia. No legislatures, courts, or police. Law and custom were the same.[2]

Most villagers relied primarily on gardening for their subsistence, though fishing, hunting, and trading were also prevalent economic pursuits. Most families kept pigs, though they were eaten only on important occasions. The horticultural technology was simple, confined primarily to the digging stick and the hand-hewn axe. Gardens were small, no larger than a woman could till, and families would move from one garden to another every few years, whenever the current plot grew less productive. The primary occupations—gardening, fishing, and hunting—related to food-getting. It was a subsistence economy, in which each household produced little more than the family could use. Members of the community interacted on the basis of relative equality.

Most communities partook of a rich and textured social, religious, and mythic life. Each Melanesian village was a separate and autonomous entity, with its own customs and its own processes for enforcing norms and resolving disputes—in other words, with its own law. Although the political autonomy of villages did not survive colonialism and statehood, Melanesian villagers still expected that they and their neighbors would practice their own customs and adhere to their own values and beliefs.

To an outsider, it might seem that Melanesian societies have a great deal in common. But Melanesians, themselves, experience their communities as exceedingly diverse. The government of Papua New Guinea (PNG) recognizes the existence within its borders of over eight hundred different languages, many of which are spoken by societies of only a few hundred or a few thousand people. Each of these languages signifies the existence of a unique culture, with its own customs, norms, and values—that is to say, with its own customary law. However, there are basic attributes of customary norms and processes that are universal, and to a great extent, those are the aspects of customary law that we will focus on in this chapter.

Customary Legal Processes

The laws and law courts introduced into Papua and New Guinea by the colonial powers were not the only, or even the first, legal norms and processes recognized by Indigenous Papua New Guineans. The village societies of precolonial Melanesia were governed by customary norms and dispute settlement processes that are very different from the legal systems imposed by the colonial powers, but perform the same basic functions of keeping order and protecting life and property.

Because farming, hunting and fishing were full-time pursuits for just about everyone, no one could be spared from the major occupations of gardening, hunting, and fishing. There was no one who worked full time as a priest or soldier or artist, and therefore no separate political or legal institutions. Law, politics and custom were the same. And yet, absent the power of the state that is manifested in constables, courts, and prisons, order was nonetheless maintained; people were convinced to do what they were supposed to do; disputes settled, usually before they erupted into bloodshed or anarchy. What made people generally willing to follow the rules, even when doing so was uncomfortable, an interruption, or even annoying?

The first Western intruders into these simple societies were flummoxed by these questions. They did not see how anyone could be prevented from robbing or killing their neighbors absent the threat of state-sanctioned punishment. Nothing in the background of the adventurers and colonizers inclined them to the cultural relativism that would be required to imagine there might be in these societies totally different, though equally sophisticated, means for maintaining the social order and resolving disagreements. It must be magic, they decided; these untutored and childlike souls held to the straight and narrow out of the fear instilled in them by their primitivistic religion. The natives were, the colonizers decided, completely under the thumb of something they started to call "the iron hand of custom."

In fact, at least three different, informal processes tend to be at work in most societies, all of which effectively ensure that people generally obey the rules: reciprocity, revenge, and resolution. These processes help to regulate behavior everywhere, not only in stateless societies. Even in a society with fully articulated governmental and legal systems, there are many areas of mutual behavior that require rules, and adherence to those rules, but do not have the enforcement power of the state's legal institutions. People must learn to get along together, to settle quarrels, to go along with the majority or the consensus, to follow the rules (whether written or not) in all situations: family, school, work, the local park, the checkout line at the supermarket. And, for the most part, people do, largely because reciprocity, revenge, or resolution, or some combination of them, are everywhere at work. The remainder of this chapter will, however, mostly limit descriptions of these processes to a Papua New Guinean context.

Reciprocity

Loani badly wanted to sleep in that night, but his friend Sao had come by earlier to say it looked like a good night for fishing, so here they were, not long after midnight, five of them, out on the water in Sao's boat. It was a long night, but productive. They came home near dawn with nets full of fish. Before they each stumbled back to their beds for a few hours' sleep, Sao divided much of the catch among the five of them and put aside the rest for other folks in the village.[3]

The people living in the hamlets and villages of pre-independence PNG found themselves in everyday life in a network of intersecting relationships that would last their entire lives. In a small village, everyone knows everyone else and depends on everyone else. And everyone relates to everyone else in a number of different roles: Loani and Sao may be members of the same family, lineage, or clan; they may be cousins, age mates, clan brothers, owner and crew on the same fishing boat, married to women from the same clan, friends, guardians of one another's children, and more. They depend on each other's help in each of these roles. Thus, for example, Sao will provide pigs or shells for the bride price when one of Loani's children is married, not because a court tells him to, but because Loani or Loani's father or uncle or cousin-brother has done the same for him. Loani will help Sao build a canoe and then serve on its crew, not just because the unwritten rules of the village say he should, but because he is expecting that Sao will someday help him to clear the land and burn the bush to put in a new garden. Reciprocity and mutual support are strong motivators in a situation where people expect to interact for at least the foreseeable future, and where their interactions are across a whole array of roles, functions, and relationships.

Reciprocity may be relatively informal, as in the case of Sao and Loani, who probably never talk about the many times in which they have helped one another, at least not in those terms. It is just what they do for each other. Reciprocity may also be formalized; the rituals that culminate in the marriage of a couple, or perhaps continue up to and after the birth of their children, consist primarily of gift exchanges between the spouses' extended families, each family attending a series of feasts prepared by one side for the other. If individuals or families were to fall down on these obligations, they would be subjected to public scorn and ridicule, and worse, to the possibility that all their future attempts to arrange marriages for other family members would fail because no one would trust them to carry through on bride price requirements.

If Sao were asked why he would be willing to give up a whole day to help Loani with the arduous work of clearing the bush for a new garden, he would probably not mention reciprocity. More likely, he would say something along the lines of "it's the right thing to do." Or even, just, "he asked me to." Most people, most of the time, articulate their obligations to family and friends, and to the other groups to which they belong, in these terms.

> In ongoing social life, relationships and interactions between individuals and groups are oriented and guided by the generalized, customary standards current in the society. . . . The very definition of a relationship—the pattern of behavioral interaction, interests, rights, obligations, and affective content, and the extent of tolerable leeways in all these—depends on such accepted standards, more or less clearly understood by the embers of the social unit. These standards carry some degree of moral imperative. . . .[4]

When custom is based on membership in a group and on the expectation that one will give to the group and get from the group in roughly equal measure, and when one adds that group members participate daily in multidimensional face-to-face relationships, custom is a very powerful motivator indeed.

Revenge

Kauba returned home to find his nephew dead, his throat cut, and a bloodstained knife lying beside the body. Kauba recognized the knife. It belonged to Tine, a distant cousin from a neighboring village. He set out immediately for that village, arriving in the early evening; Tine was not at home, and no one in the village had any idea why Kauba was there. Tine's son Hamo invited Kauba to join him in a smoke while they waited for Hamo's father to return. As soon as Hamo's back was turned, Kauba pulled out his bushknife, killed the boy, and immediately ran off home. Tine and all his kin were horrified and enraged; they pledged to seek revenge for the killing. Before a war could break out between the two villages, however, slightly cooler heads prevailed. At the urgent plea of Tine's wife, his father-in-law, a respected big man from Kauba's village, suggested to Kauba that perhaps he might send Tine and his clan a number of pigs, blankets, shells, and some money to compensate them for the loss of one of their own. After some remonstration, Kauba agreed to do so. In response, Tine's clan prepared a feast for Kauba and his clansmen, during which they gave a like number of pigs, other food, hair ornaments, and shells to Kauba and his clan.[5]

The second process that helped to ensure that life and property were respected, both within the village and with neighboring groups, was payback, a Papua New Guinean term for revenge. Men were expected to respond to an insult or physical injury by threats of revenge. The persons responsible for carrying out the revenge included not only the injured party himself, but also other members of his extended family or clan. Similarly, payback can be inflicted upon the person who caused the initial injury—or upon anyone in that person's family, clan, or village. Finally, the form and severity of the payback can be the same as the original injury—or greater.

Although the colonial authorities permitted many Papua New Guinean customs to continue, the authorities made a concerted effort to stamp out payback. It was too directly in conflict with the legal system and political order that the colonizers were attempting to impose, not to mention seemingly unalterably alien to Western customs and values. When payback resulted in the death of an individual, the courts deemed it murder, a violation of the imported Criminal Code, and punished the offenders accordingly. Judges occasionally meted out moderate sentences to Papua New Guineans convicted of crimes, not on the grounds that the offenders were doing the right thing in carrying out their society's legal norms, but on the theory that they were not yet civilized enough to understand and embrace Western law. However, the judges were more likely to be lenient in sentencing when the crime could be construed as a sudden and uncontrollable outburst of passion or as self-defense, rather than as payback. And when payback escalated into a war between villages, the police were called in to stop the fighting and to arrest the participants, who were viewed not as participating in a legitimate political action but, merely, as guilty of crimes such as assault, criminal mischief, riot, or murder.

What the colonizing authorities did not recognize was payback's function as a peacekeeping mechanism, punishing offenders and deterring them and others from further acts of violence. In large-scale societies, these functions are performed by police and prisons. Small, subsistence societies do not have the resources to support institutions whose sole function would be the arrest and detention of offenders. Payback performed that function by punishing offenders; the mere threat of payback helped deter people from committing violent acts and reconcile opponents once those acts had been committed. As Andrew Strathern noted, there were always many more threats of payback than actual acts of payback, because the possibility of payback often convinced the killers, or their kinfolk and wantoks, to look for less painful ways, such as compensation payments, to appease the injured parties.[6]

Because payback involved all of the parties' kin, failure to resolve the conflict through negotiation meant that it might escalate into full-scale tribal warfare. However violent these battles might have seemed, they were fought with spears and arrows that tended not to find their targets and usually ended when one finally did. Chris Ballard recently explained to a correspondent from *The Guardian* the constraints in precolonial social systems that helped to keep tribal fighting from resulting in multiple death tolls: "Nobody was interested in mass death. The cost of having to fork out pigs for compensation for death placed limits on what people were prepared to even envisage."[7]

The key lay in the interaction between reciprocity and revenge. Even the antagonists in a tribal war were probably related in some way, so any murder or property damage, payback, or tribal fight would ultmately require the mutual payment of compensation by each side to the other. "Even in the worst cases of warfare where entire clans were forced off their territory, casualties were pretty minimal and they were almost always fighting men [never women, children, or the elderly]," Ballard continued. "Given dense webs of social connection and strict requirements around paying compensation for deaths, random killings were considered 'truly dumb.'"[8]

Or perhaps the colonizing authorities did indeed recognize payback's role in deterring and sanctioning actions that injured persons and property. Perhaps they realized that payback competed, usually successfully, with the law they were tryng to impose. Perhaps that was among the reasons they tried to get rid of it. One of the courts' repeated criticisms of payback was that it constituted "taking the law into one's own hands." A justification for having a government is its singular ability to protect people and their property by preventing and punishing crimes. The colonizers justified colonialism to themselves by arguing that they could care for the people of PNG better than Papua New Guineans could care for themselves. But, if the people of PNG could and did deter violence and resolve crime themselves, they had no need for colonialism.

Resolution

Nia, Petli's first wife, was furious with Meri, wife number two. Meri's pigs had broken into Nia's garden that morning, eaten just about everything, and trampled what they had not eaten. Although Meri loudly protested her innocence, Nia was sure Meri had let them into her garden on purpose. The shouting match turned physical before their sisters could pull the two women apart. That afternoon, Petli called his kinfolk and neighbors together to see whether this simmering enmity between two of his wives could be settled amicably. People gathered informally, most of them sitting on the ground in front of the men's house, some on the men's house steps. Kids played, people chatted and chewed buai *(betelnut) until Petli's cousin-brother, a* big man, *asked everyone to listen to Nia air her grievances. Nia did not stop at the morning's events. She admitted she had not liked Meri from the day Petli brought her home, but Meri did nothing to ingratiate herself with the older wife. "She sits, sits, sits," Nia said, "while I work, work, work. She doesn't even help fix the old man's meals." Meri spoke next. She had an even longer list of grievances. Meri did not believe Nia's protestations of innocence when two of Meri's best bracelets were ruined or when her* bilum *(stringbag) mysteriously developed a large hole in the bottom or when friends commiserated with her for being barren. After the women had talked, Petli broke in, appealing to his* lain *(his lineage) and his neighbors, "You see how it is. They argue, argue, argue, all day. I just want some peace and quiet." Others in the group spoke up. Some recalled other incidents when the two women fell out, some blaming Nia, some Meri, some suggesting no one was to blame, these things just happen. Others implored them to get along. "You are the senior wife," one said to Nia, "it is your job to welcome the other wives, to be kind to them and to teach them the ways of the household." "You are the young one," another said to Meri, "you should show more respect to Nia." There was much discussion of rights and wrongs, of morality, of the ways of the ancestors. At one point, Nia's cousin and Meri's mother's brother almost got into a shouting match, each defending his* lain. *Petli's brother was not the only big man there, and each of them offered sage advice, as did some of the older women who also related their own tales of the troubles that ensue when new wives join a household. Nia's cousin took advantage of the opportunity to remind Petli that it was his job to keep peace and order in his household, something he had clearly failed to do. And Meri's kin mentioned that Petli could well afford a few more pigs to recompense them for their inconsolable loss of a woman who had worked diligently for their family and was now doing so for Petli. As the talk continued, Nia and Meri began, grudgingly, to agree that perhaps each had been a little hasty in blaming the other for everything that went wrong. And when Petli's cousin-brother summed up the feelings of the community—"Meri, you need to do your share of the work, you should help Nia more; and, Nia, why don't you replace Meri's bracelets and* bilum*? Most of all, you two, forgive and forget; try to get along"—the women, sheepishly, agreed. As a show of their willingness, Meri gave Nia two beautiful blankets, and Nia responded with a string of shell money for Meri. As the sun set, all the villagers enjoyed a* mumu *(a feast) prepared by the families of both women.*[9]

This third process consisted of gatherings of kin, neighbors, or clan members, occasionally of the whole village, to participate in the settlement of disputes between two or more of their members.[10] The typical pattern, when the disputing parties or someone close to them realized that their argument had grown too intense to be resolved privately between them, was for one or another of them to approach village *big men* or elders, who would call a dispute settlement meeting. Word would get around that the meeting was to be held, and by the time the big man was ready to call it to order, just about everyone in the village would be there. Some of them were actually involved with the disputants; others were simply there to be entertained. The elders or big men who had convened the meeting might get it started, but they were not overbearing leaders of the meeting, and they tended not to issue orders, especially not orders that declared one of the parties the unequivocal winner, at the expense of the other party's being viewed as the loser. The aim of a gathering of this kind was not to do that, but instead to try to convince the parties to accept a compromise that would restore good relations between them and bring peace and harmony back to the village or clan.

The achievement of these results usually required an extended course of argument, discussion, the recital by elders or onlookers of community norms (some of which conflicted with each other), the application of no small amount of pressure on both parties, and more discussion and negotiation (about all sorts of topics, eventually bringing up just about every disagreement the disputants had ever had, even those utterly unrelated to the topic of the moot). Eventually, but slowly, if all went well, and only after everyone felt they had been heard, a consensus would take shape, leading to an outcome that everyone at the meeting, especially the original disputing parties, could accept. If this happened, as it usually did, the families or clans of one or both parties would provide everyone with a meal, and gifts would be presented all around.

The ultimate goal of dispute settlement meetings was not to establish right and wrong, not to declare a winner and a loser, but to reestablish peace and harmony in the family and the village.[11] In part, this outcome and, indeed, the entire process were dictated by the limitations placed on the *big men* or others leading the meeting. They could not enforce their orders on parties unwilling to accept those orders because they had neither police nor any other state apparatus at their disposal to back them up. They had only their ability to convince the parties to agree, and that required a combination of the big man's diplomatic and rhetorical skills, the participants' own desire to remain respected and liked members of their community, and the fashioning of a compromise that would sufficiently satisfy each of the parties, so that neither felt he or she was giving up too much or that the other was gaining too much.

The dispute described here happened to involve two women, although public gatherings to discuss disputes between women were rare. Most Papua New Guinean societies, at least on mainland PNG, were (and still are) patriarchal, so disputes between women were often left to fester privately, not considered by the men in the village of enough significance to be worthy of public discussion. Moreover, disputes that might seem to involve a woman as a party (those involving adultery, for example, or rape, or accusations that bride wealth had not been paid) were instead viewed as disputes between the families or lineages of the disputing parties. The dispute between Petli's two wives would probably never have been the subject of a village gathering if Petli himself had not asked for one, and he seems to have done so not to help either wife but to give himself some peace and quiet. Since men were dominant in family and clan, these wrongs were seen as the men's affair, even though they might have been perpetrated by or against women. Similarly, although women attended most dispute settlement gatherings, their voices were often silenced.

Informal dispute settlement gatherings work best within a closed community, where everyone is equally anxious for an outcome that re-

stores harmony and good relations, because everyone has to go on for the foreseeable future interacting with everyone else in the community. For the same reasons, this kind of dispute settlement is at its most effective in resolving personal and family disputes, less so at settling disagreements of a more political nature, such as those between different villages, which have either already, or could at any moment, erupt into the violence of payback and tribal fighting. Intervillage or interclan disputes are most likely to be resolvable when there are some crosscutting ties between the disputing clans and villages—for example, if there has been intermarriage between the villages or if there is trade between them. And, as noted above, the threat of imminent violence is also effective in convincing parties to negotiate their differences, just as the promise of a negotiated settlement and a measure of compensation can convince parties to put the violence aside.

Dispute settlement gatherings vary from one area to another. Our description here is a model that, in its essentials, is practiced just about everywhere in Melanesia, but the details differ from one region to another. In one area, for example, pigs are the proper measure of exchange to cement good relations at the end of a moot; in others, participants would be more likely to exchange fine mats or shells or, these days, money. In some areas, big men play a greater role in facilitating a moot than in others. Some facilitators depend primarily on their powers of persuasion to bring parties around, others are more likely to admonish the participants and to remind them of their traditional duties. In these small differences, people find the bedrock of their customs.

The Rules of Customary Law

Customary norms differ considerably from one part of the country to another, even from one village to the next, but, as with dispute settlement processes, there is an underlying similarity that permits us to describe them in at least general terms.

Marriage and Family

Marriage tends to be a merger not only of a couple, but of their families and clans. As a result, there are many rules about who can marry whom:

some groups prefer intraclan marriages, others forbid them; some groups favor marriages between cousins, especially if the spouse is the child of the mother's brother, other groups require the bride and groom to be from more distantly related clans and families.

There are also many norms about how marriages should come about: some groups prefer that parents or other relatives arrange marriages, some prefer the couple find one another. But overall, the purpose of the rules is the same: to widen the circle of kin, to provide mutual benefits to the families of both partners, to create for everyone a new network of relationships to be called upon in time of need. The ceremonies and other activities thought necessary to validate the marriage also vary with the locality, though all involve the donation of goods (including, these days, money and other Western goods, in addition to the traditional shells, beads, pigs, woven mats, and foodstuffs) by the groom's family to the bride's, and, usually, a reciprocal ceremony, at which the bride's family in turn gives lavish gifts to the family of the groom. The amounts thought proper to be paid, the goods thought appropriate to give and receive, and the people considered to be within the circle of donors and recipients vary from one village or group to another. In some areas, after one or two such ceremonies, everyone considers the couple to be married; in others, a long series of reciprocal gift exchanges will not end until the birth of the first child, or even beyond, and the marriage is considered to still be forming, still able to be called off if either family fails to live up to its bargains.

Whatever the particulars of the exchange process, however, the meaning is the same throughout Melanesia. The initial donation is called bride price or bride wealth, because, in patrilineal societies at least, it is given by the groom's family to the bride's, and is seen as recompensing a family for the loss of a woman whose services will now be lost to her clan and gained by her spouse's clan, and the loss of her future children, who will belong to her husband's clan. Of course, at the very next gathering that involves both families, the bride's clan will give gifts in equal or greater measure to the groom's family, and no one will think this in any way obviates the purpose of the initial gift giving. Instead, this will be viewed as a statement by the bride's family of its willingness to enter into a relationship of mutual exchange, continued reciprocity, and ongoing support with the family of the groom.

The most common problems in marriage, both in traditional PNG and today, involve bride price, adultery, rape, and divorce, and all demonstrate the patriarchal nature of traditional Papua New Guinean values and laws. Failure to pay bride price is deemed an insult not primarily to the bride but to her family, so claims are to be pursued not by her but by her father and his brothers. Similarly, adultery by a woman is considered an affront to the marital rights of the men in the family, most directly, her husband and his relatives who participate in paying bride wealth. Rape, too, is viewed as an affront to a woman's husband and family, and compensation for rape is paid to them, not to the victim.

The major issue in divorce, after the return of the bride price, is custody of the children. Under customary law, children are deemed to belong to the clan as much as, if not more than, they belong to their parents. In a matrilineal society, they belong to their mother's clan; in a patrilineal society, they belong to the clan of their father. If their parents get divorced, the children are expected to remain in the custody of their clan. Since patrilineal societies are far more common than matrilineal societies in PNG, that resulted most often, in the past, in fathers gaining custody of the children, even very young children. Although PNG's marriage statutes tend to recognize most aspects of customary marriage, even including polygamy, an exception was eventually carved out in child custody cases, permitting mothers to gain custody of their young children.

Land

The set of norms defining access to land is another example of customs or rules that are roughly similar in the general outlines of their form and function throughout Melanesia, while, at the same time, differing in many specifics from one region to another. Not all Papua New Guinean societies are patrilineal (meaning, in its simplest terms, that rights over land are handed down from fathers to sons). A few Melanesian societies are matrilineal, which means rights over land are in the names of women, who inherit those rights from their mothers. However, in PNG, even the matrilineal societies are resolutely patriarchal. Although the rights of a lineage or clan to land may be traced through women, it is their brothers who actually determine which family members can use which parts of the family's land.

Because Papua New Guinean societies were traditionally subsistence economies, it was crucial that every family had access at all times to the amount of arable land necessary to feed that family. Family size and family needs varied over time. Moreover, gardens would be used only for so long as they remained productive, usually for no more than a few years; when a garden stopped producing, it was allowed to remain fallow, and the family moved on to other gardens near the village.

These economic realities resulted in a system of land law where, in direct contradiction to the land ownership rules of most Western legal systems, land was owned communally, and the rights of an individual or family to land were not deemed to be permanent. While the clan maintained hegemony over the clan's land in perpetuity or until the clan was defeated in war, those rights were similar to the territorial sovereignty of a state. The rights of a family to the exclusive or shared use or occupancy of a particular parcel of land might have rested on current family members' own prior use of that garden, on oral histories demonstrating that the family's ancestors had claimed and used that land, or on general acquiescence in the village to the family's use of that land at that time. But the single most important factor was the need that a family or individual might have for the land at any given time. Should an individual or family cease to need the land they were occupying or gardening, at least in comparison to others who might have greater need for it, the use and occupation of it might shift to members of the needier family.

Because of the shifting nature of land use, disputes over land arose with some frequency both within and between families, and might not be settled until everyone met in a dispute settlement gathering to discuss and weigh the validity of each party's claim to the land. The participants in the gathering would hear what everyone had to say and then edge the parties toward a solution. The most workable solutions were usually based upon a combination of the rules of land use and inheritance, the relative political and physical power of the two families, and the group's assessment of whose needs were more pressing or opportunities to use other land less available at the time. No settlement was entirely one sided; all the parties got something. Otherwise, it would not have been possible to reach a settlement to which everyone would agree. And a one-sided settlement would have offended the sensibilities of villagers looking always to restore harmony and balance to the village.

Injuries to Persons or Property

The Papua New Guinean approach to theft and personal injury seemed to have been the most difficult area of customary law for colonial authorities to understand or accept. Unlike the English or Australian law that the colonizers were used to, Papua New Guinean customary law did not distinguish between crimes and torts. All wrongs were met with threats of revenge, sometimes with actual acts of revenge, and eventually with compensation. No court was involved, nobody went to prison, and a very tort-like payment was often made. This led the colonial authorities to conclude that Papua New Guineans had no understanding of criminal law, a view that made it easier for the authorities to substitute their own codes and courts for customary law.

Another key difference between the approaches of custom and state law in the colonial period lay in their different perspectives on responsibility for criminal or tortious acts. One of the bedrock values of Western law is the focus on individual responsibility. In custom, however, the emphasis is on collective rights and collective responsibility. Land, for example, was viewed as belonging not to individuals but to the family or clan, and people also viewed personal property, even though it might belong to one person, as available to other family members, or even to others in the village, who might need to use it. Collective responsibility, in the areas of criminal and tort law, meant that a wrong done by a clan member was the shared responsibility of everyone in the clan, just as a wrong done to any clan member was deemed to have been done to everyone in the clan.

This led to incidents that horrified the colonial authorities, such as payback killings of a son or brother or cousin of a murderer. To the colonial magistrate, the son or brother or cousin was an innocent, and the killing of them therefore as much murder, as defined in state law, as the original killing that prompted it. But norms of collective responsibility help maintain order and stability, and even cut down on violence, in customary societies. As soon as a killing or other harm occurred, the kinsmen of the perpetrator, knowing that they would become targets of payback if they did not act quickly, would suggest that compensation be paid. Collective responsibility may indeed have deterred violence when cooler heads in the clan stepped in with suggestions about dispute settlement that prevented simmering quarrels from coming to a full boil.

Are There Customary Rules?

It was fashionable for a time to say that traditional peoples had no rules, because the way that rules could be manipulated, even, it seemed, ignored, by the participants in a moot made it seem to an outsider as if no one took the rules seriously. However, rules do exist and are taken seriously, although, as in Western law, rules are open to different interpretations and applications depending on the circumstances. In the case of Petli's wives, for example, the resolution might have been different had everyone simply agreed that the rule requiring junior wives to show respect for senior wives should be followed strictly and at all costs. But that rule was malleable enough for the village to decide, when Nia and Meri agreed to exchange gifts, that it was being followed. Further, it was not the only rule applicable to the situation. There was also a rule requiring senior wives to welcome and assist new wives. The existence of two norms that may be mutually supportive in some circumstances and openly conflicting in others is not unusual in Melanesian custom or anywhere else without a system of mutually agreed-upon norms, and in this Melanesian societies are no different from any other. Most Melanesians, like most people everywhere, lead their lives according to the norms of their society most of the time. However, if people are to be able to get along, if groups are to be able to depart from the usual way of doing things in order to meet the occasional special needs of some of their members, if societies are to be able to adapt to changing circumstances, then the rules must be malleable. And the rules in every society, the rules governing every group, are flexible; they are subject to differing interpretations so they can operate differently in different situations and solve different problems. Sometimes this can occur because a rule is general enough to cover a number of different circumstances. Sometimes this can occur because there are more rules than one, any of which can be the one that applies to a given problem. Sometimes it occurs because thinking has changed over time. This is as true of statutes and the common law as it is of the norms of Papua New Guinean societies, the unwritten rules governing the behavior of students and teachers in a classroom, the norms of family life, or the constitutions of a club or religious group.

Comparing Custom and State Law

In a large-scale society with separate institutions of government and law, the governmental bodies, including the courts and law enforcement agencies, perform the functions that moots, payback, and reciprocity performed in the small, stateless villages of PNG. Moots, in particular, may be similar, in the most general way, to courtroom proceedings in that both are gatherings intended to resolve disputes and determine the relative rights of parties. But the operation and goals of moots and state courts differ in almost every important respect.

Courts versus Moots

The Impartial Judge versus the Knowledgeable Elder

In a village moot, unlike in a state court, there are no impartial, disinterested judges; instead, there are big men or elders, who often lead the meeting but can hardly be called impartial or disinterested, since they are related to almost all the parties and usually have a strong interest in the outcome. The participants in the moot find the elders' knowledge of the parties an advantage; disputes will be resolved more justly, they believe, when the moot is led by someone who truly understands the participants and the situation. In contrast, the participants in state court proceedings believe that disputes can be fairly resolved only if the trial is presided over by a neutral party who can referee without fear or favor. To ensure judicial neutrality, they insist that judges are not even acquaintances, let alone family or friends, of the parties, and would prefer that the judges be so unversed in the case at hand that all the facts have to painstakingly presented to them.

Participants

In a court, the only participants are the judge and the lawyers. Even the parties to the case are only passive onlookers, unless their lawyers decide to call them as witnesses. No one else can participate in the proceedings, unless called as a witness, and they can be called only if their testimony is germane to the issues. However, in the moot, nearly everyone in the village will participate, not just the elders and the immediate parties, but anyone who cares to speak.

The judge is both above and at the center of trial proceedings: the parties do not talk to one another, each party talks only to the judge. Indeed, at most trials, the parties talk very little if at all; they are represented by lawyers who do most of the talking. The lawyers decide whom to call to the stand to speak, and what those witnesses and parties can say is strictly rationed by the rules of evidence, which require not only that testimony be limited to the narrow issues that are being litigated at this trial, but also that it comply with a number of other rules as well, designed to make sure that only the truth, or something that people can be satisfied is as close to the truth as one can be, is heard in the courtroom.

Evidence versus Understanding

In a court proceeding, the issues are carefully drawn and steadily narrowed; nothing extraneous to the immediate dispute is to be mentioned, and there are voluminous rules about who can do the mentioning. These rules of evidence essentially forbid anyone from testifying to anything except what they did or saw themselves. This narrow definition of the issues and of admissible evidence are intended to ensure that what judge and jury hear are as close to factually accurate as possible. In contrast, in a moot there are essentially no rules about what issues can be discussed and what can be proffered as evidence; the discussion ranges widely over every disagreement the parties and their kin have ever had. Any of the parties or anyone who has happened by, for that matter, can raise any issue or express any opinion they want to, no matter how seemingly unrelated to the matter at hand, and can do so without a shred of formal proof.

There are several reasons for these differences in evidentiary rules. One is the difference in the lack of information that judges, on the one hand, have of the parties and the dispute, contrasted with the wealth of knowledge that a big man or elder will have of everything that has gone on in the clan or village. Elders know the parties and everyone testifying; they also usually have some familiarity with the events at issue. They can rely on this experience to help them determine credibility. Because judges do not know the parties and cannot assess the credibility of the parties and their witnesses from personal experience, judges must rely on a set of rules about what can be said and who can say it, in the hopes that these will produce something that is at least reliable, if not totally accurate.

More often than not, the parties in a court case do not know one another either; they have come together in the courtroom only because of their mutual involvement in a car crash or commercial transaction gone wrong. They will be in one another's orbit only for this case and then probably never have need or reason to interact again. They owe no loyalty to one another, no bonds of family or friendship that might lean them toward telling the truth about one another. There are no assumptions about ongoing relations, and therefore no feeling that they need to preserve some modicum of generosity or respect for one another. In a court, each party will do all they can to win the case, with no regard to the rights, feelings, or needs of the other. Indeed, the rules governing lawyers in a state legal system make it a violation for a lawyer to do anything but zealously and single-mindedly represent the client, no matter how selfish, misguided, or bizarre the client's aims might be. To make up for all of this, the state legal system has developed stringent rules of evidence that are supposed to make it harder for untruths to be told and easier for the judge to sort out which of these two strangers is more likely telling the truth.

Finality versus Flexibility

The final key difference between courts and moots is their different attitudes toward the finality and permanence of their outcomes. In a state legal system, once the court has issued its decision, and the parties have exhausted the orderly series of appeals to higher courts that the law allows them, the court's decision as to that issue is final. The parties can never bring that issue to a formal court again. The outcome of a moot has a very different trajectory. The parties or anyone else with an interest is free to bring up the same dispute over and over, and parties often do. This lack of finality may be a distressing result of the village's lack of enforcement authorities. Equally likely, it may be a reflection of changing political relations. In land cases, for example, as one party's kin gain in numbers and political power, they may decide the time is ripe to press their claims again. While the lack of finality promotes uncertainty, it also provides needed flexibility. As people's need for land changes, their access to land can change as well.

A dispute settlement meeting will end when the parties are ready to accept a solution, and since their acceptance usually requires that each get something of what they wanted, most solutions are compromises. The most successful meetings end with the restoration of good feelings and harmony between the parties, their families, and the village as a whole. Because the dispute has been discussed by everyone in the family, clan, or village, its resolution is not merely what the parties want, or even what the big men or elders who are acting as mediators want; the resolution reflects the entire group's consensus about what is best for all concerned. As a result, everyone involved feels that he or she is responsible for the outcome and will work to support it.

At the end of a trial, the judge or jury delivers a verdict or decision, which is almost never a compromise and is certainly not intended to promote harmony. Most often, it is cast as a zero-sum game, in which one party wins it all and the other loses completely.

Similarities between Courts and Moots

Just about the only similarity, from a lawyer's or judge's perspective, between courts and traditional moots may be the very similar ways in which moots and courts approach the rules. In both state and customary legal systems, the rules are both known to everyone and debated by everyone, forever the same and forever changing, consistent and inconsistent, rigid and flexible. The judge in a state court knows that laws evolve and change, that each can be interpreted a dozen different ways, depending on circumstances, and at the same time, the judge accepts that his or her major responsibility in the courtroom is to apply the laws to the facts, almost as if that rule were forever unchanging and consistent. The participants in a moot understand that the rules are steadfast and binding. Indeed, everyone in attendance, especially elders and big men, continually remind everyone that village norms are sacrosanct, especially if one or both of the parties has arguably transgressed a norm. But the participants, including elders and big men, are willing to bend and reshape the rules in the interest of finding a resolution to the dispute that is fair and acceptable to the parties and that upholds the values of the community. In both cases, the rules are both unbending standards and tools to be manipulated in order for the body to achieve what it considers a just outcome.

Explaining the Differences

The major reason for the differences between moots and courts is that the outcomes that courts are expected to attain are very different from the outcomes that participants in a moot strive to achieve. A court proceeding ends by declaring one party the absolute winner and the other the loser, and in state law, winner takes all. In contrast, a dispute settlement meeting or moot ends when all of the participants have generally agreed on a compromise.

The ultimate goals of the state court system are best met by this winner-take-all approach. While one of the goals of a trial is to end the dispute between the parties, that is not the only goal, and perhaps not even the primary goal. In reaching a decision, and in demonstrating that the decision is based on no interests other than the judge's interest in applying the relevant laws to the parties' dispute, the court satisfies the goal that the government probably considers more important, which is to reinforce the legitimacy and authority of the government by demonstrating that it, and it alone, is capable of protecting persons and property and maintaining order. Every decision by a state (or colonial) court is intended to make that point.

In capitalist countries, the court process also serves the economy. Its criminal divisions do so by protecting persons and their property, but the civil arms of the courts are also key to the smooth workings of the market. At its simplest, a market economy consists of people buying and selling goods and property and entering into service and business agreements with one another. The law provides certainty and predictability. Persons buying a piece of land want to know that the ownership rights they are buying are secure, that no one can come in weeks or months or even years later and claim superior rights to the land; if the seller cannot give that assurance to the buyer, then the land will be much harder to sell and will go for a much lower price. Similarly, persons entering into an agreement to work together over a period of time want assurance that the courts will support their initial understandings of their agreement, so one party cannot suddenly and unilaterally change the rules of the relationship partway through. Courts provide the certainty, predictability, and security that the market requires by demonstrating, every time they decide a case, that there exists a body of laws, that these laws are for the most part unchanging and are available for everyone to know them, that the courts will apply those laws neutrally and disinterestedly to every case that comes before them, and that, once decided, a case about the ownership of land or personal property, or about the working of a contractual agreement, is final and cannot be ignored or overturned.

The court's goals would be impossible to achieve were it not for two factors. First, the parties are, very likely, strangers to one another; each wants to win, and neither usually wants the other to win or cares about the consequences to the other of their losing. Even if the parties know one another, they probably relate only along one vector—as parties to a contract, for example, or as shareholders of a corporation—and have no need or interest to relate to one another again once the trial is over. Second, to make sure that the loser accepts the verdict, judges can rely on the always present threat of the state's power, exemplified in its law enforcement agencies.

The moot's goals would be equally impossible of achievement were it not for the very different circumstances in which it operates. The parties do know one another and do feel a sense of mutual obligation, or at least a sense that bad relations cannot continue because what lies ahead for each of them is a lifetime in which they will continue to see one another, to work together, to rely on one another, and to relate in many ways. These intersecting, reciprocal relationships help to ensure that the parties and their kin, fellow clan members, and neighbors will agree to a consensus outcome.

Negotiation, Mediation, and Adjudication

Court hearings are only one of the methods available in state societies to parties who need to resolve their differences. Parties may choose not to subject themselves to a winner-take-all trial, but instead to try to negotiate or mediate their dispute. It has been suggested that traditional dispute settlement processes may have more in common with these informal methods of dispute resolution than with the highly structured courtroom process.

Negotiation and mediation differ markedly from adjudication. Negotiation consists of direct bargaining between two parties and will succeed only if the parties can find a mutually acceptable compromise.[12] There is no third party who can either help them achieve that end or require them to accept a solution that the third party proposes. Mediation adds a third party, the mediator, who will try to help the parties reach a solution

but who cannot impose a solution on them. Adjudication puts that third party, the judge, at the center of the action; the parties address their arguments to the judge, not to one another, and the judge, not the parties, determines the result. Both parties must accept the judge's decision, even if they disagree with it or believe that it favors one of them over the other.

Traditional dispute settlement gatherings display elements of all three of these and, at the same time, are not entirely like any of them. As in a negotiation, village moots often involve interaction between the parties directly, with both seeking to find a mutually agreeable solution, but moots differ from the purely dyadic model primarily in that other parties freely intervene in the discussion, which is often guided by a big man or clan elder, who acts somewhat as a mediator. However, dispute settlement gatherings do not entirely follow the mediation model either. The big man might suggest a solution, but he is just as likely to be the person reminding the parties of the norms that they have failed to respect, and others in the crowd are as likely as the big man or elder to suggest the resolution that everyone will ultimately accept.

Was It Law or "Only Custom"?

If you define law according to its form rather than its function, and if you believe that the only form in which legal processes can exist are in courts and law enforcement agencies established by the state, and further that the only form in which legal rules can exist are in statutes and regulations that also emanate from the state, then, you are going to decide that the precolonial societies of PNG had no law. However, if you define law according to its function, and if you further believe that the major functions of the law are to make and enforce social rules, maintain order and social cohesion, and resolve disputes, then you will most probably concede that the precolonial societies of PNG had a thriving and effective legal system. This debate, which seems purely academic today, was of great importance to the British and Australian colonizers of PNG because the answer to it would be crucial in deciding whether the colonial regime would recognize and support custom or supplant it with imported laws and courts.

The early colonizers of Papua and New Guinea were legal positivists, which is to say they firmly believed that law exists in form not function, and, equally important, that the only law and processes are those made, maintained, and enforced by the state. Added to that was their unshakable belief that Papua New Guineans were too primitive, too perpetually childlike, and above all too savage to have anything as sophisticated as a legal system. A few of the early officials and missionaries in British New Guinea, such as the two special administrators during the protectorate (1884–1888), Peter Scratchley and John Douglas, as well as Rev. James Chalmers, a longtime missionary in British New Guinea, did argue that custom, not English laws, should govern New Guineans. However, that view was not intended as praise either of custom or of New Guineans, both of which they viewed as primitive, even savage. They favored custom because they believed Papua New Guineans incapable of anything better. Hubert Murray, who served as lieutenant-governor and chief judicial officer of the Territory of Papua from 1908 until 1940, and who also argued that Papua New Guineans should be left for the most part to govern themselves by their own customary rules, believed both that custom was not law and that many of the customs he encountered were "cruel and revolting in the extreme"[13] and "hard to reconcile with any degree of sanity."[14]

A Sidebar on Theories of Conquest and Discovery

From the fourteenth century, when the earliest merchant adventurers set sail from European shores, the goals of their voyages were the extension of the power, wealth, and sovereignty of the European nations. Politicians and scholars were already debating what should be done about the native peoples unfortunate enough to find themselves in the path of European colonial expansion. The earliest international law doctrine to win acceptance among the European sovereigns, and one that persisted well into the nineteenth century, held that a conquering nation had the right to annex any territory it had acquired by conquest, but must, to the extent possible, respect and uphold the laws of the conquered people. For example, Justice William Blackstone, the preeminent British jurist, took the position that American colonies were conquered or ceded countries, and concluded:

> Our American Plantations are principally of this later sort [i.e., ceded or conquered countries], being obtained in the last century either

> by right of conquest and driving out the natives, (with what natural justice I shall not at present inquire,) or by treaties. And, therefore, the common law of England, as such, has no allowance or authority there; they being no part of the mother country, but distinct, though dependent dominions.[15]

However, the situation was very different when explorers found uninhabited lands, particularly if those lands were then settled by Europeans. When this occurred, then it was considered that the laws they brought with them, the laws of their home country, were immediately in force. The British put it most quaintly: "the common law is the birthright of every subject, carried with him wherever he goes."[16] This "doctrine of discovery" served the European powers well; it was quickly expanded to include not only lands that were totally unoccupied, but also areas of vacant land within an otherwise occupied territory. Under the doctrine of discovery, these lands could be claimed as their own by the European settlers, without having to pay compensation to possible Indigenous owners of the land. Often, of course, lands that Europeans claimed in this fashion only looked vacant or unclaimed to the encroaching Europeans, who were used to the cities, towns, and intensive agriculture of the European countryside, but they might indeed be inhabited. For example, these might be gardens lying fallow between plantings or land used for hunting or religious purposes.

Another interpretation of the discovery rule permitted European colonizers to deem as uninhabited, and therefore available for European settlement and the imposition of European law, any land occupied by people who were not Christians or who were not civilized (whatever that term might mean). It was presumed that such people had no real concept of law or of the ownership of land, and therefore, it was a service to bring them both in the form of European law.

In the early nineteenth century, Justice John Marshall, the American jurist, did not want to deprive the Native American nations of their last vestiges of political and legal autonomy, or of the right to possess and control such of their lands as were left to them. And he was equally loath to concede that the British and, after them, the Americans had conquered the Native American tribes, or that Native Americans were a soulless people whose lands could be declared uninhabited. Nor, however, did he want to require the return to Indigenous peoples of the vast tracts of land already held by generations of white settlers, indeed already developed into cities, towns, farms and industry. Beginning with his landmark decision in *Johnson v. M'Intosh*, Marshall resolved this dilemma through a compromise that modified the theory of discovery so that, in his formulation, it now provided that native peoples, while no longer fully sovereign nations, did have a measure of sovereignty that permitted them to retain their own laws until such time as Congress might act to repeal or override them. He similarly upheld their right to continue in possession of their lands but circumscribed that right by holding that the federal government could end that at its own choosing.

Later American courts declined to follow Marshall's lead,[17] and his respect for the laws and customs of the Indigenous people, however limited, was ignored in Australia, at least within its own borders, until the *Mabo* decision in 1992. The Australian state treated the Aboriginal peoples of Australia essentially as a non-people, imposing Australian law upon them and annexing their land at will. It was not a surprise that, except in matters involving land, the official stance of the Australian colonial office was to presume that the Australian common law and statutes imported into the territory were the only laws available in Papua and New Guinea and applicable to everyone, settler and native alike.

Positivism and Discovery Theory

There were two reasons, according to colonial authorities, why the colonial administration had to import laws and a legal system into PNG and could not simply permit Indigenous communities to apply their own customs. First, no one in the colonial government believed that custom was law. Second, they believed custom was un-Christian, unwholesome, and immoral. Imposing Anglo-Australian laws, courts, and jails in PNG therefore represented not only an easier and more accessible way to govern the territories, but it was also a moral imperative. In his 1930 report to the colonial office, Ralph T. Gore, an Australian jurist who became a judge in PNG's colonial courts, summarizes these views:

> The assumption of rule [by Australia] in Papua found a rudimental people. So backward were they in communal arrangement that [there did not even] exist the primitive law-giver to regulate the punishment

> for crime. . . . The matter of redress for wrong was left to the inclination of the individuals who had suffered and the punishment or satisfaction varied with the power, the will, or the opportunity of the sufferer or his adherents. No particular regard was paid to the object of punishment, very often an innocent person suffering for the crimes of another, the latter thereupon becoming free from molestation. . . . It cannot be said that there existed any generally accepted idea as to the degree of punishment except that death was the prevailing form. There being no semblance of a legal system to serve as a foundation, [the colonial] Government was not faced with the problem of choice, and the only hope for posterity was the establishment [by the colonial authorities] of a legal system of civilization to the exclusion of all else.[18]

The colonial authorities were not alone in believing that Papua New Guineans and other small, stateless societies had no legal system. Not only was that view shared by the colonizers of most European nations, but most anthropologists also agreed. In true Hobbesian fashion, they presumed that no one would comply with the norms, at least not with those that required them to make an effort or to forego something they wanted, unless they feared a punishment for noncompliance more than they disliked the burden of compliance. Unable to understand how, absent fear of the police and prisons of an overwhelmingly powerful state, a group of people could agree to obey the norms (well, most of them, at least most of the time) and settle their differences without bloodshed (well, most of them, again, at least most of the time), the earliest anthropologists presumed that it was primitive religion, and the fear of sorcery and magic that it instigated in the primitive mind, that kept the members of stateless societies in check.

It was not until the 1940s that anthropology began to recognize that law is more accurately described by the functions it performs than by the form it takes, and to entertain the notion that the dispute settlement mechanisms of stateless societies deserve to be called law. Among the first were Karl Llewellyn and E. Adamson Hoebel, not coincidentally a lawyer and an anthropologist, who jointly studied the Cheyenne, a Native American nomadic, semi-pastoral people, and other Native American tribes who had up until then been assumed by the invading U.S. forces to be without a legal system. Llewellyn and Hoebel pointed out that the Cheyenne had a very sophisticated system of customary norms and dispute settlement processes, which made each tribe able to resolve disputes and punish offenders.[19] Llewellyn and Hoebel were quickly joined by other anthropologists reporting on the numerous methods traditional, stateless societies have found for maintaining order and resolving disputes, including Inuit singing duels, Blackfoot horse raids, Jibaro head-hunting, Albanian blood feuds, and negotiations in Mexican market towns.[20]

Those initial studies focused primarily on dispute settlement processes, which are probably the most evident examples of custom performing a legal function. It was left to later studies to turn their attention to the daily lives of traditional peoples, when disputes were not occurring, and to uncover the forces that make most people comply with the norms of their group most of the time. Simon Roberts described the interwoven network of kinship responsibilities, reciprocity and exchange, and morality that impel people to do what is expected of them, even when they might not want to.[21] Sally Falk Moore brought these insights home to the United States, analyzing communities and groups (such as schools, churches, scouting troops, sororities, labor unions—even families and groups of friends) within state societies. She noted that these groups also have rules and that, although the rules are not enforced by the state, its courts, it police or prisons, nonetheless, the members of these groups—just like Pacific Islanders—obey most of the rules most of the time. And, like Pacific Islanders, they do so out of a mixture of group loyalty, reciprocity, and the desire to be (or to be seen as) a good and moral person.[22]

Custom in the Colonial Courts

For much of the colonial period, the imported courts were used primarily by the colonizers themselves as forums in which to settle their own disputes. Melanesians seldom came before the courts, and then, usually, as criminal defendants. When Indigenous people had disputes among themselves, they tended to settle them in the village using customary norms and processes. Colonialism created the crudest forms of legal pluralism. Most colonial administrations in the Pacific brought with them only those parts of their home legal system they believed would help them govern the natives.

Indigenous legal systems did not disappear, although they were deeply affected by colonialism and its aftermath. In theory and on the books, the statutes and regulations of the imposed legal system constituted the only official law of the colony, but the colonial administration, and especially its court system, was severely understaffed for most of the colonial period, As a result, the only contact most villagers had with the regime was the occasional visit of a patrol officer (called, in local parlance, a *kiap*). Travel in the country's mountainous interior was difficult and time consuming: there were few roads, so *kiaps*, together with their Indigenous bearers and police, traveled by foot through wild terrain. They had the time to visit most villages in their districts no more than once or twice a year for a few days at a time.

Except when the *kiap* was actually present, villagers continued to make use of their own customary law. Unable to provide an effective substitute for this continuing self-rule, the colonial administration allowed villagers to continue to organize their affairs according to customary law, so long as customary norms or processes did not overtly threaten the authority or aims of the colonial enterprise. The administration did not perceive any threat to its authority when Papua New Guineans regulated their social relations in regard to personal matters such as marriage, divorce, and family law, and even in regard to non-violent disputes that were solely between villagers, such as those pertaining to customary land. When it came to offenses under the Criminal Code, however, or to claims to customary land by non–Papua New Guineans, the colonial authorities stepped in whenever they could, usually applying the codes and statutes introduced into the colony from Australia rather than Indigenous customs, usages, or process.

Once a Papua New Guinean was brought into a colonial court, the case was governed by the laws imported from Australia. Further, colonial judges imported more than the common law. They also brought with them their jurisprudence and their way of approaching legal questions. That way was overwhelmingly positivist, which is to say that they believed that the only true law is a product of the state—of its legislators or judges—and that this law is best taken at face value, read and applied literally, regardless of the policies underlying its enactment or the problems it was intended to solve, or whether a literal reading helps it perform its task effectively.

Positivism was a good fit with the colonial endeavor because it produced judges who basically agreed with the goals of the colonial enterprise. Like the colonial administrators, the judges were certain that custom, since it did not arise from the state, was not law, and could, for all intents and purposes, be ignored. Indeed, they believed that an important part of the colonial mission was to civilize the peoples of PNG by weaning them from custom and acquainting them with the benefits of the British common law. This they did by occasionally referring to custom, not as an equal (or even unequal) and competing source of law, but as the dark past (and present) from whose toils the colonial courts would help Papua New Guineans escape.

The judges and magistrates believed custom to be not only different from, but also vastly inferior to, the common law. Papua New Guineans might eventually develop the sophistication necessary to know and follow the imported laws. Until that happened, however, it would be unjust to hold Melanesians to the standards set by the imported legal system. Rural Papua New Guineans, who had not had much contact with missionaries or schools, could plead custom as a defense in criminal trials, or at least as a reason for a lesser sentence, but educated Melanesians could not.

Customary Law in the Colonial Era

Colonialism ended the autonomy of village societies, putting several layers of government and administration above them, and making the imported laws and courts dominant over village custom. Customary law was affected by the colonial political and legal system in many ways, in particular:

(a) by colonial rules that limited its impact or outlawed significant aspects of it;

(b) by its relegation to second-class status within the overall colonial and postcolonial legal system, in that it became the municipal law of villages within a larger political system, rather than the highest law of sovereign political entities;

(c) by limiting its jurisdiction to only certain kinds of parties and certain kinds of disputes;

(d) by the existence of an alternative legal system (the state-imposed system) to which people could turn if not satisfied with custom; and

(e) by the example of that state legal system, upon which customary norms and customary dispute settlement processes began to model themselves.

But none of this entirely put an end to the functioning of customary legal processes in practice nor to the reliance of Papua New Guineans on customary norms. In fact, during much of the colonial period, at least into the early 1960s, the state legal system seldom imposed itself on local people. Most Papua New Guineans, most of the time, continued to settle their disputes in customary forums and to manage their lives according to the rules and relationships of custom. For the most part, if Papua New Guineans found themselves in state courts at all, it was only because they had done something that had come to the attention of the colonial authorities and that allegedly constituted a crime under state law, or because their actions had in some way directly impacted the interests of white settlers, such as an attempt to reclaim land that was now deemed to be owned by the colonial administration or by European settlers. The continuation of custom was not something that the colonial authorities overtly supported; it happened primarily because the colonial administration never had enough officers to effectively rule the large, and largely unexplored, territory, making it impossible to impose state law everywhere.

Custom, *Kiaps*, and the Native Regulations

The first brushes that most Papua New Guineans had with the state legal system were not in the courts, but through the patrols that the colonial administration regularly sent out to villages throughout the colony. There tended to be only one *kiap* on a patrol, but he was accompanied by a dozen or more bearers and constabulary, all of whom were native to PNG but recruited from districts other than the one they were patrolling. In the less accessible parts of the colony, the patrol officer and his *polis* were the only connection with the colonial authorities that most people ever had.

Kiaps were for the most part young men recruited from Australia. By the 1960s, the colonial office had begun to offer somewhat more extensive training for *kiaps,* that included some attempts at teaching cultural sensitivity, but even then, most received only a cursory introduction to their jobs before being tossed into this very foreign environment, where they found themselves asked not just to take a census or make sure the village common areas had been cleared of brush, but also to adjudicate local disputes and enforce the Native Regulations and the Criminal Code.

The advent of the *kiaps* was the first addition of a layer of law and government on top of the village itself. People who were dissatisfied with the results of a village dispute settlement gathering could bring their disputes to the *kiap* hoping an airing in this different environment would produce an outcome they preferred. Since the *kiaps* knew little of custom and would probably not have believed they should enforce it even if they did learn its rules, they tended to settle the disputes that were brought to them by means of their own rough and ready idea of common sense. There are no records on whether people actually complied with the *kiap*'s off-the-cuff decisions once he and his policemen had left the village, but the process must have been useful to some, because patrol officers continued in their official reports and memoirs throughout the colonial period to describe it being used.

The *kiap*'s word was, supposedly, law in the village. One purpose of the native police, as they were then called, who traveled with him was protection, but another was enforcement. *Kiaps* had the authority to arrest people they found to have committed offenses and bring them back to district headquarters for trial. Although *kiaps* were charged with enforcing the Criminal Code, the legislation that had the most impact on the lives of Papuans and New Guineans during the colonial period was not the Criminal Code but the Native Regulations.[23] Unlike the Criminal Code, these regulations governed only Papuans and New Guineans and were designed especially to control every aspect of their daily lives and to punish customary practices that were offensive to Europeans. The Native Regulations had something to say about nearly every aspect of the lives of Papua New Guineans, from marriage and divorce to inheritance and intestate distribution to the upkeep and cleanliness of the village. Until the mid-1960s, the regulations were ostensibly enforced by government bodies called Courts for Native Matters in Papua and Courts for Native Affairs in

New Guinea.[24] However, these courts were staffed by district officers and patrol officers, could meet anywhere, and were not bound by the rules of evidence. In other words, the *kiap*, on his own in the village (except for his phalanx of police), was the court. In fact, he was every member of the court: prosecutor, judge, and enforcement authority. There was only one role he did not fill: defense attorney. Although appeals from the *kiap*'s decisions theoretically could be taken to the supreme courts of the two territories, in practice this was rarely done.

Modernization Theory and the Movement to Supplant Custom with State Law

In the 1960s, a new international law doctrine emerged, supplanting conquest and discovery theories, and recasting the relationship of colonial powers to their subject peoples and to customary legal systems. Although the new doctrine, termed Modernization or Law and Development theory by its proponents, purported to be grounded in economics, it was the brainchild of lawyers and law professors, primarily from the United States, who set out into the developing world, especially to the colonies and emerging nations of Africa, determined to take the side of the colonized peoples against their colonial oppressors.[25] However, the result of their do-goodism was a denigration of custom as thorough as any their colonial adversaries could have envisioned.

Modernization theorists started from the premise that, once the colonies had achieved independence, the new states would not succeed politically unless they also succeeded economically, which meant modernizing their economies to compete on roughly even terms with those of the developed world, and could take advantage of the goods, services, and investment that the developed world had to offer. This, the Modernization theorists opined, meant the adoption of market economies similar to those in the United States, Europe, and Australia. And this required that custom be abandoned because everything about it supposedly stood in the way of the development of a market economy. Custom favors community, sharing, and reciprocity. Capitalism is based on individualism, self-interest and contract. At its core is the notion that the market will function fairly and efficiently only when individuals bargain out of rational self-interest. Customary law provides for rights to land and other crucial economic matters to be reopened whenever circumstances or needs change; the market economy depends on security of title: no one will willingly purchase property that they think can be taken away from them. Customary law is flexible; the rules themselves embrace change and accommodation. The market economy requires certainty. For two self-interested individuals to enter into an agreement, when neither can or will trust the other, both must trust that the rules that governed the transaction when they began will stay the same and will continue to govern their transaction as time goes on.

Modernization theory was a 1960s liberal approach to customary law. Its presumption that Indigenous peoples could, and would, attain independence and master the world economy stood in sharp contrast to earlier approaches. However, it was not as different as it first might appear. Modernization theory found a ready welcome in the PNG colonial establishment. The United Nations Trusteeship Council was already calling for the Australian government to set a timetable for an almost immediate independence for PNG. Modernization theory provided the colonial authorities with an aura of concern for the native population while, at the same time, giving them an excellent excuse for delay. It was Australia's duty, the colonial argument went, to continue to govern PNG until the natives were ready to govern themselves and to compete successfully in the economic sphere with the rest of the world, and that would happen only when their government, legal system, culture, and economy had all been modernized. And, by modernization, colonial administrators meant, as did the Modernization theorists, a government and legal system virtually identical to those of Australia. But for Papua New Guineans to become like Australians, the colonial administration predicted, would take many more generations, given the current state of almost total backwardness of PNG's customs and people. Indeed, though they only occasionally said it expressly, most colonial administrators and judges believed that independence could never happen because they could not imagine the local population, whom they saw as simple, childlike, even savage, ever attaining the sophistication and complexity with which they credited Australians.

The Derham Report: Declaring the Death of Custom

By the 1960s, the Australian colonial authorities had made contact with almost all the peoples of both Papua and New Guinea and had almost enough personnel and other resources to consider imposing direct rule throughout the territories. That put the administration in the position where it could actually implement Modernization theory by actively imposing colonial law on all Papua New Guineans and requiring that all disputes be settled in the colonial courts, rather than in informal customary gatherings or by customary means.

If there were any disputes in the colonial office or administration in the 1960s about the future of the legal system in PNG, they were not about whether to permit customary law to continue to play a major role. Had this even been proposed, it would not have been taken seriously. Instead, the dispute, if there was any, was over whether to continue for the foreseeable future to treat Papua New Guineans as guileless children and savages, as people essentially too unsophisticated to use any legal system, including that which the Australians had imported into the territories, or to begin to prepare PNG for self-government and independence, which would include applying the strictures of the imported legal system to them with no mitigation.

In 1960, the colonial office took its first, small steps toward the eventual goal of self-government and independence. It hired a consultant, the Australian constitutional law professor Sir David Derham, to advise on changes to the colonial courts and legal system in order to provide more access to Indigenous Papua New Guineans. Derham had practically no experience in or prior knowledge of colonial or customary law in general, or PNG in particular. But he was highly regarded in Australian legal circles and was probably hired more for his eminence than for his expertise.

Reforms to the imposed legal system could have gone in a number of directions. There were a few who hoped Derham would propose integrating customary law, but Derham held no brief for custom. Like the Modernization theorists, he viewed custom as nothing but a barrier to development. As Shaun Larcom phrases it: "He . . . argued that custom had no answers to the problems arising from changing methods of agriculture, commerce, and personal relations in urban environments."[26] Like the Modernization theorists, Derham believed that custom impedes economic and political development, while the introduced legal system enables it. Again, according to Larcom:

> Derham freely admitted that he was engaging in "social engineering". He saw the state criminal law as a tool to transform the economic and social structure of Papua New Guinea and called for an end to the policy of interfering as little as possible in the life of the indigenous communities. . . . He saw the courts, at all levels, as one of the institutions that would develop Papua New Guinea and enable self-government. This meant that the old colonial systems needed to be dismantled and replaced with modern ones. Derham recommended the end of legal bifurcation between the indigenous and European populations. He concluded that Papua New Guinea needed a Western justice system for all Papua New Guineans and recommended that indigenous magistrates and judges should serve in the Local and District Courts respectively.[27]

Derham was recommending the destruction of Papua New Guinean custom and culture, but unlike the more draconian of the colonial administrators, he, like the Modernization theorists, saw himself as on the side of the Papua New Guineans; he was doing it for their own good.

The Native Customs Recognition Ordinance: More Ordinance Than Recognition

The colonial office responded to the Derham report by abolishing the old Courts for Native Matters (Papua) and Courts of Native Affairs (New Guinea), and creating instead a unified court system. At the bottom-most rung, the local courts would be staffed by magistrates, who, it was envisioned, would be closer to the people and would hear many cases brought by and against Papua New Guineans. Little attempt was made, however, to staff any of the courts with Papua New Guineans, an endeavor that would have been difficult, even if the administration had an interest in doing it, since there was no university or law school in PNG at the time. Indeed, there was little public education at all, and though some of the relatively few Papua New Guineans who had managed to be educated up to high school level in the missionary schools then went to Australia or overseas for higher education, none would be directed into the study of law until the late 1960s and early 1970s.

It was assumed, in keeping with Derham's strictures, that even in the lowest level courts, the law to be applied would be primarily the imported law. The administration did accept that there would have to be some room made for the state courts to give a nod to custom, especially when dealing with natives from areas still so untouched by colonial rule that people could not be expected to have a notion of what the imported rules might require. To meet this need, the *Native Customs (Recognition) Ordinance of 1963* was enacted. It represented, in some respects, a break with Derham's proposals, in that the ordinance at least envisioned that the colonial courts would occasionally use custom, but it severely limited that use, providing at section 2 that custom included only those traditions that had been held by Indigenous Papua New Guineans "since time immemorial" and that custom could be applied in criminal cases essentially only to mitigate sentences and in civil cases only when both parties were native-born Papua New Guineans.[28]

In permitting custom to be pleaded even in limited instances, the ordinance might also be viewed, in some respects, as a step beyond positivism. For example, the ordinance permitted the courts to use custom in both criminal and civil matters, but in very limited ways.[29] However, in significant ways, it still embodied colonial attitudes denigrating custom. The ordinance provided that the courts could apply custom only in personal matters, such as customary land rights, customary marriages and divorce, and custody and guardianship of the children of customary marriages.

In criminal cases, a colonial court could not decide that a wrong under customary law was a crime; the only crimes that courts were permitted to recognize were those in the Criminal Code. The formal courts were authorized to use custom in criminal matters only to judge the reasonableness of a criminal defendant's actions or beliefs, to ascertain a criminal defendant's state of mind, and to determine criminal penalties.[30]

The ordinance further demonstrated the suspicion in which its drafters held custom by stipulating that, even in circumstances where the ordinance might otherwise permit custom to apply, the courts should not apply custom if it would result "in injustice or would not be in the public interest" or if it was "repugnant to the general principles of humanity."[31] These are not limitations that one would ever see placed upon the imported legal system. With nothing to define either of these clauses, the judges tended to interpret them according to the their own values and beliefs, so the ordinance that seemed to support custom instead became just another way in which Papua New Guineans could be judged and found wanting according to a moral system entirely foreign to them.

Positivism is grounded in the view that a norm or rule is a law only if it emanates from the state, and the ultimate proof that the Native Customs Recognition Ordinance was not at odds with positivist theories lay in its express decree that custom was not to be viewed as law. Instead, custom was treated as an issue of fact: it was to be introduced into evidence and tested for its relevance and credibility, just like any other fact that one or the other of the parties to a case might want to prove. This crucial difference from the way that the imported law would be treated had two major consequences. First, it meant that the judiciary was essentially absolved from having to determine in any case whether there was an applicable rule of custom; instead, the judge could wait upon counsel, and if they failed to mention custom, then the judge could ignore its possible existence. Second, the ordinance made it clear to one and all that, in the eyes of the state, custom, unlike the imported law contained in ordinances and judicial writings, was inferior; it was not real law.

From Colonialism to Postcolonialism— Dependency Theory

As early as the 1960s, when the colonial authorities were grudgingly preparing for some small degree of Papua New Guinean integration into the state legal system, as part of what the colonizers expected to be an exceedingly gradual ascent by Papua New Guineans toward national self-reliance and independence, there were already Indigenous movements within PNG calling for a much faster process, and for custom and the traditional values of PNG to continue to play a major role both during the colonial period and beyond. The movement had some degree of early success, especially in preserving customary land ownership rules.

At about the same time as the court structure was being reformed in the Derham model, colonial authorities had also brought forth proposed new legislation that would, for all intents and purposes, abolish customary land tenure, replacing it with a form of fee simple ownership and recorded titles like that in England and Australia. Papua New Guineans, the colonial authorities promised, would not lose their land under the new legislation; quite the contrary, they would gain more security of title. However, Papua New Guineans and their allies pushed back. In addition to preferring the communitarian nature of customary land tenure over the individualism inherent in the Western model, they recognized that, once landholding was in the Western format, its very security would make it utterly insecure for Papua New Guineans, because it would become marketable. It would be available for sale to whichever buyers presented themselves and a little cash, and thus would quickly become permanent alienated from its customary owners. The opposition forces managed to defeat the land bills. However, although the battle over land rights was won, the war for general recognition of custom as the primary law of Papua New Guinea would still be lost.

By the early 1970s, when the Australian government had joined forces with the Indigenous independence movement to push for immediate self-government, to be followed by independence within just a few years, it seemed entirely possible to some that the independent state of PNG would be able to retain many pieces of custom and customary law. Especially in the years from 1972, when, to the surprise of the Australian colonial office, the Indigenous-led Pangu party captured control of the first self-governing House of Assembly, to independence in 1975, a number of examples of custom-flavored and custom-oriented legislation were enacted, including the *Sorcery Act of 1971* (which overturned the colonial notion that anyone who believes in sorcery is by definition irrational), several land acts (which reinforced customary land tenure by making the local group, not individuals, the owners of customary land), the *Inter-Group Fighting Act of 1977* (which tried to assign group responsibility and group penalties to villages engaging in tribal warfare), the *Village Courts Act* (which created a system of trial level courts for Papua New Guineans that would apply customary law), and even the constitution itself, which stipulated in Schedule 2 that PNG's homegrown common law (called the underlying law, to differentiate it from its English model) would be largely and primarily based in custom.

However, the Modernization theorists had been correct about one thing. Customary law was not going to become the primary law of an independent PNG. Indeed, it would play only a minor role at best in the development of the legal system of postcolonial PNG. Custom would be in large part relegated, as it had been throughout most of the colonial era, to acting as the personal law for rural villagers when the state courts were felt to be too distant, either in actual miles or in their emotional distance from the problem at hand. The formal courts, for their part, continued to apply the (renamed but not significantly recast) *Customs Recognition Act*, and to ignore the constitution's attempt to have custom embroidered into the underlying law. And most Papua New Guineans, if asked, would probably opine that this is how it should be; after all, that's what they have been told, over and over.

Although Modernization theory was accurate in predicting that customary law would not be paramount, its reasons for the prediction had proven incorrect even as the theory was being spun. Customary law is not the major barrier to economic development that the Modernization theorists had opined; the major barrier to development is the market itself, at least as it operates between the former colonial powers and the postcolonial nations that become their subsidiaries. As the Latin American economist and Dependency theorist Andre Gunder Frank describes it, the continued economic success of already-developed nations depends upon the continuing underdevelopment of their former colonies.[32] The developed economies are producers of goods, money, and services, and they require two things: raw materials to turn into finished products and a market into which to sell those products. The former colonies are kept in a continuing state of economic dependence so that they will provide both: they are the source of cheap raw materials, and, because they cannot produce sufficiently inexpensive finished products on their own, their governments and people must purchase the goods that the global corporations produce. As a result, the former colonies are always on the losing end: they provide cheap labor and sell their raw materials cheaply, and then they have to buy the finished products, made from those very same raw materials, at higher prices.

The winners in this cycle are the producing nations; they buy cheaply and sell globally. And that is the one role that the former colonies can never hope to have, because they cannot compete with the metropolis in the size of the markets into which they would sell their goods or the price at which they can produce them. Attempts to set up factories in the former colonies have almost universally met with failure, because the domestic market cannot be large enough to undercut the prices of imported goods. The continuing economic dependence of the former colonies requires that they maintain a postcolonial legal system and political structure. The metropolitan nations require that the laws and legal system support a market economy, and that the rules be essentially the same everywhere that the global corporations operate. It is they, not the internal markets, who require permanent title to land and other property; it is they, not the *bizniz* people of the former colony, who want certainty and predictability in their contractual transactions.

Nevertheless, custom continues to operate in PNG in small but significant ways, despite the efforts of the colonial authorities during almost one hundred years of colonial rule to ignore it or stamp it out, and despite, as well, the subsequent actions of the postcolonial state to replace it with something that colonial era theorists and foreign investors convinced them would be better suited to the needs and interests of a developing economy. Village courts began operating in 1975 and are active throughout the country, and villagers continue to frequent them as well as informal moots and dispute settlement gatherings. For the most part, state courts still apply the imported common law, but custom does creep into common law decisions now and then, despite the unwillingness of the judges to embrace it.

Sources

Books and Articles

Azeem Amarshi, Kenneth Good, and Rex Mortimer, *Development and Dependency: The Political Economy of Papua New Guinea* (Melbourne: Oxford University Press, 1979).

Peter Balmford, "Foundation of the Monash Law School," *Monash University Law Review* 15(3/4) (1989) 139–175.

Peter Bayne, "Legal Development in Papua New Guinea: The Place of the Common Law," *Melanesian Law Journal* 3(1) (1975) 9–39.

William Blackstone, *Commentaries on the Laws of England*, vol. 1, sec. 107 (Oxford: Clarendon Press, 1765–1770).

Paul Bohannon (ed.) *Law and Warfare: Studies in the Anthropology of Conflict* (New York: Natural History Press, 1967).

Kenneth Brown, "Customary Law in the Pacific: An Endangered Species," *Journal of South Pacific Law* 3(2) (1999), (https://www.usp.ac.fj/index.php?id=13145).

Brian Brunton and Duncan Colquhoun-Kerr, *The Annotated Constitution of Papua New Guinea* (Port Moresby: University of Papua New Guinea Press, 1984) 509–516.

J. Chandler, "The Karida Massacre: Fears of a New Era of Tribal Violence in Papua New Guinea," *The Guardian*, July 23, 2019.

James D. Cockroft, Andre Gunder Frank, and Dale L. Johnson, *Dependence and Underdevelopment: Latin America's Political Economy* (Garden City: Doubleday, 1972).

John Comaroff and Simon Roberts, "The Invocation of Norms in Dispute Settlement: The Tswana Case," in Ian Hamnet (ed.), *Social Anthropology and Law*, ASA Monograph No. 14 (New York: Academic Press, 1977) 77–112.

David and Dorothy Counts, "The Kaliai Lupunga: Disputing in the Public Forum," in A. L. Epstein (ed.), *Contention and Dispute* (Canberra: Australian National University Press, 1974) 113–151.

Eve Darian-Smith and Peter Fitzpatrick (eds.), *Laws of the Postcolonial* (Ann Arbor: University of Michigan Press, 1999).

A. L. Epstein, "Moots on Matupit," in A. L. Epstein (ed.), *Contention and Dispute* (Canberra: Australian National University Press, 1974) 152–197.

John D. Finch, "Unresolved Disputes in the Eastern Highlands," presentation at the American Anthropological Association Annual Meeting, Nov. 15–19, 1989.

Raymond Firth, "The Founding of the Research School of Pacific Studies," *The Journal of Pacific History* 31(1) (June 1996) 3–7.

Peter Fitzpatrick, *Modernism and the Grounds of Law* (Cambridge: Cambridge University Press, 2001).

Miranda Forsyth, *A Bird That Flies With Two Wings: Kastom and State Justice Systems in Vanuatu* (Canberra: Australian National University Press, 2009).

Mark Galanter, "The Modernization of Law," in M. Weiner (ed.), *Modernization* (New York: Hill and Wang, 1976).

James Gibbs Jr., "The Kpelle Moot," *Africa* 33(1) (1963) 1–10.

James Gibbs Jr., "Two Forms of Dispute Settlement among the Kpelle of West Africa," in Donald Black and Maureen Mileski (eds.), *The Social Organization of Law* (New York: Seminar Press, 1973) 368–373.

P. H. Gulliver, *Disputes and Negotiations: A Cross-Cultural Perspective* (New York: Academic Press, 1979).

E. Adamson Hoebel, *The Law of Primitive Man* (Cambridge: Harvard University Press, 1954).

Ilan Kapoor, "Capitalism, Culture, Agency: Dependency Theory versus Postcolonial Theory," *Third World Quarterly* 23(4) (2002) 647–666.

Shaun Larcom, *Legal Dissonance: The Interaction of Criminal Law and Customary Law* (New York: Berghahn Books, 2015).

Stephanie Lawson, "Postcolonialism, Neo-Colonialism and the 'Pacific Way': A Critique of (Un)critical Approaches," Discussion Paper 2010/4, Governance in Melanesia Seminars, School of International, Political and Strategic Studies, Australian National University (2010).

Karl Llewellyn and E. Adamson Hoebel, *The Cheyenne Way: Conflict and Case Law in Primitive Jurisprudence* (Norman: University of Oklahoma Press, 1941).

B. Malinowski, *Crime and Custom in Savage Society* (London: Kegan Paul, 1926).

Gary Meyers and John Mugambwa, "The Mabo Decision: Australian Aboriginal Land Rights in Transition," *Environmental Law* 23(4) (1993) 1203–1247.

Sally Falk Moore, *Law as Process: An Anthropological Approach* (London: Routledge & Kegan Paul, 1978).

Sally Falk Moore, "Individual Interests and Organisational Structures: Dispute Settlements as 'Events of Articulation,'" in Ian Hamnet (ed.), *Social Anthropology and Law*, ASA Monograph No. 14 (New York: Academic Press, 1977) 159–188.

John Hubert Murray, *Papua of Today* (London: P. S. King & Son, 1925).

Laura Nader (ed.), *Law in Culture and Society* (Berkeley: University of California Press, 1997).

Laura Nader and Harry Todd (eds.), *The Disputing Process: Law in Ten Societies* (New York: Columbia University Press, 1978).

Bruce L. Ottley, "Custom and Introduced Criminal Justice," in R. W. James and I. Fraser (eds.), *Legal Issues in a Developing Society* (Port Moresby: University of Papua New Guinea Faculty of Law, 1992) 128–145.

Bruce L. Ottley, "Looking Back to the Future: The Colonial Origins of Current Attitudes toward Customary Law," in Jonathan Aleck and Jackson Rannells (eds.), *Custom at the Crossroads* (Port Moresby: University of Papua New Guinea, 1995) 97–107.

Bruce L. Ottley and Jean Zorn, "Criminal Law in Papua New Guinea: Code, Custom and Courts in Conflict," *American Journal of Comparative Law* 31(3) (1983) 251–300.

Abdul Paliwala, Jean Zorn, and Peter Bayne, "Economic Development and the Changing Legal System of Papua New Guinea," *African Law Studies* 16 (1978) 3–79.

C. Guy Powles, "Law and Government in the South and Central Pacific," *Lawasia* 1985 (1985) 110–130.

Robert Redfield, "Primitive Law," in Paul Bohannon (ed.), *Law and Warfare: Studies in the Anthropology of Conflict* (New York: Natural History Press, 1967) 15–18.

Simon Roberts, *Order and Dispute: An Introduction to Legal Anthropology* (London: Penguin, 1979).

W. W. Rostow, *The Process of Economic Growth* (New York: Norton, 1962).

W. W. Rostow, *The Stages of Economic Growth* (Cambridge: Cambridge University Press, 1971).

Peter Sack, "The Range of Traditional Tolai Remedies," in A. L. Epstein (ed.), *Contention and Dispute* (Canberra: Australian National University Press, 1974) 67–92.

Richard Scaglion, "Samukundi Abelam Conflict Management: Implications for Legal Planning in Papua New Guinea," *Oceania* 52 (1981) 28–38.

Peter Sevareid, "I Know Money, I Don't Know Human Beings: A Mano House Palaver," *Liberian Studies Journal* 17(1) (1992) 105–119.

Paul Sillitoe, "Pigs in Disputes," *Oceania* 51 (1981) 256–265.

Francis Snyder, "Law and Development in the Light of Dependency Theory," *Law & Society Review* 14(3) (1980) 723–804.

Special Issue, "Postcolonialism, Globalization and Law," *Third World Legal Studies* 1999 (1999).

Christine Stewart, "Human Rights, Custom and the Underlying Law of Papua New Guinea," presentation at conference on Law and Culture: Meaningful Legal Pluralism in the Pacific and Beyond, USP School of Law, Port Vila, Vanuatu, August 30–September 1, 2010.

Andrew Strathern, "When Dispute Procedures Fail," in A. L. Epstein (ed.), *Contention and Dispute* (Canberra: Australian National University Press, 1974) 240–270.

Marilyn Strathern, "Discovering 'Social Control,'" *Journal of Law and Society* 12(2) (1985) 111–133.

Symposium, "Colonialism, Culture and the Law," *Law & Social Inquiry* 26(2) (2001).

Symposium, "Post-Colonial Law—Uses of Theory in Law Reform Projects," *American University Journal of Gender, Social Policy & the Law* 10(3) (2002).

Walter W. Tiffany, "Disputing in Customary Land Courts: Case Studies from the Solomon Islands," *Melanesian Law Journal* 7(1/2) (1979) 99–115.

David Trubek and Marc Galanter, "Scholars in Self-Estrangement: Some Reflections on the Crisis in Law and Development Studies in the United States," *Wisconsin Law Review* 1974(4) (1974) 1062–1102.

James Weiner and Katie Glaskin (eds.), *Customary Land Tenure and Registration in Australia and Papua New Guinea* (Canberra: Australian National University Press, 2007).

David Weisbrot, Abdul Paliwala, and Akilagpa Sawyerr, *Law and Social Change in Papua New Guinea* (Sydney: Butterworths, 1982), 176–177.

Edward P. Wolfers, *Race Relations and Colonial Rule in Papua New Guinea* (Sydney: Australia & New Zealand Book Company, 1975).

Gordon R. Woodman, "Some Realism about Customary Law—The West African Experience," *Wisconsin Law Review* 1969(2) (1969) 128–152.

Jean Zorn, "Common Law Jurisprudence and Customary Law," in R. W. James and I. Fraser (eds.), *Legal Issues in a Developing Society* (Port Moresby: University of Papua New Guinea, 1992) 103–127.

Jean Zorn, "Making Law in Papua New Guinea: The Influence of Customary Law on the Common Law," *Pacific Studies* 14(4) (1991) 1–34.

Jean Zorn, "*Graun Bilong Mipela*: Local Land Courts and the Changing Customary Law of Papua New Guinea," *Pacific Studies* 15(2) (1992) 1–38.

Government Documents

David P. Derham, *Report on the System for the Administration of Justice in the Territory of Papua and New Guinea* (Canberra: Australia Department of Territories, 1960).

Ralph T. Gore, "Appendix A: The Punishment of Crime Among Natives," *Papua Annual Report 1930* (Melbourne: Government Printer, 1931).

Law Reform Commission of Papua New Guinea, *Marriage in Papua New Guinea*, Law Reform Commission Monograph No. 4 (Port Moresby: Government of Papua New Guinea: 1986).

Cases

Johnson v. M'Intosh, 21 U.S. (8 Wheat.) 543 (1823)

Mabo v. Queensland (No. 1), HCA 23, (1992) 175 CLR 1

Martin v. Waddell's Lessee, 41 U.S. 367 (1842)

Nall v. Campbell, Cowp. R. 204, 211, 212; 1 Chalm. Ann. 14, 15

R. v. Galamo Obu, unreported National Couarurt Judgment 1974, No. 76

R. v. Kauba-Paruwo [1963] PNGLR 18

State v. Emp Mek [1993] PNGLR 330

Statutes

Constitution of the Independent State of Papua New Guinea

Criminal Code Act 1974, No. 78 of 1974

Customs Recognition Act 1975 (PNG) (originally enacted as Native Customs (Recognition) Ordinance 1963, No. 28 of 1963, amended and renamed 1975)

Inter-Group Fighting Act 1977, No. 43 of 1977 (PNG)

Native Administration Regulations 1924 (New Guinea)

Native Regulation Ordinance 1908, No. 25 of 1909 (Papua),

Sorcery Act 1971 (PNG) (repealed by the Sorcery (Repeal) Act 2013, No. 7 of 2013 (PNG)

Underlying Law Act 2000, No. 13 of 2000 (PNG)

Village Courts Act 1989, No. 37 of 1989 (PNG)

Notes

1. We use the term "family" to refer both to the nuclear family (parents and their children) and the extended family (consisting, usually, of several generations—grandparents, parents, and children—and frequently of more than one married couple of the same generation, with their children). Papua New Guineans tended to live in hamlets consisting primarily of members of their extended families. We also use the term "lineage"; that refers to all the people who trace their relationship to a common ancestor, and, depending on how far back in time the ancestor is, this can be one or more extended families. In many Papua New Guinean societies, the lineage is an important political entity. We also use the term "clan" because it has often been employed in the PNG context to refer to sociopolitical groups that are larger than a lineage, but still describe their inter-relationship as having something to do with kinship. However, even among anthropologists, the term is notable more in that it does away with the negative connotations associated with the word "tribe" and less because it has any consistent meaning from one group to another.
2. Some writers on Pacific and other traditional legal systems distinguish between "custom" and "customary law." Unfortunately for consistency, however, they do so in different ways and for different reasons. There are at least three main differentiations made: (a) Some use "custom" to mean rules or norms of the Indigenous peoples, while "customary law" is saved for those customary rules that have been recognized and applied by the state courts, thereby becoming part of the formal law. This distinction is useful because readers can easily tell which the writer is referring to. Also, it points out that the adoption of custom by state courts changes the customs into something different. They cease to be the flexible and ever-changing, mostly unwritten, mostly unconsidered, norms of a culture, and become rules that courts treat as precedent. (b) Some legal scholars, however, do not like to make that distinction between "custom" and "customary law" because it is the distinction that the colonial rulers made, and they meant by it that the "customs" of Indigenous people were not "law" in any sense and, indeed, were inferior to the "laws" that the colonizers brought with them or imposed on their subjects. In opposition to that colonial view, many scholars purposely use the phrase "customary law" to refer to the unwritten norms, usages, rules, and values of the Indigenous peoples of the Pacific. Another example of this political use of the terms "custom" and "customary law" occurs in the laws of Papua New Guinea (PNG). The older Native *Customs (Recognition) Ordinance of 1963*, which requires courts to treat

the unwritten norms of the peoples of PNG as facts, not as laws, refers to those norms as "custom." The more recently enacted *Underlying Law Act of 2000*, which provides that these norms and usages are to be the primary and major source of PNG's own common law, refers to them as "customary law." (c) Colonial (and even some postcolonial) legislation and court-made laws used the term "custom" to refer only to those norms and usages of the Indigenous peoples of the Pacific that had existed since long before colonial times, since "time immemorial." At independence, the Constitution, Art. 20, expressly repudiated this usage, defining "custom" to mean the "customs and usages of the indigenous inhabitants of the country … regardless of whether … the custom or usage has existed from time immemorial." After independence, the *Customs (Recognition) Act* was revised to adopt the Constitution's new definition of "custom." (d) Finally, many lawyers, judges, legislators, and scholars use the two terms—"custom" and "customary law"—interchangeably, without paying much attention to shades of meaning. Basically, that is what we do.

3. This story is based upon material in Simon Roberts, *Order and Dispute: An Introduction to Legal Anthropology* (London: Penguin, 1979).
4. P. H. Gulliver, *Disputes and Negotiations: A Cross-Cultural Perspective* (New York: Academic Press, 1979) 74.
5. This story is based roughly on facts from *R. v. Galamo Obu*, unreported National Court judgment (1974) No. 786, and *R. v. Kauba-Paruwo*, National Court judgment (1963) PNGLR 18.
6. Andrew Strathern, "When Dispute Procedures Fail," in A. L. Epstein (ed.), *Contention and Dispute* (Canberra: Australian National University Press, 1974) 240–270.
7. J. Chandler, "The Karida Massacre: Fears of a New Era of Tribal Violence in Papua New Guinea," *The Guardian,* July 23, 2019, https://www.theguardian.com/world/2019/jul/23/the-karida-massacre-the-start-of-a-new-era-of-tribal-violence-in-papua-new-guinea. The article describes a violent raid by one Highlands clan on the village of another; the raiders were armed with assault rifles and other automatic weapons, killed ten women and six children, and then hacked their bodies into pieces. Ballard is quoted in the article, as are other PNG experts, pointing out that this kind of raid is utterly unrelated to and does not spring from the kinds of tribal fighting that occurred in precolonial PNG. It has much more to do, Chandler and her sources say, with the failed promise of the massive liquid natural gas facilities, built on the lands of these clans, which advertised it would bring wealth to the region, but instead has brought nothing but social and ecological disruption.
8. *Id.*

9. Adapted from A. L. Epstein, "Moots on Matupit," in A. L. Epstein (ed.), *Contention and Dispute: Aspects of Law and Social Control in Melanesia* (Canberra: Australian National University Press, 1974) 93–112.
10. These relatively informal meetings at which disputes are aired have been variously called "moots" or "gatherings." We use those and other terms interchangeably.
11. The return of the disputants, and indeed of the whole village, to peace and harmony is a frequently restated theme in writings about dispute settlement processes in small groups and societies worldwide. "Restoration of social balance [is] the dominant goal of intragroup dispute settlement." Peter Sevareid, "I Know Money, I Don't Know Human Beings: A Mano House Palaver," *Liberian Studies Journal* 17(1) (1992) 105. Laura Nader describes the goal of moots as "to make the balance". Laura Nader, "Styles of Court Procedure: To Make the Balance," in Laura Nader (ed.). *Law in Culture and Society* (Berkeley: University of California Press, 1997) 69–91. J. L. Gibbs states that a dispute settlement meeting ends when both parties feel satisfied. "Two Forms of Dispute Settlement among the Kpelle of West Africa," in Donald Black and Maureen Mileski (eds.), *The Social Organization of Law* (New York: Seminar Press, 1973) 368–373.
12. Gulliver defines negotiation as "a process by which parties interact in developing an agreement." P. H. Gulliver, *Disputes and Negotiations: A Cross-Cultural Perspective* (New York: Academic Press, 1979) 70.
13. John Hubert Murray, *Papua of Today* (London: P. S. King & Son, 1925) 244.
14. *Id.* at 238.
15. William Blackstone, *Commentaries on the Laws of England*, vol. 1, sec. 107 (1765).
16. Id. Quoted by Justice Story in *Nall v. Campbell.*
17. See, for example, J. Taney in *Martin v. Waddell's Lessee*, as well as the opinion of J. Story above.
18. Ralph T. Gore, "Appendix A: The Punishment of Crime Among Natives," *Papua Annual Report* 1930.
19. Karl Llewellyn and E. Adamson Hoebel, *The Cheyenne Way: Conflict and Case Law in Primitive Jurisprudence* (Norman: Univ. of Oklahoma Press, 1941).
20. These can be found in Paul Bohannon (ed.), *Law and Warfare: Studies in the Anthropology of Conflict* (New York: Natural History Press, 1967), and in Laura Nader and Harry Todd (eds.), *The Disputing Process: Law in Ten Societies* (New York: Columbia University Press, 1978).

21. Simon Roberts, *Order and Dispute: An Introduction to Legal Anthropology* (London: St. Martin's Press, 1979).
22. Sally Falk Moore, *Law as Process: An Anthropological Approach* (Oxford: Oxford University Press, 1978).
23. Native Regulation Ordinance, sec. 3; Native Administration Ordinance, vol. X, 3579, Part II.
24. *Id.*
25. Mark Galanter, "The Modernization of Law," in M. Weiner (ed.), *Modernization* (New York, NY: Hill and Wang, 1976) 153; David Trubek and Mark Galanter, "Scholars in Self-Estrangement: Some Reflections on the Crisis in Law and Development Studies in the United States," *Wisconsin Law Review* 1974(4) (1974) 1062.
26. Shaun Larcom, *Legal Dissonance: The Interaction of Criminal Law and Customary Law* (New York: Berghahn Books, 2015) 64.
27. *Id.*
28. At section 8, the ordinance further limited the civil law application of custom to cases involving the ownership and inheritance of land or water held in customary tenure, customary marriages, and family matters, transactions which the parties intended or justice required to be regulated by custom, and decisions about the reasonableness of an act or the state of mind of an actor. At section 7, the ordinance limited the criminal law application of custom to defenses: ascertaining the state of mind of a defendant, deciding the reasonableness of the defendant's acts, deciding whether the defendant was entitled to other defenses (such as provocation or self-defense), and determining the penalty. Finally, at section 6, the ordinance provided that custom could be recognized and enforced by state courts only if the custom were not "repugnant to the general principles of humanity."
29. *Id.* at sections 4 and 5.
30. This has been construed narrowly to mean that custom may be taken into account only to mitigate or aggravate a penalty prescribed by the Criminal Code, and not to permit customary penalties to be imposed: *State v. Emp Mek* [1993] PNGLR 330.
31. *Native Customs (Recognition) Ordinance* at section 3(1)(a).
32. James D. Cockroft, Andre Gunder Frank, and Dale L. Johnson, *Dependence and Underdevelopment: Latin America's Political Economy* (Garden City: Doubleday, 1972).

3 Laying the Foundations of the Colonial Legal System

The British Protectorate 1884–1888

November is one of the hottest months of the year in Port Moresby, with cloudless skies and mid-day temperatures hovering above 90 degrees Fahrenheit (32 degrees Celsius). Because of what a contemporary journalist described as the especially intense heat in November 1884, Commodore James E. Erskine of the British Royal Navy decided to schedule the landing on the beach to begin at 6:30 a.m. on the morning of November 6, assuming that the heat at that early hour would not yet be oppressive. Erskine issued a general order that the dress for the officers of the five ships under his command—the *Nelson*, the *Espiegle*, the *Raven*, the *Swinger*, and the *Harrier*—should be cocked hat, blue dress coat, and epaulettes. Erskine directed the seamen to wear white frocks and hats and the marines to wear white tunics and helmets. As a result, the numerous small landing crafts, carrying approximately 250 officers, marines, and sailors from the ships anchored offshore, presented a colorful and impressive scene, with the wooden stilt houses of the village bordering the beach and the green leaves of the banana trees on the dry brown hills in the background.

After their landing, the officers and sailors immediately marched up the hill to the one-story house belonging to the London Missionary Society, while the marines and the band waited on the beach until Erskine landed at precisely eight o'clock. The marines then presented arms and, with bayonets fixed, marched with the band to join the officers and sailors at the mission house. Waiting on the wide verandah to greet Commodore Erskine were the Rev. William G. Lawes and his wife, Fanny, who had lived and worked as missionaries in the Port Moresby area since 1874 and were in charge of the mission station; the Rev. James Chalmers, a missionary in New Guinea since 1877; Hugh Hastings Romilly, a British deputy commissioner for the Western Pacific High Commission, who had been sent to New Guinea the previous month and would remain there as an official until late 1888; Henry M. Chester, the police magistrate on Thursday Island in the Torres Strait; John F. Mann, an explorer, a surveyor, and a representative of the Geographic Society of Australasia, who was traveling on the *Nelson*; and Mr. K. R. Stuart, the son of the colonial secretary of the colony of New South Wales. The marines and sailors from Erskine's ships formed two lines in front of the house. Behind them were a number of New Guineans, as well as a few of the dozen or so traders, mostly white men, who plied their wares along the southern coast of New Guinea.

What was the purpose of gathering so many people together at a house in a place that was not yet a town, on an island unknown to all but a handful of British and Australians, and organizing the pomp and circumstance of a military display? Since the early 1870s, a small number of private individuals and government officials in Australia and New Zealand had been urging Britain to annex, or at least to declare a protectorate over, the portion of the islands of New Guinea not claimed by the Netherlands. Some of those individuals hoped for economic gain from European settlement or from the exploitation of the islands' natural resources. A few saw British control as a way to end the recruitment of New Guineans to work in virtual slavery on the sugar plantations in Queensland. By the early 1880s, however, Australian interest in New Guinea was driven largely by fears of German intervention in, and possible control of, the islands and shipping lanes just to their north. Queenslanders, in particular, were convinced that the Torres Strait (between New Guinea and northern Australia) would soon rival the Suez Canal (completed in 1869) in terms of strategic and commercial significance. Although Britain was reluctant to assume administrative and financial responsibilities for New Guinea, an intercolonial convention of its Australasian colonies in Sydney in November and December of 1883 produced pledges of financial support for British administration of the islands. In the face of pressure from its own colonies, Britain agreed to establish a protectorate over the southeastern coast and the adjacent islands as an interim measure, until permanent arrangements could be worked out for its full control of the territory. In late October 1884, Commodore Erskine was instructed to sail from Sydney to New Guinea, and on November 6, he read a statement proclaiming *a Protectorate of Her Most Gracious Majesty over a portion of New Guinea and the islands adjacent thereto.*

Erskine's speech made no mention of possible German encroachment, of European settlement, or of the islands' natural resources and trade. Instead, he justified Britain's intervention solely on humanitarian grounds: the need to protect New Guineans from unscrupulous individuals:

> Whereas it has become essential for the protection of the lives and properties of the native inhabitants of New Guinea, and for the purpose of preventing the occupation of portions of that country by persons whose proceedings unsanctioned by any lawful authority might tend to injustice, strife and bloodshed, and who, under the pretence of legitimate trade and intercourse, might endanger the liberties, and possess themselves of the lands of such native inhabitants. . . .
>
> [I now] declare and proclaim the establishment of such Protectorate over such portions of the coast and the adjacent islands as is more particularly described in the schedule hereunto annexed.[1]

Erskine concluded his proclamation speech with a declaration concerning the protection of land in the protectorate. Since the acquisition of land by colonial administrations and by individual Europeans would become a primary topic of controversy and the subject of numerous laws throughout the colonial period, the scope and unqualified terms of Erskine's first words on the subject are particularly important:

> And I hereby proclaim and declare that no acquisition of land whatsoever or howsoever acquired, within the limits of the Protectorate hereby established, will be recognized by Her Majesty. And I do hereby, on behalf of Her Majesty, command and enjoin all persons whom it may concern to take notice of this Proclamation.[2]

The Rev. Lawes then translated Erskine's proclamation speech into Motu, the local vernacular language. Lawes, along with Chalmers, had opposed an attempt by the Colony of Queensland to annex the territory in 1883, fearing that it would lead to the abduction of New Guineans to work on the Queensland sugar plantations. At that time, Lawes wrote: "We would much rather not be annexed by anybody, but if there was any probability of a foreign power taking possession of New Guinea, then let us have British rule: but as a Crown Colony, not as an appendage to Queensland."[3] When Britain declared its protectorate over New Guinea, Lawes and Chalmers supported and worked with colonial officials. In 1886, Lawes wrote optimistically: "I see no reason why British rule should not succeed in New Guinea, and prove a benefit and blessing to the native as well as to the alien race."[4]

At the conclusion of Erskine's proclamation speech, the Union Jack was raised on the mission station flagstaff, the military band played "God Save the Queen," a twenty-one-gun salute was fired from the *Nelson*, and the troops fired a series of ceremonial rifle salutes. Erskine then concluded the ceremony with brief remarks aimed at the small group of Europeans, reiterating his concern for the welfare of the Indigenous inhabitants of the territory:

> This interesting and important ceremony now formally concluded, it only remains for me, in Her Majesty's name to express the fervent hope that under the blessing of Almighty God the establishment of this Protectorate may conduce to the peace, happiness and welfare of the people of this vast territory. May the British flag which we have this day planted on these shores be to the people of this portion of New Guinea the symbol of their freedom and their liberty, and the Proclamation which I have just read, the charter of their rights and privileges. May it be to them a Protectorate in deed, as well as in name, protecting them alike from the encroachment of foreigners and the aggressive or unlawful actions of any other nationality; may the blessings of civilization and Christianity, the seeds of which have been already sown by English hands in the persons of the brave and good men present on this occasion, increase and multiply exceedingly amongst them; and lastly, as the Union Jack which has on several former occasions been hoisted on the shores of New Guinea

and the adjacent islands is on this day for the first time displayed and hoisted on New Guinea under the authority and by the command of her Most Gracious Majesty Queen Victoria, I most fervently pray that the establishment of a British Protectorate on these shores may tend to insure the integrity and inviolability of the great Australian Colonies, and promote the best interests of their people; and I trust that this important step may be attended with the happiest results, and redound to the honor of Her Most Gracious Majesty the Queen, for whom I now invite you to give three hearty cheers.[5]

A few of the New Guineans who attended the proclamation ceremony that November morning had been in contact with Europeans in the decade since Lawes, Chalmers, and a few traders began living and working in the Port Moresby area in the 1870s. However, they certainly would not have understood that a distant empire, in the name of "Her Most Gracious Majesty," was establishing a "Protectorate" over their lands. It was an indication of Great Britain's lack of concern for the wishes of New Guineans that the protectorate was established without a single New Guinean having been asked whether they wished to be "protected." Since it was the third time in eighteen months that there had been a flag-raising ceremony at the London Missionary Society house,[6] the New Guineans may well have assumed that the ceremony was just a strange ritual that white men regularly performed. All that may explain Lawes's statement, a month after the proclamation, that New Guineans had received the news of the protectorate "cordially" and that he had "never heard a whisper of distrust or discontent."[7]

Erskine had tried to explain to some New Guineans from the area around Port Moresby the meaning and consequences of a protectorate. On the day before the proclamation ceremony, he invited a group of about fifty leaders from the surrounding villages to the *Nelson*, and, after giving them ship's biscuits and boiled rice sweetened with brown sugar, he made a brief speech stating British policy for the protectorate. Erskine's speech, which was translated into Motu by Lawes, set out in greater detail than the following day's proclamation the protections the British government said it would provide to New Guineans and what it expected of them in return. In later years, that speech was considered so important that Hubert Murray, who served from 1908 to 1940 as the lieutenant-governor of the Territory of Papua (the name given to the territory when Australia assumed administration of it in 1906), wrote that it was taken to be "a fundamental part of the Papuan Constitution, which is not to be altered by legislation."[8]

> I desire, on behalf of Her Majesty the Queen, to explain to you the meaning of the ceremonial which you are about to witness. It is a proclamation that from this time forth you are placed under the protection of Her Majesty's Government; that evil-disposed men will not be able to occupy your country, to seize your lands, or to take you away from your own homes. I have been instructed . . . to give you the strongest assurance of Her Majesty's gracious protection of you, and to warn bad and evil-disposed men that if they attempt to do you harm, they will be promptly punished by the officers of the Queen. Your lands will be secured to you; your wives and children will be protected.
>
> Should any injury be done to you, you will immediately inform Her Majesty's officers, who will reside amongst you, and they will hear your complaints, and do you justice. You will look upon all white persons whom the Queen permits to reside amongst you as your friends, and Her Majesty's subjects. The Queen will permit nobody to reside here who does you injury. You will under no circumstances inflict punishment upon any white person; but if such person has done you wrong you will tell Her Majesty's officers of that wrong in order that the case may be fairly inquired into. You must know that it is for your security, and to prevent bloodshed, that the Queen sends me here to you, and will send her officers to live amongst you. And now I hope that you clearly understand that we are here amongst you as your friends. You will all keep peace amongst yourselves, and if you have disputes with each other, you will bring them before the Queen's officers who will settle them for you without bloodshed.
>
> Should bad men come amongst you, bringing firearms and gunpowder, and intoxicating liquors, you are not to buy them, and are to give notice at once to the Queen's officers, so that such men may be punished.[9]

Erskine ended his ship-board speech with a sentence that highlighted Britain's ostensibly maternal attitude toward New Guineans and the task that it was undertaking: "Always keep in your minds that the Queen guards and watches over you, looks upon you as her children, and will not allow anyone to harm you, and will soon send her trusted officers to carry out her gracious intentions in the establishment of this Protectorate."[10]

As with the proclamation ceremony the following day, there is no record of what the New Guineans on board the ship that afternoon thought of Erskine's speech, of the strange men who had come to their land in big ships, or of the concept of an absent "Queen" who guarded, watched over, and protected them "as her children."[11] New Guineans had an extensive oral tradition but were nonliterate, and the British did not consider their opinions worth soliciting or recording. However, we do know that the small group of European traders in attendance was not impressed when they heard Erskine's reference to "bad and evil-disposed men" (which they assumed referred to them) or by his bans on acquiring land and trading in certain goods. The traders attributed those statements to the fact that Erskine was "a simple dupe in the hands of the missionaries."[12]

Despite the concern in Erskine's speeches for the welfare of New Guineans and the pageantry of the proclamation ceremony itself, Britain was very reluctant to assume responsibility for the large, rugged, and almost completely unknown island of New Guinea. The Australian colonial governments were also unenthusiastic about the financial obligations they had undertaken to support Britain's administration of New Guinea and had no plans for economic activity or settlement in the new protectorate, despite their repeated petitions to London for annexation. And the very event that Australians hoped that the protectorate would prevent became public a month after the proclamation ceremony. Germany informed Great Britain that it had established a protectorate over the northeastern quarter of New Guinea and the Bismarck Archipelago on November 3—that is, three days *before* Britain had proclaimed its protectorate over the southern coast of New Guinea. To Australian colonial officials, Britain's hesitation in declaring its protectorate had invited Germany's annexation, although it is at least equally likely that Germany acted only because it knew that Britain was about to do the same. Germany's action forced Britain to expand its protectorate beyond the southern coast, and the two countries reached an agreement in April 1886 on a boundary between their territories.

The November 1884 declarations marked the beginning of formal British/German/Australian control over what, a little more than ninety years later, would become the Independent State of Papua New Guinea. One of the most striking aspects of those nine decades in Papua and New Guinea, as in all European colonies, was the imposition of many aspects of the culture of the three metropolitan colonial powers—most particularly their legal systems—on the Indigenous peoples they ruled.

Legal systems are more than codes, statutes, judicial decisions, and procedures. They embody the attitudes of public officials and private citizens alike about fairness, justice, and what constitutes the binding rules of law, as well as what roles the various types of law should play within a society. In a colonial society, the structure of the legal system and the attitudes that shape it are also determined by how and why the territory became a colony, as well as the fact that it is a colony. The legal system created in British New Guinea by the British and Australians consisted of the English common law, English and Australian statutes, and local ordinances, and was informed and interpreted by English and later Australian notions about the nature of law and its role in a colony. Except informally and unofficially, it did not include the customary norms and processes by which Indigenous Papua New Guineans governed themselves.

During the thirty-seven years between the creation of the protectorate over British New Guinea in 1884 and the beginning of Australia's formal control over the former German New Guinea as a League of Nations Mandate in 1921, those factors and influences came together to create the basis of Papua and New Guinea's colonial legal systems. While the specific contents of the colonial legal systems evolved over the decades, the systems created in those early years endured until independence in 1975—and continue to influence postcolonial law today.

Justifications for British Control of New Guinea

From the seventeenth until the mid-nineteenth century, Britain and France focused most of their attention in the South Pacific on Australia, New Zealand, and the smaller islands of Polynesia, Melanesia, and Micronesia. Contact with the islands of New Guinea during the first three centuries of British and French expansion into the Pacific was sporadic, often marked by hostility on both sides, and had no lasting effect on the lives of Indigenous people. However, officials in Australia and New Zealand grad-

ually began to take an interest in New Guinea in the mid-nineteenth century, as the waters around the islands of Melanesia became regular shipping lanes between their colonies and Britain. Beginning in the late 1860s, a few Australian and New Zealand speculators began to promote the idea that the islands could be a source of wealth based upon gold, timber, and pearl shells and could sustain European settlement. On a number of occasions, groups of merchants or adventurers formed associations with the goals of acquiring land, engaging in trade, promoting colonization, or prospecting for gold in New Guinea. However, almost all of those endeavors were abandoned due to a lack of support from the Australian colonial governments and the British Colonial Office or because they were poorly planned and organized and resulted in the death of the participants.

In the course of surveying the southern coast of New Guinea in February 1873, British naval Captain John Moresby became the first European to explore the area that he named Port Moresby. His favorable descriptions of the area led some politicians and private individuals in Australia to begin lobbying the British Colonial Office to annex New Guinea. The following year, the London Missionary Society established the first permanent mission station in Port Moresby. However, the governors of the Australian colonies were uninterested in formal involvement in New Guinea. Britain's lack of interest in the annexation of New Guinea is illustrated by a comment in a speech by Prime Minister Lord Derby that "Great Britain had already black subjects enough."[13]

Prospects for the colonization of New Guinea increased briefly in late 1877 when the discovery of gold near Port Moresby led to the first influx of Australians, most of whom had no experience with the hardships of prospecting. Since the prospectors found only a small amount of gold and many of them died of malaria and malnutrition, the gold rush era was short lived and had no immediate impact on New Guinea. However, the presence of gold, and the fact that about one hundred Australians made the trip north to try to exploit it, led some in Australia to believe that settlement was viable and that annexation was inevitable.

The gold rush saw the first unofficial attempt to impose some of the norms of English law on New Guinea. William Bairstow Ingham, an Englishman, had settled in Australia in 1873; frustrated with his job prospects there, he sailed to Port Moresby in 1878. Before he left Queensland, Ingham volunteered to serve as the unpaid representative of that colony in

New Guinea. The governor appointed Ingham the "Agent for the Government of Queensland in Port Moresby," although no specific duties or powers were contained in the appointment. Once he reached New Guinea, Ingham took himself and his appointment seriously and, although he had no legal authority or qualifications to do so, he attempted to impose his understanding of English law on the area. He carried out minor police actions, confiscated a ship that he suspected of illegal activities, deported two prostitutes, and recorded land transactions between New Guineans and Europeans. He also persuaded a group of local chiefs to petition Britain for annexation, although the colonial secretary had discouraged him from doing it.

In November 1878, Ingham sailed to Utian Island, in the Louisiade Archipelago, in what is now Milne Bay Province, to investigate the killing of Edwin Redlick, a European who had been engaged in the *beche-de-mer* trade.[14] Ingham and his small crew were killed in a surprise attack. The following year Britain sent a warship to the island to attempt to collect any remains of Ingham's papers and arrest those responsible for the killings. When they failed to identify the leaders of the attack, the British shelled the island and destroyed some huts, coconut trees, and canoes. Although no further action was taken against the islanders, the punitive raid was the first example of a method of inflicting punishment on New Guineans that would become common and controversial during the early colonial period.

The prospects for European settlement and the annexation of New Guinea were not without debate. In response to the 1877–1878 gold rush, an Australian newspaper quoted Andrew Goldie and the Rev. James Chalmers, who took very different positions about the colonization of the territory:

> It would almost seem in spite of warnings, that a rush will set-in to New Guinea, even providing no gold be discovered. It will open up a large track of new country of which very little is known. Mr. Chester writes from Thursday Island, that Mr. Goldie deplores the excitement cause[d] by his discovery of gold in New Guinea, and again warns people against going there.
>
> The Rev. Mr. Chalmers thinks the time has come for the colonisation of New Guinea; he considers a well-organized party of twenty

> men, well supplied with rations would be quite sufficient to prospect the whole of the island; he strongly deprecates any attempt at getting up a rush until something tangible is discovered.
>
> Mr. Chalmers considers New Guinea is suitable for the cultivation of sugar and cotton—an exploring party accompanied with a botanist and naturalist might pay their expenses, providing they did not discover any gold. Already two or three vessels are there, so we shall know shortly what the place shines in.[15]

Despite the optimistic statements by Chalmers, and the continuing attempts by private individuals to promote colonization, there was no investment in the islands throughout the 1870s and early 1880s and no plans by the British or Australian governments to promote white settlement or economic activities in the area. New Guinea's forbidding climate and geography, and the reputation of the Indigenous inhabitants for hostility to outsiders, presented little opportunity for trade and commerce.

A few Europeans began reaping profits from the islands in the 1860s by recruiting, tricking, or kidnapping what became an estimated eighty thousand islanders from New Guinea, the Solomon Islands, and the New Hebrides (now Vanuatu) to work as indentured laborers on sugar plantations in Queensland and Fiji. The harshness of blackbirding, and the attitude of white Queenslanders toward it and toward New Guineans, is illustrated by an 1884 case in which the seven crew members of the *Hopeful* were tried and convicted by a court in Queensland, after a four-day trial, of kidnapping New Guineans to work on the plantations. Two of the crew, Bernard Williams and Neil McNeil, were also convicted of murdering a number of New Guineans who resisted efforts to kidnap them. When the chief justice of Queensland, Sir Charles Lilley, sentenced the two men to be hanged, there were serious protests. For the first time in Queensland, the evidence of black men had been admitted in court, and white men had been sentenced to death for the murder of black men. The protests led the Queensland Executive Council to commute the sentences of Williams and McNeil to life in prison on the slender grounds that there was no proof that the New Guineans they had shot had actually died. After more than twenty-eight thousand Queenslanders signed a petition denouncing the severity of the sentences, all of the members of the crew were pardoned in 1888.

The few legal restrictions that Britain enacted to control blackbirding were largely ineffective. Missionaries, who were establishing a permanent presence in the New Guinea islands in the 1870s and taking an interest in the welfare of the Indigenous peoples, were the only group to oppose blackbirding, although the abuses of labor recruiting also drew the attention of politicians in Australian colonies other than Queensland. A debate in the Victorian Parliament in December 1872 over how to stop blackbirding produced one of the first calls by elected officials in Australia for Britain to extend control over New Guinea. During the debate, some members of the Victorian Parliament took the position that it was "imperatively necessary in the interests of humanity and civilisation" that Britain annex or declare protected territories all of the South Pacific islands between California and Australia.[16] However, the governor of Victoria, George Bowen, did not share that view and took no steps to lobby for British action.

Captain John Moresby was the first person to lay out detailed arguments for and against British annexation. In a "Supplementary Chapter" to his 1876 book on his explorations in New Guinea, Moresby asked: "How shall we treat the South Sea Islands and that part of New Guinea which is not Dutch?"[17] Moresby offered six reasons in support of British control of the islands: first, England, as represented by Australia and New Zealand, was effectively the great power closest to New Guinea and had the advantage of access and proximity; second, English subjects had settled on other Pacific islands and had established thriving industries; third, the actions of "lawless Englishmen" in the New Guinea islands required Britain to take action to repress the violence; fourth, Britain wanted the labor and raw commodities available in the islands "and we are determined to have these things"; fifth, the New Guineans "have seen so much of our heathenism that we are bound in fairness to show them something of our Christianity"; and finally, if Britain did not intervene, then other European powers would.[18]

Moresby also offered six arguments against British annexation: first, Britain already had enough land for its emigrants and would have enough for a long time into the future; second, the climate in New Guinea was so harsh that Europeans could not be manual workers; third, the English character often deteriorated "when Englishmen are brought into contact with aboriginal races"; fourth, the British Empire already was too large to permit proper administration of another remote territory; fifth, New Guineans were happy on their own and should be left alone; and finally, Britain and Australia lacked the financial resources to develop New Guinea since Britain was "saddled with the largest national debt in the world" and Australia needed all of its financial resources for its own internal development.[19] Although Moresby admitted that the arguments against annexation were strong, he spent the remainder of the chapter refuting each of them and concluded by saying that he hoped that Britain

> would take up what I conceive to be her duty, and annex New Guinea and the islands, and thus have it in her power to start right with the aborigines from the first; to prevent the first occasions of mistrust, disgust, and anger, which would at once and forever stamp an image of greed, perfidy, and cruelty, as our likeness on the native's heart.[20]

Moresby's arguments in favor of British annexation reflected the broad motives that drove European expansion during "the age of empire." Colonialism throughout the South Pacific resembled colonialism everywhere else in that it was not the result of any systematic or planned process. It occurred sporadically over the course of the nineteenth century and was the product of a complex blend of motives and actions that sometimes conflicted with each other. These included the rivalry among European states for international prestige; competition for strategic military advantage; humanitarian and religious concerns; and the need to protect existing commercial interests, insure sources of raw materials, and secure markets for manufactured goods. However, as the social and political theorist Isaiah Berlin pointed out, colonialism was not "fed just by greed or the desire for glory."[21] To gain support of everyone in the colonizing nation, it had to be justified by some central idea. The central idea that justified colonialism for a significant segment of the British public, including many of the colonizers themselves, was the white man's duty to take up the "burden" of spreading the moral and material components of what they viewed as civilisation and Christianity and protecting Indigenous people from exploitation. Britain's decision to intervene in New Guinea ultimately was motivated by neither commercial nor humanitarian interests. Instead, it was driven by strategic denial: the need to meet the threat to Australia's security and economy that Australians believed would happen if a rival or hostile foreign power acquired control of New Guinea.

By the early 1880s, Germany, Britain, and France had assembled most of their colonies in the Pacific Islands. Government officials in Australia—and particularly in Queensland—supported Moresby's argument that, if Britain did not act in New Guinea, "alien hands may reap a rich harvest that might have been ours."[22] With a population then of only three million people, its great distance from Britain, and its dependence upon the British navy for defense, Australia, itself still not independent of Britain, needed colonies of it own only for security, if that; it viewed New Guinea primarily as a buffer against German, and to a lesser extent French, expansion. In March 1883, rumors that Germany intended to annex New Guinea led the premier of Queensland, Sir Thomas McIlwraith, to send Henry Chester, the police magistrate of Thursday Island in the Torres Strait Islands, to Port Moresby with orders to claim for Great Britain the portion of New Guinea and its adjacent islands that were not under Dutch control.

Many Australians opposed the annexation, believing that McIlwraith's primary motive was to secure New Guinean labor for Queensland's sugar plantations. British Prime Minister William Gladstone also opposed further colonial expansion, and the British Colonial Office refused to approve Queensland's annexation. Lord Derby, then the colonial secretary, did not believe that Germany intended to annex any part of New Guinea. He also took the position that a colonial government such as Queensland did not have the authority to act beyond its boundaries. Nor did he share the security concerns of the Australian colonies. Derby thought the trouble and expense of assuming additional colonial responsibilities in the hostile conditions of New Guinea outweighed any potential economic or political benefits.

Despite Britain's desire not to become involved in New Guinea, support for Queensland's annexation among the other Australian colonies produced pressure to take some form of action. This led to an intercolonial convention in Sydney involving all of the Australian colonies, New Zealand, and Fiji, in November and December 1883. The members of the convention unanimously adopted a resolution stating: "That further acquisition of dominion in the Pacific, south of the Equator, by any Foreign Power, would be highly detrimental to the safety and well-being of the British possession of Australasia, and injurious to the interests of the Empire."[23] The convention supported the idea of incorporating New Guinea into the British Empire and produced a pledge by the colonial governments to submit bills to their legislatures for an appropriation of £15,000 per annum to defray the cost of establishing control over New Guinea.[24] By May 1884, the growing German commercial presence in the South Pacific in general, and in the northern part of New Guinea in particular, coupled with continuing pressure from the Australian colonies to take some action, finally convinced the British government to change its position. Britain reluctantly agreed to establish a protectorate over the southeastern portion of New Guinea. It was that protectorate that Commodore Erskine proclaimed on the morning of November 6, 1884.

Whose Laws Should Govern New Guinea? First Thoughts

During the debate over whether Britain should assert control over New Guinea, almost no attention was given to what Britain should do with the territory once Britain acquired it. Britain's options were limited by its financial and personnel resources, as well as by the fact that British officials knew almost nothing about the area, since there had been little or no contact with the people beyond a few coastal villages. They could only guess at how many people lived on the islands they would be "protecting." In addition, at the time of the declaration of the protectorate, there were only about twenty non-New Guineans living in the territory, mostly beachcombers, missionaries, and traders. Most of the traders lived on the boats that they used to travel along the coast. Neither Britain nor its Australian colonies had any plans to establish trading posts or to promote European settlement or investment in the territory.

In his 1876 book, John Moresby expressed his hope that Britain would annex New Guinea. Although Moresby did not state specifically whether that meant establishing a protectorate or a Crown Colony, he did make brief reference to what he thought should be Britain's two primary responsibilities if it did take control of New Guinea: bringing Christianity to the people and making them law-abiding.[25] Moresby's conception of law-abiding no doubt involved the introduction of English law into the territory; it was certainly not an assessment that New Guineans were failing to abide by their own customary laws and norms. In his view, the British were

> the best colonists in the world; we do not claim the merit of perfection for our laws and system of government, but we believe them to be the best extant. Our residence amongst these races, and the prevalence of our laws, are therefore rather to be desired for them according to our own belief, than the like connection with any other nation.[26]

The Rev. Chalmers, who never held an official position in the colonial administration, took a markedly different position. In 1883, he set out—but unfortunately did not elaborate upon—four broad policies that he felt should guide Britain if it annexed New Guinea. Unlike Moresby, Chalmers believed that New Guineans should be governed not by English laws but by "the laws suited for them"—although he did not specify how that would be determined.

> Let us begin by recognising all native rights, and letting it be distinctly understood that we govern for the native races, not the white men; that we are determined to civilise and raise to a higher level of humanity those whom we govern; that our aim will be to do all to defend them and save them from extermination by just humanitarian laws—not the laws of the British nation—but the laws suited for them. It will not take long for the natives to learn that not only are we great and powerful, but we are just and merciful, and we seek their good.[27]

Although Moresby and Chalmers differed on the kind of law that should apply, both seemed to believe that the British should create some kind of formal legal system for New Guineans. The British government, however, was of the opinion that the territory's protectorate status restricted Britain's jurisdiction solely to British subjects and denied it any explicit authority over New Guineans and the small number of other resident non-British subjects. The choice of protectorate status for New Guinea was not surprising since between 1880 and 1900 Britain gave all but one of its territories in Africa and the Pacific Islands that designation. However, the few people who wrote and spoke about the future of the territory of New Guinea did not distinguish between a protectorate and a colony.

Thus, the choice between introducing English law and creating laws suited for New Guineans would wait until the territory became a British colony in 1888. In the meantime, the protectorate was governed by a special commissioner, an official with the authority of a deputy commissioner of the Western Pacific High Commission. The commission's authority came from the Western Pacific Order in Council (1877), under powers derived from the *Pacific Islands Protection Act of 1872* and the *Foreign Jurisdiction Acts*. The purpose of the commission was to give Britain jurisdiction over the activities of its subjects who were traders, settlers, and labor recruiters in those western Pacific Islands that were not formally annexed or under the control of another colonial power, which included British New Guinea. The high commissioner had the authority to appoint deputy commissioners where needed in the islands. The Western Pacific Order in Council also established a High Commissioner's Court for the Western Pacific Islands in Fiji, although that court had jurisdiction only over British subjects in the designated islands. English civil and criminal law were applicable but only to British subjects.

Despite the lack of a formal legal system in British New Guinea, and with limited jurisdiction and resources, British officials developed policies and procedures for the protectorate that later would become the basis for much of the colonial legal system.

Laying the Foundation for the Colonial Legal System

An initial glance at the four years that British New Guinea was a protectorate could lead to the conclusion that the period made little, if any, contribution to the creation of the colonial legal system. There was no reception or adoption of British or Australian laws, no legislative body to enact ordinances for the territory, and no judicial system to resolve disputes or to deal with matters of law and order or issues involving land. Except for *The Murders Abroad Act of 1817*, an English statute that made it a crime for persons who were or had been crew or passengers on British ships to commit murder or manslaughter on islands not under British control or under the control of other European states, the English common law and statutes were not applicable to the protectorate. That led the deputy commissioner in New Guinea, Hugh Romilly, to lament in a letter in September 1885 that: "The natives are murdering away merrily, but in the present absurd stage of things we have no jurisdiction either to issue regulations or to punish. At present we are being successfully defied both by natives and whites."[28]

Despite the limitations, it would be a mistake to underestimate the influence the four years of the protectorate ultimately had on the creation of the colonial legal system in Papua and New Guinea. Many of the key issues that arose during the protectorate continued to challenge administrators throughout the colonial period. Although there were no English laws applicable to the protectorate, each of the special commissioners took steps that had long-term significance for the colonial legal system. They created an administrative system for governing the protectorate, established policies and procedures for the commercial or compulsory acquisition of land from New Guineans by the administration and by private parties, and tried to provide a measure of protection from exploitation for New Guineans by placing restrictions on Australians and other non-New Guineans coming into the protectorate and by banning the importation and sale of firearms, explosives, and alcohol. They also took steps—often unsuccessfully—to punish New Guineans who killed whites. They justified their actions by treating a number of statements and directives issued by Erskine and the colonial office as constituting their authority to administer the territory. These included Erskine's shipboard speech to the group of New Guinean leaders on the day before the proclamation of the protectorate; his statements during the proclamation ceremony; seven regulations that he issued on November 14, 1884 (one week after the proclamation ceremony); and the instructions from the colonial office contained in the letter given to Sir Peter Scratchley when he was appointed the first special commissioner of the protectorate in 1884. Those statements and instructions, along with the policies that the special commissioners developed to carry them out, laid the foundation for many of the ordinances enacted when New Guinea became a British Crown Colony in 1888.

The Problem of Jurisdiction

Before British officials could take any steps toward governing the protectorate, they had to determine what authority, if any, they had over the three groups of people living there: Indigenous New Guineans, British subjects (a category that included Australians), and non-British foreigners. The first statement on the extent of Britain's jurisdiction to act in New Guinea was made by British Prime Minister William Gladstone in answer to a question in the House of Commons in August 1884, three months before New Guinea became a protectorate. Gladstone took an expansive view, stating that, "within the limits of it [the protectorate], the jurisdiction of the Government will be sufficient to afford protection to the natives against lawless action, by whomsoever taken, whether by British subjects or foreigners."[29] That approach was reflected in Commodore Erskine's address establishing the protectorate, and it also shaped the long list of duties contained in the instructions that the colonial office gave to Sir Peter Scratchley in his November 17, 1884, letter of appointment as special commissioner:

> 8. . . .You should proceed to make yourself acquainted with the county, its harbours and general features; and you should lose no time in entering into friendly relations with the natives, and in endeavouring by all means in your power to inspire their confidence, and acquire their goodwill.
>
> 9. You will especially make it your duty to explain to them that Her Majesty, in taking them under her protection, has their welfare in view, and that you are sent to secure to them the safety of their persons, the enjoyment of their property, and particularly to protect them from being deprived of their lands by force and fraud. At the same time you will make it known to them that if it shall be decided to allow Her Majesty's subjects or others to purchase land, such transactions must in every case be conducted through you; that their wishes in these matters will be respected, and that the purchase money will be paid through you to them, unless in any case it shall appear desirable to apply it in their behalf for some object in which they are directly interested. You will also explain carefully, and satisfy yourself that they comprehend, that by the sale of land they deprive themselves of all further claims to it, and that it becomes the absolute property of the purchasers. In the event of any such purchases being made, it will be your duty to see that both parties agree as to the boundaries of the land, and that these boundaries are

defined by beacons or other easily recognizable marks. All such transfers should be carefully recorded in a register, and all subsequent transactions must be similarly recorded, or they will not be recognized by Her Majesty's Government.

10. You should give all proper encouragement to peaceful and legitimate trade between the natives and persons who may visit the Protectorate. . . .

11. It will . . . be your duty to prohibit all dealing with the natives in arms or ammunition, explosive substances, or spirituous liquors, and . . . to prohibit the supply of arms, ammunition, and explosive substances to natives. . . .

12. It is probable that attempts may be made to engage Laborers for Queensland, and possibly, other places, from among the natives in the Protectorate; and should such attempts be made, it will be your duty to place every lawful obstacle in their way.[30]

Three days after giving Scratchley his instructions, Lord Derby sent him his commission as "Special Commissioner for the Protected Territory in New Guinea," which required him

> to the utmost of your power, to promote religion and civilization among the native inhabitants of the Protectorate, and you are especially to take care to protect them in their persons and in the free enjoyment of their lands and other possessions, and by all lawful means to prevent and restrain all violence and injustice which may in any manner be practiced or attempted against them.[31]

Some of Scratchley's instructions required no underpinning of legal authority. However, if he was going to "secure . . . the safety" of New Guineans, protect their lands, oversee the acquisition of their land by non-New Guineans, prevent the dealing in weapons, obstruct labor recruiters, as well as "prevent and restrain all violence and injustice which may in any manner be practiced or attempted against" New Guineans, Scratchley would need jurisdiction not only over British subjects but also over New Guineans and non-British citizens living in the protectorate.

Gladstone's expansive interpretation of British jurisdiction in New Guinea caused uncertainty in the colonial office and led the permanent head of that office to seek advice from the solicitor-general and the attorney-general. In their December 11, 1884, Crown law officers' report, the two senior officials took the position that, under the *Foreign Jurisdiction Act*, Britain's declaration of a "Protectorate" over a state gave it jurisdiction only over British subjects and over the foreign affairs of the protectorate.[32] Since the purpose of the act was to give the British government the authority to establish courts and to exercise jurisdiction over British subjects in territories where Britain had the right of control but not sovereignty, it did not give Britain jurisdiction over the Indigenous people of the territory or over non-British persons. That limited view of jurisdiction squared with Britain's limited goal, in proclaiming the protectorate over New Guinea, of protecting its Australian colonies with minimum expense.

The limited scope of Britain's jurisdiction over its protectorates was based on the view that a protectorate amounted to a foreign state, and that its residents did not become British subjects simply as a result of the territory becoming a protectorate. However, other European nations, especially those seeking to become colonial powers, did not share Britain's limited view of its power in relation to areas they had declared to be their protectorates. And some legal scholars also disagreed with the British position.

Ultimately Britain's position was rejected in Australia as well. In a 1973 decision, then chief justice of the High Court of Australia, Sir Garfield Barwick, writing for the majority in *The Administration of Papua and New Guinea v. Guba and Dorija*, took the position that the law officers' approach to the protectorate "was an erroneous view,"[33] writing that:

> [T]he extent to which the Crown obtains power over British and non-British persons in a Protectorate depends very much on the purposes for which the Protectorate is proclaimed and the situation in the area of the Protectorate; particularly as regards local sovereignty or authority. The express purpose of establishing the Protectorate [in New Guinea] was to protect Papuans, both from foreigners, British subjects and, indeed, from themselves in order that they might enjoy the use of their land in peace. That purpose could not be carried out without exercising authority both over the foreigners and the Papuans as well as over British subjects. The usual purpose of the declaration of Protectorate was really absent in relation to Port Moresby, that is to say, the purpose of taking charge of external relations of the

> community occupying the Protectorate. There was little possibility of there being any external relations for Port Moresby beyond the physical exclusion of non-indigenous people who might come either forcibly or deceitfully to take Papuans' land or the Papuans themselves for use as agricultural workers elsewhere.[34]

In an attempt to resolve the contradiction between the extensive list of duties contained in his letter of appointment and the limited view of his powers to carry out those duties in the law officers' report, Scratchley stopped in Queensland on his way to New Guinea in order to seek the opinion of Sir Samuel Griffith, then the premier of Queensland and later the first chief justice of Australia. Unfortunately for Scratchley, Griffith also took a narrow view of the extent of his authority, writing that:

> General Scratchley has at present no legal jurisdiction and authority of any kind, except such as he can exercise as a Deputy Commissioner for the Western Pacific; and in particular that he has no power to make any regulations having the force of law, or to impose or collect any taxes or license fees upon exports, or imports, or otherwise to exercise any legislature or judicial functions in the Protectorate.[35]

Thus, the special commissioners of the protectorate had no jurisdiction over either New Guineans or non-British citizens living in the territory. The few measures of legal authority they possessed came from their position as deputy commissioners of the Western Pacific High Commission. As deputy commissioners, they could issue regulations governing British subjects living on Pacific islands that were not formally colonies, but those regulations had little effect in New Guinea, since there were only about twenty non-New Guineans living in the Protectorate, not all of whom were British subjects.

Establishing an Administration for the Protectorate

Scratchley's first challenge after his arrival in New Guinea was to establish an administration for the protectorate. Although Port Moresby had only seven expatriate residents, it was chosen as the seat of the administration for four reasons: it was the only place that had any permanent expatriate residents at all; it was thought to be a reasonably healthy location; it had a good harbor; and it was easily accessible to Cooktown, in the far north of Queensland, which had a telegraph station.[36] While the situation would have been difficult for any administrator, it posed special challenges to Scratchley who, as a retired general, engineer, and advisor on defense matters, had no prior experience in colonial administration. In addition, financial restrictions severely limited his ability to carry out the duties listed in his letter of appointment. His only funds were the £15,000 provided annually by the Australian colonies. Thus, Scratchley was able to hire a staff of only six persons to administer the entire territory, which was the size of England and Wales combined.

Because of the size of the protectorate, the widely scattered New Guinean population, the difficulty of travel within the territory, and the lack of financial and human resources, Scratchley decided that an administrative system based on direct rule was impossible. Instead, he took the view that "New Guinea must be governed for the natives and by the natives"[37] and considered creating a system of "indirect rule," similar to that developed by the British in the mid-eighteenth century in India and later used in some of their African and Asian colonies.[38] Under Scratchley's proposal for indirect rule in New Guinea, the colonial administration would appoint a tribal chief for each district who would be responsible for the safety of all foreigners and for the maintenance of law and order within his district.

But, Scratchley's term as special commissioner was to last barely five months, He contracted malaria and died on December 2. Few colonial officials shared his views. Anthony Musgrave, his own assistant deputy commissioner, opposed his views, a position Musgrave made public within just a few months of Scratchley's death. In an 1886 "Memorandum on Native Policy," Musgrave wrote that Scratchley's "opinions and projects regarding British New Guinea were avowedly of a tentative character, and some of those referring to a future native policy and control would, I believe, have been widely modified, if not abandoned, had he lived to gain a closer and larger experience of our aboriginal population."[39] In particular, Musgrave wrote that to pursue any policy based on the idea that "'New Guinea must be governed for the natives and by the natives,' would . . . be a costly and chimerical experiment in colonial organization, inevitably resulting in failure. It could not retard indefinitely the natural and progressive influences of civilisation."[40] Musgrave's statements reflected the beliefs of the majority of British and Australians at the time that their duty was to bring Christianity and Western civilization to New Guineans, a mission that they believed could be carried out only by direct rule. Musgrave also expressed harsh views about New Guineans and their customs that reflected those typically held by most Australians throughout the colonial period:

> Our aboriginals are savages in the first stages of barbarism, swayed by intense and degrading superstitions which involve them in ceaseless intertribal feuds and bloodshed, and the first really important protection that the natives require . . . is from each other. . . . No real tribal discipline or organization exists and to "govern by the natives" is a sheer impossibility. . . .[41]

In late December 1885, John Douglas, a politician who had served as premier of Queensland from 1877 to 1879, succeeded Scratchley as special commissioner. Two months later, Douglas prepared a memorandum to Britain's secretary of state for the colonies setting out what he thought were the requirements for the administration of the protectorate. Douglas made a major recommendation "as regards administration and legislation," aimed at giving formal recognition to the customs of New Guineans.

> [T]he Government of New Guinea must, for some years at least, be primitive and paternal, dependent much on personal influence. Native customs must be recognized; native rights must be respected. This, in any agreement made with Her Majesty's Government, should be clearly defined, and should be a fundamental article in the constitution of the new State, when the Queen's Sovereignty is confirmed.[42]

Douglas was much more specific than Scratchley had been that "New Guinea must be governed for the natives and by the natives." He called for the recognition of the customs of New Guineans to be "a fundamental article in the constitution of the new State" when the protectorate formally became a colony. Douglas's recommendations likely would have had a transformative impact on the ethos, structure, and operation of the colonial legal system. However, British and Australian officials did not accept them. Their views were much more in line with Musgrave's. Although the reality of administering New Guinea persuaded officials throughout the colonial period to give informal recognition to custom and to provide a measure of protection for customary land rights, any formal recognition of custom or customary law by the colonial legal system would have to wait eight decades.

Land Acquisition Policies Governing Colonial Administrations

There were only two buildings in Port Moresby when Scratchley arrived in August 1885: the London Missionary Society house (the site of the proclamation ceremony) and a trade store belonging to Andrew Goldie, an explorer and trader who had been in New Guinea since 1877 and had purchased or leased several large tracts of land from New Guineans. In order to carry out governmental functions, Scratchley had to acquire land and construct buildings. The instructions accompanying his letter of appointment prohibited Scratchley from incurring any building expenses until the Australian colonial government provided the necessary funds. Scratchley managed to secure those funds while in Australia on his way to New Guinea.

As a result, a few days after he arrived in the protectorate, Scratchley and Musgrave began purchasing land from New Guinean groups living in the Port Moresby area. They paid for the land in trade goods, such as hatchets, cloth, and tobacco. The land they obtained ranged in size from about one acre up to 333 acres and, according to G. Seymour Fort, who was Scratchley's private secretary, comprised "the best sites in the harbor and nearly the whole of the frontage to the sea."[43] On one portion of the land, Scratchley had constructed a two-room government house, which served as an office and his residence, a printing office, and a jail. He also set aside land for a future township and held other land as a native reserve.

The acquisition of land by the administration gave the villagers around Port Moresby their first contact with the English legal system. Unfortunately, the record is lacking in many of the details about how Scratchley and Musgrave went about procuring these lands. We know that, in some cases, they followed something vaguely approximating the requirements of English property law by calling together the Koita and Motu owners of the land and "obtaining their assent to parting with their property *in perpetuo* and thus securing a sound title for the Government."[44] However, British and New Guinean concepts about the relationships of individuals to land, who could use it, for how long, and whether it could be sold were so different that it is doubtful the two groups of negotiators understood one another. The Motuans and other tribes who lived in and near Port Moresby had no concept of individual fee simple ownership of land, nor would the notion that land could be alienated *in perpetuo* from the clan ever have occurred to them. Most likely, they believed they were loaning the use of the land to these foreigners until such time as someone in the tribe needed to use it again. At the same time, Scratchley and other special commissioners were equally in the dark about Motu concepts of group tenure and of the flexible and ever-changing nature of land use. Scratchley asked the Rev. Lawes to prepare a report on the subject, but it was not published until March 1886, three months after Scratchley died. According to Lawes:

> The land on the coast is all owned by families, each member having his own plot. They are accustomed to sell their land occasionally. A man who has but a little will beg of one who has plenty. Sometimes they loan it for one crop—a short rental really. Often, it is an absolute sale. In this case it does not revert to its original owners on the death of the purchaser, but is the property of his heirs forever. The land in the interior is probably subject to the same conditions. It is very doubtful if there is any really unowned or waste land; there is certainly none in the neighborhood of Port Moresby. From the coast range of hills, right away to the Laroge River, all belongs to the Koiapu tribe. The thick forests on the banks of the rivers and creeks, in thinly-populated districts, are the most likely to be unclaimed, as the wood is not used by the people, and is too large to be cleared for cultivation of the soil.[45]

Musgrave justified the acquisitions by stating that the land acquired by the government was not needed by its New Guinean owners since it was not in cultivation. However, New Guineans practiced sustainable shifting agriculture, creating vegetable gardens on one plot of land for five or six years and then moving to different plots, leaving the old gardens fallow for a decade or more. As a result, much of the land the administration acquired would have been used for gardens after a fallow period and the rest was probably designated for hunting and gathering.

Scratchley also procured a large tract of land, consisting of approximately half of Stacey Island, off the southeast coast in present-day Milne Bay Province, in October 1885. The island was chosen because it was thought to be a good site for a mission station. Since there purportedly was only one customary owner of that land, and the rest of his tribe recognized his individual right to it, Scratchley did not prepare a deed for the sale of the land. Instead, the Rev. Chalmers signed a statement that the New Guinean owner of the land had the sole right to it, that he parted with it voluntarily, and that he and his tribe were satisfied with the payment of trade goods consisting of an axe, three tomahawks, four knives, twelve mirrors, a bundle of hoop-iron, twenty-one pipes, cloth, and tobacco, worth a grand total of about £5.

The special commission given to John Douglas instructed him to protect New Guineans in the free enjoyment of the lands. Although it did not give him express powers to acquire land, Douglas wrote in his first annual report: "The land question is no doubt the cardinal one upon which almost everything connected with British policy within the Protectorate will turn. It is the primary consideration, both as regards the present native inhabitants and those schemes of colonization which have at various times been suggested."[46] Douglas was eager to add to the amount of land that Scratchley had acquired in the Port Moresby area and hired a surveyor from Adelaide to design and lay out a new township. By the end of 1886, the administration had obtained more than 850 acres in and near Port Moresby. Officials believed that they had purchased 552 acres of that land after negotiating with more than 1,250 New Guineans with interests in the land.

In Western law, the doctrine of waste and vacant land allows a colonizer to seize land that seems to be uninhabited or unused without having to pay for it. Although that concept does not exist in Papua New Guinean customary land law, Douglas used it to obtain an additional three hundred acres of land that he considered to be of no use to New Guineans. We will never know whether in fact the land was owned by one clan or another and used by them as hunting ground or for crops that were not being grown at that time, but Douglas felt no necessity to pay for that land. Using the doctrine, he made another acquisition of land for a cemetery in Port Moresby in 1886.

The land Douglas purchased in the area near Port Moresby, now known as Newtown, became the subject of litigation in the early 1970s. In *Administration of the Territory of Papua New Guinea v. Guba*,[47] the High Court of Australia first had to decide whether the protectorate had the power to purchase land in Port Moresby in 1886 and to enter into legal transactions with New Guineans. Writing for the court, Chief Justice Barwick held that Erskine's prohibition on the acquisition of land applied only to private individuals and did not prevent the administration from securing land by purchase or compulsion for public purposes.[48] The case also underscored the different attitudes toward the concepts of *ownership* and *sale* of land in customary law and English law, which were ignored by Scratchley and Douglas and which characterized all land transactions throughout the colonial period. The administration claimed it had ownership of the land on the basis that Douglas had purchased it on behalf of the Crown in 1886. The plaintiffs were representatives of two clans that claimed to be descended from the land's original owners. They took the position that, under the customary law of the time, their forbears had no capacity to transfer permanent and absolute ownership of the land to strangers. In its *Guba* decision, the High Court quoted Lawes's report to support the administration's contention that New Guineans understood a transaction of outright sale of their land and that the Crown had acquired the land by purchase for value, the value being the "trade mutually agreed" between the representatives of the Crown and the clan.[49] In giving its support to the policy that customary land had been available to non-Papua New Guineans, the High Court determined that English law and not the law of the traditional owners governed the land transaction, even though English law had not been adopted in the protectorate and was not the law of the clans who owned the land.

The acquisition of land by Scratchley and Douglas appeared to conflict with the earlier assurances to New Guineans given by Erskine in his November 1884 shipboard speech preceding the establishment of the protectorate, in which he promised the assembled New Guineans "your lands will be secured to you." Erskine was more specific and comprehensive the following day in his proclamation speech, when he declared: "no acquisition of land, whensoever or howsoever acquired, within the limits of the Protectorate hereby established, will be recognized by Her Majesty." Finally, one of the regulations Erskine issued a week after the proclamation stated that "[n]o settlement or acquisition of land is on any account to be permitted."[50] However, Erskine did not state whether he intended that prohibition on the acquisition of land to apply to the colonial administration as well as to private individuals. The ambiguity in Erskine's statements became moot when the colonial office gave Scratchley his instructions along with his letter of appointment as special commissioner. Those instructions prohibited the acquisition of land from New Guineans by private individuals but not by the administration. In the absence of language prohibiting acquisitions by the administration, Scratchley and Douglas adopted a policy (which was codified once New Guinea became a colony) that gave them the right to acquire land from New Guineans, subject to some conditions. In doing so, the special commissioners established the three methods that administrators would use throughout the colonial period to secure land in New Guinea: "purchase" from the Indigenous owners of the land; a declaration by administrators that the land was "waste and vacant"; and compulsory acquisition of the land.

Land Acquisition Policies Governing Private Purchasers

During the protectorate, the special commissioners had to deal with requests by private individuals to purchase land from New Guineans. Erskine's unequivocal statements against the alienation of land were superseded by the instructions given to Scratchley with his commission of appointment in 1885. Those instructions began the often-conflicting policies of protecting New Guinean land rights while, at the same time, promoting trade and settlement by encouraging Europeans to acquire land for their own use. Instruction No. 9 mandated that, if New Guineans wanted to sell their land to Europeans, they had to submit the terms of the sale to Scratchley for his approval, and the purchase price had to be paid through him. The instruction also directed Scratchley to make sure that the New Guineans understood that, by "the sale of the land," they gave up "all further claim to it" and that it became "the absolute property of the purchasers."[51] As in the cases of acquisition by the administration, giving up "all further claims" to land was a concept unknown to New Guineans. Under virtually all customary land tenure systems in New Guinea, land belonged collectively to the members of the clan—it might be loaned to others briefly for a specific purpose or to meet changing needs, but it could not be alienated. The administration's warnings to New Guineans that they were alienating the land permanently was probably so incomprehensible to them that they would not have understood it. How and to what extent individual expatriates could acquire land in the territory was a subject that became the topic of numerous ordinances after New Guinea became a British Crown Colony in 1888.

Scratchley and, after him, Douglas also had to decide how to deal with the few expatriates who claimed that they already had purchased or leased land from New Guineans before the proclamation of the protectorate. An example of the confusion in these transactions was the supposed acquisition of approximately twelve thousand acres of land in 1883 along the southern coast in the Kabadi district by Andrew Goldie and J. B. Cameron. Goldie claimed that the local owners had fully discussed the transactions, had voluntarily agreed to a deed transferring the land, and had received cloth and tobacco worth about £120 as payment. Goldie said that he did not intend the acquisition to be an "out-and-out purchase," but only a way of insuring his prior claim over the land. However, Cameron took the view that the purchase was a final sale.

Scratchley investigated all of the claims by whites that New Guineans had sold their land to them. In most cases, including Goldie's, he determined that there was no legal basis to permit the transfer of the land. Other traders claimed a prescriptive right to lease land, based on their long occupancy or exploration of it. For example, Goldie also claimed to have leased the rights to graze animals on another large tract of land for twenty years. The terms of the lease, an annual payment of £50, were described as "very equitable" since the land was "at present not utilized . . . at all" and was "lying waste and contains no garden or villages."[52] The lease also gave Goldie the right to erect buildings and cultivate the land and to cut timber for building or fencing. Scratchley investigated those claims as well and gave Goldie and Ah Gim, a Chinese trader on Suau Island, permission to occupy administration land and to construct a house and store in place of the land they had leased. Although Scratchley planned to introduce a system of land registration for persons who purchased or occupied land, his early death delayed the development of the register.

Douglas also was unsympathetic to land acquisition claims—past and future—by individual expatriates. In 1886 the administration decided to remove expatriate settlement from the Hanuabada area adjacent to Port Moresby. In exchange for his property, the administration offered Andrew Goldie six blocks in the new township. However, after a dispute with Anthony Musgrave, Goldie was compensated with £300 and given fifty acres outside of Port Moresby and three allotments in the town on which he built a store in January 1887. In 1888, Theodore Bevan sought a land concession of 254,000 acres as recognition for his explorations in the protectorate. Douglas refused his request, and those of other individuals and syndicates, stating that he had no authority to make any such grants of land. Douglas also feared that expatriate acquisition of large tracts of fertile land would leave New Guineans without land for their own food production and would require physical force to acquire and defend, which the administration did not have.

The policies toward the acquisition of land formulated by Scratchley and Douglas were based on two foundations that would be codified in land ordinances throughout the colonial period: recognition of the land rights of New Guineans and restrictions on the alienation of land to expatriates. While the details of the land acquisition policies would vary over the years, these key factors remained constant and led to a situation that would be unusual in the colonial world. At the end of the colonial period, 97 percent of the land in Papua New Guinea remained in the hands of Indigenous owners. The 3 percent of the land that was owned by the government or was under long-term lease to expatriates included not only the administrative centers but also some of the best and most productive land in the country. Whether it should be returned to local control was a matter of considerable contention. However, unlike in many colonies, Papua New Guinea did not experience the concentration of much of its land in the hands of a few large estates owned by whites, resulting in a dispossessed and landless Indigenous population left to work on those estates as tenants.

Protecting New Guineans from Harm and Exploitation

The special commissioners seemed to take seriously Erskine's declaration that they try to protect New Guineans from exploitation by foreigners. Based on two of the regulations that Erskine issued in November 1884, Romilly banned the import and sale of firearms, explosives, and alcohol into New Guinea. He also tried to put a stop to blackbirding by prohibiting labor recruiters from taking New Guinean workers out of the protectorate; he oversaw the repatriation of almost 650 New Guineans who had been taken to work on the sugar plantations in Queensland; and he provided compensation (in the form of trade goods) to the relatives of over 190 New Guinean men who had died while working on plantations in Queensland.

There was almost no economic activity by the British or Australians during the protectorate and no plans to encourage European settlers. Regulations promulgated by Romilly and Scratchley prohibited non-New Guineans from entering the protectorate without a permit. Theodore Bevan, who arrived in Port Moresby in late 1884, later wrote that Romilly

> interrogated us as to our intention, and stated that we had no right to be there at all; that under the proclamation no settlement of any kind would be allowed; and further characterized the reported prevalent idea in Australia of future settlement being permitted as, in his opinion, *very delusive*.[53]

However, Romilly permitted Bevan to land and to remain in Port Moresby for five or six weeks on the condition that he leave when the ship on which he arrived departed. Although Scratchley later granted permits to several private companies and individuals to trade in New Guinea, he rejected a number of applications to explore the territory, some on the grounds that they were underfunded, others because he felt that the applicants would harm relations with New Guineans.

Like Romilly, Scratchley did not hesitate to deport non-New Guineans whose presence he considered to be a threat to peace in the villages in which they were living. Often because the expatriate was sexually harassing or assaulting women. For example, in November 1885 Scratchley convened a court of inquiry at Hula, west of Port Moresby, aboard the administration's ship to try two men, Guise and Currie, on charges of "interfering" with New Guinean women. The two men previously had been deported by Romilly, but had returned. Although the New Guinean witnesses failed to provide sufficient evidence to convict the men of crimes, Scratchley issued an order of prohibition, under clause 27 of the Western Pacific Order in Council, requiring them to leave the protectorate. Clause 27 prohibited foreign residents in New Guinea from remaining if the high commissioner considered their presence to be "detrimental to the peace and good order of the Pacific Islands."[54] Although Scratchley did not have that authority, the isolation of New Guinea permitted him to act decisively and without repercussions.

Tribal Fighting

In his report on British New Guinea for 1886, John Douglas wrote that his officers had "acquired a very considerable influence over the neighboring native population, and that this has been exercised with very beneficial results in repressing the intertribal atrocities which are the normal incidents of New Guinea life in its savage state."[55] Despite that initial note of optimism, the success of the special commissioners in preventing tribal fighting was actually quite limited. In a letter written in December 1887, Romilly referred to Erskine's shipboard speech to New Guinean leaders in which he told them that they must keep the peace among themselves; if they had disputes with other tribes, they were to come to government officials who would settle them without bloodshed. Romilly wrote that, as a result of that order, a number of groups of New Guineans had come to him with accounts of members of their tribes being killed by other tribes and asking for his help. However, a frustrated Romilly noted that: "I have no power, either legal or physical, to punish their aggressors, and so I am in the disagreeable position of having to act illegally or break the most solemn promises."[56] Although the British and Australians became more aggressive in dealing with tribal fighting once New Guinea became a colony, inter-group conflicts lasted throughout the colonial period and have continued since independence.

New Guinean Resistance: Killing Expatriates

Of all the issues that arose during the protectorate, the special commissioners viewed the deaths of expatriates as the most serious. In his shipboard speech to New Guinean leaders the day before the establishment of the protectorate, Erskine emphasized that "under no circumstances" were they to "inflict punishment upon any white person." Instead, if any white man harmed a New Guinean, they were to inform government officers immediately and those officers would investigate their complaints and see that they received justice. Nevertheless, a number of expatriates did die at the hands of New Guineans during the four years of the protectorate. Officials investigated many of those deaths and in some instances managed to capture suspects. In other cases, officials conducted punitive raids and used British naval ships to shell and burn villages, exacting indiscriminate revenge. However, in the majority of cases, the lack of resources and of the jurisdiction to arrest and prosecute New Guineans meant that officials decided they were unable to do much of anything at all about the killings.

Romilly was the most cautious official when dealing with the killing of expatriates. Three months after the protectorate was established, he learned that an expatriate couple, along with the entire crew of their boat, had been killed. However, Romilly wrote that he would "do nothing till we know more."[57] In fact, no more was ever done. That same month, the captain and some crew members of a ship belonging to the British navy were attacked while on shore and forced to retreat to their ship. The ship then fired on the New Guineans. Anthony Musgrave, who was then deputy commissioner, doubted the legality of causing damage to New Guineans and ordered the ship to withdraw. A month later, Musgrave sought permission to punish some New Guineans for killings in Amazon Bay. Romilly refused him permission, fearing that Musgrave lacked the forces to do so successfully and that the protectorate lacked jurisdiction over New Guineans. He summed up the situation in 1886 when he wrote about the killing of a ship captain and two other men: "[I]n the present state of affairs, before the Queens's sovereignty has been proclaimed, we have no legal right to issue regulations or to punish."[58]

Scratchley spent a large portion of his three months in New Guinea exploring the country and used that time to investigate reports of the killing of expatriates. In some cases, he was unsympathetic to the traders or labor recruiters who were killed, believing that they provoked New Guineans by their actions. In an October 1885 diary entry, Scratchley wrote:

> I am satisfied that these traders are often reckless, unscrupulous, brutal, and piratical. They cheat the native and are apt to appeal to their revolvers. I cannot feel any sympathy for such men. They go where they have no business to. They are a thorn in my side, and I do not think the life of any white man should be risked in avenging their deaths.[59]

While not condoning the killing of expatriates, many missionaries—who lived with New Guineans, often for long periods of time—were prepared to defend the New Guineans. In a paper prepared at the request of Scratchley in 1885, the Rev. Lawes wrote:

> I know of no case in which it can be said with certainty that the natives were the first aggressors. Instead of being described as "savage," "hostile," and "treacherous," they should, in justice be spoken of as kindly disposed and friendly on their first intercourse with white men, but generally suspicious and watchful.[60]

In a speech in Queensland in June 1888, Lawes said that "each [New Guineans and Europeans] considered the other cannibals and worth watching—and the conflicts that had arisen had usually been the result of mutual misunderstanding and suspicion."[61] Lawes believed that New Guineans had good reason to be suspicious of expatriates, given the New Guineans' history of harsh treatment by whites. The close relationship and mutual sympathy between missionaries and New Guineans resulted in a shared suspicion between missionaries and expatriate settlers that continued throughout the colonial period.

Scratchley's assessment of the killing of expatriates was reflected in the conclusions he reached after investigating six cases that had occurred in the two years before he arrived in New Guinea. He concluded that those killings fell into two classes: first, expatriates who were killed for their individual crimes against the customs of New Guineans, such as interfering with local women, unjust dealing, or ignoring tribal warfare; and second, expatriates who were victims of vengeance in response to the forced labor trade. In all six of those cases, Scratchley concluded the victims had been guilty of either "direct or indirect aggressive provocation" or had recklessly disregarded warnings. He declined to take action against any of the New Guineans involved.

Despite Scratchley's lack of sympathy for those particular victims, he did not assume that the death of every expatriate was provoked. In some cases, he conducted an investigation but was unable to find those responsible. In other cases, where villagers refused to surrender suspects, he sometimes resorted to punitive methods. In October 1885, a group of New Guineans killed a young fisherman named Fred Miller. Miller operated a smoke house on an island, in what now is Milne Bay Province, and employed a number of New Guineans to help him cure the fish. Scratchley went to the village where the killing occurred and questioned a number of men. Two villagers from the island admitted killing Miller because one of their relatives had died on a sugar plantation in Queensland and the compensation required by their custom had not been paid to them. To appease the spirit of the dead relative, the two villagers killed the first European they saw. One of the murderers, a man named Diavari, voluntarily came on board one of the navy ships, confessed to the killing, and offered to make compensation in the form of some arm-shells, a basket, and some tobacco.

Diavari's actions were the first example of what would become a serious and recurring problem throughout the colonial period: the conflict between the rules of the British criminal law system and the customary norms and processes of New Guineans. Scratchley believed he had an obligation under British law to punish Diavari for killing Miller, even though there were no criminal statutes in force in the protectorate, no judges to conduct a trial, and no British jurisdiction over New Guineans. Diavari just as firmly believed that it was a justified killing under customary law, and the proper response was that the killer and his relatives offer appropriate compensation, such as arm-shells or pigs, to the victim's family or community. Diavari was doing what was expected of him by his community, none of whom had any idea that there were harsher ways of resolving the matter when a person was killed. Diavari and all of his relatives and fellow villagers must have been surprised and confused when the commander of the navy ship detained him and sent him to Port Moresby. There, Diavari had the distinction of being the first person held in the jail built by Scratchley. Diavari worked on public works projects in the town for a year and then was returned to his village. Unfortunately, his interpretation of his experience with the British legal system is not known.

The approach taken by Scratchley in dealing with Diavari laid the foundation for what later would become the practice of judges when dealing with cases involving New Guineans accused of acts such as tribal fighting, sorcery, payback killings, and cannibalism, which amounted to serious crimes under British law but not under customary law. The colonial administration arrested and prosecuted New Guineans for acts that violated British law in order, the authorities said, to demonstrate to villagers that their customs were not acceptable to the colonial regime. A defendant never was adjudged innocent on the grounds that he had been doing what custom required him to do. At the same time, however, Scratchley and later the colonial judges believed it would be a mistake to subject Papuan and New Guinean defendants to the maximum sentence under British law for their crimes because they were still ignorant of the laws they had broken.

All too frequently, Scratchley found that his officers could not identify or apprehend the perpetrator. In those situations, it became common for the administration to exact punishment from the defendant's entire village. For example, when villagers refused to surrender a second suspect in the Miller case, Scratchley retaliated by sending Romilly and his forces to burn entire towns. Romilly, who then was the deputy special commissioner responsible for the area where the killing occurred, wrote with some regret about the incident and about the reasons New Guineans killed men such as Miller:

> We have got as far as East Cape on our tour of inspection, and now we have got to go all the way back to Port Moresby for coals and provisions. We have been burning towns and smashing canoes, and other police work. We all hate it, and feel very mean while we are doing it. The natives have sworn to kill every white man, and they have killed a good many. They say they were stolen by Queensland ships, and half their men died in Queensland, and they must have revenge.[62]

The Miller case is an example of actions that belie one of the enduring myths of New Guinea's colonial history: that the establishment of British and Australian rule was without the violence that characterized colonization in India, Africa, and Asia. Beginning with the British navy's response to the death of William Bairstow Ingham in late 1878, the frustration of not being able to discover or arrest individual New Guineans alleged to have committed crimes led officials on a number of occasions to mount punitive expeditions. An example of what one scholar has called "naval justice"[63] occurred after the killing of a trader named Webb and his New Guinean wife at Milport Harbor in 1884. The captain of a Royal Navy vessel sent to investigate was unable to obtain any evidence, and his ship left after New Guineans attacked it. The following year, two other warships, led by Scratchley, returned to the area and shelled the villages on the hills surrounding the bay. These actions were taken despite the fact that Scratchley later wrote that Webb was "a horrible brute; he had often burned down villages, shot boys for stealing tobacco, and he compelled his wretched wife to go with him."[64] Scratchley's private secretary concluded: "Webb had borne a very bad character for brutal and dishonest dealings with the natives." However, he felt that the shelling was "the only punishment possible."[65] In 1944, Lewis Lett, a historian and long-time resident of New Guinea, wrote:

> This massacre was as fully justified as such a thing could be. Webb's record was a black one. For years he had been the maker of his own laws; laws which tended always to his own advantage at the expense of the natives. Rough, unprincipled, cruel, he paid no more than the inevitable price for his period of dominance.[66]

The comments of Romilly and Scratchley's secretary about the response to the killings of Miller and Webb indicate that the myth that violence was not part of government policy was propagated by the very men who perpetrated it. The photographer John W. Lindt, who also was part of the search party for Miller's killers, described the shelling of the village not as violence but as a "fracas" and concluded that "I do not think a single native was hurt. . . . in fact, the Commanders never intended to take life, but simply to administer a wholesome lesson."[67] Lewis Lett defended Scratchley's punitive actions on the grounds that "in justice it must be admitted that no other form of punishment was possible. There was no police force in those days; there was no power behind the laws for the very good reason that there was no New Guinea law in existence; nor had the Special Commissioner power to make any."[68] At the same time, however, he admitted that using navy ships to fire upon and burn villages

> was probably the least effectual [punishment] that could have been devised, and its result was merely to raise in the natives a spirit of resentment and defiance, while the war vessels upon which they had looked with a good deal of apprehension were stripped of their terrors and became mere annoyances and objects of more or less contemptuous dislike.[69]

Immediately after engaging in the punitive actions in the Miller case, Scratchley sailed to another island to investigate the murder of a trader named Reid. When he learned that Reid had been "a lawless fellow, who for a long time set all native rules and mere common decency at nought," Scratchley concluded that his bad conduct had been the cause of the killing and decided to take no further action.[70]

The Miller and Reid cases, along with other investigations, led Scratchley to two conclusions about the killing of expatriates. The first was that "the Government cannot be responsible for the protection of irresponsible traders, who cruise from place to place in vessels insufficiently manned, whose defenceless position and the possession of trade which they injudiciously expose, are almost invariably a source of incitement to the native to attack them."[71] Scratchley felt that the traders came to the country to pursue their own desire for profit and with full knowledge of the risks they faced. Scratchley's second conclusion was that this form of vigilantism—using navy ships to shell coastal villagers as a punishment—was not the answer to the killing of Europeans, since it risked killing innocent villagers, embittered relations, and in most cases was ineffective since the villagers simply retreated inland when they saw a warship approaching. Scratchley wrote:

> Men-of-war vessels are not suited for the purpose of administering justice and punishing outrages on the New Guinea coast; that under the peculiar condition for which they are required, they combine the least amount of efficiency with the greatest display for force.[72]

The Rev. Chalmers, who accompanied Scratchley on a number of his investigations, also objected to the burning of village houses, writing that "[i]n acts of this kind, innocent and guilty suffer alike; this is certainly not being in harmony with John Bull's love of fair play."[73]

Douglas also realized that he did not have the legal authority or the resources to arrest and punish New Guineans who killed expatriates, but he also used punitive expeditions to avenge such deaths. In September 1886, New Guineans killed John C. Craig, a ship captain and trader, along with seven non-New Guinean crewmembers. In response, Douglas made a bold statement to the admiral in charge of the Australia Station, the British naval command responsible for the area around Australia: "The future civilization of the Protectorate will depend very much on the determination of the rulers to make their power felt and respected; to do so in moderation, but decisively."[74] Douglas sent the administration official responsible for the Eastern Division, Henry O. Forbes, to investigate the killings and to arrest the perpetrators and recover the weapons and other stolen property. Although Forbes and the private traders he hired to assist him failed to arrest the killers of Craig, they captured other suspects and recovered some of the firearms taken when Craig was killed. They also burned three villages as punishment. Douglas agreed with the type of punishment inflicted on the New Guineans but criticized the excesses of its application. The historian John Mayo described the episode as an example of "the complete absence of any considered policies in the Protectorate for dealing with indigenous attacks on foreign traders."[75] The following year, Douglas ordered a punitive raid to avenge the killing of a South Seas Island missionary teacher and five New Guineans. The raid resulted in the killing of five New Guinean and the wounding of four others. That same year, Douglas went to Moresby Island to punish five villages for killing some Chinese men. He used the navy to bombard and burn villages and canoes and fired into the New Guineans who had gathered near the shore. Douglas gave a justification for that punitive raid in his 1887 annual report, which could have served as the justification employed to make all such raids seem less barbaric and violent than they actually were:

> It is necessary that the white man should, under proper limits, assert his power, and I should not myself hesitate to take life in order to vindicate justice, but I am most desirous to avoid not only the appearance, but the reality of practices which are as barbarous as those of the native themselves.[76]

The Protectorate: A Brief Assessment

When the British declared a protectorate over the southeastern portion of the islands of New Guinea in November 1884, they intended it to be a temporary status. Formal annexation would come only when, and if, Britain and its Australian colonies could agree on a plan to finance the administration of the territory. Although financial, personnel, and jurisdiction limitations restricted the reach of the administration to Port Moresby and small government stations at Motu Motu, Rigo, and Samarai, the four years of the Protectorate were an important period for the development of New Guinea's colonial legal system. It was during that brief time that the special commissioners, acting without a formal legal system, developed policies and practices that would be of paramount importance throughout the colonial period: first, the colonial authorities would recognize New Guinean ownership of their land and regulate the alienation of it to expatriates, but British law and not Papuan or New Guinean customary law would govern both the principles of land ownership and the validity of land transactions; second, the employment of New Guinean labor by expatriates would be permitted but it too would be regulated by the administration; and third, killings and other acts considered by the administrations to be serious crimes would be punished. The policies of the special commissioners during those four years laid the foundation for the ordinances and procedures that became the formal colonial legal system once New Guinea became a British Crown Colony.

Sources

Books and Articles

David Armitage, *The Ideological Origins of the British Empire: Ideas in Context* (Cambridge: Cambridge University Press, 2000).

The Australian Handbook 1886 (London: Gordon and Gotch, 1886).

The Australian Handbook 1888 (London: Gordon and Gotch, 1888).

Chris Ballard, "Exploration of Interior New Guinea, 1725–1876," in Margaret Jolly, Serge Tcherkézoff, and Darrell Tryon (eds.), *Oceanic Encounters: Exchange, Desire, Violence* (Canberra: Australian National University Press, 2009) 221–258.

Denver Beanland, *The Queensland Caesar: Sir Thomas McIlwraith* (Tingalpa: Boolarong Press, 2013).

Wilfred N. Beaver, *Unexplored New Guinea* (London: Seeley, Service and Co., Ltd., 1920).

Peter Bellwood, *Man's Conquest of the Pacific: The Prehistory of Southeast Asia and Oceania* (Oxford: Oxford University Press, 1979).

Isaiah Berlin, "Notes on Prejudice," *The New York Review of Books* (October 18, 2001) 12.

Theodore F. Bevan, *Toil, Travel, and Discovery in British New Guinea* (London: Kegan Paul, Trench, Trübner and Co., 1890).

Peter Biskup, Brian Jinks, and Hank Nelson, *A Short History of New Guinea* (Sydney: Angus and Robertson, 1968).

David Blair, *Cyclopedia of Australasia; or Dictionary of Facts, Events, Dates, Persons, and Places Connected with the Discovery, Exploration, and Progress of the British Dominions in the South from the Earliest Dawn of Discovery in the Southern ocean to the Year 1881* (Melbourne: Fergusson and Moore, 1881).

James Boutilier, "Papua New Guinea's Colonial Century: Reflections on Imperialism, Accommodation, and Historical Consciousness," in Deborah B. Gewertz and Edward L. Schieffelin (eds.), *History and Ethnohistory in Papua New Guinea* (Sydney: University of Sydney Press, 1985) 7–25.

Stephen R. Bown, *Merchant Kings* (New York: Thomas Dunne Books, 2010).

Stephen R. Bown, *1494: How a Family Feud in Medieval Spain Divided the World in Half* (New York: Thomas Dunne Books, 2012).

Brisbane Courier, "A Visit to New Guinea," *Brisbane Courier*, May 20, 1885, 2.

George Brown, *Pioneer Missionary and Explorer: An Autobiography* (London: Hodder and Stroughton, 1908).

Ian C. Campbell, *A History of the Pacific Islands* (Berkeley: University of California Press, 1989).

The Capricornian, "Annexation of New Guinea," *The Capricornian*, March 18, 1876, 17.

James Chalmers, *Adventures in New Guinea* (London: The Religious Tract Society, 1886).

James Chalmers, *Pioneering in New Guinea* (London: The Religious Tract Society, 1887).

Henry M. Chester, *Narrative of Expeditions to New Guinea* (Brisbane: Government Printer, 1878).

William B. Churchward, *Blackbirding in the South Pacific* (London: Swan Sonnenschein and Co., 1888).

Frank Coffee, *Forty Years on the Pacific: The Lure of the Great Ocean* (New York: Oceanic Publishing Co., 1920).

John Conley, "Australia in New Guinea Prior to Annexation," *Journal of the Royal Historical Society of Queensland* 6(2) (1960) 424–434.

C. Kinloch Cooke, *Australian Defences and New Guinea* (London: MacMillan and Co., 1887).

Matthew Cooper, "On the Beginnings of Colonialism in Melanesia," in Margaret Rodman and Matthew Cooper (eds.), *The Pacification of Melanesia* (Ann Arbor: University of Michgan Press, 1979) 25–41.

Peter Corris, "Blackbirding in New Guineas Waters, 1883–1884," *Journal of Pacific History* 3(1) (1968) 85–105.

Michael Crowder, "Indirect Rule—French and British Style," *Africa: Journal of the International Africa Institute* 34(3) (1964) 197–205.

John Darch, *Missionary Imperialists? Missionaries, Government, and the Growth of the British Empire in the Tropics, 1860–1885* (Eugene: Wipf and Stock Publishers, 2009).

Darling Down Gazette, "Rev. W. G. Lawes's Lecture," *Darling Down Gazette*, June 13, 1888, 3.

George Collingridge De Tourcey, *The First Discovery of Australia and New Guinea* (Sydney: W. Brooks, 1906).

F.W.S. Cumbrae-Stewart, "First Attempts at Settlement in New Guinea," *Journal of the Royal Historical Society of Queensland* 1(3) (1917) 155–184.

Edward W. Docker, *The Blackbirders: The Recruiting of South Seas Labor for Queensland, 1863–1907* (Sydney: Angus and Robertson, 1970).

Hugh Edward Egerton, *A Short History of British Colonial Policy* (London: Meuthuen & Co., 1897).

James Erskine, *Narrative of the Expedition of the Australian Squadron to the South-East Coast of New Guinea* (Bathurst: Robert Brown and Associates, 1885).

Michael H. Fisher, "Indirect Rule in the British Empire: The Foundations of the Residency System in India (1764–1858)," *Modern Asian Studies* 18(3) (1984) 393–428.

James Anthony Froude, *Oceana or England and Her Colonies* (London: Longmans, Green Co., 1886).

Donald Craigie Gordon, *The Australian Frontier in New Guinea: 1870–1885* (New York: AMS Press, 1968).

James Griffin, Hank Nelson, and Stewart Firth, *Papua New Guinea: A Political History* (Richmond: Heinemann, 1979).

William E. Hall, *A Treatise on the Foreign Powers and Jurisdiction of the British Crown* (Oxford: Clarendon Press, 1894).

Peter Hastings, *New Guinea: Problems and Prospects* (Bathurst: Robert Brown and Associates, 2nd ed., 1973).

Allan Michael Healy, "Native Administration and Local Government in Papua 1880–1960) (unpublished Ph.D. diss., Australian National University, March 1962).

Eric Hobsbawm, *The Age of Empire: 1875–1914* (New York: Pantheon, 1987).

Jeremy Hodes, "John Douglas, Special Commissioner to New Guinea, 1886–1888," *Queensland History Blog* (December 21, 2011) http://queensland history.blogspot.com/search/label/John%20Douglas.

K. R. Howe, *Where the Waves Fall* (Homolulu: University of Hawai'i Press, 1984).

Harry Jackman, "Sir Peter Scratchley: Her Majesty's Special Commissioner for New Guinea," *Journal of the Papua and New Guinea Society* 3 (1969): 46.

Rudi W. James, "Land Law and Policy in Papua New Guinea," *Papua New Guinea Law Reform Commission* Monograph No. 5 (Port Moresby: Government Printer, 1985).

Henry Jenkyns, *British Rule and Jurisdiction Beyond the Seas* (Oxford: Clarendon Press, 1902).

R. B. Joyce. "Australian Interest in New Guinea before 1906," in W. J. Hudson (ed.), *Australia and Papua New Guinea* (Sydney: Sydney University Press, 1971).

R. B. Joyce, *Sir William MacGregor* (Oxford: Oxford University Press, 1971).

Biama Kanasa, "Borders Across Rivers: Problems with the Creation of the Anglo-German Border Across Gira, Eia, Wuwu, and Waria Rivers, 1884–1909," *Transforming Cultures eJournal* 1(2) (June 2006), http://epress.lib.uts.edu.au/journals/TfC.

Joseph King, *W. G. Lawes of Savage Island and New Guinea* (London: The Religious Tract Society, 1909).

Diane Langmore, *Tamate A King: James Chalmers in New Guinea 1877–1901* (Melbourne: Melbourne University Press, 1974).

Diane Langmore, "James Chalmers: Missionary," in James Griffin (ed.), *Papua New Guinea Portraits: The Expatriate Experience* (Canberra: Australian National University Press, 1978) 1–27.

Diane Langmore, *Missionary Lives 1874–1914* (Honolulu: University of Hawai'i Press, 1989).

W. G. Lawes, "The Condition of New Guinea," *Sydney Morning Herald*, March 11, 1886.

W.G. Lawes, "New Guinea and Its People," *Popular Science Monthly* 20 (1882) 324–332.

J. D. Legge, *Australian Colonial Policy* (Sydney: Angus and Robertson, 1956).

Cuthbert Lennox, *James Chalmers of New Guinea* (London: Andrew Melrose, 1902).

Lewis Lett, *The Papuan Achievement* (Melbourne: Melbourne University Press, 1942).

C. C. Lewis, *The Plantation Dream: Developing British New Guinea and Papua 1884–1942* (Canberra: Journal of Pacific History, 1996).

John W. Lindt, *Picturesque New Guinea* (London: Longmans, Green Co., 1887).

Richard Lovett, *James Chalmers: His Autobiography and Letters* (London; The Religious Tract Society, 1902).

Adelaide Lubbock, "Owen Stanley in the Pacific," *Journal of Pacific History* 3(1) (1968) 47.

Charles E. Lyne, *New Guinea: An Account of the Establishment of the British Protectorate Over the Southern Shores of New Guinea* (London: Sampson, Low, Marston, Searle & Rivington, 1885).

Samuel Macfarlane, *Among the Cannibals of New Guinea* (Philadelphia: Presbyterian Board of Publication and Sabbath School Work, 1888).

Robert F. Maher, *New Men of Papua* (Madison: University of Wisconsin Press, 1961).

John F. Mann, *First Report on New Guinea* (Sydney: Turner and Henderson, 1889).

John F. Mann, *Continuation of Mr. Mann's Report on New Guinea* (Sydney: Turner and Henderson, 1890).

John Mayo, "A Punitive Expedition in British New Guinea, 1886," *Journal of Pacific History* 8(1) (1973) 89–99.

John Mayo, "From Protectorate to Possession: British New Guinea 1884–88," *Australian Journal of Politics and History* 21(3) (1975) 54–69.

Robert J. Miller, "The International Law of Colonialism: A Comparative Analysis," *Lewis & Clark Law Review* 15 (2011) 847–922.

Clive Moore, "The Life and Death of William Bairstow Ingham: Papua New

Guinea in the 1870s," *Journal of the Royal Historical Society of Queensland* 14(10) (1951) 414–432.

Clive Moore, *Kanaka: A History of Melanesian MacKay* (Port Moresby: Institute of Papua New Guinea Studies, 1986).

Clive Moore, "Queensland's Labor Trade and the Annexation of New Guinea in 1883," in Sione Latukefu (ed.), *Papua New Guinea: A Century of Colonial Impact 1884–1984* (Port Moresby: The National Research Institute and University of Papua New Guinea, 1989) 1–18.

Clive Moore, *New Guinea: Crossing Boundaries and History* (Honolulu: University of Hawai'i Press, 2003).

Alan Moorehead, *Fatal Impact* (New York: Harper and Row, 1966).

John Moresby, *New Guinea & Polynesia: Discoveries & Surveys in New Guinea and the D'Entrecasteaux Islands* (London: John Murray, 1876).

William P. Morrell, *Britain in the Pacific Islands* (Oxford: Oxford University Press, 1960).

Sankar Multhu, *Enlightenment Against Empire* (Princeton: Princeton University Press, 2003).

George M. S. Muroa, "Legal Aspects of Compulsory Acquisition of Land in Papua New Guinea" (unpublished master's thesis, University of Tasmania, 1987).

John Hubert Murray, *Papua or British New Guinea* (London: T., Fisher Unwin, 1912).

Hank Nelson, *Papua New Guinea: Black Unity or Black Chaos* (Ringwood: Penguin Books, 1974).

Hank Nelson, *Black, White and Gold: Gold Mining in Papua New Guinea, 1878–1930* (Canberra: Australian National University Press, 1976).

Douglas Oliver, *Black Islanders* (Honolulu: University of Hawai'i Press, 1991).

Nigel Oram, "Land and Race in Port Moresby," *Journal of the Papua and New Guinea Society* 4(1) (1970) 5–13.

Nigel Oram, *Colonial Town to Melanesian City* (Canberra: Australian National University, 1976).

Peter Overlack, "German New Guinea: A Diplomatic, Economic and Political Survey," *Journal of the Royal Historical Society of Queensland* 9(4) (1973) 128–152.

Peter Overlack, "Queensland's Annexation of Papua: A Background to Anglo-

German Friction," *Journal of the Royal Historical Society of Queensland* 10(4) (1979) 123–138.

Francis Taylor Piggott, *Nationality: Naturalization and English Law on the High Seas and Beyond the Realm* (London: William Clowes & Sons, 1907).

W. D. Pitcairn, *Two Years Among the Savages of New Guinea* (London: Ward & Downey, 1891).

Jennifer Pitts, *A Turn to Empire: The Rise of Imperial Liberalism in Britain and France* (Princeton: Princeton University Press, 2005).

Wilfred Powell, *Wanderings in a Wild Country: Or Three Years Amongst the Cannibals of New Britain* (London: Sampson, Low, Marston, Searle & Rivington, 1883).

Max Quanchi, "The Invisibility of Gospel Ploughmen: The Imaging of South Seas Pastors in Papua," *Pacific Studies* 20(4) (1997) 77–101.

Margriet Roe, "A History of South-East Papua to 1930" (unpublished Ph.D. diss., Australian National University, 1961).

Hugh H. Romilly, *The Western Pacific and New Guinea* (London: J. Murray, 1886).

Hugh H. Romilly, *From My Verandah in New Guinea: Sketches and Traditions* (London: David Nutt, 1889).

Hugh H. Romilly, *Letters from the Western Pacific and Mashonaland, 1878–1891* (London: David Nutt, 1893).

Jane Samson, *Imperial Benevolence: Making British Authority in the Pacific Islands* (Honolulu: University of Hawai'i Press, 1998).

Deryck Scarr, *Fragments of Empire: A History of the Western Pacific High Commission, 1877–1914* (Canberra: Australian National University Press, 1967).

Gavin Souter, *New Guinea: The Last Unknown* (Sydney: Angus and Robertson, 1970).

Regis Tove Stella, *Imagining the Other: The Representation of the Papua New Guinean Subject* (Honolulu: University of Hawai'i Press, 2007).

Ian Stuart, *Port Moresby: Yesterday and Today* (Sydney: Pacific Publications, rev. ed. 1973).

Pamela Swadling, *Papua New Guinea's Prehistory: An Introduction* (Port Moresby: Gordon and Gotch, 1981).

Sydney Morning Herald, "New Regulations for New Guinea," *Sydney Morning Herald*, December 20, 1884, 10.

The Telegraph, "Prospects in New Guinea: The Rev. W. G. Lawes Interviewed," *The Telegraph*, December 24, 1884, 2.

Nicholas Thomas, *Islanders: The Pacific in the Age of Empire* (New Haven: Yale University Press, 2010).

Nicholas Thomas and Richard Evans, *Bad Colonists* (Durham: Duke University Press, 1999).

James P. Thomson, *British New Guinea* (London: George Philip and Son, 1892).

John Waiko, *A Short History of Papua New Guinea* (Oxford: Oxford University Press, 1993).

John M. Ward, *British Policy in the South Pacific* (Sydney: Australasian Publishing, 1950).

Michael Waterhouse, *Not a Poor Man's Field* (Canberra: Halstead Press, 2012).

William T. Wawn, *The South Sea Islanders and the Queensland Labor Trade* (London: Swan Sonnenschein and Co., 1893).

June L. Whittaker, Noel G. Gash, John F. Hookey, and Roderic J. Lacey, *Documents and Readings in New Guinea History: Prehistory to 1889* (Milton: Jacaranda Press, 1975).

Martin J. Wiener, *An Empire on Trial: Race, Murder and Justice Under British Rule, 1870–1935* (Cambridge: Cambridge University Press, 2009).

W. Allen Young, *Christianity and Civilization in the South Pacific: The Influence of Missionaries upon European Expansion in the Pacific during the Nineteenth Century* (London, 1922).

Government Documents

The Annual Register: A Review of Public Events At Home and Abroad for the Year 1884 (1885) 432–434.

Annual Report on British New Guinea (Brisbane: Government Printer, 1886).

Annual Report on British New Guinea (Brisbane: Government Printer, 1888).

"British New Guinea: Mr. H. O. Forbes' Report," in *Journal of the Legislative Council of New South Wales*, vol. 42, part I (1887).

"British New Guinea: Report for the Year 1886 by Her Majesty's Special Commissioner for the Protected Territory," in *Journals and Printed Papers of the Federal Council of Australasia*, vol. II (January 16 to February 9, 1888).

"The Condition of New Guinea—Report by the Rev. W. G. Lawes," *British New Guinea: Report for the Year 1888 by Her Majesty's Special Commissioner for the Protected Territory*, in *Journals and Printed Papers of the Federal Council of Australasia*, vol. II (January 16 to February 9, 1888).

"Correspondence on the Subject of the Proposed Annexation of New Guinea and with Reference to the Principle of Contribution by the Colonies Interested in the Scheme," in *Journal of the Legislative Council of New South Wales*, vol. 226, part I (1876).

"Correspondence on the Subject of the Proposed Annexation of New Guinea, Enclosure," in No. 1, 3, 4 (1876), at https://www.flickr.com/photos/queenslandstatearchives/30611795851/in/photostream/.

John Douglas, "Memorandum by the Special Commissioner for the Protected Territory of British New Guinea," *British New Guinea: Report for the Year 1886 by Her Majesty's Special Commissioner for the Protected Territory*, in *Journals and Printed Papers of the Federal Council of Australasia,* 51 Vic. 1888, vol. 2 (January 16 to February 9, 1888).

G. Seymour Fort, *British New Guinea: Report on British New Guinea from Data and Notes by the Late Sir Peter Scratchley, Her Majesty's Special Commissioner* (Melbourne: Government Printer, 1886).

"Labor Trade in the Western Pacific," a *Dispatch from the Honorable the Secretary of State for the Colonies, Transmitting Copy of a Report on the Subject of the Labor Trade in the Western Pacific* (1882), at http://www.parliament.vic.gov.au/papers/govpub/VPARL1882-83No31.pdf.

"Major-General Scratchley's Instructions," *South Australian Weekly Chronicle*, January 10, 1885, 12.

"Memorandum by Assistant Deputy Commissioner Musgrave Respecting Acquisition of Certain Government Lands (9th November 1886)," *in Journals and Printed Papers of the Federal Council of Australasia,* vol. II (January 16 to February 9, 1888).

"Memorandum by Assistant Deputy Commission on the First Purchase of Government Lands in British New Guinea, (8th September 1885)," *British New Guinea: Report for the Year 1886 by Her Majesty's Special Commissioner for the Protected Territory*, in *Journals and Printed Papers of the Federal Council of Australasia,* vol. II (January 16 to February 9, 1888).

"Memorandum by Mr. Deputy- Commissioner Romilly, Addressed to His Excellency the Special Commissioner," in *British New Guinea: Report for the Year 1887, by Her Majesty's Special Commissioner for the Protected*

Territory (1887) at http://www.parliament.vic.gov.au/papers/govpub/VPARL1888No32.pdf.

"New Guinea Protectorate: Dispatches and Other Papers Relating to Establishment and Administration," in *Journals and Printed Papers of the Federal Council of Australasia,* vol. I (49 Vic. 1886, January 25 to February 6, 1886).

"New Guinea," *Northern Territory Times and Gazette,* May 25, 1878, 1.

"Protected Territory of New Guinea," in *British New Guinea: Report for the Year 1886 by Her Majesty's Special Commissioner for the Protected Territory,* Appendix D, 20 at http://www.parliament.vic.gov.au/papers/govpub/VPARL1887No25.pdf.

Report of the Proceedings of the Intercolonial Convention, Held in Sydney in November and December, 1883 (1883).

"Report of Special Commissioner British New Guinea," in *Journal of the Legislative Council of New South Wales, Second Session of 1887,* vol. 42, part I (1887).

Victorian Legislative Assembly Hansard, 12 December 1872, 2364–2370.

Case

The Administration of Papua and New Guinea v. Guba and Dorija [1973] 47 A.L.J. 621

Statutes

Foreign Jurisdiction Act 1890 (Great Britain)

The Murders Abroad Act 1817 (Great Britain)

New Guinea and Pacific Jurisdiction Contribution Act (1884) (Great Britain)

Pacific Islands Protection Act of 1872 (Great Britain)

Notes

1. Charles E. Lyne, *New Guinea: An Account of the Establishment of the British Protectorate Over the Southern Shores of New Guinea* (London: Sampson, Low, Marston, Searle & Rivington, 1885) 7–8.
2. *Id.* at 8.
3. Richard Lovett, *James Chalmers: His Autobiography and Letters* (London: The Religious Tract Society, 1902) 238.

4. "The Condition of New Guinea. Report by the Rev. W. G. Lawes," *Sydney Morning Herald*, March 11, 1886, 4.
5. Charles E. Lyne, *New Guinea: An Account of the Establishment of the British Protectorate Over the Southern Shores of New Guinea* (London: Sampson, Low, Marston, Searle & Rivington, 1885) 8–9.
6. The first ceremony took place in April 1883 when Queensland attempted to annex New Guinea on behalf of Britain. The second occurred on October 23, 1884, when, as a result of a misunderstanding concerning his instructions, Hugh Romilly raised the British flag and declared a protectorate over New Guinea. Romilly's actions were ignored by Erskine, who explained to the New Guineans that it was a "preliminary" to the official ceremony. Charles E. Lyne, *New Guinea: An Account of the Establishment of the British Protectorate over the Southern Shores of New Guinea* (London: Sampson, Low, Marston, Searle & Rivington, 1885) 2. A few days after the November 6, 1884, proclamation ceremony, Romilly wrote to his mother, "I made rather an ass of myself" by raising the flag early. However, he concluded that "it did not make much difference, as [Erskine] did it all over again when he arrived." Hugh H. Romilly, *Letters from the Western Pacific and Mashonaland, 1878–1891* (London: Davit Nutt, 1893) 202.
7. "Prospects in New Guinea: The Rev. W. G. Lawes Interviewed," *Telegraph*, December 24, 1884, 2.
8. John Hubert Murray, *Papua or British New Guinea* (London: T. Fisher Unwin, 1912) 74.
9. Erskine's speech is reprinted in Charles E. Lyne, *New Guinea: An Account of the Establishment of the British Protectorate Over the Southern Shores of New Guinea* (London: Sampson, Low, Marston, Searle & Rivington, 1885) 4.
10. *Id.*
11. *Id.*
12. Theodore F. Bevan, *Toil, Travel, and Discovery in New Guinea* (London: Kegan Paul, Trench, Trubner and Co., 1890) 15.
13. "Annexation of New Guinea," *The Capricornian*, March 18, 1876, 179.
14. The primary use of *beche de mer*, more colloquially known as sea cucumber, is in Chinese medicines and cuisine.
15. "New Guinea," *Northern Territory Times and Gazette*, May 25, 1878, 1.
16. *Victorian Legislative Assembly Hansard*, 12 December 1872, 2364–2370.
17. John Moresby, *New Guinea & Polynesia: Discoveries & Surveys in New Guinea and the D'Entrecasteaux Islands* (London: John Murray, 1876) 295.
18. *Id.* at 295–296
19. *Id.* at 296–297.

20. *Id.* at 303.
21. Isaiah Berlin, "Notes on Prejudice," *The New York Review of Books,* October 18, 2001, 12.
22. John Moresby, *New Guinea & Polynesia: Discoveries & Surveys in New Guinea and the D'Entrecasteaux Islands* (London: John Murray, 1876) 296.
23. "The Right Hon. The Earl of Derby to the Administrator Sir. A. H. Palmer, K.C.M.G. (Queensland)," *Report of the Proceedings of the Intercolonial Convention, Held in Sydney in November and December 1883* (1883) 13.
24. *Id.* at 13–14. This resulted in *The New Guinea and Pacific Jurisdiction Contribution Act (1884)* (48 Vic. 7).
25. John Moresby, *New Guinea & Polynesia: Discoveries & Surveys in New Guinea and the D'Entrecasteaux Islands* (London: John Murray, 1876) 304.
26. *Id.* at 296.
27. Cuthbert Lennox, *James Chalmers of New Guinea* (London: Andrew Melrose, 1902) 126–127.
28. Hugh H. Romilly, *Letters from the Western Pacific and Mashonaland, 1878–1891* (London: David Nutt, 1893) 265.
29. "New Guinea Protectorate: Dispatches and Other Papers Relating to Establishment and Administration," in *Journals and Printed Papers of the Federal Council of Australasia,* vol. I (49 Vic. 1886, January 25 to February 6, 1886) 51.
30. "Major-General Scratchley's Instructions," *South Australian Weekly Chronicle,* January 10, 1885, 12.
31. "New Guinea Protectorate: Dispatches and Other Papers Relating to Establishment and Administration," in *Journals and Printed Papers of the Federal Council of Australasia,* vol. I (49 Vic. 1886, January 25 to February 6, 1886) 76.
32. *Foreign Jurisdiction Act 1890* (Great Britain) section 1.
33. *Administration of Papua and New Guinea v. Guba and Dorija* at 635.
34. *Id.*
35. C. Kinloch Cooke, *Australian Defences and New Guinea* (London: MacMillan and Co., 1887) 273–274.
36. James Griffin, Hank Nelson, and Stewart Firth, *Papua New Guinea: A Political History* (Richmond: Heinemann, 1979) 11–12.
37. G. Seymour Fort, *British New Guinea: Report on British New Guinea from Data and Notes by the Late Sir. Peter Scratchley, Her Majesty's Special Commissioner* (Melbourne: Government Printer, 1886) 26.
38. Michael Crowder, "Indirect Rule—French and British Style," *Africa: Journal of the International Africa Institute* 34(3) (1964) 197.
39. Anthony Musgrave, "Memorandum on Native Policy in Her Majesty's Protected Territory of New Guinea," in *British New Guinea: Report for*

the Year 1886 by Her Majesty's Special Commissioner for the Protected Territory, Appendix D, 20.

40. *Id.*
41. *Id.*
42. John Douglas, "Memorandum by the Special Commissioner for the Protected Territory of British New Guinea," *British New Guinea: Report for the Year 1886 by Her Majesty's Special Commissioner for the Protected Territory*, in *Journals and Printed Papers of the Federal Council of Australasia*, vol. II (51 Vic. 1888, January 16-February 9, 1888) 640.
43. G. Seymour Fort, *British New Guinea: Report on British New Guinea from Data and Notes by the Late Sir. Peter Scratchley, Her Majesty's Special Commissioner* (Melbourne: Government Printer, 1886) 8.
44. C. Kinloch Cooke, *Australian Defences and New Guinea* (London: MacMillan and Co., 1887) 281–282.
45. "The Condition of New Guinea—Report by the Rev. W. G. Lawes," *British New Guinea: Report for the Year 1886 by Her Majesty's Special Commissioner for the Protected Territory*, in *Journals and Printed Papers of the Federal Council of Australasia*, vol. II (January 16 to February 9, 1888) 36.
46. *Annual Report on British New Guinea* (1886) 8.
47. [1973] 47 Australian Law Journal 621.
48. *Id.* at 629.
49. *Id.* at 630.
50. "New Regulations for New Guinea," *Sydney Morning Herald*, December 20, 1884, 10.
51. "Instruction No. 9, Major-General Scratchley's Instructions," *South Australian Weekly Chronicle*, January 10, 1885, 12.
52. "A Visit to New Guinea," *The Brisbane Courier*, May 20, 1885, 2.
53. Theodore F. Bevan, *Toil, Travel, and Discovery in British New Guinea* (London: Kegan Paul, Trench, Trubner and Co., 1890) 11 (emphasis in the original).
54. G. Seymour Fort, *British New Guinea: Report on British New Guinea from Data and Notes by the Late Sir. Peter Scratchley, Her Majesty's Special Commissioner* (Melbourne: Government Printer, 1886) 42–43.
55. "Report of Special Commissioner British New Guinea," in *Journal of the Legislative Council of New South Wales, Second Session of 1887*, vol. 42, part I (1887) 6.
56. Hugh H. Romilly, *Letters from the Western Pacific and Mashonaland, 1878–1891* (London: David Nutt, 1893) 297.
57. *Id.* at 211.
58. *Id.* at 255.

59. *Id.* at 337.
60. "The Condition of New Guinea. Report by the Rev. W. G. Lawes," *Sydney Morning Herald*, March 11, 1886, 4.
61. "Rev. W. G. Lawes's Lecture," *Darling Down Gazette*, June 13, 1888, 3.
62. Hugh H. Romilly, *Letters from the Western Pacific and Mashonaland, 1878–1891* (London: David Nutt, 1893) 268.
63. R. B. Joyce, *Sir William MacGregor* (Oxford: Oxford University Press, 1971) 127.
64. C. Kinloch Cooke, *Australian Defences and New Guinea* (London: MacMillian and Co., 1887) 350.
65. G. Seymour Fort, *British New Guinea: Report on British New Guinea from Data and Notes by the Late Sir. Peter Scratchley, Her Majesty's Special Commissioner* (Melbourne: Government Printer, 1886) 51.
66. Lewis Lett, *The Papuan Achievement* (Melbourne: Melbourne University Press, 1942) 27.
67. John W. Lindt, *Picturesque New Guinea* (London: Longman Green and Co., 1887) 91.
68. Lewis Lett, *The Papuan Achievement* (Melbourne: Melbourne University Press, 1942) 29.
69. *Id.*
70. John W. Lindt, *Picturesque New Guinea* (London: Longmans, Green and Co., 1887) 92.
71. G. Seymour Fort, *British New Guinea: Report on British New Guinea from Data and Notes by the Late Sir. Peter Scratchley, Her Majesty's Special Commissioner* (Melbourne: Government Printer, 1886) 13.
72. *Id.*
73. Cuthbert Lennox, *James Chalmers of New Guinea* (London: Andrew Melrose, 1902) 137.
74. John Mayo, "A Punitive Expedition in British New Guinea, 1886," *Journal of Pacific History* 8(1) (1973) 91.
75. *Id.* at 99.
76. *Annual Report on British New Guinea* (1887), quoted in John Hubert Murray, *Papua or British New Guinea* (London: T. Fisher Unwin, 1912) 79–80.

4 Establishing Legal Authority

British New Guinea 1888–1906

The precarious financial situation that British New Guinea faced when it became a protectorate in 1884 grew much more serious in 1886 and early 1887, when South Australia, Fiji, New Zealand, and Tasmania ceased contributing to the £15,000 annual fund for administering New Guinea. That financial crisis along with the need to provide a more effective administration for the territory led to a colonial conference in London in April and May 1887. At the conference, Great Britain agreed to annex New Guinea, in return for Queensland undertaking to guarantee £15,000 per year for ten years to cover the costs of administering the territory. New South Wales and Victoria each agreed to contribute one-third of that amount to Queensland. That arrangement was consistent with the general view in Britain at the time that colonies should pay for themselves and not be a burden on the Crown. The terms of the agreement were incorporated into *The British New Guinea (Queensland) Act of 1887*. The act gave the governor of Queensland nominal supervision over the administrative, financial, and legislative affairs of the territory, subject to a vague requirement that he consult with New South Wales and Victoria on "all matters other than those of ordinary administration." However, Britain retained the ultimate right of veto over affairs in the colony through its colonial office. Britain issued the necessary letters patent on June 8, 1888, and on September 4, 1888, the area that would later be called Papua, but which the British government referred to as British New Guinea, formally became a Crown Colony.

Britain appointed William MacGregor, a 41-year-old Scottish-born physician, as the first Administrator of its new colony. MacGregor had extensive experience in colonial administration, having held positions in the colonial service in the Seychelles, Mauritius, and Fiji. He arrived in Port Moresby on the morning of September 4, 1888, and held the formal annexation ceremony later that afternoon. As with the proclamation of the protectorate four years earlier, the ceremony involved a band and an honor guard of sailors and marines from the British navy. On the veranda of the government house, MacGregor read the royal proclamation and gave a short speech. He was surrounded by naval officers from the small British warship that had brought him to Port Moresby, as well as by seven non-New Guinean residents of the territory, including H. H. Romilly, the Rev. and Mrs. William G. Lawes, and Andrew Goldie, all of whom had been present four years earlier for the proclamation of the protectorate. Although about two hundred of the New Guinean residents of the area were also present for the ceremony, they were not invited to join the whites on the verandah. They had had no voice in the decision to surrender their land and sovereignty to the British Crown. Their consent to annexation was considered irrelevant. Few, if any, New Guineans understood the meaning of the change of the status of their land, and no real attempt had been made to inform them about it.

Like Erskine four years earlier, MacGregor set out Britain's goals for New Guineans in his brief proclamation speech: "The Queens's Sovereignty here will be a guarantee that every effort will be made to educate the native race; to impart to them the great and sublime truths of the Christian religion; to teach them to value and respect law and order, and to appreciate justice."[1] With those words, MacGregor signaled Britain's intention to do something the special commissioners had been unable to do during the four years of the protectorate: create a formal legal system for the colony that would apply both to expatriates and New Guineans.

The Jurisdiction and Structure of the Colonial Administration

The designation of New Guinea as a Crown Colony brought an end to the limited jurisdiction that made it difficult for Britain to enforce its rules during the protectorate. Britain's authority now formally extended to everyone in the colony: British subjects, non-British residents, and New

Guineans. The governmental structure for the new colony was established by *The British Settlements Act of 1887* and the letters patent. The act applied to any "British settlement" that was a "British possession," but which had not been acquired by cession or conquest, and where, as the preamble stated, there was "no civilised government." The act permitted Britain to administer such a possession without a representative legislature. In the case of British New Guinea, such a legislature would have been inconceivable in 1888, given the tiny expatriate population and the lack of any tradition in British colonial practice of giving the Indigenous population of a colony any role in formulating government policy.

The letters patent created a complex system of colonial administration, with responsibilities divided among Britain, Queensland, and officials in New Guinea. This provided for an Administrator (renamed lieutenant-governor after 1895), who was appointed by the British government, but who was required to follow the instructions of the governor of Queensland on all important matters. The letters patent also established an Executive Council and a Legislative Council. The Executive Council, which was an advisory body, consisted of the Administrator, the chief judicial officer, the government secretary, and a resident magistrate. The Administrator was required to consult with the Executive Council on all important matters, except those where the operation of the administration would be prejudiced by consultation or where the matter was too urgent to wait for the council to meet. The Legislative Council, whose function was to enact ordinances for the colony, consisted of the members of the Executive Council as well as between two to five additional members appointed by the Administrator. The failure to require elections for the members of the Legislative Council became a controversial issue among expatriates in the colony in the years immediately after Australia assumed control in 1906. The majority of the appointed members of the Legislative Council continued to be government officials until the 1960s, and New Guineans had no representatives on either council until 1951.

The Colonial Legal System

Although MacGregor's proclamation stated that Britain would make "every effort" to bring education and Christianity to New Guineans, he did not use any of the £15,000 annual allocation for either of those purposes. Instead, he left both religion and education to the missionaries. He did, however, actively pursue the third goal, teaching New Guineans "to value and respect law and order, and to appreciate justice." That offered him an opportunity to reconsider the two different positions articulated earlier in the decade by John Moresby and James Chalmers: introducing English laws and procedures or enacting laws best suited for New Guineans and local circumstances. Not surprisingly, since MacGregor was a long-time member of the colonial service, he believed that it was his duty to introduce what he considered the superior values of the English legal system into the colonies, MacGregor did not reopen that debate. Instead, he relied on section 2 of *The British Settlements Act of 1887*, which gave colonial officials the authority

> to establish all such laws and institutions, and constitute such courts and officers, and make such provisions and regulations for the proceedings in the said courts and for the administration of justice as may appear . . . to be necessary for the peace, order, and good government of Her Majesty's subjects and others within any British settlement.

MacGregor established the structural basis of a colonial legal system that lasted throughout the colonial period and consisted of three components: first, laws imported from England and Australia, including the English common law and principles of equity, as well as English and Queensland statutes and procedures; second, locally enacted ordinances, which, in most cases, were copied from or modeled on Queensland legislation; and finally, a set of *Native Regulations*, which applied only to New Guineans.

English Law

One of the earliest pieces of legislation enacted by the Legislative Council in British New Guinea was *The Courts and Laws Adopting Ordinance (Amended) of 1889*, which established Queensland and English laws as the basis of the legal system in the colony. Section 2 adopted 167 acts and statutes of Queensland, as they were in force on September 17, 1888. This wholesale adoption was not without its critics. Queensland Governor-General Sir Anthony Musgrave (the uncle of Anthony Musgrave, the government secretary in British New Guinea) opposed importing Queensland laws into New Guinea, arguing that those laws were "altogether premature and inapplicable to the present condition of the territory where the great mass of the inhabitants are native savages, and those of European extraction do not number as many as 30."[2] The second set of laws adopted for British New Guinea under the 1889 reception ordinance was "[t]hose portions of the Acts, Statutes and Laws of England" that were in force in Queensland on September 17, 1888, and which could be adopted by ordinance in British New Guinea.[3] Finally, section 4 of the reception ordinance adopted "[t]he principles and rules of common law and equity that for the time being shall be in force in England . . . so far as the same shall be applicable to the circumstances of the Possession." This included both civil and criminal law, despite the very different circumstances of the colony.

Musgrave was correct that British New Guinea neither needed nor could afford the elaborate legal system that MacGregor and his Legislative Council had introduced. As Musgrave pointed out, there were only about thirty non-New Guineans in residence, most of them government officials, missionaries, traders, and miners. This small number was spread out along the southern coast of New Guinea and on the adjacent islands and had little contact with each other. In addition, the limited financial and human resources available to MacGregor meant that his administration had almost no ability to persuade New Guineans to abandon their customary legal systems and to govern their lives according to the alien Queensland and English laws. Without a continuous presence in the villages, the colonial administration could not apply even its criminal laws, unless New Guineans reported crimes to an official. Despite those limitations, colonial officials still took it for granted that it was both their right and their duty to introduce English laws and procedures into the colony.

In his *Commentaries on the Laws of England*, first published in the 1760s, William Blackstone wrote:

> Plantations or colonies, in distant countries, are either such where the lands are claimed by right of occupancy only, by finding them desert and uncultivated, and peopling them from the mother country; or where, when already cultivated, they have been either gained by conquest, or ceded to us by treaties. And both these rights are founded upon the law of nature, or at least upon that of nations.[4]

This classification had its basis in the international law of the era and was incorporated into British law and practice through a long series of cases beginning with *Calvin's Case*,[5] decided in the Court of Exchequer in 1608. Blackstone went on to say that, in the case of colonies "gained by conquest or ceded to [Britain] by treaties," the preexisting local laws remained in force until changed by the English Parliament or by colonial officials. However, if English subjects "discovered" and settled an "uninhabited" country, then "all the English laws then in being" were considered to be in force there, since such laws were "the birthright of every subject." Since the British encountered only sporadic and isolated incidents of armed resistance to their assertion of control over British New Guinea, and since there was no single government in place in Papua that represented all or even a significant number of Papuans, there were no treaties ceding the territory to Britain. It is not clear that the British would have made treaties with the Papuans in any case. The British treated British New Guinea as "claimed by right of occupancy only." Thus, like Australia, British New Guinea was in the anomalous position of being considered a previously uninhabited territory "discovered and planted by English subjects," despite having been inhabited for more than fifty thousand years by a large Indigenous population.

English subjects carried their laws with them to "deserted and uncultivated" colonies, as British New Guinea was deemed to be. Blackstone did qualify the scope of this somewhat: "colonists carry with them only so much of the English law as is applicable to their own situation and the condition of an infant colony."[6] In British New Guinea, that limitation also was included in *The Courts and Laws Adopting Ordinance (Amended) of 1889*. The ordinance adopted English and Australian statutes and the English common law and equity "as far as the same shall be applicable to the circumstances of the Possession."[7] In practice, however, there is no record of the British ever refusing to enforce a common law rule or statute on the grounds that it was not applicable to the circumstances of New Guinea. The limitation certainly did not serve as a mechanism for promoting the formal recognition of customary law. The British never questioned the legitimacy of imposing English law on the people in their colonies without their consent. Instead, the doctrine of circumstantial applicability was a recognition of the fact that the British might have to make some pragmatic modifications in order for the English legal system—with its need for an elaborate system of courts, professional lawyers, law reports, and treatises—to operate in colonies where courts met infrequently and lawyers and legal materials were scarce.

The decision to import the English legal system into British New Guinea also reflected the prior practice of the colonial office in dealing with its colonies in Africa, Asia, the Caribbean, and other parts of the Pacific. The almost identical reception ordinances enacted throughout the British colonies made the principles of English common law, the doctrines of equity, and the statutes of general application, which were in force in England on a given date, the basis of the legal systems of Great Britain's possessions throughout the world. The Gold Coast Colony (now Ghana) *Supreme Court Ordinance of 1876*[8] was the first of the reception ordinances in Africa and served as a model for other colonies, including British New Guinea. Section 14 of that ordinance stated: "The common law, the doctrines of equity, and the statutes of general application which were in force in England on the date when the colony obtained a local legislature . . . shall be in force with the jurisdiction of the Court."

In British New Guinea, the *Courts and Laws Adopting Ordinance (Amended) of 1889* followed this model. There was no mention in the ordinance about what role, if any, the colonizers envisioned for customary law. Since it was one of the goals of the British that New Guineans eventually would accept Western rule and, with it, the English legal system, the silence of the reception ordinance regarding customary law can be interpreted as a rejection of any role for it in the colonial legal system. Although the drafters of the reception ordinance understood that colonial officials would be unable for the foreseeable future to apply English laws to New Guineans, they did not believe that the norms and processes of customary law constituted a legal system and certainly not one that could take the place of English law.

An alternative interpretation of the failure of the reception ordinance to expressly provide any role for customary law lies in the provision that English and Queensland law applied only to the extent they were "applicable to the circumstances of the Possession." That provision can be interpreted to mean that, given the very different circumstances, customs, and lifestyles of New Guineans, English and Queensland law did not apply to them. The effect of that interpretation of the reception ordinance's silence on the role of customary law would have been to create two distinct legal systems for British New Guinea: English law for the non-New Guinean community and customary law for New Guineans.

In a speech in London in 1895, which included a discussion of the creation of the colonial legal system, William MacGregor discussed these two possible explanations for the reception ordinance's failure to recognize custom. According to MacGregor, he had been forced to consider from the beginning of his administration whether the colony should follow solely English criminal law, under which punishment was exacted by the state solely to the individual wrongdoer, or whether the colony should have also adopted the customary practices of compensating victims and assigning blame not only to the actual wrongdoer but also to the extended family.[9]

While MacGregor admitted that officials had given unofficial recognition to customary practices during the protectorate, it was "undesirable to revert to the antiquated system" since it was "not in harmony with the spirit of modern legislation"[10] because custom encouraged crime by allowing a wrongdoer to escape punishment if he paid the victim, which was an incentive for the powerful to oppress the weaker; and its recognition would not create confidence in and respect for the administration. These were the reasons successive generations of colonial officials gave for their refusal to afford customary law official recognition in the formal legal system. Their refusal reflected more than the colonizers' misunderstanding of the nature and effects of custom. Their profound antagonism toward custom also reflected their view that the colonial endeavor would succeed only if the colonizing authority were seen to be the sole source of order and sole protector of life and property. MacGregor concluded his speech by stating:

> It is now clear that the Papuan, with his keen sense of justice and active intellect, can be made to understand our system; he is learning fast that punishment must be applied by the Government, that it overtakes only the guilty individual, and that it cannot be compounded for by any payment.[11]

Despite his insistence that English law should reign supreme, MacGregor recognized that his colonial service was stretched too thin to handle anything more than the most serious crimes. His administration made no attempt to require all New Guineans to follow English law nor did it seek to interfere with custom in civil or domestic matters such as marriage, divorce, adoption, the distribution of property after death, and land tenure. As a result, although totally unofficially, two parallel legal systems did exist in the colony throughout the colonial period.

Local Ordinances

The Legislative Council had the power to enact ordinances for the colony during the almost ninety years of colonial rule and introduced legislation dealing with every subject that touched the lives of New Guineans and expatriates. Among the ordinances were ones dealing with adoption, automobiles, cattle brands and theft, cemeteries, child custody, companies, contracts, courts, criminal law and procedure, dangerous drugs, debtors and creditors, divorce, electric power, employers' liability, evidence, firearms, fishing, gambling, gifts to religious and charitable institutions, health, immigration, import duties, inheritance, labor, land, livestock, marriage, medicine, mining, motor traffic, parasitic diseases affecting trees and plants, posts and telegraphs, printers and newspapers, prisons, the protection of wild birds, public hospitals, revenue, timber, the sale of liquor, sorcery, superannuation, trading in human remains, vaccinations, where villages could be built, wills, and workers' compensation. Although many of the ordinances were copied from, or based upon, the corresponding laws of Queensland, others were unique to New Guinea.

During the first year of MacGregor's administration, the Legislative Council adopted eleven ordinances. Among them was *The Courts and Laws Adopting Ordinance of 1888*, which established a judicial system in British New Guinea. The highest court in the colony was the Central Court, presided over by the chief magistrate, who had the same authority as a judge of the Supreme Court of Queensland.[12] Although the Central Court nominally was based in Port Moresby, it could hold sessions wherever necessary. An example of this was a sitting of the court on Dobu Island in the present-day Milne Bay Province, in 1891, at which a New Guinean was convicted of the murder of a Chinese trader. MacGregor wanted to hold the trial on Dobu, rather than where the crime had occurred, to induce more local people to attend. The trial is said to have drawn an audience of six to seven hundred New Guineans, although only a few of them were able to hear all the testimony and even fewer, if any, would have understood the proceedings.

The Central Court acted as the criminal trial court and also heard appeals from summary courts with limited civil and criminal jurisdiction and from the Warden's Court, which heard disputes involving rights to land and mining tenements. There was a right of appeal from the Central Court to the Supreme Court of Queensland in civil cases if the amount in question exceeded £100. In criminal cases, such an appeal was possible if the defendant received a sentence of more than three months imprisonment. However, during the ten years that MacGregor was Administrator, there were no appeals.

In 1889, the Legislative Council enacted the *Criminal Procedure Ordinance* for the colony. Following English procedure, the ordinance provided that a criminal case could not be brought in the Central Court unless a magistrate had investigated it. Criminal procedure in British New Guinea differed from that in England and Australia in two important areas. First, because of the absence of lawyers in the colony, anyone who was not a witness in the trial could represent the accused. Second, there were no jury trials, either in criminal or civil cases. MacGregor rejected jury trials because of the small number of whites in the colony and because he believed that New Guineans inevitably would be biased in favor of their own clans or lineages. The lack of jury trials for expatriates would become an issue after Australia assumed control in 1906.

Native Regulations

Although New Guineans nominally were subject to the same introduced laws and ordinances that applied to whites in the colony, MacGregor mandated there also be a set of regulations specifically aimed at New Guineans, "set out in language as simple as possible."[13] The *Native Affairs Ordinance of 1889* established a native administration board, consisting of the Administrator, at least two members of the Legislative Council, and other persons nominated by the Administrator. The function of the board was to advise the Administrator on matters affecting New Guineans and enact regulations applicable only to New Guineans. The first set of Native Regulations were based on those in Fiji. In 1894, MacGregor wrote that the regulations of most use to his administration were those that prohibited theft, spreading false reports and threats, adultery, and sorcery. The anti-sorcery regulation of 1893 is a good example of the paternalistic attitude and form that the regulations took:

(1) White men know that sorcery is only deceit, but the lies of the sorcerer frighten many people. The deceit of the sorcerer should be stopped.

(2) It is a forbidden act for any person to practice or to pretend to practice sorcery.

(3) It is a forbidden act for any person to threaten any other person with sorcery whether practiced by himself or by anyone else.

(4) Any person who practices sorcery or who procures another person to do so or who threatens anyone with sorcery may be tried by a magistrate. If a native is found guilty of any of the above offenses he may be sentenced by a European magistrate to imprisonment not exceeding three months, or by a native magistrate to imprisonment not exceeding three days, and will be made to work without payment.

Since it was impossible to produce evidence in sorcery prosecutions, other than the belief on the part of the victim that it had occurred or boasts by the practitioner, Wolfers later asked how it was possible for a magistrate to convict and sentence a person for the offense. In Wolfers's eyes, the fact that the colonial administration took sorcery seriously made it an ally of the sorcerers.

The major purpose of the Native Regulations was to interfere in everyday village practices in order to socialize New Guineans into becoming more like Australians and to solicit free labor from them on the administration's behalf. Regulations ranged from prohibitions on the burial of the dead in villages to injunctions against the careless use of fire. In addition, New Guineans were required to build and maintain roads, clear land for gardens, cut grass and trees, dig wells, plant coconut and other trees, repair houses, support their wives and children, improve village sanitation, keep water channels clear, and send their children to school, even though there were no government-run schools at the time and very few mission schools. Violations of the Native Regulations, of which there were many, were punished with a fine or a jail sentence. In 1896–1897, for example, 202 cases were reported; they included charges as varied as: failing to report for road building, stealing, breach of the burial regulation, adultery, assault, sorcery, and spreading false reports.

Governing the Crown Colony

The challenges confronting the administration of the Crown Colony remained almost identical to those that had plagued the protectorate. The administration had to stretch its limited financial resources and personnel to manage, explore, and extend colonial control over the colony, while maintaining order among the members of the small expatriate community, and managing, training, and protecting New Guineans.

Unlike the special commissioners during the protectorate, the Crown Colony also had to respond to growing demands from Australians that it provide them with incentives to settle in the colony, establish plantations, and hire New Guinean laborers. In carrying out those tasks, MacGregor had what one author called "practically a free hand to enact ordinances, while working within limits which were defined by the British Government on the one side and the principal Australian Colonies on the other."[14] His free hand was due to the fact that, after New Guinea became a Crown Colony, British and Australian officials had very little interest in the details of the administration of their distant, undeveloped, and largely unknown possession.

Establishing an Administrative Structure

The first challenge facing MacGregor—as it had challenged Scratchley during the protectorate—was establishing a workable administrative system for the Crown Colony. Like Scratchley before him, MacGregor was constrained by the £15,000 per year that was allocated for running the colony, which did not increase during the decade of his administration. Consequently, MacGregor was forced to look elsewhere for additional revenue but with few obvious potential sources. New Guineans engaged in subsistence agriculture, the first plantations were not even established until about 1890, and most of the coastal traders carried on itinerant businesses from their ships. At MacGregor's urging, the Legislative Council enacted a series of ordinances imposing a tariff on goods brought into New Guinea. While items such as alcohol and tobacco were subject to the tax, most items—meat, flour, unsweetened biscuits, machinery, building materials, furniture, and agricultural implements—were admitted free of any tariff. Despite the large number of exceptions, the tariffs raised between £2600 and £10,000 per year and became the principal source of additional revenue for the administration.

The limited financial resources available to MacGregor meant that he was able to hire only a small staff. As a result, many colonial officials held more than one position. For example, Francis P. Winter, a Queensland barrister, who had been the attorney-general of Fiji, became both chief judicial officer and deputy administrator in 1888. Charles Monckton, who served as a resident magistrate in New Guinea from 1897 to 1907, described Winter as:

> widely read, a profound thinker possessed of a singular charm of manner, simple and unaffected to a degree. Winter was a man that fascinated every one with whom he came in contact. I don't think he ever said an unkind word or did a mean action in his life. Every officer in the Service, then and later, took his troubles to him, and every unfortunate out of the Service appealed to his purse.[15]

MacGregor's first official act was to divide the colony into divisions—two at first, but four by 1898—with a "resident magistrate" in charge of each division. Those officials were, according to Wolfers, "the sole local personification of the government."[16] They not only had administrative and police powers, and the authority to initiate prosecutions, but also judicial powers, although they had no legal training or experience, as magistrates of the Court of Petty Sessions and the Court for Native Matters. The main task of the resident magistrates was to conduct "government by patrol." Those patrols were meant not only to familiarize the official with his division and its people, but also to make the presence and policies of the colonial administration known to New Guineans and, later, to determine whether those policies were being followed. In a speech at the end of his tenth year in the colony, MacGregor said that, because of his financial limitations and the large size of the colony, it had been possible for his administration only "to establish certain centres and to work outwards from these.... There still remain large areas in the far interior that have not yet been visited by any European."[17] Contact occurred slowly and, in 1912, John Hubert Murray, the lieutenant-governor, estimated that half of the colony remained unexplored.

Although Scratchley had earlier proposed giving New Guineans a formal role in the colonial administration, his early death and the opposition to his plans by colonial officials meant that they were not implemented. As a result, New Guineans played no significant roles in the administration until the late 1960s. However, MacGregor took three steps that gave New Guineans a limited role in the administration. Two of those steps proved successful, while the third did not.

In 1890, the Legislative Council passed an ordinance creating an Armed Native Constabulary under the supervision of the resident magistrates.[18] The constabulary was in keeping with the British practice in India and other colonies of using Indigenous men to do its fighting and policing. Constables accompanied the resident magistrates, acting as interpreters, explaining the purpose of the patrol and the nature of the colonial power to villagers, protecting the resident magistrate when angry villagers attacked, and enabling enforcement of the resident magistrates' orders. The constabulary initially was composed of two Fijian noncommissioned officers, twelve Solomon Islands constables, and eight New Guineans. By 1899 the number of New Guineans in the constabulary had risen to 110 men, and by 1915 to 316 men. While the majority served for only one or two years, a few made it their career. Despite some initial criticism of the performance of the constabulary from villagers and colonial officials, the constabulary came to play an indispensable role in government patrols, particularly of the Highlands, during the late 1920s and 1930s.

MacGregor's second step toward giving New Guineans a small role in the colonial administration was the creation of village constables. Most coastal New Guinean societies were not ruled by hereditary chiefs, but by big men who came to power through the force of their rhetoric, their negotiating skills, their ability as fighters, and their ability to marshal others when needed. But to colonial officials, expecting all primitive people to be ruled by hereditary chiefs, it looked as if village societies had no government. As a result, officials did not rely on big men to act as or to appoint village constables, but instead themselves appointed random villagers to those positions. The constables were not expected to govern in any real sense; their major function was to act as the administration's representatives at the local level, passing on the administration's orders and making sure they were obeyed. Village constables also supplemented the native constabulary, which never was large enough to maintain a continued presence in every village. In selecting village constables, one journalist wrote that MacGregor possessed

> the faculty of getting unexpected results from all sorts and conditions of men. He would make magistrates out of the least likely material, and even turn so-called native murderers into capable village constables. Under these conditions of native life in New Guinea, the constable became the chief, or so far as the equivalent that "Government" as embodied in his august person could command obedience under all difficulties.[19]

Village constables were given a uniform, £1 annual pay, a pair of handcuffs, and a brass badge. Officially, they had the responsibility of enforcing the Native Regulations and ensuring that the people in the villages carried out the instructions of the resident magistrates on such matters as building and maintaining rest houses and roads, planting crops, and promoting public health, such as burying the dead. It is not clear what deference, if any, villagers actually paid to village constables.

Initially, it was the responsibility of missionaries and settlers to explain the Native Regulations to the village constables. However, the administration also began translating the penal provisions of the regulations into Motu, the most widely spoken *lingua franca* along the southern coast. By 1893 the regulations dealing with stealing, injuries to persons, burial of the dead, false reports and threats, destroying coconut trees, and adultery had been translated into Motu.

Although they had no express authority to do so, some village constables also mediated minor disputes in their villages. In addition, they reported serious matters and crimes to the resident magistrates, who visited villages during their periodic patrols. By the end of MacGregor's administration in 1898, there were 202 village constables. Writing after he left New Guinea, MacGregor stated that he considered the village constables and Armed Native Constabulary, to be "[t]he two finest and best institutions I left in New Guinea."[20]

MacGregor's other attempt at involving New Guineans in the colonial administration was the amendment of the *Native Board Ordinance of 1889* to permit the creation of Native Magistrates' Courts to handle cases arising under the Native Regulations.[21] Resident magistrates and persons appointed by the administration presided over those courts, which were not bound by the common law rules of evidence. There was no appeal from the decision of those courts. The 1890–1891 *Annual Report* for British New Guinea reported that J. B. Cameron, the resident magistrate for the Western Division, had appointed two New Guinean men, Gamia, the chief of the Mowatta, and Duba, the chief of the Turi Turi, as native magistrates, with the authority to decide "petty cases only." Cameron referred to them as "very intelligent men."[22] Two years later, Bingham Hely, the new resident magistrate of the division, wrote in the *Annual Report* the following evaluation of the work of Gamia and Duba:

> Of the native magistrates, Duba . . . is the best. He carries more respect among the various tribes than Gamia, although he is perhaps not so intelligent. The latter has been rather spoilt by receiving too much trade and having too much license allowed him. Not a single person in Gamia's village has ever been brought before me by him on any charge whatsoever, although I don't doubt that there has been cause. Whereas Duba keeps a sharp lookout and has been instrumental in enabling me to deal with three cases of adultery and one of assault in his village. I had received information from various native sources which led me to suppose that Gamia was not indisposed to pass over offenses in the Mawatta village for consideration received.[23]

By the following year, Hely had revised his opinion of Duba downward and had suspended Gamia from his position.

> Duba, the native magistrate at Turi Turi, is a weak man, and his constables are lazy. . . . The native magistrate Gamia, however, during the year, went from bad to worse, tampering with women and doing much damage to the Government influence. On the 30th March I suspended Gamia from his office of native magistrate and chief, for tampering with the wife of one of the constabulary.[24]

Two years later, Hely had entirely lost confidence in Duba, writing: "Of the Ture Ture native magistrate and his police I cannot say much that is good. Duba is a very decent man, but a weak one, and is absurdly frightened of 'puri puri' [sorcery]."[25] It is possible that the choice of a different man might have produced a better result. It also is likely that neither Duba nor Gamia received sufficient training. It is certain that whatever the colonial administration wanted them to do and whatever policies the administration expected them to implement would have been very different from Indigenous ideas about what a "big man" should do. As a result of the disappointment with Gamia and Duba, the program was discontinued. No New Guinean was appointed a magistrate again until the late 1960s. One academic said about it:

> The failure of the experiment in native magistrates in effect meant that MacGregor gave up his aim of carrying out a system of indirect rule in British New Guinea. Why did he give up so easily? Perhaps in view of the circumstances under which he worked it was remarkable that he attempted at all. However, it is likely that his Victorian prejudices and assumptions, which conflicted with his concern for native culture and which MacGregor never seemed to resolve himself, were a determining factor in his precipitate retreat from his aim of indirect rule.[26]

Whatever the expectations about the authority and role of native magistrates, they were not participating in indirect rule. The British colonial institution permitted local people to rule themselves, with colonial officers limiting their interference primarily to advice and counsel. The village constables in New Guinea were not empowered to govern their villages; their only task was to ensure that orders from the colonial office were passed on to their village and then were obeyed.

Exploitation versus Economic Development: Land and Labor

As set out in the letters patent from the British government in 1888, two of the primary goals for the Crown Colony were the protection of New Guineans and their lands and the economic development of the colony. However, the goal of economic development would require acquiring land from New Guineans and making it available to expatriate settlers to establish plantations. Those plantations would need a steady supply of New Guinean workers to carry out the physical labor Europeans felt they were incapable of performing in the tropics. These two stated goals of the letters patent—protecting New Guineans and the reality of needed land and labor—created conflicts that lasted throughout the colonial period. Colonial officials enacted a series of local ordinances to help them effect an uneasy balance between these two goals.

Seeking a Balance: Land

The first of Britain's goals in New Guinea was articulated by MacGregor at a meeting in Hobart, Tasmania, in 1886, two years before he became Administrator of British New Guinea. MacGregor spoke of the need to protect the lands of New Guineans: "[N]othing more exasperates a coloured race—or, for that matter, any race . . . than being dispossessed of their hereditary lands. Were that system once introduced, the consequences would be a long train of murders, reprisals and revenge, and finally a war of extermination."[27] MacGregor's view was reflected in the 1888 letters patent, which restated the policy developed by Scratchley during the protectorate of prohibiting private individuals from purchasing land in New Guinea, except from the government or from those who already had purchased the land from the government. The Legislative Council soon codified that policy in the *Land Regulation Ordinance of 1888*. Section 1 of the ordinance made it an offense, punishable by a fine of £100 or imprisonment for up to one year, for any person to purchase land, or any interest in land, from New Guineans. Section 2 prohibited New Guineans from selling their land to anyone except the Administrator.

The prohibition on private individuals acquiring land directly from New Guineans remained a constant in land legislation throughout the colonial period. That prohibition represented a very different attitude toward land in New Guinea from the one taken by authorities in Australia. When Britain established its first settlement in the New South Wales colony (which extended to what are now the states of Queensland, Victoria, and Tasmania) in 1788, it based its claim on the legal fiction that most of the continent was *terra nullius*; that is, it belonged to no one, despite the presence of hundreds of thousands of Indigenous Australians living there. One justification that Britain gave for the designation was that, although Indigenous Australians felt a deep kinship and an obligation toward the land, they had no cultural concept of land ownership as the term was used in the laws of England. Moreover, Indigenous Australians were hunter-gatherers. They trod very lightly on the land, leaving none of the physical evidence of occupation and use that settlements, farms, and gardens do. Crown ownership remained the law in Australia until 1992 when, in *Mabo v. Queensland*, the High Court at last recognized "native title" to land.[28]

The British did not declare the land in New Guinea to be *terra nullius*; instead, they expressly recognized that New Guineans lived there and had rights over land, which the colonizing power was bound by international law to respect. While never expressly articulated, there were at least two reasons why the British attitude toward land ownership in New Guinea differed from that in Australia. First, the colonial authorities were more likely to understand and recognize the relatively permanent villages and gardens in New Guinean societies as evidence of a system of land ownership. Second, Britain seized the land in Australia in order to make it available as a penal colony and then settler colony. However, there was no need or desire on the part of Australians or other expatriates for large amounts of land in New Guinea. Unlike Australia, which was seen as suitable for farming and for grazing cattle and sheep, the rugged terrain and equatorial climate of New Guinea were seen as unsuitable for those purposes and for significant white settlement.

The *Land Regulation Ordinance of 1888* prohibited individuals from purchasing land directly from New Guineans but allowed the colonial administration to do so if the New Guinean owners wanted to sell or lease it and the Administrator was convinced that the land was "not required nor likely to be required" by its New Guinean owners. Such a determination could be difficult to make since it often was not clear which group had the rightful claim to the land. By permitting the Administrator to make that determination and setting no guidelines for the exercise of his discretion, the ordinance almost guaranteed that he would find that the land in question was "not required."

The *Land Regulation Ordinance of 1888* was silent on whether the Administrator could transfer the land he acquired from New Guineans to white settlers and, if so, what the terms of any transfer would be. While many New Guineans were willing to let outsiders use their lands for limited purposes such as hunting or planting gardens—a courtesy similar to that extended to members of neighboring clans or villages—the idea of transferring all rights to their land in perpetuity was not something they would entertain or allow.

The ordinance's silence on the topic of land sales met with criticism from some Australians, particularly those who had been interested in exploiting the colony economically; they argued that MacGregor was too protective of New Guineans and was keeping potential settlers out of the colony. In response to that criticism, and in an attempt, in MacGregor's words, "to procure settlers,"[29] the Legislative Council enacted the *Crown Grants Ordinance of 1889,* which expressly permitted the Administrator to transfer Crown land (land acquired by the Administrator since 1888) to prospective settlers and, more importantly, to give them permanent and complete ownership rights to the land. The ordinance placed only two conditions on transfers of land to private parties: first, in keeping with standard British practice, it reserved all minerals under the land to the Crown, and second, it prohibited grants of land until a licensed surveyor had charted it. Since there were no surveyors in the colony until 1896, the first grants did not become effective until then. The Legislative Council also enacted the *Real Property Ordinance of 1889*, which adopted from Queensland the *Real Property Act of 1861* and the *Real Property Act of 1877* and introduced the Torrens Title land registration system of conveyancing into New Guinea.

In another attempt to draw expatriate settlers to the colony, the Legislative Council enacted the *Crown Lands Ordinance of 1890*, easing the ability of the administration to acquire land for private individuals by giving the Administrator the authority to take possession without compensation of so-called waste and vacant land and sell it or lease it to settlers as well. Under the ordinance, the determination of whether land was waste and vacant was left to the Administrator who merely had to show that the land "was not used or required or reasonably likely to be required" by New Guineans "for building, agricultural or other industrial purposes." MacGregor was not above using what one scholar has termed "verbal bullying" in order to persuade an unnerved chief to "voluntarily" grant land to the administration.[30]

The 1890 ordinance also required the Administrator to issue a Crown grant for any lands acquired by expatriates "on fair terms" before the declaration of the protectorate in November 1884. Although the purchase of land by private individuals directly from New Guineans was prohibited after that date, the 1890 ordinance permitted the Administrator to use his discretion in deciding whether to make a Crown grant for land acquired between 1884 and 1888.

The land ordinances adopted by the Legislative Council in 1889 and 1890 marked a shift away from the highly protective aspects of the 1888 ordinance and toward an attempt to attract settlers to the colony. However, few expatriates were willing to come to New Guinea, and by the middle of 1891 MacGregor was forced to admit that

> [f]urther experience and more extended knowledge of the country has only confirmed the opinion formerly expressed that any plan for systematic settlement of an agricultural population of Europeans in the country is inadmissible. It is highly improbable that people of European descent could ever perform continuous manual Labor in the field there, unless it were at a high altitude on the great mountain ranges; and from these, produce could not be removed to the coast save at ruinous expense.[31]

MacGregor believed that good land was available throughout the country for the cultivation of tobacco, tea, coffee, vanilla, bananas, and coconuts, but that the "class of man" suitable for work in the conditions of the colony would be "difficult to obtain."[32] Although he did not abandon his goal of attracting settlers, MacGregor articulated a new goal for New Guineans in a speech in London in February 1895. He wanted to encourage the Indigenous population to adopt expatriate-style economic activity and, "side by side with the planter, it is hoped that the native will become a useful cultivator on his own account," explaining that:

> The laws affecting natives recognize and preserve their rights; but while this has been done, sight has never been lost of the fact that they must be pushed or led into economic activity. The laws of the Possession are not framed with the object of keeping the native caged up in a reserve; but with the view of making him a useful and industrious peasant proprietor in his own country, with ownership in the soil and with commercial rights equal to those of the European settler.[33]

The administration sought to accomplish that goal, at least in part, through the Native Regulations. The Legislative Council added a provision requiring New Guineans to plant coconut trees and other cash crops on their land.

Australia suffered through an economic depression in the 1890s. As a result, few people were willing or able to incur the costs associated with moving to New Guinea and taking up allotments of land in the largely unknown colony. In the 1895–1896 *Annual Report*, MacGregor reported that no grants of Crown land had been issued that year and "no European planting on a scale of any importance has been started."[34] That led him to turn to private syndicates, which offered to invest in the colony, in return for large tracks of land. In March 1898, for example, the Legislative Council approved the *British New Guinea Syndicate (or Company) Ordinance of 1898*, which permitted the British New Guinea Syndicate to acquire 250,000 acres of land at the price of two shillings per acre. The goals of the syndicate were to explore and open up the land, to plant rubber trees and other tropical produce, and to explore for mineral deposits. The size of the land grant provoked opposition from Australian trading companies, such as Burns Philp, which had interests in New Guinea, as well as from the governments of Victoria, New South Wales, and Queensland. As a result, the British government rescinded the arrangement, leaving those three Australian colonial governments to settle the question of compensation with the syndicate. A number of other syndicates also sought to acquire large allocations of land in New Guinea, but their offers lapsed or were withdrawn due to insufficient financial support. To better manage this process, the colonial administration established a Department of Lands and Survey in 1898 to deal with applications for land in New Guinea. However, the financial and physical risks of the colony meant that only a few individual expatriates were willing or able to take up the challenge. While the Crown held almost one million acres in 1906, expatriate settlers had made only a few applications for the land.[35]

Seeking a Balance: Labor

Labor was a second area in which the introduced law and ordinances demonstrated the administration's conflicting views of its responsibilities. As with land, a primary focus of labor relations was on protecting New Guineans. The 1888 letters patent called for an ordinance prohibiting New Guineans from being removed from the territory or from one part of it to another.[36] In response the Legislative Council enacted *The Natives Removal Prohibition Ordinance of 1888*, which prohibited the removal of New Guineans from the colony or taking New Guineans more than ten miles from their home districts, except for education, religious purposes, government service, or to work on a boat operating within the boundaries of the colony.

The restrictions in the ordinance initially provoked no opposition from expatriates because there was almost no demand for New Guinean labor. However, attitudes about labor in the colony (but not the demand for it) were beginning to change. Pressure from miners and from those who hoped to establish plantations impelled the administration to draft legislation that attempted to maintain the protections of New Guineans from the worst forms of exploitation, while making labor available for plantations and the goldfields.

The Legislative Council replaced the 1888 ordinance with the *Native Labor Ordinance of 1892*, which retained the prohibition on removing New Guineans from the colony but loosened restrictions on work within the colony. If a worker was hired for more than a month, or employed more than twenty-five miles from his home, a resident magistrate had to approve the contract and satisfy himself that the laborer was willing to enter into the contract and that he would be treated fairly, duly paid, and returned to his home at the end of the contract. The ordinance also restricted labor contracts to a maximum of twelve months and allowed employers to hire New Guineans under an oral contract without the consent of a resident magistrate if the period did not exceed one month and the worker was not taken more than twenty-five miles of his home. The following year, criminal sanctions of up to one month in jail were adopted for workers who deserted their employment.

The administration justified the changes in the 1892 ordinance on two grounds: first, there no longer was a risk in permitting laborers to be taken from one district to another, and second, the more New Guineans from one district came into contact with those from other districts, the more they would understand the way the administration worked and the less suspicious they would be. The new ordinance did not attract significant controversy, perhaps because few potential employers came to New Guinea during the 1890s, so the demand for New Guinean labor to work on plantations was not significant.

During the final two years of MacGregor's administration, the Legislative Council lifted almost all restrictions on employing New Guineans as laborers. With the 1897 and 1898 ordinances, MacGregor declared the south coast of the colony settled and allowed New Guineans to be employed without a written contract, unless they were going to be taken more than sixty miles from their home villages. The labor ordinances reflected British common law concepts when that was in the interests of the employer but ignored those concepts where it was not. For example, the ordinances followed British contract law in viewing labor contracts as arms-length transactions between persons with roughly equal information, knowledge, and bargaining power. In the case of British New Guinea, that was an obvious fiction. Contracts were utterly outside the knowledge and experience of New Guineans, who lived in an economy characterized by reciprocity rather than self-interested bargaining. Nor were local people in a position to bargain over salary, terms of employment, or working conditions.

The ordinances departed from British common law notions of contract in that they were not treated as purely personal transactions, enforceable only in civil courts. Instead, the ordinances provided for a fourteen-day jail term or loss of wages if a laborer did not carry out his assigned tasks in a reasonable manner. Anyone who assisted a laborer to desert his employer was also liable to criminal penalties. There was no penalty for an employer who did not keep his terms of the labor contract.

Still the administration was not willing to permit the recruitment of New Guineans to work on the sugar plantations of Queensland. In a paper presented to the Royal Colonial Institute in 1895, MacGregor said there were "insurmountable obstacles" to such employment, since New Guineans would not go voluntarily, and forcing them to go "would be an outrage to which neither Queensland nor Australia would ever consent." In addition, taking laborers to Queensland would deprive settlers in New Guinea of the labor they needed for their plantations, or as MacGregor put it: "What planter would care to commence operations in British New Guinea if the available Labor were removed to Queensland?" He concluded that:

> [t]he development of New Guinea requires that its population remain and work in their own country. . . . Political foresight and considerations of humanity combine to show clearly that the natives of the Possession should not be removed elsewhere for any purpose in their present condition and in the undeveloped state of their own country.[37]

The Challenge of Law and Order

The biggest challenge that MacGregor's administration faced was the imposition of British criminal law. The first ordinance enacted by the Legislative Council was the *Arms, Liquor, and Opium Prohibition Ordinance, 1888,* which built on similar policies adopted by the special commissioners during the protectorate. The ordinance prohibited expatriates from supplying, and New Guineans from possessing, firearms, ammunition, explosives, intoxicating liquor, or opium. The Administrator could give firearms to New Guineans only for purposes of self-defense or hunting for food. The prohibition on owning firearms, ammunition, and explosives was meant partly to prevent an escalation in the weaponry used by New Guineans in tribal fighting and to prevent them from using firearms against administration officials and expatriates. This ordinance was met with criticism in Australia. One Queensland newspaper wrote that MacGregor gave too much deference to missionaries and New Guineans and that the ordinances stifled "the legitimate trade of white men."[38]

Establishing British concepts of law and order proved difficult because, according to Chief Judge Francis Winter, "[t]he natives of British New Guinea possess ideas of their own on the subject of justice, which, . . . in certain respects differ widely from ours." In the 1897–1898 *Annual Report,* Winter noted three key philosophical differences: the New Guinean belief in collective responsibility for the actions of individuals; the unwillingness of New Guineans to agree that the administration had a right to intervene in matters that did not affect foreigners; and the inflexibility and disinterestedness of British justice.[39]

The administration and New Guineans particularly disagreed about which kinds of killings were justified and which were not. To the British, killings carried out on behalf of the state—such as killings by police in the line of duty or by soldiers during war—were justified. So too were some killings in self-defense or in defense of others. New Guineans might not have agreed that any of those were justified. They did, however, condone payback killings, those that occurred during tribal fighting, or the killing of sorcerers, all of which were deemed unjustified and attracted criminal liability under British law.

Tribal fighting and the killing of sorcerers posed particular problems, although MacGregor occasionally was able to use his position as Administrator to negotiate an end to fighting between tribes. The administration was more concerned about the killing of whites by New Guineans than about New Guineans' killing one another. The *Annual Reports*, books, and newspaper articles published during the late 1880s and 1890s contain numerous reports of efforts to capture New Guineans suspected of the murder of whites. In some of those cases, colonial officials succeeded in arresting the suspects, who then were tried in the Central Court and, if convicted, were imprisoned or sentenced to death. Murder investigations and attempts to make arrests often led to fighting between the Armed Native Constabulary and New Guineans, during which New Guinean villagers—the guilty and the innocent alike—were shot and killed.

Of the murders that occurred during MacGregor's ten-year administration, the one that received his administration's greatest attention, the Ansell case, led to the first criminal trial in the Central Court, and the first public executions. In mid-November 1888, just two months after he became Administrator, MacGregor received a report that Edward Ansell, the captain of the copra-trading schooner *Star of Peace*, had been killed in Chads Bay, near Samarai in the eastern part of the colony. One of Ansell's two crew members had also been killed, and the other crew member had escaped with injuries. Villagers took goods, including arms and ammunition, from the ship before burning it. About two weeks later, the resident magistrate at Samarai traveled by navy ship to the area to investigate. In the deserted village, he found a number of houses containing articles taken from the ship. He also found Ansell's body and buried it at sea. MacGregor stated that, in the administration's view, "[t]here seems to be no doubt that this was a cold-blooded murder, prompted by a desire for plunder, and there now remains the question of how this is to be adequately punished."[40] He decided to go to Chads Bay himself, arrest those involved in the killings, take them to Samarai, and try them in the Central Court.

In his 1975 book on race relations in colonial Papua New Guinea, Wolfers quotes two colonial historians, Lewis Lett and J. D. Lange, who criticized MacGregor for being too quick to use force against New Guineans in order to show the power of his administration. However, MacGregor believed he was adopting the less punitive of two possible responses:

> I am extremely anxious that punishment for the murder should overtake the actual perpetrators, which would have a great effect on

> these people, especially if the penalty were carried out in their own locality. A general punishment inflicted on the natives of the district—such as fining them, burning their houses and driving them to the bush—will never, I fear, stop these murderous attacks on Europeans by natives of New Guinea, and of course any such form of punishment would now be illegal here, and could not be justified unless if were found after earnest endeavour that ordinary legal punishment could not be applied.[41]

It is doubtful that anyone had communicated these views to the New Guineans living in and near the site of the killings. A search party spent two months in the Chads Bay area and was attacked by New Guinean villagers who used spears and stones. MacGregor's response was not to use the same order of force; instead, he ordered the constabulary to fire on the villagers, killing four and wounding a number of others. MacGregor wrote a few weeks later that the incident was not without its benefits: "This encounter is much to be regretted on account of the loss of life arising from it; but it produced immense moral effect, and without it the natives would have remained impressed with the belief that we dared not contend with them."[42]

Assisted by some members of another clan, MacGregor and his party managed to capture a number of men they suspected of taking part in the killings. When members of one village boasted that they had given shelter to one of the alleged murderers and vowed that they would kill MacGregor if he attempted to arrest the man, MacGregor invited some of the leaders of that village to his ship, where he held them captive until the suspect was apprehended. By early January 1889, eleven accused had been brought to Samarai and committed for trial—the first one held in the new colony.[43] The trial and executions were conducted quickly. On January 18, 1889, at a trial attended by about two hundred New Guineans, Chief Judicial Officer Francis Winter presided as the judge and Basil Thomson, MacGregor's private secretary, acted as the prosecutor. There was no defense counsel to represent the eleven defendants. Instead, Judge Winter cross-examined the witnesses on behalf of the accused. The trial lasted only one day, at the end of which four of the men were sentenced to death, five were sentenced to imprisonment for twelve months, and one was sentenced to imprisonment for eighteen months. Judge Winter acquitted only one person. The death sentence was scheduled to be carried out a week later.

The death sentences were referred to the Executive Council in Port Moresby for review. Surprisingly, Judge Winter (who was a member of the Executive Council) argued that the death sentences, which he had imposed, should be commuted. He gave a number of reasons for his view: it was the first case tried in the colony; New Guineans should see that it was better to submit to the law than to be driven out of their homes and exposed to the dangers of pursuit by the administration; the four defendants probably did not realize the serious nature of the crime they were committing under English law; and all the villagers near where the killings occurred were implicated in the murders in some way.[44] MacGregor argued in opposition:

> . . . I could not ignore the fact that the murder of white men engaged in peaceable and lawful calling has become so common as almost to be a custom of the country; that this was a case in which there was a deliberate, carefully prepared, and widespread conspiracy to rob and murder, and I knew that there is a common belief among natives here that no severe punishment could overtake them. It was also my opinion that the exercise of the prerogative of mercy would be misunderstood, and the mere fact of trying these men would not act as a deterrent in the future unless the law was allowed to take its course. It appeared to me that these people should at once, as well for their own sake as for the safety of white men in these parts, be taught a hard lesson that killing is murder, and the punishment for it death.[45]

The Executive Council voted 2–1 to uphold the death sentences. To make the greatest possible impact on New Guineans, one of the men was hanged at Samarai, another at Ahioma, and the two others were hanged at the site of Ansell's death. According to MacGregor's reports, about three hundred New Guineans witnessed each of the hangings. In his report to the governor of Queensland, MacGregor summed up what he hoped New Guineans would learn from the case:

> It is not unreasonable to hope and expect that this case, now finally disposed of, has produced an impression on the native mind that will, to their great good, prove deep and lasting. There can be no doubt

> that they now recognize in these districts that a new power, armed with authority, is established among them, and they will before long begin to feel its advantage.[46]

According to historian Hank Nelson: "MacGregor found the decision to hang people difficult and distasteful; but he believed that one harsh lesson was a quicker and ultimately less bloody way to a more law-abiding society."[47] Although more than four hundred New Guineans were charged with murder during MacGregor's administration, executions rarely were carried out. In his biography of MacGregor, R. B. Joyce wrote:

> During MacGregor's ten years of office 418 Papuans were charged with murder and two-thirds of these cases were brought to trial. A verdict of guilty was returned in 138 cases, for all of which the death sentence was imposed. In only eleven cases was the death sentence carried out, however, all for murders committed before June 1894.[48]

Of those eleven, nine had been convicted for killing whites, one for killing a Chinese man, and one for killing another New Guinean. Members of the colonial administration, and especially MacGregor, produced many documents, leaving us with a clear and detailed record of how they viewed those killings. Unfortunately, we do not have a record of what the New Guinean defendants and other villagers believed. We do not know what, if anything, Ansell or his crew members might have done to provoke the attack on their ship. All we know is that no one in the colonial administration at the time seems to have asked. Nor can we surmise what the provocation, if any, might have been, because the other thing we know is that expatriate and New Guinean views about what might justify killing were very different.

A short time after the Ansell case, a second trial starkly highlighted the differences between the British and New Guineans on the topic of justified homicide. Two New Guineans, members of the Manukolo clan, were convicted of murdering and another of aiding and abetting the murder of a New Guinean woman and four children belonging to another group, the Veburi. Manukolo and Veburi were enemies of long standing, at least since members of the Veburi ambushed and killed twenty Manukoloans some years earlier. The Manukoloans were constantly on the lookout for opportunities to kill Veburi, and Manukoloans suspected that the Veburians also were working sorcery against them. For the Manukolo and other clans, the killing of women from an enemy group was seen as legitimate strategic warfare, since it reduced the ability of that group to reproduce and increase the number of its warriors.

The murder occurred in October 1888, and in March of the following year, MacGregor went to Manukolo, arrested three men, and took them to Port Moresby for trial. Robert Hunter, a government official who spent many decades living and working in New Guinea, represented the three men. Hunter argued that the men were ignorant of English law, had been following their custom, and had dealt with a grievance against the Veburi as any New Guinean would be expected to do. His arguments fell on deaf ears. Judge Winter told the defendants that New Guinea was now an English possession and they were now subject to English law. Since the men had confessed to the killings during the committal proceedings, he convicted them and sentenced them to death.[49]

While deciding whether to approve the death sentences, MacGregor received a petition from Hunter and four missionaries asking for leniency for the men. The petition repeated Hunter's arguments at trial that the killings were part of a tribal war that had been going on at the time New Guinea became a British possession. In killing the women and children, the three men had been acting according to a customary obligation and putting into practice customary concepts of retributive justice. They stressed that the men had never heard of Queen Victoria and had no idea they were now subject to English law.

Following the approach taken by Scratchley in the Miller case in 1885, MacGregor decided that, because New Guinea had become a British colony, he had an obligation to uphold the conviction of the three men. However, because the men had not even been aware of the imposition of English law, let alone its detailed requirements, he reduced the death sentence to fourteen years in prison for the two men convicted of the actual murders and to five years in prison for the man convicted of aiding and abetting the killings. MacGregor had decided that, before New Guineans could be held guilty of murder to the same degree as expatriates, they had to be aware of and understand English law. Although in his view the trial itself was a form of "enlightenment" and a first step toward that goal, the procedure still was completely unintelligible to New Guineans.

The Work of the Crown Colony Courts

New Guineans were far more likely to appear in the colonial courts as criminal defendants than as parties to civil suits. Officials believed that public trials would somehow educate New Guineans into British ideals of law and order and justice, although they made no attempt to explain the reasoning behind the laws or procedures that were used. Those procedures were in many important respects different not only from New Guineans' customary processes but also from the procedures in effect in England or Australia. For example, there was no independent judiciary in British New Guinea. The judge of the Central Court, Francis Winter, was also a member of the Executive Council and the Legislative Council. The magistrates who heard cases brought in the Court of Petty Sessions, the Small Debts Courts, Wardens' Courts, and the Courts of Native Matters were resident magistrates, officials in charge of administering the various divisions in the colony. Thus, the administrative, legislative, and judicial functions of the colonial administration often were combined in the same person.

Between the small size of the expatriate population and the New Guinean population's lack of interest in utilizing the alien courts, there were very few civil cases before the courts in the eighteen years that British New Guinea was a Crown Colony. In 1889–1890, for example, there were only two civil proceedings in the Central Court; one was an action for goods sold and money lent and the other an application for administration under the *Intestacy Act*. By 1896–1897, the number of civil cases had risen only to eleven, nine of which involved intestate estates or probate and two appeals from Wardens' Courts. In 1902–1903, the Central Court heard forty-nine civil cases, with forty-seven involving intestacy and probate and two being applications to appoint guardians for children. The civil cases heard by the Court of Petty Sessions were limited to matters of debt, with an occasional claim for damages. In 1902–1903, for example, the Courts of Petty Sessions heard twenty-three cases, all involving debts. There were at least three reasons for the relative absence of civil cases: the expatriate population was very small and scattered; the simple economy did not give rise to many commercial disputes; and New Guineans rarely brought their disputes to the colonial courts for resolution.

The Courts of Native Matters did hear some civil claims by and against New Guineans. In 1902–1903, there were thirty-one such cases, involving a variety of subjects: land, the destruction of property, debt, the restoration of property, payment for food, and payment for services.[50] In 1903, the court in the Western Division heard a claim brought by an unmarried New Guinean woman against the father of her child to recover the cost of providing food for the child. The father, who was married to another woman, admitted the parentage of the child but refused to contribute to its support. Although there is no report of the outcome of the case, it shows that a few New Guineans at least were beginning to resolve disputes by resorting to the colonial courts rather than relying on custom and traditional dispute settlement.

The vast majority of the cases heard by the courts were criminal cases, in which New Guineans were the defendants. In 1891–1892, for example, criminal trials in the Central Court involved twenty-eight New Guinean men, all of whom were charged with murder, sedition, manslaughter, or rape. The court acquitted only three of them, and sentenced twenty-one to death. The death sentence, however, was carried out in only one case. In the other cases, Judge Winter commuted the sentence to a term of imprisonment. In cases that did not involve murder, no physical punishment was imposed; instead, work on government projects in Port Moresby occupied the prisoners' time before they were returned to their villages.

In cases in which Winter commuted the death sentences, defendants usually had acted in furtherance of a customary obligation to pay back earlier injuries to their families or clans. For example, in a murder trial in 1891–1892, a son claimed that he was obligated to "take payment" in blood from a neighboring tribe for the murder of his father many years earlier. In a second case that year, three persons killed a member of their own clan thought to have caused the death of one of their relatives by sorcery. In a third case, two men were convicted of an attack on someone whom they thought had caused the death of several people by sorcery. In another case, six men were convicted of raping two women from a neighboring clan as payback for an old grievance. In another trial, eight men were convicted of murdering members of a nearby village, again in retaliation for an interclan dispute. Finally, a Chinese merchant was murdered as payback for a relative in the previous generation who had been killed by a white man. The accused men in all six of those cases were reported to have admitted committing the crimes.

Summary criminal cases made up the overwhelming majority of cases heard in the Courts of Petty Sessions and the Native Magistrates' Court. In 1897–1898, for example, there were 393 criminal cases dealt with in these lower courts. The offenses included larceny, assault, breach of the *Labor Ordinance*, breach of the *Arms and Liquor Ordinance*, drunken and disorderly conduct, insulting language, trespass, breach of the *Roads Ordinance*, spreading false reports, adultery, destroying coconut trees, sorcery, and theft. In the vast majority of those cases, the defendants were convicted and sentenced to a short term in jail.

The *Annual Reports* did not stipulate the race of defendants in criminal cases until after New Guinea became an Australian colony in 1906. However, other records suggest that almost all of the defendants were New Guineans. For example, in his *Annual Report* for 1891–1892, MacGregor praised the expatriate population for being "remarkably law-abiding for people in such circumstances" and pointed out that, during the first four years of the colony, only one expatriate had been charged with murdering New Guineans. In that 1889 case, the court dismissed the charge as baseless. In the 1897–1898 *Annual Report*, Judge Winter reviewed the administration of justice in the colony during the previous ten years and concluded that the criminal offenses committed by whites were so few and so minor "that it is not worthwhile to touch upon them."[51] According to MacGregor, "[t]he total exemption of Europeans from this category of criminals supplies the best proof that could be adducted that the general character of the Europeans in the country has been good."[52] However, the good character of whites in New Guinea during those years is subject to debate. Wolfers and others recount numerous instances of sexual and physical assaults by white men against New Guineans in general, and New Guinean women in particular. Harsh treatment of New Guinean workers and domestic servants was generally accepted, and it not infrequently escalated into assault. That only a small number of criminal cases was brought against perpetrators was the result of the unwillingness of the colonial administration to risk the publicity, the loss of prestige, and the loss of cooperation that such prosecutions would cause.

Instead of prosecuting them, the administration quietly deported disruptive expatriates back to Australia.

The Le Hunte Administration

The financing agreement between Britain and its Australian colonies expired in 1898, at the time that the Australian colonies were moving toward federation, leaving the position of New Guinea unclear. The British colonial administration and its legal systems remained in force, pending the decision on Australia's future.

That same year, MacGregor resigned as lieutenant-governor, and the British Colonial Office appointed George R. Le Hunte as his successor. Le Hunte, who had held administrative positions in a number of British colonies since 1875, served in New Guinea from March 1899 until May 1903. During those four years, the colonial legal system continued to evolve. In 1900, on the basis that some areas of the colony had become sufficiently pacified to permit New Guineans access to firearms, the Legislative Council amended the *Arms, Liquor and Opium Prohibition Ordinance of 1888,* enabling resident magistrates to issue annual permits to New Guineans to possess and use guns and ammunition. In addition, the amendment provided for issuing permits to mixed-race persons and non-New Guineans to purchase liquor. Possessing firearms or liquor without a permit continued to be punishable by a fine of at least £20 or three months in prison.[53]

Land and labor legislation also changed during Le Hunte's administration, although Australians still were reluctant to settle in New Guinea. In a continuing effort to attract expatriate settlers to the colony, the *Land Ordinance of 1899* provided that any offer by the administration to sell or lease parcels of areas of land of 640 acres (one square mile) should be advertised in England, Australia, and New Zealand for six months before the land could be sold. By mid-1900 the colonial administration held over 440,000 acres of Crown land, while less than 20,000 acres had been granted to settlers. Resistance to settlement was not the only reason why so little land had been alienated: the administration rejected most applications for large tracts of Crown land because Australian companies feared competition for scarce markets if new plantations were successful.

With few Australians taking up land in New Guinea, there was little demand for labor. By 1900, only about four thousand New Guineans were employed, most of them on plantations, in gold mining, working for traders, or as domestic servants. The *Native Labor Ordinance of 1900* consolidated previous labor laws and provided for the licensing of recruiting agents and the appointment of inspectors who could cancel or vary labor contracts. There were two provisions in labor contracts that the inspectors could not alter without the consent of the resident magistrate before whom the laborers were hired: the place at which the men were to be paid at the end of their term, and the requirement that, at the end of their twelve-month contract period, men could not be rehired without first returning them to their home villages. The ordinance also provided that New Guineans could face imprisonment and lose wages for refusing to work or for desertion.

By the time of the Le Hunte administration, there already were hints of labor unrest. In the 1903–1904 *Annual Report*, the resident magistrate for the Eastern Division wrote that "[t]he majority of natives working in the Eastern Division now have little or nothing to complain of with regard to the treatment they receive at the hand of their respective employers. Of course there are one or two exceptions, but these only go to prove the rule."[54] The workers must have had something to complain about because, in the next paragraph, the resident magistrate called for stiffer penalties in the labor ordinance to deal with the problem of desertion:

> Cases of desertion have occurred, and they seem to, in many cases, require more fitting punishment than the law at present allows. A native servant who deserts his master at a very awkward moment for no other reason that a whim of his deserves, in my opinion, more than a month's imprisonment, and I think that if the law allowed a longer term in gaol than the period above-mentioned, desertions of this nature would soon be a thing of the past.[55]

The official went on to blame desertions on "knowing natives" who had too much contact with expatriates "and not profited thereby, who makes a practice of deserting without a cause, and it very often happens that he also influences other native servants, who would not think otherwise of doing so, to desert with him."[56] Questions about the treatment of plantation workers and consequent desertions would become major issues for the colonial administration in the following decade.

The most important addition to the colonial statutes during Le Hunte's administration was the reception into New Guinea of Queensland's 1899 *Criminal Code*. The code, drafted by Sir Samuel Griffith, who would become Australia's first chief justice following federation, was intended as a progressive codification of the Anglo-Australian common law of crimes as well as incorporating a number of related statutes, and all in one volume—making it suitable for areas without large numbers of lawyers, judicial officers, and law libraries. While a significant achievement, the suitability of the *Criminal Code* to the very different circumstances of New Guinea was very much open to question. Nevertheless, it was adopted by ordinance in British New Guinea in 1902 without the qualification of circumstantial applicability that applied to the English common law and equity.

Although legislation governing land, labor, and criminal law continued to change during the Le Hunte administration, the administration's dismissal of customary law and its role in the colonial legal system did not change. Shortly before he retired in 1898, MacGregor asked Winter to prepare a document clarifying the role of custom in British New Guinea. In his report, Winter recognized that Papuans did not understand English notions of individual guilt and punishment. He also acknowledged that colonial officials did not understand New Guinean ways of thinking and their elaborate social obligations. However, he reached the same conclusions about the role that custom should play in the colonial legal system that Scratchley had advocated more than a decade earlier. Since the English legal system was "superior," English law and not customary law should govern the colony, even in the Courts for Native Matters. The only place for custom was as a potentially mitigating factor in determining the sentences New Guineans should receive for violations of English criminal law.[57]

The enforcement of law and order was a significant issue throughout Le Hunte's four years as lieutenant-governor. In 1900–1901, for example, 101 persons, almost all of them New Guineans, were tried in the Central Court for criminal offenses. The range of offenses included murder and manslaughter but also arson, desecration of a burial site, assault, indecent assault, larceny, jail breaking, perjury, and abusing a girl under the age of ten. Only seventeen of the persons tried were discharged or found not guilty. The crime that drew the most attention during Le Hunte's administration—the murder of missionaries James Chalmers, Oliver Tomkins, and ten New Guinean Christians on April 8, 1901, by villagers on Goaribari Island, in the Gulf of Papua—did not result in anyone being arrested or charged. Instead, the response by Le Hunte and his successor to the murders had deadly consequences both for New Guineans and for the colonial administration that extended beyond Le Hunte's time.

Rejecting the London Missionary Society's plea against reprisals, Le Hunte led a punitive expedition in May 1901 that resulted in the death of twenty-four New Guineans on Goaribari Island, the burning of ceremonial houses, and the destruction of war canoes. The killings and destruction were criticized widely in Britain and Australia. Le Hunte led a second expedition in March 1902, in which he negotiated a peace agreement with the Goaribari islanders and returned with Chalmer's skull. However, in early March 1904, Le Hunte's successor, Christopher Stansfield Robinson, led a third expedition to Goaribari Island with the intention of arresting the murderers. Robinson was a young Brisbane barrister who had been appointed acting Administrator (but not lieutenant-governor), as well as chief judicial officer in June 1903. Unfortunately, Robinson's mission led to the islanders firing arrows at his ship. The members of the Armed Native Constabulary responded by firing about 250 rounds from their rifles. At least eight New Guineans were killed, some apparently shot by Robinson himself.

News of the killings at Goaribari Island produced another round of strong criticism in Australia, especially from religious organizations, and Robinson was suspended from his position. On the morning of June 20, 1904, just days after he had been informed that the Australian government had appointed a Royal Commission of Inquiry to investigate the Goaribari events, Robinson, who was suffering from malaria and depression, shot and killed himself near the flagstaff in front of government house in Port Moresby. He was only thirty-two years old and had served as acting Administrator for just one year. The report of the Royal Commission blamed Robinson for the shootings. It concluded that he suffered from a "temporary loss of self-controlling reason, to which strong excitement too often leads."[58] In 1932, the European community erected a memorial to

Robinson in Samarai. The inscription on the base of the obelisk, which has survived World War II and decades of neglect, reads:

> He was an able governor, upright man and honest judge. His aim was to make New Guinea a good place for white men. He was as well-meaning as he was unfortunate and as kindly as he was courageous.

With the death of Robinson, the position of chief judicial officer became vacant. John Hubert Murray, a forty-two-year-old Australian-born and Oxford-educated barrister, who was bored practicing law in the country towns of western New South Wales, successfully applied for the position. Murray arrived in Port Moresby in September 1904 and held the position, and later the office of lieutenant-governor, until his death thirty-six years later.

In contrast to the Goaribari tragedy was the administration's handling of the 1901 killing of Amideo Gullianetti, the assistant resident magistrate at Mekeo in the Central Division, who was shot and killed while asleep in his room by escaped prisoners. Two of the prisoners were captured that night and the others a short time later. At their trial, Judge Winter acquitted all but two of the men. The two men he convicted were the instigator of the crime and the man who actually committed the murder; each received prison sentences of fourteen years. The sentences upset the expatriate community in Port Moresby, which had expected that the New Guineans would receive the death penalty. In a case the following year, the armed constabulary arrested six men from a tribe that had killed and eaten two men from another tribe. Although none of the men arrested had taken part in the murders, they had participated in eating the bodies. Judge Winter sentenced them to jail only "for a short term of imprisonment," since there was no evidence that cannibalism had taken place on the island where the killings had occurred in the previous twelve years.[59]

The continuing shortage of personnel, coupled with the challenging geography of the colony, frequently prevented officials in Le Hunte's administration from arresting New Guineans for tribal fighting or for murdering expatriates, whose deaths often resulted from their lack of understanding of New Guinean customs or from interfering with New Guinean women. His administration relied on the Armed Native Constabulary to maintain law and order, often by resorting to punitive raids. In November

1900, the constabulary, led by the resident magistrate for the Western Division, fought a group of Tugeri from Dutch New Guinea who had crossed the border to raid and kill villagers. The police sank five canoes, and about thirty Tugeri were shot or drowned. In 1902, the constabulary led by Charles A. Monckton, the resident magistrate for the North-Eastern Division, shot and killed several members of the Doriri, who had been attacking other tribes. Later that year, Monckton led another punitive expedition against the Dobodura, who also had been attacking other tribes. According to Monckton's report, "a good many" Dobodura were killed and others "subsequently made peace."[60] Although the spate of raids and killings resulted in widespread criticism within New Guinea and in Australia, Le Hunte did not discipline or remove the officers who led the punitive patrols. The Australian Minister for External Affairs later justified the lack of disciplinary action, saying that the rule in the colony was that "life is never to be sacrificed except in self-defence, and this rule never has been departed from, so far."[61] Since, the killing of all the New Guineans had occurred in "self-defence," according to the official version of events, no one was criminally liable.

The End of British Rule in New Guinea

With the establishment of the Commonwealth of Australia in January 1901, the nation's new Parliament passed a resolution affirming its readiness "to accept British New Guinea as a Territory of the Commonwealth."[62] Letters patent were issued in March 1902 to place British New Guinea under the authority of Australia. However, protracted debate in the Australian Parliament over whether to ban completely the sale of alcohol in the territory and whether to end freehold grants of land delayed enactment of a legal basis for its administration. It was not until November 1905 that the Australian Parliament enacted the *Papua Act*, which went into effect in September 1906.

In eighteen years of rule in New Guinea, Great Britain had established no more than nominal control over the protectorate. The shortage of financial and personnel resources meant that actual contact with the Indigenous population was sporadic at best, limited to the narrow confines of the south coast and the islands. However, British rule did have one lasting effect. Although the British legal system had little impact at the time, it was to become the basis of the colonial legal system and, indeed, would ultimately prevail over custom to become the state law of the Independent State of Papua New Guinea.

Sources

Books and Articles

Adelaide Observer, "British New Guinea," *Adelaide Observer*, January 24, 1903.

B.F.S. Baden-Powell, *In Savage Isles and Settled Lands* (London: Richard Bentley and Son, 1892).

Wilfred N. Beaver, *Unexplored New Guinea* (London: Seeley, Service, and Co., 1920).

Peter Biskup, Brian Jinks, and Hank Nelson, *A Short History of New Guinea* (Sydney: Angus and Robertson, 1968).

William Blackstone, *Commentaries on the Laws of England*, vol. 1 (Oxford: Clarendon Press, 1765–1770).

Manning Clark, *A Short History of Australia* (New York: Mentor, 1969).

Ronald G. Crocombe (ed.), *Land Tenure in the Pacific* (Suva: University of the South Pacific Press, rev. ed., 1987).

Tom Dutton, *Police Motu* (Port Moresby: University of Papua New Guinea Press, 1985).

Examiner, "British New Guinea," *Examiner*, August 22, 1902, 8.

Thomas P. Fry, "The Life and Work of Lieut.-Col. Sir. John Plunkett Murray, B.A.," *Journal of the Royal Historical Society of Queensland* 3(6) (1947) 405–438.

H. J. Gibbney, "The Interregnum in the Government of Papua, 1901–1906," *Australian Journal of Politics and History* 12(3) (1966) 341–359.

Peter Hastings, *New Guinea: Problems and Prospects* (Melbourne: Cheshire, Australian Institute of International Affairs, 1969).

W. J. Hudson (ed.), *Australia and Papua New Guinea* (Sydney: Sydney University Press, 1971).

W. J. Hudson (ed.), *New Guinea Empire: Australia's Colonial Experience* (Melbourne: Cassell Australia, 1974).

R. B. Joyce, "The British New Guinea Syndicate Affair of 1898," *Journal of the Royal Historical Society of Queensland* 5(1) (1954) 771–793.

R. B. Joyce, *Sir William MacGregor* (Oxford: Oxford University Press, 1971).

R. B. Joyce, "William MacGregor: The Role of the Individual," in Kenneth S. Inglis (ed.), *The History of Melanesia* (Canberra: Research School of Pacific Studies, Australian National University, and Port Moresby: University of Papua New Guinea Press, 1971) 33–44.

R. B. Joyce, *Samuel Walker Griffith* (Brisbane: University of Queensland Press, 1984).

Alan Kerr, *A Federation in These Seas* (Canberra: Attorney General's Dept., 2009).

Henrika Kuklick, *The Savage Within: The Social History of British Anthropology, 1885–1945* (Cambridge: Cambridge University Press, 1991).

J. D. Legge, *Australian Colonial Policy* (Sydney: Angus and Robertson, 1956).

Lewis Lett, *The Papuan Achievement* (Melbourne: Melbourne University Press, 1942).

Lewis Lett, *Sir Hubert Murray of Papua: Statesman and Empire Builder* (Sydney: Collins, 1949).

D. C. Lewis, *The Plantation Dream: Developing British New Guinea and Papua 1884–1942* (Canberra: The Journal of Pacific History, 1996).

Nancy Lutton, "C. A. W. Monckton: Reprobate Magistrate," in James Griffin (ed.), *Papua New Guinea Portraits: The Expatriate Experience* (Canberra: Australian National University Press, 1978) 48–74.

"Sir W. MacGregor's Discoveries in New Guinea," *The Scottish Geographical Magazine* 6 (1890) 245–254.

Kenneth Mackay, *Across Papua* (London: Witherby and Co., 1909).

Peter Maiden, *Missionaries, Headhunters and Colonial Officers: British New Guinea and the Goaribari Affray 1860–1907* (Rockhampton: Central Queensland University Press, 2003).

Lucy Mair, *Australia in New Guinea* (London: Christophers, 1948).

J. R. Mattes, "The Sources of Law in Papua and New Guinea," *Australian Law Journal* 37 (1963) 148.

John Hubert Murray, *Papua or British New Guinea* (London: T. Fisher Unwin, 1912).

Hank Nelson, "Miners, Laborers and Officials on the Lakelamu Goldfield of Papua," *Labor History*, No. 25 (November 1973) 40–52.

Hank Nelson, "The Swinging Index: Capital Punishment and British and Australian Administrations in Papua and New Guinea, 1888–1945," *Journal of Pacific History* 13(3) (1978) 130–152.

Hank Nelson, "Changing the Label," in Sione Latukefu (ed.), *Papua New Guinea: A Century of Colonial Impact* (Port Moresby: The National Research Institute and the University of Papua New Guinea, 1989) 19–36.

Hans Jürgen Ohff, *Disastrous Ventures: German and British Enterprises in East New Guinea up to 1914* (Melbourne: Plenum Publishing Australia, 2015).

Christina Oke, "The Native Administrations of MacGregor, Murray and Hasluck in Papua/New Guinea: Continuity and Contrast," *University of Wollongong Historical Journal* 1(1) (1975) 7–41.

Nigel Oram, *The Western Motu Area and the European Impact: 1872–1942*, in Sione Latukefu (ed.), *Papua New Guinea: A Century of Colonial Impact* (Port Moresby: The National Research Institute and the University of Papua New Guinea, 1989).

Robin S. O'Regan, "The Reception of the Common Law and the Authority of Common Law Precedents in the Territory of Papua and New Guinea," *International and Comparative Law Quarterly* 19(2) (1970) 217–228.

W. D. Pitcairn, *Two Years Among the Savages of New Guinea* (London: Ward and Downey, 1891).

B. N. Primrose, "The Papua Bill: Australian Colonial Policy?" *Australian Journal of Politics and History* 19(2) (1973) 205–223.

The Queenslander, "British New Guinea: The Labor Question," *The Queenslander*, April 20, 1895, 725.

Henry Reynolds, *The Law of the Land* (Ringwood: Penguin, 2nd ed., 1992).

Henry Reynolds, *Aboriginal Sovereignty* (Sydney: Allen & Unwin, 1996).

Charles G. Seligmann, *The Melanesians of British New Guinea* (Cambridge: Cambridge University Press, 1910).

Richard Semon, *In the Australian Bush and on the Coast of the Coral Sea* (London: MacMillan, 1899).

R. T. Shand, "The Development of Cash-Cropping in Papua and New Guinea," *Australian Journal of Agricultural and Resource Economics* 7(1) (1963) 42–54.

George W. Stocking Jr., *Victorian Anthropology* (New York: Free Press, 1987).

George W. Stocking Jr., *After Taylor: British Social Anthropology 1888–1951* (Madison: University of Wisconsin Press, 1998).

Ian Stuart, *Port Moresby: Yesterday and Today* (Sydney: Pacific Publications, rev. ed., 1973).

Sydney Morning Herald, "New Guinea," *Sydney Morning Herald*, July 3, 1889, 4.

Sydney Morning Herald, "The Papuan Dependency: Report of Mr. Atlee Hunt," *Sydney Morning Herald*, November 1, 1905, 9.

Telegraph, "British New Guinea," *Telegraph*, October 16, 1891.

J. P. Thomson, *British New Guinea* (London: George Philip and Son, 1892).

John Waiko, "Australian Administration under the Bindandere Thumb," in Sione Latukefu (ed.), *Papua New Guinea: A Century of Colonial Impact* (Port Moresby: The National Research Institute and the University of Papua New Guinea, 1989) 75–108.

Nii Lante Wallace-Bruce, "Two Hundred Years On: A Reexamination of the Acquisition of Australia," *Georgia Journal of International and Comparative Law* 19(1) (1989) 87–116.

Frank Welsh, *Australia: A New History of the Great Southern Land* (New York: Overlook Press, 2004).

F. J. West, "Captain Barton of Papua," *South Pacific* 7 (May–June 1954) 858–862.

Francis West, *Hubert Murray: The Australian Pro-Consul* (Melbourne: Oxford University Press, 1968).

Western Mail, "Mr. Atlee Hunt's Visit: An Interesting Report," *Western Mail*, November 4, 1905, 33.

Osmar White, *Parliament of a Thousand Tribes* (Melbourne: Wren, 1972).

Francis P. Winter, "Notes on a Government Expedition under Dr. J. A. Blayney, Capt. J. R. Barton, and Mr. A. E. English to the Main Range, British New Guinea," *Queensland Geographical Journal* (new series) 16(16) (1900–1901) 63–69.

Edward P. Wolfers, *Race Relations and Colonial Rule in Papua New Guinea* (Sydney: Australia and New Zealand Book Co., 1975).

Government Documents

Annual Report for British New Guinea 1888–1889 (Brisbane: Government Printer, 1889).

Annual Report for British New Guinea 1889–1890 (Brisbane: Government Printer, 1890).

Annual Report for British New Guinea 1890–1891 (Brisbane: Government Printer, 1890–1891).

Annual Report for British New Guinea 1892–1893 ((Brisbane: Government Printer, 1892–1893).

Annual Report for British New Guinea 1893–1894 ((Brisbane: Government Printer, 1893–1894).

Annual Report for British New Guinea 1895–1896 (Brisbane: Government Printer, 1895–1896).

Annual Report for British New Guinea 1897–1898 (Brisbane: Government Printer, 1898).

Annual Report for British New Guinea 1902–1903 (Brisbane: Government Printer, 1903).

Annual Report for British New Guinea 1903–1904 (Brisbane: Government Printer, 1904).

"The Colony of New Guinea," in *The Australian Handbook* (London: Gordon and Gotch, 1888) 539–546.

Commonwealth Bureau of Census and Statistics, *Official Year Book of the Commonwealth of Australia*, 1901–1907 (Canberra: Commonwealth Bureau of Census and Statistics, 1908).

Atlee Hunt, "Report on British New Guinea, 1905," *Commonwealth Parliamentary Papers* (Brisbane: Government Printer, 1905) 5–7.

William MacGregor, *Handbook of Information for Intending Settlers in British New Guinea* (Brisbane: Government Printer, 1892).

William MacGregor, "British New Guinea," *Proceedings of the Royal Colonial Institute* 24 (1892–1893) 289–313.

William MacGregor, "British New Guinea," *Proceedings of the Royal Colonial Institute* 26 (1894–1895) 193–239.

William MacGregor, "British New Guinea," *Proceedings of the Royal Colonial Institute* 30 (1898–1899) 238–270.

"New Guinea Natives," *The Register*, June 15, 1903, 3.

T. H. Hatton Richards, "British New Guinea," *Proceedings of the Royal Colonial Institute* 24 (1892–1893) 299–300.

Royal Commission, "Report of the Royal Commission on the Affray at Goaribari Island, British New Guinea, 6 March 1904," *Commonwealth Parliamentary Papers*, No. 42 (Brisbane: Government Printer, 1904).

M. Staniforth Smith, *Handbook of the Territory of Papua* (Melbourne: Government Printer, 1906).

Cases

Blankard v. Galdy, 91 Eng. Rep. 356 (1694)

Calvin's Case, 77 Eng. Rpt. 379 (1608)

Campbell v. Hall, 20 St. Tr. 239 (1744)

Mabo and Others v. Queensland (No. 2), [1992] 175 CLR 1

Statutes

Armed Native Constabulary Ordinance 1890 (British New Guinea)

Arms, Liquor, and Opium Prohibition Ordinance 1888 (British New Guinea)

The British New Guinea (Queensland) Act 1887 (Great Britain)

British New Guinea Syndicate (or Company) Ordinance 1898 (British New Guinea)

The British Settlements Act 1887 (Great Britain)

The Courts and Laws Adopting Ordinance 1888 (British New Guinea)

The Courts and Laws Adopting Ordinance (Amended) 1889 (British New Guinea)

Criminal Procedure Ordinance 1889 (British New Guinea)

Crown Grants Ordinance 1889 (British New Guinea)

Land Ordinance 1899 (British New Guinea)

Land Ordinance 1906 (British New Guinea)

Land Regulation Ordinance 1888 (British New Guinea)

Marriage Ordinance 1912 (British New Guinea)

Native Affairs Ordinance 1889 (British New Guinea)

Native Board Ordinance 1889 (British New Guinea)

Native Labor Ordinance 1892 (British New Guinea)

Native Labor Ordinance 1900 (British New Guinea)

The Natives Removal Prohibition Ordinance 1888 (British New Guinea)

New Guinea Act 1920 (Australia)

Papua Act 1905 (Australia)

Real Property Ordinance 1889 (British New Guinea)

Roads Ordinance 1888 (British New Guinea)

Supreme Court Ordinance 1876 (Gold Coast)

Notes

1. *Annual Report on British New Guinea* (Brisbane: Government Printer, 1889–1890), Appendix A, 2.
2. R. B. Joyce, *Sir William MacGregor* (Oxford: Oxford University Press, 1971) 182.
3. *Annual Report on British New Guinea* (Brisbane: Government Printer, 1889–1890), Ordinance No. VI of 1889, section 3.
4. William Blackstone, *Commentaries on the Laws of England*, vol. 1 (Oxford: Oxford University Press, 2016) 76.
5. 7 Coke Report 1A, 77 E.R. 377 (1608).
6. William Blackstone, *Commentaries on the Laws of England*, vol. 1 (Oxford: Oxford University Press, 2016) 77.
7. *The Courts and Laws Adopting Ordinance (Amended) of 1889*, sections 2 and 3.
8. Ordinance No. 4 (1876), reprinted in *Ordinances of the Gold Coast Colony, In Force June 1898* (1898) 9.
9. William MacGregor, "British New Guinea," *Proceedings of the Royal Colonial Institute* 26 (1894–1895) 193.
10. *Id.* at 218.
11. *Id.*
12. *The Courts and Laws Adopting Ordinance of 1888*, section 7.
13. "British New Guinea," *The Telegraph*, October 16, 1891, 6.
14. C. Brunsdon Fletcher, *The New Pacific: British Policy and German Aims* (London: Macmillan and Co., 1917) 143.
15. Charles Arthur Whitmore Monckton, *Some Experiences of a New Guinea Resident Magistrate* (London: John Lane, 1921) 12.
16. Edward P. Wolfers, *Race Relations and Colonial Rule in Papua New Guinea* (Sydney: Australia and New Zealand Book Co., 1975) 19.
17. William MacGregor, "British New Guinea," *Proceedings of the Royal Colonial Institute* 30 (1898–1899) 244–245.
18. *Armed Native Constabulary Ordinance* (Ordinance No. 1 of 1890), in *Annual Report on British New Guinea* (Brisbane: Government Printer, 1889–1890) 6.
19. C. Brunsdon Fletcher, *The New Pacific: British Policy and German Aims* (London: Macmillan and Co., 1917) 141–142.
20. William MacGregor, "Introduction," in John Hubert Murray, *Papua or British New Guinea* (London: T. Fisher Unwin, 1912) 27.
21. *Native Affairs Ordinance of 1889.*
22. *Annual Report for British New Guinea* (Brisbane: Government Printer, 1890–1891) Appendix I, 78.

23. *Annual Report for British New Guinea* ((Brisbane: Government Printer, 1892–1893) Appendix I, 39.
24. *Annual Report for British New Guinea* ((Brisbane: Government Printer, 1893–1894) Appendix I, 50, 52.
25. *Annual Report for British New Guinea* ((Brisbane: Government Printer, 1895–1896).
26. Christina Oke, "The Native Administrations of MacGregor, Murray and Hasluck in Papua/New Guinea: Continuity and Contrast," *University of Wollongong Historical Journal* 1(1) (1975) 7, 13.
27. R. B. Joyce, "William MacGregor: The Role of the Individual," in Kenneth S. Inglis (ed.), *The History of Melanesia* (Port Moresby: University of Papua New Guinea, 1971) 35.
28. *Mabo and Others v. Queensland (No. 2)* [1992] 175 CLR 1.
29. William MacGregor, "British New Guinea," *Proceedings of the Royal Colonial Institute* 26 (1894–1895) 216.
30. Andrew James Connelly, "Counting Coconuts: Patrol Reports from the Trobriand Islands Part I: 1907–1934" (unpublished master's thesis, California State University, Sacramento, 1987) 35.
31. *Annual Report on British New Guinea* (1890–1891) xxii.
32. *Id.*
33. William MacGregor, "British New Guinea," *Proceedings of the Royal Colonial Institute* 26 (1894–1895) 217.
34. *Annual Report on British New Guinea* ((Brisbane: Government Printer, 1895–1896) xxxiii.
35. Ronald G. Crocombe (ed.), *Land Tenure in the Pacific* (Suva: University of the South Pacific Press, rev. ed., 1987) 341–342.
36. Letters Patent, dated June 8, 1888, section XIII.
37. "British New Guinea: The Labor Question," *The Queenslander*, April 20, 1895, 725.
38. Hank Nelson, "The Swinging Index: Capital Punishment and British and Australian Administrations in Papua and New Guinea, 1888–1945," *Journal of Pacific History* 13(3) (1978) 130.
39. *Annual Report on British New Guinea* (Brisbane: Government Printer, 1897–1898) Appendix J, 69–70.
40. "Dispatch Reporting Murder of Captain by Natives of Chads Bay," *Annual Report on British New Guinea* (Brisbane: Government Printer, 1888–1889) Appendix K, 16.
41. "Dispatch Reporting Murder of Captain Ansell by Natives of Chads Bay," *Annual Report on British New Guinea* (Brisbane: Government Printer, 1888–1889) Appendix K, 17.
42. "Dispatch Reporting Steps Taken to Effect Capture of Murder of Captain

Ansell," *Annual Report on British New Guinea* (Brisbane: Government Printer, 1888–1889) Appendix K, 18.

43. "Dispatch Reporting Trial of Murders of Captain Ansell," *Annual Report on British New Guinea* (Brisbane: Government Printer, 1888–1889) Appendix K, 22.
44. "Dispatch Reporting Trial of Murders of Captain Ansell," *Annual Report on British New Guinea* (Brisbane: Government Printer, 1889–1889) Appendix K, 24.
45. *Id.*
46. *Id.*
47. Hank Nelson, "The Swinging Index: Capital Punishment and British and Australian Administrations in Papua New Guinea, 1888–1945," *Journal of Pacific History* 13(3) (1978) 132.
48. R. B. Joyce, *Sir William MacGregor* (Oxford: Oxford University Press, 1971) 184–185.
49. "New Guinea," *The Sydney Morning Herald*, July 3, 1889, 4.
50. *Annual Report on British New Guinea* (Brisbane: Government Printer, 1902–1903) 10.
51. *Annual Report on British New Guinea* (Brisbane: Government Printer, 1897–1898) Appendix J.
52. *Id.* at xi.
53. Ordinance No. III of 1900.
54. *Annual Report on British New Guinea* (Brisbane: Government Printer, 1903–1904) Appendix B.
55. *Id.* at 26.
56. *Id.* at 26.
57. "Memorandum by the Chief Judicial Office on the Administration of Justice, in Connection with the Natives of the Possession, during the Past Decade," *Annual Report on British New Guinea* (Brisbane: Government Printer, 1898) Appendix J.
58. "Report of the Royal Commission on the Affray at Goaribari Island, British New Guinea, 6 March 1904," *Commonwealth Parliamentary Papers* (No. 42, 1904) 16.
59. "British New Guinea," *Examiner*, August 22, 1902, 8.
60. "British New Guinea," *Adelaide Observer*, January 24, 1903, http://trove.nla.gov.au/ndp/imageservice/nla.news-page18986443/print.
61. "Fighting in Papua," *The Mercury*, December 25, 1913, 5.
62. Motion made by Australian Prime Minister Edmund Barton in the Commonwealth Parliament on November 12, 1901, in Alan Kerr, *A Federation in These Seas* (Canberra: Attorney General's Department, 2009) 23.

5 Constructing a Colonial Legal System

The Territories of Papua and New Guinea 1906–1921

With the adoption of the *Papua Act* in 1905, the Commonwealth of Australia took formal possession of British New Guinea, renaming it the Territory of Papua. As on previous occasions, the change in the colony's status was marked by ceremony and a speech, this time given by Francis R. Barton, who had arrived in British New Guinea in 1899 after having been an officer in the West Indian Regiment. In British New Guinea, he served first as the private secretary to Le Hunte, then as the resident magistrate for the Central Division, and finally as acting lieutenant-governor from 1904–1907. Barton addressed his remarks upon his appointment as acting lieutenant-governor to the "European residents, visitors, and others."[1] At that time, the population of Port Moresby consisted of only sixty-six expatriates, about a dozen houses, and five buildings used by the government. As had previous colonial administrators, Barton also made a short address to the "native inhabitants of the Territory of Papua," which was translated into Motu.

The Papua Act and the Colonial Legal System

Although the *Papua Act* changed the colony's political status, it had little effect on its administrative or legal systems. For administrative purposes, the Territory of Papua retained the system of government it had as a British Crown Colony. It continued to be governed by a lieutenant-governor, who now was appointed by the governor-general of Australia, rather than by the British. Article 122 of the Australian Constitution authorizes the Commonwealth Parliament to make laws for any territory "placed by the Queen under the authority of and accepted by the Commonwealth, or otherwise accepted by the Commonwealth." Since Australia viewed Papua as being "under" its administration "but not included in it,"[2] the *Papua Act* delegated the power to makes laws "for the peace, order, and good government of the Territory" to the Legislative Council in Papua. That body was composed (as it had been during the period of British rule) of the six members of the Executive Council (including the lieutenant-governor) and three nonofficial members appointed by the governor-general. The Legislative Council had the power to make ordinances for the "peace, order and good government of the Territory."[3] Any ordinance passed by the council had to be sent to the lieutenant-governor for his assent. An ordinance also required the ultimate approval of the governor-general of Australia, who could disallow it within three months of its submission.

The *Papua Act* retained all of the introduced laws and local ordinances in effect in the territory. Similarly, the courts in the territory at the time the act went into effect—the Central Court, the Court of Petty Sessions, the Warden's Courts, and the Native Magistrates' Courts—as well as their jurisdiction, practice, and procedure, remained in force. Appeals from the Central Court were transferred from the Supreme Court of Queensland to the High Court of Australia, but appeals were very rare during the remaining colonial period.

Customary law continued to play no formal role in the colonial legal system after Australia assumed control of Papua. For example, there was no mention of customary marriage in the *Marriage Ordinance*, enacted in 1912. Under section 11 of the ordinance, marriages could be performed only by a minister of religion, a district registrar, or an authorized justice, and only after specified formalities had been met. The ordinance stated that every such marriage was legal and valid for all intents and purposes and that "no other marriage shall except as hereinafter provided be valid for any purpose."[4] Although both expatriates and Papuans could marry according to the procedures of the ordinance, very few Papuans did so, and no attempt was made to compel them to comply with the formal legal requirements.

Despite the ordinance's express words to the contrary, the omission of any mention of customary marriage in the 1912 *Marriage Ordinance* was most probably interpreted to mean that the ordinance was meant to apply only to expatriates, leaving Papuans to follow their own customary law marriage processes. That interpretation is supported by the fact that it would have been impossible, in practice, to enforce the requirements of the ordinance against the much larger Papuan population. Since customary marriages were assumed to pose no threat to the colonial administration's policies and preserved social stability in the villages, they were a classic example of the type of customary law practice that Murray thought should be tolerated, at least until they died out of their own accord due to European influence. In addition, since there was no mention of customary marriages in the *Marriage Ordinance*, no ordinance in Papua sought to regulate customary divorce.

The presumed non-applicability of the requirements of the *Marriage Ordinance* to Papuans is supported by other legislation in Papua that expressly recognized customary marriages. For example, the Native Regulations permitted a deserted wife in a customary marriage to claim maintenance; the regulations also created the offense of adultery with the wife of another man.[5] The regulations defined a wife as "any woman that by the customs of the natives is regarded as or reputed to be the wife of a man."[6]

The Future of Papua: Attitudes and Policies

The transfer of British New Guinea caused the Australian government to re-examine its policies with respect to the economic development of the territory, the treatment of its Indigenous inhabitants, and the nature and content of the colonial legal system.

Although Papua had been a British possession for more than twenty years, the territory still was largely unknown to Australian officials. There was a serious lack of communication and understanding between expatriates and Papuans, in large part the fault of expatriates who believed that Papuans must adopt the English language, English law, and English customs rather than expatriates learning Papuan languages, culture, or ways of doing things. The vast majority of colonial officials, traders, planters, miners, and missionaries believed in a system of racial hierarchy with whites at the top as the superior race. Africans, Asians, and Melanesians were classified as subject or backward races who were biologically, intellectually, and morally inferior to the white race. To expatriates, Papuans were living both as "noble savages," in primitive innocence, and in a Hobbesian world in which life was "poor, nasty, brutish and short." Expatriates, by and large, were white; Papuans were brown. And whites at the time were confident that their racial superiority was the reason they had discovered what they considered the universal truths of culture, government, morality, religion, and law. They assumed that their racial superiority and knowledge of those truths was what made them economic, political, and military powers and gave them the right to rule and control non-white peoples.

Atlee Hunt, the secretary and permanent head of Australia's Department of External Affairs, became frustrated by his lack of information about conditions in Papua and made an official visit to the territory in July 1905. It turned out, however, that he learned more about the expatriate community in Papua than about Papuans. Hunt met with groups of expatriate residents who voiced their dissatisfaction with conditions in the territory: the deteriorating morale among officials and other white residents following the suicide of Christopher Robinson; the inefficiency of the Barton administration; the difficulty in recruiting Papuan laborers; the need to tax Papuans as an incentive for them to work on plantations; and the need for protection and encouragement for miners. Some residents also gave Hunt a petition asking that Australia provide for elected representation on the Legislative Council and for expatriates to have trial by jury. Although Hunt had some sympathy for the complaints raised by the white residents, and the taxation of Papuans was adopted in 1918, he was not prepared to recommend either elections for the Legislative Council or jury trials.

In his October 1905 report on his visit to Papua, Hunt was critical of the British, writing that "no definite policy for the government of New Guinea has ever been laid down." To remedy that, he set out, in one long and complex sentence, integrated goals for the territory and the use of its land and labor which amounted in part to a restatement of the policies in place during MacGregor's administration:

> To encourage the development of the country under the European auspices by the employment of imported capital to be expended under European direction, employing native Labor, and at the same time to extend the influence of the Government until the whole Possession is brought under control.[7]

However, unlike MacGregor, Hunt made no mention of protecting Papuans and their lands from expatriates. Instead, he insisted that Papuans were "growing lazier" because they were not being kept "well-occupied." Australia owed a duty to Papuans "to give them the advantages of civilization, divesting them so far as we are able from the evils that too often follow in their train." That duty required a shift of major emphasis by Australia. Hunt believed it necessary to compel Papuans to become laborers on expatriate-owned plantations. His proposals would require amendments to the land ordinance to make it easier for expatriates to obtain land and a new taxation ordinance that would coerce Papuans into working on those plantations.[8]

In response, the Australian government established a Royal Commission of Inquiry in August 1906, chaired by J. A. K. MacKay, "to inquire into and report upon the present conditions, including the methods of Government of the territory now known as British New Guinea, and the best possible means for their improvement."[9] The commission took testimony at various centers throughout the territory over a three-month period. Although it made no explicit recommendations about the colony's legal system, the commission's attempt to formulate a distinct Australian policy for the territory had repercussions for future land, labor, and taxation legislation. In his testimony before the commission, Murray was critical of Barton and of the policies and conduct of the Barton administration. Murray testified that the Barton administration had placed too much emphasis on protecting Papuan interests and not enough on helping expatriates, making it difficult for settlers to obtain land and laborers.

In its February 1907 report, the commission restated much of what Hunt had recommended and what had long been the goal of colonial administrators in the territory: the encouragement of expatriate settlement and the establishment of plantations, on which Papuans would perform the physical work. The commission concluded that a few years of labor on plantations would rescue Papuans from what it termed their "slothful decadence" and promote their physical well-being.[10] In order to provide Papuans with the incentive to work on the plantations, the commission proposed the imposition of a head tax on Papuans. Only one proposal in the commission's report failed to gain the support of the colonial officials. The commission recommended that "all unalienated Papuan land be declared Crown land." The administration did not adopt that proposal, and officials never again raised it. Finally, after hearing criticism from planters, traders, and miners, the commission recommended the reorganization of the public service and that Barton not be appointed lieutenant-governor. In his place, the Australian government appointed Hubert Murray.

New Directions in Land Laws

Most of the land laws adopted in Papua since 1888 had sought to accomplish the potentially conflicting goals of protecting the land rights of Papuans while encouraging settlers to come to the colony. Murray continued those policies. In his review of the Australian administration of Papua from 1907 to 1920, he stated that Australia had a duty to develop the natural resources of the territory, which included an obligation to help expatriate settlers, making land and labor available to them, as well as by maintaining law and order. At the same time, Murray wrote, Australia considered the protection of Papuans from the most egregious forms of exploitation by expatriates to be of paramount importance. In light of the widespread criticism that Murray was receiving at the time from whites, particularly in Port Moresby, it is not surprising that he concluded that his policy of protecting Papuans was "not likely to lead to popularity or to win applause from the people at large."[11]

There was almost no expatriate agricultural activity in Papua in 1906, and conditions were not promising for economic development. Gold accounted for more than half of the exports, although there were only about two hundred miners remaining in the territory and they were not prospering. There were only about a dozen expatriate-owned plantations in operation, and the total area under cultivation was only 1,467 acres.[12] The new Australian colonial administration enacted the *Land Ordinance of 1906,* which retained the prior prohibition on Papuans selling, leasing, or otherwise disposing of their land to anyone except the administration.

The ordinance made a major change in the policy adopted in 1889 by repealing the provision permitting the administration to make grants in fee simple to expatriates of the land it acquired from Papuans. From 1906 on, expatriates were permitted only to lease Crown lands from the administration, although the term for the leases—periods up to ninety-nine years—was the equivalent of ownership, and the rent was waived for the first ten years, after which, the amount of rent would depend on whether and how much the land was improved. In the period between the enactment of the ordinance and the outbreak of World War I in 1914, the amount of Crown land increased to over one million acres, of which expatriates held 26,500 acres as freehold and 332,400 acres as leasehold. By 1914 the number of expatriate-owned plantations had grown to almost two hundred, with 24,700 acres under cultivation for crops.[13] In the years prior to World War I, however, gold and not agricultural products continued to dominate Papua's small export trade.

New Directions in Labor Laws

The increase in expatriate-owned plantations led to a shortage of labor by 1912 and calls for the colonial administration to make recruitment of workers easier for plantations and mining. Those demands led the administration to enact the *Native Labor Ordinance of 1907,* which increased the period for which a plantation worker could be indentured to three years and mine workers for up to eighteen months. Although the ordinance offered some small protection to Papuans by providing that no one could recruit workers without a license, it vitiated that protection by providing that employers could recruit their own workers without a license, provided the workers were being hired for three months or less. Papuans hired for more than three months had to be taken to a resident magistrate or other official who was supposed to explain the terms of the written contract to them and approve the terms and conditions of the employment and repatriation. The resident magistrate also had to be satisfied that the worker was freely entering into the contract, would be fairly treated, and would be returned to his home at the end of the employment. No Papuan worker could be taken out of the territory or more than forty miles from his home. A Papuan who signed a labor contract, but who refused to work or deserted, was subject to a fine or a jail term ranging from one to three months.

In its 1907 report, the Royal Commission recommended a head tax be imposed on Papuans to induce them to take up paid employment. Murray's administration enacted the first tax ordinance in 1917, which imposed a tax of 10 shillings per year on "native Laborers" who were employed by expatriates and £1 per year "on natives other than native Laborers." The tax applied to all Papuan males between the ages of sixteen and thirty-six, except those who were members of the Armed Native Constabulary, village constables, mission teachers, or students, unfit for work, or had four or more children. Murray defended the ordinance, saying that it served three important purposes: first, it provided the labor that expatriate plantation owners required; second, it engaged Papuans in work in ways that would give them the "habits of industry"; and finally, it provided money for education, native plantations, and health. The regulations issued under the ordinance directed that this tax revenue be directed to grants to missions for education; the establishment of "native plantations"; the study of anthropology; medical care for Papuans; and village improvements.[14] Murray and the newspapers reported improbably that the tax was popular among Papuans.

Supposedly in keeping with the Royal Commission's view that Papuans should be encouraged "in habits of industry," but more likely to obtain free labor for administration infrastructure projects, the Legislative Council passed *The Encouragement of Industry Ordinance* in 1908. The ordinance required all Papuan males "between prescribed ages" to work without pay for one month each year on a government plantation, public road, or native reserve. There was an exemption for Papuans who were government employees, mission students or teachers, or were cultivating approved crops. The penalty for not complying with the ordinance was imprisonment with hard labor for up to six months. The vast majority of whites in Papua, including Murray and some missionaries, supported the ordinance. However, it encountered serious opposition in Australia and England from officials and church leaders who thought that the ordinance had gone too far. They feared that, in an attempt to secure cheap labor for the administration, it had introduced "forced labor" and "legalized slavery" into Papua.[15] Responding to these concerns, the Australian governor-general decided not to approve the ordinance, and it never went into effect.

Murray tried to reassure critics that labor in Papua was "entirely voluntary."[16] During the following decade, however, many expatriates in Papua and some Australians argued that a form of "forced labor" should be introduced in the territory, since they had "undertaken to develop Papua" and Papuans would "not work unless some form of compulsion is put upon them."[17] Newspapers in Australia printed stories that referred to Papuans as "the hulking, lazy native"[18] and spoke repeatedly of "Labor problems,"[19] "native Labor questions,"[20] and a "lack of Labor,"[21] and asked: "Should native Labor be exploited?"[22] A 1912 article discussed the reluctance of Papuans to work on plantations and lamented that Papuans "laugh at the white man and would infinitely prefer to fritter away their lives in their own villages to toil and hew upon the most liberally managed plantations ever known."[23]

One reason for the reluctance of Papuan men to take jobs as laborers on plantations and on the goldfields was the fear of abuse and neglect by their supervisors, a charge that whites vocally denied. A 1909 newspaper article quoted an Australian, who had returned from a visit to Papua, as saying "[e]very bit of local evidence was against the allegation of the natives being badly treated by their employers."[24] A report in 1912 suggested that accounts of the abuse of workers was "an unfair prejudice" and that "it is almost impossible to ill-treat the boys here."[25]

However, one of the most famous cases of the pre–World War I period in Papua occurred in 1913 when an expatriate resident of Port Moresby, George Bernasconi, was prosecuted for assaulting a Papuan plantation laborer for desertion. Bernasconi, a plantation manager, had a prior conviction for neglecting a sick worker who died, and was charged with assault causing bodily harm, which involved hanging the young man by his neck from a rafter. After a trial, presided over by Murray, Bernasconi was found guilty and sentenced to twelve months imprisonment. One Australian newspaper reported the trial under the headline: "Is There Slavery in Papua?"[26] Bernasconi's appeal to the High Court of Australia was dismissed, and he served almost nine months in jail in Port Moresby.

After Bernasconi's release from jail, the Executive Council issued an order prohibiting him from employing Papuan workers or working for anyone in a position where he would supervise Papuan workers. One Australian newspaper viewed this restriction as "very unfair" and tied the case to broader complaints about the treatment of expatriates by the colonial administration:

> This only goes to show how British justice is meted out to residents of Papua. In no other part of the world would a British subject, after having served the penalty of the law for any crime, be called upon to suffer another and worse penalty—that of the taking away of his livelihood. When will the whites here receive British justice? It seems not until we have elected representatives.[27]

The number of Papuans working for expatriates grew to 8,610 in 1918–1919 but then fell to 6,397 the following year. One reason given for the decrease was the difficulty of planters in obtaining rice to feed their workers. There also were continuing allegations of harsh treatment of workers. Although vigorously denied by planters and their supporters, the ill treatment of Papuan plantation workers led in May 1918 to Papua's first strike. Twenty-eight workers from the Itikinumu plantation, owned by the British New Guinea Development Company (the largest company in Papua), left their jobs and walked thirty miles to Port Moresby to protest harsh conditions at the plantation: overwork, lack of food, a requirement to work on Sunday, and beatings by managers. A magisterial report, released in 1920, confirmed what it called "an ugly picture . . . of the treatment of natives" on the plantation.[28] However, the report went on to state that it hoped the abuses represented "only an isolated case." Although the British New Guinea Development Company tried to prosecute the workers for desertion, an investigation by the Native Affairs Department dismissed the company's complaint and canceled the workers' contracts. Protracted negotiations between Murray and the head of the company failed to reach a solution, and no steps were taken to punish the company men responsible for the ill treatment. By 1922, a combination of factors, including labor problems and bad business decisions, forced the British New Guinea Development Company into voluntary liquidation and reorganization.

The Administration of Justice

When Hubert Murray arrived in Port Moresby in 1904, he was not only the sole judge on the Central Court, but also a member of both the Executive and Legislative Councils. Since there were no other barristers, solicitors, or legally trained magistrates in the colony, he also served as the administration's legal advisor and legislative draftsman. Murray provided legal advice—without a fee—to private individuals who asked him. Remarkably, Murray saw no conflicts of interest in fulfilling all of those roles and even stated publicly that, as judge, he did not consider himself bound by any legal opinions that he gave. In 1910, Murray's judicial responsibilities were eased somewhat when Charles E. Herbert, a judge of the Northern Territory in Australia, was appointed deputy chief judicial officer of Papua, a post he held until 1928. In addition to serving as the second judge on the Central Court, Herbert also was a member of the Executive and Legislative Councils.

Ten days after beginning his duties in New Guinea, Murray heard his first case as a judge, a murder prosecution that forced him to confront local custom and its role in the imposed criminal law. Murray later described briefly the conflict between customary obligations and the Criminal Code arising in that case, which involved the killing of a New Guinean by two other men. When Murray asked the court interpreter why one of the two accomplices had become involved, he received the following explanation:

> "It is the New Guinea custom, sir," said the Court interpreter. . . . He was a highly civilised man for a Papuan; he spoke English well—not pidgin English—and he could read and write. I had asked him why some man, who had absolutely no connection with the matter in dispute, had joined in committing a murder. "It is the New Guinea custom, sir," he replied; "if a man asks you to join in killing another man you cannot refuse." "But," I objected, "if someone asked you to come and kill a man surely you would not go?" "Yes, sir," was the reply, "I should certainly go if he asked me."[29]

It did not take Murray long to recognize that, in the majority of the murder cases he heard, there was no criminal responsibility from the New Guinean point of view. Killing was mandated in many situations and even praiseworthy when it involved carrying out a duty expected of a person in that society. Even understanding this, Murray could not give up the belief that his job was to introduce Western culture to Papua and that the full application of English criminal law was necessary to accomplish that change.

Even more important, Murray believed unreservedly that government should be the sole determiner of criminal law: the "first and most obvious duty of any Government was the protection of life and property and the maintenance of order and administration of justice."[30] This led him to accept the two basic conclusions that Winter reached in his 1898 memorandum about the role of custom: first, there was no question that English criminal law should apply to Papuans and, second, customary law should not be considered a competing body of law but merely as one of the factors to be considered when imposing sentences in criminal cases. In cases in which Papuans raised a custom-related defense to a charge of murder, Murray usually imposed a custodial sentence of one to seven years, depending on the amount of contact the defendant and his clan had had with the administration. In the case of Papuans from more settled areas, and who were aware of how serious the colonial administration considered their crimes, Murray did not hesitate to impose the death penalty. One such case occurred in 1915 when a Papuan man, who had been rejected by a young woman, took out his frustration by killing the first person he and a companion met on a road about twenty miles from Port Moresby. Murray convicted both men for murder, and they were hanged.

Murray's goal was for all criminal activity to be punished only by the official courts and only according to the rules set out in the Criminal Code. He did not intend to permit Papuans to mete our punishments according to customary law and processes; nor would he allow the punitive raids and reprisals that had been one of Le Hunte's reactions to crime. Murray also placed restrictions on the use of deadly force by the Armed Native Constabulary. In instructions issued in October 1909, Murray stated that there were only three circumstances in which a constable would be justified in taking the life of another: in self-defense; in order to prevent the escape of a person who had been arrested or was sought for arrest for a serious offense such as murder; and when necessary to overcome forcible resistance to an arrest. Moreover, those exceptions should be relied upon only "when all other means have failed" rather than as a matter of general practice.[31] Although Murray's instructions did not entirely eliminate police shootings, they did reduce the number of villagers killed, since officials knew they would be required to explain any deaths that occurred during patrols. Murray took pride in the fact that his administration mounted no punitive expeditions: "If a man was murdered, the murderer was arrested and punished. The authorities did not punish the village or the tribe. . . ."[32]

Criminal matters continued to make up the overwhelming number of cases coming before the courts. In 1913–1914, for example, 187 persons (all Papuans) were tried in the Central Court for a wide variety of charges: willful murder, murder, attempted murder, manslaughter, rape, uttering, deprivation of liberty, forgery, breaking and entering, corruption of a witness, affray, receiving stolen property, malicious damage to property, escaping from custody, accessory before the fact, perjury, obstructing the police, stealing, arson, incest, improper interference with a corpse, assaulting a superior officer, and desertion (by a member of the constabulary). One hundred and nineteen Papuans were convicted, and sixty-eight, or 36 percent of those charged, were acquitted. Of those convicted, ten were sentenced to death, but in all but one case, Murray commuted the death sentences to prison terms. The procedure followed in criminal cases in the Central Court led Murray to write:

> I am inclined to think that very few innocent Papuans were convicted; after a few months in gaol the truth generally comes out, and I can only recall one case where it appeared likely that the prisoner was innocent. On hearing that there were doubts as to his guilt, I sent him word that if he liked I would reopen the case, but he took a very philosophical view of the matter, and said that he was learning so many useful things in gaol that he would sooner finish his sentence.[33]

The colonial administration devoted considerable effort to trying to arrest Papuans who killed each other, members of the constabulary, or expatriates. The murders occurred for a variety of reasons: ordinary quarrels, jealousy, tribal fighting, ritual killings, the desire for social distinction, compliance with demands of local etiquette, and revenge ("payback") for a previous murder or for a person having performed sorcery. Because of the social unrest posed by sorcery, particular efforts were also made to arrest and prosecute its alleged practitioners, although writers at the time said it was extremely difficult to prove a case against accused sorcerers because witnesses were afraid to testify against them. The difficulty in arresting, trying, and convicting Papuans was not limited to sorcery cases. The efforts of the administration were hindered by lack of manpower, by the difficulty in finding the suspects, and by the difficult terrain of the colony.

Although whites believed otherwise, there were very few murders of expatriates by Papuans. Between 1907 and 1920, only five whites were killed by Papuans, and none after 1915. Four of the killings involved a miner shot by one of his Papuan employees; an elderly market-gardener killed for ritual reasons; a mineralogist who ventured into an area of the country not previously visited by whites; and a government officer shot with an arrow while trying to arrest some Papuans suspected of murder. The fifth murder was the result of an expatriate's lack of respect for Papuan customs. In 1914, villagers in the Sogeri area near Port Moresby killed Harry Ballot, a recent immigrant from Russia, for killing some pigs that belonged to them. The *Annual Report* noted that Ballot probably did not realize the value that Papuans attached to pigs. Five Papuans were convicted of Ballot's murder, three of whom were hanged, while the other two were sentenced to prison terms. Murray wrote that it was "usual" to hang a Papuan convicted of murdering a white. He justified the punishment as necessary "for the protection of the small white community."[34]

The Colonial Legal System and the Expatriate Population

By the second decade of the twentieth century, the Australian colonial administration had established control along almost the entire southern coast of Papua. The interior of the country still was largely unknown to expatriates and would remain so for many years. World War I significantly reduced the ability of the administration to conduct patrols, since one-third of Murray's staff left the colony to enlist in the army. Hank Nelson has estimated that the expatriate population of Papua in 1906 was only about seven hundred persons.[35] By the beginning of World War I in August 1914, however, the expatriate population had risen to almost 1,200 persons, with 453 in Port Moresby.[36] The journalist Osmar White gave a very negative description of Port Moresby and its inhabitants at the time it became an Australian colony in 1906:

> Port Moresby was a tiny, poverty-stricken outpost of European rule on the fringe of a vast and savage wilderness. Its inhabitants, Government servants and otherwise—following the tradition of earlier colonization of the deep tropics—were either refugees from the irksome restraints of their own social order or would-be exploiters of

> the "lesser breeds." The town dwellers were mainly alcoholics, eccentrics, or little men disguising their lack of social and intellectual status behind a front of starched tropical drill.
>
> . . . The centre of social life in this isolated, malarial place was an appalling tavern near the waterfront where the riff-raff of the Pacific occasionally came ashore and engaged in bloody brawls. Its centre of commercial life was a tumbledown trade store given over mainly to the buying of sandalwood and the selling of cheap grog.[37]

It is not surprising that Port Moresby's residents, and the small expatriate population scattered throughout the rest of Papua, made little, if any, use of the elaborate English legal system. However, over the next decade, as Port Moresby's population grew, its residents became less raffish, and it came to resemble any small Australian country town. By early 1914, the town had two banks; two butchers and two bakers; Catholic and Protestant churches; an open-air cinema; a choral society; a community hall, a freezing plant for ice and frozen meat, general stores, two hotels lit by gas and electricity and with running water and fresh food; a public library; a number of motor vehicles; sporting facilities and competitions for cricket, tennis, shooting, and horse racing; a supply of fresh water; and a wireless telegraph service. A biweekly steamer service had been established between Port Moresby and Sydney.

The first two decades of the twentieth century also saw the arrival in Port Moresby of two people whose work would present Papua to a wider world and shape how that world perceived the territory and its inhabitants: Beatrice Grimshaw, who wrote a number of popular works of nonfiction, as well as adventure novels set in Papua, came to Port Moresby in 1907. Her writings were intended to promote white settlement in Papua by romanticizing life on the plantations there and portraying Papuans as noble and mysterious savages. The anthropologist Bronislaw Malinowski arrived seven years later. Malinowski's fieldwork in the Trobriand Islands resulted in a number of influential books that changed the emerging field of anthropology and the way many people viewed custom.

The expatriate residents of Port Moresby were not litigious. Intestacy matters still formed a large part of the work of the Central Court, and Murray wrote in 1912 that "civil cases are very few and do not present any particular points of interest, being of much the same kind as in other parts of the world."[38] That view is borne out by the Central Court's civil work in 1913–1914, which consisted only of issuing five writs representing total claims of £1,806, hearing and disposing of three motions and petitions (the nature of which were not specified in the *Annual Report*), and granting one divorce.

Occasionally more contentious matters did arise. In 1911, the *Papuan Times and Tropical Advisor,* the first newspaper in the territory, began to be published in Port Moresby. Its publisher, W. C. Bruce, along with a number of other residents in Port Moresby, strongly opposed Murray because of his testimony against Barton before the 1906 Royal Commission and the perception that he favored Papuans at the expense of expatriates. Bruce used his newspaper to campaign for electing expatriate members to the Legislative Council, the right to trial by jury for whites, and revision of the native labor regulations. In 1918, the collector of customs won a libel action against Bruce, forcing the newspaper out of business. The following year, the colonial administration brought suit against the British New Guinea Development Company for more than £11,000, the value of the administration's vessel that had been sunk following an explosion during repairs in Port Moresby Harbor. That same year, a company called Pacific and Papua Produce brought suit against the administration, alleging that it failed to issue a certificate of title in fee simple for certain islands in the Conflict Group (in present-day Milne Bay Province) that it had an option to purchase. However, the Australian government concluded that the provisions of the *Papua Act*, which barred freehold estates in any land in Papua, superseded the grant.

Administrators in Papua continued to boast that expatriates rarely were brought before the courts as defendants in criminal cases. In 1912, Murray wrote that it "very rarely happens that a European prisoner is brought before [the Central Court]—for the white community in Papua is one of the most law-abiding in Australasia."[39] The following year, Judge Herbert stated in an interview: "There is very little trouble with the whites. In the three years [that he had been a judge in the colony] there have been only three instances in which Europeans have been concerned."[40] However, a few cases did involve prosecutions of expatriates. In early 1909, Murray acquitted a missionary charged with manslaughter in the death of a student who attended the mission school. When the student admitted giving the missionary's wife trouble and using bad language, he was given twenty strokes with a strap in front of the entire school. The student did not appear to be seriously hurt. A month later he became ill, could not eat, and died a short time later. An Australian newspaper claimed that the student's death was the result of mumps.

The 1917–1918 *Annual Report* noted that, of the 158 persons committed for trial for criminal offenses during that year, only three were expatriates. However, the report did not mention the nature of the offenses for which the Europeans were charged. Two of the men were convicted and one was acquitted. In 1919–1920, five expatriates were among the 140 persons brought before the Central Court on indictments. Again, however, no mention was made of the charges against them, only that three of the men were convicted and one was acquitted.

A few criminal prosecutions of whites provoked controversy within the white community in Papua. In 1904, an expatriate named Steve Wolfe was convicted of murdering a Papuan and sentenced to death. Although his sentence was commuted to three years imprisonment, the conviction led to unsuccessful demands to reopen the case. The trial also renewed demands from expatriates for jury trials and raised questions about the weight that a judge should give to the testimony of a Papuan against a white. In response to those concerns, the Legislative Council enacted the *Jury Ordinance of 1907*, which provided that the trial of an expatriate charged with a crime punishable with death should take place before a jury of four expatriate men. In addition, if a court imposed the death penalty, it could not be carried out unless the Executive Council reviewed the sentence and the Administrator issued a warrant for the execution. In the end, no expatriates were executed in Papua for crimes during the entire colonial period.

Although the *Jury Ordinance* gave expatriates the right to a jury trial in capital cases, the absence of juries in noncapital cases remained an issue. The conviction of plantation manager George Bernasconi for the assault on one of his workers was an opportunity for many expatriates in Port Moresby to criticize Murray's administration and express their distain for Papuans in general, since Bernasconi's convicted rested in part on the testimony of a Papuan. D. C. Lewis, who analyzed the trial and its aftermath summarized it as follows:

> As Murray had suggested in his remarks about the tendency of settlers, if unchecked, to reduce "natives" to slavery, white men in the

> predicament of settlers would readily see the laws as basically having application between "civilized" men whose societies had developed them. Otherwise as in Papua, they thought, laws should exist primarily to protect the white resident. Only in time—and certainly not yet, it could seem—should Papuans be allowed something approaching legal equality.... Until the twenties planters generally ... were inclined to give their peers charged with an offense the benefit of the doubt.[41]

At the request of Bernasconi's solicitor, Murray reserved for the High Court of Australia the question of whether he had correctly refused Bernasconi's request for a jury trial. In 1915, the High Court held that Chapter III, section 80, of the Australian Constitution, which provided for jury trials for indictable offenses, had no application to the territories and Bernasconi and other whites were not entitled to a jury trial in noncapital cases.[42]

The Trust Territory of New Guinea

German New Guinea was an Imperial German Protectorate for thirty years (1884–1914). The protectorate consisted of the northern half of the island of New Guinea as well as the adjacent islands of New Britain, New Ireland, and Bougainville. German New Guinea came to an end at the outbreak of World War I. At Britain's request, the Australia Naval and Military Expeditionary Force (ANMEF) seized control of the colony's capital, Rabaul, on September 13, 1914, and Germany's military forces in New Guinea surrendered eight days later. For the next seven years, ANMEF governed the territory and promulgated its ordinances. Since ANMEF's object was merely to keep the colony going during the war, all laws in German New Guinea remained in force so long as they did not interfere with military or strategic interests. The military and the courts continued to apply German laws and procedures relating to land, taxation, and other matters to everyone in the colony. However, the military administration also imposed punishments that were outside the law. An example of this occurred in October 1914, when a group of German residents on New Ireland attacked a British minister who they believed was a spy. The Australian forces arrested the Germans, and, rather than try them in a court, the Australian general in charge ordered the Germans flogged in a public square in Rabaul in the presence of all adult white males. When the Australian Parliament questioned the legality of the general's order, the minister for defense promised that such acts would not happen again.

At war's end, under Article 119 of the Treaty of Versailles, "Germany renounce[d] in favor of the Principal Allied and Associated Powers all her rights and titles over her overseas possessions." The new League of Nations assumed control of Germany's former territories. Article 22 of the League of Nations Covenant created a mandate system to govern the former German colonies that were "inhabited by peoples not yet able to stand by themselves under the strenuous conditions of the modern world." Article 22 also stated that the "well-being and development of such peoples" was "a sacred trust of civilisation" that "should be entrusted to advanced nations."

The League of Nations established three classes of mandates based upon "the stage of the development of the people, the geographical situation of the territory, its economic conditions and other similar circumstances."[43] Mandated territories deemed to be the most developed received Class A status. Germany's Pacific Islands colonies were designated as Class C Mandates, "owing to the sparseness of their population, or their small size, or their remoteness from the centres of civilization."[44] In December 1920, the League of Nations made the former German Protectorate of New Guinea a Class C Mandate of Australia. In keeping with the attitude prevailing at the time, that European nations assumed the right to impose their laws on colonial peoples, the mandate stated that these areas could "best be administered under the laws of the Mandatory as integral portions of its territory,"[45] and Article 2 of the mandate governing New Guinea specifically permitted Australia to apply its laws to the territory, "subject to such local modifications as circumstances may require."

In August 1919, Australia established a Royal Commission to make recommendations concerning the administration of New Guinea under the mandate. The Royal Commission was chaired by Hubert Murray and also included Atlee Hunt (the secretary of the Department of Home and Territories) and Walter Lucas (general manager of the trading company, Burns Philp). In the commission's final report, Hunt and Lucas, who supported the promotion of Australian business in the territory, proposed that German nationals be deported from New Guinea and that all German-owned plantations and businesses be expropriated and sold to

Australians. In his minority report, Murray disagreed, supporting protections for New Guinean laborers and the amalgamation of New Guinea and Papua into a single administrative unit. Concerned that amalgamation would give Murray influence over New Guinea as well as Papua, the Australian government adopted the views of Hunt and Lucas, and New Guinea remained a separate territory. The issue of amalgamation arose again in early 1939 when the Australian government feared that New Guinea could become a target of German or Japanese military interest and appointed a three-person committee to study merging the territories. Although not a member of that committee, Murray opposed amalgamation at that time, as did the public service, the trading companies, and many planters, fearing that it would bring Papua under the League of Nations Mandate.

In 1920, the Australian Parliament passed the *New Guinea Act*, authorizing the Australian governor-general to accept the Mandate of German New Guinea for Australia, and in May 1921, civilian rule began. The legislation stated that "the Acts of the Parliament of the Commonwealth shall not be in force in the Territory unless expressed to extend thereto, or unless applied to the Territory by ordinance made under this Act."[46]

In 1921, the Australian Parliament also enacted the *Laws Repeal and Adopting Ordinance*, providing that all German laws ceased "to extend or apply to, or be in force in the Territory of New Guinea" and creating a legal system for New Guinea similar to that in Papua. The revocation of German law was not complete, however, since section 4(1) specified that it did not affect "any existing status or capacity, or any right, title, obligation or liability." Section 6 preserved the "rights, titles, estates, claims or interests," which were vested or contingent when the ordinance was adopted. As a result, whites who owned land under German land law retained their ownership.

In addition to revoking German law, the *Laws Repeal and Adopting Ordinance* adopted a number of Australian Commonwealth laws, including legislative acts adopted by the military administrator from 1914 to 1921; the Queensland Criminal Code and other Queensland statutes; a number of imperial statutes and laws; and fourteen Papuan ordinances and regulations. The ordinance also adopted "[t]he principles and rules of common law and equity."[47] Unlike the Papuan reception ordinance, however, the New Guinean ordinance contained a date by which the Queensland and English statutes, Papuan ordinances, and the English common law and equity would be measured: May 9, 1921. Finally, as in Papua, the statutes, ordinances, and common law were adopted only if they were "applicable to the circumstances of the Territory, and [were] not repugnant to or inconsistent with the provisions of any Act, Ordinance, Law, regulation, rule order or proclamation having the force of law that has been or may hereafter be expressed to extend to or be applied to or made or promulgated in the Territory."[48]

The decision by Australia to introduce the English common law and English and Australian statutes into New Guinea was based on the same attitudes that guided British officials earlier in Papua. They believed that the colonial mission required them to make New Guineans adopt Western law and culture. Although not explicitly mentioned, there was another reason: in order to take advantage of the perceived economic opportunities in the territory and fulfill what it saw as its civilizing mission, Australia encouraged expatriates to come to New Guinea, take over German plantations, and, hopefully, settle permanently in the territory. The government presumed it would be easier to attract people willing to come to the territory, settle down, marry, have children, establish businesses, enter into contracts, buy and sell property, and make wills if there was a familiar legal system underpinning those activities—especially since that legal system supported the ownership and conduct of market-oriented business ventures.

While the British and Australians agreed on the introduction of English and Australian law into Papua and New Guinea, they took different approaches in their attitude toward the role of custom. The reception ordinance in British New Guinea had contained no provision recognizing customary law. Conversely, the New Guinea *Laws Repeal and Adopting Ordinance* expressly recognized custom as part of the territory's colonial legal system. According to section 10 of the ordinance:

> The tribal institutions, customs and usages of the aboriginal natives of the Territory shall not be affected by this Ordinance and shall, subject to the provisions of the Ordinances of the Territory from time to time in force, be permitted to continue in existence in so far as the same are not repugnant to the general provisions of humanity.

Although this provision recognized custom as a source of law, it did not describe what role, if any, custom would play in New Guinea's colonial legal system or how courts should ascertain and apply custom if it became an issue in a case. Both of those questions would remain central throughout the colonial period for the Legislative Council and for the courts when, with their limited knowledge of custom, they were called upon to decide disputes involving New Guineans. The approach that administrators and judges took to custom in New Guinea, as well as in Papua, reflected the broader attitudes of colonial officials toward Papuans and New Guineans, colonial policy, the establishment and maintenance of law and order, economic development, and the encouragement of Australian businesses and settlements.

The End of the Beginning

The establishment of the League of Nations Mandate over New Guinea and the enactment of the *New Guinea Act of 1920* finally gave Australia what it had coveted since 1884: administrative control over both Papua and New Guinea. The enactment in Papua of the *Courts and Laws Adopting Ordinance 1888* and the *Papua Act* of 1905, and in New Guinea of the *New Guinea Act* of 1920, and the *Laws Repeal and Adopting Ordinance* of 1921, created the framework for the colonial administration and legal systems of Papua and New Guinea that would continue in force, with only minor changes, until January 1942.

Despite that vast legal structure, Australia's knowledge of Papua and New Guinea and its people—and its actual control over them—were still almost non-existent. It was not until after World War I that Australia began to take steps to extend its control over all the Indigenous peoples of Papua and New Guinea and to find a way to fashion the territories into economically productive settler colonies. The colonial legal systems would play key roles in Australia's attempt to achieve both of those goals.

Sources

Books and Articles

The Advertiser, "Boy Suspended from a Rafter," *The Advertiser*, March 12, 1915, 6.

The Age, "The Future of Papua," *The Age*, March 18, 1911, 6.

The Age, "Papuan Administration," *The Age*, October 18, 1920, 7.

Auckland Star, "Judiciary Slavery," *Auckland Star*, December 23, 1908.

Wilfred N. Beaver, *Unexplored New Guinea* (London: Seeley, Service, and Co., 1920).

Peter Biskup, Brian Jinks, and Hank Nelson, *A Short History of New Guinea* (Sydney: Angus and Robertson, 1968).

F. S. Burnell, *Australia versus Germany* (London: G. Allen & Unwin, Ltd., 1915).

Manning Clark, *A Short History of Australia* (New York: Mentor, 1969).

Andrew James Connelly, "Counting Coconuts: Patrol Reports from the Trobriand Islands Part I: 1907–1934" (unpublished master's thesis, California State University, 1987).

Ronald G. Crocombe (ed.), *Land Tenure in the Pacific* (Suva: University of the South Pacific Press, rev. ed., 1987).

Tom Dutton, *Police Motu* (Port Moresby: University of Papua New Guinea Press, 1985).

C. Brunsdon Fletcher, *The New Pacific: British Policy and German Aims* (London: Macmillan and Co., 1917).

Thomas P. Fry, "The Life and Work of Lieut.-Col. Sir. John Plunkett Murray, B.A.," *Journal of the Royal Historical Society of Queensland* 3(6) (1947) 405–438.

Ralph T. Gore, *Justice versus Sorcery* (Brisbane: Jacaranda Press, 1965).

Beatrice Grimshaw, *The New New Guinea* (London: Hutchinson, 1910).

Beatrice Grimshaw, *Guinea Gold* (New York: Moffat, Yard and Co., 1912).

Basil Hall, "Amalgamation and a Mandate," *The Australian Quarterly* 11(3) (Sept. 1939) 88–95.

Peter Hastings, *New Guinea: Problems and Prospects* (Melbourne: Australian Institute of International Affairs, 1969).

Hermann J. Hiery, *The Neglected War* (Honolulu: University of Hawai'i Press, 1995).

W. J. Hudson (ed.), *Australia and Papua New Guinea* (Sydney: Sydney University Press, 1971).

W. J. Hudson (ed.), *New Guinea Empire: Australia's Colonial Experience* (Melbourne: Cassell Australia, 1974).

Colin A. Hughes, "The Legislative Councils of Papua-New Guinea," *Parliamentary Affairs* 12(20) (1958) 209–229.

Kalgoorlie Miner, "Native Labor Questions," *Kalgoorlie Miner*, May 18, 1909.

J. Scott Keltie (ed.), *The Statesman's Year-Book* (New York: Macmillan and Co., 1916).

Alan Kerr, *A Federation in These Seas* (Canberra: Attorney General's Dept., 2009).

August Ibrum K. Kituai, *My Gun, My Brother* (Honolulu: University of Hawai'i Press, 1998).

Henrika Kuklick, *The Savage Within: The Social History of British Anthropology, 1885–1945* (Cambridge: Cambridge University Press, 1991).

Eugenie Laracy and Hugh Laracy, "Beatrice Grimshaw: Pride and Prejudice in Papua," *Journal of Pacific History* 12(3) (1977) 154–175.

J. D. Legge, *Australian Colonial Policy* (Sydney: Angus and Robertson, 1956).

Lewis Lett, *The Papuan Achievement* (Melbourne: Melbourne University Press, 1942).

Lewis Lett, *Sir Hubert Murray of Papua: Statesman and Empire Builder* (Sydney: Collins, 1949).

D. C. Lewis, *The Plantation Dream: Developing British New Guinea and Papua 1884–1942* (Canberra: The Journal of Pacific History, 1996).

Nancy Lutton, "C. A. W. Monckton: Reprobate Magistrate," in James Griffin (ed.), *Papua New Guinea Portraits: The Expatriate Experience* (Canberra: Australian National University Press, 1978) 48–74.

"Sir W. MacGregor's Discoveries in New Guinea," *The Scottish Geographical Magazine* 6 (1890) 245–254.

Kenneth Mackay, *Across Papua* (London: Witherby and Co., 1909).

S. S. MacKenzie, *The Australians at Rabaul* (Sydney: Angus and Robertson, 1941).

Lucy Mair, *Australia in New Guinea* (London: Christophers, 1948).

Bronislaw Malinowski, *Crime and Custom in Savage Society* (New York: Harcourt, Brace and Co., 1926).

J. R. Mattes, "The Sources of Law in Papua and New Guinea," *Australian Law Journal* 37 (1963) 148.

R. R. McNicoll, "Sir Walter McNicoll as Administrator of the Mandated Territory," in Kenneth S. Inglis (ed.), *The History of Melanesia* (Port Moresby: University of Papua New Guinea, 1969) 113–134.

The Mercury, "The Hulking, Lazy Native," *The Mercury*, September 20, 1910, 3.

The Mercury, "Fighting in Papua," *The Mercury*, December 25, 1913, 5.

Charles Arthur Whitmore Monckton, *Some Experiences of a New Guinea Resident Magistrate* (London: John Lane, 1921).

Charles Arthur Whitmore Monckton, *Last Days in New Guinea: Being Further Experiences of a New Guinea Resident Magistrate* ((London: John Lane, 1922).

John Hubert Murray, *Papua or British New Guinea* (London: T. Fisher Unwin, 1912).

Hank. Nelson, "European Attitudes in Papua, 1906–1914," in Kenneth S. Inglis (ed.), *The History of Melanesia* (Port Moresby: University of Papua New Guinea, 1969) 593–623.

Hank Nelson, "Miners, Laborers and Officials on the Lakelamu Goldfield of Papua," *Labor History* 25 (November 1973) 40–52.

Hank Nelson, "The Swinging Index: Capital Punishment and British and Australian Administrations in Papua and New Guinea, 1888–1945," *Journal of Pacific History* 13(3) (1978) 130–152.

Hank Nelson, "Changing the Label," in Sione Latukefu (ed.), *Papua New Guinea: A Century of Colonial Impact* (Port Moresby: The National Research Institute and the University of Papua New Guinea, 1989) 19–36.

Observer, "Judge Herbert of Papua," *Observer*, January 18, 1913, 37.

Hans Jürgen Ohff, *Disastrous Ventures: German and British Enterprises in East New Guinea up to 1914* (Melbourne: Plenum Publishing Australia, 2015).

Christina Oke, "The Native Administrations of MacGregor, Murray and Hasluck in Papua/New Guinea: Continuity and Contrast," *University of Wollongong Historical Journal* 1(1) (1975) 7–41.

Nigel Oram, *The Western Motu Area and the European Impact: 1872–1942*, in Sione Latukefu (ed.), *Papua New Guinea: A Century of Colonial Impact* (Port Moresby: The National Research Institute and the University of Papua New Guinea, 1989).

Robin S. O'Regan, "The Reception of the Common Law and the Authority of Common Law Precedents in the Territory of Papua and New Guinea," *International and Comparative Law Quarterly* 19(2) (1970) 217–228.

Susan Pedersen, *The Guardian: The League of Nations and the Crisis of Empire* (Oxford: Oxford University Press, 2015).

B. N. Primrose, "The Papua Bill: Australian Colonial Policy?" *Australian Journal of Politics and History* 19(2) (1973) 205–223.

The Queenslander, "The Traveller: A Trip to Papua—III," *The Queenslander*, May 9, 1914.

Henry Reynolds, *The Law of the Land* (Ringwood: Penguin, 2nd ed., 1992).

Henry Reynolds, *Aboriginal Sovereignty* (Sydney: Allen & Unwin, 1996).

C. D. Rowley, *The Australians in German New Guinea 1914–1921* (Melbourne: Melbourne University Press, 1958).

Charles D. Rowley, "The Occupation of German New Guinea 1914–1921," in W. J. Hudson (ed.), *Australia and Papua New Guinea* (Sydney: Sydney University Press, 1971) 57–73.

Peter Sack and Bridget Sack, "Land Law and Land Policy in German New Guinea," in Kenneth S. Inglis (ed.), *The History of Melanesia* (Port Moresby: University of Papua New Guinea, 1969) 101–112.

R. T. Shand, "The Development of Cash-Cropping in Papua and New Guinea," *Australian Journal of Agricultural and Resource Economics* 7(1) (1963) 42–54.

George W. Stocking Jr., *Victorian Anthropology* (New York: Free Press, 1987).

George W. Stocking Jr., *After Taylor: British Social Anthropology 1888–1951* (Madison: University of Wisconsin Press, 1998).

Ian Stuart, *Port Moresby: Yesterday and Today* (Sydney: Pacific Publications, rev. ed., 1973).

Sydney Morning Herald, "Papua. II. An Introspection. The Native Labor Question," *Sydney Morning Herald*, January 22, 1912, 5.

Sydney Morning Herald, "Papua. II. Treatment of Natives. Magisterial Report," *Sydney Morning Herald*, April 29, 1920, 6.

Telegraph, "Natives of Papua. Labor Problems," *Telegraph*, March 7, 1911, 8.

Telegraph, "Life in Papua. Progress of Territory. Lack of Labor," *Telegraph*, December 18, 1912.

Truth, "Is There Slavery in Papua," *Truth*, April 29, 1920, 7.

Truth, "Papuan Pars. Opening of the Legislative Council," *Truth*, August 29, 1915, 12.

John Waiko, "Australian Administration under the Bindandere Thumb," in Sione Latukefu (ed.), *Papua New Guinea: A Century of Colonial Impact* (Port Moresby: The National Research Institute and the University of Papua New Guinea, 1989) 75–108.

Frank Welsh, *Australia: A New History of the Great Southern Land* (New York: Overlook Press, 2004).

F. J. West, "Captain Barton of Papua," *South Pacific* 7 (May–June 1954) 858–862.

Francis West, *Hubert Murray: The Australian Pro-Consul* (Melbourne: Oxford University Press, 1968).

The Western Australian, "Papua's Principal Problem," *The Western Australian*, March 25, 1912, 8.

Osmar White, *Parliament of a Thousand Tribes* (Melbourne: Wren, 1972).

Edward Wolfers, *Race Relations and Colonial Rule in Papua New Guinea* (Sydney: Australia and New Zealand Book Co., 1975).

Worker, "Should Native Labor be Exploited," *Worker*, August 15, 1912.

Michael W. Young, *Malinowski: Odyssey of an Anthropologist 1884–1920* (New Haven: Yale University Press, 2004).

Government Documents

Annual Report for the Territory of Papua 1921–1922 (Melbourne: Government Printer, 1922).

Royal Commission on Late German New Guinea, *Interim and Final Reports*, Commonwealth Parliamentary Paper No. 29 (1920).

M. Staniforth Smith, *Handbook of the Territory of Papua* (Melbourne: Government Printer, 1906).

Case

The King v. Bernasconi, 19 C.L.R. 629 (1915)

Statutes

The Encouragement of Industry Ordinance 1908 (British New Guinea)

Jury Ordinance 1907 (British New Guinea)

Land Ordinance 1906 (British New Guinea)

Laws Repeal and Adopting Ordinance 1921 (Australia)

Marriage Ordinance 1912 (British New Guinea)

Native Labor Ordinance 1907 (British New Guinea)

New Guinea Act 1920 (Australia)

Papua Act 1905 (Australia)

Notes

1. H. N. Nelson, "European Attitudes in Papua, 1906–1914," in Kenneth S. Inglis (ed.), *The History of Melanesia* (Port Moresby: University of Papua New Guinea, 1969) 593.
2. Commonwealth Bureau of Census and Statistics, *Official Year Book of the Commonwealth of Australia*, 1901–1907 (Canberra: Commonwealth Bureau of Census and Statistics, 1908) 57.
3. *Id.* at section 36.
4. *Id.* at section 18.
5. *Native Regulations* (Papua), Regulation 84.
6. *Id.* at Regulation 77(4).
7. Atlee Hunt, "Report on British New Guinea, 1905," *Commonwealth Parliamentary Papers*, 5–7. "The Papuan Dependency: Report of Mr. Atlee Hunt," *Sydney Morning Herald*, November 1, 1905, 9.
8. Atlee Hunt, "Report on British New Guinea, 1905," *Commonwealth Parliamentary Papers*, 11, 28. "Mr. Atlee Hunt's Visit: An Interesting Report," *Western Mail*, November 4, 1905, 33.
9. Kenneth Mackay, *Across Papua* (London: Witherby and Co., 1909) 5 (quoting from the letters patent establishing the commission).
10. Ian Stuart, *Port Moresby: Yesterday and Today* (Sydney: Pacific Publications, rev. ed., 1973) 84.
11. "Papuan Administration," *The Age*, October 18, 1920, 7.
12. Peter Biskup, Brian Jinks, and Hank Nelson, *A Short History of New Guinea* (Sydney: Angus and Robertson, 1968) 76.
13. "The Traveller: A Trip to Papua—III," *The Queenslander*, May 9, 1914, 29.
14. *Annual Report, Territory of Papua, 1921–1922* (Melbourne: Government Printer of the State of Victoria, 1921) 19.
15. "Judiciary Slavery," *Auckland Star*, December 23, 1908.
16. John Hubert Murray, *Papua or British New Guinea* (London: T. Fisher Unwin, 1912) 348.

17. "The Future of Papua," *The Age*, March 18, 1911, 6.
18. "The Hulking, Lazy Native," *The Mercury*, September 20, 1910, 3.
19. "Natives of Papua. Labor Problems," *Telegraph*, March 7, 1911, 8.
20. "Native Labor Questions," *Kalgoorlie Miner*, May 18, 1909.
21. "Life in Papua. Progress of Territory. Lack of Labor," *Telegraph*, December 18, 1912.
22. "Should Native Labor be Exploited," *Worker*, August 15, 1912.
23. "Papua's Principal Problem," *The Western Australian*, March 25, 1912, 8.
24. "Native Labor Questions," *Kalgoorlie Miner*, May 18, 1909.
25. "Papua. An Introspection. II. The Native Labor Question," *Sydney Morning Herald*, January 22, 1912, 5.
26. "Is There Slavery in Papua?" *Truth*, November 22, 1914, April 29, 1920, 7.
27. "Papuan Pars. Opening of the Legislative Council," *Truth*, August 29, 1915, 12.
28. "Papua, Ill-Treatment of Natives. Magisterial Report," *Sydney Morning Herald*, April 29, 1920, 6.
29. Francis West, *Hubert Murray: The Australian Pro-Consul* (Melbourne: Oxford University Press, 1968) 37–38.
30. "Papuan Administration," *The Age*, October 18, 1920.
31. August Ibrum K. Kituai, *My Gun, My Brother* (Honolulu: University of Hawai'i Press, 1998) 139–140.
32. "Papuan Administration," *The Age*, October 18, 1920.
33. John Hubert Murray, *Papua or British New Guinea* (London: T. Fisher Unwin, 1912) 228.
34. *Id.* at 212.
35. H. N. Nelson, "European Attitudes in Papua, 1906–1914," in Kenneth S. Inglis (ed.), *The History of Melanesia* (Port Moresby: University of Papua New Guinea, 1969) 593.
36. "Papuan Pars," *Truth*, March 22, 1914.
37. Osmar White, *Parliament of a Thousand Tribes* (Melbourne: Wren, 1972) 53.
38. John Hubert Murray, *Papua or British New Guinea* (London: T. Fisher Unwin, 1912),197.
39. *Id.* at 198.
40. Observer, "Judge Herbert of Papua," *Observer*, January 18, 1913, 37.
41. D. C. Lewis, *The Plantation Dream: Developing British New Guinea and Papua 1884–1942* (Canberra: The Journal of Pacific History, 1996) 129.
42. *The King v. Bernasconi*, 19 C.L.R. 629 (1915) .
43. *Interim and Final Reports of Royal Commission on Late German New Guinea, Commonwealth Parliamentary Paper No. 29* (1920).
44. *Id.* at 227.
45. *Id.*

46. *New Guinea Act*, section 13.
47. *Id.* at section 16.
48. *Id.*

6 The Colonial Legal Systems in Operation

Administration and Economic Development 1921–1942

With the establishment of the League of Nations Mandate over New Guinea and the enactment of the *New Guinea Act of 1920*, Australia finally achieved what it had coveted since 1884, administrative control over both Papua and New Guinea. Unlike Britain's establishment in Papua of a protectorate and later a Crown Colony, there was no flag-raising ceremony on May 9, 1921, the day Australian civil administration officially began in New Guinea. However, the lack of formalities and speeches did not mean that Australia lacked goals for the mandate that would shape the content and operation of the colonial legal system throughout the two decades between the world wars.

The first statements of the policies that Australia intended to pursue in New Guinea came in two recommendations of a 1919 Royal Commission: expropriation of all German-owned property in the territory and deportation of most German nationals. Those actions were intended to further two broader goals that Australia had for New Guinea: using it as a security barrier against potential invasion from Asia and as a source of employment and potential wealth for Australian settlers. However, Article 2 of the League of Nations Mandate for New Guinea stated that Australia had to do more than further its own interests; it required the government to "promote to the utmost the material and moral well-being and social progress" of the local inhabitants.

In response to the mandate, Australian Prime Minister William Morris "Billy" Hughes set out in a speech in 1920 the ambitious terms of what he called "the work ahead" in New Guinea: "To establish law and order throughout the territory; to maintain schools everywhere for the education of the natives; to provide for the sanitation of all the villages; to examine thoroughly all the possibilities—agricultural, mineral, and timber—and to construct roads and perhaps railroads."[1] However, since financial resources and experienced personnel were limited, Hughes concluded his speech with the candid admission that, for the foreseeable future, "all Australia can hope to do is to give adequate facilities for the development of the territory and to make reasonable provision for improving the condition of the natives."[2]

Australia's recognition of its limitations can be found in the *New Guinea Act of 1920*; the section on guarantees contained very few promises of positive action. Instead, it restated the list of the prohibitions required by the League of Nations: no slave trade or forced labor; no trafficking in arms or ammunition; no sale of intoxicating liquor to New Guineans; no military or naval bases; and no military training of New Guineans except for police purposes. The only addition was a subsection guaranteeing (a) freedom of conscience (although that right was made subject to any legislation required to maintain public order and morals), and (b) freedom of worship (necessary because of the presence of missionaries from numerous Christian denominations). Australia's financial focus found further expression in its promotion of the economic interests of plantation owners and gold miners during the interwar years. As was the case during the earlier periods of German rule, that priority shaped the approach of the colonial legal system toward land and labor.

When civil administration began in New Guinea in May 1921, Papua had already been an Australia colony for fifteen years, although Australia had taken little interest in Papua's internal affairs and would continue its neglect throughout the interwar years. As a result, Hubert Murray, who continued to serve as lieutenant-governor until his death in February 1940, received little interference from the Australian government and was pretty much free to set and pursue his own policies.

Murray's stated policies for Papua put more emphasis on the welfare of Papuans than the colonial office's policies for New Guinea seemed to do. In practice, however, they differed little. His 1925 book, *Papua of To-Day*, invoked Article 22 of the League of Nations Covenant and its declaration that the mandates were the "sacred trust of civilization." To Murray, that obligation should apply to all colonies, not only to mandates, and marked "the abandonment of the theory that a colony is to be regarded merely as a business proposition, and the native inhabitants merely as 'assets' to be utilized for the purpose of this business."[3] Instead, the "interests of the native" would be considered of the "first importance."[4] But, "first" means different things to different people. Murray explained to Australians who might otherwise be worried about the interests of Australian plantation owners and business people, that the "interests of the native" can be compatible with economic development for expatriates. That led him to adopt Frederick Lugard's concept of a *dual mandate* that had become the basis of British rule in Africa. To Murray, Australia had a dual responsibility in administering Papua: promoting the development of the colony's economy, based on plantations owned and managed by Australians and using Papua labor, while, at the same time, protecting Papuans and their land from the most blatant forms of exploitation by the expatriates. Murray saw no conflict between between the best interests of Papuans and the development of a modern economy, owned primarily by Australian companies and settlers. In his view, the best thing that his administration could do for Papuans would be to introduce them to western economic and legal models. He fully accepted the dominant colonizing belief that Papuans were still at a "primitive" stage of development and that their "backwardness" was due to their lack of historical interaction with the "higher races of Europe and Asia."[5] But the fact that Murray supported the interests of Papuans, even to that extent, enraged Australian planters and businessmen. That tension shaped the colonial legal system throughout the 1920s and 1930s.

In addition to creating economic conditions that the colonial administrations hoped would attract Australian settlers to the colonies, the colonial legal systems served as the personal legal system for those who came to Papua and New Guinea. Although the number of settlers increased during the interwar years, it remained small—at its height, about 1600 in

Papua and 4500 in New Guinea. Some of those residents came to the territories intending to spend their lives as plantation owners. Others came for business purposes, to work for the administrations, or to serve as missionaries for a few years or with the intent of returning to Australia when they retired. All of them wanted a legal system with which they were familiar. They looked to the colonial legal systems to provide them with rules and procedures to govern their personal lives and business affairs and to resolve their disputes.

Although promoting the economic development and interests of the colonialist population were important goals of the administrations in Papua and New Guinea in the years between the wars, they were not their only goals. Beginning in the mid-1920s, the administrations in both territories sought to expand the scope of their control over the Indigenous population and began to send patrols to explore the unknown (to Australians) Highlands region. As a result, colonial officials came into contact with tens of thousands of people they previously did not know existed, but who had lived in the area for thousands of years. The extension of contact, and assertion of nominal control over large areas and numbers of people, raised a number of questions that also played a major role in shaping the colonial legal systems throughout the 1930s: How should the administrations control and govern the indigenous population that was vastly larger than Australians had expected it to be? What role, if any, could Papuans and New Guineans play in the administrations? What recognition, if any, should the colonial legal systems give to the customary norms and processes of Papuans and New Guineans, particularly in criminal cases?

In this chapter, we will examine three of the major functions of the colonial legal systems in the years between the wars: creating the administrative structure to govern Papua and New Guinea; providing the legal means and justifications for its economic policies; and serving as the personal legal systems of the colonial population. In the next chapter, we will focus on the use of the colonial legal systems to bring under previously unconquered parts of the Indigenous population under administration control and to aid generally in governing the territories.

The Colonial Administrations and the Colonial Legal Systems

Papua's system of colonial administration, set out in the *Papua Act of 1905*, did not change during the interwar years, although the colony's population, which expanded considerably between 1907 and 1923, reacted as if it had. Many expatriates fiercely criticized Hubert Murray's land and labor policies during those years. In their view, he pampered the Papuans and favored Indigenous interests over those of the expatriates. Port Moresby residents unsuccessfully petitioned Prime Minister Hughes in 1920 to replace Murray with Miles Staniforth Smith, a former official in the Papuan administration and an open critic of Murray. However, the following year, the Australian Minister for Home and Territories visited Papua and submitted a report to the Cabinet that was favorable to Murray. Murray's position strengthened from the mid-1920s onward as his books, articles, and speeches enhanced his international reputation as one of Britain's leading authorities on colonial administration. Even his harshest critics were silenced after he was knighted in 1925.

The structure of Papua's judicial system changed very little during the 1920s and 1930s. The highest court (the Central Court) was renamed the Supreme Court in 1935 and appeals from that court transferred from the Supreme Court of Queensland to the High Court of Australia. Just three men served as judges on the Central Court/Supreme Court during the entire interwar period: Hubert Murray himself (1904–1940), Charles Herbert (1910–1928), and Ralph T. Gore (1928–1962). There continued to be no separation of powers between the administration and the judiciary in Papua, even though this was considered essential in Australia. Nowhere is this better illustrated than in the person of Judge Charles Herbert, who, in addition to being a Central Court judge, was also a member of the Executive and Legislative Councils, drafted the ordinances and regulations that he then interpreted as a judge, and served as acting lieutenant-governor when Murray (who also was chief judge) was away from the colony.

In New Guinea, Article 2 of the League of Nations Mandate gave Australia the power to choose its own administrative system, and it chose something very similar to that already operating in Papua. Under the *New Guinea Act of 1920*, the chief administrative official was the Administrator, who was appointed by the Australian prime minister and who had essentially the same powers as the lieutenant-governor in Papua. New Guinea also enjoyed administrative stability between 1921 and 1942, with only three persons serving as Administrator: Evan Wisdom, Thomas Griffiths, and Walter McNicoll. All of them had been military officers during World War I, and Wisdom and Griffiths also had served during the war as British military administrators of New Guinea. The Administrators faced the same financial problems that had confronted officials in Papua since the beginning of the colonial period: Australia had little interest in New Guinea, other than making sure that no other country could control it, and the Australian government wanted the mandate to be as financially self-sufficient as possible. Wisdom faced a challenge similar to the one Murray had faced earlier: he had to deal with plantation owners and German missionaries whose attitudes about how the territory should be administered reflected the German colonial period. All three of the Administrators also had to deal with the negative attitudes of plantation owners and managers toward New Guineans and their occasional maltreatment of their workers.

Unlike Papua, the New Guinea administration had no Executive Council or Legislature Council until 1933. Instead, the *New Guinea Act of 1920* gave the Australian governor-general the power to "make Ordinances having the force of law in the Territory" subject to disapproval by Parliament.[6] In November 1932, Australia amended the act to create an Executive Council (composed of the Administrator, eight administration officials, and one nonofficial member) and a Legislative Council (composed of the Administrator, the eight official members of the Executive Council, and seven nonofficial members nominated by the Administrator to represent the interests of businessmen, miners, planters, and missionaries). As in Papua, the Legislative Council had the authority to make ordinances "for the peace, order and good government of the Territory."[7] An ordinance required the ascent of the Administrator and had to be forwarded to the Australian governor-general, who could disallow it. Again, as in Papua, there were no popular elections for the Legislative Council during the interwar years and no New Guinean members. That was consistent with the practice in Britain's colonial possessions throughout Africa and

Asia, where neither the Indigenous populations nor the expatriates had a voice in choosing their officials.

Article 2 of the League of Nations Mandate also gave Australia the authority to apply its laws to New Guinea. The *Laws Repeal and Adopting Ordinance,* which went into effect on May 9, 1921, stated that all German laws ceased to apply in the mandate. In their place, the ordinance adopted statutes from the Australian Commonwealth, the military administration, Queensland, and Papua, as well as the rules of the common law and equity in force in England on that date. The ordinance provided that all Crown lands passed to Australia and that estates and interests in land held by persons from the German government or from the British military administration continued to be held from Australia on the same terms. However, in a major change from Papua, the ordinance specifically recognized the customs and usages of New Guineans and stated that they were not affected by the ordinance and could continue so long as they were "not repugnant to the general principles of humanity."[8]

The *New Guinea Act of 1920* did not create a judiciary for the mandate. That was left to the *Judiciary Ordinance of 1921*, which abolished all courts created by German law and by the military administration and established a judicial system similar to that in Papua. The ordinance created a Central Court, which in 1934 was renamed the "Supreme Court of the Territory of New Guinea."[9] The Central Court initially consisted of two judges: Chief Judge David Wanliss (1921–1937) and Karl Drake-Brockman (1921–1924). However, a 1924 ordinance abolished all judgeships in New Guinea except that of the chief justice. In February 1928, that law was repealed, and Frederick Beaumont Phillips, who had been serving as a stipendiary magistrate in New Guinea, was appointed to the Central Court. He remained a judge in New Guinea, and later Papua New Guinea, until his retirement in 1957. Philip L. Griffiths, a barrister who had been solicitor-general of Tasmania, was appointed acting chief judge in 1938 and then judge in 1939. He became acting chief judge again in October 1940 and died in Tasmania in June 1945. As in Papua, the judicial systems in New Guinea also consisted of District Courts, Courts for Native Affairs, and Wardens' Courts, which had jurisdiction over matters relating to mining. Although appeals from decisions of the Central Court/Supreme Court could be taken to the High Court of Australia, that rarely happened because of the expense involved.

The Colonial Economies and the Colonial Legal Systems

At first, Australia believed that its goal of making both Papua and New Guinea as economically self-sufficient as possible could be achieved by plantations that would export copra, rubber, hemp, and timber. To that end, the Papuan administration continued in force ordinances specifying how land could be acquired from Papuans and regulating the working conditions of Papuans employed on plantations. In New Guinea, Australia sought to build a plantation economy not by acquiring land from New Guineans but by expropriating the plantations that had been established during the period of German rule and selling them to persons of British descent (especially returned Australian servicemen) who, it was hoped, would settle in the territory with their families and manage the plantations.

New Guinea: Expropriation and Deportation

Shortly after the signing of the Treaty of Versailles in June 1919, and more than a year before the League of Nations ratified Australia's mandate over New Guinea, Australian Prime Minister Hughes told Parliament that "the national safety is assured now that the great rampart of islands [New Guinea]" is under Australian control.[10] Government officials and newspapers spoke optimistically of the economic potential that the well-developed system of plantations in the New Guinea territory held for Australians willing to settle there. The legal system was a handy mechanism for expropriating those plantations from German ownership and transferring them to Australians.

Under Article 120 of the Treaty of Versailles, both "movable and immovable property" belonging to Germans in New Guinea passed to the Australian government. Article 297(b) of the treaty gave Australia the power to "retain and liquidate the property rights and interests" of German nationals and companies in the mandate. Those provisions received support from the majority report of the 1919 Royal Commission, which recommended that Australia expropriate all German-owned plantations and sell them to non-Germans, liquidate all German businesses and replace them with Australian firms, and expel all German residents from the mandate. The Australian government adopted those recommendations, and the British military administrator of New Guinea, Brigadier-

General Thomas Griffiths, "proclaimed" the *Expropriation Ordinance* in September 1920. In April 1921, Brigadier-General Evan Wisdom, who succeeded Griffiths as British military administrator, "enacted and proclaimed" the *Deportation Ordinance.* Since the ordinances had not been enacted by the Australian government, they were not valid once New Guinea became a mandate. However, Australia saw the ordinances as furthering its security by eliminating a foreign influence in New Guinea and removing a group of people (German nationals) who might become a threat to Australia in the future. The ordinances also promoted Australia's economic goals by permitting it to seize German plantations and other property without compensation and to sell them to Australians. The expropriation of German property received legal force in the mandate in June 1921 when an ordinance was enacted pursuant to the *Laws Repeal and Adopting Ordinance of 1921.*

Under the *Expropriation Ordinance,* all German residents (except for missionaries) in New Guinea were required to turn over their land and personal property to the Administrator. The Administrator appointed a public trustee (later known as the custodian) to hold the property. He also created a four-member Expropriation Board to manage the expropriated real property, which included approximately 268 plantations, 20 large stores, workshops, shipping facilities, and other businesses. Once German property was turned over to the board, no one working on it could quit or be discharged without permission of the board. The failure to obtain the board's permission made a person liable for a fine of £100 or six-months imprisonment. The stiff penalty was an admission that, although Australia was supposed to be expelling the German residents of New Guinea, it was unable to manage their expropriated property without their help.

Because the former German plantations were the foundation of New Guinea's economy during the 1920s, the power given to the Expropriation Board to deal with issues of land, labor, and finance made the board more important than the administration. Its power also made it controversial from the start, especially since its chairman, W. H. Lucas, was also the president of Burns Philp, one of the two largest trading companies in the Pacific islands. Many feared that those companies would use their connections with the mandate's administration to further tighten their control on plantation trade.

But the management of the plantations and businesses caused the Expropriation Board numerous problems. As the former German owners were deported, the board hired young and inexperienced Australian returned servicemen to manage the properties. Most of them knew little about agriculture, and nothing about growing coconuts or managing large groups of New Guinean laborers. In addition, many of the New Guinean workers refused to renew their employment contracts and returned to their villages. The neglect of copra production and export and the support services they sustained led to widespread allegations in Australian newspapers of mismanagement of the expropriated plantations, as well as claims of fraud and theft of expropriated property. One newspaper published an exposé of what it called "expropriation evils," while another referred to the government's control of plantations as a "ghastly failure."[11] The press also made allegations against administration officials for permitting forced labor and the flogging of New Guinean workers by the police. In response to what one newspaper called the "sensational charges against officials responsible for the administration of New Guinea," the paper stated that it was "against the national consciousness to condone excesses of this kind." However, the paper then offered its view of New Guinean workers and the treatment of them: "We are aware that the native of tropical lands is incurably lazy and often tricky and treacherous. Therefore, he must be dealt with firmly. Still, there ought to be some other way of inflicting punishment than by flogging."[12]

In response to widespread criticisms of the board, the Australian government asked Colonel John Ainsworth, the former chief native commissioner of Kenya, to visit the mandate in 1924 to study all aspects of its administration. Ainsworth's report went beyond matters affecting New Guineans and included recommendations that the Expropriation Board cease acting as plantation owners and traders and sell the properties it managed, since it had become a dominant economic power in the mandate and was keeping private capital out of the territory.[13] The administration began selling or leasing expropriated properties in late 1924. Sale of the properties, which was restricted to Australian returned servicemen or persons who were British subjects by birth, was completed in 1927. However, as with the young Australians initially hired by the board to manage the plantations, most of those buyers knew little or nothing about tropical agriculture.

Although the board offered the plantations for sale at generous prices, most of the returned servicemen lacked the financial resources required even for the deposit. In order to obtain the funds, some of them agreed to serve as "dummies" for one of three large companies—Burns, Philp & Co., W. R. Carpenter Pty. Ltd., and the Melanesia Company Ltd.—that loaned them the purchase money in return for their turning over the management of the plantations to the companies. The companies could have purchased the plantations in their own names but would have had to pay twice the deposit and repay the balance in half the time as individual purchasers. Although the practice of using so-called "dummies" led to government investigations, little or nothing was done to put a stop to it.

When the price of copra collapsed in 1927, followed by worldwide depression two years later, the plantation economies in neither Papua nor New Guinea could meet the administrations' hopes. It became impossible for many of the individual purchasers of plantations to repay their loans. They filed for bankruptcy and returned to Australia. Many of the properties were taken over by Burns, Philp & Co. or W. R. Carpenter, which came to dominate the New Guinea plantation economy in the 1930s. The complete collapse of the territorial economies was averted only by the discovery of gold in the mid-1920s, which became the largest export from Papua and New Guinea throughout the 1930s.

The deportation of German nationals from New Guinea began in December 1920, when they were ejected from their properties, jobs, and homes without notice. German nationals subject to the *Deportation Ordinance* were permitted to take only £50 with them when they left. According to the Treaty of Versailles, it was the obligation of the German government to compensate its nationals for their property losses in New Guinea. Still, many Australians came to view the treatment and mass deportation of the German residents as too harsh. One district officer in New Guinea referred to it not as expropriation but as "looting" and "unjust and hate-breeding."[14]

Land Ordinances in Papua and New Guinea

When Murray became lieutenant-governor of Papua in 1908, he viewed it as one of the duties of his administration to encourage the establishment of plantations that would be owned and managed by persons of European descent. However, the stagnant economy of the 1920s was not the only reason for a sharp decline in the interest of returned servicemen and others to come to Papua and establish plantations. One of the reasons was the Australian *Navigation Act*, which raised the cost of agricultural exports from Papua and New Guinea by requiring that they be shipped through a port in Australia before being sold abroad. In addition, although Australia's population reached 6.4 million people in 1930, men experienced at farm work were not willing to go to Papua when there was land available in Australia. Finally, there was a shortage of Papuan laborers, since many were understandably reluctant to give up the familiarity of village life for the regimentation and harsh working conditions on foreign-owned plantations far from their villages.

Many of the Australians who had come to Papua to establish plantations became disappointed in their financial prospects. They blamed Murray for the failure of their hopes. Their principal complaints were that, despite abundant land for plantations, the administration was too particular in inquiring whether the Papuans required the land and that there was too much delay in dealing with land applications. Murray viewed the criticisms as inevitable with any policy that sought to provide even minimal protections to traditional owners of the land.

In New Guinea, the *Laws Repeal and Adopting Ordinance of 1921* repealed German law and replaced it with English and Australian law, except for the property rights acquired under German law, which continued to be valid. The following year, the *Land Ordinance of 1922* adopted the approach used in Papua for future acquisitions of land: Private parties would not be permitted to buy or lease land from New Guineans; only the Administrator could acquire land from New Guineans. As in Papua, the ordinance also permitted the administration to take land that appeared to be "waste or vacant." Unlike in Papua, the governor-general of Australia then could sell the land the administration acquired, subject to any conditions he thought fit. As in Papua, the administration could lease the land it had acquired for a period up to ninety-nine years. Two years later, the *Lands Registration Ordinance of 1924* brought all lands that had been under the German system of titles into freehold titles under the Australian Torrens title system of land registration. The administration continued to have the power to make freehold grants of land until 1962.

Although the language of the land ordinances in Papua and New Guinea placed strict controls on the acquisition of land by the colonial administrations, many of those controls were little more than symbolic. When the administrations in either territory wanted land, officials put pressure on traditional owners to sell the land to them at low prices or declared it "waste or vacant." A careful assessment of the current or future needs of local owners for the land rarely occurred. In addition, the administration and local owners often disagreed about whether the land was waste and vacant. The gardening methods used by Papuans and New Guineans let areas of land lie fallow for a number of years for conservation purposes. Papuans and New Guineans did not consider that land was waste or vacant. However, the decisions of colonial officials, rather than those of traditional owners, determined whether land was waste or vacant.

The land ordinances in Papua and New Guinea also permitted the administrations to acquire land by compulsory acquisition for public purposes, such as airfields, cemeteries, and schools. In 1941, those provisions in the various land ordinances in Papua led to litigation that ultimately was decided by the High Court of Australia. In 1937, a group of Papuans living near Port Moresby had leased approximately fifty acres of land to the administration for a term of ten years at an annual rent of £15. According to one Papua New Guinean legal scholar, the owners of the land agreed to the lease on the understanding that the land would be returned to them with whatever improvements were made to the land at the end of the lease. The administration then built the first civilian airfield on the land. By 1939, the administration had constructed a single runway, with concrete drains and parking areas, and had enclosed the entire area with a fence. The airfield, which served Port Moresby, had become known as the Kila Kila Aerodrome. The administration also erected buildings used as a radio and meteorological station and a customs and quarantine office. In addition, a number of companies constructed buildings on the land, which they used for servicing the airplanes. The value of the improvements was estimated to be £6,200.

After work on the land was completed, the Papuan administration enacted the *Lands (Kila Kila Aerodrome) Acquisition Ordinance of 1939*, authorizing the administration's compulsory taking of the land, along with another thirty-eight acres near the aerodrome. Presumably, this after-the-fact legislation was done to avoid having to pay rent on the land and to prevent having to return the land at the end of the lease. However, section 3 of the ordinance required that the administration pay compensation for the land based on the manner set out for land compulsorily taken under the *Lands Acquisition Ordinance of 1914*. In deciding the value of the land, Justice Ralph Gore did not consider the value of the improvements on the land. He held that they were not part of the land and would be useless to the Papuans. The buildings probably would not remain if the administration returned the land to the Papuans. Justice Gore concluded that the land had no potential for Papuans except for gardens and assessed compensation at £454, less than 10 percent of its assessed value.

The Papuan owners of the land appealed the decision to the High Court of Australia. R. D. Bertie, an Australian lawyer who had been practicing in Port Moresby for more than twenty years, represented them. In the High Court, the administration took the position that Papuans did not own the land in fee simple; any rights they might have had to the land depended solely on custom and on the promise made by Commodore Erskine in 1884 that "Your lands will be secured to you." Since the Papuans did not own the land, they were not entitled to the value of the improvements.

The administration had good reason to expect it would prevail in this case, because, at that time, and for many years afterward, Australian law did not recognize that the Indigenous peoples of Australia had any ownership rights in their ancestral lands. However, in a unanimous decision, the High Court held that the Papuans' title to the land was a "communal usufructuary title equivalent to full ownership of the land."[15] The difference between the application of Australian law to customary land ownership in Australia itself and in Papua may have been based upon the judges' belief that Papuans differed from Aboriginal Australians, in that Papuans were gardeners, relatively settled in long-maintained villages, rather than nomadic hunters and gatherers. Or perhaps it was easier to grant land rights far from home. Going even farther, the court ordered that the Papuan owners had to be compensated on the same basis as if the administration had acquired the land from an expatriate and that the value should include any improvements on the land, such as buildings, that were permanently attached to the land.

The restrictions on alienation contained in the land ordinances, together with the lack of interest on the part of Australians in settling in Papua or New Guinea, meant that less than 5 percent of customary land was alienated during the colonial period, preventing Papuans and New Guineans from becoming landless tenant farmers, a fate that befell Indigenous people in parts of Asia and Africa.

Labor Legislation

Although the colonial administrations continued their efforts to attract Australians to settle in Papua and New Guinea, it was accepted "wisdom" that persons of European descent were not well suited for physical labor in tropical climates. Papuan and New Guinean men performed all of the manual labor on plantations. Although some Papuans and New Guineans had worked for short periods over the years on plantations, they naturally preferred village life with their families to the regimentation and loneliness of wage labor far from home. More importantly, Papuans and New Guineans had no real need of the jobs because they had very few expenses that could be paid for only in money. As a result, there was not a steady enough supply of labor in the interwar years to meet the demand. In an effort to provide that labor, the colonial administration in Papua adopted the *Native Taxes Ordinance* in 1918, and the administration in New Guinea enacted a similar ordinance in 1921. In Papua, the ordinance imposed a "head tax" on all Papuan males between the ages of sixteen and thirty-six years old. The amount of the tax varied by districts but could not exceed 10 shillings per year for laborers. In the case of Papuan males who were not laborers, the tax could be up to £1 per year and could be paid in money or in kind. Failure to pay the tax could result in imprisonment for up to six months. Five categories of people were exempt from the tax: members of the Armed Native Constabulary; village constables; persons unfit for work; a man supporting four or more children by a single wife; and mission teachers and students.

The stated purpose of the tax was to raise money that could be used for the education of Papuans or for other purposes benefiting them, such as hospitals and village improvements. However, the real goal of the tax was to coerce Papuan and New Guinean men to take jobs as plantation laborers, despite the fact that forced labor was nominally prohibited in Papua and New Guinea and the colonial administrations repeatedly denied that such a practice existed in their territories. The few other paying jobs open to them were limited to serving in the Armed Native Constabulary or police force, or working on boats, as stevedores, or as domestic servants.

Thus, there was little alternative to avoid jail but to work on the plantations or in the goldfields in order to earn money to pay the tax. Although Murray repeatedly stated that the interests of Papuans were of the "first importance," he defended the tax ordinance on the basis that the interests of Papuans would be best served by integrating them into the western economy. In particular, he said, working on plantations or the goldfields was ultimately in the best interests of Papuans, since it gave them discipline and educated them in work habits that they could use for their own benefit when they returned to their villages. Of course, no one asked Papuans if they agreed with that assessment.

Throughout the 1920s and 1930s, almost all plantation owners and gold miners used indentured labor, under statutes that required the laborer to work for a specific period of time and the employer to house, feed, and pay his wages. There also was a system of nonindentured labor (also referred to as "free labor") that was not subject to statutory requirements or conditions. However, the majority of employers preferred indentured labor, which continued in both territories until World War II, even though the British government recommended abolishing it in the colonies. Murray viewed indentured labor as "a necessary evil"[16] but defended it as a means of ensuring a steady and reliable supply of workers for the plantations and goldfields. Murray, like others in the colonial service, believed Papuans and New Guineans lacked the ability to understand the need for continuous work for an extended period of time. They further justified indentured labor as necessary to protect Papuan and New Guinean workers from the supposedly greater exploitation they might encounter under casual employment.

Since indentured labor was based on a written contract between the employer and the workers, the terms of that contract were crucial. The labor ordinances tried to strike a balance, at least on paper, between the demands of the plantation owners and miners and the need to protect Papuans and New Guineans from exploitation, but even on paper the balance very much favored the employers. Although the labor ordinances varied slightly between Papua and New Guinea, they dealt with four broad topics: labor recruiting; the requirements for a worker to sign a labor contract; the obligations of the employer; and the duties of the workers and penalties for violations of the contract.

Labor Law and Policy in Papua

In the years between the wars, the Papuan *Native Labor Ordinance* governed all aspects of labor involving Papuans. The ordinance permitted employers to recruit workers themselves or use a licensed recruiter. The indenture of women was not permitted, except as house servants. Labor contracts had to be in writing and signed before a magistrate or other government official who had to be satisfied that a number of conditions were met, including that the worker had entered into the contract voluntarily and there was no reason to suspect the worker would be treated unfairly; the worker was physically fit for the job; the pay was fair; the worker would be housed and fed; and the worker would be returned to his home by his employer at the end of the contract. Employers also were supposed to provide medical care and to keep a medicine chest, stocked with necessary drugs and first aid equipment. A magistrate could terminate a labor contract based on unjust or harsh treatment of the worker. The wages for indentured plantation workers were set at 10 shillings per month and 15 shillings for those working in the goldfields. The term of indenture could not exceed three years on plantations or eighteen months on the goldfields.

Although an employer could terminate a worker at will, breach of an employment contract by a Papuan was a crime, not a civil matter. An indentured laborer who refused to perform work, neglected his duties, or deserted because of harsh working conditions, could be convicted summarily and punished by a fine or a jail term. Murray correctly characterized the use of criminal penalties as "really rather like slavery." He added, however, that the abolition of indentured labor "would be ruinous to both employer and employed in Papua. . . . [O]ur task is to make it work as harmoniously as possible."[17] The depression in 1930 led to a decline in the number of indentured workers in Papua to slightly over 5,000 in 1933, but by 1939 the number had risen to 16,984.

Throughout the 1920s and 1930s, planters continued to criticize Murray's labor legislation and policies, accusing him of pursuing pro-Papuan policies that threatened the prosperity of plantations. They considered the labor ordinances that controlled the recruitment and employment of laborers, prohibited imported labor and forced labor, and restricted corporal punishment to be too rigid and attacked Murray for being anti-expatriate. They wanted to be able to hire women, boys under the age of fourteen, and entire families in order to create a permanent labor force living close to their plantations. Murray refused their demands and stated that he did not want Papuans to be turned from what he called "peasant proprietors," into a "race of Laborers, men and women divorced from village life, and dependent on the plantation for their very existence."[18]

Labor Law and Policy in New Guinea

The plantation system was more extensive in New Guinea than in Papua, which created more demand for labor. There were a number of labor ordinances in New Guinea, culminating with the *Native Labor Ordinance of 1935–1939*. Not surprisingly, the Australian under-secretary for external affairs termed New Guinea's labor ordinance "the most complete, liberal, humane and efficient of the British Empire."[19] The ordinance applied to all employment of New Guineans by settlers, except casual employment, New Guineans living within twenty miles of the place of employment, and New Guineans working as day laborers and for not more than three months. On its face, the language of the ordinance was very protective of those workers. Recruitment was permitted only for employment within the mandate, and there were strict limitations on taking New Guineans out of the territory. Laborers had to be in good health, of full physical development, and over twelve years old. Although women could not be recruited, an exception was made in the case of married women, who could work in the same place as their husbands. This was seen as a way to induce more men to become plantation laborers. Labor recruiters had to be licensed, and the administration could prohibit them from recruiting labor from villages where too many men had already signed up.

The ordinance contained a number of other requirements for the protection of workers: employment had to be voluntary; the worker had to understand the nature of the engagement; and the workers had to be treated fairly and be properly fed and housed. The ordinance also required employers to provide medical assistance to their employees, including sick rooms, a hospital if the employer had more than one hundred employees, and a qualified doctor if there were more than five hundred workers. New Guineans had to be examined by a medical officer and appear before a district officer for approval and registration of their contracts before they could begin work. The minimum pay was 5 shillings a month for men and

4 shillings for women. No more than a third of that amount could be paid at the end of each month. The balance was paid at the end of the contract period, which ordinarily was three years.

Finally, the labor ordinance prescribed the amount of food rations, the conditions of housing and the cooking arrangements to be provided by employers. Working hours on plantations could not exceed ten hours a day, and workers were not required to work on Sundays. Employers were required to provide blankets, a bowl, a spoon, and a locked box. Employers were not permitted to punish employees, except by withholding the weekly ration of tobacco, and that had to be reported to the district officer. Anyone who assaulted or mistreated a laborer was subject to a fine of £50 pounds or imprisonment for up to six months.

The Reality of Labor Conditions

Perhaps the language of labor ordinances in Papua and New Guinea seemed to protect workers from exploitation and abuse. But employers in both territories were able to flout the requirements with impunity. Some recruiters used force or fraud to induce villagers into signing contracts. Regulations concerning the length of the contract, minimum wages, hours of work, and working conditions were often ignored. There were frequent prosecutions of employers in the courts for violating the labor regulations. However, violators received only warnings or small fines. Desertion by a worker, which carried a penalty of three months in prison, was the most common offense tried in the district courts.

The labor abuse that received the most attention was corporal punishment of workers. In 1921, Sir Joseph Cook, the acting prime minister of Australia, reacted angrily to allegations that flogging had been used at the order of a magistrate in Papua.[20] The newspaper reporting the story had defended flogging as common punishment for a number of offenses in other Pacific Islands under British administration, since jailing Indigenous defendants was regarded as expensive and ineffective. Foremen and planters should be able to use flogging on plantations to keep "the irresponsible natives in order," the newspaper said. Flogging, the newspaper insisted, was the form of punishment Papuans feared most.[21]

In New Guinea, flogging had been a common method of punishment used by German planters, and Australian newspapers frequently carried stories about the severe floggings of laborers for trivial offenses. Although the Australian military administration generally prohibited flogging by private individuals after 1914, it was retained, even after New Guinea became a mandate, as a penalty for a variety of criminal offenses: arson, assault, attempted murder, desertion from employment, housebreaking, insubordination, murder, perjury, robbery, and theft, and serious offenses against women. In November 1921, Prime Minister Hughes defended it in the case of New Guineans who were caught near the homes of white women. However, he said if a private individual were found to have flogged a New Guinean, he would be prosecuted.[22]

Rabaul Strike of 1929 and Its Aftermath

The failure of the colonial administration in New Guinea to look after the interests of workers led to the first workers' strike in Rabaul, New Britain, on January 2, 1929. The strike was not the result of the harsh conditions on plantations; instead, it was precipitated by the low wages paid to urban workers and an effort to secure a basic wage of £12 a month. That night, almost all of the three thousand New Guinean workers in Rabaul (seamen, police, house boys, as household workers were then called, and others) quietly left their jobs and walked to the Catholic and Methodist missions outside town. They did not report to work the next morning. The New Guineans hoped that the missionaries would mediate their wage demands. Unfortunately, that did not happen. Some of the strikers held out for two or three days, but by the morning of January 3, the strike had ended, and most of the workers had returned to Rabaul.

Although there was no wage increase, the attempt itself was significant. The strike was the largest collective action by Papuans or New Guineans until after World War II. The fact that three thousand men took part in the action showed that, for the first time, New Guineans from different parts of the territory, from different groups and speaking different languages, could come together for a common goal. The strike was also a complete surprise to the expatriate residents of New Guinea in general and Rabaul in particular and increased their deep insecurity. The common belief that Indigenous people were incapable of organized and concerted action led Administrator Evan Wisdom to blame outside influences, such as communists or agitators. In March 1929, the official commission established to investigate the origins of the strike assigned the major blame to "the advice given by foreign coloured sailors" and two

New Guineans: Sumsuma and Sergeant-Major Rami.[23] Sumsuma had been born in New Ireland and was the captain of a motor schooner owned by a company based in Rabaul. At the time of the strike, he was probably the highest-paid New Guinean in the territory, earning up to £12 a month, when most New Guineans working for wages received 5 shillings a month.

In order to protect themselves from what they feared was an imminent massacre by New Guineans, the residents of Rabaul turned to the colonial legal system, as well as to extra-legal measures. Criminal charges were brought against many of the strikers, resulting in harsh penalties. Twenty-one men were sentenced to three years imprisonment, and twelve men were sentenced to twelve to eighteen months. Hundreds of others were sent to jails in remote areas or to work in the goldfields. Sumsuma was among those sentenced to three years imprisonment, during which he received severe beatings from his guards that left him with permanent scars. Extra police were called in from Australia, and expatriates armed themselves. Many employers either fired their workers or beat or flogged them when they returned to work. Evan Wisdom played down reports of floggings, saying: "Probably what has happened is that one or two impetuous employer[s] have laid a stick across a tender part of a few natives' anatomies."[24] Although Wisdom promised that, if any white person administered regular floggings to New Guineans, he would be charged, no prosecutions were brought. There also was no more labor unrest until after World War II.

Law and Colonial Society

The major purpose of the colonial legal systems was to serve the interests of the expatriates in Papua and New Guinea. Although their number increased between the war years, it remained small—at its height, about 1,600 persons in Papua and 5,000 in New Guinea. Some of them came to the territories as settlers, intending to spend the rest of their lives working on plantations. Others came for a few years to work for the administrations, for business purposes, or to serve as missionaries with the intent of returning to Australia when they retired. While in the territories, all of them wanted a legal system with which they were familiar, and which would provide them with security and protect their property and business interests. They looked to the colonial legal systems to provide them with rules and procedures to govern their personal lives and business affairs, to resolve their disputes, and to protect them from one another and from Papuans and New Guineans.

Once they had settled in Papua or New Guinea, whether for the short or long term, whites developed what anthropologists would describe as small-scale societies. Throughout the colonial period, cultural anthropologists focused their ethnographic research primarily on small-scale Indigenous societies in Africa, Asia, and the Pacific Islands. They examined how factors such as population, networks of family and social relationships, geography, and economics shaped the way those societies functioned. Those factors are also the key to understanding the societies that the expatriates created in Papua and New Guinea and the ways in which they interacted with colonial law.

Anthropologists have described the traditional societies in Papua and New Guinea as small, separated, and parochial. Those terms also describe Port Moresby, Rabaul, and the other towns the expatriates established. Their communities in Papua and New Guinea shared a number of similarities with Indigenous societies. Both consisted of small populations, living in geographically separated and often isolated communities, built around networks of face-to-face relationships, requiring the need for cooperation, with simple economies, and an absence of either great wealth or serious poverty.

While figures for the expatriate population in Papua and New Guinea vary depending upon the source, all sources agree that it remained very small until after World War II. According to the Australian Bureau of Statistics, the April 1921 census in Papua recorded the "non-Indigenous" population of the colony as consisting of 2,078 persons (1,408 men and 670 women). Of that number, 1,343 were classified as "Europeans," with the remainder listed as Asian or "half-caste" in the census report.[25] Due in part to the Great Depression, by the time of the 1933 census in Papua, the "European" population had fallen more than 10 percent to 1,148 persons (677 men and 471 women).[26] The expatriate population was very young, with the 1933 census indicating that 30 percent of what it termed the "non-Indigenous population" were under the age of twenty—not likely to enter into business transactions or to be otherwise involved in matters requiring use of the legal system.[27] However, by June 1940 (the last time before the war that a census was taken in Papua), the "European" population in the colony had risen to 1,822 (1,201 men and 621 women).[28]

The expatriate population in New Guinea during the interwar years was also small, although larger than in Papua. The 1921 New Guinea census showed that there were 1,288 (1,006 men and 282 women) "Europeans." The census also listed 1,816 Asians (of whom 1,424 were Chinese) and 69 identified as "half-caste."[29] With the deportation of German nationals in the early 1920s, the "white population" fell by 50 percent to 1,550 in 1928, of whom more than half were British subjects. The number of Chinese also fell but only slightly, to about 1,300.[30] However, by 1933, the number of "Europeans" in the territory had almost tripled to 3,191 persons.[31] The June 1939 census showed that the "European" population had risen to 4,608.[32] The last prewar census in New Guinea was taken in June1940 and showed that, with the threat of war, the European population had declined to 4,399.[33] Thus, the total population listed as "European" in Papua and New Guinea at its height during the 1920s and 1930s was about 6,300 persons.

The geography of Papua and New Guinea was also influential in shaping Indigenous and expatriate societies. During the 1920s and 1930s, the expatriate population was dispersed throughout the mainland of the territories, on the numerous islands, on government and mission stations, and on the goldfields. It was not until the late 1950s that half the expatriate population lived in towns. Steep mountains, dense jungles, strong rivers, marshes, and scattered islands made travel and communication difficult and served to isolate the various communities. The lack of roads outside the few towns meant that expatriates had to travel by foot, boats, and later airplanes between the government and mission stations, plantations, and towns. Although there were 194 cars and trucks in Papua in 1934, there was only one road suitable for motor traffic in the vicinity of Port Moresby, and it extended only twenty-five miles out of the town. Geography prevented easy contact among expatriates and made resorting to courts almost impossible for people who did not live in the few towns. The increase in civil litigation between expatriates beginning in the late 1950s can be explained, in part, by the increase in the urban population where there was greater access to the courts.

During the interwar years, the two largest expatriate communities were Port Moresby and Rabaul. At the time of the 1921 census, 313 expatriates lived in Port Moresby, which at the time was very much a frontier town. During the 1920s, Port Moresby's atmosphere gradually changed as it grew and attracted a more settled population, consisting, in addition to government employees, of representatives of a few trading companies, bank employees, a dentist, a photographer, bakers, publicans, residents of a boardinghouse, craftsmen, and casual laborers. Many Australian newspapers carried a regular column entitled "Papuan Notes," describing events in the town, such as formal balls, amateur theatricals, meetings of the library association, and sports such as cricket, "ladies' cricket," tennis, and golf. In his history of Port Moresby, Ian Stuart described the town during the 1930s:

> Whereas previously it had been a hot-bed of intrigue, strife and bitter argument, it now was as a pleasant little community of some 500 expatriates, who, while divided somewhat by class and other social distinctions, and also by whether they worked for the Administration or did not, managed to live together through an economically depressed and depressing period reasonably happily and harmoniously, united in the hope that the rich gold finds in New Guinea would soon be repeated in Papua.[34]

In the early part of the 1900s, Samarai, in the eastern islands of Papua, also served as an administrative and commercial center. Although it declined in importance beginning in the 1920s, Samarai remained a destination for tourists and was the seat of a Catholic bishop. Its amenities included three pubs and three stores, government buildings, private residences, athletic fields, one hospital for expatriates and one for Papuans, and electric lights. According to the census, it had in 1932, a "European" population of 214 persons (116 men and 98 women).

Rabaul, the capital of New Guinea, had a population larger than Port Moresby, with what the 1929 census called the "white population" numbering about 780 persons[35] and the 1940 census putting that population at 709.[36] Based on his research using issues of the *Rabaul Times* newspaper from 1937, one Papua New Guinean scholar has described the town as dominated entirely by its expatriate residents—in particular, its white residents, who tended to keep themselves as separate from Chinese and other nonwhite expatriates as they did from Papuans and New Guineans. (A telling example of white domination of Papua New Guinea's small expatriate societies is the widespread use, in that time and place, of the term "European" to mean expatriate.) Their primary goal was to make the town a little European empire in the tropics, where they could live in comfort and peace without integrating the Indigenous or Asian populations into the community in any way.[37]

Because the few towns in Papua and New Guinea were very small, their expatriate residents knew each other and were part of networks of face-to-face social and commercial relationships arising out of their work, churches, and sports. This made the resolution of disputes and the avoidance of litigation more important than in large communities in Australia, where people usually could keep out of one another's way after litigation.

Although there were significant similarities between the white and Indigenous societies, there also were important differences. Within Indigenous societies, the only division of labor was between men and women. In most Indigenous societies in Papua and New Guinea, there was no nobility, no warrior class, no priestly class, no commercial class, and no governing class. Although the white population was small and primarily middle-class, its members were divided into five broad occupational categories: government officials and employees; plantation owners, their managers, and assistants; goldminers; missionaries; and persons engaged in business (such as traders, store owners, hotel and pub owners, and their employees). While exact figures for the number in each occupational group are not available, the 1933 census in Papua put the number of what it termed "breadwinners" engaged in public administration and professional occupations at 578, the number in "agricultural industries" at 169, and the number in "commercial occupations" at 154. In New Guinea, the 1933 census put the number of "breadwinners" at 3,494, of whom 23 percent (804 persons) were engaged in public administration and professional occupations (including missionaries), 15 percent (527 persons) worked in mining, and 12 percent (420 persons) were engaged in agriculture.[38] There are no statistics on the exact number of missionaries; it was estimated in June 1941 that there were about 600 Catholic and Protestant missionaries in New Guinea.

Expatriates shared much the same attitude toward Papuans and New Guineans, but the differences in their goals in coming to the territories produced conflicts among them as well. Administration officials and plantation owners bitterly distrusted each other's values and goals, while missionaries often found themselves at odds with town people or plantation owners. The differences were rooted in their different personal backgrounds and lifestyles. Administration officials and missionaries criticized plantation owners for exploiting and mistreating Indigenous labor; in turn, plantation owners viewed administrators as overly protective of Indigenous land and labor. Missionaries were distrusted both by plantation owners and by people in the towns because missionaries had close relationships with Papuans and New Guineans, were more sympathetic to them, and were less likely to observe the hierarchical canons of colonial society.

Other sources of tension among expatriates arose from class differences and boredom. These manifested themselves in rivalries, personal jealousies, suspicions, and malicious gossip. Mixed with the heavy consumption of alcohol that was a favorite pastime for many expatriates, conflict was almost inevitable. Prior to the 1920s, this often resulted in bar fights among expatriate men. It was only after a significant number of expatriate wives and children began to arrive in Port Moresby in the mid-1920s that the town shifted from a frontier mentality toward greater concern with imitating middle-class Australian suburban respectability. However, the presence of expatriate wives did not always prevent conflict. As in colonial Africa, much of expatriate social life in the towns revolved around clubs, dances, dinner parties, sports, and amateur theater. The presence of a small number of expatriate wives in a sea of men, most of whom were single, led to gossip and disputes about real or imagined marital infidelities. While this sometimes resulted in "petitions for dissolution of marriage," more often it led to a change of postings, after which the cycle repeated itself.

The distrust and difference seldom found its way into the courts. Like the small-scale societies that characterized Indigenous culture, the small community of expatriates most often resolved their disputes through informal, extralegal means. For example, Ian Downs recounted a case in which the long-simmering hostility between a magistrate (an Irishman) and a planter (who had been a soldier in the British army) resulted in a brawl and threats from both parties of lawsuits. However, Downs wrote he was able to keep the matter out of court and restore peace by threatening to reveal some of what he knew about their private affairs to the police.

Downs quoted another magistrate as saying that "a little legitimate blackmail is better than a day of justice."[39]

Civil Cases in the Colonial Communities

The colonial courts were called upon to deal with many aspects of life (and death), as well as to resolve those disputes that could not be resolved informally. Courts provided the framework for the regulation and structure of expatriates' personal and business relationships. Although the colonial communities in Papua and New Guinea were small and scattered, individuals used the law in the same way that they used the legal system in Australia: to establish the rules they would follow for marriage and divorce; buying and selling property; entering into and enforcing contracts; forming and operating companies; declaring insolvency when those businesses failed; and settling their estates when they died.

Most of the expatriates were Australians, transplanted to Papua or New Guinea for a relatively short time. It is not surprising that most of the ordinances enacted in the territories in the 1920s and 1930s dealt with subjects of importance in Australia—business associations, contracts, electricity, liquor, motor vehicles, the public service, superannuation, wills—and were copied directly from, or based substantially upon, Australian legislation. However, some legislation was unique to situations in the territories. An example of this was the Papuan *Matrimonial Causes Jurisdiction Ordinance of 1910*, which, unlike its Australian source, did not permit divorce in the case of an expatriate married to a Papuan or a mixed-race person. Attempts to repeal the restriction in 1941 were opposed on the grounds that such a change would result in too many applications for divorce, so the provision was carried over into the new *Matrimonial Causes Ordinance* enacted that year. One reason for the prohibition on divorce was that many expatriate men lived in Papua for only a few years and then returned to Australia. The administration feared that some of those men would marry Papuan women while living in the colony and then divorce them before returning home. The administration believed that the restriction both discouraged interracial marriages, which were frowned upon in the expatriate communities, and protected Papuan women from being divorced and left without support by their departing expatriate husbands. It did not seem to have occurred to the administration that expatriate men might not feel the need of marriage in order to live with Papuan women—and leave them unsupported.

Civil litigation remained rare in Papua and New Guinea. In a statement made in 1912 that would remain valid throughout the colonial period in both territories, Murray wrote that "civil cases are very few and do not present any particular points of interest, being of much the same kind as in other parts of the world. Nearly all of the work of the court is in its criminal jurisdiction."[40] Murray's statement is borne out by the *Annual Reports* of the two territories. In 1926–1927, for example, the Central Court of Papua sat only six times, and its civil work consisted of only thirty-one matters, including one petition for dissolution of marriage, one for admission to practice by a Queensland barrister, and one for insolvency. That same year, the *Annual Report* listed only seventy-five matters heard by the Central Court. Two of those involved divorce, and twenty-six involved probate or intestacy.

The *Annual Reports* of Papua during the 1930s did not contain statistical reports on the work of the courts. However, the 1936–1937 *Annual Report* of New Guinea indicated that the nature and volume of the civil work of the renamed Supreme Court had not changed greatly from a decade earlier, even though the population had nearly tripled. With an expatriate population of about 4,200, the report listed ninety civil matters handled by the court, including four for divorce and forty for probate and intestacy.

The work of the civil courts in New Guinea differed from that in Papua. A major part of the work of the Supreme Court in New Guinea consisted of probate and administering intestate estates, due primarily to the fact that an estimated one-third to one-half of all expatriates living in New Guinea were Australian married couples who owned plantations. In Papua, most expatriate residents were single, male government officials, missionaries, or commercial employees who spent a few years in the colony and then returned to Australia to marry, retire, or continue their careers. They were less likely to die in Papua, less likely to arrive with a family, and less likely to involve the courts in winding up their estates or their marriages.

Commercial litigation in Papua and New Guinea was limited by the nature of the economies of the territories. Throughout the colonial period, the territories were primarily plantation economies, heavily dependent upon the export of copra, coffee, tea, and gold. Until the Bougainville copper mine opened in the late 1960s, the territories had marginal economies, with exports never exceeding $60 million in a year. Port Moresby and Rabaul acted as export funnels to Australia since there were no local manufacturing or secondary industries to process the plantation crops. The small commercial population of the towns was service based. Most commercial cases revolved around breaches of contract and debt.

Another factor that contributed to how the courts and the law functioned in the territories was the lack of lawyers. Throughout the 1920s and 1930s, there were at least two lawyers in private practice in Papua: R. D. Bertie and J. P. Guinane. Both lived in Port Moresby and represented individuals and companies in their disputes with each other and with the administration, as well as representing individuals charged with crimes. Ralph Gore served as the Crown law officer in Port Moresby from 1924 until his appointment as a Supreme Court judge in 1928. E. B. Bignold succeeded Gore as Crown law officer, served throughout the 1930s, and was appointed a judge of the Supreme Court of Papua and New Guinea after World War II. Although the Papuan *Annual Reports* stated that one solicitor had been admitted to practice before the Central Court each year between 1925 and 1928, the reports did not list the names of those solicitors, and there is no mention in newspaper articles or government publications of anyone other than Bertie and Guinane practicing law in Papua.

In New Guinea, there were a number of lawyers in private practice in Rabaul beginning in the 1920s and, after 1934, in Wau (the site of the goldfields). There were no other lawyers outside those two centers. One Rabaul solicitor was convicted in 1933 of stealing £800 in trust money from Guinea Airways and sentenced to four years imprisonment with hard labor. Before his arrest and trial, he had been adjudged bankrupt and had fled to the mountains in New Britain to avoid prosecution. Searchers found him living among the Indigenous population.

Although there were few appeals from Papua or New Guinea to the High Court of Australia, the appeals that were taken involved a variety of subjects: commercial and mining suits; disputes over the winding up of companies; a claim by a wife for maintenance; an appeal by an assistant resident magistrate against his reduction in rank and salary; an appeal about whether the Australian Parliament had the power to enact a law requiring an Australian state court to recognize the process of a court in New Guinea; and appeals of criminal convictions and sentences. Only two of the appeals had a sizable effect on the colonial legal systems.

In 1934, Reginald James Sutherland was convicted in New Guinea of stealing gold from his employer and sentenced to four years imprisonment. He was deported to Sydney to serve his sentence. Sutherland appealed his conviction to the High Court, arguing that the evidence was not sufficient to convict him and that he was entitled to be tried before a jury. The High Court found that the evidence was sufficient to support his conviction. The court held that the *Papuan Criminal Procedure Ordinance of 1889*, which had been adopted in New Guinea, excluded trial by jury. Although some provisions of the Queensland Criminal Code adopted in New Guinea made reference to trial by jury, laws that were adopted in the territory were done so only to the extent that they were applicable to the territory. The High Court held that trial by jury was not applicable to New Guinea.[41] Thus, as in Papua, there was no right to a jury trial in New Guinea, except in capital cases.

The second appeal involved Doris Regina Booth, one of the most remarkable expatriates living in the territories at that time.[42] Trained as a nurse, she married a soldier, Charles Booth, who had been a prospector in Papua before the war and became a plantation manager for the Expropriation Board in 1920. Doris Booth became a shareholder in four trade stores and a licensed labor recruiter. In 1924 she secured a miner's right to prospect for gold. She worked at Bulolo while her husband prospected at Edie Creek. She also established a hospital and cared for those suffering from dysentery. The Booths sold their mining leases in 1927, and Doris Booth became a director of Morobe Gold Ltd. By the late 1920s, the marriage began to fail, and Doris Booth sought to take control of the family's business from her husband. He then sued her in the Central Court of New Guinea in 1933, seeking restitution of property. At the time, New Guinea had no law that explicitly protected a married woman's property rights. Judge Frederick Phillips held that legislation passed in 1921 superseded the common law principle of male control of joint property and ruled in favor of Doris Booth. Her husband appealed to the High Court of Australia, which upheld Judge Phillips. Perhaps spurred by the *Booth* case, the colonial administration enacted the *Status of Married Women Ordinance* in 1936, which gave wives control over their property. The Booths never divorced, and Doris Booth became a successful mine manager and company director. In 1951 she became the first woman member of the new Legislative Council, a position she held until 1957.

Criminal Cases in the Expatriate Communities

Cases of willful murder, murder, manslaughter, bodily harm, rape, riot, and stealing made up the vast majority of the criminal cases heard by the superior courts of the two territories in the years between the wars. Papuans and New Guineans most often were the defendants in those cases. However, in a few instances, expatriates were charged with serious crimes. Table 1 (compiled from the territories' *Annual Reports*) lists the total number of persons charged with criminal offenses in the Central Courts/ Supreme Courts in selected years. The numbers in parentheses represent the number of expatriates charged.

TABLE 1. SUPREME COURTS OF PAPUA AND NEW GUINEA

Criminal Charges

Year	Papua	New Guinea
1921–1922	134 (2)	—
1923–1924	178 (1)	—
1925–1926	169 (1)	125 (6)
1927–1928	203 (1)	111 (9)
1929–1930	293 (3)	154 (12)
1933–1934	n/a	165 (2)
1935–1936	n/a	101 (18)

The *Annual Reports* did not list, on a regular basis, the specific offenses with which expatriates were charged. However, a few examples of criminal cases in Papua involving them and the sentences they received (where known) are as follows:

- the attempted murder of another expatriate (for which the defendant received a sentence of one year imprisonment with hard labor);
- arson of a dwelling house;
- interfering with the wife of a Papuan;
- willful damage of property (for which the defendant received a sentence of three months in jail); and
- being a prohibited immigrant (for which the defendant was sentenced to two months imprisonment).

In New Guinea, criminal cases against expatriates involved:

- stealing from employers;
- arson;
- the rape of a New Guinea woman;
- seizing a ship and attempting to murder its captain (the defendant was convicted and sentenced to four years imprisonment);
- drunkenness and fighting with police (for which the three Australians received a sentence of two years imprisonment with hard labor);
- violation of immigration laws (a ship captain was convicted, fined £1730, and sentenced to six months imprisonment);
- assault on New Guineans (a fine of £40 and one year imprisonment);
- theft of gold (which resulted in a sentence of twenty-one months imprisonment); and
- depriving New Guinean laborers of their liberty. (In a 1929 case, Chief Judge David Wanliss imposed a fine of £150 on an expatriate, stating that, in the future, offenders would be sentenced to imprisonment because of the harm to Australian prestige and the risk of bloodshed. In a 1936 prosecution for breach of the same law, Chief Judge Wanliss did sentence an expatriate to two years in prison.)

Although the administrations occasionally charged expatriates with assaulting Papuans or New Guineans, the courts rarely imposed anything more than a modest fine on those convicted and in many of cases imposed no penalty at all. The administrations were more likely to deport expatriates accused or convicted of serious offenses to Australia, rather than prosecute or jail them in Papua or New Guinea and run what they saw as the risk of lowering white prestige in the eyes of Papuans and New Guineans.

The colonial administrations took a lenient approach toward most-crimes committed by expatriates, although they did prosecute offenses they considered highly serious. In 1936, Gallfred Mervyn Collins Ffrost was charged with unlawfully killing a New Guinea. Ffrost fled to Queensland, and in January 1937, the New Guinea administration sought to have him returned to Rabaul to stand trial. Ffrost argued that the League of Nations Mandate for New Guinea did not permit the application of the Queensland Criminal Code there. The governor-general of Australia had the power to make ordinances for New Guinea and, Ffrost argued, could apply commonwealth law but not state law. The High Court held that the power to return Ffrost to New Guinea was under the *Fugitive Offenders Act*, an imperial statute, and returned him to New Guinea. [43] In November 1937, Judge Phillips found Ffrost not guilty of unlawful killing but convicted him of assault causing bodily harm and sentenced him to six months in prison.[44]

Four other cases involving expatriates illustrate the type of cases the administrations prosecuted and the range of punishments they received. In January 1922, Reginald Ellis Chancellor, a planter and trader, was convicted by the Central Court in Port Moresby of taking a young Papuan woman away from her village against her will, detaining her on his plantation for several weeks against her will, and forcing sex on her while she was detained on his plantation. When she ran away, one of Chancellor's Papuan employees brought her back. Chancellor argued that he had arranged with the young woman's relatives for her to come to his plantation after another expatriate man had abandoned her. Although Judge Charles Herbert convicted Chancellor of the charges, he stated that he was sorry "to see a man such as the accused in this position, and he would give him a sentence very light in comparison with that which he might have imposed."[45] He sentenced Chancellor to only six months in prison with hard labor on each count, with the sentences running concurrently. The leniency of that sentence can be seen when it is compared with another case, decided the same day, in which Judge Herbert sentenced a young teenage

Papuan boy to twelve months imprisonment and a whipping for "an attempted offense" (the exact nature of which was not given) involving the young daughter of the Papuan boy's employer.

The second case occurred in New Guinea in 1935 when an expatriate was convicted of having "assaulted natives, doing them grievous bodily harm." In one instance, the accused had a New Guinean man tied to a post and then struck him twice on the nose with his fist and then with a pair of pincers. As a result, he broke off one of the man's teeth. The expatriate was sentenced to imprisonment for one year and ordered to pay a £40 fine.[46]

In 1936, George Roberts, a cattleman working on a plantation near Samarai, was charged with the murder of a Papuan man, who had been working with him. At the trial, two Papuans testified that they had seen Roberts strike the deceased in the face and kick him several times before riding away on horseback. Justice Ralph Gore convicted Roberts of manslaughter but sentenced him to only eighteen months imprisonment. Although Robert's wife sought to have her husband deported to Australia to serve his sentence, the administration refused to do so.[47]

Finally, the most highly publicized criminal case involving an expatriate during the interwar years occurred in New Guinea in early 1936 when Ludwig Schmidt, a German national, was convicted on three separate counts of the murder of several New Guinean men in 1934. At his trial, Schmidt's sole defense was that he had intended only to frighten the men. Chief Judge Wanliss convicted Schmidt of murder and sentenced him to death. Schmidt chose not to appeal his conviction or sentence to the High Court of Australia, although he had the right to do so. Schmidt became the first and only expatriate hanged in New Guinea during the colonial period. The willingness of the court to impose the death penalty may have been influenced by the fact that Schmidt was a German.[48]

Surprisingly, one group of expatriates who occasionally found themselves charged with serious crimes, both against each other and against Papuans and New Guineans, were missionaries. Here again, their sentences tended to be very light. In April 1936, a young Catholic priest from the Netherlands, Father Anthony Cranssen, pleaded guilty, at the suggestion of his solicitor, to sending an armed party of New Guineans to attack two Lutheran missionary teachers and burn down their houses. The offense occurred in an uncontrolled area of the Highlands in which the colonial administration had no presence. Chief Judge Wanliss sentenced the priest to five years imprisonment with hard labor and deported him to Sydney to serve his sentence. The perceived severity of Cranssen's sentence resulted in an appeal to the High Court of Australia, which, in August 1936, held that the five-year sentence was out of proportion to the seriousness of the offense and substituted a sentence of six months imprisonment. In his dissent, Justice Starke wrote that it was important that the High Court not do anything that would weaken the authority of the New Guinea court in the eyes of New Guineans.[49]

A few weeks prior to its decision in the Cranssen case, the High Court refused an application for appeal by Henry Foege, a Lutheran missionary in New Guinea, who had been sentenced to two years imprisonment by Chief Judge Wanliss for having unlawfully deprived a New Guinean of his liberty. However, in 1936, the New Guinea colonial administration reduced Foege's sentence and ordered his release on October 1 of that year. The administration justified his decision by saying it was consistent with the usual practice applied to prisoners deported to Australia and that the missionary was eligible for a reduction in his sentence for good behavior.[50] Finally, also in August 1936, Chief Judge Wanliss found another missionary not guilty of killing a New Guinean.[51]

Although the most serious cases against expatriates were prosecuted in the superior courts, most of the criminal charges brought against them were for violations of the summary offenses ordinances and were handled by the district courts. Table 2 is compiled from figures taken from the *Annual Report* for New Guinea; figures for Papua are not available.

TABLE 2. DISTRICT COURT OF NEW GUINEA

Criminal Charges against Expatriates

Year	New Guinea
1927–1928	183
1929–1930	213
1933–1934	119
1935–1936	208

Among the offenses that resulted in the prosecution of expatriates were assault, drunkenness, gambling, fraud (passing valueless checks), negligent driving resulting in collisions, offensive behavior, stealing, permitting liquor to be served in a hotel after hours, traffic offenses, and breaches of the labor ordinances governing the hiring and working conditions of Papuans and New Guineans. The penalty for these offenses was a fine or jail for nonpayment or for repeated offenses. Only in cases of stealing did the district courts sentence expatriates to jail, and in such cases, defendants often were sent to Australia to serve their sentences.

Conclusion

Our topic in this chapter has been the ways in which the Australian legal system was changed and adapted to meet the particular governance and economic development aims of the colonial administration during the years between the two world wars. The primary focus of the chapter has been the functions that the colonial legal system performed for the expatriate communities of Papua and New Guinea. We will continue in the next chapter to discuss the colonial legal system in those two decades, but that chapter's focus will be on the role that the imported legal system played in the lives of Indigenous Papua New Guineans and on the relations between colonial law and custom.

Sources

Books and Articles

Advocate, "To Have Portion of Sentence Remitted," *Advocate*, September 9, 1936, 7.

Advocate, "Population Figures," *Advocate*, January 26, 1942, 4.

Argus, "Not Guilty of Killing Native," *Argus*, November 6, 1937, 15.

Ballarat Star, "Flogging Natives," *Ballarat Star*, September 26, 1921, 1.

Barrier Miner, "The Governor-General Given Reception at Rabaul," *Barrier Miner*, July 17, 1929, 1.

Percy Chatterton, *Day That I Have Loved* (Sydney: Pacific Publications, 1974).

Arthur Kent Chignell, *An Outpost in Papua* (London: Smith, Elder & Co., 1911).

Daily Telegraph, "Clean This Up!" *Daily Telegraph*, June 29, 1923, 4.

Bill Gammage, "The Rabaul Strike, 1929," *Journal of Pacific History* 10(3) (1975) 3–29.

Basil Hall, "Amalgamation and a Mandate," *The Australian Quarterly* 11(3) (1939) 88–95.

Herald, "New Guinea Scandal," *Herald*, June 28, 1923, 17.

Benedict Y. Imbun, "Labor Relations in Papua New Guinea: A Historical Review of Literature 1920–2006," *Labor and Management in Development Journal* 8 (2007) 1–13.

Charles F. Jackson, *Native Labor Law and Practice in Papua* (Sydney: Law Book Company of Australasia, 1924).

Brian Jinks, Peter Biskrup, and Hank Nelson (eds.), *Readings in New Guinea History* (Sydney: Angus and Robrtson, 1973).

Kalgoorlie Miner, "New Guinea Mandate," *Kalgoorlie Miner*, September 10, 1920, 4.

Roderic Lacey, *Our Young Men Snatched Away: Laborers in Papua New Guinea's Colonial Economy, 1884–1942* (Port Moresby: University of Papua New Guinea, 1983).

Lewis Lett, *The Papuan Achievement* (Melbourne: University of Melbourne Press, 1942).

Lewis Lett, *Sir Hubert Murray of Papua: Statesman and Empire Builder* (London: Collins, 1949).

C. D. Lewis, *The Plantation Dream: Developing British New Guinea and Papua 1884–1942* (Canberra: The Journal of Pacific History, 1996).

Lithgow Mercury, "Brutal Employer Is Sentenced at Rabaul," *Lithgow Mercury*, March 20, 1935, 1.

A. McLennan, "The Population Problem in Australian New Guinea," *The Australian Quarterly* 10(1) (1938) 44–52.

R. R. McNicoll, "Sir Walter McNicoll as Administrator of the Mandated Territory," in Kenneth S. Inglis (ed.), *The History of Melanesia* (Port Moresby: University of Papua New Guinea Press, 1971) 113–134.

Mercury, "New Guinea's Population," *Mercury*, April 23, 1928, 10.

Hubert Murray, *Australian Policy in Papua* (Port Moreby: Government Printer, 1930).

Hubert Murray, *The Machinery of Indirect Rule in Papua* (Port Moresby: Government Printer, 1935).

Hubert Murray, *Native Labor in Papua* (London: Anti-Slavery and Aborigines Protection Society, 1929).

Hubert Murray, *Papua of To-Day: An Australian Colony in the Making* (London: P. S. King and Son, 1925).

Northwestern Courier, "Mr. Hughes Speech," *North Western Courier*, October 2, 1919, 3.

Christine Oke, "The Native Administrations of MacGregor, Murphy and Hasluck in Papua/New Guinea: Continuity and Contrast," *University of Wollongong Historical Journal* 1(1) (1975) 7–41.

Gabriel Olakunle Olusanya, "The New Guinea Mandate: Australia's 'Sacred Trust'" (master's thesis, University of British Columbia, 1961).

Susan Pedersen, *The Guardians: The League of Nations and the Crisis of Empire* (Oxford: Oxford University Press, 2015).

Queenslander, "New Guinea. Provisions of the Ordinance," *Queenslander*, April 1, 1922, 32.

Noah Riseman, *Defending Whose Country? Indigenous Soldiers in the Pacific War* (Lincoln: University of Nebraska Press, 2012).

Ralph Shlomowitz, "The Internal Labor Trade in Papua (1884–1941) and New Guinea (1920–1941): An Economic Analysis," *Journal de la Societe des Oceanistes* 42(82–83) (1986) 177–181.

D. W. Smith, *Labor and Law in Papua New Guinea* (Canberra: Australian National University Press, 1975).

Ian Stuart, *Port Moresby, Yesterday and Today* (Sydney: Pacific Publications, rev. ed.,1973).

Sun, "N. Guinea Law," *Sun*, August 19, 1936, 18.

Sydney Morning Herald, "Rabaul Strike. Alleged Floggings," *Sydney Morning Herald*, January 7, 1921, 12.

Sydney Morning Herald, "New Guinea. Flogging Incidents. Mr. Hughes Explains," *Sydney Morning Herald*, November 22, 1921, 9.

Sydney Morning Herald, "Murder of Natives," *Sydney Morning Herald*, March 26, 1936, 11.

Roger G. Thompson, "Making a Mandate: The Formation of Australia's New Guinea Policies 1919–1925," *Journal of Pacific History* 25(1) (1999) 68–84.

G. W. L. Townsend, *District Officer: From Untamed New Guinea to Lake Success, 1921–46* (Sydney: Pacific Publications, 1968).

Townsville Daily Bulletin, "A Samarai Case," *Townsville Daily Bulletin*, June 9, 1936, 2.

John Dademo Waiko, *A Short History of Papua New Guinea* (Oxford: Oxford University Press, 1993).

Warwick Daily News, "Control of New Guinea," *Warwick Daily News*, July 17, 1923, 4.

Francis West, *Hubert Murray: The Australian Pro-Consul* (Melbourne: Oxford University Press, 1968).

West Australian, "New Guinea's Population," *West Australian*, September 14, 1934, 15.

Government Documents

Commonwealth Parliamentary Debates, vol. 136 (November 2, 1932) 1762–1782.

Commonwealth Bureau of Census and Statistics, *Census of the Commonwealth of Australia 4 April 1921, Census Bulletin No. 4 Territory of Papua.*

Commonwealth Bureau of Census and Statistics, *Census of the Commonwealth of Australia 30 June 1933, Census Bulletin No. 5 Territory of Papua.*

Commonwealth Bureau of Census and Statistics, *Census of the Commonwealth of Australia 4 April 1921, Census Bulletin No. 8 Territory of New Guinea (Mandated Area).*

Parliament of the Commonwealth of Australia, *Interim and Final Reports of the Royal Commission on Late German New Guinea* (1920).

Parliament of the Commonwealth of Australia, *Report to the League of Nations on the Administration of New Guinea, from September 1914 to 30 June 1921.*

Territory of New Guinea, Annual Report, 1926–1927 (Melbourne: Government Printer, 1927).

Territory of Papua, Report for Year 1926–1927 (Melbourne: Government Printer, 1927).

Territory of Papua, Report for Year 1937–1938 (Melbourne: Government Printer, 1938).

Yearbook of Australia, 1940.

Cases

Booth v. Booth (1934–1935) 53 C.L.R. 1

Cranssen v. The King (1936) 55 C.L.R. 509

Ffrost v. Stevenson (1937) 58 C.L.R. 528

Geita Sebea v. Territory of Papua [1941] 67 C.L.R. 544

Sutherland v. The King (1934) 52 C.L.R. 356

Statutes

Criminal Code (Papua; New Guinea) (*amended and adopted 1974 as the Criminal Code Act 1974, No. 78 of 1974* (PNG))

Deportation Ordinance (Australia)

Expropriation Ordinance (Australia)

Fugitive Offenders Act (Great Britain)

Judiciary Act 1903–1969 of Australia

Judiciary Ordinance 1921–1938 (New Guinea) (*amended and adopted 1975 by Constitution, Section Sch. 2.6 and Schedule 5, Part 1* (PNG))

Lands Acquisition Ordinance 1914 (Papua)

Lands (Kila Kila Aerodrome) Acquisition Ordinance 1939 (Papua)

Land Ordinance 1922 (New Guinea)

Lands Registration Ordinance 1924 (New Guinea)

Laws Repeal and Adopting Ordinance 1921 (New Guinea)

Marriage Ordinance 1912–1936 (Papua)

Matrimonial Causes Jurisdiction Ordinance 1910–1941 (Papua)

Native Administration Ordinance 1921 (New Guinea)

Native Administration Regulations 1924–1963 (New Guinea)

Native Labor Ordinance 1935–1939 (New Guinea)

Native Labor Ordinance (Papua)

Native Regulation Ordinance 1908, No. 25 of 1909 (Papua)

Native Regulations 1939 (Papua)

Native Taxes Ordinance of 1918 (Papua)

Navigation Act (Australia)

New Guinea Act 1920 (Australia)

Papua Act 1905 (Australia)

White Women's Protection Ordinance 1926, No. 2 of 1926 (Papua)

Notes

1. "New Guinea Mandate," *Kalgoorlie Miner*, September 10, 1920, 4.
2. *Id.*
3. John Hubert Murray, *Papua of To-Day: An Australian Colony in the Making* (London: P. S. King and Son, 1925) 210–211.
4. *Id.* at 214.
5. *Id.* at 219.
6. *New Guinea Act* (No. 25 of 1920) section 14.
7. *An Act to Amend the New Guinea Act* (No. 51 of 1932) sections 19–33.
8. *Laws Repeal and Adopting Ordinance of 1921* (No. 1 of 1921) section 10.
9. *Judiciary Ordinance* (1921–1938) sections 6–10.
10. "Mr. Hughes Speech," *North Western Courier*, October 2, 1919, 3.
11. See "Clean This Up!" *Daily Telegraph*, June 29, 1923, 4; and "New Guinea Scandal," *Herald*, June 28, 1923, 17.
12. "Control of New Guinea," *Warwick Daily News*, July 17, 1923, 4.
13. John Ainsworth, *Report on Administrative Arrangements and Matters Affecting the Interests of Natives in the Territory of New Guinea* (Melbourne: Government of the Commonwealth of Australia, 1924).
14. G. W. L. Townsend, *District Officer* (Sydney: Pacific Publications, 1968) 28.
15. *Geita Sebea v. Territory of Papua*, (1941) 67 C.L.R. 544, 557.
16. Hubert Murray, *Native Labor in Papua* (London: Anti-Slavery and Aborigines Protection Society, 1929) 4.
17. *Id.*
18. *Id.* at 6.
19. "New Guinea. Provisions of the Ordinance," *Queenslander*, April 1, 1922, 32.
20. "Flogging Natives," *Ballarat Star*, September 26, 1921, 1.
21. *Id.*
22. "New Guinea. Flogging Incidents. Mr. Hughes Explains," *Sydney Morning Herald*, November 22, 1921, 9.
23. Bill Gammage, "The Rabaul Strike, 1929," *Journal of Pacific History* 10(3) (1975) 3, 26.
24. "Rabaul Strike. Alleged Floggings," *Sydney Morning Herald*, January 7, 1921, 12.

25. Commonwealth Bureau of Census and Statistics, *Census of the Commonwealth of Australia 4 April 1921, Census Bulletin No. 4 Territory of Papua*, 14.
26. Commonwealth Bureau of Census and Statistics, *Census of the Commonwealth of Australia 30 June 1933, Census Bulletin No. 5 Summary for the Territory of Papua*, 8.
27. *Id.* at 3.
28. *Yearbook of Australia, 1941*, 229.
29. Commonwealth Bureau of Census and Statistics, *Census of the Commonwealth of Australia 4 April 1921, Census Bulletin No. 8 Territory of New Guinea (Mandated Area)* 13.
30. "New Guinea's Population," *Mercury*, April 23, 1928, 10.
31. *Yearbook of Australia, 1940*, 266.
32. *Id.*
33. *Id.* at 236.
34. Ian Stuart, *Port Moresby: Yesterday and Today* (Sydney: Pacific Publications, rev. ed., 1973) 116.
35. "The Governor-General Given Reception at Rabaul," *Barrier Miner*, July 17, 1929, 1.
36. "Population Figures," *Advocate*, January 26, 1942, 4.
37. Jeremiah Tetaga, "Reflections from the *Rabaul Times*: The Rabaul Community in 1937," *Yagl-Ambu: Papua New Guinea Journal of the Social Sciences and Humanities* 1(2) (1974) 135–139.
38. "New Guinea's Population," *West Australian*, September 14, 1934, 15.
39. Ian Downs, *The Last Mountain: A Life in Papua New Guinea* (Brisbane: University of Queensland Press, 1987) 257.
40. Hubert Murray, *Papua or British New Guinea* (London: T. Fisher Unwin, 1912) 197.
41. *Sutherland v. The King*, (1934) 52 C.L.R. 356.
42. *Booth v. Booth*, (1934–1935) 53 C.L.R. 1.
43. *Ffrost v. Stevenson*, (1937) 58 C.L.R. 528.
44. "Not Guilty of Killing Native," *Argus*, November 6, 1937, 15.
45. "Native's Abduction," *Newcastle Sun*, March 9, 1922, 5.
46. "Brutal Employer Is Sentenced at Rabaul," *Lithgow Mercury*, March 20, 1935, 1.
47. "A Samarai Case," *Townsville Daily Bulletin*, June 9, 1936, 2.
48. "Murder of Natives," *Sydney Morning Herald*, March 26, 1936, 11.
49. *Cranssen v. The King* (1936) 55 C.L.R. 509.
50. "To Have Portion of Sentence Remitted," *Advocate*, September 9, 1936, 7.
51. "New Guinea Law," *Sun*, August 19, 1936, 18.

7 The Colonial Legal Systems and Papua New Guineans

Contact, Control, and Customary Law 1921–1942

Extending control throughout Papua and New Guinea was a major goal of the British, German and Australian administrations from the beginning of the colonial period. However, it was not until the late 1920s that Australians were aware of just how large that task would be. Convinced that no one could, or did, live in the rugged mountain ranges that formed the seemingly impassible spine of the main island, the colonial presence was limited until 1930 to the coasts and the islands. Even in the coastal areas, the only sustained contact between colonizers and Papuans or New Guineans was on the plantations and mission stations and in Port Moresby and Rabaul, the administrative and business centers of the territories.

It was not the colonial administration that first extended contact beyond the coast and islands. It was, instead, gold prospectors who in the late 1920s first explored the Highlands, the large and mountainous area in the center of the country, prompting the colonial office to assign patrol officers (*kiaps*) to do the same. Those explorations, which continued until the outbreak of World War II and then resumed in the early 1950s, introduced colonialists to the verdant Highlands valleys, inhabited, it turned out, by hundreds of thousands of Indigenous people. The extension of nominal rule to the people in the Highlands raised the question of how—or even whether—a colonial administration with severely limited funds and personnel, could govern this very large population over whom the administration had, at best, only limited sway. The answers to that question were shaped not only by financial restraints but perhaps even more by the condescension and paternalism that characterized the attitudes of Australians and other westerners towards Papuans and New Guineans.

Australian Attitudes Toward Papuans and New Guineans

The views that expatriates held about Papuans and New Guineans were not unique to those two territories. The expatriates were the heirs to European beliefs about non-Western people that can be traced to the 1500s and to the earliest efforts to justify the African slave trade. During the eighteenth century, many European philosophers, including David Hume, Immanuel Kant, and Voltaire, adopted the theory of polygenism, the idea that there is more than one "human race" and that the races have different origins. Combining polygenism with Darwin's theory of biological evolution, Herbert Spencer's popular writings about social Darwinism and survival of the fittest, and the work of naturalists such as Georges Cuvier, most nineteenth-century Europeans believed that there was a hierarchy of distinct human races. With Caucasians on the top as the master race, they classified Africans, Asians, and other darker peoples as "backward" or "subject" races. Europeans were confident that their racial superiority had led to their discovering what they believed to be the universal truths of government, law, morality, and religion. They also assumed that racial superiority was what made them economic, political and military powers and thus gave them the right to rule non-Caucasian peoples.

No more than a handful of the expatriates in Papua and New Guinea had any knowledge of the theories of Hume, Kant, Voltaire, or Cuvier. However, the ideas of those men had become the basis of accepted European thought about race. In addition, most of the expatriate men in Papua and New Guinea had grown up reading the "boy's own" fiction and nonfiction adventure books and magazines that were popular in England and Australia from the mid-nineteenth century until the mid-twentieth century. Many of those works extolled the idea of the superiority of the British and the inferiority of Britain's dark-skinned colonial subjects. One of the most popular of the authors was George Alfred Henty. In his 1884 novel, *By Sheer Pluck*, a schoolboy saves several of his fellow students from drowning. The grateful father of one of those students arranges for him to accompany Mr. Goodenough, a famous naturalist, on an expedition to Africa. When they arrive at the Gold Coast colony (now Ghana), Goodenough describes the Africans they see in the racial terms reflecting European thinking that remained dominant well into the twentieth century:

> "They are just like children," Mr. Goodenough said. "They are always either laughing or quarreling. They are good natured and passionate, indolent, but will work hard for a time; clever up to a certain point, densely stupid beyond. The intelligence of an average negro is about equal to that of a European child of ten years old. . . . Living among white men, their imitative faculties enable them to attain a considerable amount of civilization. Left alone to their own devices they retrograde into a state little above their native savagery."[1]

Most expatriates in Papua and New Guinea knew nothing about the culture of the Indigenous inhabitants nor did they have any interest in learning about the people or their cultures. The racial attitudes of the times led them to a near unanimous belief that Papuans and New Guineans were living in a Hobbesian world in which life was "poor, nasty, brutish and short." In such a state of nature, there was no property or justice; only personal violence and tribal warfare. Like the character in Henty's novel, Australian officials and other expatriates frequently used the terms "childlike" and "savage" to describe Papuans and New Guineans. In 1932, when the Australian Parliament debated legislation to establish the first Legislative Council in New Guinea, some Labor members unsuccessfully sought to include a provision that would have created seats on the new council specifically for New Guineans. In opposing the provision, other members stated:

> The native races are of a distinctly primitive type. . . . His mentality is that of the average lad of from 14 to 16 years of age. They are called boys and are essentially boys. . . . The best way in which to describe the culture of the natives is to say that practically speaking they are people of the Stone Age . . . having the mentality of children, they cannot be expected to go beyond that. . . . The present intellectual

> development of the natives generally may well be such that they could not be entrusted with the control of the ordinary activities of the territory.[2]

Those views were held not only by government officials, plantation owners, and traders, but even by missionaries, who had the closest and most sustained contact with Papuans and New Guineans. In his 1924 memoir, *An Outpost in Papua*, Arthur Kent Chignell, an Anglican priest and missionary in Papua, wrote that life was lonely for missionaries because "friendship is not possible with the coloured folk." The reason for that was what he described as

> the inevitable and ever-present difference between the civilized man, whose ancestors have been more or less outwardly "respectable" for centuries, breaking out into savagery merely in places, and only now and then, and the real savages whose "respectability" and enforced conformity to some of the ways of civilisation have been adopted very lately and rather unwillingly, and maintained only with great difficulty. These men were cannibals twenty years ago; and if the Government and the missionaries went away tomorrow it would not be long before some of them would begin spearing the people and burning the villages up and down the coast, as they and their fathers used to do in the old days.[3]

Notwithstanding their feelings of racial superiority, expatriates were frightened of Papuans and New Guineans. A tiny minority in both territories, expatriates feared that the locals would rise up against them. That explains, in part, the harshness of their response to the peaceful strike by workers in Rabaul in January 1929. Expatriates also were afraid that, cut off from Western civilization, they too could descend to the same level as the "savages." Joseph Conrad's 1902 novella, *The Heart of Darkness*, set the tone for that fear with his story about the descent into madness of a European in the Belgian Congo (now the Democratic Republic of Congo), who became too closely associated with Africans. Expatriates believed they had to keep both a psychological and physical distance from local people or risk the same fate of "going native." Other than at sporting events, there was virtually no social contact between the races until the late 1960s. It was not until after World War II that Papuans and New Guineans were even invited to administration functions.

The physical separation of expatriates from Papuans and New Guineans during the 1920s and 1930s also applied, at least formally, to marriage and cohabitation. In New Guinea, the *Marriage Ordinance* prohibited the marriage of "a native with any person other than a native" without the express permission of a district officer.[4] In Papua, marriages and cohabitation between expatriate men and Papua women had occurred since the beginning of British rule. Between 1892 and 1940, there were thirty-seven such marriages (the youngest Papuan bride was only thirteen years old). However, only fourteen of those marriages took place after Australia assumed control of Papua in 1906, and none occurred after 1924. In part, that was due to the increased number of white women in Papua beginning in the 1920s and the change in the type of expatriate men who came to Papua. Traders, miners, and seamen gave way to businessmen and planters who often brought their wives and families. After 1906, Hubert Murray made it clear that his field officers should remain aloof from Papuans and that their behavior should never bring them "down to the native level." Government officials who cohabited with Papuan women were asked to resign their posts. However, those attempts to ban sexual relations between expatriates and Papuans and New Guineans were not entirely successful, as evidenced by the sizeable mixed-race populations in both territories.

Murray was the person who wrote the most about Papuans and New Guineans during the 1920s and 1930s. Like other expatriates, Murray believed in the superiority of Europeans and their civilization. However, as a result of his administrative and judicial experiences in Papua, as well as his study of anthropology and colonial administration, Murray's views about Papuans were slightly more nuanced than those of his contemporaries. Two years before he died in 1940, Murray summed up his attitude when he wrote that "the best Papuans are superior to the worst Europeans, but . . . Europeans as a whole have an innate superiority over Papuans."[5] At the same time, Murray wrote that "the truth" was a Papuan was not "half devil and half child"; instead, he was a man with

> a man's passions and a man's power to hate and love, but he is a very ignorant man, and he is a man whose customs and ways of thought are strange to us, even in the rare instances in which we try to understand them. And if we must use the method of analogy, we should argue not from the child but from the peasant.[6]

Murray viewed Papuans and New Guineans as naturally inferior to whites. In the very long run, he believed they were capable of being "improved" but never to a point where they would be the equals of whites. At the same time, however, they could not remain as they were: they had to embrace Western civilization or die out. The colonial administration, therefore, had to adopt as a goal the education of Papuans and New Guineans in Western concepts, standards, and institutions as a replacement for their own inferior culture. In Murray's view, it was crucial that the replacement of traditional cultures with Western norms happen slowly. He feared that if there was excessive or in his view unjustified interference with traditional societies happened too quickly or in excess, those societies would they would collapse immediately.

The range of expatriate attitudes toward Papuans and New Guineans—from "childlike" to "inferior" to "savages" to capable of being "improved"—impacted the content and operation of colonial law in three areas: the policies of the colonial administrations governing native administration; the ordinances adopted by the territories' Legislative Councils; and the recognition given to custom by colonial courts.

Policies Affecting Native Administration

From the beginning of the colonial period everywhere, British officials were confronted with the question of how to govern the people they ruled. Basically, they had two options: direct rule (i.e., government by colonial officials) or indirect rule (i.e., allowing the Indigenous population to govern itself as far as possible through existing leaders and local power structures). Based on British practice in India and the influence of Frederick Lugard, a colonial governor in Nigeria, many British colonies were using indirect rule by the 1920s. In the British colonial system Indigenous people were afforded some degree of political power and self-direction, within a framework of oversight and supervision by colonial officials.

As with all things, Murray tried in this area, too, to satisfy the demands of white settlers and business interests, while giving lip service to a more enlightened colonial policy. While he wrote that indirect rule would have been the preferable system for Papua, like most other Australians at the time, he wrongly believed that Papuans had "no Chiefs, no Councils, no

Courts, no Administrative machinery of any kind, nothing but a very problematic 'collective unconsciousness.'"[7] To his mind, that made effective indirect rule impossible in Papua, making it necessary, he believed, to adopt direct rule. Not surprisingly, colonial officials in New Guinea held the same views.

Colonial officials gave Papuans and New Guineans no positions on the Legislative or Executive Councils of the territories in the two decades between the wars. Papuans and New Guineans took no part in making the policies and laws that governed them. The colonial administrations also refused to establish courts presided over by Papuans or New Guineans that would have enabled them to apply their own customary laws and processes to resolve disputes. No Papuan or New Guinean served on any of the Legislative Councils until 1951 or on the official colonial courts until 1967, less than a decade before independence, when the first Indigenous local court magistrates were appointed.

In practice, however, the limited reach and resources of the administration meant that colonial officials were forced to permit Papuans and New Guineans to play some small roles in governance and dispute resolution. During the period of German rule in New Guinea, officials had given limited authority to New Guineans by appointing *luluais* to help administer the laws of the German colonial administration and to help keep order in the villages. Although *luluais* were required to bring serious disputes and breaches of the law to the attention of German patrol officers, they had the power to resolve every day village disputes, such as those about money, pigs, or other customary goods. If local people were unhappy with the decision of the *luluais*, they could appeal to the German patrol officer.

After the establishment of the mandate, the Australian administrations nominally retained the *luluais* but took away their formal judicial powers. *Luluais* became law enforcers instead of law deciders. In his 1924 report on New Guinea, Colonel John Ainsworth recommended the restoration of *luluai* courts. His proposal was rejected. Australian colonial officials believed New Guineans were not ready for that responsibility, assuming that such courts would result only in favoritism and corruption. However, the 1927 *Annual Report* for New Guinea acknowledged that a number of *luluai* in New Britain and New Ireland continued to sit "as a kind of court" to hear minor complaints. The report stated that colonial officials realized "the importance of fostering these native institutions and tribunals and encouraging the natives to take a more active part in the management of their own affairs."[8] Unofficial courts also existed, both with and without administration approval, on Bougainville.

Although Murray did not create Indigenous courts in Papua, he did establish what were called "village councils" near Port Moresby. The councils, whose members were elected by the people of the villages, were meant to form a communications bridge between the administration and the villagers, as well as to serve as a forum for making suggestions for the improvement of village life. Although not officially sanctioned to do so, members of some of the village councils also exercised judicial and quasi-judicial functions. By 1927, the council in Hanuabada, a large village near Port Moresby, was settling minor disputes. Although the council had no statutory powers or formal means to enforce its decisions, it provided a local, quasi-governmental forum in which Papuans could discuss and resolve their disputes.

In the Trobriand Islands, where there were traditional chiefs, colonial officials appointed village councilors in the early 1930s. They were given the power to discuss and decide civil claims, including land ownership, matters relating to the *kula*, and the repayment of bride price on divorce. In the late 1920s and 1930s, village councils were also established in parts of the Morobe District.

Murray's biases about Papuans were evident in his mixed feelings about their potential to decide cases in formal courts. In the late 1930s he wrote that he hoped Australians eventually could "hand over petty acts of administration and trivial native cases to Papuans." It would be difficult, he continued, to find Papuans "of sufficient intelligence to try a case"; the problem would be in finding men with sufficient "strength of character" not to be influenced by family or village considerations and who were not afraid of sorcery.[9] Murray did appoint a group of Papuan men in 1929 to sit in Port Moresby with the Australian district court magistrates as lay assessors, but not to decide cases, merely to advise the district court magistrates on matters of custom in cases involving Papuans.

The colonial administration in Papua eventually judged the assessor system unsuccessful and canceled it. District court magistrates had a low opinion of assessors. Some magistrates thought that Papuans were not intelligent enough to assist in deciding cases, while others thought the scheme was impractical until more Papuans understood English, the language of the courts. Colonial officials never gave the assessors decision-making powers, even though they had been appointed to advise on cases involving custom.

The limited role given to assessors was in keeping with the legal positivism of Murray's administration. Customary rules were seen as facts, not laws, which were outside the knowledge of the expatriate district courts magistrates. The role of the Papuan assessors was to advise the magistrates on those facts, which they then would consider, along with other facts, in reaching their decisions. The magistrates were not formally required to consult the assessor and often did not. None of the Papuans who were appointed lay assessors were considered to be ready to take over responsibility for a court when civil government ceased in 1942, and no effort was made to revive the assessor program after the war.

Colonial Legislation

The territorial Legislative Councils enacted ordinances dealing with a wide variety of topics during the 1920s and 1930s. However, few of those ordinances had any effect on the lives of Papuans or New Guineans, who, for most purposes, were governed by the *Native Regulations* in Papua and the *Native Administration Regulations* in New Guinea. Although the regulations were a means of enforcing administrative policies, they became so complex that in 1925 Hubert Murray wrote that they formed "so portentous a mass of prohibitions and penalties that one wonders how a native, who in ninety-nine cases out of a hundred has not learnt to read, can ever hope to steer clear of them." However, Murray defended the regulations on the grounds that "most of them deal with matters with which the native has been familiar from childhood."[10] A better explanation is that they reflected the fear expatriates had of the numerically superior Papuans and New Guineans and the consequent desire to control every aspect of the lives of the local population. That fear intensified after the Rabaul strike of January 1929 as the white residents of the town became preoccupied with what was known locally as the "Black Peril." According to one scholar, "many of Rabaul's Europeans thought of the town's white community as a garrison under siege. They never doubted that those around them would cheerfully cut their throats if it could be done."[11] In that atmosphere there was a demand not for the establishment of the Anglo-Australian system of criminal justice but for a more draconian system of laws, backed by criminal sanctions, to meet those fears and desire for control.

Through the use of fines and jail sentences, the native regulations kept Papuans and New Guineans segregated from expatriates and in a subordinate position. The regulations were enforced by Courts for Native Matters (in Papua) and Courts for Native Affairs (in New Guinea), staffed by *kiaps*. Although appeals from their decisions theoretically could be taken to the Central Courts/Supreme Courts of the two territories, in practice that rarely happened. For most Papuans and New Guineans, the decisions of the magistrates of the native courts were "the law." However, the large number of cases in the courts for native affairs shows that Papuans and New Guineans either were, as Murray suggested, unaware of the regulations and thus unable to avoid violating them or were not as subservient as they were expected to be. Many of the regulations conflicted with precepts of the people's own customary law. When a choice had to be made about which to follow, most Papuans and New Guineans opted for following custom.

During the 1920s, as the expatriate population in Port Moresby and Rabaul increased, more Papuans and New Guineans were recruited to work in the towns' shops, on the wharfs, and as domestic servants. New regulations were enacted to exclude, segregate, and control Papuans and New Guineans in the towns. In Port Moresby, for example, the regulations prohibited most Papuans from living within the town limits, but not from working there during the day. Although New Guineans were permitted to live in Rabaul, regulations prescribed the areas where they could live, resulting in segregated communities. To the expatriate residents of those towns, who feared the superior number of Papuans and New Guineans, exclusion and segregation were justified because of their belief that local people carried diseases and were likely to attack women if given the opportunity. In New Guinea, regulations made it an offense for New Guineans living in towns to be absent from the living quarters assigned to them by their employers between 9:00 p.m. and daybreak without the written consent of their employers. The regulations also prohibited "all noise, shouting, beating of drums, and dancing" in towns and villages between 9:00 p.m. and daybreak. In fact those were the most frequent offenses heard by the Courts of Native Affairs in New Guinea; they carried a fine of £1 (equal to two months wages for a New Guinean) or two months in jail.

Other regulations in Papua and New Guinea also punished activities that were not prohibited to expatriates. For example, regulations made adultery an offense for Papuans and New Guineans, but not for expatriates. In New Guinea, a conviction for adultery could result in a fine of £3 or six months in jail. Other regulations sought to control Papuans and New Guineans by prohibiting conduct and activities that were considered disrespectful or annoying to expatriates such as using "threatening, abusive, insulting, jeering or disrespectful language to any European"; behaving in a "threatening, abusive, insulting or disrespectful manner towards any European"; begging for "money, tobacco or other property from a European"; and loitering in towns. Regulations in New Guinea prohibited playing games or riding a bicycle on any street in Rabaul unless authorized in writing. Other regulations prohibited spreading false reports, using threatening and obscene language, being absent from a tribal village, deserting wives and children, touting, gambling, or attending or taking part in a *singsing* (traditionally a ceremonial dance, but, in colonial parlance, any party involving music) without permission of the district officer. A regulation in Papua even prohibited locals from acting in films.

The administrations also used the native regulations to criminalize customary practices that conflicted with their policies. For example, ostensibly in the interest of improving public health in Papua and New Guinea, regulations made it an offense to "bury the body of any person in the ground underneath any house, or in or near any occupied village, or keep the dead body of any native after it has reached a stage of decomposition in or near any occupied village."[12] Since many customary practices prohibited by the native regulations quite literally went underground in order to avoid prosecution, the administrations believed that they had been successful in changing traditional practice.

One of the most important customary practices prohibited by the native regulations was sorcery. Colonial officials wanted to stamp out sorcery because, they said, it caused arguments and payback and led to many of the murder cases heard by the courts. Expatriates were deeply offended by sorcery. Some saw it as conflicting with the Christianity that the missionaries were trying to spread. Others viewed it as conflicting with the scientific explanations that, in the age of rationalism, had come to be as important a belief system to some Westerners as religion was to others. Belief in sorcery was, and still is, widespread in Papua New Guinea, offering a nonreligious and nonscientific explanation for sudden illness, death, or misfortune. Threats and bribes were the only means, short of murder, available for people to protect themselves against sorcery. If that failed, the person suspected of practicing sorcery could be the victim of a retaliatory attack, which often resulted in death and which might, in turn, set tribes against each other.

In Papua, section 80 of the *Native Regulations* stated: "Sorcery is only deceit, but the lies of the Sorcerer frighten many people and cause great trouble, therefore the Sorcerer must be punished." The regulation made it an offense, subject to fine of £3 or up to six months in jail, to practice or pretend to practice sorcery; to threaten any person with sorcery (whether practiced by himself or another person); to procure or attempt to procure another person to practice or pretend to practice or assist in sorcery; to possess any implements or charms used in sorcery; or to accept payment or presents in the form of food or otherwise when the intention of making such payments or presents was to propitiate a sorcerer.

The regulations did not stamp out sorcery. Some officials believed this was because the penalties were too lenient. A jail sentence of no more than six months for sorcery, they suggested, may have prevented Papuans from giving information against sorcerers. Papuans might have feared that a convicted sorcerer would return to the village in a few months and seek revenge against those who betrayed him or her. It is equally likely, however, that the belief in sorcery was too deeply held to be wiped out with a couple of regulations.

Unfortunately, there are no contemporaneous written records of what Papuans or New Guineans thought of the native regulations. Sir Maori Kiki, who published the first autobiography by a Papua New Guinean in 1968 and who served as deputy prime minister in the first government of the independent state, wrote that the regulations showed that the colonial administrations considered Papuans and New Guineans "to be irresponsible and treated us like children."[13] An example of this was the regulation that prohibited Papuans and New Guineans from wearing clothes on the upper part of their bodies without government permission. Percy Chatterton, a missionary who served in Papua from 1924 until his death in 1985, wrote that the regulation (not repealed until 1939) may have originated out of genuine health and hygiene concerns, but it quickly became a means of preventing "them" (Papuans and New Guineans) from wearing the same kind of cloths as "us" (expatriates).[14] The regulation produced an embarrassing result, Chatterton wrote, when a young government officer ordered Papuan women entering a church on a Sunday morning to remove their brightly patterned dresses.

The colonizers' racism and fear and their resulting desire for control were translated into a number of ordinances, backed by criminal sanctions, which differed significantly from the criminal laws in Australia. The most notorious example of such legislation was the *White Women's Protection Ordinance*, which applied in Papua between 1926 and 1958. A similar ordinance was drafted in New Guinea in 1937, although the administration dropped it in favor of amendments to the Criminal Code, which had the same effect.

Reported attacks on a white woman and a young girl by Papuans in Port Moresby in August 1925 led many whites to see sexual motives as the reason. That interpretation certainly was not unique to Papua, since the fear of the rape of white women by native men was a powerful, pervasive, and often exaggerated force in all British colonies. In a book published the same year, Murray took the position that attacks on women and girls were rare and did not involve any intent to commit rape.[15] Historian Amirah Inglis found evidence that supported Murray's view and concluded that the situation in no way merited such drastic actions. Her study of court records from 1918 to 1924 showed only three cases of indecent assault upon small children and four cases of indecent assault upon women. None of the cases revealed any intent to rape.[16] However, in December 1925, two more assaults on white women were reported, so despite the facts and Murray's opposition, public reaction led him, however reluctantly, to introduce the *White Women's Protection Ordinance*. The ordinance made it an offense punishable by death for anyone to commit or attempt to commit the crime of rape upon a European woman or girl. It also provided that anyone who "unlawfully and indecently assaults a European woman or girl" was liable to life imprisonment "with or without whipping which may be inflicted once, twice or thrice."[17]

Inglis noted two "extraordinary features" about the ordinance. The first was the distinction as to the race of the victim. English and Australian laws never made racial distinctions about the victims of rape and other sexual assaults, and penalty did not depend upon the race of the victim or the offender. Murray justified limiting the ordinance to white women in Papua in a dispatch to the Australian government in these remarkable terms:

> Doubtless there are native women who set the highest value on their chastity, but they are the exception, and the rape of an ordinary native woman does not present any element of comparison with the rape of a respectable white woman, even where the offence upon the latter is committed by one of her own race and colour.[18]

The second "extraordinary feature" of the ordinance was its provision for the death penalty for rape, with no alternative. At the time, New South Wales and Victoria were the only two Australian states that made death the penalty for rape, and Victoria's law included mitigating circumstances that could prevent the death sentence. Moreover, the ordinance mandated the death penalty for attempted rape, an offense that was at that time classified as a misdemeanor in all states except Queensland.[19]

Despite the harsh penalties, the number of assault cases involving white women actually increased in the years following its enactment. Although the death penalty was imposed by the Central Court of Papua after a conviction in 1929, it was commuted by the Labor government in Australia, which opposed capital punishment generally. The only execution under the ordinance occurred in January 1934 after a Papuan was convicted of the rape of a European girl.

The Role of Custom in the Colonial Legal Systems

The attitudes, ideology, and beliefs of colonial officials toward Papuans and New Guineans also influenced the limited roles that customary law and processes were allowed to play in the colonial legal systems. To expatriates, their possession of Western civilization meant that they were guided by reason while Papuans and New Guineans acted solely in response to childlike or savage emotions. Murray wrote more about Indigenous customs than any other colonial official of the time. While varying slightly in degree over the decades, he was consistent in his general attitude toward local customs and did not vary greatly from those of colonial officials in New Guinea.

Murray was critical of many of the customary beliefs and practices of Papuans. He referred to "the strange medley of customs . . . some of [which] appear . . . to be simply foolish, but others are cruel and even revolting, and all appear . . . to be utterly meaningless"; he also wrote that many customs were "hard to reconcile with any degree of sanity" and "so utterly senseless that one can hardly imagine that they ever had any real meaning." At the same time, Murray strongly believed that Papuans were "in fact, quite sane. They go about their business in the ordinary way, they make gardens, build their houses, and look after their children, just like anyone else."[20]

In this, as in most areas relating to Indigenous people, Murray took what must have seemed at the time a middle ground. He took the position that, while the colonial administration would be working to eventually replace Papuan custom with Western law and religious beliefs, neither could it "contemptuously ignore" customs as "the beastly devices of the heathen, and dismiss those who practice them as either children or devils."[21] It was the duty of the administration to try to understand the "motive" for the customs in order "to take effective steps to modify [the] mode of thought" that gave rise to them and carry out their mission to improve the Indigenous people. Murray admitted that such understanding would be difficult, since the basis of most customs was elusive to whites, and it suited him to believe that in most cases Papuans themselves did not know the derivation or were likely to make up an answer aimed at pleasing the questioner. Murray distinguished between customs that were "cruel and revolting in the extreme," which should be opposed and stamped out by the administration, and others that should be tolerated and even encouraged out of a need to promote stability in village societies. However, he believed that even this latter class of custom eventually would wither and die out as a result of European influence, to be replaced by a belief in Christianity and superior western ways.[22]

The Legislative Councils in both territories enacted ordinances dealing with a wide variety of subjects in the 1920s and 1930s. Although custom played no express role in those ordinances, in areas of life that affected only Papuans and New Guineans, such as marriage, adoption, divorce, and succession, the colonial administrations created *de facto* dual legal systems by permitting Indigenous people to continue to follow their customary practices. An example of this was the legislative approach to customary marriage. In Papua, there was no mention of customary marriage in the *Marriage Ordinance of 1912–1935*. According to that ordinance, marriages could be performed only by a minister of religion, a district registrar, or an authorized justice, and only after the prescribed formalities were met. The ordinance stated that every such marriage was a legal and valid marriage for all intents and purposes and "no other marriage shall except as hereinafter provided be valid for any purpose."[23] Although open to them, few Papuans married according to the procedures of the ordinance, and the administration made no attempt to compel them to comply with its requirements.

The omission of any mention of customary marriage in the *Marriage Ordinance* can be interpreted in two ways. First, the requirements of the ordinance can be viewed as applying only to expatriates, leaving Papuans to follow their own customary procedures for marriage. That view is likely, especially given the lack of clergy and government officials in Papua. It also would have been impossible to expect every Papuan to meet the requirements of the ordinance. Customary marriages posed no threat to the administration's policies, and even enhanced stability in the villages, making them the type Murray had in mind when he said some should be tolerated until they died out of their own accord. The presumed nonapplicability of the requirements of the *Marriage Ordinance* to Papuans also is supported by the *Native Regulations,* which permitted a deserted "wife" to claim maintenance and created an offense of adultery with a "wife" of another man. The regulations defined a "wife" as "any woman that by the customs of the natives is regarded as or reputed to be the wife of a man."[24] Thus, although the *Marriage Ordinance* in Papua made no specific reference to customary marriages, the silence of the ordinance, coupled with the language of the *Native Regulations* and the failure to the administration to interfere with them, gave implicit recognition to such marriages.

In New Guinea, by way of contrast, the *Marriage Ordinance* was expressly made not to apply "to any marriage both of the parties to which are natives."[25] Customary marriages were recognized by the *Native Administration Regulations*, which provided that every marriage between New Guineans in accordance with the custom prevailing in the group to which the parties to the marriage or either of them belonged was valid. Under the

New Guinea regulations, the Administrator could forbid a customary marriage if the woman objected to the marriage and had been educated in expatriate or Western surroundings or acquired such habits to the extent that, in the opinion of the Administrator, it would be a hardship to compel her to conform to custom. There are no surviving records indicating whether the Administrator ever exercised this power.

The New Guinea regulations contained another difference from those in Papua. They expressly provided that every dissolution of marriage between New Guineans should be recognized according to the custom of their group. In a case in which the husband and wife belonged to clan or kin groups with differing customs, the validity of the divorce was determined according to the custom prevailing in the group to which the wife belonged. Following dissolution, the party who by custom had the duty of maintaining the children of the marriage was required to support them in accordance with that custom, and failure to do so would amount to an offense.

The Role of Custom in Criminal Cases

Unlike the ordinances dealing with civil matters, the Criminal Codes were applied to Indigenous people. No effort was made to modify those codes, which were basically copies of the Queensland Criminal Code, or to adapt them to local customs or circumstances. Papuans and New Guineans, who committed acts defined as offenses under the codes, could be indicted, tried, convicted, imprisoned, and even executed. The fact that the particular act in question was not an offense according to custom, that an exculpatory excuse or justification was available in custom, or that custom might even have compelled the performance of that act, had no bearing upon the liability of the accused.

The conflict between the Criminal Codes and custom was sharpest in cases of murder. Murray chronicled the various types of custom-related killing he had encountered in Papua, all of which resulted in prosecutions under the colony's Criminal Code. According to Murray, the most common motive for murder was payback for a previous killing or tribal war, which was an integral part of customary life—even an obligation—in many Papuan and New Guinean societies. Murder also could result, Murray wrote, from a desire to enhance the social position of the murderer.

Whites believed that, in some Papuan clans, young men won the right to wear certain ornaments (the *heera* in the Motu language) signifying warrior status and a means of winning the favor of the young women in the village, only by killing someone from another clan or village. In a number of clans along the Papuan coast, Murray insisted it was the custom to try to kill an enemy in order to celebrate the building of a men's house or a seagoing canoe. In some societies, according to Murray, twins were killed at birth. Children also might be killed if there was a danger of drought or lack of food. In other societies, if a mother died, her child might be buried alive with her if there was no one to nurse and care for the child. According to Murray, it was the custom among one tribe in Papua, on the death of a chief, to kill one of his wives or a small child to accompany him to the next world and cook for him. Anthropologists have not been able to verify any of these claims.

Sorcery was another area of conflict between the Criminal Codes and custom and a frequent motive for murders. The killing of sorcerers presents a good example of the conflicting position in which colonial officials and judges found themselves. According to Murray, who dealt with many such cases in his role as chief judge:

> On the one hand you have the murderer, posing triumphantly and confidently as a public benefactor, for has he not rid the world of an incarnate fiend, who was causing the death of innocent men and women? And on the other hand you have the poor friendless old woman, who was brutally murdered for an imaginary reason. One can appreciate the argument of the murderers, but the murdered demand our sympathy, and had a right to our protection.
>
> Native custom would loudly claim that the murderer should be praised, and perhaps rewarded, for his public service. But, if the victim had friends in the village or belongs to another community, there would certainly be an equally loud counterclaim; and a demand no less insistent would be made that the witch's life should be atoned for, either by another life, or by payment of the recognized price in pigs or native wealth.[26]

Another area in which the Criminal Codes and custom conflicted was in their disparate approaches to certain sexual practices. The British and

Australian societies of the time were extremely prudish about sex, very different from the more open attitudes of many Pacific cultures. For example, the Criminal Codes abhorred premarital sex, and defined sexual relations with girls under the age of sixteen as "unlawful carnal knowledge." However, in village societies, marriageability was based upon the apparent stage of physical development of the young woman, not on chronological age, and sexual relations with a young woman of "marriageable age" was not unlawful in many Papuan and New Guinean societies, where sex was treated as a permissible or even necessary prelude to marriage. Similarly, homosexual acts were an integral part of the ritual of initiation of young men in many societies. However, because the Criminal Codes, formulated in Australia where homosexuality still was against the law, prohibited sexual acts between persons of the same sex, these initiation rites could result in prison sentences of up to fourteen years.

There was also a difference between the codes and custom in their basic theories of criminal responsibility. The Criminal Codes were based upon the English concept of individual responsibility, assuming that individuals acted after forming a conscious intent and then implementing that intent free of pressure from family, ethnic group, ideals, or emotions. However, Papuans and New Guineans believed, as do many non-Western peoples, in communal responsibility and support; the idea of individuals free from mutual responsibility to the family and clan or unable to count upon the family and clan when needed was as foreign to Papuans and New Guineans as collective responsibility was to Westerners. Like other Westerners, Murray believed that the "sense of individual responsibility should be encouraged."[27] At the same time, he realized that was the area in which "[p]erhaps we deviate most widely from Papuan ideals." He believed collective responsibility to be unthinkable in an English court and, in keeping with the philosophy of legal positivism, added that "if the Papuan ever advanced so far as to establish a court, he would have realized it as well as we."[28]

The colonial administrations did not officially recognize the traditional methods by which conflicts involving custom were often resolved, notably the village moot or gathering, where parties could be reconciled, and balance and order within a community restored through discussion, negotiation, compromise, and consensus. The very spirit of moots, let alone the process, directly conflicted with the formal adversarial proceedings of trials. Moots continued to exist at the village level throughout the colonial period. Papuans and New Guineans did not willingly use the formal colonial courts, where proceedings were not conducted in their language but in English, and where the procedure, the rules of evidence, and the role of witnesses or the judge were so different from village moots. In the Supreme Courts, the Australian judges and barristers continued to follow the British practice of conducting trials in wigs and gowns, a practice that must have been extremely uncomfortable in Papua and New Guinea's tropical climate.

Trials conducted by colonial magistrates and judges also differed from customary proceedings in the scope of their focus. Fundamental to English procedure is the narrowing of the legal issues until they encompass only the immediate dispute or harm, no matter how many other interactions the parties may have had. This focus omitted all that was most crucial to Papuans and New Guineans: the historical and social context in which the act took place, the relationships between the parties, other transactions or disputes that might have occurred between them or between their kinsmen, and the obligations on the person and his kin group to act. In his study of a murder and assault that took place in the Mount Hagen area of the Western Highlands, anthropologist Andrew Strathern noticed that what was important to the Supreme Court was of little significance to the local people. While the court focused on whether the accused had the necessary intent and premeditation, the people in Mount Hagen were interested in the social background of the events, including questions of revenge and compensation for an earlier death.

In criminal cases, the magistrate or judge could sentence a convicted person to imprisonment or impose a fine payable to the administration. In most Papuan and New Guinean communities, however, payment of a mutually agreed amount of money, pigs, shells, and other food and goods as compensation to the victim, and his kin could be accepted as satisfaction for a harmful act. Frequently both the wrongdoer and the victim, as well as the families of both, compensated one another to affirm that their relationship was again on mutually respectful terms. The Western practice of imprisoning wrongdoers was not a part of the customary law of Papuan and New Guinean societies, and its use by the colonial courts did not accomplish the goal of restitution that was an essential part of customary law. As a result, relatives of the victim and even those of the offender felt that the courts concentrated on issues of minor importance that either were irrelevant to the resolution of the dispute or, in cases of imprisonment, actually impeded a customary settlement.

The colonial courts in Papua and New Guinea ignored custom when determining the guilt or innocence of a defendant. However, they sometimes attempted to minimize the harshness and injustice of the Criminal Codes by imposing reduced sentences based on the degree of contact that a Papuan or New Guinean defendant had had with the administration, missionaries, or urban areas. According to the judges, if there had been little contact, the defendant could not be expected to realize that murder was a crime and thus must be given a more lenient sentence. In 1925, Murray wrote:

> The sentences passed on convicted murderers vary very much. The murder of a white man is generally punished with death, and a native murder with a term of imprisonment, varying from life to the rising of the Court, according to the circumstances of the case, and particularly according to the standard of civilization which the accused has reached. A native of the Port Moresby villages would be, and indeed has been, hanged for a native murder, for he knows the law as well as a white man; whereas a native less familiar with our ways might get a term of five or seven years imprisonment, and another, who had hardly been brought under control, might get off with six months, and a thoroughly untaught savage might receive only a nominal sentence.[29]

Kiaps, the Courts of Native Affairs, and Custom

Despite the formal importance of the English common law and statutes, the ordinances enacted by the legislative assemblies, and the decisions of the courts, for the vast majority of Papuans and New Guineans colonial law consisted of what *kiaps* acting informally or as magistrates of the courts of native affairs, told them it was. Each *kiap* was responsible for maintaining order and a semblance of colonial administration in his assigned area. Based in towns or on government stations, *kiaps* did a regular circuit of the villages under their authority by foot patrol, making journeys through the bush lasting weeks or months at a time, accompanied by members of the Armed Native Constabulary and bearers. The most detailed pictures of patrols, the work of *kiaps*, the cases they heard as magistrates, and the role of custom in those cases come from the reports they filed after each patrol. An examination of the surviving reports shows that there were four types of patrols. Their work ranged from making contact with previously unknown groups to applying colonial laws and resolving disputes using local custom.

The first type of patrols included those made into areas that had not been contacted previously by the administration. Although such patrols began with the establishment of colonial rule, the most organized and well known of them took place during 1930s. Their purpose was exploration and contact with people previously unknown to colonial authorities and who, at that point, were unaware that Papua and New Guinea had been colonized.

Once contact was established in an area, the second type of patrol would be mounted. On these, the *kiap* attempted to consolidate and strengthen the influence of the administration. Often, it took numerous patrols to accomplish that goal. *Kiaps* did not enforce the native regulations or hold formal court sessions on those patrols. Instead, they used an amalgam of custom and their own schoolboy notions of fair play to resolve disputes. Many *kiaps* had learned that it was not enough just to deal with the immediate problem or to punish wrongdoers, since most disputes, and particularly tribal wars, were only the most current manifestation of feuds that had long histories involving larger groups. In his report of a patrol in the Simbu region of the Highlands in January 1940, Ian Downs wrote:

> In these cases it is not sufficient to settle payments merely for the current killing but it is necessary to adjust the original injury which caused the vendetta to commence no matter how many years ago. When this is done the native groups concerned cannot have any moral excuse for continuing the vendetta.[30]

In another incident also in the Simbu, Downs imposed extrajudicial physical punishment on those involved on both sides, reporting that: “All the natives in all the groups concerned were caned as this part is not under the same control as the areas within the base camps. The next offence will invoke the N.A.R. [Native Administration Regulations.]"[31]

In the third type of patrol, the *kiap* was sent to investigate specific serious incidents, such as murders, tribal fighting, fights on plantations, or raiding and thefts from missions and mining camps. In most instances, the purpose of such patrols was to arrest the suspects and bring them back to the patrol station for a district court hearing and, if there was enough evidence, a trial.

Once an area had been explored and its people had been contacted and come to recognize the authority of the colonial administration, the final type of patrol commenced. Those involved regular visits (usually once or twice a year) to collect taxes, record the census, check on public health and treat illnesses, check rest-houses, inspect gardens, recruit plantation laborers, inspect and order the building of roads, and inform the villagers of administration policies. It was during those visits that *kiaps* not only acted as magistrates for the courts for native matters but also as prosecutor and defense counsel as well, and then, having found the offender guilty, as the person who punished him for his infractions of the native regulations or for failing to carry out prior orders. If the offense was more serious and jail was the punishment, the *kiap* would take the offender back to the government station to serve his sentence. In very serious cases in which a person was accused of murder or rape under the Criminal Codes, the *kiap* would arrest the person and take him back to the government station to await trial at the next circuit of the Supreme Court.

Unfortunately, most patrol reports do not describe in any detail the number or types of criminal cases heard. Typical of the report entries are those that stated simply: "Held C. N. M" (*i.e.*, Court of Native Matters). However, a few reports do mention, although without discussion, the wide variety of offenses handled by the kiaps: assault, failing to appear for the census, incest, indecent behavior, labor desertion, neglect of duty, sorcery, spreading false reports, stealing, threatening language, and unlawfully wearing clothes.

Villagers frequently asked *kiaps* to resolve individual and group disputes. Papuan and New Guinean customary law does not distinguish between criminal and civil matters, but English law does, so if a *kiap* wanted to resolve a dispute, he had to classify it as civil so he could justify resolving it without following the rules and procedures in the native regulations and Criminal Codes. Although the disputes raised a broad range of issues, the patrol reports rarely discussed them in detail, merely referring to them as "trivial complaints." However, an examination of the patrol reports reveals that most of the disputes involved matters that would have been very important to villagers. These included: bride price, pigs destroying gardens, divorce, debts, and land boundaries. Since those cases involved matters of custom about which the *kiaps* had no knowledge, they sometimes insisted that the village elders or entire village sit down in council and make their own decision, which the *kiap* then confirmed as the judgment of the court. More often, the *kiap* decided the matter himself. Very occasionally, if the parties requested it, the *kiap* held something like a formal court, gave an opinion, and made a written record.

The native regulations gave *kiaps* broad powers to deal with civil disputes. In Papua, they could hear "any matter which is the subject of a claim by one person against another," except those dealing with the ownership of land, water, or reefs and claims for bride price. The most common disputes brought to *kiaps* were about land and bride price. Since all civil disputes involved issues of custom, the native regulations in both territories permitted or directed *kiaps* to take custom into consideration in dealing with them. That was not done out of any respect for custom but out of concern that, if disputes were not resolved to the satisfaction of the parties in the village, they could lead to unrest and even tribal warfare. Thus, Regulation 134 of the *Native Regulations* in Papua provided that:

> [A] Magistrate may use his discretion as to taking notice of matters that are civil claims. The chief object the Magistrate should keep in view is to appease quarrels and disputes about property and rights, real or imaginary, and to prevent as much as possible the strong taking advantage of the weak.

In New Guinea, Regulation 57(2) of the *Native Administration Regulations* went further and treated custom as law, specifically directing courts to "take judicial notice of all native customs and give effect to them, save in so far as they are contrary to the principles of humanity or conflict with any law or Ordinance in force in the territory." Regulation 57 also required administration officers to "make themselves acquainted by all means in their power with the native customs in their district" and to "reduce such customs to writing and keep a copy of them in the district office." However, the perpetual shortage of field staff, their frequent transfer from one district to another, and the average *kiap's* lack of appreciation for the cultures and customs of New Guinea made it unlikely that *kiaps* would learn much about local customs. One district officer voiced his criticism of Regulation 57 in a report:

> [A]ll field staff were now instructed to gather and record all possible information concerning systems of native land tenure,... and to learn as much as possible of the native people and their way of life.
>
> All very sound, of course.... Unfortunately, in our infant administration in New Guinea, postings were left to the Staff Clerk in Rabaul who had field staff playing musical chairs all over the Territory. It was impossible in the short period any officer remained at any one station to do very much more than perform the routine tasks necessary to keep a Station functioning. There was little time, even for the most enthusiastic and interested officer, to learn more about native customary life than what was immediately apparent in his District.
>
> Even from these instructions to learn more about native matters there was one curious omission. There was no request to inquire into native customs relating to tribal and village methods of dealing with offences and their punishments....[32]

That is as a good a place as any to leave this discussion of the interwar period in Papua and New Guinea. In the following chapters, we will discuss the changes brought to the territories by the multiple impacts of World War II.

Sources

Books and Articles

Paula Brown, *Highland Peoples of New Guinea* (Cambridge: Cambridge University Press, 1978).

Paula Brown, *Beyond a Mountain Valley: The Simbu of Papua New Guinea* (Honolulu: University of Hawai'i Press, 1995).

Ivan F. Champion, *Across New Guinea: From the Fly to the Sepik* (London: Constable and Co., 1931).

Percy Chatterton, *Day That I Have Loved* (Sydney: Pacific Publications, 1974).

Arthur Kent Chignell, *An Outpost in Papua* (London: Smith, Elder & Co., 1911).

Brenda Johnson Clay, *Unstable Images: Colonial Discourse on New Ireland Papua New Guinea 1875–1935* (Honolulu: University of Hawai'i Press, 2005).

Bob Connolly and Robin Anderson, *First Contact: New Guinea Highlanders Encounter the Outside World* (New York: Penguin Books, 1987).

Ian Downs, *The Last Mountain: A Life in Papua New Guinea* (Brisbane: University of Queensland Press, 1986).

Bill Gammage, "The Rabaul Strike, 1929," *Journal of Pacific History* 10(3) (1975) 3–29.

George Alfred Henty, *By Sheer Pluck* (London and Glasgow: Blackie & Son, 18–84).

Amirah Inglis, *The White Women's Protection Ordinance: Sexual Anxiety and Politics in Papua* (London: Sussex University Press, 1975).

Amirah Inglis, *Karo* (Canberra: Australian National University Press, 1982).

Brian Jinks, Peter Biskrup, and Hank Nelson (eds.), *Readings in New Guinea History* (Sydney: Angus and Robertson, 1973).

Mathias Kin, *My Chimbu* (Lexington: Self-Published, 2018).

August Ibrum Kituai, *My Gun, My Brother: The World of the Papua New Guinea Colonial Police, 1920–1960* (Honolulu: University of Hawai'i Press, 1998).

Michael Leahy, *Exploration into Highland New Guinea 1930–1935* (Tuscaloosa: University of Alabama Press, 1991).

Lewis Lett, *The Papuan Achievement* (Melbourne: University of Melbourne Press, 1942).

Lewis Lett, *Sir Hubert Murray of Papua: Statesman and Empire Builder* (London: Collins, 1949).

Robert F. Maher, *New Men of Papua: A Study of Culture Change* (Madison: University of Wisconsin Press, 1961).

Albert Maori Kiki, *Kiki: Ten Thousand Years in a Lifetime* (Melbourne: Cheshire Publishing, 1968).

Peter M. Munster, "A History of Contact and Change in the Goroka Valley, Central Highlands of New Guinea, 1934–1949" (unpublished PhD diss., Deakin University, 1986).

Hubert Murray, *Australian Policy in Papua* (Port Moresby: Government Printer, 1930).

Hubert Murray, *The Machinery of Indirect Rule in Papua* (Port Moresby: Government Printer, 1935).

Hubert Murray, *Papua of To-Day: An Australian Colony in the Making* (London: P. S. King and Son, 1925).

Christine Oke, "The Native Administrations of MacGregor, Murphy and Hasluck in Papua/New Guinea: Continuity and Contrast," *University of Wollongong Historical Journal* 1(1) (1975) 7–41.

Gabriel Olakunle Olusanya, "The New Guinea Mandate: Australia's 'Sacred Trust,'" (unpublished master's thesis, University of British Columbia, 1961).

Noah Riseman, *Defending Whose Country? Indigenous Soldiers in the Pacific War* (Lincoln; University of Nebraska Press, 2012).

C. D. Rowley, *The New Guinea Villager* (New York: Praeger, 1966).

Ian Stuart, *Port Moresby, Yesterday and Today* (Sydney: Pacific Publications, rev. ed.,1973).

Roger G. Thompson, "Making a Mandate: The Formation of Australia's New Guinea Policies 1919–1925," *Journal of Pacific History* 25(1) (June 1999) 68–84.

G. W. L. Townsend, *District Officer: From Untamed New Guinea to Lake Success, 1921–46* (Sydney: Pacific Publications, 1968).

Townsville Daily Bulletin, "A Samarai Case," *Townsville Daily Bulletin*, June 9, 1936, 2.

John Dademo Waiko, *A Short History of Papua New Guinea* (Oxford: Oxford University Press, 1993).

Francis West, *Hubert Murray: The Australian Pro-Consul* (Melbourne: Oxford University Press, 1968).

Edward P. Wolfers, *Race Relations and Colonial Rule in Papua New Guinea* (Sydney: Australia and New Zealand Book Co., 1975).

Government Documents

Territory of New Guinea, Annual Report, 1926–1927 (Melbourne: Government Printer, 1927).

Territory of Papua, Report for Year 1926–1927 (Melbourne: Government Printer, 1927).

Territory of Papua, Report for Year 1937–1938 (Melbourne: Government Printer, 1938).

Yearbook of Australia, 1940.

Statutes

Criminal Code (Papua New Guinea) (*amended and adopted 1974 as the Criminal Code Act 1974, No. 78 of 1974* (PNG))

Judiciary Ordinance 1921–1938 (New Guinea) (*amended and adopted 1975 by Constitution*)

Marriage Ordinance 1912–1936 (Papua)

Matrimonial Causes Jurisdiction Ordinance 1910–1941 (Papua)

Native Administration Ordinance 1921 (New Guinea)

Native Administration Regulations 1924–1963 (New Guinea)

Native Regulation Ordinance 1908, No. 25 of 1909 (Papua)

Native Regulations 1939 (Papua)

White Women's Protection Ordinance 1926, No. 2 of 1926 (Papua)

Notes

1. George Alfred Henty, *By Sheer Pluck* (London and Glasgow: Blackie & Son, 1884, 1933) 118.
2. *Commonwealth Parliamentary Debates*, vol. 136 (November 2, 1932) 1762–1782.
3. Arthur Kent Chignell, *An Outpost in Papua* (London: Smith, Elder & Co., 1911) 69–70.
4. *Marriage Ordinance* (1935–1936) section 14.
5. *Territory of Papua, Report for Year 1937–1938* (Melbourne: Government Printer, 1938) 20.
6. Hubert Murray, *Papua of To-Day: An Australian Colony in the Making* (London: P. S. King and Son, 1925) 231.
7. Hubert Murray, *The Machinery of Indirect Rule in Papua* (Port Moresby: Government Printer, 1935) 3.
8. *Territory of New Guinea, Annual Report*, 1926–1927 (Melbourne: Government Printer, 1927).
9. Hubert Murray, *Indirect Rule in Papua* (Port Moresby: Government Printer, 1929) 10–11.

10. Hubert Murray, *Papua of To-Day: An Australian Colony in the Making* (London: P. S. King and Son,1925) 64.
11. Bill Gammage, "The Rabaul Strike, 1929," *Journal of Pacific History* 10(3) (1975) 3, 19.
12. *Native Regulations* section 102(1) (New Guinea).
13. Albert Maori Kiki, *Kiki: Ten Thousand Years in a Lifetime* (Melbourne: Cheshire Publishing, 1968) 91.
14. Percy Chatterton, *Day That I Have Loved* (Sydney: Pacific Publications, 1974) 11–12.
15. Hubert Murray, *Papua of To-Day: An Australian Colony in the Making* (London: P. S. King and Son, 1925) 94.
16. Amirah Inglis, *The White Women's Protection Ordinance: Sexual Anxiety and Politics in Papua* (London: Sussex University Press, 1975) 64–65.
17. *White Women's Protection Ordinance* section 4.
18. Amirah Inglis, *op.cit.* at 72.
19. *Id.* at 73.
20. *Territory of Papua, Report for Year 1926–1927* (Melbourne: Government Printer, 1927) 120.
21. *Id.*
22. Hubert Murray, *Papua of To-Day: An Australian Colony in the Making* (London: P. S. King and Son, 1925) 244–246.
23. *Marriage Ordinance of 1912–1935* section 18.
24. *Native Regulations* (1924) sections 77(1), 77(4) 84.
25. *Marriage Ordinance* section 5A.
26. Hubert Murray, *Australian Policy in Papua, op. cit.* at 244.
27. *Territory of Papua, Report for Year 1926–1927* (Melbourne: Government Printer, 1927) 124.
28. Hubert Murray, *Indirect Rule in Papua* (Port Moresby: Government Printer, 1929) 10–11.
29. Hubert Murray, *Papua of To-Day: An Australian Colony in the Making, op.cit.* at 85–86.
30. Paula Brown, *Beyond a Mountain Valley: The Simbu of New Guinea* (Honolulu: University of Hawai'i Press, 1995) 132–133 (quoting Ian Downs).
31. *Ibid.*
32. G. W. L. Townsend, *District Officer: From Untamed New Guinea to Lake Success, 1921–46* (Sydney: Pacific Publications, 1968) 119.

8 World War II and Its Impact

Papua and New Guinea in the 1940s

War Changes Everything

World War II brought changes that would reverberate throughout Australia's postwar attempts to reintroduce civilian rule. Japanese forces occupied East New Britain, Bougainville and parts of the north coast and islands, beginning in January 1942 and, despite Allied attempts to dislodge them, the Japanese occupation continued until war's end. Although Australian women and children were evacuated from Rabaul and the surrounding plantations just before the Japanese invasion, Australian men, both military and civilians, were not, and they, together with the Chinese and Indigenous populations, suffered heavy casualties.

The war caused widespread devastation to the colonial infrastructure in Papua and even greater destruction in New Guinea. Between Allied bombings and ruins that the Japanese forces left behind when they evacuated near war's end, Rabaul was almost completely destroyed; other colonial towns and outposts were also severely damaged. Plantations were left to go to seed; many were bombed or strafed. Destruction to the gardens, hunting grounds, and villages of rural Papuans and New Guineans was even more widespread, with villages burnt to the ground and slow-growing crops like coconut palms machine-gunned into uselessness. The worst damage to the Indigenous economy was probably the most insidious. The Australian forces (which were usually referred to by the acronym ANGAU) pressed thousands of young Papuan and New Guinean men into service; by the time the war in the Pacific was declared over, many had been away from home for five years or more. The prolonged absence of so many young men caused much hardship for those left behind. New garden land was not cleared; an entire age cohort went uninitiated.

The war severely undermined the fiction of Western authority and power that had supported and sustained colonial rule, not only for the Australians in Papua and New Guinea, but for the British and other colonial empires throughout Asia and the Pacific. From Singapore down to Port Moresby, Indigenous people had seen how easily, and completely, the Japanese had driven out their formerly invincible colonial masters. And, though the Japanese were not brown like Pacific Islanders, neither were they white. The lesson could not have been clearer: to the extent that colonialism had depended on the myth of white power and white superiority, that myth was shattered, at least in the eyes of the colonized. As the war drew to a close, colony after colony, all around the world, declared independence. Closest to Papua and New Guinea, Indonesia waged a bloody armed struggle for independence from the Netherlands, beginning with the Indonesians' unilateral declaration of their independence in 1945 and ending in 1949, when the Dutch capitulated.

If the war did not immediately and completely overturn the colonial situation in Melanesia, it did much to change Papuans' and New Guineans' perceptions about how, as colonized subjects, they should be treated. The American armed forces arrived in New Guinea with many soldiers who looked very much like Melanesians. At that time, the United States was still practicing apartheid, even in the armed forces, but Papuans and New Guineans did not know that. To them, black American soldiers seemed to be treated, and to treat everyone around them, including Melanesians, with extraordinary equality. African Americans lived in barracks just like those that the white soldiers inhabited, wore the same clothes that whites did, drove jeeps, ate Western food off of Western tables, had access to cash and goods, and did many other things denied to Papuans and New Guineans by their Australian overlords. Any Melanesian who saw that, or heard about it, did not want a return to the kind of race relations practiced in Papua and New Guinea before the war.

Even some of the Australian soldiers treated Papuans and New Guineans differently from the way that planters and administration officials had acted toward them before the war. On the one hand, ANGAU used its emergency war powers to conscript as many Indigenous men as it needed and to keep them working, and away from home, for years. Although wartime service by Melanesians was supposed to be voluntary, there were Australian officers who filled their quotas at the point of a gun, and who were not above whipping Indigenous men who tried to leave the service. At the same time, the Australian forces included many soldiers who were new to Melanesia and had not been indoctrinated into prewar colonial stereotypes, and who saw no harm in treating Indigenous men at least genially, especially when they proved to be invaluable in bearing wounded soldiers in stretchers across jungle or mountain terrain, or finding food for starving troops who had no idea what in a tropical jungle was edible and what was not.

The good feelings toward Papuans and New Guineans continued even after the war. Australian machismo is laced with masculine sentimentality, and the Papuan and New Guinean stretcher bearers were celebrated throughout the 1950s in countless paintings, stories, and ballads (almost all of questionable artistic merit). The following is an example that sublimely sums up the unique postwar amalgam of gratitude, sentimentality, and condescension:

Many a mother in Australia,
When the busy day is done,
Sends a prayer to the Almighty
For the keeping of her son,
Asking that an Angel guide him
And bring him safely back
Now we see those prayers are answered
On the Owen Stanley track,
For they haven't any halos,
Only holes slashed in the ears,
And with faces worked by tattoos,
With scratch pins in their hair,
Bringing back the wounded,
Just as steady as a hearse,

Using leaves to keep the rain off
And as gentle as a nurse.
Slow and steady in bad places,
On the awful mountain track,
And the look upon their faces,
Makes us think that Christ was black.[1]

If the poem itself is not mawkish enough, its anonymous ANZAC Day scribe went on to inform us that the ballad was penned by one "Sapper Bert Beros at 4 am one morning on the Kokoda Track. . . . It may never have been printed," he cannot resist adding, "but for the fact that an officer sent a copy home to his mother." No matter how problematic the sentiment, it was nevertheless emblematic of the deep reservoir of good feelings toward Papuans and New Guineans that the war had engendered among many Australians.

The First Post-War Decision: To Stay or To Go

Australia's decision to retain control of Papua and New Guinea after World War II was not a foregone conclusion. There seemed, in fact, many good reasons for Australia to get out of the colonial business as quickly as possible. Staying would be very expensive. The war had ravaged the territories, destroying towns and plantations, and the rebuilding costs would be enormous. Nor did it seem any more likely than it had since the beginnings of the colonial era that the territories would ever repay that investment. Neither Papua nor New Guinea was amenable to the kinds of plantations that Australian settlers might want to own, the kind that could make a profit; the gold fields seemed to have been played out, and, in the 1950s, Papua and New Guinea's vast wealth in oil and other minerals remained undiscovered.

Moreover, anticolonial sentiment was building all across the world, and was soon to find a focus in the United Nations, especially in the Trusteeship Council and the Decolonization Committee of the General Assembly. India, Great Britain's largest colony, celebrated its independence on August 15, 1947, exactly two years after the surrender of Japan ended World War II in the Pacific. Pro-independence groups were forming in other colonies throughout Asia, Africa, and the Pacific, spurred by India's example, and by the war itself, which had demonstrated that their colonial masters were not as invincible as they had portrayed themselves.

There was just one policy interest militating in favor of Australia's staying the course as a colonial power in Papua and New Guinea, and that was Australia's national security. If World War II had taught Australia anything, it was that the Japanese had been prevented from a full-scale invasion of the Australian mainland only by the intruding New Guinea land mass. The enemy had changed—it was no longer the Japanese; now it was a specter called "World Communism." But, for Australia at any rate, the threat was still from Asia, so Papua and New Guinea still served, in the minds of most Australians, as an important bulwark against invasion.

But the problem faced by postwar governments was how to explain and justify their decision to retain the colonies. The world—at least as represented by the Trusteeship Council and Decolonization Committee of the United Nations—was pressing for an explanation, as were those in Australia who believed the colonial experiment should come to an end. The opportunities that colonies usually provide for settlement, mining, and business would have proven a satisfactory answer, at least to some, except that these colonies provided little, if anything, of those. In the absence of economic gain and in the face of ever-increasing costs, another reason had to be found. It just was not good enough, given the current trend of world opinion toward anticolonialism, to admit that security was the only, or even the major, reason for keeping an entire nation in thrall.

The Directorate Tries to Change Colonial Policy

The Labor Party's first post-war pronouncements on its colonial policy, and even some of its actions in regards to the colonies, suggested there would be a change from Australia's pre-war emphasis on white settlement to a policy aimed more at supporting Indigenous development. But, either because of opposition from the party's leadership or because Labor was replaced in office too soon after the war to bring any of its policies to fruition, little in the way of change ultimately occurred.

At first, things looked hopeful. Even before the end of the war, the progressive, more academic wing of the party had gathered itself around General Thomas Blamey and Colonel Alfred Conlon, in what came to be known as the Army Directorate of Research and Civil Affairs, established ostensibly to determine how to prepare Papua and New Guinea for the transition from military to civilian rule. In fact, the directorate—whose members included Ian Hogbin, John Kerr, Isa Leeson, James McAuley, James Plimsoll, Marie Reay, W. E. H. Stanner, Harold Stewart, and Camilla Wedgwood, all prominent academics, most of them anthropologists with extensive experience and expertise in the territories and in Indigenous Australia—went much further, producing plans for the governance of the territories, and laying out a program that would have led to a very different Papua and New Guinea.

Some of what they proposed came into existence—for example, the joint administration of the two colonies under a combined public service, and the creation of a Legislative Council and laws for the territories separate from those governing mainland Australia. Some of it, such as provisions for a much better educated colonial public service, came into being only partially. More generally, though, what they had most wanted was a totally different attitude toward the territories. The prewar Australian emphasis on its own self-interest, which translated into support for planters, traders, miners, and other white settlers—sometimes at great cost to Papuans and New Guineans—should be replaced, they argued, by an emphasis on "the paramountcy of native interests." In particular, the focus should be on reestablishing normal village life, even at the cost of Australian business: "If native welfare is to be closely conserved, the possibilities of purely commercial investment, and employment of natives, may be relatively small."[2] Unfortunately, this was achieved more in lip service than in reality.

But the situation was not so simple. Australians with no real ties to Papua and New Guinea and no economic interests there might have supported reforms that would better suit the interests of Papuans and New Guineans; but the great majority of plantation owners, miners, steamship and trading company executives, returning *kiaps*, and even many missionaries did not, arguing instead for a return to prewar, pro-settler policies. The directorate "had no machinery" to put any of its proposals into effect.[3] Its only recourse lay in appeals to the Labor Party, and Labor, it turned out, was a weak reed, especially in its choice of a minister to oversee the territories. In 1943, then Prime Minister John Curtin, who died in office on July 5, 1945, had moved E.J. (Eddie) Ward, an ardent unionist, from the labor portfolio, which Ward loved and in which he felt comfortable and competent, to the newly created dual Ministry of Transport and

External Territories. Ward was out of his depth with the external territories portfolio; he experienced the move as a demotion, made even more galling in 1945, when, on Curtin's death, he lost his bid for leadership of the party (and therefore the prime ministership) to Ben Chifley. Ward had neither the time for the territorial ministry nor the inclination to play an active role in reforming the policies of the colonial administration.

Planters, Patrol Officers, and Colonel Murray

A number of the directorate's more specific proposals did get introduced in the years immediately after the war, primarily because the first postwar Administrator of the territories, Colonel J. K. Murray, believed strongly in them:

> . . .the colony struggled to establish the hospitals and schools, the farming projects, the co-operative societies and the local government councils that featured in the plans of the Directorate of Research. These were genuine innovations, but introduced not through the formal channels of the Department of External Territories, but directly from Port Moresby, through such people as the Administrator J. K. Murray, who had worked in the Directorate. To that extent, the Directorate's influence continued long after it was disbanded in 1946; it helped to create a climate for reform and provided a number of specific, innovative proposals.[4]

Ward appointed Murray to be the postwar Administrator of both Papua and New Guinea, continuing the war-created precedent of administering the two territories as one. This was also in line with what the directorate had proposed. Murray (no relation to Sir Hubert, and not much like him, either) wanted to effect many changes in Papua and New Guinea. His main aim was to administer the colony in the interests of the Indigenous population. Wolfers quotes him saying in 1946 that "a new spirit, new ideas, new demands and standards" seemed to have spread through the Indigenous community during the war, and "I do not propose to attempt, even if I could hope to succeed, to stifle that spirit so that European employers can return to the standards of a vanished world."[5]

Despite these brave words, Murray only partly succeeded. He introduced many changes, but had intended to do much more. There are various opinions about why his success was limited. He was a principled administrator, with a strong sense of what he wanted done in and for Papua and New Guinea. Most likely, he failed because he did not have sufficient support from Canberra, and none from his own district officers, most of whom had served before the war and had the attitudes to prove it. But history is written by the winners, in this case the conservative Liberal-Country coalition. Murray's successors, who were intent on rolling back the changes he had made, took the position that he was uptight and unapproachable, not a bloke or a mate (the terms Aussies would use for the kind of guy who would be admired by the rough and ready men who made up the colonial public service).

This Liberal-Country critique of Murray came to be so widely accepted that, in more recent years, even writers like Allen Healy, who are very critical of what the Liberal-Country administration did in Papua and New Guinea, believe that Murray was an amiable failure. Healy wrote that Murray was "sensitive to the need for change," but "lacked the necessary experience for the job. The tradition of amateur control continued."[6]

Within the territory, Murray's most vociferous adversaries were Australian planters and businessmen. Returning to Papua and New Guinea after spending the war years safe in Australia, they discovered that the world they remembered was much changed. Plantations that their indentured workers had struggled to carve out of the jungle were, essentially, jungle again. Few plantations or commercial buildings had survived the war. And, thanks to the Labor government, which had ended the servitude of all those Indigenous men who had served far from home throughout the war, the workers needed to build it up again had gone home to their villages. The private sector let their views be known, vocally, in *Pacific Islands Monthly*, in letters to Canberra, and in interviews with any Australian journalist who happened by. It was the considered and deeply held opinion of the planters and businessmen that Australia's main purpose in colonizing Papua and New Guinea, perhaps its only purpose, was to provide economic opportunities for "good Australians" like themselves. The war had not changed these opinions, nor their essential belief that it was still possible to carry out these aims.

Murray might still have succeeded had he gotten the necessary backing from Canberra and been granted the time to nurture a public service that shared his views. Unfortunately for him, and for the immediate future of

Papuans and New Guineans, the planters' views were pretty widely shared by most of the officers who had staffed Australia's colonial service before the war—and who made up the bulk of the officers available to Murray at war's end. Despite his criticisms of Murray, Healy best sums up the forces arrayed against him:

> While Murray sketched vague new objectives giving priority to indigenous involvement and development, he lacked the political understanding and support from Canberra that might have enabled him to overcome the inertia stemming from four decades of the "Murray tradition" (the *other* Murray). The post-war return to senior positions in the Papua New Guinea bureaucracy of the pre-war officials meant that Murray spent his time on in-fighting rather than reform; his departmental heads and older field staff were advocates of a continuation of white dominance. The problem was exacerbated by the transfer, to Papua New Guinea officialdom, of Australian bureaucratic practices, particularly a late retiring age (65) and promotion by seniority; these ensured near-stagnation in outlook and methods at a critical time.[7]

Failed Attempts to Create a New Public Service

Murray would have liked to recruit an entirely new colonial service, made up of people who did not share the supremacist values that had characterized the service before the war. He especially hoped to attract men with some education, particularly in anthropology, and he hoped to give them training in British and other indirect methods of colonial rule. But post-war exigencies made these hopes all but impossible to achieve. Even with a Labor government in power, enthusiasm for significant change was hard to marshal. Murray and his supporters had to compromise severely on their desire to overhaul the educational process for new recruits.

The major opponents in the dispute over how to train new recruits were Alfred Conlon, who got involved in the dispute when he was appointed in 1942 to head the newly formed Army Directorate of Research and Civil Affairs, and J. R. Halligan, Secretary of the Department of External Territories. They were opposites in almost every way. They had dissimilar public service backgrounds and equally dissimilar experiences of the territories. Halligan had begun his career in New Guinea in the 1920s and had been in charge of training cadets in the 1930s. Conlon came later to the territories, and most of his experience was during the war. Put in charge of training soldiers who administered civilians in wartime Papua and New Guinea, he set up the Army School of Civil Affairs in 1944, modeled on British and American army schools, and staffed by a team of young intellectuals, including anthropologists, many of whom would go on to do distinguished and seminal anthropological studies in Papua and New Guinea.

The directorate was intended to research and develop proposals for the postwar administration of the territories. Conlon and his staff

> felt that the pre-war objectives [for the territories] had been skewed, and that after the war the prime focus should be on the processes of acculturation rather than white-centred economic development.[8]

The staff of the directorate believed that Papua and New Guinea would be best governed by men and women who were deeply educated in the culture, economics, history, and political situation of the territories, in large part because they believed that only people with that kind of understanding could implement the sort of administrative changes they were proposing. Halligan and his supporters preferred short-term practical training. They viewed academic approaches as unnecessary, a waste of time, and predicted it would result in officers who coddled the natives too much. Halligan's views won out. The ministry instituted a short, almost entirely practical course, with relatively little "theoretical" (i.e., cultural, anthropological) learning. There was also a longer course that field officers could come back and take after forty-six weeks of service, but that too was made more "practical" and less thoughtful than Conlon would have wanted. Few officers ever came back to take it.

One might have expected that a Labor government would favor the directorate's proposals, especially since Labor had started its postwar administration of the territories with sturdy speeches promising that their focus in governing the territories would be on aiding Papuans and New Guineans, and not on supporting white business interests.

Murray had been a member of Conlon's team before becoming Administrator of the territories, and he succeeded at implementing a few of the directorate's proposals. However, neither Murray nor Conlon had the authority on their own to implement most of the proposals, especially their plans for improving the training of the public service. To do that, action was required from Canberra, where Halligan was actively opposed to changing anything from the way it had been done when he served in New Guinea in the 1920s. And, on the issue of education, Halligan had Ward on his side. A number of historians have described the debate over the education of the public service primarily as a personality conflict, and it is probably true, as many have written, that Conlon was young and brash and did not realize the importance of lobbying in Canberra for his proposals. It was equally true that Halligan was slow and cautious, hesitant to put his name to any new proposal, and that Ward was massively uninterested in his territorial portfolio. But it would be a mistake to believe that key trends were solely the result of the temperament and personalities of individual leaders, and that major policy choices depended entirely on the strategic alignments of individual bureaucrats and politicians. To a much larger extent, the key decisions reflected economics and the ideology that characterized Australia in the 1950s.

A major reason for the failure of Conlon's innovative suggestions was economic: faced with critical shortages of personnel, the territories could not afford the resources and time that longer educational programs would require. Another major reason was rooted deeply in Australian culture, which was at that time distinctly anti-educational and anti-intellectual. Drawing very strongly on the British empiricist tradition, the overarching myth of the Australian colonial service was of the self-taught, almost instinctively canny *kiap*, whose education came from experience and not from books; who, time after time, won out, alone and single handed, over thousands of natives, purely on the strength of his good, pure Aussie reactions, untainted by weak ideas like schools and systems. A third reason was a combination of economic and ideological: the directorate had proposed a kind of training that would, they hoped, produce a public service very different from the one that had existed before the war, a public service dedicated to serving the local population. Their opponents, including Halligan, preferred a public service cast in the prewar image, dedicated to making Papua and New Guinea safe for Australian settlement and business interests.

The training center was originally established in Canberra, on the grounds of the Australian Royal Military College. Since that was close to the proposed site of the new Australian National University, the directorate took heart, thinking they had secured an academic base for the curriculum. In March 1946, the school was transferred to civilian control and renamed the Australian School of Pacific Administration (ASOPA). But when ASOPA was relocated from Canberra to Sydney in May 1947, the directorate members must have known they had lost. Nor was ASOPA integrated into Sydney University, where it had been before the war. Recruits were not required to have very much schooling, and the staff "were people with limited relevant education and even less relevant experience," Allen Healy reports. The courses were not very critical, serious, thorough, or deep, but they taught recruits what the conservatives wanted them to learn. Healy continues:

> Very largely, they simply reinforced the metropolitan assumptions and preconceptions which had, from the beginning, determined the nature of the colonial administration. . . . The young men coming into the service were being pre-programmed in the "[Hubert] Murray tradition." This meant that the initial attempts to introduce indigenous local government to Papua New Guinea were doomed from the beginning.[9]

The conflict over the education of recruits was symbolic of the kinds of conflicts going on as the war drew to a close and in its aftermath over every aspect of governance and administration of the territories. The outcome of those conflicts would have deep and long-term effects, because it produced a generation or more of public servants ill-equipped to deal with a new era in colonial relations. However, it probably did not have much of an immediate impact, because it did not involve a sizeable number of territorial officers. The postwar colonial service was not very successful at attracting good recruits. It had trouble recruiting anyone at all, and those it did manage to attract tended to be young, with very limited education. There was more than enough work in Australia, which itself had much postwar reconstruction to do, so the best and the brightest, and the least infected by prewar colonial values, found good jobs closer to home and, for the most part, did not apply to go to the territories. Instead, Murray found his service staffed heavily by older *kiaps* who had been in Papua or New Guinea before the war, and who did their best to undermine his new strategies at every opportunity.

Labor's Labor Policy

Although Murray's and Conlon's aims got little support from Canberra, Labor's single greatest achievement in Papua and New Guinea during that era did come directly from Canberra—and it happened almost immediately after the end of the war. As one of his first postwar actions, on October 15, 1945, Ward signed a declaration that canceled all Papuans' and New Guineans' labor contracts, sending home all the men who had worked for ANGAU during the war. And, shortly after that, Ward promulgated a new regulation that ended, or at least significantly ameliorated, the civilian indenture system as well. It was through that system that planters had gotten their laborers, and, in the stroke of a pen, Labor permitted every indentured worker to go home if they wanted to. Almost all of them, thousands of them, wanted to. Ironically, some were prevented from going quickly only because the same regulation had ended the indentures of the men who worked the coastal and island boats that would have taken them home.

Not surprisingly, the one place where an actual piece of the Labor Party's progressive agenda was turned into government policy was in labor relations—probably because that was something Ward, a former union official and minister for Labor, knew and had heartfelt beliefs about. There was great opposition, especially among the plantation owners, to ending the indenture system. Even Halligan wrote glowingly in favor of indenture, arguing that it "developed 'character' and the 'habit of industry,' provided instruction in sanitation and personal hygiene, exposed workers to discipline and law and order, illustrated to them the 'principles of contract,' and established the habits of a 'regular life' as against an irregular one."[10]

As far as many of the planters were concerned, even the prewar system had not gone far enough in support of management. In their view, "the Labor organization of a typical plantation in the Territory [was] at a considerable disadvantage when compared with a typical plantation in Malaya or other comparable tropical country," since in the latter, rubber planters could bring in whole families and put them all to work.[11]

But Ward held uncharacteristically firm, or perhaps acted so quickly that no one had time to change his mind. In his landmark study of race relations in colonial Papua and New Guinea, Wolfers points out that not only did the government allow all wartime laborers to return home to their villages when civil administration was restored—but as a symbol of its commitment to change, the first announcement that all existing labor contracts had been canceled was made directly to the general public, over the radio, and in Motu:

> Against the protests of the planters . . . the government then scrapped the penal provisions in the Native Labor Ordinance. . . . The pay for indigenous laborers was made uniform and raised to fifteen shillings per month [from 10 in Papua and 5 in New Guinea] . . . the minimum age for employment was raised to sixteen [from 14 for laborers and 12 for domestic workers] . . . and the period of indenture was limited to one year [from 4 in Papua and 7 in New Guinea].[12]

Equally important, the ordinance did away with the criminal penalties for workers who left their employ early. However, it continued to make it illegal for "outsiders" (i.e., union organizers) to "create disaffection towards their employers"—an odd provision to find in a Labor-backed statute.[13]

There are differences of opinion about why so many workers went home as quickly as they could once the indentures were canceled. One thing on which all writers agree is that many of them had been forced by ANGAU to serve long past the date that their original indentures were supposed to have concluded. Beyond that, the answer seems to depend on one's perspective on race and colonialism. *Pacific Islands Monthly*, in those days a mouth piece for plantation and trading interests, reported, angrily, "In the view of Ward-ism, it is much more important that Fuzzy-Wuzzy shall be sent singing across the kunai ridges, than that gold shall be dug out of the Bulolo and the Watut."[14] Another planter reported that his "leading boss-boy" told him he was going home because there was plenty of food to be had in the villages: "You pay us our money, but we cannot buy anything with it—it is no good to us."[15] Lucy Mair, who reported on postwar conditions for the directorate, would agree that given the postwar shortages money was probably not much use to laborers, but she also reported that there was very little of either food or money in many of their villages. Wartime bombings, wartime theft of their crops by marauding Japanese and Australian soldiers, requisitions by ANGAU of what crops were left, all exacerbated by the long absence of most of the able-bodied men and boys, had left many villages hovering on the brink of starvation. It is most probable, though something the planters would never imagine, that men who had been away for years, missed their families, and that word had reached them that they were badly needed at home.

The planters and companies predicted that the end of the indenture system would lead to their economic ruin, and for a few months the "European economy came to a standstill."[16] But, to the Labor government, the fact that so many Papuans and New Guineans chose to go home confirmed that "the indenture system was obviously disliked by Papua New Guineans and ought to be abolished."[17] Ward "defended his policy as a stand against exploitation by the big companies which had previously had 'a throttle-hold on the Territories.'"[18] And, over the next few years, the stream of available workers once again increased to a level satisfactory to planters and traders.

However, whether that was a success of a free (non-indentured) labor system is open to question. Peter Fitzpatrick has argued persuasively that indenture had not in fact been abolished, that only the terminology had changed:

> ...this abolition of the [indentured labor] system and its replacement by the "agreement system" amounted to little more than a change in name. The basic structure of the system (especially the repatriation provisions) remained unchanged, [and even the supposed repeal of] most of the penal provisions, such as those requiring workers to be diligent and not to desert, [was not entirely accurate]. To a considerable extent, at least initially, the system "survived by bluff"; officials would act as if the penal provisions still existed, and the worker, not having heard otherwise, would usually fall into line. Further, an alternative type of sanction was then introduced; this involved a simple type of court action whereby on certain grounds, an employer (and, on other grounds, a worker) could apply to the court to have the employment contract terminated and to have "damages" paid out of the worker's deferred pay. The grounds included such as being absent from work for more than seven days, and "exerting a bad influence on his fellow workers".... [T]he average number of court orders of this type made annually [in New Guinea] in favour of employers was 549 (the average number a year in favour of workers was five).[19]

Fitzpatrick's views were supported by contemporary observers, even by those not otherwise inclined to favor Labor's policies. Brian Essai observed in 1961 that, although the stringent prewar system had been ameliorated, what remained in the 1950s could still not be called a system of employment totally free of government oversight and control:

> . . . the principal changes that have been made since the war are designed to shape a course towards the ultimate adoption of a universal free Labor. . . . With regard to penal sanctions, moderate fines have been substituted for gaol sentences. . . . It is . . . important to remember that although the indenture system has been abolished, the majority of natives in the Territory have still not reached the stage when they can work without some form of written agreement approved by the Administration.[20]

Planters and other business people wanted the prewar indenture system to continue because they believed they would be unable to get, or keep, local workers without it. There were two major arguments made in support of the need for an indenture system. The more racist argument—but one frequently read in the pages of *Pacific Islands Monthly* and similar outlets—was that Papuans and New Guineans were inherently lazy, and would not work unless forced to, or would work only enough to satisfy their immediate want for cigarettes or alcohol, and would quit as soon as those needs were met. The second argument was a more polished version of the first. McAuley was among its proponents, pointing out that no one takes on employment unless they need to and so long as Papuans and New Guineans continued to meet all of their needs from their abundant, subsistence economy, they would not need other work. If the administration considered it important for Papuans and New Guineans to take and keep paying jobs, then the choices were either indenture or the creation of incentives, such as trade goods, taxes, school fees, and other imposts that only money could buy.[21]

Through the end of the war, indentured workers had come primarily from the coastal regions. In the postwar period, the flow of workers from the coast declined significantly, partly in response to the end of the indenture system but mainly because fewer unskilled and uneducated workers were available from these areas that had long been colonized. However, just as the flow of workers from the coast and islands was drying up, the Highlands region was being brought under Australian control for the first time, and that area contained hundreds of thousands of men unskilled at Western forms of employment. Fitzpatrick noted that

> Any foreseeable risk in "abolishing" the indenture system was more than off-set by the opening of the Highlands—the greatest Labor frontier of them all. The Highlands Labor Scheme was . . . a massive recruiting operation run by the colonial administration. Although the scheme did not formally come into operation until the end of 1951, it had, effectively, been operating on a trial basis for two years before that. By the . . . end of 1950, 14 percent of the indentured workforce had been supplied through the Highlands Labor Scheme; within a further fifteen years, more than half the indentured or "agreement" workforce was supplied through the Scheme.[22]

The "free" or non-indentured labor force grew very slowly throughout the 1950s, from 33,927 in 1950 to 41,746 in 1960. That might have been because, as the planters direly predicted, Papuans and New Guineans simply did not want to work; more likely, however, it was because global economics, and the abundance of available land in Australia, continued to keep Papua and New Guinea's plantation sector relatively small. By 1961, counting indentured workers and "free" workers together, only about 5 percent of the total population was in the labor force, whereas the mean for developed countries is 40 percent. As far as Papuans and New Guineans were concerned, their economy continued to be primarily subsistence.

Summing Up Labor's Impact

Labor was voted out of office in 1949, only four short years after war's end. Although the party's more progressive wing attempted to instigate significant changes in colonial policies and in the makeup of the colonial administration, it did not have the unwavering support from party leadership that was needed in order for changes to be implemented in the face of objections from planters, businessmen and the entrenched public service. The party's single success at bringing new laws into force came, not surprisingly, in the area of labor regulation. And then in 1949, time ran out.

Sources

Books and Articles

ANZAC Day Commemoration Committee of Queensland, www.anzacday.org.au.

Leo Austen, "Cultural Changes in Kiriwina," *Oceania* 16(1) (1945) 15–61.

Peter Biskup, Brian Jinks, and Hank Nelson, *A Short History of New Guinea* (Sydney: Angus and Robertson, 1968).

I. C. Campbell, "Anthropology and the Professionalisation of Colonial Administration in Papua and New Guinea," *The Journal of Pacific History* 33(1) (1998) 70–90.

I. C. Campbell, "The ASOPA Controversy: A Pivot of Australian Policy for Papua and New Guinea 1945–49," *The Journal of Pacific History* 35(1) (2000) 83–99.

Donald Denoon, *A Trial Separation: Australia and the Decolonisation of Papua New Guinea* (Canberra: Australian National University, Pandanus Books, 2005).

Brian Essai, *Papua and New Guinea: A Contemporary Survey* (London: Oxford University Press, 1961).

Peter Fitzpatrick, "Rather Like Slavery: Law and Labor in the Colonial Economy in Papua New Guinea," *Crime, Law and Social Change* 4(1) (1980) 77–95.

James Griffin, Hank Nelson, and Stewart Firth, *Papua New Guinea, a Political History* (Richmond: Heinemann Educational Australia, 1979).

Allen M. Healy, "Monocultural Administration in a Multicultural Environment: The Australians in Papua New Guinea," in J. J. Eddy and J. R. Nethercote (eds.), *Colony to Coloniser: Studies in Australian Administrative History* (Sydney: Hale & Iremonger, 1987) 207–224.

Brian Jinks, "Australia's Post-war Policy for New Guinea and Papua," *The Journal of Pacific History* 17(2) (1982) 86–106.

James McAuley, "Australia's Future in New Guinea," *Pacific Affairs* 26(1) (1953) 59–69.

Colonel J. K. Murray, "In Retrospect: Papua-New Guinea 1945–1949 and Territory of Papua and New Guinea 1949–1952" *Australian Journal of Politics and History* 14(3) (1968) 320–341.

Hank Nelson, "The Return to Rabaul 1945," *Journal of Pacific History* 30(2) (1995) 131–153.

Edward P. Wolfers, *Race Relations and Colonial Rule in Papua New Guinea* (Sydney: Australia and New Zealand Book Co., 1975).

Statute

Native Labor Ordinance 1941 (Papua)

Notes

1. Reprinted by the ANZAC Day Commemoration Committee of Queensland, on their website www.anzacday.org.au.
2. Brian Jinks, "Australia's Post-war Policy for New Guinea and Papua," *The Journal of Pacific History* 17(2) (1982) 94.
3. *Id.* at 99.
4. *Id.* at 99–100.
5. Edward P. Wolfers, *Race Relations and Colonial Rule in Papua New Guinea* (Sydney: Australia and New Zealand Book Co., 1975) 120.
6. Allen M. Healy, "Monocultural Administration in a Multicultural Environment: The Australians in Papua New Guinea," in J. J. Eddy and J. R. Nethercote (eds.), *Colony to Coloniser: Studies in Australian Administrative History* (Sydney: Hale & Iremonger, 1987) 218.
7. *Id.*
8. *Id.* At 219.
9. *Id.* at 219–220.
10. Brian Jinks, "Australia's Post-war Policy for New Guinea and Papua," *The Journal of Pacific History* 17(2) (1982) 98.
11. Brian Essai, *Papua and New Guinea: A Contemporary Survey* (London: Oxford University Press, 1961) 46.
12. Edward P. Wolfers, *Race Relations and Colonial Rule in Papua New Guinea* (Sydney: Australia and New Zealand Book Co., 1975) 121–122.
13. *Id.* at 122.
14. James Griffin, Hank Nelson, and Stewart Firth, *Papua New Guinea, a Political History* (Richmond: Heinemann Educational Australia, 1979) 103.
15. *Id.*
16. *Id.*
17. *Id.*

18. *Id.*
19. Peter Fitzpatrick, "Rather Like Slavery: Law and Labor in the Colonial Economy in Papua New Guinea," *Crime, Law and Social Change* 4(1) (1980) 84–86.
20. Brian Essai, *Papua and New Guinea: A Contemporary Survey* (London: Oxford University Press, 1961) 44.
21. James McAuley, "Australia's Future in New Guinea," *Pacific Affairs* 26(1) (1953) 59–69.
22. Peter Fitzpatrick, "Rather Like Slavery: Law and Labor in the Colonial Economy in Papua New Guinea," *Crime, Law and Social Change* 4(1) (1980) 85–86.

9 Re-establishing Authority/ Remaking Administration

Papua and New Guinea in the 1950s

Had the Australian Labor Party continued in power, Australia might have divested itself of its territories at some point during the 1950s, but, Labor was defeated in 1949 by a conservative coalition made up of the Liberal Party and the rural-based Country Party, which remained in office for the next twenty-two years. Robert Menzies, leader of the Liberal Party and Australia's prime minister before the war, became prime minister again, and would continue in office until 1966. Menzies understood the need both to cultivate friends among Australia's traditional allies, most of whom were anti-colonial, and at the same time, to retain backbench support, which meant holding onto the external territories for as long as possible. As a result, in justifying his colonial policy, Menzies emphasized preparing Papua and New Guinea for eventual independence by developing their economic and political skills and institutions. But he set no date for independence, permitting his colonial administrators to presume that event would not be until far into the future.

The colonial policies of the Liberal-Country coalition that Menzies led were the product of the so-called white Australia policy, a network of beliefs, policies and laws that enshrined white exceptionalism as a basic tenet of Australian political and social life. In order to understand the way that the ideology of white Australia shaped Australia's colonial policies and its relations to other nations in the region, we must start this chapter with a brief theoretical detour.

Where Prejudices Intersect

Kimberlé Crenshaw, an African American sociologist and law professor, coined the term "intersectionality" to refer to situations where people are subject to more than one source of discrimination and stereotyping. Her primary example was American black women, like herself, who were doubly discriminated against, both for being women and for being black. Crenshaw's major contribution to studies of race, class, and gender was her insight that the prejudice aimed at people who are members of more than one subordinated group is not just greater than the prejudice aimed at the members of any of these groups; it is qualitatively different. She honed this insight reviewing cases in which the U.S. Supreme Court had refused to rule that discrimination was involved when black women were fired. The court had separated the characteristics, saying that it would find for the plaintiffs either if the companies had fired every black employee or if they had fired every woman. Of course, the companies had done neither, so the court held that plaintiffs had not succeeded in proving that discrimination was involved in their terminations. What Crenshaw looked at, however, and what the court had failed to see, was that the companies had fired every black woman employee. If the court had realized that black women constituted their own subordinated group, different from either blacks or women generally, then the court might have recognized that discrimination had occurred and the women might have received the remedies they deserved.

Papuans and New Guineans were also doubly subordinated in the Australian view. First, Papua New Guineans are black, while most Australians—especially those with any power—are not only white, but acutely conscious of the specialness and privilege of whiteness in a corner of the world that is overwhelmingly brown and black. Second, Papua and New Guinea's Melanesian cultures were vastly different from Anglo-Australian culture, and different in ways that many Australians found simultaneously thrilling and frightening, beckoning and off-putting. In the following sections of this chapter, we will discuss the colonial policies created by the intersectionality of these particular racial and cultural differences, policies that were best characterized by condescension and paternalism. Australian policy in Papua and New Guinea was firmly embedded in the belief that Papuans and New Guineans must be changed, and that there was only one direction in which that change should occur. It was the Australians' particular duty to make black and brown Papuans and New Guineans as much like white Australians as possible.

The view generally accepted by white Australians was that Papua and New Guinea were darkly primitive places with people mired in the Stone Age, little better than children, irrational, violent, and amoral—if not downright immoral. This perspective was shared even by those who liked Papuans and New Guineans. For example, returning soldiers and the popular press still celebrated the "fuzzy wuzzy angels," Papuans and New Guineans who during World War II had carried wounded Australian soldiers through the jungle to hospitals and safety. That goodwill might have resulted in a more respectful colonial policy, were it not condescending. The very use of the patronizing term "fuzzy wuzzy" to describe grown men who had risked (and lost) their lives in the service of Australia suggests an underlying prejudice that colored every decision Australia was to make about its colonies.

This was hardly surprising. In the 1950s, the "white Australia" immigration policy was still officially the law of the land, as well as reflecting the sentiments of most Australians, a product of both white supremacist views and an allied existential fear of the peril of being overrun by neighboring populations. Gathered under the "white Australia" rubric were a number of laws and policies, including restrictions on the immigration, or even visits, to Australia of Asians and Pacific Islanders. This was designed, as Prime Minister John Curtin said in 1942, to ensure that Australia would "remain forever the home of the descendants of those people who came here in peace in order to establish in the South Seas an outpost of the British race."[1] Conflicting policies and interests—including an impetus toward increasing the population through immigration, and the interest of ex-service men in having their Asian wives join them in Australia—caused significant cracks to develop in its façade during the 1960s, but it was not until 1973 that "white Australia" was formally erased from the legal system.

The white Australia policy reflected an essentialist view of race and encouraged white Australians to view their own culture (which they believed to be the best of British culture) as unconditionally superior to those of Asia and the Pacific, and to view Asians and Pacific Islanders as not only culturally, but perhaps also as genetically, inferior. Australians tended to be social Darwinists, who saw Pacific Islanders on a scale that put them significantly behind Australians in their social and intellectual development, but who might (or might not) someday in the distant future achieving something like cultural parity. These essentialist views were shared by Australians of all political leanings, from those who wanted to help Papuans and New Guineans develop, to those who saw Papuans and New Guineans as inferior, good only to be servants or unskilled laborers.

Ensuring the Safety of Mainland Australia

Writing in 1955 in *Pacific Affairs*, Norman Harper, a leading foreign policy expert of the time, explained Australia's unusual foreign policy position: "Australia constitutes a white outpost in a predominantly Asian area. Unlike the Western imperial powers, she cannot cut loose from Asia."[2] At the same time, Harper wrote, Asian nations have become stronger, independent, more assertive, and anti-Western, and some were possibly Communist.

Australia quickly came to view Indonesia as the major threat to its security. Indonesia had gained its independence from the Netherlands in 1949, just before the Liberal-Country coalition came to power in Australia. Early in 1950, Indonesia gained control of the Aru and Tanimbar Islands, which are close to Australia, and was claiming sovereignty over the western half of Australia's bulwark, the island of New Guinea. Indonesia was anticolonial; it threatened, or at least Australians believed that it threatened, to elect a Communist government at any moment, and it was, or so the Australian press portrayed it, antiwhite. If New Guinea was to form a barrier against invasion, then its western flank could not be occupied by a potential invader. Given those fears, it was no surprise that the Australian government vehemently opposed the transfer of authority over half of the island of New Guinea from the Dutch to the Indonesians, although Australians like James McAuley, who styled themselves as experts in foreign affairs, disagreed:

> There is a strong body of opinion in Australia favouring either continuance of Dutch control or the substitution of an Australian trusteeship.... There is also a fear that a regime of Indonesian nationalists in Western New Guinea would stimulate subversive tendencies on the Australian side; this possibility, however, must not be exaggerated, since communication across the border is not at all easy, and the example of Indonesian nationalism will take effect rather through what the advanced natives of Rabaul and Port Moresby will read in the newspapers (when they have sufficient schooling to read the newspapers) than through closer contacts with Western New Guinea, where in any case the Indonesians would appear as masters of the Papuans, and less wealthy masters than the whites—a fact that counts for much in native estimation.[3]

Conservatives argued strongly that Australia had to be a party to any decision about Western New Guinea, that the Indonesian claim to sovereignty over it was "inadmissible" and "that 'the Government of Indonesia, being unstable and politically immature, is not capable of assisting the native peoples of New Guinea in the way required.' In addition, . . . Indonesia would be a hostile and aggressive neighbor. . . ."[4]

In a speech in August 1950, Australian Minister for External Affairs and External Territories P. C. Spender went even further, stating categorically that Indonesia has no "valid claim" to Western New Guinea, because the whole of New Guinea is "not in any way geographically part of Indonesia" but is part of the "Australian continental group":

> . . . the people of Dutch New Guinea are the same people as inhabit Australian New Guinea and Australian Papua . . . they are of approximately the same degree of social development, with the same background, customs and traditions.... Dutch New Guinea is accordingly an integral part of New Guinea as a whole. . . . The people have no racial affinity with the peoples of Indonesia.[5]

Spender did not stop there. Papuans in Dutch New Guinea, he said, should not have promises of immediate independence dangled before them; they should be treated in the same way that Australia treated Papua New Guineans:

> Their future should only be determined when they are able—which cannot be for a number of years—to speak politically for themselves. It will require long administrative experience and resources of scientific skill and personnel to enable the peoples of Dutch New Guinea to be gradually led to the concepts of democratic self-government.[6]

In those speeches, Spender made his and his government's interests apparent. One concern was that, should the Indonesians convince the Papuans of Western New Guinea that they were now independent, the thirst for independence would infect Australia's colonies as well. Another worry revealed in that statement was Australia's fear for its own security:

> If the claim of Indonesia to Dutch New Guinea were conceded to any degree at all, it would be but a matter of time, no matter how genuine may be assurances to the contrary, when the claim will be pushed further, so as to include the Trust Territory of Australian New Guinea and its people. . . . Experience has shown to Australians how strategically vital to Australian defence is the mainland of New Guinea. . . . [O]ne cannot disregard the ever-increasing Communist pressure in Asia. Communism has not got any foothold yet in Australian New Guinea. Australia is determined in so far as it can to ensure that it will not.[7]

China, where the Communist Party won control in 1949, was also very much feared, and that trepidation extended even to the small Chinese community in New Guinea. Despite overwhelming evidence that the New Guinea Chinese were traders and business people to the core, their nationality alone made them suspect, and one of the white settlers in New Guinea called for all settlers to be armed against the Chinese. McAuley pointed out that the natives of Papua and New Guinea seemed utterly uninterested in Communism, a situation that, he predicted, would change only if Australians were to "display unnecessary alarm," which "[would] naturally convince the more attentive natives that Communism is an interesting and potent force."[8]

If Australia regarded its Asian neighbors with suspicion, Asian attitudes toward Australia were, in return, similarly distrustful. What Asians noticed most prominently about their southern neighbor was the white

Australia policy, especially the restrictions it placed on Asians settling in, or even visiting, Australia. Australia and New Zealand, the only countries dominated by a white majority, and the only ones that still looked to Europe for their legitimacy and identification, were anomalies in the region. Although both had been colonies of England, they were pointedly not invited to a major conference of newly independent nations from Africa and Asia, which was held at Bandung, Indonesia, in 1955. The organizers announced that they were excluding Australia and New Zealand, in large part because of Australia's racial makeup and policies (as a result, the conference organizers were criticized in the Australian press for being "racialist"), and partly because of Australia's position on Western New Guinea. The resolutions passed by the conferees included one condemning "colonialism in all its manifestations" (although the condemnation did not extend to Indonesia's dubious acquisition of Western New Guinea).

The Intersectional Dilemma: Racist Policies Gradually Give Way, But Cultural Stereotypes Do Not

In the 1950s, the vast majority of Papuans and New Guineans still lived in villages and pursued a traditional, subsistence lifestyle. The very small number of Papuans and New Guineans who lived in towns worked for Australians, some for the colonial administration as police officers or clerks, and some for companies, often as domestic servants. The Australians created an intricate system of ordinances and regulations intended to preserve this rural-urban separation. For example, in 1953,

> the Papuan Native Regulations were amended to bring them into line with their counterparts in New Guinea by making it illegal for a Papuan to remain within a town for more than four days without employment, unless he or she were there to attend a hospital or court, were awaiting a passage home after the ending of a Labor agreement [or had permission from a magistrate or police officer to be there].[9]

That regulation was strengthened in 1957, with new rules permitting *kiaps* who came upon Papuans and New Guineans who were away from their home areas to order them to return home. The regulations also kept those Papua New Guineans who were in the towns separate from, and subservient to, the white population. Whites blamed resident locals for all sorts of social ills and were advised by an Anglican mission doctor to "keep natives away from your house at night. They are infectious [with malaria] just as a case of scarlet fever, except that the 'germ' needs a mosquito to carry it from the native to you."[10]

As for those Papuans and New Guineans permitted to stay in town, most of the regulations seemed to be aimed at keeping them in their place. The native regulations contained any number of discriminatory rules, such as those prohibiting Papuans and New Guineans from buying alcoholic drinks or even from entering public bars, and new rules kept being promulgated, further limiting what Papuans and New Guineans could do. In 1952, for example, it became illegal in New Guinea—as it had been in Papua since 1922—for a Papuan or New Guinean to be in another Indigenous employee's quarters without the employer's permission.[11] In 1953, Papuans and New Guineans were forbidden from having any weapons, other than tomahawks, axes, or knives, and those only if required for their work. After 1953, films that had already passed inspection by Australian censors could be imported into Papua and New Guinea without further censorship, but only for white audiences; films could not be shown to Papuans and New Guineans without a special permit until 1962, when censorship of films to all audiences was reinstated. Wolfers notes that the only grounds for censoring films were supposed to be blasphemy, obscenity, and the like, but that "even after 1962, films were generally censored on racial, rather than moral, grounds."[12] The censorship difference between films for white audiences and those for Papuans and New Guineans was important, because it was not until 1958 that the regulations requiring separate seating for whites and Papuans and New Guineans at all public meetings and places of entertainment were lifted. If Papuans and New Guineans thought that, during the 1950s, they could make up for their lack of access to movie theaters and other white entertainments by having their own parties, they were often disappointed. An ordinance enacted in 1952 made it unlawful to "make a noise by shouting, beating a drum or dancing during the curfew hours."[13]

There were some bright spots. In 1946, the clothing regulations were reformed to permit New Guineans to wear Western-style clothes, a prohibition that had been lifted in Papua only in 1941. However, as the regulation insisted, it was still unlawful for a Papuan or New Guinean to wear

Western garb if it was "dirty, wet or insanitary." Also in 1946, shopkeepers were, for the first time, required to sell to locals and to charge them and whites the same prices, although shopkeepers could still require that Papuans and New Guineans not enter their stores, but make all their purchases "from a shutter at the side."[14] In 1955, the curfew regulations, which had at one time prohibited Papua New Guineans from being out in public at any time in any of the colonial towns without a pass from their employer, were reduced, to the hours between 11 p.m. to 5 a.m.

In the 1950s, as had been the case earlier, Australians did not refer to the Indigenous population as Papuans or New Guineans. Sometimes, an Australian would use an Indigenous person's tribal affiliation, such as Goilala or Chimbu. Most often, however, Australians referred to Papuans and New Guineans as "natives," *kanaka* (or, more disparagingly, *bush kanaka*), or *boi* (a term used for men of every age; the female equivalent was *meri*, and Papuan and New Guinean children were called *pickaninis*). The use of the term *boi* was banned from official government documents in 1947. When official use of the term "native" was banned in 1956, a great many Australians confessed themselves perplexed about why Papuans and New Guineans would object to such an "innocuous" term. Simogun, one of the three Indigenous members of the Legislative Council, all of whom had been chosen because of their pro-administration attitudes, was quoted as saying in response that:

> ...We are Natives of this country, but the European is not called a Native he is called after the name of his country, and we ask ... that this custom of calling us Native now cease and we be known as Papuan men, New Guinea men, or Papuan women, New Guinea women.[15]

Although the new rules might have succeeded in erasing the offending terms from official documents, they continued to be widely used in conversation and unofficial documents well into the 1970s. And, indeed, Wolfers notes, in 1969 the administration had to remind colonial officers again that they were not supposed to use *boi* "when speaking or writing of or to indigenes" and should not be addressed as *masta*.[16]

The ambiguity of ordinances related to rape and sexual abuse demonstrated the racial myths that dominated thinking in the colonial period. The *White Women's Protection Ordinance*, forbidding a Papuan or New Guinean male from approaching a white woman, had been in place since

1926, but no similar protection had existed for Papuan and New Guinean women. Indeed, rather than protecting Papuan and New Guinean women from unwanted sexual advances by white men, many Australians blamed the women for what happened to them. A handbook for Lutheran missionaries at the time advised that "Missionaries must beware of becoming too friendly with the opposite sex. The native has very strong sexual drives which [she] often is unable to control."[17]

It was assumed by many Westerners that sex with Indigenous women was part of their colonial due. That imbalance was addressed, though certainly not righted, in the 1950s by an administration anxious to appear to be fair and concerned. But the first legislation to be enacted, in 1951, did not expressly bar white men from having sex with Papuan and New Guinean women, as the *White Women's Protection Ordinance* had done in regards to Indigenous men. Instead, it put the onus on Indigenous women, making it unlawful for them to be in "premises occupied by any person other than a native between the hours of six o'clock in the evening and six o'clock in the morning" unless the woman's husband was with her. Cyril Belshaw describes weekend evenings in Hanuabada, a large Papuan village within the boundaries of Port Moresby, with its narrow walkways jammed with white men coming into the village in search of sex.[18]

That problem was addressed in 1954, with a new regulation prohibiting any non-Papua New Guinean from entering a village during curfew hours. Belshaw's research suggests, however, that the ordinance was not strictly enforced. And barring white men from the villages did not bar them from taking Indigenous women into their homes. Meanwhile, in 1958, the *White Women's Protection Ordinance* was repealed, so that, finally, it was not unlawful for a Papuan or New Guinean male and a consenting white woman to have sex.[19]

Despite all of this, there were some marriages (or liaisons so extended that they took on many of the aspects of a marriage) between whites and Papuans and New Guineans in the 1950s—almost all involving a white man and a Papuan or New Guinean woman. According to at least one white man who had married a local woman, "The old contention was that when you take a native girl for a wife you inevitably go down the scale instead of bringing them up."[20] Andrew Lind led a team in the late 1960s that interviewed about thirty-five interracial couples, some of whom had married not long after World War II. Lind notes that intermarriage, while still uncommon in the 1950s, happened slightly more frequently than it had prewar:

> The war was undoubtedly "a kind of watershed in the development of race relations in New Guinea", in which it became increasingly possible to accept the marriage of a European man with a native woman as at least tolerable for some people, if still incomprehensible to most "normal" people. [21]

Still, Lind found, couples who entered into mixed-race marriages in the 1950s tended to be "a bit of the rebel and the non-conformist and [to have] a disposition to strike out on new ventures" because:

> . . .the social definitions of mixed racial marriages have been modified with the passage of time, diminishing in the severity of their disapproval notably during [the 1960s]; but there still remain and there are likely to continue to be for a long time strong collective sentiments adverse to inter-racial marriage in both the European and native communities.[22]

Although the disapproval of intermarriage decreased during the 1960s, it did not entirely disappear, and the partners in such marriages found that they and their children remained perpetual outsiders, at least in relation to Australian society:

> A few Papua New Guineans "made it" in colonial society, especially after World War II, though it is doubtful whether they ever became fully accepted members of it. . . . Persons of mixed race origins, immigrants from other Pacific Islands and Asian countries, and their descendants, lived in a social limbo between the two main castes.[23]

These couples were venturesome not only in marriage but in other parts of their lives as well. Lind found that "much of the more significant economic development, notably in the Highlands, had been carried out by European [men] who in their pioneering activities have dared to oppose traditional expectations by taking native wives."[24] The husband tended to be the dominant partner in those marriages. Not surprisingly, their wives' submissiveness was one of the reasons these men gave for preferring a mixed marriage over a marriage to an Australian or another white woman:

> I can tell you this [one of Lind's informants told him], if I had my life to live over again, I wouldn't be married to a European. With my wife now, there is nothing that I can't do. Everything I do, even though it's dead wrong, it's dead right. And you know that is a very pleasant atmosphere to live in. . . .[25]

It is a pity that none of Lind's interviewers were women. The Papuan and New Guinean wives might have opened up more to a woman, especially to another Indigenous woman, and one would like to have had the wives' views, not just about their relations with their spouses, but also about the role that the wives had in their husbands' economic success.

Another Kind of Diversity: Different Versions of Racism

There were differences among Australians, but not in their view that Papuans and New Guineans were less than their equals. Just about every Australian in Papua and New Guinea believed that; the differences came in the varying attitudes toward the people whom they all agreed were inferior. Some Australians believed that Papuans and New Guineans were genetically inferior, that no amount of education or assistance would ever make them the equals of white Australians. Some believed that Papuans and New Guineans could, possibly, develop to be the equal of whites, but that it would take much effort on the part of helpful Australians, and many years.

Paternalism was the approach of almost all Australians, Labor or Liberal-Country, planter, missionary, or politician. The idea of paternalism was already undergoing enough criticism in international circles for the Australian government to be somewhat embarrassed by it, or at least to see a need to justify it, as Sir Paul Hasluck, the Minister for Territories from 1951 to 1963, endeavored to do:

> We should remember that paternalism in its true nature is good. Paternalism should not be accepted as a term of abuse or criticism.

> At the same time, we need to be aware, as all fathers need to remind themselves, that the paternal attitude is only good for small children so long as they need the protection and the guidance of their parents.[26]

Most Australians involved in the colonizing of Papua and New Guinea in the 1950s agreed with Hasluck that Papuans and New Guineans were still "small children," and that, therefore, to look down on them, especially if one did so in a kindly way, was not discriminatory or racist. Australians insisted on this in every report to the Trusteeship Council. Of course, one might expect the truth to be a bit varnished in that setting, but similar sentiments were expressed in many places where it is more likely that the writer was saying what he believed.

Racism, however, is a term with different definitions. Australians argued that they were not racist because Papuans and New Guineans truly were inferior to them, at least culturally, at least at that moment, and so it was not racist to say they were inferior, nor was it racist to treat them paternalistically, even condescendingly. Nor was it racist to maintain a society separate from theirs from which even their educated few were barred. To outside observers however, these attitudes amounted to the very essence of racism. Wolfers quotes "a cautious Indian observer":

> For the people of New Guinea the good Australian Administrator has sympathy, even affection, but no sense of affinity. The "paternalism" strikes one as fairly genuine and there is pride and satisfaction at the achievements of the "native". But there is no concept, dream even, of a multiracial society.[27]

Those Australians who had to deal with outsiders, such as foreign ministry officers, knew that Australia had to tread warily around these differing expectations of the proper relations between people of different cultures and races. In 1950, P. C. Spender, the minister for external territories, wanted to ensure that members of the United Nations not receive information or opinions that might give rise to criticism of Australia's role as a colonial power, and instructed government field officers to do what they could to prevent the presentation of petitions by Indigenous people to the United Nations Visiting Mission that toured New Guinea in 1950.[28]

Even in this atmosphere, there were

> some dramatic, if symbolic, gestures towards the building of a multiracial society. In 1944, the [Labor] Minister for External Territories (E. J. "Eddie" Ward) refused to allow himself to be carried ashore from a boat by some Papuans. He preferred to take off his shoes and wade—a gesture that was widely derided by expatriates at the time, and not repeated by one of his successors as Minister for External Territories (C. E. Barnes) who allowed himself to be carried ashore by Papuans in 1969. In 1946, some Papuans visited government house for tea, and earned the then Administrator of the Territory (Colonel J. K. Murray) the title of which he is now reputedly most proud—"Kanaka Jack". For some time, the old-time settlers, the "B4s" boycotted government house in protest against even such token integration.[29]

Proving that, as with President Richard M. Nixon's visit to China, breakthroughs of that radical a nature can be done safely only by members of the conservative party, there was some, but less, fuss when Sir Donald Cleland (Colonel Murray's successor as Administrator, and an appointee of the Liberal-Country coalition government) invited a few token Papuans to a large, diplomatic reception at government house. In her memoir, Lady Rachel Cleland recalls this as one of the government house's proudest moments. Remarkably, however, there is no other mention of socializing with Papua New Guineans in a memoir that is exhaustively detailed about her social engagements.

Many Australians, exemplified by public servants like Sir Donald and Lady Cleland, grew very fond of Papua and New Guinea and its inhabitants, and were committed to their betterment. That kindness, however, was always laced with condescension. They liked Papuans and New Guineans, but they did not respect them; they liked them in the same spirit in which one likes small children or kittens. Lady Cleland's memoir of her years as the Administrator's wife demonstrates her fondness for the people of the country, but, over and over, it also demonstrates her blindness to their maturity, ability, and intelligence.

The Clelands and those like them believed that Papuans and New Guineans could be educated and become fully responsible Australians. But they saw Papuans and New Guineans as currently being so far from that ideal that it would take many generations for them to catch up. In the meantime, all one could do was to be kind, and to offer them education, a little at a time. Lady Cleland tells a story about finding her cook sitting outside the cookhouse one day, appearing to be very unhappy. She was a kind person; she sincerely liked her cook. She asked him what the matter was. He told her that he felt he had no future, that he would always be nothing but a kitchen boy, and that he wished for more. Lady Cleland was perplexed: she, too, could see no future for him other than as a kitchen boy, but she did not understand why he was feeling so upset about it. That was what Papuans and New Guineans were—kitchen boys. What more could he expect?

Another example of the condescension of even the most sympathetic of public officers was provided by David Fenbury. His concern for Papuans and New Guineans is demonstrated by the task he took on in the 1950s. He was almost solely responsible for convincing the administration to create a new kind of home rule for Papuans and New Guineans. He called them local government councils, elected bodies that were to be given many of the powers of a town council, and that were to take Papuans and New Guineans a sizeable step closer to political self-sufficiency. Fenbury also campaigned, though less successfully, in favor of promoting Papuans and New Guineans to judgeships in the Courts for Native Affairs and Courts for Native Matters. His support of these institutions, in the face of considerable opposition from his more conservative colleagues, demonstrates that Fenbury believed, when many around him did not, that Papuans and New Guineans were capable of running an independent polity.

And yet his writings about Papua and New Guinea were laced with racism. In a talk to the Waigani Seminar in 1969, for example, he tried to strike a note of jaunty "boys-will-be-boys" humor by referring to Papuans and New Guineans as "little"; "morose little survivors"; "scruffy little Kaulons"; and "two miserable little Kasalea men."[30] For a speech given to an academic conference, it was remarkably lacking in insight or analysis. The only attempts at elucidating Papuan and New Guinean culture resulted in sentences like this: ". . .the primitive's philosophy is ever disconcertingly callous."[31]

Many of the Australian planters and business people in Papua and New Guinea and more than a few public servants were even more negative toward Papuans and New Guineans. They believed local culture to be inferior not only at the moment, but forever. In their minds, Papuans and New Guineans were, not just by their culture, but by their very natures, less intelligent, less reasonable, and less mature than whites—perhaps even less human.

It served their purposes, both economic and social, for Papuans and New Guineans to be considered inferior. They did not want to see Papuans and New Guineans in positions any higher than house servant or plantation laborer. They did not want Papuans and New Guineans living in town, unless they were in the *boi haus* or the barracks. They derided any attempts, whether by the missions or by the administration, to improve the lot of Papuans and New Guineans, especially if the improvements seemed in any way to suggest that a local person was capable of personal development. Still, many of the members of this group made firm friends among Papuans and New Guineans whom they cared for very deeply. Invariably, however, they saw these friends as exceptions.

The view that Papuans and New Guineans were inferior was shared by another group. It was made up of men who viewed Papua and New Guinea as their very own vast, savage, romantic playground, a magical and difficult territory that existed mainly for their personal enjoyment, to afford them adventures out of which they could spin stories that would impress the folks at home. Many of the swashbuckling romantics were *kiaps*, and most of them wrote books about their exploits.

Often, the second group (those who believed Papuans and New Guineans barely capable of rational thought) and the third group (the swashbucklers) were combined in one person. J. K. McCarthy, for example, who began his long career in Papua and New Guinea as a cadet in 1927—and with the exception of a few years during World War II remained there as a colonial public servant until after the elections for the first House of Assembly—wrote a memoir that focused heavily, and with the obvious delight of the raconteur, on the most outlandish of New Guinean exploits, including, of course, cannibalism and head-hunting, and not omitting descriptions of the rites used for everything from warding off bad spirits to curing warts. McCarthy himself figures centrally in all of his stories as a greatly wise and civilized man, amused at the antics of the natives, but always tolerant, because they are so exotic, and childish, and wrong.

The 1950s: Liberal-Country Takes Over—and Settles In for the Long Term

Labor's tenure in government in Australia (and, therefore, its role in shaping Papua and New Guinea), which had begun in 1941, came to an abrupt end after the December 1949 election, when the conservative Liberal-Country coalition secured a narrow victory. The new government moved almost immediately to alter the administration of the territory. A new Ministry for Territories was created, to oversee Papua and New Guinea, as well as Australia's Northern Territory, which had Australia's largest Indigenous population. Prime Minister Robert Menzies appointed Paul Hasluck, a Liberal Party MP, to head the new ministry. Hasluck was in many ways the opposite of his predecessor Eddie Ward, and not only because Hasluck was an academic (in particular, a historian), a patrician, and a conservative. He was Ward's opposite in action, too; he exercised full control of the affairs of the territories, right down to the mundane details. During the Labor years, J. K. Murray, the Territorial Administrator in Port Moresby, had been the driving force in the administration, with Canberra acting more as a secondary influence, occasionally in support but more often as a brake on the Administrator's enthusiasm. During Hasluck's twelve years in the ministry, however, everything emanated from his office in Canberra. Murray was quickly replaced by Donald Cleland, who proved to be an expert at carrying out his minister's wishes.

The government preached, and probably desired, Indigenous economic development in Papua and New Guinea, if for no other reason than so the territories would begin producing their own revenues and stop being a drain on government finances. But, the style and values of the government—and probably of most Australians at that time—made it almost impossible for Indigenous development of any kind, economic or political, to occur.

The Australian Colonial Style: Top-Down Management

Australians saw their mission in the territories as one of educating a backward people to the point where they could govern themselves. Col. J. K. Murray had suggested that some kind of self-determined change in the status of Papua and New Guinea was likely in the foreseeable future. But even his own minister, Eddie Ward, did not subscribe to that view. In a 1948 speech, Ward said:

> How quickly can a million and a half people, most of them naked or in loincloths, be brought up to a decent civilized standard? It's too big a job to be done in a few years, too big to get done in a generation. But we've made an interesting start.[32]

Ward's successor Hasluck spoke of an even longer time line. In his view, it would be a century, at least, perhaps much longer, before Papuans and New Guineans would have evolved to the point where they could govern themselves. Hasluck's view was more geological than historical:

> We will see a better educated native people, a more politically conscious and politically active native population who, very gradually, over a number of generations, will take an increasing interest both in running their own enterprises and in taking a share in their own government. [But . . .] those days may be far away—they may be more than a century in the future. . . .[33]

Hasluck believed that Papuans and New Guineans had to be uplifted by being introduced to the values inherent in two important Australian institutions - Christianity and the law. This would take a very long time, but it was a key part of the Australian responsibility, in his view, to resist the kind of accelerated decolonization taking place elsewhere in the world. Papuans and New Guineans could have a positive role in their own administration only when they had learned to exercise authority in accordance with Australian concepts, values, and procedures; in the meantime, they were in an indefinite learning phase.[34]

It never occurred to the Australians who had anything to do with colonial policy that there might be a particularly Papuan and New Guinean path to economic, political, and social development—or that such a path might be different from, and yet just as valid as, the Australian path. The brand of ethnocentric social Darwinism that held sway in Australia at the time took, as one of its major premises, that social evolution is a one-way, one-lane road. They believed that every culture wends its way along an almost preordained route, growing ever more intelligent, ever more sophisticated, culminating finally in the great apotheosis of Western society. James McAuley, a poet, diplomat, and student of colonial affairs, was among the most thoughtful men of his generation, and yet even he believed that there was only one path to development for everyone, not least for Papuans and New Guineans:

> . . .the direction of culture change in New Guinea must be a one-way assimilation of native life to Western culture as represented by Australia. There is not in New Guinea that hard resistant core of an alien religious-social order which sets limits to acculturation among Islamic peoples, for instance. The indigenous traditional cultures are parochial, variegated, extremely primitive and very fragile. On the one hand they lack the durability which codification and organization give to civilized traditions; and, on the other hand, none of their distinctive peculiarities seems able to survive under close contact with modern civilization: not only material equipment and techniques, traditional arts and crafts and pursuits, but also the fundamental world view, the ceremonial life, the body of customary law relating to basic personal and property relations, the characteristic forms of social organization, the local languages, seem bound to be more or less completely effaced as time goes on. . . . Where old things give way to new, the new things adopted will be Western. . . . This is so even in the absence of any deliberate policy of acculturation, but Australianization could become a part of conscious policy, influencing not only the manner and matter of native education but also the administration of native affairs generally.[35]

It was therefore not part of the Australian worldview to consider moving Papuans and New Guineans onto a different path; Australians were convinced that, even if they were given a choice, this was the only possible path, and therefore the one that Papua New Guineans would eventually have made for themselves.

The only difference the colonizers might make was to hasten the process, to make it occur somewhat sooner than it otherwise might. Even with Australian assistance, however, it would take a very long time. The Hasluck administration adopted Hubert Murray's view that Papuans and New Guineans could "grow up" under Australian tutelage. But, since

Hasluck, like most Australians of his time, believed Papuans and New Guineans to be in a very primitive stage of development, the conclusion drawn was that it would take a very, very long time for that growth to occur. It might, indeed, take forever. Healy's take on Hasluck is pretty devastating:

> He had absolutely no experience of colonial government; and, if his writings may be taken as indicators, he read nothing in the way of comparative colonial administration. But he was convinced that if he set a course for Papua New Guinea towards a model society (as in Hubert Murray's day, an idealized Australia), he was fulfilling a moral trust by insisting that New Guineans conform to all the paradigms appropriate to the ultimate goal. Any notion of cultural pluralism was automatically excluded from the shaping of administrative institutions.... Within Australia he came to be regarded as the fount of all wisdom on colonial matters, even across party political boundaries.[36]

By the 1950s, the official position became one of eventual and gradual assimilation. If they were to develop, Papuans and New Guineans had to adopt Western political, social, and legal institutions. Only then would it be possible for them to begin assuming positions of responsibility and self-rule. Hasluck wrote:

> ...in the nature of things ... self-government cannot come until the two races in New Guinea have solved that major problem of living and working together. It is certain that the problem cannot be finally solved until the native peoples have advanced to a point where a large majority of them can, in fact, participate in management of the life, industry, and politics of the country. That is a long way ahead. It may be, as I have said, more than a century ahead....[37]

Hasluck does not explain his statement that "the two races" will continue to live together, and different interpretations can be drawn from it. He might have meant that Papua and New Guinea would remain, forever, an Australian overseas possession. It seems more likely, however, that he envisioned Papua and New Guinea eventually becoming, as he said in that same speech, "a part of Australia, like the Northern Territory." At a later date, he said he "looked forward to a free, close and permanent association between the two countries; perhaps New Guinea would even become a State of Australia, like New South Wales or Queensland."[38]

Hasluck did not envision that Australia would ever leave Papua and New Guinea to its own devices. For him, it seems, one of the reasons why Papuans and New Guineans had to take a decidedly Australian path to development was because Australians and Papua New Guineans would always be politically linked. He was not clear—or, more likely, he changed his mind from time to time—about the nature of that linkage, but he was firm in the belief that Australians would continue to live forever in Papua and New Guinea and participate in its government. As a result, in governing the territories in the 1950s Hasluck said that the administration had two problems:

> The first is essentially a problem of race relations, in that a way has to be found in which peoples of different standards of living and cultural habits can live in harmony with each other and with respect for each other's rights and dignity. The second is the problem of employing native people to an increasing extent in the Public Service so that . . . they can be trained to assume responsibility when the eventual goal of self-government is attained.[39]

Note again, Hasluck's use of that key word "eventual."

Policies and Practice: The Public Service and Political Development in the 1950s

Many of those who observed the colonial experience in Papua and New Guinea concluded that a major reason for the failure of most attempts at Indigenous development during the period was that even a hint of initiative on the part of Papua New Guineans was met with resistance by the colonial administration. Wolfers, for example, says,

> The primary aim of all colonial administrations in Papua and New Guinea until the 1960s was neither "development" nor "preparation" but control. . . . And the long-term debilitating effects of this policy upon the political advancement of Papua New Guineans were often neither intended nor foreseen.[40]

The Public Service: Bureaucracy

There are many governing styles that colonial administrations can choose, and many goals they can adopt for the nations they have colonized. And the two go together. The quality, education, aims, and administrative structure of the colonial civil service will have much to do with whether the administration's goals are met—and will suggest whether policymakers were serious in the first place about trying to meet their stated goals. One bit of evidence that strongly suggests the Australian government was not truly serious about helping Papuans and New Guineans to develop a self-sustaining political and economic structure was the defeat of postwar efforts to create a more professional colonial service, one that would have been better able to carry out the kind of development that the Australian government said it wanted for the territories. Another bit of evidence was the way in which infrastructure improvements in the territories were allocated: although Canberra poured considerably more money than it had prewar into building roads and government stations, hospitals, and aid posts, and supporting a huge public service sector, the construction seemed to lead much more toward the comfort of white folks and not toward real development for Papuans and New Guineans.

Under the Liberal-Country administration, the public service in and about Papua and New Guinea grew ever larger and more complicated:

> Pre-war, Papua and New Guinea were expected to pay for themselves; [New Guinea did] while Papua struggled along with an annual subsidy from Australia averaging about £45,000. After the war, by contrast, Australia poured money, materials and white officials into the islands. . . .[41]

But the increasing expenditures did not lead to greater efficiency. Even Donald Cleland, an administrator of exceeding tact, who was hardly ever heard to utter a criticism of his superiors, complained that with some department heads reporting to him, others reporting directly to Canberra, and some with no clear idea of where they should report, it was extremely difficult to put any program into effect, let alone to get departments to work together.

But the confusion in Port Moresby served the ministry's aims. Under Hasluck's direction, control of both the general policies and day-to-day action decisions affecting the territories shifted from administrators and district officers in Papua and New Guinea itself to politicians and public servants in Canberra. Hasluck was a details man, and he had the time to devote to it. Unlike the earlier postwar ministers, who also held other portfolios, and ones they considered of more importance than Papua and New Guinea, external territories was Hasluck's sole portfolio. Still, the centralization of all decision making in Hasluck's office might have been another reason for the slow pace of development in the 1950s. Administrators in Moresby had to reduce every problem, large or small, to a memo, and then send the memo to Canberra, where it would move slowly upward through the bureaucratic hierarchy, until it eventually reached Hasluck himself.

Finally, the policies of the Liberal-Country coalition were themselves a major factor in the slow pace of development. Hasluck, a university lecturer, came to his job with little experience of colonial administration, but he refused to learn from those with know-how. He would not pay attention to anything the British had done, he said, because Papua and New Guinea was *sui generis*. There was no other place like it: "New Guinea is neither a colony nor a territory; it is the experimental stage of something which the world has not yet seen . . . a guardianship," Hasluck said.[42]

Hasluck insisted that the entire country had to rise at the same time. There could be, for example, no primary schools until the administration was prepared to finance primary schools everywhere. There could be no high schools until every Papuan and New Guinean child had been educated through primary school. Hasluck even frowned upon sending promising students overseas, on the grounds that none should go until all could go. He refused to educate a small group of people, arguing that he did not want to create an elite. It was, he said, small groups of educated elites who were causing anticolonial uprisings in other parts of the world. Too much education created "native demagogues."[43] Since he believed that Australians would always remain in Papua and New Guinea, Hasluck aimed to create a situation in which they would be safe and their interests would be respected. As a combined result of these policies, there were few educational opportunities for Papuans and New Guineans throughout the 1950s.

Education in the 1950s—or the Lack of It

There had been precious few schools prior to the war, and by 1960 there were not that many more. Westerners have a penchant to credit (and blame) individuals rather than parties or systems for successes (or failures). It became common in Australia to blame W. C. Groves, the director of education for Papua and New Guinea for the failure to recruit sufficient teachers or build sufficient schools in the period. However, the department need not have hired him as its director, and, once it became apparent, as it quickly did, how timorous he was, and how slowly he would proceed, he could have been replaced. Better men (like J. K. Murray) were replaced, but Groves stayed in office for years. One has to assume he was doing in the educational sphere exactly what was wanted—i.e., practically nothing.

The Health Service in the 1950s

The health service was an exception to the otherwise slow pace of development in the 1950s. At the end of World War II, there were only a couple of hospitals in all of Papua and New Guinea, primarily military facilities that had been built during the war. There were very few doctors available, and only a handful of aid posts to serve the vast rural areas. Owing partly to the malnutrition brought about by wartime shortages, and partly to the importation by waves of soldiers of germs formerly unknown in New Guinea, disease was rife. John Gunther was appointed assistant administrator for health services. He was energetic and proficient, and he did not let rules or red tape stand in his way. For example, hearing that there were in Australia a number of refugee doctors from various European countries who were not allowed to practice medicine because of their lack of the English-language skills that would enable them to pass the Australian medical exams, Gunther recruited them to work in Papua and New Guinea. He also trained Papuans and New Guineans to serve as medical personnel, especially in rural aid posts.

Some Australians complained about Gunther's methods. They were even more critical of the use of Papuans and New Guineans as medical personnel than they were about the European doctors. Most writers today credit the health service's successes entirely to the force of John Gunther's personality, and there is no doubt that is a large part of the explanation. Equally important, however, was the willingness of Canberra (that is, of Hasluck and his departmental secretary) to acquiesce in what Gunther proposed. Canberra was willing to support Gunther in opening hospitals and extending medical care, because, in Hasluck's view, medicine was a social service graciously delivered by the administration to needy Papuans and New Guineans. Where Hasluck drew the line was when Gunther wanted to send a few Papuans and New Guineans to the school for Pacific Island medical assistants that had recently been established in Fiji. Their enrolment would have implied they were capable of learning fairly complicated concepts, and that was hard for many Australians to accept, so it was easier to deny Papua and New Guinea trained medical personnel than to deal with the political blowback at home and among Papua and New Guinea's expatriate planters and business people.

The debate over the capacities of Papuans and New Guineans was often hidden in arguments that seemed to be about something else. For example, Brian Essai published *Papua and New Guinea: A Contemporary Survey* in 1961, an odd little pro-administration book that got most of its facts right but seems confused about others. Essai wrote that, in addition to the *luluai* and *tultul*, government-appointed village officers responsible for keeping order and carrying out administration decisions, most villages also had a "medical *tultul*," an orderly trained to do simple medical procedures and appointed on the recommendation of a medical officer. Essai wrote, "Administration policy is to replace medical *tultuls* by 1961 with native medical assistants who have graduated from one of the medical training schools in the Territory and are employed by the Department of Health."[44] But that was not administration policy, and there were no medical training schools in the Territory. He may have been referring here, however obliquely, to what must have been arguments between local whites and John Gunther about the status of Papuans and New Guineans who were trained in medicine.

Political "Development"—Why It Did Not Happen

The administration's plans for political development grew out of its view that all forms of Papuan and New Guinean development should be in the direction of making the territory and its people as much like Australia and Australians as possible, as well as its wish that development proceed exceedingly slowly.

In keeping with these policies, the administration's political development program at first consisted only of appointing Papuans and New Guineans to represent the administration in each village. In Papua, the village officials were called village constables; in New Guinea, they were called *luluai* and *tultuls*, and given brimmed caps as insignia of office. The administration was supposed to appoint a *luluai* for each village. According to the ordinance, the *luluai's* powers included "the maintenance of law and order, sanitation, hygiene, maintenance of roads, etc."[45] What that meant in practice was that the *luluai* conveyed the administration's instructions on those matters to the village. Essai wrote that *luluai* were "usually" nominees of the people "with natural authority and good standing in the community."[46] *Tultuls* were assistants to the *luluais* and were also administrative appointments. In some areas, the administration also named what they called paramount *luluai,* to oversee the work of the *luluai* in several villages.

The terms *luluai* and *tultul* were borrowed from German New Guinea, but the borrowing pretty much stopped at the names. The German regime in New Guinea, like those of the British in India and Africa, was indirect and gave local people a great deal of leeway in running their own affairs, especially at the local and village level; the German colonial administrators had viewed these village-level appointments as a first step toward locally managed governments that would combine German ideas about republican polities with New Guinea's traditional governmental forms. To this end, they empowered villagers to select headmen and constables from among their own. The Australians had no intention of supporting that kind of democratic initiative. Although they insisted that they intended Papuans and New Guineans to learn about democracy, and to remain colonized only until they did gain such an understanding, the administration's form of rigidly top-down autocracy would not have given local people much information about what democracy was supposed to be about, nor any experience in operating democratic institutions:

> relations between government and governed in Papua and New Guinea were not in any meaningful sense "political". The systems of "native administration" . . . were systems of structured dependence. . . . Village officials were expected to ensure that the lawful orders made by (white) administration officers were obeyed and peace was kept between patrols; that taxes were collected; that villages were cleaned; and that government policies were otherwise adhered to. They "led" only as cheerleaders for developmental projects proposed by foreign government officials. . . . Government officers always retained the

> right to intervene directly in any area of indigenous community life. Village officials were only occasionally consulted by government officers, and then only when the latter chose. If the villagers did not obey these officers, they might be gaoled. . . .[47]

The *luluai* and *tultul* system that the Australians created was not particularly effective. It is doubtful whether villagers, particularly those far from government stations, paid any attention at all to these supposed official leaders, except during a *kiap*'s infrequent visits to the village. Even Essai, who usually took the administration's side of things, concluded that, "Generally, the system of native administration, through indigenous authorities has not been successful." Local officials, Essai said, had not been granted the kinds of police powers, nor did they possess the hereditary status, that would enable them to enforce their orders, "and therefore couldn't succeed unless they happened to have strong personalities and happened to get Government backing."[48]

The administration and local people saw the problem of village governance from very different perspectives. Whether their villages were organized around semi-hereditary chiefs (as in the Trobriand Islands and other coastal and island areas), or around leaders that Australians and anthropologists called "big men," who rose to power through the skills at oratory, mediation, or war, villagers believed that they already had adequate and functioning systems of governance. Although Australian administrators could not see it, these systems were essentially democratic. Indeed, they were more democratic than Australia's periodic elections, and considerably more democratic than the top down, autocratic rule imposed by Australia on PNG. Big men could not succeed without the support of the clan or village. Even hereditary chiefs depended for their political power on the continuing consent of their people; if a consensus in favor of a chief fell away, he had no choice but to retire. Because these kinship and clan-based political systems were so different from the institutions of government they had at home in Australia, the colonial administrators were unshakeable in their belief that villagers had no political system worth preserving, or even adapting. And that whatever they did have, it was not democratic.

The administration also wanted different things of village government than Papuans and New Guineans did. *Luluai* and *tultul* were admonished to see to it that an Australian standard of hygiene was met, that roads were built, and that tribal fights were stopped. None of these strange, imported notions were of any interest to village people. In addition, the administration wanted to unify the territories into a single political whole, with villages as mere parts of that greater system:

> The problem . . . is to evolve a system of government for a primitive country whose population is at widely varying cultural levels, and whose distribution and social organization do not favour the growth of large political units. . . . The system of administration adopted by the Government is, in effect, to foster a series of centralized native authorities by appointing village officials and endowing them with certain powers and jurisdiction over tribal areas.[49]

This may well have been the concept most bewildering to Papuans and New Guineans. It was also the one most likely to undermine their way of life. Roads and aid posts could be accommodated, and might even prove to be useful. But the end of villages as independent political entities meant a change of unthinkable magnitude.

A first step in the process of integrating Papuan and New Guinean polities into larger entities was the introduction of local government councils. The notion behind such councils—another Australian reworking of a British colonial idea—was that Papuans and New Guineans gradually could be introduced both to the concept of representative self-government, and to the notion that they were now part of a political entity larger than the clan or village, through their participation in the councils each of which would have authority over a geographical grouping composed of several villages, and be made up of popularly elected members. As envisioned, especially by David Fenbury, who had spent several months in Africa learning the British system, the councils would finance themselves and their projects by raising taxes, and would have the authority to build roads, schools, health care facilities, and other infrastructure as well as make rules for village life. Fenbury even imagined a tribunal, connected to each local government council, which would hear disputes among local people.

The idea of local government councils was met with mixed reactions. More conservative *kiaps* and commissioners saw the councils as adversaries in the quest for village allegiance, and therefore condemned them as inherently dangerous and wrongheaded. But the powers in Canberra, and therefore in Port Moresby, were behind the idea and even provided funds. For the most part, Papua New Guineans embraced the new governmental bodies. In a move contrary to the administration's usual autocratic style, Fenbury and his staff created an educational campaign, which they mounted wherever they thought local people were ready for local government councils, and did not actually introduce councils until the people in area had learned about them and requested one.

The work of the councils varied, depending more on the kinds of infrastructural support received from the administration than on the skills of the councilors, most of whom were ready and able to do a good job, if they received sufficient training about what that meant. In Hanuabada, for example, a village that had gradually found itself surrounded by the town of Port Moresby, people had been exposed over many years to the workings of the colonial administration. Many Hanuabadans worked in government offices in Port Moresby. As a result, councilors were ready to carry out their work effectively from the day they were first elected, and had plenty of excellent ideas about projects that their council could undertake. When the *kiap* seconded to assist the council was sympathetic and respectful, the council worked effectively and efficiently. Too often, however, the resident *kiap* would expect that all Papuans, including those sitting around the council house, were there only to do what he told them to, and the work of the council would grind to a halt as he argued about whether he would let them do one project or another.

The effectiveness of different councils also seems to have depended upon how much groundwork had been laid prior to their introduction. A comparison of two councils, one of which had been established after a period of education and another which—for reasons having more to do with administration office politics than anything about the villagers themselves—was constructed hastily and without much prior education or consultation, is instructive. Not surprisingly, the former council operated effectively, represented its constituents fairly, and generally did a good job for them. The latter broke down into factions, with the dominant faction led by a local big man who used his office as yet another means of obtaining power and status, and making other villagers believe themselves beholden to him.

Hasluck's solemn belief was that gradualism was forced upon him by the slowness and backwardness of his Papuan and New Guinean charges. And it was true that his was not the first administration to presume that it would take generations to develop Papua and New Guinea. Hubert Murray had preached it. Eddie Ward, the Labor minister for external territories, had said much the same. Across party lines, Australians were uniformly agreed that Papuans and New Guineans were far behind the average Australian not only in technology, but also in culture, civilization, values, beliefs, education, and intelligence, and even in morals and the ability to reason. Equally, all were agreed that the inevitable future for Papuans and New Guineans was to become as exactly like Australians, in all those respects, as any brown people could be. No one, at least no one other than anthropologists who wrote in any public way about Papuans and New Guineans in the 1940s and 1950s, believed that there was any aspect of local culture equal to that of Australian, or any aspect of it particularly worth saving.

Local government councils promised—even if they did not always deliver—a measure of self-rule. At higher political levels, however, no one in the territories—neither Australian settlers nor Papuan and New Guinean villagers—enjoyed much in the way of self-rule. During the 1950s, Papuans and New Guineans gradually were given more glimpses of the democratic process. A Legislative Council was created after the war to advise the Administrator, but the Administrator had the authority to ignore that advice, which he often did; nevertheless its existence alone suggested a gradual retreat from autocracy. In the first postwar Legislative Council, convened in 1951, only three of the twenty eight seats were reserved for Papuans and New Guineans. The appointment of Papuans and New Guineans to the Legislative Council, even in such small numbers and with such a limited role, was not met with universal approbation.

But, the presence on the council of Papua New Guineans was not the only contentious issue about its formation and work. Although it had been billed as a step towards democratic self-rule for the territories, there was little about it that supported self-determination, even by white settlers. The Papuan and New Guinean representatives were not the only members chosen by the Administrator; so were the vast majority of the other members of that first council as well.

The Legislative Council's lack of power was but one aspect of the absence of democracy from the colonial experience. The major example was the operation of the colonial administration itself: secretive, top-down, autocratic, with a minister and Administrator giving orders and expecting them to be obeyed rather than seeking advice and consensus. As Wolfers has written, "Colonial government is essentially bureaucratic government; it tends to transform every political problem into a technical problem to be dealt with by administrators." Australians told Papuans and New Guineans that they were to develop a political system like that of Australia, but, since Papuans and New Guineans were all but entirely denied access to mainland Australia, local people could be excused if they believed that democracy meant the autocratic and bureaucratic model that the administration employed in the territories.

Uprisings and Revolts

One of the enduring myths of the Australian colonial era was that the Australian colonizers seldom, if ever, resorted to violence, and, correspondingly, that once the benefits of pacification were explained to them, Papuans and New Guineans were so happy to come under colonial control that there were few if any uprisings or revolts. Both of these beliefs are partly true but both are also mostly false. Their continued currency among both Australians and Papua New Guineans has led to a situation in which many Australians believe they need take no responsibility for what has happened in Papua New Guinea since it became a nation, putting the blame on Papua New Guineans themselves for the political and economic problems that were actually caused or exacerbated by colonial rule. At the same time, Papua New Guineans have largely accepted the same false notions, internalizing the belief that they did nothing to earn independence and that their failures at democratic government and development are entirely their own, a product of being poor learners during the beneficent colonial period.

Among the steps that the colonial administration took to ensure that Papuans and New Guineans would not find a way to an organized revolt, or even to broach early independence, were ordinances that all but outlawed trade unions and made it illegal for trade unions, cooperatives, or local government councils to engage in party political activity. The administration also went out of its way to quash attempts by Papua New Guineans to promote village level economic development, branding the leaders as trouble makers or accusing them of fomenting rebellion.

The Highlands—A Case in Point and a Special Case

There were great differences—in culture, norms, social structures, and systems—among the many regions, tribes, clans, and ethnic groups that made up the variegated fabric of Papua and New Guinea. There were differences, as well, in their experiences of colonialism. The peoples who inhabited the vast Highland valleys, six thousand feet above sea level, and hidden from the outside world until the 1930s, were perhaps the most different of all. They had settled their valleys at least ten thousand years earlier, well before any of the coastal or island cultures had arrived in New Guinea. They were of a different ethnic mix from coastal or island peoples. And their culture was different in many ways from those of coastal Papua and New Guinea: more egalitarian, more warlike, more prone to display.

Although first to settle New Guinea, they were the last to come under the colonial yoke. For coastal and island peoples, the colonial era lasted almost a hundred years, so that when independence was finally achieved in 1975, there were probably few people alive who remembered life before the Australians had invaded. For much of the Highlands, however, the entire colonial experience—from first encounter through pacification and the incursion of missionaries, and on to the construction of roads, patrol posts, and aid stations—was telescoped into little more than a decade. From there to independence was barely another fifteen years. That did not make it easier for Highlanders; it just made it more intense.

Australians had not found their way into the Highland valleys until the 1930s, and had visited very little of that vast, heavily populated region when World War II brought a halt to further adventures. It took some years for the money, men, and material to become available again to push into the Highlands, so first contact between Australians and many Highlands groups did not happen until the 1950s, and for a few villages, even later. Australians were at first convinced that they had found a potential "white highlands," like the fabled Rift Valley of Kenya, where the climate was perpetually temperate, the soil rich, and land for white people could be had for the taking.

There was a rush for plantations when they were first offered in 1952. But it quickly became evident that the New Guinean and Kenyan Highlands were very different, and that the Kenyan plantation economy could not easily be transplanted to New Guinea's less welcoming plateaus. Unlike the sparsely populated Kenyan Highlands, New Guinea's upland valleys were heavily populated, and Highlanders were not averse to fighting settlers—and each other—so besides the continuing threat of violence, land titles would always be uncertain. Moreover, the understandable tendency of Highlanders to fight back when Australians encroached led the colonial administration to declare many great swathes of territory "uncontrolled," which meant they were off limits not only for settlement, but even for brief visits by any whites other than *kiaps*, a situation that prevailed for significant parts of the Highlands well into the 1960s.

So, while people in other parts of Papua and New Guinea were being asked to experiment with local government councils, Highlanders were meeting white men for the first time and were being told that they could no longer engage in tribal fighting or revenge killings. These customs had been key cultural components in most Highlands societies for millennia, providing social control, political advancement, a source of meaningful activity for otherwise restless young men, and a way to forge (and undo) alliances and to gain (and lose) land. Given how deeply payback and war were woven into the fabric of Highlands societies, it is worth discussing how easily Highlands cultures gave them up, or at least cut back on them for a time.

Australians credit their patrol policies with the fairly rapid pacification of the Highlands. Joachim Gorlich has analyzed the pacification process from the descriptions provided by the *kiaps* who patrolled among the Kobon, a Highlands people whose territory is in the upland regions of what is now Madang Province. The colonial administration employed a three-step process to achieve what Gorlich terms "a monopoly on violence."[50] First was initial contact, followed by occasional patrols by *kiaps* and police, usually as a reaction to homicide reports that had filtered out to the nearest patrol post. Finally, the occasional patrol became a routine administrative visit, every few weeks or months, during which the *kiaps* would not only hunt down offenders, but also appoint village *luluai* and *tultuls*, conduct censuses, and collect taxes. Pacification is the routine name for this process in official and almost all other descriptions of what happened. The Australians were not saying that violence is wrong *per se*; instead they were saying what every state says to its subjects: violence is right only when it is done by the state, and only by the state. And, indeed, guns were major tools in the *kiaps'* campaign to end tribal violence, as demonstrated by an excerpt that Gorlich quotes from a *kiap's* log:

> . . .the patrol officers, whose aim was to build co-operative social relationships, also announced to the Kobon that committing violent acts against other people was forbidden. Any infringement of this rule would result in violence from the patrols. The verbal order to refrain from violence was given reinforcement by demonstrations of the power of firearms: "Long talk given on policies, etc. . . . Two large pigs brought in and these shot before crowd. All dispersed after flag ceremony at 6 pm as heavy rain again started."[51]

The message conveyed by the dead pigs was hardly equivocal. The Australians were not signaling that any and all violence is bad; they were demonstrating that only they, the representatives of the government, were allowed to use violence. And, of course, Highlanders did not have access to guns at that time, so it also showed that the violence available to the *kiaps* was much stronger than anything Papuans and New Guineans could muster.

Its monopoly on the use of force gave the colonial administration not only great power, but also greater legitimacy, as the state became the only party with the power to settle disputes and punish those who disobey the rules against violence. Prior to that first Australian patrol into the mountains south of Madang, the Kobon policed themselves. They used payback and war, or the threats of payback and war, as their means for resolving disputes and punishing offenders. Once Australian rule was cemented, the Kobon could no longer police their members with the same degree of effectiveness and had to depend on the colonizers to do it for them. They were being deprived not only of access to violence, but also of their sovereignty and their ability to govern themselves.

The Kobon (and other Highlanders) were large in number, and administration patrols were few and far between. Yet in a matter of a few years, the incidence of tribal wars and payback had been significantly reduced in the Highlands, a situation that was to remain until self-government. The colonial administration liked to take all the credit for this, and *kiaps* and police do deserve much credit, but there were many reasons for the success of pacification. At first, certainly, the mysterious and frightening killing power of the *kiaps*' guns was a key factor, especially when the guns were turned not on pigs but, as happened more frequently than anyone cares today to recall, on people. Another important factor was the native police, who (often unbeknownst to unsuspecting *kiaps*) were instrumental in cajoling, bribing, beating, and terrorizing villagers into submission. Yet another factor was internal to Highlands politics, since self-policing was tiring, dangerous, and limiting. For a while, at least, the willingness of somebody else to do this work probably seemed like a welcome respite. Like most colonial subjects, the Highlanders quickly became experts at manipulating the colonial authorities to do what they wanted done. But, the major cause was probably what Franz Fanon has termed the psychopathology of colonization, the tendency of colonized peoples to accept the colonizers' view of themselves as dependent and inferior.

Promoting Economic Development (or Not)

It is possible that the biggest barrier to the economic development of Papua and New Guinea was created by the Australian colonizers themselves. Too often, attempts by Papuans and New Guineans to improve their economic condition were shut down by the administration. Australian policymakers insisted that it would take many generations for Papuans and New Guineans to reach a stage where they could meet the political, economic, and cultural demands of self-determination. But whenever local efforts might prove that wrong, district officers reacted by undermining, and even closing down, homegrown attempts of Papuans and New Guineans to create their own economic development projects.

The "Tommy Kabu" Movement

The administration's destruction of the so-called "Tommy Kabu movement" is a case in point. Kabu (which means "the man who owns things") was born Koiva Aua in the early 1920s in the Purari Delta, which the colonizers had dubbed the Gulf District. Sometime in his teens, he joined the Royal Papuan Constabulary as a native constable and spent World War II in Cairns. Though not in the navy himself, Kabu (who was called "Tommy" by the Australians) worked as an orderly for Lieutenant-Commander Norman Pixley and became very close to the Pixley family, accompanying them on holidays and moving with them to Brisbane for a time. He was "by all accounts, popular with the Australians, making a name for himself as a clean-living and dignified man who spent long hours reading the Bible."[52] As the war neared its end, however, the Australian government ordered all Pacific Islanders in the country to an internment camp in Queensland, where "the officer in charge of the camp, an ex-New Guinea planter, possibly a subscriber to the old orthodoxy of white prestige, reportedly beat Kabu for being 'cheeky.'"[53]

Kabu, like all the non-whites in the camp, was subsequently repatriated to his homeland. He could have reentered the constabulary, but he chose instead to return to the Purari Delta, intending to bring economic prosperity and independence to his home area by putting into effect the principles of business and industry he had learned in Australia. He intended to start a series of companies, all of which would be co-owned by any Purari who wanted to subscribe. According to historian Anthony Yeates, he wanted to do this in the way businesses operated in Australia, with as little government interference as possible. His first venture was to be the transport of local produce, such as sago and vegetables, for sale in Port Moresby, but the fledgling company ran into difficulties when the first ship it purchased to transport the produce burned before it had even left the seller's anchorage. Although the seller had agreed to refund the purchase price, the company never saw the money, because the administration stepped in and spent the next several years oddly arguing that the money should go back to the individual subscribers rather than to the company.

That was only one of the roadblocks that *kiaps* and others in the administration put in the way of every venture that Kabu and the Purari villagers attempted to start. Local *kiaps* tended to be more suspicious of Kabu than higher-ranking officials were, but the hatred and fear of the local *kiaps* was all that was needed to make it virtually impossible for the villagers to accomplish anything. Yeates cites three main reasons for the enmity with which the *kiaps* treated Kabu. First, Australian patrol officers did not rule by consultation and consensus; *kiaps* gave orders and expected, in Yeates's words, "to be both obeyed and respected." In their view, any Papuan who got above himself, by thinking he could run a business or do other things that were the sole purview of Australians, was insufficiently obedient and respectful. Second, patrol officers did not believe they were

in Papua and New Guinea to promote economic development; their role, they believed, was "that of enforcer of the peace and regulator of compliance and control." They saw Kabu's actions not as courageous and intelligent attempts at economic self-reliance, but as threats to their status and, by extension, to the power and authority of the administration. Finally, despite the promises of the Labor government to promote Indigenous enterprise, most *kiaps* sided with expatriate planters and business people, whose monopoly over production and trade in Papua was threatened by local enterprises like that of Kabu and his supporters.

Eventually, the administration termed Kabu's project a cargo cult, withdrew what little support they had ever provided, and arrested him. Since Australians could not believe that Papuans and New Guineans were capable of sophisticated economic thought or enterprise, they presumed that the projects had to be something else, something much simpler and more sinister. The idea of cargo cults appealed to Australians' paternalism: the cargo cult label turned Tommy Kabu's project from the complex socioeconomic vision it was, into the betel-nut-fed daydream of a typically primitive, superstition-ridden native. For the colonizers, it felt much better to be able to shake their heads and laugh, than to have to admit that they were dealing with people of great acumen, who were perfectly capable of moving from the "Stone Age" to independence in less than a generation. And putting potential leaders in prison on trumped-up charges was a lesson to all their followers, or to anyone else who might be foolish enough to promote similar economic ventures.

A Sidebar on "Cargo Cults"

The administration was not entirely incorrect in its perception that Indigenous Papuan and New Guinean attempts at economic development, like the Tommy Kabu movement, differed significantly from the free-market, individualistic, and entrepreneurial model that the Australians were attempting to transplant. But not all of the homegrown attempts at economic achievement were cargo cults. Even those mystical, religious movements that did deserve the name might have served a number of useful purposes for their members if the administration had let them be. Cargo cults were millenarian semi-religious organizations, often fueled by the belief that the whites' power and goods had been magically bestowed upon them, and that Papuans and New Guineans could have access to the same goods and powers by following the magical formula prescribed by cult leaders. A number of cargo cults attracted broad membership from across different villages or regions, and seemed able to withstand administrative attempts to shut them down for quite some time. The administration feared cargo cults, and often arrested and jailed the leaders, as well as taking other steps aimed at suppressing these organizations. To an extent, the colonial administration was probably correct in suspecting so-called cargo cults of presenting a potential threat to peace and good order. Even if the cargo cults were not intended to be directly antagonistic to colonial rule, they often involved what sociologists refer to as passive or covert resistance to the administration.

One way to view cargo cults is as an attempt by Indigenous people to foresee coming transformations and to prepare themselves to take advantage of them. People might have begun by trying out more mundane economic development activities like planting coffee or cocoa palms. When those did not work, or did not work rapidly and completely enough, or when the people were blocked by overly zealous colonial officials from pursuing them, people often tried to achieve the same end in different ways—for example, by dancing, marching, venerating the dead, and other quasi-religious activities. These activities, which seem pointless to observers from other cultures, may actually be useful in drawing people into the more practical aspects of the economic endeavor and ensuring solidarity and group support, which are necessary if the economic schemes are to succeed. While accepting that cargo cults did exist in the 1950s and afterward, one can still regret that name because the term has come to have a pejorative, even condescending, meaning, which obscures the creativity, hard work, and genuine skill that often characterized them.

Conflicting Attitudes

The Australians' quick suspicion of homegrown economic development projects was also due to the Liberal-Country style of colonial administration. Patrol officers expected to be "both obeyed and respected."[54] *Kiaps* never asked villagers what the village might need; instead, they ordered villagers to do what the patrol officer decided was good for them. It was a totally top-down, authoritarian form of rule. It brooked no opposition, and every divergence from the patrol officer's orders, no matter how small or sensible, was viewed as opposition and an affront to the patrol officer's authority. Part of this attitude came from the *kiaps'* lack of education for their demanding roles. With little preparation, they were thrown alone into what to them must have seemed a forbidding wilderness, where they were told to keep order over hundreds, maybe thousands, of people, most of whom spoke languages they could not understand and had customs they could not fathom. Despite outward braggadocio, most patrol officers must have been frightened a lot of the time: frightened of losing control, frightened of being killed, or just frightened of being laughed at and ignored. Their only safety, as they saw it, was in insisting on obedience from these people at all times.

Moreover, the patrol officers were not entirely incorrect in believing that projects like those of Tommy Kabu and his followers posed a threat to them and, ultimately, to colonial rule. Merely by demonstrating that they could do it on their own, the Papuans and New Guineans involved in these projects were, whether they intended to or not, undermining the basic justifications for continued Australian control, especially when some of the projects proved more successful than those the administration had tried to impose.

The Liberal-Country Government and "Bizniz"

The Liberal Party's founders self-consciously styled their movement after the classical liberalism of mid-nineteenth-century Britain, which had supported individual civil liberties, light touch government, and the rule of law as vehicles for the business success of the then-emerging English entrepreneurial class. Given that emphasis, it is not surprising that the Liberal-Country administration supported the Australian planters, traders, and other expatriate businessmen of Papua and New Guinea, but one might have expected the party also to support attempts by Papua and New Guinea's budding Indigenous entrepreneurs to forge their own businesses. Why that did not happen can be traced primarily to racism, and to the abiding wish of those in the dominant group to retain their dominance and the perquisites that go with it.

Like Labor, the Liberal-Country coalition came to power saying that its primary aim in ruling Papua and New Guinea was the protection and improvement of the Indigenous population. However, the coalition differed from Labor in that it had a business-oriented agenda for that improvement. The interests of Australians in Papua and New Guinea would be protected and supported on the grounds that these businesses would employ and eventually train Papua New Guineans, but the administration would also endeavor to develop the skills and abilities of Indigenous business people. But white Australian stereotypes about Papuans and New Guineans left the government unsure about how to create Indigenous business enterprises, or even if it could be done. Australian writing during this period are full of comments about Papuans and New Guineans being "Stone Age" men, so far removed from any modernity, any sense of what market economics were about, that it would take centuries before they could hope to take part. When Sir Albert Maori Kiki, a leading Papua New Guinean politician, businessman, and writer of the 1970s, titled his autobiography *Ten Thousand Years in a Lifetime*, he was doing so partly with tongue in cheek, an ironic tip of the cap to the Australians who were convinced it would take that many millennia to fashion a man like him.

Papua and New Guinea's Indigenous economy was also blamed for the inability to get locals to participate in externally imposed development schemes or even to accept employment on plantations or in town. Most Papuans and New Guineans participated in their village's abundant subsistence economy. Shifting horticulture, together with some hunting, fishing, handicrafts, and trading, produced an ample and comfortable lifestyle for villagers, leavened only by the society's inability to counter the dire effects of continual warfare and, especially among infants, of disease. Australians argued that the existence of the subsistence economy made it difficult for businesses to maintain a stable work force. Planters and planners both said that once a worker had enough money for the limited things that money could buy in the village, the worker tended to disappear until the next time a bit of cash was needed.

It is not uncommon for business interests to blame the traditional economy and social structure of preindustrial societies for their supposed failure to develop into a market economy. Papua and New Guinea's kinship system also came in for a share of the blame. Papuan and New Guinean social systems were characterized by vast and complex webs of mutual and multivalent reciprocity, which contributed to order and cohesiveness by making sure that villagers could depend upon one another for help and support. The most obvious examples of reciprocity at work were the feasts given by successful men, during which a great many pigs and other valuables would be given away to relatives and associates, who would, by those gifts, then be bound to loyalty and to performing similar tasks for the givers. Another example was the great *kula* rings, involving huge trade networks up and down the Papuan coast and out to the islands, through which villagers gained access to shells, pots, mats, and other needed goods, that were available in areas other than their own. The traders formed reciprocal partnerships with people on their routes, so that the goods changed hands not just according to some monetary scheme, but as putative gifts that were given and received.

These relationships were simplified, in the bar and poolside chatter of Australian planters and district officers, into something they crudely called "the *wantok* system." (*Wantok* is a Tok Pisin word for relatives and friends who speak the same language — i.e., one talk.) To those who wanted Papuans and New Guineans to become Australian-style workers, the *wantok* system was nothing but a primitive barrier to development. Papuans and New Guineans, it was said, cannot save as Australians do because everything they earn is immediately "stolen" by their *wantoks*. Consequently their businesses fail. A common story, probably apocryphal, but told so often that every Australian believed he or she knew someone to whom it had happened, was of the Papuan or New Guinean who tried to start a trade store, only to have it fail, because his *wantoks*—as was their traditional right—took everything off the shelves for themselves without paying for it. These stories were both the result of and contributed to the condescending attitude that Australians exhibited toward Papuans and New Guineans. Myths like this one served both to convince the administration that Indigenous economic development would be a long time coming and that the only way to promote it was to tear down traditional economic and social structures and replace them with something more in keeping with a market economy. In an odd, and even morose, article published in 1950, James McAuley wrote that there was a conflict inherent in Australian attempts to import capitalist development into the territories; the only way to get a sufficiently large and committed labor force, he wrote, is to make the "natives" want a Western mode of life; they must be convinced to "acquire Western wants and ambitions."[55] But, once they have those wants and ambitions, he continued, they will not be able to satisfy them, even if they join the labor force, because there is no way that they could get paid enough or advance fast and far enough. So, he concluded, the attempt to introduce capitalism will lead only to unrest and perhaps even to revolutions, such as those occurring at the time in many African colonies.[56]

The unrest in Africa was a major topic of discussion in Australian political circles in the 1950s, as were the dangers supposedly posed to Australian national security by the twin threats of Asia and communism. The need to forge a strong Papua and New Guinea to protect Australia against potential aggressors from within and without was seen in the 1950s as axiomatic. McAuley's worries that Papua and New Guinea could not be strong without economic development to make it self-sustaining, but that economic development would inevitably lead to unrest, were widely shared, especially in key public policy journals like *Pacific Affairs*, which were widely read by academics and government policymakers. McAuley's own 1950 article in that journal was part of this discussion, arguing that the best way for Australia to defend itself against Asian expansion and communist insurgency would be for Australia to make Papua and New Guinea more of a settler-planter colony, while educating and supporting Papuans and New Guineans to take part in business ventures led by Australian settlers. Even McAuley, who was considerably more liberal than the Liberals in power, assumed that Australians would always remain the bosses, and Papuans and New Guineans the workers.

McAuley's aim in writing the article was to convince Liberal-Country leaders that economic development could indeed occur in Papua and New Guinea, something Australians were not quite sure they believed. The main reason development had not happened, he said, was that Papua and New Guinea were poor in resources: ". . .the development of New Guinea will be restricted by the generally poor soils, the limited opportunities for irrigation on a significant scale, the huge area of mountains, the rushing rivers, vast swamps, and scattered islands."[57]

Still, McAuley blamed the lack of development primarily on Australian policies. It could not be denied, he said, "that less development has taken place in New Guinea than was possible." But the reason was that both the territory and Australia were underdeveloped, both required large investments of capital, equipment, and labor in order to develop, and, perhaps most telling, given the similarities in climate and topography, development often led to competition between planters in PNG and planters in

Australia, as demonstrated by the "well-known instance of the inhibition of sugar-growing in Papua to preserve the monopoly of Queensland growers. Territorial products have, with trifling exceptions, received no preference in Australia."[58]

Australians of the time tended to put the blame for the difficulty in promoting Papua and New Guinea's economic development on Papuans and New Guineans themselves, describing them as men mired in the Stone Age, centuries away from the ability to comprehend modern business aims and methods. One of McAuley's aims was to refute these kinds of arguments, but he did admit that the current educational level of Papuans and New Guineans also contributed to the lack of development, because it resulted in an "unsatisfactory Labor supply."[59]

There have been, McAuley wrote, many suggestions for solving the labor problem: "Some employers favour the introduction of Asian Labor; but this would be opposed by Australian public opinion. . . ." There had also been proposals to forcibly remove Papuans and New Guineans from their scattered villages into "proletarian communities attached to industrial sites. . . . Whether this programme could be justified on moral or cultural grounds is a question that would receive a variety of answers. . . ."[60]

McAuley was a prescient forecaster in noting that the most likely engine for economic development in Papua and New Guinea would be the creation of large-scale mining projects. He was also correct in pointing out that this would mean that outsiders would manage the heights of Papua and New Guinea's economy, leaving to locals only secondary roles as workers in big industries under European ownership and management. Papuans and New Guineans, McAuley said, would prefer small-scale enterprises, individual or communal, that they could own and run. He concluded, however, that the most likely development would be large scale—not only mining, but also timber and agriculture—because technically and financially, that would be the most efficient.

Although everyone agreed that development was sorely needed, both to counter outside threats to Australian national security and to lessen the territories' ever growing strain on finances, the 1950s were characterized by considerably more talk than action. The administration could not decide whether its major support should be for expatriate, larger-scale development or for smaller-scale Indigenous development. Both came with risks. The major risk of relying on Australians and other expatriates to develop the economy, or so it seemed at the time, was that it would not happen, that there would not be sufficient interest, as there had not been to that point. World opinion favored Indigenous development, and the sinking fortunes of Australian plantations seemed to lead to that conclusion as well. But much as Australians feared aggression from their Asian neighbors to the north and west, they equally feared the unrest that they were sure would result from the inequalities and unfulfilled desires that Indigenous development would bring.

So, through most of the 1950s, the administration proceeded by doing not quite enough for either Australian settlers or Papuans and New Guineans. In the end, events would decide the controversy. The discoveries of copper, gold, and oil made large-scale development, owned and managed by foreign investors, inevitable. The burgeoning political power of Papuans and New Guineans themselves took choices about small-scale, locally owned ventures out of the policymakers' hands. But neither of those came to fruition until the 1970s.

The Function of Colonial Law in the 1950s: Promoting Political Development (or Not)

To govern Papua and New Guinea, the Australian Parliament, the Ministry for External Territories, the Administrator, with the sometime advice and support of his Legislative Council, and every territorial department, produced acts, ordinances, regulations, and orders almost too numerous to count. The plethora of official rules was probably far in excess of what territories of fewer than two million needed, but the abundance of laws, covering every conceivable situation, had a number of effects, some intended, some not, some salutary, some not. First, the rules provided a sense of order and legitimacy to the colonial enterprise.

Their existence did direct *kiaps*, and those in the home offices in Port Moresby and Canberra as well, on their duties, telling them what to do and when to do it, and, even more importantly, what not to do. To the extent *kiaps* and other administrators followed the rules, higher officials could have confidence that their plans and programs for the territory were being put into operation in the ways they envisioned. The rules achieved a purpose even when (as often happened) *kiaps* did not know about them, or ignored them, or even disobeyed them, since their very existence allowed politicians, higher government officials, and even the public, to believe that plans and programs were being carried out.

But the multiplicity of official rules, their seemingly orderly compilation into neatly compartmentalized rows of typeface, is yet another demonstration of the governing style of the Liberal-Country coalition in the 1950s. Allen Healy has described that style as meticulously detailed, neat, almost obsessively organized, brooking no opposition, and containing no independent thought. While the existence of field regulations that covered almost every eventuality a *kiap* might meet probably kept many a youthful, inadequately trained *kiap* from committing acts even more outrageous than many of them did, the plethora of rules, combined with the top-down public service that they supported, also prevented independent spirits, especially those from within the local population, but also those in the colonial service itself, from doing the kinds of innovative things that would have brought to Papua and New Guinea an earlier, less officious, and more human-centered kind of development.

The laws also had their darker side. Much is touted about the so-called rule of law, at least when that law is Western law: the way that it purportedly promotes equality and forbids favoritism; and the way that it provides for order and predictability, thereby facilitating the eventual success of an economy catering to efficient and profitable business enterprises. But a blind adoration of the rule of law—an insistence that all laws be obeyed at all times—overlooks the possibility that some laws might be bad ones. The "white Australia" policy, for example, was a creation of immigration and related laws. As for the territories, there were too many ordinances and regulations in effect in Papua and New Guinea in the 1950s that discriminated against Papuans and New Guineans, kept them from achieving any kind of economic, political, or social success, and generally maintained them in a position subordinate to that of their colonial overseers.

For the Australian administration in Papua and New Guinea, the years following World War II were a time of reestablishing Australian authority over the territories. The law played a pivotal role in this endeavor. The war had been a time of fear and trauma for Papua and New Guinea, and for Australia as well. Japanese forces held the north coast of Papua and New Guinea for much of the war, and an enemy invasion of the Australian mainland was averted only by the impenetrable nature of the mountains in the Highlands of Papua and New Guinea, and many small heroic acts of Papuans, New Guineans and Australians alike.

The immediate postwar years were hardly less fraught, at least for colonialists, as colonies throughout the world began to argue for independence. The army had managed the administration of the territories during the war, but almost as soon as the war ended, civilian authorities sought to resume control. The only questions were what the newly reestablished colonial enterprise would look like. Would the territories continue to be managed as one, as had been the case during the war? Would new laws and regulations, as well as newly created courts and legal structures, involve Papuans and New Guineans more in political and legal processes, paving the way toward early self-government and independence? Would colonial officers receive a deeper education in Papuan and New Guinean cultures and social systems? These questions were often summed up at the time in what was seen as the overarching question: would the territories be run for the benefit of Papuans and New Guineans or for the benefit of Australian planters, businessmen, and politicians?

The Papua and New Guinea Act of 1949

The political battles over these issues resulted in the *Papua and New Guinea Act of 1949*, which was in most respects a victory for the more conservative factions that expected Papua and New Guinea to remain an Australian colony for the foreseeable future. Basically, the act provided for Papua and New Guinea to be jointly administered, for the continuation of indefinite Australian rule, and for little if any participation by Papuans and New Guineans in any aspect of colonial rule, least of all in the legal system.

Constitutionally, Papua and New Guinea had to be treated differently in order to bring both of them under the act. Papua was a colony, fully within the sovereign powers of Australia. New Guinea, however, having begun its colonial existence as a German colony, was a United Nations Trust Territory, so any changes to its administration had to be negotiated by Australia and the UN Trusteeship Council, and approved by the General Assembly. Their agreement was codified in Article 6 of the act, which provided for the continuation of the trusteeship, but also permitted Australia to govern its two Papua and New Guinea territories together and to apply the laws of the Australian Commonwealth in New Guinea.

The commonwealth government had greater authority to legislate for Papua and New Guinea than it did for Australia, where its power was constitutionally limited by the enumerated powers of the Australian states. Australia's legislative authority over both Papua and New Guinea was plenary; that is, it was unlimited as to subject matter and not constrained by any of the prohibitions or guarantees of the Australian Constitution.

The act provided for three governmental entities for Papua and New Guinea: a chief executive (who came to be called the Administrator), an Executive Council (which advised and assisted the Administrator), and a Legislative Council. Under the act, the commonwealth delegated its legislative power to the Legislative Council. However, the commonwealth could continue to legislate for Papua and New Guinea, and the Legislative Council was not permitted to enact any ordinance that would conflict with commonwealth legislation.

The Legislative Council

The Legislative Council consisted of twenty eight members, of whom sixteen were so-called official members and twelve nonofficial. The official members were colonial officers, appointed by the governor-general of the commonwealth, on the nomination of the Administrator. Official members held office until their appointments were revoked. The nonofficial members consisted of three elected and nine appointed members. They held office for three years unless removed earlier. The elected members were from three regions, but all were white. The appointed members were supposed to be three from missions, three Indigenous Papuans and New Guineans, and three others. Altogether, of the twelve nonofficial members, only five had to be from New Guinea, and only three had to be Indigenous.

All ordinances passed by the Legislative Council had to be sent first to the Administrator. He could assent to the legislation or deny it, but in either case the ordinance then went to the governor-general for assent. Even after the Administrator and the governor-general had both assented, the ordinance was not yet in effect; it first had to be approved by both houses of the Australian Parliament. The act did contain some restrictions on legislative powers, mostly aimed at the paternalistic protection of Papuans and New Guineans. For example, the Legislative Council could not institute a slave trade or forced labor, and could not end the ban on liquor for Indigenous people.

According to historian Donald Denoon, the council was "more decorative than effective. It did not enact legislation; it merely advised the Administrator, and he was free, as was the Minister, to ignore its advice, a response, or should we say lack of response, that both frequently adopted."[61] Nor was it likely that the council would have done anything radical, even if it had been granted more power. For much of the 1950s, the majority of members were colonial officials who, for all intents and purposes, worked for the Administrator. Of the unofficial members, most were appointed by the Administrator, and it is unlikely he would choose people who fundamentally disagreed with him. Finally, the elected members tended to represent plantation and business interests, not the developmental needs or aspirations of Papuans and New Guineans.

Although the number of nonofficial members was increased gradually through the 1950s, the majority on the council remained white until 1961 and almost always voted with the Administrator. The only serious disagreement between the government and the nonofficial members did not occur until 1959, when the whites on the council opposed the administration's plans to impose an income tax. The tax would, of course, impact whites most, as they were essentially the only people in Papua and New Guinea earning enough money to pay significant taxes. When the Administrator instituted the tax over their opposition, the three elected members (all of whom were white) resigned, and appealed to the Australian High Court, arguing that enactment of the tax had been unlawful because it was done without three elected members in office. The High Court sided with the administration.

The elected members lost the tax battle, but they may have won the legislative war, because by the time a new council was convened in 1961, its makeup had been changed. For the first time, nonofficial members outnumbered the official ones. However, given that prior to 1961 the nonofficial members, both elected and appointed, had mostly represented Papua and New Guinea's white business and plantation classes, the 1961 changes may have been a case of regretting what you wish for, because the number of Papuans and New Guineans on the new council was made equal to that of whites. There were twelve elected members on the new council, of whom six were to be Papuan and New Guinean and six were to be white, and only ten official members, of whom five were to be Papuan and New Guinean and five to be white.

The Legislative Council may have given a very small number of Papuans and New Guineans a limited window into the workings of the colonial administration, but it did not provide a road to self-government. Its activities, its very existence, was "invisible to village people," and, as such, it was basically just another example of Hasluck's top-down method of governing the territories.[62] Another new institution, local government councils, introduced in 1956, promised to educate more Papuans and New Guineans into something more akin to democracy.

Local Government Councils

Any adult Papuan or New Guinean, male or female, could stand for election to a local government council and vote in those elections. Introduced into Papua and New Guinea by the *Native Local Government Councils Ordinance of 1949–1957*, they were elected bodies handling governmental matters, and thus the first opportunity that most Papuans and New Guineans had to participate in something like Australian-style democracy and self-governance. Each council represented an area that encompassed several villages, making them also the first governmental institution to stand between the villages and the central administration. Councils were granted some meaningful powers, including the ability to raise taxes, and to use that money to repair roads, build aid posts and schools, and buy trucks for transporting produce to market. Papuans and New Guineans adopted the new institution with relish:

> By 1960 people all over the Territory were asking that councils be established in their districts. At first it was thought that some of these areas would not be able to find enough money to pay council tax, but the people were very keen to have councils. By the middle of 1960 there were 36 councils in the Territory, representing 250,000 people.[63]

This suggests that Papuans and New Guineans took very easily to self-government. Commentators disagree, however, about how successful the local government councils actually were. Biskup, Jinks, and Nelson paint a darker picture:

> Not all councils were successful; some councilors did not understand their jobs, so they relied on patrol officers to do much of the work.... Some did not understand the difference between their own local government and the Administration; they thought that the local government councils had to do exactly as the Administration told them. This was not so. The Administration wanted the people to take the initiative and do things of their own accord.[64]

This assessment was not shared by other commentators. Belshaw, for example, described the Hanuabadan villagers as sophisticated political actors, who, if left to their own devices, adeptly utilized their local government council to do the things that needed to be done. Their work was, however, continually impeded by authoritarian and officious *kiaps*, who mistakenly believed they knew better than any Papuan or New Guinean would.[65]

And Wolfers noted that the one thing the administration did not want was for Indigenous people to take the initiative:

> ... the Australian government was more concerned with securing support for its policies than with fostering indigenous initiative.... Local government councils were little more than extensions of the administrative arm of the government.... The government ... saw itself as having to explain its politics to Papua New Guineans, rather than consult, negotiate, or compromise with them....[66]

The structure, history, and culture of the Australian colonial administration make it likely that Belshaw's and Wolfer's assessments are more accurate than the picture of hapless natives painted by Biskup, Jinks and Nelson. Everything about the Australian style of governance suggests that the administration would have been unlikely to support much in the way of Indigenous initiative, either in local government councils or elsewhere.

The initial proposals for the creation of local government councils were derived from the British model of indirect rule. The British essentially allowed their Asian and African possessions to govern themselves, with the colonial administrators taking only an advisory role. But administrators in Papua and New Guinea had not been trained to be advisors. Used to the top-down, autocratic model, "the great majority of . . . officials made no secret of the fact that they regarded local government as a totally unwarranted intrusion on their powers and functions."[67]

The Australian administrators could not envision a world in which Papuans and New Guineans would be left free to make their own decisions. From the start, the councils were hemmed about with restrictions and subjected to constant oversight by colonial officials. The ordinance itself made this clear: in an uncanny foretelling of the form that the Papua New Guinea Constitution would take, it was drafted based on Australian models. It was huge, long, and difficult for anyone but a lawyer to read; it contained elaborate oversight provisions, and required a form of local government that was too Australian and too complicated, deriving absolutely nothing from traditional, Papuan and New Guinean ways of self-rule (or indeed, even from British indirect rule).

The local government councils could have done any of three things: (1) they could have taught Papuans and New Guineans how to be just like Australians, by copying Australian models of democratic government; (2) they could have given Papuans and New Guineans a chance at a Papua and New Guinean-style home rule, using traditional leaders and processes as much as possible; or (3) they could have been used by the administration as just another way of making sure the orders they came up with were obeyed. Colonial officials said the councils were intended to do the first, and now and then, especially in more experienced and self-assertive areas, like Port Moresby and Rabaul, they did. But they certainly did not do the second, and nobody at the time thought for even a minute that they should. Local government councils were totally based on an Australian model; there was nothing of Indigenous culture about them, at least in the way they were planned and administered by the government. For the most part, they did the third:

> . . . the councils were viewed by the government as training grounds where the councilors could be instructed in the elements of Australian ideas and methods—as many of the councilors came to understand and resent, despite their lack of education. . . . [T]heir prime function was to facilitate the implementing of central edicts, not to question or modify those edicts, still less to have any role in local

> policy formulation. The councils, in short, became further mechanisms for continuing white dominance.[68]

The councils became yet another channel for the administration to make sure Papuans and New Guineans were doing what the administration wanted them to do.

Finding a Role (or Not) for Customary Law in the Introduced Legal System

For most of the colonial period, there were effectively two legal systems operating in Papua and New Guinea—the official system of courts and laws imported into the territories by the colonial administration, and the customary laws and legal processes by which Papuans and New Guineans ordered their societies and resolved disputes. The *Papua and New Guinea Act of 1949* made explicit the power of the Commonwealth of Australia to import its own law and legal institutions into Papua and New Guinea. If one presumed that the legal system in Papua and New Guinea was exactly as described in the act, then one would assume that imported laws and courts had totally replaced custom.

The court hierarchy in the 1950s began, at the top, with the possibility of appeals to the High Court of Australia and from there to the Judicial Committee of the British Privy Council in London. The highest court in Papua and New Guinea was the Supreme Court, which was both a trial court of limited jurisdiction and a mid-level appellate court. Judges on the Supreme Court, all of whom were white, were drawn primarily from the ranks of retired or minor judges from Australia. They conducted trials and heard appeals from the magistrates' courts, which were the midlevel trial courts. The lowest rung on the judicial ladder was occupied by the Courts for Native Affairs, which, as the name implies, heard cases from and (primarily) about Papuans and New Guineans.

But the assumption in the statute that Papua New Guineans and expatriates would generally be subject to the same legal system was belied by the reality. For the most part, the formal courts and laws continued through the 1950s to apply primarily to whites, while Papuans and New Guineans continued to resolve the great bulk of their disputes on their own, using customary law and legal processes. The major reasons for this, however, were not respect on the part of the colonial judiciary for custom, but a lack of courts and lawyers outside of the major urban areas, coupled with the administration's belief that it would be unfair to subject locals to the imported law until they were more educated in its sophisticated concepts and values.

The lack of formal recognition of custom meant that Papuans and New Guineans could never be sure when the imported law might be applied to them. Nor, with small exceptions, did they have any real power to choose. Occasionally, when a *kiap* came through their village, dissatisfied disputants might bring to the *kiap* an argument that would otherwise have been resolved in a customary dispute settlement gathering. They were forsaking custom in the hope of achieving a more favorable outcome. But, for the most part, it was the *kiap*, the courts, and the police who determined whether Papuan and New Guinean disputes would be decided in customary ways or brought into the state legal system. And the choice to move a Papuan or New Guinean's case from customary law to state law was itself based on state law, not on customary law or process.

Usually, the only time Papuans and New Guineans were brought into state courts was as defendants in actions that constituted crimes under state law. At least during the 1950s, there were very few if any lawsuits in which a Papuan or New Guinean was a plaintiff. If the development of Papuans and New Guineans had been a major aim of the colonial system, it would have been useful to involve Papuans and New Guineans in the courts, not only as defendants or plaintiffs, but as clerks, bailiffs, magistrates and judges. Given that the colonial administration provided almost no primary or secondary education for Papuans and New Guineans, training them to be magistrates or judges would have involved a major commitment of time, effort, and resources—but bringing them in as assessors would have been possible. This did start to happen, primarily in Port Moresby, under a few magistrates, but it did not get far.

Magistrates' Courts: Papuans and New Guineans as Assessors

For a dozen years before World War II, Papuans and New Guineans had served as assessors, a subordinate but still important role in magistrates' courts. In the late 1930s, Sir Hubert Murray had written that he hoped

Australia eventually could "hand over petty acts of administration and trivial native cases to Papuans."[69] Although he did not think it would be difficult to find Papuans "of sufficient intelligence to try a case," he believed it would be all but impossible to find men with sufficient "strength of character" who would not be influenced by family or village considerations and who were not afraid of sorcery.[70]

In 1929, Murray had selected a group of Papuans to sit with the district court magistrates in Port Moresby and act as lay assessors. The goal was to train these Papuans to preside eventually over native courts. Murray wrote:

> In July 1929 the advisability of using native assessors in native cases was suggested to Magistrates with the view eventually—perhaps only in the distant future—of establishing native courts under native magistrates. The views of the Magistrates were not encouraging. Some seemed of the opinion that the native was not intelligent enough; others that the scheme is impracticable until a knowledge of English is more widespread. In the majority of the magisterial districts little progress has been made, but here and there . . . results have been encouraging.[71]

Although the Papuan assessors regularly sat with the magistrates in the early 1930s and advised them on matters of custom and compensation, their authority was limited to making suggestions to the magistrate. They were never given real decision-making powers, and the program was discontinued at the beginning of World War II before any of the assessors were felt to be qualified to preside over a court. No effort was made to revive the program after the war.

It seems that colonial officials saw no conflict between their belief that Papuans and New Guineans were not suited to the bench, while at the same time allowing Papuans and New Guineans to engage in customary dispute settlement gatherings that took up the same kinds of family, land, and inheritance disputes that magistrates and judges regularly heard in court. The role of Papuan assessors was to advise Australian magistrates on issues of fact, not of law. That included customary rules, which were treated in the courts as facts, not law. Thus, magistrates could simultaneously appreciate the superior knowledge that Papuans might have of custom, while maintaining their own sense of superiority in being the only ones learned enough to state and apply the law. No locals actually served as a magistrate on any of the colonial courts until 1967, when the first Papuan and New Guinean local court magistrates were appointed.

Courts for Native Affairs: "For" But Not By Papuans and New Guineans

The Courts for Native Matters in Papua and Courts for Native Affairs in New Guinea were staffed by district commissioners and *kiaps*. They were supposed to "take into account, as far as possible, indigenous usages, rights and local customary law, except where it is contrary to the principles of humanity or conflicts with the law of the Territory."[72]

Although the colonial administration permitted rural Papuans and New Guineans to resolve many family and personal disputes using customary practices, such as dispute settlement gatherings, the administration refused to formally recognize customary methods of dispute resolution or to establish courts presided over by Papuans or New Guineans that would apply customary law and processes. As early as 1924, a British official with experience in Kenya, who had been invited to New Guinea to advise on policy, recommended the establishment of courts that would be presided over by Papuans and New Guineans and that would apply customary law. The administration rejected the proposal, arguing that Papuans and New Guineans were not ready for this responsibility and that such courts would result in corruption. The *Papua and New Guinea Act of 1949* provided for the establishment of village courts, and in December 1949, a *Native Village Council Ordinance* was enacted, but no courts were created under its aegis.[73] In the 1950s, Fenbury argued for the establishment of native courts, on the British colonial model, where "indigenes could administer their own law."[74] Fenbury thought them a necessary complement to local government councils, arguing that they would replace the "illicit" tribunals that Papuans and New Guineans continued to use. However:

> Hasluck personally delivered the coup de grace to the proposal by insisting that only Australian officials were in a position to define what was law and what was not. Law he said, "is a gift we brought them.... The law is the Queen's law."[75]

Despite the administration's general opposition to the formal creation of native courts, it did allow some local initiatives to operate. Murray had created councils in the 1920s in the villages near Port Moresby. Council members were elected by the people of the villages, and were intended both to provide a forum for the discussion of village issues and to exercise some judicial functions. According to Belshaw, by 1927, the Hanuabada council was successfully settling minor disputes.[76] In the Trobriand Islands, colonial officials set up a body of village councilors in each district in the early 1930s. They decided civil claims, including land ownership, issues arising from the *kula* trade, the payment due to a man and his family on the remarriage of his divorced wife, and similar matters. In their *1926–1927 Annual Report*, colonial officials acknowledged that there were a number of unofficial tribunals in New Britain and New Ireland, staffed by New Guineans who "sat as a kind of court to hear minor complaints." The report stated that officials realized "the importance of fostering these native institutions and tribunals and encouraging the natives to take a more active part in the management of their own affairs."[77]

By the end of the 1950s, however, Papuans and New Guineans were being prosecuted for operating their own courts. In a 1961 case, four Papuan men were convicted of setting up "false courts" and imposing punishments. Chief Justice Alan Mann called the actions of the accused "a serious offence and one very dangerous to society." Mann held, however, that the five months the accused had spent in custody awaiting trial was for a number of reasons more punishment than their actions deserved: the defendants had "acted in good faith, on reasonable grounds and with the concurrence of their people"; the lack of patrol officers left the accused "inadequate guidance and advice"; the official courts were "grossly understaffed and inadequately provided for"; the accused held positions of responsibility in the community that might lead to confusion about their powers "which they deemed essential for the protection of their people"; and "[t]here have been many cases in the Territory where men occupying positions of the kind occupied by these men have been officially allowed or directed to settle disputes."[78]

Custom in the Supreme Court: Changing Views about the Responsibility of Papuans and New Guineans

In the postwar years, small but significant changes began to take place in the way judges of the Supreme Court treated Papuan and New Guinean defendants. Judges began to recognize that the courts had a role to play in the colonial enterprise aimed at developing Papua and New Guinea—which meant, first, developing Papuans and New Guineans—so one saw the first glimmerings of a judicial attempt to make the punishment fit not just the crime, but also the criminal. One of the aims of criminal trials became the education of Papuans and New Guineans into the values and mores of the Australian legal system.

The major form that this education took was for Papuan and New Guinean defendants to be found guilty, but then to have the charges reduced and the sentence lessened based on a defense such as self-defense, provocation, or mistake of fact. The judges found the defense of provocation particularly suited to their purposes. In order to establish that the events leading to a killing amounted to provocation, section 271 of the Criminal Code required the accused to prove to the court that he had been so provoked by:

> any wrongful act or insult of such a nature as to be likely when done to any ordinary person, or in the presence of an ordinary person to another who is under his immediate care, to whom he stands in a conjugal, paternal, filial, or fraternal relation, or in the relation of a master or servant, to deprive him of the power of self-control, and to induce him to assault the person by whom the act or insult is done or offered.

The construction of the "ordinary person" test in terms suitable to Papua and New Guinea posed a particular challenge for the colonial courts. In England, the courts defined the ordinary person as a reasonable person, not easily roused, seldom inclined to emotion—in other words, a typical Englishman. The Papua and New Guinea courts held that the "ordinary person" concept had to be modified to meet local circumstances. Cases in which a killing resulted from adultery provided an opportunity. In English law at that time, only the act of finding the spouse in the midst of committing an adulterous act was deemed sufficient provocation to cause an "ordinary person" to lose self-control. The English courts did not consider the mere confession of adultery sufficient to provoke the ordinary Englishman. Indeed, under the English common law of the time, words alone could never constitute provocation; there had to be an act.

The modification of the provocation doctrine began with a 1957 case from the Goilala region of the Papuan Highlands. The defendant killed a man who had committed adultery with the defendant's sister-in-law. The defendant had not seen any evidence of the adultery, but killed the victim with a blow from an axe when the man admitted the adultery to him and made a remark that angered him. Chief Justice Mann held that there was sufficient evidence of provocation under the Criminal Code to reduce the crime from murder to manslaughter. In reaching his decision, the chief justice held that, in the context of the society in which the defendant lived, with its customary relationships and obligations, words alone could amount to provocation and cause a reasonable villager to lose self-control.[79] The chief justice also cited the customary duties of a man to his sister-in-law when her husband was absent from the village. These customary obligations made the sister-in-law the ward of the accused and made him responsible for her care and protection.

The term "ordinary person" now had a more nuanced meaning; it meant "an ordinary person in the environment and culture of the accused."[80] The court distinguished the ordinary Englishman from the ordinary Papuan or New Guinean, primarily on the basis that the court deemed Papuans and New Guineans to be inherently more excitable, less reasonable, less in control of their emotions, than Englishmen.

For example, in a fight between two clans in a remote part of the Chimbu District in the New Guinea Highlands, the defendant, who had received a blow on the head that stunned him momentarily, grabbed a bow and arrow from a fellow clansman and shot and killed his fleeing attacker. It was obviously not self-defense, but, the defendant argued the blow to his head had constituted provocation. Chief Justice Mann agreed, stating: "[A]ny able-bodied Chimbu in the remote area where this fight occurred, would be likely, indeed very likely, in similar circumstances, to lose his power of self-control to the extent of shooting an arrow at his fleeing attacker."[81] In deciding that the defendant had been provoked, the chief justice took into account his lifestyle and the values of his community, but what weighed most heavily was the defendant's lack of education and employment outside his own remote area, his limited contact with the colonial administration, and the absence of any mission influence.

Although the Supreme Court was willing to give an expansive interpretation to the defense of provocation, the judges drew the line at payback. They were willing to treat leniently Papuans and New Guineans who acted in the heat of passion, but were not prepared to deal kindly with persons who, in their perception, flouted the state's monopoly over the means of punishment by attempting to exact retribution themselves.

The defense of provocation served the court well. It squared with the European image of Papuans and New Guineans as excitable people, quick to anger and childlike in their inability to control their emotions and behavior. Because the provocation defense was contained in the Criminal Code, the court felt itself safely within the framework of legal positivism in applying it. Although the court responded with some creativity in fashioning the defense's application to Papuans and New Guineans, it did so incrementally and without straying far from the precedents. Moreover, the court favored the provocation defense over others contained in the Criminal Code because the defense merely reduced the charge from willful murder to manslaughter, whereas other defenses, such as self-defense or mistake of fact, absolved the accused entirely of criminal responsibility. Finally, because the defense focused on the emotional or mental state of the defendant, and not on the defendant's community obligations, it allowed the court to fashion a defense based upon local circumstances without having to expressly adopt or accept local custom as law.

Summing Up the 1950s

In the 1950s, the colonial administration attempted to reestablish its authority over a colony that it expected would remain under Australian rule for another century or more. Perhaps because of the winds of independence that were blowing from the United Nations Trusteeship Council and other colonies around the world, the Australian administration became, if anything, more colonial than ever. But the structure it believed it was remaking to last a century would last barely another fifteen years. To explain the gulf that existed between the administrators and Papuans and New Guineans, Wolfers quotes a telling paragraph, written by John Stuart Mill in 1861:

> Foreigners do not feel with the people. They cannot judge, by the light in which a thing appears to their own minds, or the manner in which it affects their feelings, how it will affect the feelings or appear to the minds of the subject population. What a native of the country, of average practical ability, knows as it were by instinct, they have to learn slowly, and after all imperfectly, by study and experience. . . .

> They are feared, suspected, probably disliked by the population; seldom sought by them except for interested purposes; and they are prone to think that the servilely submissive are the trustworthy. Their danger is of despising the natives; that of the natives is of disbelieving that anything the strangers do can be for their good.[82]

Mill would probably have understood the Papua and New Guinea of the 1950s very well.

Sources

Books and Articles

Leo Austen, "Cultural Changes in Kiriwina," *Oceania* 16(1) (1945) 15–61.

Australian Broadcasting Commission, "100 Years: The Australia Story: Episode 2: Rise and Fall of White Australia" (originally broadcast March 21, 2001; https://www.kanopy.com/product/100-years-australian-story-rise-and-fall-white-australia).

Cyril Belshaw, *The Great Village: The Economic and Social Welfare of Hanuabada, an Urban Community in Papua* (London: Routledge & Kegan Paul, 1957).

Peter Biskup, Brian Jinks, and Hank Nelson, *A Short History of New Guinea* (Sydney: Angus and Robertson, 1968).

Sir Donald Cleland, "An Administrator Reflects," *History of Melanesia, Second Waigani Seminar* (Port Moresby: University of Papua New Guinea Press, 1969) 209–228.

Kimberlé Crenshaw, "Mapping the Margins: Intersectionality, Identity Politics, and Violence against Women of Color," *Stanford Law Review* 43 (6) (1991) 1270–1271.

Ronald Crocombe, "Local Government in New Guinea," *The Journal of Pacific History* 3(1) (1968) 131–134.

Donald Denoon, *A Trial Separation: Australia and the Decolonisation of Papua New Guinea* (Canberra: Australian National University, Pandanus Books, 2005).

A. L. Epstein, R.S. Parker and Marie Reay, *The Politics of Dependence: Papua New Guinea 1968* (Oxford: Taylor & Francis, 1971).

Brian Essai, *Papua and New Guinea: A Contemporary Survey* (Melbourne: Oxford University Press, 1961).

Frantz Fanon, *Black Skin, White Masks* (Paris: Editions de Seuil, 1952).

D. M. Fenbury, "Meeting the Mokolkols, New Britain 1950–51," *History of Melanesia, Second Waigani Seminar* (Port Moresby: University of Papua New Guinea Press, 1969) 153–176.

Joachim Gorlich, "The Transformation of Violence in the Colonial Encounter: Intercultural Discourses and Practices in Papua New Guinea," *Ethnology* 38(2) (1999) 151–162.

James Griffin, Hank Nelson, and Stewart Firth, *Papua New Guinea, a Political History* (Richmond: Heinemann Educational Australia, 1979).

Norman D. Harper, "Security in the Southwest Pacific," *Pacific Affairs* 24(2) (1951) 170–176.

Norman D. Harper, "Australia and Southeast Asia," *Pacific Affairs* 28(3) (1955) 203–220.

Paul Hasluck, "A Policy for New Guinea: Address by the Minister for Territories" Address to the William McGregor Club, Sydney, 20 November 1951 (Canberra: The Australian Institute of International Affairs, The Australian National University Library, 1951).

Paul Hasluck, "Australia's Task in Papua and New Guinea," Seventh Roy Milne Memorial Lecture, Perth, 1956 (Canberra: The Australian Institute of International Affairs, The Australian National University Library, 1956).

Allen M. Healy, "Monocultural Administration in a Multicultural Environment: The Australians in Papua New Guinea," in J. J. Eddy and J. R. Nethercote (eds.), *Colony to Coloniser: Studies in Australian Administrative History* (Sydney: Hale & Iremonger, 1987) 207–224.

Brian Jinks, "The Establishment of Local Government in the Northern District," *The Journal of the Papua and New Guinea Society* 2(1) (1968) 27–32.

Liberal Party of Australia Website, http://www.liberal.org.au/The-Party/Our-History.aspx.

Andrew W. Lind, "Inter-Ethnic Marriage in New Guinea," *New Guinea Research Bulletin*, no. 31 (Port Moresby: New Guinea Research Unit of the Australian National University, 1969).

Lucy Mair, *Australia in New Guinea*, 2nd ed. (Melbourne: Melbourne University Press, 1970).

Albert Maori Kiki, *Kiki: Ten Thousand Years in a Lifetime; A New Guinea Autobiography* (London: Pall Mall Press, 1968).

James McAuley, "Defence and Development in Australian New Guinea," *Pacific Affairs* 23(4) (1950) 371–380.

James McAuley, "Australia's Future in New Guinea," *Pacific Affairs* 26(1) (1953) 59–69.

J. K. McCarthy, *Patrol into Yesterday: My New Guinea Years* (Melbourne: Cheshire Press, 1963).

Nancy McDowell, "A Note on Cargo Cults and Cultural Constructions of Change," *Pacific Studies* 11(2) (1988) 121–134.

J.A. Miles, "Local Administration in British New Guinea and Papua," *South Pacific* 10(1) (1959) 61–73.

Colonel J. K. Murray, "In Retrospect: Papua-New Guinea 1945–1949 and Territory of Papua and New Guinea 1949–1952" *Australian Journal of Politics and History* 14(3) (1968) 320–341.

Nigel Oram, *Colonial Town to Melanesian City: Port Moresby 1884–1974* (Canberra: Australian National University Press, 1976).

R. S. O'Regan, "Ordinary Men and Provocation in Papua and New Guinea," *International and Comparative Law Quarterly* 21(30) (1972) 551–557.

Stephen W. Reed, "New Guinea," in E. T. Thompson and E. C. Hughes (eds.), *Race: Individual and Collective Behavior* (Glencoe: Free Press, 1958) 277–281.

C. D. Rowley, *The New Guinea Villager: A Retrospect from 1964* (Melbourne: Cheshire, 1965).

Garry Trompf, *Cargo Cults and Millenarian Movements: Transoceanic Comparisons of New Religious Movements* (Berlin: Mouton DeGruyter, 1990).

David Weisbrot, "Integration of Laws in Papua New Guinea: Custom and the Criminal Law in Conflict," in David Weisbrot, Abdul Paliwala, and Aki Sawyer (eds.), *Law and Social Change in Papua New Guinea* (Sydney: Butterworths, 1982) 59–103.

F. J. West, "Colonial Development in Central New Guinea," *Pacific Affairs* 29 (2) (1954) 161–173.

Edward P. Wolfers, *Race Relations and Colonial Rule in Papua New Guinea* (Sydney: Australia and New Zealand Book Co., 1975).

Anthony Yeates, "The Patrol Officers and Tom Kabu," *Journal of Pacific History* 40(1) (2005) 71–90.

Government Documents

Report of the Administration of the Mandated Territory of New Guinea 1926–1927 (Melbourne: Government Printer, 1927)

Territory of Papua Annual Report, 1930–1931 (Melbourne: Government Printer, 1931)

Territory of Papua Annual Report, 1937–1938 (Melbourne: Government Printer, 1938)

Cases

R. v. Bogina et al. (1961) PGSC 10

R. v. Hamo Tine [1963] PNGLR 9

R. v. Koruapu of Lupila (1957) PGSC 11

Statutes

Native Administration Regulations 1924–1968 (New Guinea)

Native Labor Ordinance 1941 (Papua)

Native Local Government Councils Ordinance 1949 (PNG)

Native Regulation Ordinance 1908, No. 25 of 1909 (Papua)

Native Village Councils Ordinance 1949 (PNG)

Papua and New Guinea Act 1949 (Australia)

White Women's Protection Ordinance 1926, No. 2 of 1926 (Papua) (*repealed 1958*)

Notes

1. Quoted in Australian Broadcasting Commission, "100 Years: The Australia Story: Episode 2: Rise and Fall of White Australia," originally broadcast March 21, 2001.
2. Norman D. Harper, "Security in the Southwest Pacific," *Pacific Affairs* 24(2) (1951) 170–171.
3. James McAuley "Defence and Development in Australian New Guinea," *Pacific Affairs* 23(4) (1950) 372–373.
4. *Id.*
5. *Id.*
6. *Id.*
7. *Id.*

8. *Id.* at 373–374.
9. Edward P. Wolfers, *Race Relations and Colonial Rule in Papua New Guinea* (Sydney: Australia and New Zealand Book Co., 1975) 130.
10. *Id.*
11. *Id.* at 129.
12. *Id.*
13. *Id.* at 128.
14. *Id.* at 122.
15. *Id.* at 130.
16. *Id.*
17. *Id.* at 135.
18. Cyril Belshaw, *The Great Village: The Economic and Social Welfare of Hanuabada, an Urban Community in Papua* (London: Routledge & Kegan Paul, 1957) 238–239.
19. Edward P. Wolfers, *Race Relations and Colonial Rule in Papua New Guinea* (Sydney: Australia and New Zealand Book Co., 1975) 135.
20. Andrew W. Lind, "Inter-Ethnic Marriage in New Guinea," *New Guinea Research Bulletin*, no. 31 (Port Moresby: New Guinea Research Unit of the Australian National University, 1969), 18.
21. *Id.* at 15–16.
22. *Id.* at 18.
23. Edward P. Wolfers, *Race Relations and Colonial Rule in Papua New Guinea* (Sydney: Australia and New Zealand Book Co., 1975) 2.
24. Andrew W. Lind, "Inter-Ethnic Marriage in New Guinea," *New Guinea Research Bulletin*, no. 31 (Port Moresby: New Guinea Research Unit of the Australian National University, 1969) 20.
25. *Id.*
26. *Id.* at 126.
27. Edward P. Wolfers, *Race Relations and Colonial Rule in Papua New Guinea* (Sydney: Australia and New Zealand Book Co., 1975) 127.
28. *Id.* at 126.
29. *Id.* at 121.
30. D. M. Fenbury, "Meeting the Mokolkols, New Britain 1950–51," *History of Melanesia, Second Waigani Seminar* (Port Moresby: University of Papua New Guinea Press, 1969) 171.
31. *Id.*
32. James Griffin, Hank Nelson, and Stewart Firth, *Papua New Guinea, a Political History* (Richmond: Heinemann Educational Australia, 1979) 103.
33. Paul Hasluck, *Australia's Task in Papua New Guinea* (Canberra: Australian Institute of International Affairs, 1956), 222.
34. Allen M. Healy, "Monocultural Administration in a Multicultural Environment: The Australians in Papua New Guinea," in J. J. Eddy

and J. R. Nethercote (eds.), *Colony to Coloniser: Studies in Australian Administrative History* (Sydney: Hale & Iremonger, 1987) 220.

35. James McAuley, "Australia's Future in New Guinea," *Pacific Affairs* 26(1) (1953) 67.
36. Allen M. Healy, "Monocultural Administration in a Multicultural Environment: The Australians in Papua New Guinea," in J. J. Eddy and J. R. Nethercote (eds.), *Colony to Coloniser: Studies in Australian Administrative History* (Sydney: Hale & Iremonger, 1987) 68.
37. Sir Paul Hasluck, *Australia's Task in Papua New Guinea* (Canberra: Australian Institute of International Affairs, 1956) 228.
38. Peter Biskup, Brian Jinks, and Hank Nelson, *A Short History of New Guinea* (Sydney: Angus and Robertson, 1968) 135.
39. Brian Essai, *Papua and New Guinea: A Contemporary Survey* (Melbourne: Oxford University Press, 1961) 67.
40. Edward P. Wolfers, *Race Relations and Colonial Rule in Papua New Guinea* (Sydney: Australia and New Zealand Book Co., 1975).
41. Brian Jinks, "Australia's Post-war Policy for New Guinea and Papua," *Journal of Pacific History* 17(2) (1982) 86.
42. Paul Hasluck, "A Policy for New Guinea: Address by the Minister for Territories" Address to the William McGregor Club, Sydney, 20 November 1951 (Canberra: The Australian Institute of International Affairs, The Australian National University Library, 1951) 227.
43. Paul Hasluck, *Australia's Task in Papua New Guinea* (Canberra: The Australian Institute of International Affairs, The Australian National University Library, 1956) 228.
44. Brian Essai, *Papua and New Guinea: A Contemporary Survey* (Melbourne: Oxford University Press, 1961) 38.
45. *Id.* at 37.
46. *Id.*
47. Edward P. Wolfers, *Race Relations and Colonial Rule in Papua New Guinea* (Sydney: Australia and New Zealand Book Co., 1975) 7.
48. Brian Essai, *Papua and New Guinea: A Contemporary Survey* (Melbourne: Oxford University Press, 1961) 38.
49. *Id.* at 37.
50. Joachim Gorlich, "The Transformation of Violence in the Colonial Encounter: Intercultural Discourses and Practices in Papua New Guinea," *Ethnology* 38(2) (1999) 153.
51. *Id.* at 155–156 (quoting a 1961 patrol report).
52. Anthony Yeates, "The Patrol Officers and Tom Kabu," *The Journal of Pacific History* 40(1) (2005) 74.
53. *Id.*
54. *Id.* at 72.

55. James McAuley, "Defence and Development in Australian New Guinea," *Pacific Affairs* 23(4) (1950) 380.
56. *Id.*
57. *Id.* at 375–376.
58. *Id.* at 376.
59. *Id.*
60. *Id.* at 378.
61. Donald Denoon, *A Trial Separation: Australia and the Decolonisation of Papua New Guinea* (Canberra: Australian National University, Pandanus Books, 2005) 17.
62. *Id.*
63. Peter Biskup, Brian Jinks, and Hank Nelson, *A Short History of New Guinea* (Sydney: Angus and Robertson, 1968) 152.
64. *Id.* at 153.
65. Cyril Belshaw, *The Great Village: The Economic and Social Welfare of Hanuabada, an Urban Community in Papua* (London: Routledge & Kegan Paul, 1957).
66. Edward P. Wolfers, *Race Relations and Colonial Rule in Papua New Guinea* (Sydney: Australia and New Zealand Book Co., 1975) 8.
67. Allen M. Healy, "Monocultural Administration in a Multicultural Environment: The Australians in Papua New Guinea," in J. J. Eddy and J. R. Nethercote (eds.), *Colony to Coloniser: Studies in Australian Administrative History* (Sydney: Hale & Iremonger, 1987) 220.
68. *Id.*
69. *Territory of Papua Annual Report, 1937–1938*, 21.
70. *Id.*
71. "Native Assessors," *Territory of Papua Annual Report, 1930–1931.*
72. Brian Essai, *Papua and New Guinea: A Contemporary Survey* (Melbourne: Oxford University Press, 1961) 72.
73. *Papua and New Guinea Act of 1949–1950,* section 63.
74. Brian Essai, *Papua and New Guinea: A Contemporary Survey* (Melbourne: Oxford University Press, 1961) 221.
75. *Id.* at 222.
76. Cyril Belshaw, *The Great Village* (London: Routledge & Kegan Paul, 1957) 211–226.
77. *Territory of Papua Annual Report, 1930–1931,* 28.
78. *R. v. Bogina et al.*, Supreme Court No. 216 (August 1961) 1.
79. *R. v. Koruapu of Lupila*, Supreme Court No. 104A (July 22, 1957).
80. *R. v. Hamo Tine* (1963) PNGLR 9, 16.
81. *Id.* at 17.
82. Edward P. Wolfers, *Race Relations and Colonial Rule in Papua New Guinea* (Sydney: Australia and New Zealand Book Co., 1975) 8.

10 Change Comes to the Colony—at Last

Papua and New Guinea in the 1960s

In 1960, Paul Hasluck, who had been Australia's minister for territories for almost a decade, predicted that Papua New Guinea (PNG) would remain under Australian rule for at least another thirty years. Hasluck had been a micromanaging minister, unwilling to delegate any aspect of colonial administration. But, even as he was making that prediction, PNG, Australia, and their places in the world were changing. By the end of the decade, PNG was rushing toward self-government; independence followed with, what might have seemed after so many years as a colony going nowhere, surprising haste. Perhaps to make that possible, Hasluck had by 1963 been shunted to another ministry and, eventually, upstairs to become governor-general of Australia.

For most of the 1960s, however, his forecast seemed to be holding. The path to independence for PNG, if even there was one, was neither sure nor straight. Afterward, it became fashionable to describe independence as a foregone conclusion, propelled by Australian self-interest, with Papua New Guineans swept along into a political future they may not have wanted nor been ready for. In this telling of the story, most if not all of the credit for convincing Australia that the time for PNG's independence had arrived, is usually given to a United Nations Trusteeship Council mission led by Sir Hugh Foot (Lord Caradon), which visited PNG in 1962. But this narrative omits the nuances that add up to a truer story. Although the Foot Committee's report did provoke considerable comment, Australia's major response to it for most of the decade was to institute the kinds of cosmetic changes that would allow Australia to maintain the status quo, doing only what it took to convince the UN that progress was being made. Those modest changes, however, had a consequence that Hasluck, in explaining his opposition to secondary or tertiary education for Papua New Guineans, had darkly foreseen: it produced a small, but vocal and charismatic group of leaders who prompted Australia to accelerate the self-determination schedule, perhaps by decades.

During the 1960s, the Australian administration did accomplish two of its major goals for a postcolonial PNG. It ensured that so-called self-determination would result not in a seventh Australian state, but in a separate nation. At the same time, it ensured that PNG's political and legal systems would faithfully replicate the Australian models, precluding not only any reference to U.S. or Asian precedents, but also any possibility of creating governmental or legal structures based on PNG's own traditions. In this chapter, we recount first the disparate forces and events that moved PNG in just over a decade from a colonial backwater to the edge of self-government. We will then circle back to describe the role that law was made to play in PNG in the period. In the 1960s, colonial judges and administrators continued to replicate Australian bureaucratic and legal models, although often in a watered-down form. They believed that they were doing good, that they were helping Papua New Guineans adopt the social and ethical values of Australia and limiting the adverse economic effects that independence might otherwise have had on Australian nationals and expatriate companies.

Political—and Other—Developments in the 1960s

The Foot Committee was not the first mission sent by the United Nations Trusteeship Council to evaluate Australia's performance in caring for the mandate. Emissaries from the U.N. had arrived in Port Moresby periodically over the years, read the reports that the Australian Department of Territories had prepared for this purpose, announced that all was well, and quickly returned home to New York. But now, as numerous countries in Africa and the Pacific had achieved their independence and were joining the United Nations, the organization's stance toward trust territories was changing, and the Trusteeship Council actually expected countries charged with the trust to do their job. The Foot Committee was shocked by what it found in PNG in 1962. Not only had the Australian colonial administration done very little in the political sphere to enable Papua New Guineans to govern themselves in a modern nation-state, but they had accomplished even less in other key areas. According to the administration's own report

> only 73,000 people (12 per cent of those of working age) earned wages, 17,000 in government and 56,000 in private enterprise (mainly plantations). Of the half-million children of school age, only one-quarter were at school [and only] 3,000 in post-primary education.[1]

The same report revealed that, in a country of 2 million people, there were only a handful of hospitals, and the few paved roads that existed were in and around the few major towns. Since the major functions of the towns were to serve Australian administrative and business interests, it was clear that the roads had been constructed for the convenience of the colonizers and not for the development of Indigenous people. The Foot Committee called for improvement in all these areas and, in particular, for the administration to set target dates for self-government and independence.

The Australian government's view was that self-government should follow, not precede economic and social change, and, "since they could imagine no way to speed up the lethargic pace of economic development, they assumed that political change must also be glacial."[2] One reason for the slow pace of economic and social development in PNG was lack of funds. From the time it became evident that PNG was not a hospitable place for Australians settlement or plantations—which was, the colonizers at the time believed, the only way that the colony could hope to pay for itself—the Department of Territories had to beg for every penny that an unwilling government would begrudge it. There was never enough money for roads, schools, or hospitals, let alone for the salaries of the district commissioners and *kiaps*—for all the things the territory needed if it was to keep its citizens alive, well, and productive.

There were two other reasons for what the Foot Committee called an almost criminal lack of attention on the part of Australian authorities to the basic developmental and infrastructural needs of PNG. First, the racism that was systemic to the Australian national consciousness—and had led Australia to treat its own Indigenous population very poorly and to declare Australia off-limits to any immigrant who was not white—had Australians convinced that Papua New Guineans were primitive and unworthy. Most Australians agreed that it would take decades, a century, or maybe longer, for Papua New Guineans to be sophisticated enough, reasonable enough, moral enough, to rule themselves. If it was going to take that long anyway, if nothing could speed it up, then there was no reason to waste good money giving Papua New Guineans advanced things—such as education—that they could not use.

Second, while Australians at home prided themselves on being egalitarian, as colonizers they were strictly hierarchal. Members of the administrative bureaucracy, from *kiap* on up, took any sign of initiative on the part of a local person as insolence, and a prelude to insubordination and revolt. Papua New Guineans were permitted to engage in cash cropping, copra, or coffee production, and to operate trade stores or any other kind of economic enterprise only if the administration had organized and approved it. When Papua New Guineans tried to do it for themselves, the administration put as many barriers in their way as it could, even to the point of driving them out of business. The administration's fear of initiative also led to the remarkable situation in which, as late the mid-1960s, there was only one high school and no institutions of higher learning in PNG. Hasluck explained that he wanted everyone to be brought up the educational ladder at the same time, so he refused to create more high schools until there were primary schools for everyone, and intended to establish no universities—nor even to allow Papua New Guineans to go overseas to university—until there were high schools all over the territory. His reason, he said, was that if a few Papua New Guineans were educated, they would become troublemakers. Within a few years, a handful of students at a newly opened college would prove him right; they would form a club that would evolve into a political party advocating self-determination and independence. But that prescience does nothing to make up for the generations who unfairly lost out on education.

There had already been some small movements toward economic development and self-government before the Foot Committee's visit. The administration had begun in the 1950s to introduce Local Government Councils into villages, with the intention that these elected bodies would eventually replace both traditional big men and *kiaps*. As of 1962, however, only 350,000 people were covered by Local Government Councils, and the extent to which the councils actually were democratically elected, or had any power, or had in any way usurped the roles either of big men or *kiaps*, was debatable. There also had been small attempts to introduce self-determination at the national level, with the introduction in 1951 of the Legislative Council, ostensibly to advise the Administrator. The Administrator was authorized to appoint all twenty-eight members of the council, with sixteen of the twenty-eight being administration officers. Of the rest, three were from the missions, three represented the planters, another three represented business and commercial interests, and only three were Indigenous Papua New Guineans. In 1961, even before the Foot Committee's visit, the number of Indigenous members was increased to seven. Despite its name, however, the Legislative Council did not legislate; its only role was to advise the Administrator, and he was entirely at liberty to ignore that advice. Since it had no power, and its members were mostly appointed, not elected, it is hard to see how the council was in any meaningful way a precursor of anything resembling self-government.

In the half dozen years following the Foot Committee's visit, the administration instituted changes designed to demonstrate that it was making progress toward self-government, while making sure that the changes were small enough, and controlled enough, so that real self-government would remain well in the future. The Legislative Council was transformed in 1963 into a House of Assembly, with fifty-four members, ten of whom were officials selected by the Administrator and forty-four of whom were elected. Of those elected, ten seats were reserved for expatriates, and thirty-four were open to Papua New Guineans and expatriates. Australians won only six of the thirty-four open seats, with twenty-eight Papua New Guineans successfully entering PNG's first elected legislative body. With that majority, Papua New Guineans could have controlled the House if they had been learned enough in foreign ways to understand its procedures or its purpose, if they were able to overcome regional differences and band together, and if its processes had been simpler, more streamlined, and less foreign. Instead, the first House of Assembly resembled nothing indigenous to Papua New Guinean homegrown methods of governance; it was modeled solely after Australian political institutions, right down to the language (English), the rules of debate (complicated and parliamentary), and even the clothing (a tailor was flown in from Sydney to provide the members with appropriate suits). Australians took the inability of Papua New Guineans to cope with the complexities of House procedure as yet another sign of a lack of sophistication. It never occurred to the Australians that, if they had been thrust into an important moot or ceremony in a Papua New Guinean village, with everyone speaking in a language they barely understood and constantly referring in shorthand to arcane symbols and rituals, they also would have been completely lost.

The administration's decision to impose that process, in all its convoluted detail, probably did not have the flummoxing of Papua New Guinean members as its primary purpose. More likely, it was done because the Australians knew no different model. Told by the UN to create a legislature, that is what they came up with. Told to prepare PNG for self-government, they prepared it for a government very much in the image of their own. Whether those institutions had any relevance to PNG was never a question than anyone in the administration seriously considered. Because they believed that nothing in Papua New Guinean culture or society was worth anything—and, in particular, because they believed that Papua New Guineans had no political or legal structures worth preserving—it never occurred to them that the House might be modeled on anything closer to home for its local members.

The imposition of Australian procedures served the administration well, at least in the first House of Assembly. Not a single piece of legislation opposed to the administration came out of the first House. Not that it would have mattered. If this was supposed to copy Australian forms and processes, so that Papua New Guineans might learn them and adopt them for themselves, they copied only the forms and not the substance. If this was democracy, it was of an extremely controlled and limited—almost nonexistent—variety. The Administrator could overrule anything the House proposed, and if he did not, the Minister for Territories would.

Still, Papua New Guineans might have been able to learn more quickly how to navigate the foreign procedures of the House of Assembly if their educations had been sufficient. In 1964, there were still only a few secondary school graduates, all from mission schools or overseas, and less than a dozen with university degrees, all from Australian or European universities. This situation was changing, however. Australia had at last begun to build a workable infrastructure in PNG. By 1968, the number of secondary school graduates had increased exponentially, and there were several dozen Papua New Guineans with university degrees. The University of Papua New Guinea (UPNG) was in the planning stages, and though it would not take in its first class until 1971, an Administrative College had opened in Waigani, Port Moresby, in 1964, and a teacher's college in Goroka three years later. There were improvements in other areas, too. By 1968, more hospitals had been built in urban areas, as well as additional health outposts in rural areas, and roadwork was proceeding apace. Work on the Highlands Highway, which would at last connect the central spine of the country with the coast, had begun earlier but was seriously pursued in the 1960s. All of these developments brought Papua New Guineans from different regions together, and introduced them to the ideas of freedom and self-determination that were sweeping the developing world. When Alexander Pope wrote that "a little learning is a dangerous thing," he had not meant that it would make Papua New Guineans dangerous to their Australian masters, but the quotation fits.[3]

By the time the second elected House of Assembly was convened in 1968, an independence movement had been born. It took root in a number of places—most notably in Waigani at the Administrative College. Although still very small, the newly formed political party, named Pangu (an acronym standing for "Papua and New Guinea United"—at the time a remarkable and radical notion), managed to elect ten of its members to the House (eight Papua New Guineans and two Australians). And they had done it in a way new to PNG, by going village to village, campaigning heavily in their regions, educating villagers about what colonialism and independence and economics and politics were all about. In the Sepik (where Michael Somare and Pita Lus campaigned), in Morobe (where a young Australian named Tony Voutas quit his job as a *kiap* to run as a Pangu candidate), and elsewhere as well, they created an informed and engaged electorate, the biggest threat to tyranny there can be.

Voutas recalled his campaign, tromping alone from village to village. It was a great change from the patrols he had led as a *kiap*; this time, he truly was alone. Although *kiaps* are romanticized in the Australian imagination as solitary transmitters of civilization to the bush, in fact they traveled with great teams of Papua New Guineans, who served as bearers and police. Campaigning, Voutas carried his own pack and had no protection. He would enter a village, and if no one was there to greet him, he would sit down on the ground where moots and *sing-sings* (ceremonial dances) were held, pull a few sticks out of pack, and start to fashion a *buang* (a possum trap). The villagers, at first wary, then condescending—"*Em man hia, em i no kiap; em rubbis iting*" ("This man here, he's not a *kiap;* he's a nobody")—would gather round to find out what this strange bloke was doing, and soon there would be a conversation about the best ways to catch possums, about whether there were possums in this area, and about what to eat in the absence of possums. That discussion eventually would lead to dinner and to political discussions that went on well into the night.

In the second House, unlike the first, a substantial share of the Papua New Guinean members understood the imposed system. Of the sixty-two Papua New Guinean members, twenty-six had never had any schooling, but at least eight had been educated through high school. And members from disparate regions of the country were finding unity in a way that had not happened before. They had been educated, usually of necessity, at places far from home. They had learned from teachers and books things that nobody in their home villages had ever heard of; they had each seen a world that was unlike anything their village families had ever encountered. As a result, they were beginning to have more in common with one another than they once might have believed possible. Their common wish for better treatment for Papua New Guineans, expressed through Pangu, gave them the vehicle they needed to come together.

The second House was fractious and angry. Pangu members presented motion after motion, and each time, whatever the topic, it was voted down by a coalition of official members, expatriates who represented planter and business interests, Highlanders who did not want independence to come until they had a chance to catch up to their coastal colleagues, and a few other Papua New Guineans. At the time, it must have seemed, to Pangu members at least, like a frustrating and never-ending war of words with a colonial administration promising self-government, and then going back on its promise by brazenly stomping down any attempts at local initiative. David Hay, who was the Administrator at the time, denied that this was official policy, but he "conceded that several

European members did oppose every Pangu proposal," and "Perhaps some of this rubbed off onto some Official Members."[4] In a classic example of blaming the victim, Hay added, "Pangu complicated the situation by reason of the fact that they regarded themselves as the opposition and behaved as such."[5] Obviously, whatever lessons about democracy the Australians had intended this experimental parliament to teach Papua New Guineans, they had not included forming political parties, opposing government policies, representing their constituents, or even occasionally winning a vote.

The coalition of European and official members saw to it that the House passed no legislation that would seriously undermine colonial authority, but those victories came at a cost. Michael Somare, Cecil Abel, Paul Lapun, and the other Pangu members took away from the second House the realization that they could find dignity and success for Papua New Guineans only by freeing it from Australian rule. And a good many Australians—even some in the administration—must have realized, seeing the ill feeling in that House, that do whatever they could, they could not stave off self-government and independence for much longer.

There is today much disagreement about whether independence was forced by the Australians on an unwilling and mostly unready PNG, or whether Papua New Guineans themselves took control of the process, shortening the colonial era by years or decades. Certainly, there were good reasons on both sides for wanting independence. But, just as certainly, there were good reasons why many Papua New Guineans might not want it, at least not right away. It is much easier to ascertain what most Australians believed, since the evidence of pollsters and journalists remains, than it is to speculate on what the majority sentiment might have been on the Papua New Guinean side. The absence of infrastructure made widespread opinion polling unfeasible. The best that can be surmised is that, despite Australia's belated push in the 1960s to construct infrastructure, increase primary education, and have everybody vote (in 1962 and 1967) for House of Assembly candidates, most Papua New Guineans probably had very little idea what colonialism was all about or what independence would entail, beyond its immediate effect on their own villages.

Those few Papua New Guineans (and they probably numbered well under one thousand) who did have some idea of what independence would mean—either because they had managed to get a high school education or, in a very few cases, attend university, or because they had aligned themselves with a Christian mission, or because they had worked for the administration, one of the trading firms, or an expatriate family as a house boy—were split. Those whose route to knowledge came through education tended to favor an early end to colonialism. Those who got there by working for expatriates tended to want the expatriates to stay in power a little longer; this was especially true of Highlanders, who believed that their region, which had been brought into the fold much later than the coastal regions, needed more time under the protection of the colonial powers in order to catch up to the coast. Those connected to the missions were divided.

Most Australians probably ignored the PNG question. If they thought about it at all, their main response would probably focus on their fear of an Asian takeover if Australia could not control the barrier island to its north. Moreover, when the Australian press mentioned PNG, it tended to be yet another story about cannibals and head-hunters, so most Australians probably still shared Hasluck's condescending view of Papua New Guineans. They would presume that it was Australia's grim duty to hang on for centuries, laboriously building one schoolhouse at a time. Finally, as historian Hank Nelson has pointed out, sentimental memories of World War II battles in Rabaul and along the Kokoda Track probably convinced some Australians that they ought to be good to the "fuzzy-haired angels" who had heroically helped the allied soldiers, although ingrained attitudes meant again that for most Australians, being good meant staying there and helping this backward and benighted people to survive, rather than helping them achieve their freedom.

By the mid-1960s, there was even division within the Liberal-Country Party coalition, with most still staunchly in favor of keeping the colony, while at the same time remaining equally strongly opposed to funding it adequately. Those with a better ear were realizing that the reasons Australia should rid itself of its colonies had grown vastly more compelling than any reasons there might be for staying. This latter group included then Prime Minister Robert Menzies. The Labor Party, at that time in opposition—although there were already signs that the next election would bring a Labor victory—was totally in favor of early independence. Although Charles Barnes, Hasluck's successor as minister of territories, was still saying, as late as 1968, that independence would not come before the end of the century, Gough Whitlam, then leader of the opposition in the Australian Parliament, stated in 1969 that, if Labor won the next general election, self-government would come to the territories by 1972 and independence by 1976. At the time, that prediction must have seemed an impossible daydream; in the event, independence occurred a year earlier than Whitlam had prophesied.

PNG had ceased to serve any real strategic purpose for Australia. At least from the 1930s, when the bottom fell out of the global copra market, it had been clear that neither Papua nor New Guinea would ever succeed as plantation colonies. It was not even clear that Australia needed colonies for that purpose—in those days, there was more than enough excess land on the Australian mainland to take care of its entire population, and then some. The strategic importance of the islands as bulwarks against an Asian invasion of the Australian continent had always seemed self-evident, an axiom proven ever more strongly when, but for the battles fought in New Guinea in World War II, the Japanese would have reached mainland Australia. Hank Nelson has pointed out that PNG provided a bulwark, even if only psychological, not only against military invasion from Asia, but also against immigration. "White Australia" was not simply a racist catchphrase; it was Australia's romanticized vision of itself as a hardy band of Anglo-Celts, far from home, but still true blue. It was the policy that had guided everything Australia did, from its prohibition on Asian or Melanesian immigration, to its creation of military alliances with nations on the other side of the globe, to its decision to pack up the butter and other goods it produced and ship them for sale halfway around the world.

All this was changing by the late 1960s. First, with the Indonesian takeover of the western half of the island from the Dutch in 1963, PNG ceased to function effectively as a military barrier:

> To share a long land border with the benign Dutch was one thing; it was another to share it with a turbulent Indonesia led by Sukarno, who was proclaiming leadership of the unaligned nations, buying arms from Russia and living dangerously with the Communist party.[6]

An army intent on invading Australia could do so as easily from the western half of the island, now controlled by Indonesia, as it could from the half still under Australian domination. Nor did it help Australia's sense of security when Great Britain and the United States, its two supposed allies and defenders against Asian encroachment, backed the transfer of West Papua to Indonesia. The Liberal-Country government was beginning to realize that these two former protectors could no longer reliably be counted on to be there should Australia need them. With no one to protect it against potential enemies in the region, Australia had better make sure it had none.

Economic changes, too, supported the Australian government's new perception that the country's best course lay in making itself part of Asia. By 1966, Great Britain was seriously considering joining the European Economic Union, which would put an end to the preferential economic treatment that Australia, New Zealand, and other commonwealth nations had enjoyed, and that had made it economically worthwhile to trade with England rather than within the region. Trade with Britain declined over the decade from one-third of Australia's exports to one-tenth, while trade with Australia's former enemy Japan grew, so that by 1966, Australia was exporting as much to Japan as to Britain, and by the end of the decade, exports to Japan were double those to Britain.

Remaking itself to become part of the Asian Pacific region meant giving up the White Australia policy; it meant welcoming visitors, even immigrants, from southern Europe, Asia, and the Pacific; and most importantly from our perspective—and for that matter, from the perspective of the Asian and Pacific nations who had been colonized by the British and other European powers—it meant giving up Australia's status as a colonial power by giving up its colonies.

Despite all these strong reasons, Australia hesitated. It took two disparate events, at opposite sides of the island, to push the Australian government into agreeing to a timetable that would result in an independent PNG within three years. The first was the late 1972 slaying of Rabaul District Commissioner Jack Emanuel, who had been sent on special assignment to negotiate with the Mataungan Association—an organization formed among the Tolai people of the Gazelle Peninsula who resented the expatriate domination of the local plantation economy. Although the perpetrators were easily caught and a show trial quickly followed, it was evident that this was not an ordinary murder. It had been carefully planned by the leaders of the village, the entire community was involved in it, and it occurred in response to the villagers' belief that the colonial administration, of which Emanuel was the local symbol, had perpetrated a series of injustices on them.

The administration might have ignored the warning bells sounded by the Emanuel affair. What it could not ignore was a more resounding, though bloodless, coup—the Papua New Guinean takeover of the third House of Assembly, in April 1972. This chapter (and the decade) began with Sir Paul Hasluck, when he was still minister for territories, reaffirming his rock-hard belief that self-determination for PNG was many generations in the future. It is appropriate, then, to end this part of the chapter with another Hasluck moment. Shunted upstairs to the governor-generalship, a post of much pomp (for which he had always expressed great hatred), but no power (which he seems always to have assumed was his due), he was brought in to give the opening address to that third House of Assembly. He spoke, as if to backward children, listing for them what they had to do in order to bring development to their poor, primitive population, and admonishing them that all this would take time, that one foot must be placed slowly and carefully in front of the other so that all would proceed at a measured pace. It was as if the momentous events of the decade had not happened.

Hasluck had barely finished speaking when Pangu party leader Michael Somare stood up to call for the historic vote that took the House and eventually the nation out of the hands of the Australian administration forever. The matter on which he was asking the House to vote—choosing the committee that would select which members would be ministers—might not seem earthshaking. But it was, in many ways. It was the first time, in three Houses of Assembly, that a Papua New Guinean, other than one who had been chosen and groomed by the administration to be the speaker, took control of the debate. Second, the issue itself took on importance since, up until that moment, the administration had assumed it still controlled the departments and it would decide which members served as their ministers. Third, and this was another first, Somare's motion carried—and by a sizeable majority.

Christine Stewart, at that time married to Tony Voutas and also a member of Pangu, remembered the politicking that had gone on deep into the night before that first sitting. Since Pangu had not won an absolute majority, the Australian and official members assumed that the administration would again win every vote. It never occurred to them that, after ten years of experience with Houses of Assembly, Papua New Guineans might have learned the system. It never occurred to them that Papua New Guineans might be ready to put regionalism aside, at least as long as it took to defeat their common enemy. It also never occurred to them that, through that long night, members of Pangu were meeting with Julius Chan and his People's Progress Party, nonaligned members, and others, to form a coalition. And it certainly never occurred to them that Papua New Guineans would have come up with a method to help their less educated colleagues not only find their way through the arcane nature of parliamentary procedure, but use it against itself.

As Stewart tells it, Pita Lus, member from Maprik and a Pangu member since the second House, spent the night going from member to member. House of Assembly rules specified that votes were recorded by having members stand. According to Stewart, what Lus instructed them to do was: "*Lukim Maikol tasol. Em bai sanap, yu bai sanap wantaim. Em bai sindaun, yu tu yu mas sindaun.*" "Just look at Michael (Somare). When he stands up you stand up. When he sits down, you also must sit down." The coalition members did this, and the vote was 55–42.[7] The coalition had a clear majority; the official members and their allies would not be able to block legislation in the third House. At least in this area, the era of Australia's dominance in PNG had ended. Only a violent turning back of the clock could have reasserted it, and, with a new world watching, Australia was not prepared to do that.

The Uses of Law in the 1960s

Throughout the 1960s, the decade that turned out to be colonialism's last, the administration and its courts did their best to entrench a Western-style legal system. They did so in part because they believed it was not only the best of all possible legal systems, but that in PNG it was the only legal system. The colonizers believed that an independent PNG would survive only if it and its citizens were remade to become as much like Australians as it was possible to make them—and they believed the law was an excellent vehicle for this educational process. Most of all, they did it so they could give up their political control of PNG secure in their belief that the economy that served Australian settlers and expatriate companies would continue to enjoy all the protections that the Western legal system provided.

Torts and Land Claims

The decade of the 1960s saw the first significant attempts by Papua New Guineans to make use of the imported courts to achieve their own goals. For almost the first time, a small but significant number of Papua New Guineans entered the courts not just as defendants in criminal cases, but as plaintiffs in suits against expatriate individuals and companies. The two areas where this occurred most often were in personal injury claims by Papua New Guinean individuals against foreign companies and in attempts by Papua New Guinean groups to reclaim land that had been taken from them.

Papua New Guineans' experience as plaintiffs in Western courts was mixed. On the negative side, the judges in both torts and land cases tended to rule against the plaintiffs or to give them monetary awards that were much less than what an expatriate might have received for a similar claim. On the positive side, however, Papua New Guinean plaintiffs did gain confidence in their ability to participate strategically in introduced institutions and to gain something from that participation.

Torts—"Let Them Take Care of Themselves"

There are substantial differences between the attitudes to compensation for personal injuries of traditional Papua New Guinean societies and the approach taken by the English common law. There are four areas of potential conflict between the two systems of law. First, in Papua New Guinean societies, there is a broad range of acts that can result in a demand for the payment of compensation. While some of those acts fit the common law and Criminal Code categories of tort law and criminal law, their scope is much broader and does not distinguish between "civil" and "criminal" wrongs. They include acts that cause personal injury, property damage, or death (such as assault, sorcery, and damage caused by children and animals); the interference with rights to land (such as trespass, stealing from gardens or trees, interfering with hunting and fishing rights); the interference with sexual rights (adultery or sexual relations with a girl "marked" for marriage to someone else); the violation of customary obligations (such as a brother's obligation to provide for his sister, the obligation of a husband to pay money to his wife's family at the birth of each child); using defamatory, insulting, or obscene language; and the breach of taboos (i.e., calling in-laws by their names, failing to keep status or dignity within the family, and incest).

Second, under the English common law, most liability in tort depends upon a showing of "fault" in the form of intent or negligence. Customary compensation systems, however, are based on strict or "no-fault" liability. Causation determines liability for compensation, not the moral culpability of the actor.

Third, unlike common law personal injury suits, which are purely private claims between the injured party and the person alleged to have caused the injury, the "plaintiff" and "defendant" in PNG are conceptually much broader. The parties are integral parts of groups based upon kinship, marriage, and descent. Underlying these relationships is the rule of reciprocity, which means that a person must provide assistance to certain others who must reciprocate in a specified manner. The result of this arrangement is that an injury to one member of the group is regarded as an injury to the entire group. Similarly, an injury caused by one member of a group is regarded as an injury for which every other member of the group is equally responsible.

Finally, in most Papua New Guinean societies, compensation traditionally was determined through some kind of dispute settlement gathering or discussion. This negotiating process drew its efficacy from kinship ties, the skill of group leaders, the threat (and sometimes the use) of force, and the existence of a shared value system. Since customary compensation systems were only one aspect of the complex intra- and intergroup relations, the response to injuries depended upon the relationship between the wrongdoer and the victim, as well as other disputes between them or their kinsmen. The purpose of compensation was to restore harmony to that relationship since it affected the entire group. For example, customary compensation systems would consider whether stealing, assault, or adultery involved a friend, a clan brother, or someone from another village. If the parties were interrelated, it might be treated as a breach of their reciprocal relationship, which could be settled through compensation at a ceremonial exchange. The amount of the compensation could be increased if clan brothers were involved since other members of the clan might express a greater degree of outrage. However, if the act was between two persons from different villages or groups, it might be necessary to employ some kind of retaliatory action before, or even instead of, compensation.

Throughout the colonial period, the administration viewed the Criminal Codes as an integral part of their attempt to maintain order and as a means to educate Papua New Guineans in European values. Successive administrations went out of their way to arrest, try, and punish those who violated the codes. However, the administration saw no strategic interest in becoming involved in claims for compensation for these violations. In the view of the administration, compensation claims were mere matters of private law. This meant that so long as its courts could also try the perpetrator for his crime, the administration generally did not stand in the way of compensation claims. However, it also meant that the administration did not support the compensation process; it would never substitute compensation for the sentence imposed by the court nor generally take the payment of compensation into account in fashioning an appropriate sentence.

Although the administration was willing to leave compensation for private injuries to custom and traditional processes, Papua New Guineans frequently brought their claims to the courts for native affairs. Magistrates in those courts were not limited to the English common law. They had the power to take a number of different approaches to the claims. They could mediate the case according to what they thought was fair; alternatively, they could determine and apply the relevant custom, or they could leave the resolution of the claim to traditional village processes.

In 1959, the Supreme Court decided its first tort case brought by a Papua New Guinean. During the next seventeen years, the courts would hear about a dozen more. There were a number of reasons for the decision by some Papua New Guinean plaintiffs to move their claims for compensation from the traditional sector into the formal courts. First, the colonial administration established a public solicitor's office in 1958. The public solicitor and the other lawyers in the office had as their sole charge the representation of Papua New Guineans before the courts. Although the office was understaffed and mainly devoted its resources to providing defense counsel in criminal cases, the public solicitors could also file civil suits. In all of the 1960s tort cases, the Papua New Guinean plaintiffs were represented by lawyers from the public solicitor's office.

Second, the defendants in the cases discussed here were Westerners or Western-owned companies. The presence of a non-Papua New Guinean defendant brought the case outside the reach of traditional dispute settlement processes; at the same time, it made a civil suit more attractive since the defendants were highly unlikely to acquiesce in claims by Papua New Guineans for compensation absent a trial in state court under Western law. Third, in all but one of the tort cases, the circumstances of the injury were not connected to traditional village pursuits, but instead were caused by motor vehicle, airplane, or work-related accidents. This made them seem simultaneously outside the traditional rules of custom and inside the rules of common law that were familiar to the Australian public solicitors. Finally, the lawyers in the public solicitor's office viewed these cases as fitting especially strongly within the common law mold, because, to their minds, the injury had been to an individual and not to a kinship group, so suit could be brought on behalf of the injured individuals rather than for the benefit of the entire clan or extended family.

All the cases involved injuries that would result in lowered employment prospects for the plaintiff. In England and Australia, plaintiffs in cases of this sort are often awarded large sums, because the courts calculate years and years of wages that the plaintiffs would have earned but for their injuries. The Australian judges who sat on the PNG Supreme Court, however, declined to award much in lost wages. Papua New Guineans, they said, were insulated from economic loss because of the cooperative nature of traditional society, which meant that everyone in the village could expect other villagers to help care for their needs. Besides, the judges said, Papua New Guineans' economic losses would not be very large anyway, because they lived in a subsistence economy and the standard of living within the villages was low.

Plaintiffs in the tort cases can be divided into three categories, depending on their age and lifestyle: a group of cases involved adults living, and likely to go on living, in a traditional village environment; another group involved children living in villages near Port Moresby; the third group consisted of Papua New Guineans who had moved out of traditional villages to live permanently in towns and take jobs in the commercial sector. The way that judges decided how much plaintiffs in each of these groups should be awarded demonstrates that supposedly neutral and disinterested judges were very much directed by the beliefs and biases that they brought with them to PNG.

The first group of cases was brought by injured adults living in a traditional village environment. The judges denied members of this group much of any recovery for future economic loss, based upon two mistaken beliefs that the judges held about village life: first, that the work done in a subsistence economy has no monetary value, and second that the family and clan provide for everyone.

It is true that the cash income of villagers was quite small, but the food and goods they produced had a substantial value that the court could have translated into monetary equivalents. A villager's injury or death produced real economic loss to the injured person or surviving relatives in two ways: first, the injured person was no longer able to work in the gardens, the source of food for subsistence, reciprocity, and sale; and second, the injured person was prevented from leaving the village to earn more money in the urban sector.

When dealing with women plaintiffs, the court added yet another mistaken belief. The judges held that by definition women could not suffer an economic loss, because everything belonged to their husbands. Even if a woman's work in the garden and home did have a monetary value, the judges said, she suffered no loss of future value because she could not sell her labor; she was obligated to work in her husband's gardens.

The judges applied the same standard when the plaintiffs were children who lived in the village. Just as they had with adults, the judges held that children whose injuries might prevent them in the future from taking advantage of educational or employment opportunities in urban areas would still be able to rely on their villages for support and would suffer no economic loss.

Given that the plaintiffs were children, the judges might have taken into account that they would become adults in a very different PNG. Change was already happening, but the judges did not seem to notice that the subsistence economy was disappearing from villages in and around Port Moresby, that the "social security" traditionally provided by clans and families was lessening, and that there were increasing opportunities for employment in the modern sector.

Beyond asserting that Indigenous plaintiffs could depend on their clan and family to support them, the Supreme Court judges did not deal effectively with all aspects of the group character of Papua New Guinean society. They failed to recognize that group responsibility went both ways: an injury to one member would result in a loss to the entire group. Since the judges admitted that the group supported an injured member, it should have occurred to the judges that the court should reimburse the group for the extra burden, caused by a member's injury, and for the additional loss of that person's future earnings and contributions to the group. Given the common law's emphasis on individual rights and individual responsibility, however, it is not surprising that village and kinship groups were not made parties to the tort cases and did not present evidence about the monetary value of the support they could be called upon to provide, or that they stood to lose, in the future.

The only cases that the judges treated differently involved claims by persons who had left the village and taken commercial or government jobs in urban areas. These cases raise a question different from the village cases, but also from any that would have confronted a judge in Australia or England. These plaintiffs were employed and but for their injuries would have continued to be employed, so as with any other wage earner, the injury had lost them considerable amounts in future income. But, what if, once they were injured, their only recourse was to return to the village? In those circumstances, to what extent should the lower costs of living in the village and the traditional support they could claim from clan members lower the damages they would otherwise have been awarded? Unfortunately, the Supreme Court gave no clear answer about the role that village life and customary support should play in calculating damages. In one case, the low amount of damages awarded by the judge seemed to represent a considerable reduction based on the lower village living standard while, in another case, the judge made no reduction.

A related problem for the Supreme Court involved claims by young wives who were living in urban areas at the time of their husband's death. Without her husband's urban income to support her, each wife had to return to her family in the village. In an odd reversal from the cases involving village women, the judges treated these plaintiffs in the same way they treated Australians. The judges recognized that the young women might have preferred not to return to the village standard of living, and based the award of damages on the loss of the husband's present and potential earnings in the cash economy. However, the judges did subtract some money, based on the possibility of remarriage, and then subtracted more on the theory that, had their husbands lived, custom would have required some of the future earnings to go to members of the extended family instead of the wives.

The tort cases teach a sad lesson. They demonstrate the drawbacks in admonishing judges to take local circumstances into account, and then not giving those judges full and accurate information about those circumstances. Applying their own preconceptions and the biases ingrained in them by their Australian and British legal educations, the judges viewed local circumstances solely as a reason for making the awards less than what plaintiffs would have obtained in an ordinary Australian court. There is irony in this, but it is a sad one.

Land Claims—Not Giving Back

The establishment of a settler colony requires the total or partial removal of the Indigenous population from those areas that settlers wish to make their own. Removal can be by war, banishment, legal decree, or (as in Australia) by creating a legal fiction that the Indigenous inhabitants simply were not there. The Australian administration removed Papua New Guineans from only about 5 percent of the land, but it was generally the most valuable land, either because it was fertile or because it became towns and cities. Although the Australians gained some land by force, and some by deeming it waste and vacant, much of the land was supposedly purchased from its Indigenous owners by the Australian colonial authorities. Unfortunately, these purchases of customary land were not governed by customary law, but by the imported law.

Papua New Guineans did not consider these purchases either valid or permanent. Customary law did not allow it. Under custom, land could not be sold away from the clan, and even within the clan the right to use it was never permanent. Households and families had the exclusive use of land only for so long as no one else in the clan needed it more than they. Land was the basis of the people's subsistence and cultural identity. It was not a commodity to be bought and sold.

Under the law that the Australians imported into PNG, however, land was available to purchase, and for their money purchasers received the sole and permanent right to use the land however they wanted, to keep it or sell it, develop it or ignore it, whether they needed the land or not, forever. The stark difference between customary law and the imported law was not reconcilable. The only question was which would apply, and the administration and the settlers presumed that it was the law they had brought with them.

In the 1960s, Papua New Guineans began to bring to the colonial courts their long-festering dissatisfaction over lands that had been taken from them. Their claims were only occasionally successful, and even when Papua New Guineans did win, the courts did not return their land to them. Instead, the judges decided that the land had been too long in Australian hands to be returned, and that the local claimants should receive monetary compensation for the loss of the land instead. Moreover, in calculating the amount of that compensation, the courts for the most part held that Papua New Guineans should not receive an award based on the value of the land at the time of the lawsuit, when it had become a successful plantation or part of a large urban center, but instead based on its much lower value when it was a subsistence plot first taken from its Indigenous owners.

Papua New Guineans lost most of the land cases. They lost not only because the imported legal system recognized land purchases that customary law did not, but also because many of the rules of the imported legal system were weighted against the Indigenous people and in favor of the alien expropriators. For example, when Papua New Guineans and colonial officials told conflicting stories about how and whether the land had been purchased, the rules of the imposed legal system favored the foreigners. The stories told by Papua New Guineans came from memory and oral histories; the stories told by the colonial officials were based on written documents—and following the dictates of the imported law, the judges relied on written documents, rather than on oral histories, to evaluate the conflicting stories. The rule in favor of documentation immediately privileged the invaders over those whose land has been taken.

The judges did not discuss the untruths and inaccuracies that frequently crept into those early documents. One reason the invaders were not always truthful was that they had to report back to bureaucrats in their home countries, not all of whom agreed with the idea of taking, or even of purchasing, land from the natives. So, the expatriates wrote what they believed they were expected to say, justifying this to themselves on the basis that the officials in Berlin or Canberra would simply not understand the difficulties of making a new life in such an unwelcome environment.

Other imported rules also privileged the settlers, including the requirement that ownership be recorded under Australia's Torrens Title land registration system. The Torrens Title system provides that registration is final and incontrovertible proof of ownership. Once an owner has registered a parcel of land, this ownership cannot be disturbed, even by proof of defects further back in the chain of title. Torrens Title was introduced into Australian law in order to make it easier and more profitable to buy and sell land, by doing away with the time-consuming title investigations and lawsuits that, in other jurisdictions, slowed down the sales and purchases of land, and that left buyers uncertain whether they had good title.

The Torrens Title system, of course, was never intended to deal with the injustice of Australia's failure to recognize native title, but, it was at least putatively fair in those limited circumstances in which buyers and sellers were operating on relatively equal footing—circumstances that did not exist in PNG at that time. This meant that the attempts by Papua New Guineans to bring into court evidence that their land was stolen from them went for naught because, wrapping themselves in the mantle of the law, the courts informed them that the land in question was registered and that ownership disputes that arose prior to registration could no longer be entertained. There were many parcels of alienated land that did not show up in the registries, however, but Papua New Guinean claimants fared no better in these cases, because the judges invented various legal fictions that enabled them to treat the land as if it had been registered, even when available evidence suggested it had not been.

This was particularly the situation in relation to land in New Guinea, which had for a time been under German control and was the most encroached upon by settlers. After World War One and the Treaty of Versailles stripped Germany of its overseas colonies, and Australia took over the formerly German colony, Australia enacted statutes providing for a double expropriation. Land that the Germans had expropriated from its native owners was in turn expropriated from the Germans. The plan was to register this land under Torrens Title in the name of a new colonial officer invented for the occasion, the custodian of expropriated properties, who would in turn auction it off to Australians, mostly returned servicemen.

The only concession to Papua New Guinean traditional owners was the provision that the commissioner of native affairs had to be notified before this registration took effect. But, the commissioner's brief did not suggest that he should return land to New Guineans because they might need it, or because it was their country, or even because it was simply the right thing to do. Rather, the commissioner's only role was to investigate the documents and notations in the Germans' files and registries, in order to make sure that the initial expropriations of the land had complied with the German law in effect at the time. No thought was given to the possibility that all of the land taken by the Germans rightfully should be returned to its traditional owners.

The whole complicated property exchange had barely started when the Second World War intervened, and the land title documents from the 1920s that might have shown which land had been fairly purchased and which had not, mostly disappeared in one conflagration or another, casualties of the fighting that raged across that area. The wholesale destruction of all of the written evidence might have given the Australian administrators the opportunity to do the right thing and return the land to its traditional owners under customary law. Instead, the colonial administration set itself the task of reconstructing the lost documents and registering the land in the name of various Australian settlers—or, if none could be found, then in the name of the custodian of expropriated properties.

In order to carry out this work, the registrars, commissioners, and courts had to rely on documentary evidence that was spotty and inconclusive. To make any sense of the evidence at all, the courts had to make numerous inferences and assumptions that often involved fairly large leaps from the available documents, and the courts almost inevitably made those leaps to support the foreign takers of the land, rather than the Papua New Guineans who had lost it. In many cases where no real evidence of registration existed, the courts decided that registration must have occurred, and must have occurred properly, solely based on the shaky assumption that colonial administrators always acted efficiently, properly, lawfully, and most importantly, quickly.

But the laws that the settlers had enacted for themselves were not simple; registration required a number of steps, all of which had to be shown to have occurred in order to prove that the land had been registered in the name of its new owners. For the courts, the existence of a number of steps just meant more opportunities for wild surmise. In the case of *In Re Wangaramut*, at least one of the key steps—advertisement in the *Gazette* by the director of native affairs—not only failed to be proven, but on the contrary, the Papua New Guinean plaintiffs could show definitively through the *Gazettes* for that period, that it had not occurred. Perversely, the court decided that all of the steps needed for registration must have occurred prior to the date that advertising in the *Gazette* became a requirement—which meant that everything required had been done in about fourteen months. There is much evidence that nothing so complicated and demanding was ever done in New Guinea in the 1920s (or since, for that matter) in such a short time. Colonial officers were few on the ground and had very inadequate office assistance or equipment, and mail service was slow or nonexistent, so even routine tasks took far longer than a mere fourteen months to be completed. For example, in *In Re Tonwalik*, the court reported on an attempted land registration that took at least four years to process—and, even then, it had only reached the point at which a draft certificate of title had been prepared. Twenty years later, the Australian who believed he was the lawful landowner sought to get a copy of the title, and found that the registration had never in fact been completed beyond the draft certificate stage.

Another way that the judges found to reject the land claims of Papua New Guineans was to deny them the protection of common law doctrines that were available in Australia, such as adverse possession. Under this doctrine, registered landowners can lose title to their land if a third party occupies the land uninterruptedly for a significant period of time. There were cases in PNG in which the occupiers laid claim to land, but did not police all of the borders, or even ignored the land for years, returning decades later to discover Indigenous people living there, hunting, fishing, and even growing cash crops. Counsel for the local people figured that, since the imported legal system had taken so much from their clients, it ought to give a bit back now and then. They argued that the Indigenous people had satisfied all of the elements of the doctrine of adverse possession, and according to Western law should now be regarded (again) as the rightful owners of the land. However, the colonial courts cynically decided that this part of land law, alone among all the others, had not been received in PNG.

Keeping Custom in Its (Very Small) Place: Making the Law as Australian as Possible

The more progressive elements in the colonial administration welcomed the participation of Papua New Guineans in the introduced legal system, and starting in 1960, the administration took steps to increase that participation. The old Courts for Native Affairs and Courts for Native Matters were abolished, and the formal court system was restructured to create new courts at the lowest level of the judicial hierarchy primarily to hear cases of relatively small value brought by Papua New Guineans, usually against other locals. However, the integration of the Indigenous population into the legal system did not include the integration of that population's native legal rules and processes, at least not to any meaningful extent. Instead, for the most part the new courts were to apply the introduced statutory and common law, and were to be staffed by magistrates trained in the imposed legal system.

David Derham Reinvents the Papua New Guinea Courts

The administration took the first step in the process of integrating Papua New Guineans into the legal system when it hired University of Melbourne Law Professor David Derham to consult on the reworking of the colonial legal system. Derham started from the premise that the goal of the colonial administration ought to be to create a unified nation out of the disparate and often conflicting cultures of Papua and New Guinea, and then hand over control of that nation to an Indigenous-led government. Among the challenges facing the administration in moving toward that goal was "[t]he relation between the law that courts know and the customs of the communities served by that law."[8] This challenge was at the heart of the recommendations in Derham's report. A unified nation, he insisted, required a unified legal system, and that system could not include custom.

Derham listed a number of reasons why it would be "inappropriate" for a Papua New Guinean nation to give a major role to custom. It would be difficult, he argued, to distinguish between customs that were mere habits or ingrained behavior and those which were followed out of a sense of obligation. Only the latter, he seemed to suggest, could rank as laws. And even if a custom did carry an obligation to conform, was the duty owed to the community as a whole or to a subgroup within it? Besides, many customs varied from one community to another. Custom provided little in the way unity across the entire nation, and and laws of a unified nation, Derham preached, should themselves be uniform. Derham also viewed most customs less as rules regulating conduct than as methods for deciding how disputes would be resolved. Forgetting the vast pages of English language statute books given over to the myriad rules of evidence and procedure, Derham opined that rules about process were not eligible to be considered "law." Most importantly, he argued that Indigenous customs could not meet the needs of changing communities:

> [T]he customs of the numerous distinct indigenous communities may be quite well suited to enable them to survive as subsistence, agricultural and hunting communities. They are not appropriate to enable larger communities to develop, to deal with problems that involve more than one community or to solve problems raised by contact with European agriculture, manufacture and commerce, or even European influence in personal relations increasingly spread by the various missions.[9]

Derham predicted that among the many problems that would confront the courts in the future if custom were to be part of the nation's legal system would be cases involving Papuans and New Guineans from different communities with conflicting customs, the breakdown of custom as a result of European influence, and the participation of Papuans and New Guineans in business ventures for which there were no suitable customary rules.

Derham concluded that the debate was not "a question of all or nothing," and that some issues should be decided by a national legal system while others could be handled at the local level by custom. Without specifying what subjects fell into each group, he wrote:

> It may be assumed that a wise government will take account of well-established customs in making general laws and will assume that interference with local customs must be justified by considerations that necessarily override local interests.[10]

The Derham report called for a number of reforms to the court structure, all aimed at integrating Papua New Guineans into the imported legal system. In particular, he recommended the abolition of the Courts for Native Affairs and Native Matters. These courts, staffed primarily by *kiaps*, rather than by trained judges or magistrates, had existed solely to adjudicate alleged breaches of the Native Regulations and to hear the occasional dispute between Papua New Guineans. Derham suggested that they be replaced by lower level courts that would be staffed by trained magistrates and would hear cases involving both the Papua New Guinean and the expatriate population. With few exceptions, these courts would apply the imported law.

White People Talking to Themselves: "Debate" in the 1960s over the Future of Custom in Papua New Guinea

Public discussion of the role that custom should have in the legal system of an independent PNG did not begin with Derham, but it certainly gained momentum after 1963, when he published a law review article justifying and explaining his recommendations for the creation of an integrated court system. That discussion would continue for the next decade, but although the subject would deeply impact Papua New Guineans, the debate occurred primarily among whites. Papua New Guineans may have been talking about the issue avidly and intelligently among themselves, but their viewpoint was not included in scholarly journals, or heard at conferences, or even broached very loudly in government or in universities until 1973. By that time, try as they might, there was little Papua New Guineans could do to alter the consensus that had already been reached about the very limited role that custom would be allowed to play in the legal system of their nation. It would be their legal system in the sense that it would govern them, but it would not be theirs in the sense that they had much to do with shaping it.

In the 1960s, attitudes toward the colonial enterprise were changing, as movements toward self-determination and independence gained ground. Change could be felt even in PNG. Of course, most of the prominent members of the administration and the judiciary continued to insist that independence was decades off in the future, and to argue equally strongly for the retention of the imported legal system even after independence finally occurred. For example, then Secretary for Law W. W. Watkins defended the English legal system in PNG and the judges who applied it:

> The traditional complaints against the complexity of the law are easy to make and usually attract applause; but in the Territory, over the last eighty years, the law has been satisfactorily administered in line with the Common Law of England which is so constructed and so flexible to accommodate consideration of, and give full effect to, the customs

and principles of conduct of the native people, so far as they do not conflict with humanity.

> The Judges who have administered the law in this Territory have been men of dedication, with breadth of vision, and they have been sensitive to the fact that they were adapting the law to the conditions and mode of life of the indigenous people. No indigenous person has even been punished or convicted without full consideration of all the circumstances, including his native background and mode of life and the customs applicable to him.[11]

Watkins no longer spoke for everyone, however. Attitudes were changing, even within the administration and the business sector. *Kiaps* like Tony Voutas and entrepreneurs like Barry Holloway joined Pangu and ran for election to the House of Assembly as party members. The establishment of UPNG brought a number of academics to the country with experience of the independence movements in Africa and Asia, many of whom supported early independence for PNG. As one might expect, legal experts, such as the members of the UPNG law faculty, as well as lawyers from the public solicitor's office and the law department were about the only people among this new pro-independence group to pay much attention to the future of the legal system in general, and to the future role of custom in particular. And, despite their respect for Papua New Guineans and their support for independence, many of them did not argue for custom to play a major role.

Instead, most of them believed that they could best support Papua New Guineans by following Derham in recommending the establishment of a single, unified system of law in which English law would continue to be supreme, but ensuring that Papua New Guineans would have a role in that system equal to that of whites. Derham's recommendations were echoed by Jack Goldring and Peter Bayne, who were members of the UPNG law faculty. Both respected the intelligence, acumen and abilities of their Papua New Guinean students and colleagues; neither shared the disdain and condescension that characterized the typical Australian approach to PNG. As a result, both were strong supporters of early independence for PNG; and both argued that an independent PNG should have a single legal system, run by expatriate and Indigenous people alike, and equally applicable both to "advanced" and to so-called "primitive" areas.[12] But, both argued that the only law that could bridge that gap was introduced Western law. For those who could not accept Western laws, Goldring recommended education. A major concern for Derham and Goldring was that PNG's legal system continue to support the demands of foreign investors and settler businessmen for a market economy. Since custom had not dealt expressly with modern capitalism and an export-oriented economy, they believed it was inappropriate to the financial needs of the new nation.

For Bayne, customary law had other shortcomings that would make its use as the governing law in the formal legal system problematic. First, PNG societies were undergoing rapid social change, rendering traditional dispute settlement methods ineffective. Second, the lack of clarity about customary rules and the variation of customs between communities made it impossible to know which customary law to apply in many cases. Third, some of the principles and practices of custom (such as payback killings and the attitude that women were inferior) conflicted with the social policies of the government. Finally, custom could not provide solutions to problems of modernization, development, and economic relations with foreign countries and companies.

Derham, Goldring, and Bayne did not argue that custom should be abandoned entirely. In common with other academic commentators, they took the position that it should continue to be used in specific areas, primarily in personal and family matters, such as land tenure, marriage, and intestate succession, where the disputes were between Papua New Guineans and did not involve expatriate individuals or companies.

By the 1960s, there were enough commercial enterprises in PNG to support a small private legal profession. By and large, these lawyers favored neither early independence nor an integrated legal system, let alone the introduction of custom into the legal system in which they practiced. Members of the judiciary and the administration's lawyers tended to agree with them. Former Supreme Court Justice R. A. Smithers, for example, argued that there were some matters "such as marriage, land tenure, and succession in which custom or traditional law must always be the primary law."[13] But he argued just as strongly against recognizing customary criminal laws, believing instead that the imported Criminal Code be applied, even where it prohibited killings that customary law would require, such as payback killings and the killing of sorcerers. For Justice Smithers, preventing such killings was a necessary step in developing the nation.

Very few whites supported the notion of giving custom a major role in the state legal system. Among the exceptions were William Lalor, the public solicitor, and T. E. (Tos) Barnett, an academic and advisor to the administration. Both would become justices of the Supreme Court after independence. Lalor argued that the legal system of the new nation should be a fusion of PNG custom with those parts of English law that are suited to the circumstances of PNG "so that there is one coherent whole or at least clear bodies of law clearly applicable to given parties or persons."[14] The members of all sectors of the legal profession would have to look carefully at the colonial legal system to determine what were the essentials of the English common law that had been adopted and what were the rules and principles that were devised peculiarly for the local circumstances of England or Australia, because only the former should be retained.

Instead of arguing that bits of custom be integrated into the introduced legal system or operate alongside of the formal legal system, Lalor argued that the introduced system should be integrated into a legal system that was primarily based on custom. Lawyers would have to "master the application of customary law and its fusion with the body of common and statute law."[15] The very procedure of the courts should change, Lalor said, to better suit the circumstances of the cases brought before them. Lalor was unusual among white commentators in suggesting that custom could even govern market transactions:

> I would suggest that there is a great need to devise new forms [of business organizations] whereby traditional modes of association are given legal recognition and whereby the mutual rights of the members can be ascertained and enforced.[16]

Barnett also focused on the shortcomings of the imported English legal system and advocated for much of it be replaced by customary rules. To those like Derham, who claimed that the diversity of custom made its recognition unworkable, Barnett replied that these arguments stemmed from a lack of understanding of what custom is and how it evolves. (These arguments also fail to recall that the English common law itself developed over time through the recognition and rationalization of local and regional variations.) In Barnett's view, the PNG courts had failed most dramatically in refusing to recognize customary rules of criminal law and in their unwillingness to come to grips with the kin-group as a legal entity. Barnett wanted a new generation of Indigenous lawyers to develop their own courts that would be open to, run by, and understood by Papua New Guineans and that would apply laws reflecting the mores and social realities of everyone in the country.

The Native Customs (Recognition) Ordinance

In 1963, the administration made its first official statement about the role that custom would play in the newly integrated colonial courts, and while custom was given some recognition, it was not afforded even as much of a role as scholars like Derham, Goldring, and Bayne had recommended. And, it was allowed even this limited role because the administration believed that Papua New Guineans would be unable to understand the imported law for some time to come and would have to be governed at least in part by custom. In the interim, magistrates and judges would need a road map for when and how custom should be applied. While the magistrates and *kiaps* in the Courts for Native Affairs and Native Matters had developed their own practices for dealing with custom, there was no legislative statement about when and to what extent custom should be enforced—nor even a legislative definition of "custom." In 1963, the PNG Legislative Council enacted the *Native Customs (Recognition) Ordinance*, based on similar legislation in the British Solomon Islands Protectorate and in the African Gold Coast colony (now Ghana). The ordinance was a directive to all courts, including the Supreme Court, and dealt with the enforcement of custom in criminal and civil cases.

The ordinance defined what it called "native custom" as

> the custom or usage of the aboriginal inhabitants of the Territory obtaining in relation to the matter in question at the time and the place in relation to which that question arises, regardless of whether or not that custom or usage has obtained from time immemorial.[17]

While that definition corresponded in large part with the definitions of custom found in domestic English law, the last clause went beyond the European stereotype of customary societies and their customs as unchanging. The clause did not require that a particular custom have existed without interruption from time immemorial, as is the requirement in English domestic law. The flexibility of the clause was recognition that custom was not static but dynamic, and that eighty years of colonialism had left an impact.

The Native Regulations had given the Courts for Native Affairs the discretionary power to apply custom if, when, and how they wanted to, but the *Native Customs (Recognition) Ordinance* made it mandatory for courts to use custom in the circumstances listed in the ordinance: "[Custom] shall be recognized and enforced by, and may be pleaded in, all courts."[18] The use of custom, however, was subject to three broad limitations. First, the existence and nature of custom had to be determined as though they were matters of fact, not law.[19] This was a codification of Austinian legal positivism, which defined law as only those rules emanating from state entities, such as legislatures and courts. In practice, the difference was substantial. When parties to litigation raise a point of law, they do not have to gather evidence to prove that the law exists. If the parties tried to introduce a rule of custom, however, they would have to offer evidence to prove its existence, just as they would any other fact in the case. The ordinance did lessen this burden somewhat by providing that courts would not be required to follow the strict rules of procedure or evidence in deciding whether a custom existed. Instead, the courts could consider any "relevant evidence," including hearsay and statements of opinion.[20] In addition, courts could inform themselves by referring to books, treatises, reports, or statements of local government councils or persons called by the court, without having to wait for counsel to find these for them.

Section 6 of the ordinance contained four more limits on the use of custom. That section stated that custom could be taken into account only if it was not "repugnant to the general principles of humanity"; it was not inconsistent with any legislation in the territories; its recognition and enforcement would not result in "injustice" or be contrary to the "public interest"; and, in cases involving the welfare of children under the age of sixteen, "its recognition and enforcement would . . . be in the best interests of the child." Those four limitations were basically a restatement and elaboration of the provision on the recognition of custom in section 10 of the New Guinea reception ordinance. However, the question of whether a particular custom fell into one of those categories was never fully addressed by the courts in PNG. The experience in PNG and in British Africa, where the enforcement of custom was subject to similar restrictions, indicates that the criteria for rejecting custom more often reflected the values of the colonial judge than they did either the values of the people whose lives were regulated by the custom or any disinterested examination of the issue.

Finally, the enforcement of custom was subject to specific limitations in criminal and civil cases. In criminal cases, the ordinance stated that courts could take custom into account for five specific purposes, which went a little beyond the prevailing judicial practice of taking custom into account only in sentencing. The courts could use custom as an indication of the state of mind of a defendant; the reasonableness or otherwise of a defendant's act, default, or omission; the reasonableness of an excuse; the extent of the penalty to be imposed; and whether to proceed to the conviction of a guilty person. The section concluded with a broad catchall that permitted courts to take custom into account when, if the court did not do so, "injustice will or may be done to a person."[21]

Custom could also be taken into account by the courts in civil matters. The ordinance permitted custom to govern ten broad types of cases: the ownership of customary land; the ownership or rights in the sea, or reef or lake, including fishing rights; the ownership by custom of rights to water; the interest in customary land whether on death or on the birth of a person; trespass by animals; marriage, divorce or the right to custody of children under a customary marriage; a transaction which the parties intended should be regulated by custom; the reasonableness of an act, default, or omission; the existence of a state of mind; and whenever not taking custom into account would result in injustice to a person. Those situations reflected the types of cases that had come before the Courts for Native Affairs and Native Matters and that were beginning to arise before the higher courts.

Judges rarely invoked the ordinance by name in their decisions, but the ordinance did seem to have some small but positive effects. In criminal cases, the judges appear to have been influenced by the ordinance to move beyond their previous practice of considering custom only in sentencing and instead began to take custom into account when interpreting provisions of the Criminal Code, such as those relating to provocation or self defense. Similarly, in tort cases, the ordinance was expressly cited only once in the years before independence, but its influence was felt when judges decided on the amount of damages in accident cases by referring not only to Western categories, such as lost wages, but also to customary rights to support from the village, traditional rights to village income, and obligations of support among clan members.

Although the ordinance mandated that courts pay attention to certain customary rules, it did not adopt the key facets of customary legal process. This might have been its greatest failing. For example, the ordinance did not alter the rules of procedure and evidence in criminal trials. These would continue to be adversarial proceedings, led by a judge and resulting in winner-take-all determinations of guilt or innocence for the individual accused, rather than the wide-ranging negotiated settlement discussions common to customary processes. Similarly, the ordinance did not deal with the fact that Papua New Guineans made no sharp distinction between criminal law and civil law, and nothing in the ordinance recognized group liability or group injuries. Instead, liability for criminal or tortious acts continued to be premised totally on individual responsibility, and the punishments (fines or imprisonment) were imposed only on the individuals charged and payable only to the state, rather than to the injured clan or family. There was no recognition that compensation was an integral part of the resolution of the harms caused by persons in Papua New Guinean communities—unless the prohibition on the Supreme Court awarding compensation in criminal cases constituted recognition of a sort.

Changes to Other Ordinances to Add a Little Custom

Changes were made in a number of other ordinances as well, primarily to define for Supreme Court judges which private transactions or family matters should be governed by custom and what the limits on that would be. Some of the changes simply involved repealing discriminatory legislation, such as the large parts of the Native Regulations that prohibited customary practices. New ordinances also were enacted, which gave formal recognition to customary practices, particularly in areas of family law. An example of this was the *Matrimonial Causes Ordinance of 1963*, which dealt with divorce, annulment, judicial separation, maintenance, and custody, and which stated specifically that nothing in the ordinance applied to customary unions—suggesting not only that the rules about who could marry would be governed by custom, but that the divorce of a couple married according to custom would also be determined by custom. The *Wills, Probate and Administration Ordinance of 1966* originally repealed the provisions of the Native Regulations that had provided for customary rules to govern the succession of property, without substituting anything in its place. As a result, the principles of English succession law governed estates in Papua New Guineans until 1970, when an amendment to the ordinance brought custom back in every case except those in which a Papua New Guinean had made a will.

The colonial administration was willing to recognize a number of customs, but it was unwilling to leave them entirely outside the scrutiny of the courts. Beginning with the *Native Customs (Recognition) Ordinance*, these ordinances recognized customary practices within the framework of the colonial legal system, but at the same time gave the courts the power to prohibit or circumscribe them in certain situations. The *Marriage Ordinance of 1964* is an example. The ordinance contained detailed requirements for entering into a valid marriage that were based on the requirements in force in Australia. In addition, the ordinance stated that:

> a native [other than one who already has entered into a valid marriage under the ordinance] may enter, and shall be deemed always to have been capable of entering, into a native customary marriage in accordance with the custom prevailing in the tribe or group of natives to which the parties to the marriage or either of them belong or belongs.[22]

In many parts of PNG, custom permitted men to have more than one wife. The effect of the ordinance was that a Papua New Guinean man could marry as many women as his circumstances and applicable custom allowed, but as soon as he entered into a marriage recognized by the formal law, he could no longer add more wives. Many men were caught unawares by this ruling. They believed they had merely acquiesced to having their wedding in a church, only to discover later, when they were told that a church wedding was a marriage under the ordinance, that they could legally have no more wives.

Two sections of the *Marriage Ordinance* demonstrated the drafters' suspicion that the main purpose of customary law was to force women into marriage against their will. Section 57(1) gave local court magistrates the power to intervene and prohibit a customary marriage where the woman objected to the marriage and "excessive pressure has been brought to bear to persuade her to enter into the marriage" or where "in the circumstances it would be a hardship to compel her to conform to custom."

Under section 53(3), if a customary marriage already had been entered into in violation of those conditions, the local court magistrate, at the request of the woman, could annul the marriage and adjust property rights as though the marriage had been dissolved according to custom.

The Criminal Code and the Courts—Turning Papua New Guineans into Australians

Many Papua New Guinean criminal defendants found themselves in the untenable situation of having to choose between violating the imported criminal law or going against the dictates of custom. Payback killings, for example, were punishable crimes under the imported codes, but understood to be obligations under customary law. Similarly, the family of a man or woman whose spouse had committed adultery was encouraged to seek revenge or recompense from the adulterous spouse and from the lover and the lover's clan and kin. Faced with these cases, colonial judges did not treat them as raising an issue involving a conflict of laws, as they would, were a defendant from, say, Belgium to have done an act in an Australian territory that was unlawful under Australian law but would be considered an obligation under Belgian law.

The judges did not believe that custom was law, nor did they respect its dictates. Still, the colonial judges did sometimes resort to custom to help defendants in criminal cases. To the judges, the fact that defendants followed custom demonstrated that they were too primitive and too uncivilized to understand the full import of the law and of their behavior. The primary use of custom in criminal cases was remedial. The judges applied "custom" not because they thought it better than the imported codes, or even as good as the codes, or even as real law, but as a method to mitigate the harshness of a heavy sentence imposed for crimes such as murder. In the previous chapter, we noted that judges in the 1950s often used the statutory defenses to criminal charges in this way, and in order to do so, occasionally changed or extended the reach of those defenses. For example, the judges permitted Indigenous defendants to raise the defense of provocation in more situations than an Australian would be permitted to use it. The judges continued to do this in the 1960s, and their use of the defenses grew more varied and complex, in keeping with their recognition that the lives of Papua New Guinean defendants were changing.

Under section 66 of the Criminal Code, an accused person who raises the defense of provocation has to show that the conduct of the victim constituted a

> wrongful act or insult of such a nature as to be likely, when done to an ordinary person, or in the presence of an ordinary person to another person who is under his immediate care, or to whom he stands in a conjugal, paternal, filial, or fraternal relation . . . to deprive him of the power of self-control, and to induce him to assault the person by whom the act or insult is done or offered.

The effect of a finding of provocation is to reduce the charge of murder to manslaughter. A number of criminal cases during the 1960s and early 1970s raised the question whether an act of adultery or a confession of adultery was a "wrongful act or insult" sufficient to deprive an "ordinary person"—at least, an ordinary Papua New Guinean person–of self-control and constitute provocation for a killing. In England, it would not; generally, English law required that a defendant could establish provocation only if the defendant had actually caught the adulterous spouse engaging in the act. The PNG courts, however, generally held that either adultery or the confession of adultery could be a "wrongful act or insult" and that the subsequent discovery that it had been going on or a confession made after the fact could amount to provocation.

One reason the judges of the PNG Supreme Court were willing to treat a subsequent discovery or a confession of adultery as a "wrongful act or insult" was their belief that adultery was taken more seriously by married couples and their extended families in PNG societies than in England or Australia. In a study published in 1975 of Papua New Guinean attitudes toward the sexual offenses in the Criminal Code, British anthropologist Marilyn Strathern found that, because of the great social disruption caused by adultery, it often led to disputes, court action, or even tribal fighting. Under the customary law of most PNG societies, anyone who interfered with the sexual rights of another committed an offense both against that person and against that person's kin. In an affair involving a married woman, those societies would consider both the woman and her lover to be offenders and would include, among the offended parties, the innocent spouse and the kin of both the wife and her wronged husband, since kin had significant political and economic interests in the marriage.

Customary resolution of the dispute would involve a choice among or combination of divorce, reconciliation, compensation payments, and violent retaliation against the adulterers or their kin. The judges took these customary rules into consideration in deciding whether a defendant's violent response to a confession of adultery had been provoked.

But the major quandary for the judges was the Criminal Code requirement that the wrongful act or insult could constitute provocation only if it was sufficient to provoke "an ordinary person." Certainly, the English courts had long held, no upstanding (ordinary) English man would be provoked by a mere admission of adultery. But the judges were quite convinced that Papua New Guineans were not at that level of self-control. Moreover, there were so many differences among Papua New Guineans—including tribal differences, regional differences, gender differences, differences between rural and urban people, between educated and uneducated, traditional and modern, missionized and unmissionized—that no single standard could capture the ordinary Papua New Guinean person in the same way that the English could use "the man on the Clapham omnibus" as a universal standard. The judges dealt with the problem of diversity by developing different definitions of the ordinary person depending upon the culture and environment of the defendant and the extent of the defendant's assimilation into urban society.

A key characteristic to which the judges often looked in distinguishing the ordinary person in one culture and environment from one in another tribe or district was the personality or temperament that the judge believed to be typical of persons in that community. In *R. v. Yande-Piaua*, the judge held that an ordinary Eastern Highlander could rely on the defense of provocation even though defendant had used an axe to kill a person who was totally unarmed and whose provocative act was to have punched the accused on the chin. According to the judge:

> I must apply the normal test by reference to a village native living as he is required to do in his primitive environment. Such a person is "culturally conditioned" to immediate reaction and especially so to sudden attack. He is conditioned to the presence of lethal weapons always at the ready and to the fact that survival requires, and has required throughout the experience of his people, readiness for immediate attack or escape. In this kind of society matters can be talked

> about afterwards but there is no time to arrive at a fully considered decision as to the course to be taken.
>
> In the circumstances, I am satisfied that the ordinary peaceful (so far as this can be applicable) citizen, living in a cultural environment of the accused man, could be expected, almost to the point of certainty, to behave in the circumstances just as the accused did behave.[23]

In elaborating this localized standard, the judge distinguished not only among villages and tribes but also among Papua New Guineans who had obtained what the judge referred to as "sophistication," acquired through education, a move to one of the urbanized areas of the country, or through conversion to Christianity. In *R. v. Manga Kitai,* the accused, originally from a rural village, had been in Port Moresby, the national capital, for a few months when he was alleged to have committed a crime. The judge held that, for such transient visitors to the city, the standard remained that of the ordinary villager from the accused's home area.

However, in *R. v. Moses-Robert*, the accused, although originally from a rural village, had lived in Port Moresby for a number of years and was employed in a semi-skilled occupation. The judge labeled the accused a "sophisticated native" but added:

> [T]his is far from saying that I must view his conduct in the light of a civilized European. I must make due allowance for the fact that such a person as accused may be more easily deprived of self-control than an ordinary European.[24]

In effect, the judge had created a further refinement of the ordinary person test: that of the "ordinary native Papuan living and working in Port Moresby."[25]

Two beliefs underpin the Supreme Court's application of different standards of the ordinary person to rural and to urbanized Papua New Guineans. First, the judges believed that increased self-control was an inevitable by-product of urbanization and education. That view would later be criticized by Bernard Narokobi, when he was a judge of the National Court, endeavoring to apply custom and a much more nuanced view of Papua New Guinean circumstances. He wrote of the attitude common to the expatriate judges:

> The [ordinary person] standard varies according to the degree of sophistication of the accused. An educated, urbanized and missionized person is expected to show a higher degree of self-control than a person from an area where contact with the West is minimal. This approach, whilst humane in its outcome, is in my view paternalistic. It assumes that Papua New Guineans are primitive and that in due course, when they are educated out of their cultural enslavement, they will behave like Englishmen in a Papua New Guinean setting.[26]

Second, the judges viewed traditional Papua New Guineans as lacking in those moral qualities that Christians believe are the exclusive property of the converted, including the ability to abstain from violent retaliation. As a result, the judges demanded a different kind of behavior from missionized Papua New Guineans, even those with few other attributes of Westernization, than it did of those who had not been exposed to the teachings of the new religions. This was illustrated by the decision in *Secretary for Law v. Witrasep Binengim*, in which the defendant had been convicted of the willful murder of her husband after inciting her lover to do the killing. On appeal, the Supreme Court increased her sentence from 2.5 years to 9.5 years, in large part because of her Christianity:

> She is not primitive. She can read and presumably write. She lives at Telefomin within five minutes walking distance from the administrative center and two minutes from the mission station. Her husband was pastor in the Baptist Church and she herself received instruction in the local Mission Pastor Training Scheme. She had worked as a domestic for two years and had recently been employed as a manageress of the Mission Children's Hostel. All these factors weighed heavily against her on the question of sentence.[27]

Under section 266(2) of the Criminal Code, a "wrongful act or insult" may also amount to provocation if it is done "in the presence of an ordinary person to another person who is under his immediate care, or to whom he stands in a conjugal, paternal, filial, or fraternal, relation."[28] Just as the judges defined "ordinary person" in terms of local conditions in PNG, they recognized that, because of the nature of extended family relationships in PNG, the term "filial" could not be limited to father–son relationships. Instead, the judges looked to customary notions and held that the term could include brothers-in-law, first cousins, nephews, and even sons of cousins. Similarly, in the case of sorcery, the judges broadened the class of persons at whom the sorcery could be directed to include "the accused or . . . some person to whom the evidence discloses the accused stood in a protective or obligatory clan relationship."[29]

In each of these cases—as in almost all the cases in which custom and the Criminal Code came into conflict—the judges used their perceptions of custom to soften the otherwise harsh and inflexible penalties of the code, but not entirely to absolve Papua New Guineans from its enforcement. In doing so, the judges had two aims. First, the judges felt condescendingly that it was a kindness to show mercy to rural, un-Christianized Papua New Guineans who were still in the grip of custom, because they were too primitive to fully grasp the nature and seriousness of their transgression. Second, the judges believed it was their job to educate and socialize the population, and that by applying the Criminal Code to Papua New Guineans, but not too strongly, they were fulfilling this obligation.

Conclusions—To Date

This chapter brings the narrative up to 1972, to what turned out to be nearly the end of Australia's colonial rule in Papua New Guinea. The decade was characterized by two very different movements. On the one hand, the Australian government in Canberra, the territorial administration in Port Moresby, and courts in both places were trying to ensure that when PNG did get its independence, it would be a country as much in the image of Australia as politicians, administrators, and judges could make it. At the same time, however, Papua New Guineans were for the first time acting as agents in shaping their own futures. The results of these great opposing waves would play themselves out from 1972 to 1975, as PNG prepared itself for independence. And almost half a century into independence, the clash between Melanesian and western values, between customary law and the introduced legal system, between reciprocity and a market economy, continues to define PNG, as it does many another post-colonial nation.

Sources

Books and Articles

T. E. Barnett, "Law and Justice Melanesian Style," in Anthony Clunies-Ross and John Langmore (eds.), *Alternative Strategies for Papua New Guinea*, 3d Ed. (Melbourne: Oxford University Press, 1973) 59–85.

Peter Bayne, "The Future of Traditional Law," *Melanesian Law Journal* 2(2) (1974) 276–282.

B. J. Brown, *Fashion of Law in New Guin*ea (Sydney: Butterworths, 1969).

B. J. Brown, "Outlook for Law in New Guinea," *Oceania* 41(4) (1971) 244–254.

Donald Chalmers, David Weisbrot, and Warwick Andrew, *Criminal Law and Practice of Papua New Guinea* (2nd ed., Sydney: Law Book Co., 1985).

Ron Crocombe, "Australia's Own History of Apartheid in Papua New Guinea," www.onlineopinion.com.au (October 24, 2006), reproduced at http://garamut.wordpress.com (August 19, 2009).

"Custom," in *Halsbury's Laws of England*, vol. 12 (4th ed.) (London: Butterworth's, 1973–1987).

Donald Denoon, *A Trial Separation: Australia and the Decolonisation of Papua New Guinea* (Canberra: Pandanus Books, 2005).

David Derham, *Report on the System for the Administration of Justice in the Territory of Papua and New Guinea* (Canberra: Government of the Commonwealth of Australia, 1960).

David Derham, "Law and Custom in the Australian Territory of Papua and New Guinea," *University of Chicago Law Review* 30(3) (1962) 495–506.

A. L Epstein, *Contention and Dispute: Aspects of Law and Social Control in Melanesia* (Canberra: Australian National University Press, 1974).

Peter Fitzpatrick, *Law and State in Papua New Guinea* (London: Academic Press, 1980).

Bill Gammage, "Police and Power in the Pre-war Papua New Guinea Highlands," *The Journal of Pacific History* 31(2) (1996) 162–177.

John Goldring, "Just Law for Primitive Society?" *Sydney Law Review* 6(3) (1971) 371–381.

J. A. Griffin, "Conflict of Inheritance Law and Custom in Nuigini," *Melanesian Law Journal* 1(1) (December 1970) 29–39.

J. A. Griffin, Hank Nelson, and S. Firth, *Papua New Guinea: A Political History* (Richmond: Heinemann, 1979).

Paul Hasluck, *A Time for Building: Australian Administration in Papua and New Guinea 1951–1963* (Melbourne: Melbourne University Press, 1976).

International Committee of Jurists, *The Rule of Law in an Emerging Society: Report of the Proceedings of the Papua and New Guinea Conference, Port Moresby, September 7–14, 1965* (Sydney: International Committee of Jurists,1970).

Samson Kaipu, "Are Papua New Guinean Wives Like Australian Wives?" *Melanesian Law Journal* 2(2) (1974) 274–275.

Sione Latukefu (ed.), *Papua New Guinea: A Century of Colonial Impact 1884–1984* (Port Moresby: National Research Institute and University of Papua New Guinea, 1989).

J. R. Mattes, "Legislative Council of Papua and New Guinea," *Australian Law Journal* 37(6) (1963) 176–180.

J. R. Mattes, "House of Assembly for Papua New Guinea," *Australian Law Journal* 38(5) (1964) 159–163.

Bernard Narokobi, "Adaptation of Western Law in Papua New Guinea," *Melanesian Law Journal* 5(1) (1977) 52–69.

Patrick Gerald Nash, *Some Problems of Administering Law in the Territory of Papua and New Guinea: Inaugural Lecture* (Port Moresby: University of Papua New Guinea, 1967).

Hank Nelson, "Liberation: The End of Australian Rule in Papua New Guinea," *The Journal of Pacific History* 33(3) (2000) 269–280.

Nigel Oram, *Colonial Town to Melanesian City: Port Moresby 1884–1974* (Canberra: Australian National University Press, 1976).

Robin S. O'Regan, *The Common Law in Papua and New Guinea* (Sydney: Law Book Co., 1971).

Robin S. O'Regan, "Ordinary Man and Provocation in Papua New Guinea," *International and Comparative Law Quarterly* 21(3) (1972) 551–557.

Bruce L. Ottley and Josephine Millott, "Compensation for Economic Loss: The Search for Standards in Papua New Guinea," *Melanesian Law Journal* 2(2) (1974) 178–205.

Bruce L. Ottley and Jean Zorn, "Criminal Law in Papua New Guinea: Code, Custom and the Courts in Conflict," *American Journal of Comparative Law* 31(2) (1981) 251–300.

Alexander Pope, *An Essay on Criticism* (London: W. Lewis, 1711).

Peter Sack, "Law, Custom and Good Government: The Derham Report in Its Historical Context," in Sione Latukefu (ed.), *Papua New Guinea: A Century of Colonial Impact 1884–1984* (Port Moresby: National Research Institute and University of Papua New Guinea, 1989) 377–397.

R. A. Smithers, "Law in the Territory of Papua and New Guinea," *Melbourne University Law Review* 4 (1963) 212–237.

Marilyn Strathern, *Women in Between* (Boston: Rowman & Littlefield, 1972).

David Weisbrot, "Integration of Laws in Papua New Guinea: Custom and the Criminal Law in Conflict," in David Weisbrot, Abdul Paliwala, and Aki Sawyer (eds.), *Law and Social Change in Papua New Guinea* (Sydney: Butterworths, 1982) 59–103.

Edward P. Wolfers, *Race Relations and Colonial Rule in Papua New Guinea* (Sydney: Australia and New Zealand Book Co., 1975).

Anthony Yeates, "The Patrol Officers and Tom Kabu," *Journal of Pacific History* 40(1) (June 2005) 71–90.

Michael W. Young, *Fighting with Food: Leadership, Values and Social Control in Massim Society* (Cambridge: Cambridge University Press, 2009).

Jean Zorn and Peter Bayne (eds.), *Foreign Investment, International Law and National Development: Papers Presented at the Seventh Waigani Seminar, April–May 1973* (Port Moresby: University of Papua New Guinea Press, 1973).

Jean Zorn and Peter Bayne (eds.), *Lo Bilong Ol Manmeri: Crime, Compensation and Village Courts* (Port Moresby: University of Papua New Guinea Press, 1973).

Government Document

Paul Hasluck, *Report of the Minister of the Territories*, Australian Government Document A 425 61/1785 (1963).

Cases

Custodian of Expropriated Property v. Director of District Administration (In Re Tonwalik) (1969–1970) PNGLR 110

Director of District Administration v. Custodian of Expropriated Property (In Re Wangaramut) (1969–1970) PNGLR 410

Director of Native Affairs v. Green (1964) PNGLR 24

Gaudi Kidu v. Port Moresby Freezing Company (1967–1969) PNGLR 466
Guba Kevau v. Steamships Trading Company, Ltd., Unreported No. 151 (1959)
Mary Gugi v. Stol Commuters Pty. Ltd. (1972) PNGLR 34
Iapidik v. Green (1964) PNGLR 178
Largo Gerebi v. Joseph Tomonoi, Unreported No. 695 (1972)
Maraipa-Daeni v. Bagari-Dubere, Unreported No. 301 (1963)
McCarthy v. The Public Curator of Papua New Guinea, Unreported No. 335 (1962)
Ogan Bal v. Ninkama Bomai, Unreported No. 696 (1972)
R. v. Domara-Saope & Others (1967–1968) PNGLR 71
R. v. Iglis Lu'umbat of Kulwango, Unreported No. 405 (1966)
R. v. Kini Abu, Unreported No. 576 (1970)
R. v. Koruapa of Lupila, Unreported No. 104A (1957)
R. v. Manga Ki (1967–1968) PNGLR 1
R. v. Moses-Robert (1965–1966) PNGLR 180
R. v. Noboi-Bosai & Others (1971–1972) PNGLR 271
R. v. Rumints Gorok (1963) PNGLR 81
R. v. Yande-Piaua (1967–1968) PNGLR 482
R. v. Zariai-Gavene (1963) PNGLR 203
Secretary for Law v. Witrasep Binengi (1975) PNGLR 172
Smerdon v. Raquel (1973) PNGLR 3
Tolain, Tapalau, Tomaret, Towarunga and Other Villagers of Latlat Village v. Administration of the Territory of Papua and New Guinea (In re Vulcan Land) (1966) PNGLR 232

Statutes

Courts and Laws Adopting (Papua) Act 1975, No. 38 of 1975 (PNG)
Criminal Code Act 1974, No. 78 of 1974 (PNG)
Laws Repeal and Adopting (New Guinea) Act 1975, No. 41 of 1975 (PNG)
Marriage Ordinance of 1964, No. 8 of 1964 (PNG)
Matrimonial Causes Ordinance of 1963, No. 18 of 1964 (PNG)
Native Administration Regulations 1924–1968 (New Guinea)
Native Customs (Recognition) Ordinance, No. 28 of 1963 (amended and renamed in 1975 the Customs Recognition Act 1975) (PNG)
Native Regulation Ordinance 1908, No. 25 of 1909 (Papua)
Wills, Probate and Administration Ordinance 1966, No. 13 of 1966 (PNG)

Notes

1. Donald Denoon, *A Trial Separation: Australia and the Decolonisation of Papua New Guinea* (Canberra: Pandanus Books, 2005) 28, citing Australian Government Document A425 61/1785, which includes the report of the Ministry for Territories and explanatory letters from Hasluck to Prime Minister Menzies.
2. *Id.*
3. Alexander Pope, *An Essay on Criticism* (London: W. Lewis, 1711).
4. Donald Denoon, *A Trial Separation: Australia and the Decolonisation of Papua New Guinea* (Canberra: Pandanus Books, 2005) 57, quoting Australian Government Document 68/55632, Part II, Administrator to Department, June 2, 1969.
5. *Id.*
6. Hank Nelson, "Liberation: The End of Australian Rule in Papua New Guinea," *The Journal of Pacific History* 33(3) (2000) 271.
7. Christine Stewart, email, June 21, 2018: "It was just magic, the thunder of the coalition members (it only got sorted at 3 am the previous night) roaring to their feet with Somare, to the total bewilderment of the government-appointed members and the cronies … still gives me a thrill to remember it. And the rest was history."
8. David Derham, "Law and Custom in the Australian Territory of Papua and New Guinea," *University of Chicago Law Review* 30(3) (1963) 495.
9. *Id.* at 505.
10. *Id.* at 506.
11. International Committee of Jurists, *The Rule of Law and the Administration of Justice in an Emerging Society: Report of the Proceedings of the Papua and New Guinea Conference, Port Moresby, September 7–14, 1965* (Sydney: International Committee of Jurists, 1970) 107.
12. John Goldring, "Just Law for Primitive Society?" *Sydney Law Review* 6(3) (1970) 371.
13. R. A. Smithers, "Law and the Territory of Papua and New Guinea," *Melbourne University Law Review* 4 (1963) 212.
14. International Committee of Jurists, *The Rule of Law and the Administration of Justice in an Emerging Society: Report of the Proceedings of the Papua and New Guinea Conference, Port Moresby, September 7–14, 1965* (Sydney: International Committee of Jurists: 1970) 89.
15. *Id.* at 90.
16. *Id.* at 91.

17. *Native Customs (Recognition) Ordinance*, No. 28 of 1963, section 4.
18. *Id.* at section 6(1).
19. *Id.* at section 5.
20. *Id.* at section 5(2).
21. *Id.* at section 7.
22. *Marriage Ordinance 1964*, No. 8 of 1964, section 55(1).
23. *R. v. Yande-Piau* (1967–1968) PNGLR 482, at 487.
24. *R. v. Moses-Robert* (1965–1966) PNGLR 180, at 185–186.
25. *Id.* at 186.
26. Bernard Narokobi, "Adaptation of Western Law in Papua New Guinea," *Melanesian Law Journal* 5(1) (1977) 58.
27. *Secretary for Law v. Witrasep Binengim* (1975) PNGLR 172, at 177.
28. *R. v. Noboi-Bosai & Others* (1971–1972) PNGLR 271.
29. *Id.* at 283–284.

11 Moving to Independence

Papua New Guinea 1972–1975

From "Not in Our Lifetimes" to "Quickly, Quickly!"

Decolonization seemed a long way off in the 1960s, with most politicians and administrators suggesting that independence for Papua New Guinea would not come "in our lifetimes," or at least not for "the next thirty years," but more likely would be "a century off."[1] However, sentiment shifted rapidly in both PNG and Australia, as well as overseas, in the early 1970s as more and more colonies and trusteeships became independent under the supervision and prompting of the United Nations. The ethos was changing from Western countries assuming that colonialism was natural and part of their due, to an increasing belief that it was morally wrong and outdated, and needed to be eliminated in the modern world. It became fashionable among Papua New Guinean nationalists in the early 1970s to bemoan the indignity of being what they called "a colony of a colony", referring to Australia's own historically deferential relationships with Great Britain and the United States.

The victory of the strongly pro-independence Pangu Party in 1972's House of Assembly elections created great impetus for a change in status, and this was virtually assured by the election of the Whitlam Labor government in Australia in December 1972. As early as 1960, Gough Whitlam had called for PNG independence to be granted in a decade, and in January 1970, Whitlam, then leader of the opposition, had made a heavily publicized visit to PNG, prompting more public interest and debate about the fate of the territory. Shortly after Labor's election victory—ending twenty-three years of conservative coalition rule—Whitlam reaffirmed his commitment to the decolonization process, "not just because it is Australia's obligation to the UN but because we believe it wrong and unnatural that a nation like Australia should continue to run a colony."[2] Taken together, Pangu's stirring victory and the softening attitude of the colonial power toward independence created a powerful and ultimately unstoppable momentum.

Despite the great disparity between Western and traditional societies—in terms of culture, linguistics, norms and mores, social organization, geography, and fundamental notions of fairness, responsibility, justice, and punishment—the colonial authorities in PNG nevertheless transplanted into Papua New Guinea a truncated form of Western laws and courts with little or no adaptation to local customs, usages, or sensibilities.

The most favorable characterization of Australia's colonial-era governance of PNG is that it amounted to benign neglect, although it was sometimes more cruel than benign—and as is usually the case with harsh regimes, the behavior of the colonial administration and colonists was perfectly legal. Peter Fitzpatrick has argued with force in his 1980 book that in pre-independence PNG, law was, and was perceived to be, the cutting edge of the colonial administration. With few resources, little infrastructure, few longer-term goals, and little vision, the Australian administration took as its principal tasks not the development of the colony's educational and economic systems, but the general maintenance of order and the provision of labor for plantations and mines. In common with British colonialism in Africa and Asia, the Australian administration justified stern and culturally inappropriate measures on the basis that this was necessary to impose the rule of law.

It is not surprising then that in the early 1970s, as nationalist sentiment grew among Papua New Guineans and the pressure for self-government and independence intensified, there were frequent and powerful expressions of discontent from leading political figures about the imposed legal system. And given the central role of that law in both the ideological underpinning and the actions of the colonial administration, it is not surprising that those same leaders were keenly aware of the relationship between control of legal institutions and the maintenance of power. Thus, the debate about the future of the legal system figured very prominently in the lead-up to independence.

John Kaputin, the first PNG Minister for Justice, was among those who made the connection, as in the following statement made in his inaugural policy speech at a 1973 legal gathering:

> The truth is that law has been used throughout the ages as an instrument of domination and oppression by the ruling classes. . . . In this country, the law was an instrument of colonialism and a means whereby the economic dominance of the white man was established over us. In other words, the law was not [a] universal and abstract principle; it was specific and it made numerous distinctions between the white and the black. And not only did it deprive us of our land, but forced us to work for expatriate plantation owners to whom the law gave our lands.[3]

Kaputin subsequently reiterated these sentiments in a stinging article in 1975 that declared the inherited legal system to be "a colonial fraud". Around the same time, the then Chief Minister (later to be Prime Minister) Michael Somare expressed the following unequivocal view of the urgent need for law reform and development:

> We are facing, at this very moment, the need to devise a system of laws appropriate to a self-governing, independent nation. The legal system that we are in the process of creating must ensure the orderly and progressive development of our nation. But, in addition, it must respond to our own needs and values. We do not want to create an imitation of the Australian, English or American legal systems. We want to build a framework of laws and procedures that the people of Papua New Guinea can recognise as their own—not something imposed on them by outsiders.[4]

The Constitutional Planning Committee

Once it was clear that a genuine push for independence had commenced, Papua New Guinean leaders needed to think seriously about the constitutional arrangements that would make independence a reality. Those leaders were unimpressed with recent decolonization processes they had observed, in which their African counterparts visited London to meet with the British authorities, who then dispensed a largely standardized constitution. The independence constitutions of Nigeria, Kenya, Uganda, Mauritius, and Zimbabwe all emerged from such Lancaster House Conferences.

Instead, Papua New Guinean leaders—especially those in Chief Minister Michael Somare's ruling Pangu Party—insisted upon devising a truly homegrown ("autochthonous") constitution developed by Papua New Guineans themselves, one that would be creatively infused with a PNG sensibility. Toward this end, a Constitutional Planning Committee (CPC) was established in 1972, with a brief to start from first principles, engage in widespread consultation, and develop a distinctively Papua New Guinean blueprint for the new, independent social charter.

All sixteen members of the CPC were senior, influential PNG politicians, strategically drawn from around the country, including, among others: Michael Somare (chair), Father John Momis (deputy chair), Opposition Leader Tei Abal, Deputy Chief Minister Dr. John Guise (later to become governor-general), Minister for Justice John Kaputin, and Deputy Opposition Leader Paul Langro. The CPC also had seven "Visiting Special Consultants," all of whom were eminent judges, lawyers, or scholars, including justices of the High Courts of Tanzania and Trinidad and Tobago; a fellow of the UN's International Legal Centre; professors of political science from Manchester University (UK), Queen's University (Canada), and the University of PNG (Nigel Oram); and Yash Ghai, an eminent Kenyan law professor who was then a fellow at Sweden's Uppsala University.

The CPC also had its own executive officer (Seaea Avosa) and a legal officer (John Ley), both of whom were Papua New Guinean, seven secretarial staff, and three Australian academic advisers. Importantly, Bernard Narokobi, then a legal officer in the public solicitor's office, was added at the insistence of Father Momis, who was concerned about the lack of Papua New Guineans among the group of advisors. Despite being relatively junior, Narokobi—who went on to become the first chair of the PNG Law Reform Commission, a justice of the PNG Supreme Court, and a speaker of the PNG Parliament, as well as a major legal and philosophical writer—was a dynamic thinker and a passionate advocate for customizing the legal system by integrating it with Melanesian values and understandings, rather than simply rolling on with Western laws and institutions after independence. In the words of the CPC itself, its mission was as follows:

> At this stage of our political history we must all be concerned with the vital but difficult task of building a nation. True nation-building, however, especially in a land with peoples as diverse as ours, cannot be achieved by the central government imposing its will through bureaucratic processes. That would be a mere continuation of the old colonial system, an exchange of masters, in which the gap between "they", the government, and "we", the "people", remained as large and unbridgeable as ever. True nation-building can come only through the active and meaningful involvement of the people in their own development.[5]

Following on from the statements of Kaputin, Somare, Narokobi, and others, the CPC set itself the goal of reestablishing the primacy of Melanesian ways in all facets of law, governance, business, and family relations. In a florid passage in its final report usually attributed to Narokobi, the CPC likened colonialism to a huge tidal wave "submerging the natural life of our people."[6] In the aftermath—having achieved self-government and independence—the task of the people is to sift through the debris and the detritus and to rebuild society

> not on the scattered good soil the tidal wave of colonisation has deposited but on the solid foundations of our ancestral land. We must take the opportunity of digging up that which has been buried. We must not be afraid to rediscover our art, our culture and our political and social organizations.[7]

This was neither a cry of despair nor a call to nihilism, but rather an optimistic message, suggesting an opportunity for a fresh start. In so doing, the first point of reference in rebuilding should be placed upon traditional ways, social obligations, and customary laws, but leaving open the option of selecting the most appropriate and effective new (Western) institutions, techniques, and technologies to add to the mix—as Melanesian societies already had been doing for many years.

In order to accomplish these ambitious goals, the CPC set out its approach to consultation and consensus:

> With the assistance of our staff, and, from time to time visiting specialist consultants, discussion was wide-ranging but no substantive decisions were made. From May to August 1973 we toured the country; by

> dividing into two groups, we visited almost every sub-district, holding over one hundred public meetings attended by an estimated 60,000 people. Our major deliberations took place at meetings during the period October 1973 to February 1974, and a number of draft chapters based on our decisions were prepared. Finally, in the months from March to June 1974, we had a number of full meetings with the Cabinet and there were also several less formal consultations. Drafting proceeded, accompanied by some revision and refining of our recommendations as the full pattern of the Constitution emerged.[8]

In May 1973, a Joint Communiqué was issued by Australian Minister for External Territories W. L. Morrison and Chief Minister Michael Somare, following a request from the CPC for discussions, setting out a two-stage process for achieving self-government, "which will be completed by the adoption of its home-grown Constitution in the House of Assembly and the passing of enabling legislation in the Australian Parliament."[9] The Communiqué expressed the agreement that:

- In December 1973, formal self-government would be achieved through amendments to the Papua New Guinea Acts passed by the Australian Parliament, so that the legislation "will then reflect in law the present situation of virtual self-government."
- In February 1974, the CPC would table its final report in the PNG House of Assembly, with a draft Constitution providing "for all major aspects of the system of government [including] provisions for the transition to independence."
- In April 1974, the House of Assembly would hold a special session "to consider and adopt the Constitution."
- In May 1974, the Australian Parliament would consider further amendments to provide for the approval of PNG's Independence Constitution, request the assent of the governor-general, and submit the Constitution to the PNG House of Assembly for ratification at its June meeting.

Following extensive consultation across the whole of PNG, the CPC produced a statement of National Goals and Directive Principles—with the tone, content, and style (not to mention rumors at the time) strongly suggesting Bernard Narokobi had a major hand in its drafting. The CPC

Report explained that the process of constitutional development and nation-building required a road map, both to ensure that all decisions would reflect traditional values and understandings, and to "provide a yardstick against which government performance can be judged."[10] As the CPC wrote, this process was intended to be transformational:

> [B]y transferring power into the hands of the people of this country, it gives us a chance to define for ourselves the philosophy of life by which we want to live and the social and economic goals we want to achieve. If the Constitution is to be truly the fundamental charter of our society and the basis of legitimate authority, it should be an instrument which helps to achieve these goals and not one which obstructs. Our Constitution should look towards the future and act as an accelerator in the process of development, not as a brake. It should be related to the national goals that we leaders of this country are enunciating. We have therefore framed our recommendations for the proposed Constitution with these goals in mind.
>
> Now is the historic moment in our search for identity and self-fulfilment to take the necessary measures to make substantial changes in all of our institutions, to create new ones and to redirect development when things are fluid and tractable. But for us to know clearly what measures should be taken, our objectives must be clearly established.[11]

The CPC also had close regard to the "Eight Improvement Aims" (often referred to as "the Eight Point Plan" or "the Eight Aims") that had been unanimously adopted by the PNG House of Assembly, and that explicitly set out the intended commitment to development based upon "the ideas of Equality, Self-Reliance and Rural Development."[12] Specifically, the Eight Aims called for:

- a rapid increase in the proportion of the economy under the control of Papua New Guinean individuals and groups, and in the proportion of personal and property income that goes to Papua New Guinea;
- more equal distribution of economic benefits, including movement toward equalisation of incomes among people and toward equalisation of services among different areas of the country;

- decentralisation of economic activity, planning and government spending, with emphasis on agricultural development, village industry, better internal trade and more spending channelled to local and area bodies;
- an emphasis on small-scale artisan, service and business activity, relying where possible on typically Papua New Guinean forms of economic activity;
- a more self-reliant economy, less dependent for its needs on imported goods and services and better able to meet the needs of its people through local production;
- an increasing capacity for meeting government spending needs from locally raised revenue;
- a rapid increase in the active and equal participation of women in all forms of economic and social activity; [and]
- government control and involvement in those sectors of the economy where control is necessary to achieve the desired kind of development.[13]

The CPC sought to provide a blueprint aimed at achieving—or in the view of many CPC members, *restoring*—an egalitarian society, based on widespread participation and a consensus-style approach to governance and dispute resolution. From the Eight Aims, the CPC developed a statement of National Goals and Directive Principles (NGDPs) that it proposed "should be incorporated in the Constitution."[14] The CPC noted that the NGDPs

> are broader and more comprehensive than the Aims in that they provide for the full development of our people, whereas the Aims emphasize the economic aspects of our society. The Goals and Principles are generally consistent with the Aims but are more specifically aimed at achieving a free and just society in Papua New Guinea.[15]

In particular, the NGDPs cover the following areas:

- **Integral human development**: calling upon "every person to be dynamically involved in the process of freeing himself or herself from every form of domination or oppression so that each man or woman will have the opportunity to develop as a whole person".[16] The NGDPs expressly recognized that achievement of this goal would require a good educational system; the active encouragement of sciences and culture; and improvements in public health and nutrition. Importantly, the NGDPs also recognized that it would be essential to promote the "moral, cultural, economic and social standing of the Melanesian family," as well as ensuring that development take place "primarily through the use of Papua New Guinean forms of social and political organization."

- **Equality and participation:** including the creation of political structures enabling "effective, meaningful participation by our people in that life, and in view of the rich cultural and ethnic diversity of our people for those structures to provide for substantial decentralization of all forms of government activity"; making every effort to "achieve an equitable distribution of incomes and other benefits of development"; equalization of services in all parts of the country; facilitating "the organization and legal recognition of all groups engaging in development activities"; ensuring participatory and representative democracy; endeavoring to achieve universal literacy in English or in one of the lingua francas (Melanesian Tok Pisin and Hiri Motu), or one of the eight hundred local languages (*tok ples*); and "recognition of the principles that a complete relationship in marriage rests on equality of rights and duties of the partners."
- **National sovereignty and self-reliance:** calling for "economic development to take place primarily by the use of skills and resources available in the country either from citizens or the State and not in dependence on imported skills and resources"; the State to regulate the national economy, especially "major enterprises engaged in the exploitation of natural resources"; and vigilance in resisting any contract, treaty, or other arrangements leading to "substantial dependence upon or influence by any country, investor, lender or donor."
- **Natural resources and environment:** including the land, sea, air, flora, and fauna, must be conserved and used for the collective benefit of all citizens and preserved for future generations.

- **Papua New Guinean ways:** ensuring that development will be achieved "primarily through the use of Papua New Guinean forms of social, political and economic organization." The NGDPs recognized that, after a long period of colonialism, this would require "a fundamental re-orientation of our attitudes and the institutions of government, commerce, education and religion towards Papua New Guinean forms of participation, consultation, and consensus, and a continuous renewal of the responsiveness of these institutions to the needs and attitudes of the People." The NGDPs further called for the recognition that the "cultural, commercial and ethnic diversity of our people is a positive strength," and that fostering "respect for, and appreciation of, traditional ways of life and culture, including language" is needed in order to unleash the dynamism creatively necessary for development. Finally, the NGDPs called for the continuation of traditional villages and communities as viable units, with steps to be taken "to improve their cultural, social, economic and ethical quality."
- **Basic rights:** all persons in PNG are entitled to the fundamental rights and freedoms, including "life, liberty, security of the person and the protection of the law; the right to take part in political activities; freedom from inhuman treatment and forced labor; freedom of conscience, of expression, of information and of assembly and association; freedom of employment and freedom of movement; and protection for the privacy of their homes and other property and from unjust deprivation of property." The inclusion of these basic rights and freedoms, modeled on those in the International Covenant on Civil and Political Rights, is particularly notable in that Australia is among the only liberal democracies without a constitutional bill of rights.
- **Basic social obligations**: while enjoying individual rights and freedoms, Papua New Guineans have corresponding obligations to respect and act in the spirit of the constitution; participate actively in the development of the country; protect the country and safeguard its wealth, resources, and environment; respect the rights and freedoms of others; contribute as required by law

to the revenue raising necessary for national advancement; and, respect and support their parents and their children.

The completion and tabling of the CPC Report and the attached draft constitution represented an important milestone, but it was not the end of the debate. Although he chaired the CPC, Michael Somare had serious concerns about some of the recommendations, including the basis of citizenship in a newly independent PNG, and the nature and status of provincial governments—a sensitive issue at that time with a number of actual and potential secessionist, separatist, and protest movements, as well as divisive cargo cult activity, threatening to tear apart the fragile new state in its infancy. With the political leaders mainly preoccupied with these controversial and existential issues, the NGDPs passed with little discussion and no dissent.

The Independence Constitution of 1975

The CPC intended the new constitution to be a fundamental decolonizing agent. The constitution that finally emerged on Independence Day, September 16, 1975, was highly ambitious and rich in detail, innovations, and complexities. But, it contained only some of what the CPC had wanted. Its 166 pages, 275 sections, and five schedules deal not only with the standard constitutional topics of the distribution of governmental powers and the nature of the various state institutions, but also with such matters as:

- basic human rights and social obligations;
- a national leadership code for politicians and public officials;
- eligibility for citizenship;
- the independent offices of the ombudsman, public solicitor, and public prosecutor;
- courts and tribunals;
- the Public Service and the uniformed services;
- the supervision of public finances;
- emergency powers—which are prescribed in great detail in Part X;
- the role of the courts in developing an "underlying law" (i.e., a uniquely Melanesian jurisprudence based on custom); and

- the establishment of permanent law reform and constitutional review bodies.

As that list suggests, although the document contained some of the CPC's design for a Melanesian renaissance, it was even more a product of the liberal legalism of that time. Ironically, the constitution incorporated many progressive features regarding human rights and civil liberties, affirmative action, government accountability, and judicial creativity that had not yet been implemented by many of the metropolitan legal systems intended to serve as best practice role models.

All this activity occurred in the early 1970s, at the height of the modernist project in law and politics, which believed in the socially transformative power of Big Law—in which almost every problem was deemed to be a legal problem, and every solution required more law: charters of rights, codification, omnibus legislation, specialized courts and tribunals.

As a consequence, postcolonial PNG inherited the then-fashionable Strong State—a system heavily promoted in the 1970s and 1980s by both metropolitan states and influential developing countries such as Tanzania. It was not the intent of the colonial power—nor would it have been possible—to leave PNG with a perfectly modulated legal system, balancing the best of custom with the best of common law. As a "soft" colonial authority, in its own perception at least, Australia believed at the time that it was leaving PNG with the beginnings of a gold standard political and legal system, mirroring its own sensibility. This included, or so the Australians believed:

- formal Western courts operated by expert professionals;
- a Westminster system of responsible government, with a touch of federalism in response to separatist pressures in Bougainville and elsewhere;
- an adversary system of politics and political parties;
- a liberal economy—although, being the 1970s, with much more state intervention and ownership (mines, airlines, banks, and so on) than is accepted as best practice in our current, more conservative and more pro-capital era; and
- a large, permanent public service to administer most of the above.

The departing Australian administration sought to leave an independent PNG that would be much in its own image. Progressive Australians argued at the time that it would be paternalistic to deliver any less than this for PNG—and many Papua New Guineans, though not those on the CPC or in many corners of academia and the public service, believed that too.

Within this highly detailed Western-style constitution, however, there are also powerful statements of philosophy and programmatic provisions echoing the CPC and calling upon the courts—now accorded the central role they lacked during the colonial era—and other institutions to transform the inherited colonial legal order. It may be that this disjunction reflected that the framers of the constitution felt unable to conceptualize or articulate how the new legal order would operate, but hoped to provide the spur and the means to achieve a transformation of the legal order in the years after independence.

Section 9 of the constitution provides that the laws of PNG consist of:

(a) the Constitution;

(b) the Organic laws;

(c) the Acts of Parliament;

(d) Emergency Regulations;

(e) laws made under or adopted by or under this Constitution; or any of those laws, including subordinate legislative enactments made under this Constitution or any of those laws; and

(f) the underlying law, and none other.

Section 37(2) provides that no one "may be convicted of an offence that is not defined by, and the penalty for which is not prescribed by, a written law." This means that purely customary offences may not give rise to criminal liability in the courts, even in the village courts—although the village courts may punish a breach of a lawful order made with regard to a customary law, insofar as this amounts to contempt of court.

One great deficiency in the constitution is that it does not itself declare and provide for the development of the underlying law. Instead, section 20 provides for Parliament to enact a law doing that. There are so-called transitional provisions in Schedule 2 of the constitution, which are meant to guide the courts in their development of the underlying law until Parliament provides statutory guidance. According to section 21, the purpose of the transitional provisions is "to assist in the development of our indigenous jurisprudence, adapted to the changing circumstance of Papua New Guinea." Schedule 2.1 provides that "custom is adopted, and shall be applied and enforced, as part of the underlying law except in respect of any custom that is, and to the extent that it is, inconsistent with a Constitutional Law or a statute, or repugnant to the general principles of humanity." This provision is similar in terms to the colonial-era *Native Customs (Recognition) Act of 1963*, section 6, which also imposed two further qualifications: that the custom may not contravene the public interest and that it not adversely affect the welfare of a child.

Schedule 2.1(3) also provides that an act of Parliament may: (a) provide for the proof and pleading of any custom; (b) regulate the manner in which, or the purpose of which, custom may be recognized, applied, or enforced; and (c) provide for the resolution of conflicts of custom.

Schedule 2.2 adopts the principles and rules of the common law and equity of England in existence at the time of independence, notwithstanding statutory revision, as the other main source of the underlying law, unless:

(a) they are inconsistent with a constitutional law or statute; or

(b) they are inapplicable or inappropriate to the circumstances of the country from time to time; or

(c) in their application to any particular matter they are inconsistent with custom as adopted by [Schedule 2.1].

Schedule 2.2's adoption of the laws of England—and not the common law and equity of Australia—was an intentional swipe at the erstwhile colonial master. But while the common law is made subject to a judicial determination of its circumstantial applicability and appropriateness, it is assumed, unlike the position with customary law, that there will be no clash between common law and "the general principles of humanity."

An affirmative duty is placed on the national judicial system, particularly on the Supreme and National Courts, to formulate an appropriate rule as part of the underlying law where neither custom nor the common law is applicable. In formulating such a rule of underlying law, under Schedule 2.3, the court must have regard to:

(a) in particular, the National Goals and Directive Principles and the Basic Social Obligations;

(b) Division III.3 (Basic Rights);

(c) analogies to be drawn from relevant statutes and custom;

(d) the legislation of, and to relevant decisions of the courts of, any country that in the opinion of the court has a legal system similar to that in PNG;

(e) relevant decisions of courts exercising jurisdictions in or in respect of all or any part of the country at any time; and

(f) the circumstances of the country from time to time.

The PNG Law Reform Commission is also given a special responsibility under Section 21(2) of the constitution to report to the Parliament and the national Executive Council from time to time on the development of the underlying law (section 21 and Schedule 2.13–2.14).

In keeping with the CPC's vision, an affirmative duty was placed on the national judicial system, especially the superior courts, to formulate an appropriate rule of underlying law in circumstances in which neither custom nor the common law are seen to be applicable. According to Schedule 2.3, when formulating a rule of underlying law, the court must have regard to: (a) the NGDPs and the basic social obligations; (b) the basic rights enumerated in the constitution; (c) analogies to be drawn from relevant statutes and customs; (d) relevant decisions of the courts of any country with a similar legal system; and (e) relevant decisions of courts exercising jurisdiction in all or any part of the country, and to "the circumstances of the country from time to time."

Schedule 2.4 charges the courts with ensuring consistency and developing the underlying law "as a coherent system in a manner that is appropriate to the circumstances of the country from time to time." Schedule 2.5 provides that in their annual report to Parliament (mandated under section 187), the judges shall "comment on the state, suitability and development of the underlying law, with any recommendations as to improvement that they think it proper to make."

It remains controversial to this day whether the highly prescriptive and detailed constitution that emerged was faithful to the vision of the CPC.

Many members of the CPC and advisers such as Bernard Narokobi envisaged a document that would do no more than set out the broad general principles upon which the new nation would be governed and that could be progressively developed over time, similar to the approach adopted in the U.S. Constitution.

But, the final version of the constitution was drafted out of Chief Minister Michael Somare's office by expatriate parliamentary draftsmen and lawyers. Historian Donald Denoon has written that the Secretary of Law Bill Kearney and the Chief Parliamentary Draftsman Joe Lynch were concerned that the CPC had made "radical proposals that would cast too great a strain on society," and tried to soft pedal them as much as they could, leading Deputy CPC Chair Father John Momis to say that Lynch "continually misunderstood clear drafting instructions."[17] After five contentious drafts, heated debates and calls for Lynch's sacking, a compromise was finally reached under which the NGDPs were approved, making time for even more contentious issues, such as parliamentary and executive oversight (through a Leadership Code and a powerful Public Accounts Committee), the vexed issues of citizenship and decentralization, and the process for amending the constitution in future.

Speaking at the United Nations on the eve of independence, Father Momis accused Somare and the Australians of stripping the constitution of most of its homegrown, distinctive, and creative features, preferring instead the comfort of the familiar (colonial) institutions.[18] Journalist Donald Woolford has similarly characterized the conflict in this way:

> Basically the committee was . . . prepared to take institutional risks . . . [while] the government preferred the safety of the status quo. The conflict was at least partly one between visionaries and pragmatists. It was also one between those who thought power should be dispersed and those with whom power resided. And it is a rare government that will agree to a dilution of its own power. Somare's government was not willing; and government had the power of patronage and the lobbying skill to produce the numbers it needed to ensure that in most cases, pragmatism won.[19]

One important, adverse consequence of this tilt to pragmatism at the expense of creative lawmaking and nation-building was relegation of the

NGDPs to the preamble of the constitution. This may have provided the goals with some prominence, except that they were expressly rendered non-justiciable under section 25(1) of the constitution. In other words, the interpretation of the NGDPs, or their application to disputes that came before the courts, could not be considered or tested by a court of law or decided on legal principles—leaving them as no more than aspirational statements. Given the intended central role of the courts in creatively developing an underlying law based on custom, the non-justiciable nature of the NGDPs effectively removed them from this transformational effort.

It was unfortunate that the drafting of the constitution was not given to a Papua New Guinean Thomas Jefferson—perhaps Bernard Narokobi, who wrote beautifully and poetically for the CPC and for many years afterward about the kind of country PNG could become. Instead, it became a project for expatriate bureaucrats—legislative drafters, who approached the task as if fashioning a complicated piece of tax legislation. The result was a document far too long, disappointingly dry, and much too detailed. In essence, PNG's founding fathers wound up choosing perspiration over inspiration and aspiration, at least in the justiciable (and therefore most important) parts of their new nation's constitution.

Sources

Books and Articles

Don Aitkin and Edward P. Wolfers, "Australian Attitudes Towards the Papua New Guinea Area Since World War II," *Australian Outlook* 27(2) (1973) 202–214.

Peter Bayne, "Legal Policy-Making," in John A Ballard (ed.), *Policy-Making in a New State: Papua New Guinea 1972–1977* (St. Lucia: University of Queensland Press, 1981) 133–156.

Donald R. C. Chalmers, "A History of the Role of Traditional Dispute Settlement Procedures in the Courts of Papua New Guinea," in David Weisbrot, Abdul Paliwala, and Aki Sawyerr (eds.), *Law and Social Change in Papua New Guinea* (Oxford: Butterworths, 1982) 169–189.

Donald R. C. Chalmers, David Weisbrot, Salamo Injia, and Warwick Andrew, *Criminal Law and Justice of Papua New Guinea* (3rd ed., Sydney: Law Book Co., 2001).

William Clifford, Louise Morauta, and Barry Stuart, *Law and Order in Papua New Guinea* (Port Moresby: Institute of National Affairs Discussion Paper No. 16, 1984).

Donald Denoon, *A Trial Separation: Australia and the Decolonisation of Papua New Guinea* (Canberra: Australian National University Press, 2005).

Lise M. Dobrin and Alex Golub (eds.) "Symposium: The Legacy of Bernard Narokobi and the Melanesian Way," *Journal of Pacific History* 55(2) (2020) 149–303.

Ian Downs, *The Australian Trusteeship 1945–75* (Canberra: Australian Government Publishing Service, 1980).

Peter Fitzpatrick, *Law and State in Papua New Guinea* (London: Academic Press, 1980).

Peter Fitzpatrick, "The Political Economy of Law in the Post-Colonial Period," in David Weisbrot, Abdul Paliwala, and Aki Sawyer (eds.), *Law and Social Change in Papua New Guinea* (Sydney: Butterworths, 1982), 25–55.

Graham Freudenberg, *A Certain Grandeur: Gough Whitlam in Politics* (Melbourne: Penguin Books, 1987).

Paul Hasluck, *A Time for Building: Australian Administration in Papua and New Guinea 1951–1963* (Melbourne: Melbourne University Press, 1976).

Patrick Kaiku, "Make PNG's National Goals Relevant Again," DevPolicyBlog (September 18, 2019), https://www.devpolicy.org/make-pngs-national-goals-relevant-again-20190918/.

John Kaputin, "The Law—A Colonial Fraud?" *New Guinea* 10 (1) (1975) 4–15.

John Kaputin, "Ministerial Policy Statement," *Memo*, 1973, 1–2.

Ronald J. May, *Micronationalist Movements in Papua Guinea* (Canberra: Australian National University Press, 1982).

Bernard Narokobi, "Adaptation of Western Law in Papua New Guinea," *Melanesian Law Journal* 5(1) (1980) 52–69.

Bernard Narokobi, *The Melanesian Way* (Port Moresby: The Institute of Papua New Guinea Studies, 1980).

Nick O'Neill, "The Judges and the Constitution—The First Year," *Melanesian Law Journal* 4 (2) (1976) 242–258.

Bruce Ottley, "Reconciling Modernity and Tradition: Papua New Guinea's *Underlying Law Act*," *Australian Law Reform Commission Reform Journal* 80 (2002) 22–25 and 70–71.

Abdul Paliwala, Jean Zorn, and Peter Bayne, "Economic Development and the Changing Legal System of Papua New Guinea," *African Law Studies* 16 (1978) 21–27.

Abdul Paliwala, "Law and Order in the Village: The Village Courts," in David Weisbrot, Abdul Paliwala, and Aki Sawyer (eds.), *Law and Social Change in Papua New Guinea* (Sydney: Butterworths, 1982) 191–217.

Bruce Pascoe, *Dark Emu: Aboriginal Australia and the Birth of Agriculture* (London: Scribe, 2018).

Peter Sack, "'Law' and 'Custom' in Papua New Guinea: Separation, Unification or Co-operation," Paper Presented at the Commission on Folk Law and Legal Pluralism Conference, Sydney, Australia, August 16, 1986.

Michael Somare, "Law and the Needs of Papua New Guinea's People," in Jean Zorn and Peter Bayne (eds.), *Lo Bilong Ol Manmeri* (Port Moresby: University of Papua New Guinea Press, 1974) 14–18.

Michael Somare, *Sana: An Autobiography of Michael Somare* (Port Moresby: Niugini Press, 1975).

David Weisbrot and Abdul Paliwala, "Lawyers for the People: Reviewing Legal Services in an Independent Papua New Guinea," *Melanesian Law Journal* 4(2) (1976) 184–210.

David Weisbrot, "Integration of Law in Papua New Guinea: Custom and the Criminal Law in Conflict," in David Weisbrot, Abdul Paliwala, and Aki Sawyer (eds.), *Law and Social Change in Papua New Guinea* (Oxford, 1982) 59–103.

E. Gough Whitlam, *The Whitlam Government 1972–1975* (Ringwood: Penguin Books, 1985).

Donald M. Woolford, *Papua New Guinea: Initiation and Independence* (Brisbane: University of Queensland Press, 2013).

Jean Zorn and Jennifer Corrin Care, "Everything Old is New Again: The Underlying Law Act of Papua New Guinea," LawAsia (2002) 61–97.

Government Documents

Department of Provincial Affairs, *Report of the Committee to Review Policy and Administration on Crime, Law and Order* (the "Morgan Report") (Port Moresby, Papua New Guinea: Department of Provincial Affairs, 1983).

Papua New Guinea Constitutional Planning Committee, Final Report (Port Moresby, Papua New Guinea: Constitutional Planning Committee, 1974) (also accessible at http://www.paclii.org/pg/CPCReport/Cap1.htm).

Papua New Guinea Law Reform Commission, *Declaration & Development of Underlying Law* (Working Paper No. 4, 1976).

Papua New Guinea Law Reform Commission, *Taking Customs, Perceptions and Beliefs Into Account* (Working Paper No. 6, 1977).

Papua New Guinea Law Reform Commission, *Customary Rules of Succession* (Occasional Paper No. 3, 1977).

Papua New Guinea Law Reform Commission, *Adultery* (Report No. 5, 1977).

Papua New Guinea Law Reform Commission, *Role of Customary Law in the Legal System* (Report No. 7, 1977).

Papua New Guinea Law Reform Commission, *Customary Compensation* (Report No. 11, 1980).

Cases

Constitutional Reference No. 1 of 1977 (1978) PNGLR 295.

The State v. Paul Pokolou (1983) Unreported, National Court Judgment No. 404

Supreme Court Reference No. 4 of 1980 (1981) PNGLR 265, at 292–293

Tabo Sipo v. Mukara Meli (1980) Unreported, PNG National Court No. 240

Statutes

Business Groups (Incorporation) Act 1974, No. 59 of 1974 (PNG)

Constitution of the Independent State of Papua New Guinea

Customs Recognition Act 1975 (PNG) (*enacted in 1963 as Native Customs (Recognition) Ordinance 1963, No. 28 of 1963, amended and renamed 1975*)

Inter-Group Fighting Act 1977, No. 43 of 1977 (PNG)

Land Disputes Settlement Act 1975, No. 25 of 1975 (PNG)

Land Groups (Incorporation) Act 1974, No. 64 of 1974 (PNG)

Postgraduate Legal Training Act 1972, No. 7 of 1973 (PNG)

Underlying Law Act 2000, No. 13 of 2000 (PNG)

Village Courts Act 1973 (PNG) (revised as *the Village Courts Act 1989, No. 37 of 1989* (PNG))

Notes

1. Don Aitkin and Edward P. Wolfers, "Australian Attitudes Towards the Papua New Guinea Area Since World War II," *Australian Outlook* 27 (August 1973) 206; Paul Hasluck, *A Time for Building: Australian Administration in Papua and New Guinea 1951–1963* (Melbourne: Melbourne University Press, 1976).
2. E. Gough Whitlam, *The Whitlam Government 1972–1975* (Ringwood: Penguin Books, 1985) 93.
3. John Kaputin, "Ministerial Policy Statement," *Memo*, 1973, 1–2.
4. Michael Somare, "Law and the Needs of Papua New Guinea's People," in Jean Zorn and Peter Bayne (eds.), *Lo Bilong Ol Manmeri* (Port Moresby: University of Papua New Guinea Press, 1974) 14.
5. Constitutional Planning Committee, *Final Report* (1974) (hereafter CPC Report), ch. 1, para. 13. The CPC Report is available online at http://www.paclii.org/pg/CPCReport/Cap1.htm.
6. CPC Report, ch. 2, paras. 13–15.
7. CPC Report, ch. 2, para. 98.
8. CPC Report, ch. 1, para. 3.
9. CPC Report, iv.
10. CPC Report, ch. 2, para 6.
11. CPC Report, ch. 2, paras. 5–6.
12. CPC Report, ch. 2, para. 8.
13. CPC Report, ch. 2, para. 7.
14. CPC Report, ch. 2, para. 9.
15. CPC Report, ch. 2, para. 9. All quotations in the text following this reference are from the CPC Report, ch. 2 and ch. 5.
16. CPC Report, ch. 2, para. 13.
17. Donald Denoon, *A Trial Separation: Australia and the Decolonisation of Papua New Guinea* (Canberra: Australian National University Press, 2005) 121.
18. *Id.* at 124.
19. Donald M. Woolford, *Papua New Guinea: Initiation and Independence* (Brisbane: University of Queensland Press, 2013) chapter 10.

12 Epilogue

Using the Past to Understand the Present 1972 and After

In a 1980 National Court case, five years after independence, Justice Bernard Narokobi reiterated his view that the constitution was intended to be fundamentally transformational, writing that:

> The Constitution did intend a new start in life. Its goals and directive principles made it quite clear that a new vision for the nation was intended. If Independence meant nothing more than maintaining unequal laws, it would not have been worth attaining. If the Constitution did not set out the highest ideals and standards for the Legislature, the Executive and the Judiciary, the whole process of creating a home-grown Constitution would have been worthless.[1]

In the years following independence, Narokobi proved to be an indefatigable advocate for establishing a new legal order built on Papua New Guinean ways, but augmented by the finest ideas, laws, and procedures from the West, believing that consciously melding the best of different traditions would produce the strongest society. In his own life, Narokobi combined the best of Melanesian and Western cultures. He had been educated in Catholic mission schools and eventually rose to become the head of the National Catholic Council of Papua New Guinea; he graduated with a law degree from the University of Sydney and believed in the rule of law and in human rights; at the same time, he was a powerful champion for elevating customary ways to be the primary source of law in the modern nation; he deeply believed in the spirit world and often said that traditional sorcery (*sanguma*) still operated.

In late 1975, Narokobi took office as the first chair of the new Papua New Guinea Law Reform Commission, a body specifically charged (among other things) with helping to develop the underlying law. Schedule 2.14 of the constitution sets out this special function of the commission in the following terms:

> In addition to its other functions and responsibilities under any law, it is a special responsibility of the Law Reform Commission to investigate and report to the Parliament and to the National Executive on the development, and on the adaptation to the circumstances of the country, of the underlying law, and on the appropriateness of the rules and principles of the underlying law to the circumstances of the country from time to time.

Narokobi took a multifaceted approach to this task, launching a formal inquiry into the fundamental role and recognition of customary law. The central recommendation in the ensuing report was that the government should repeal the colonial-era *Native Customs (Recognition) Act of 1963* and replace it with an Underlying Law Bill (which was attached to the report), designed to facilitate the declaration, integration, and development of customary laws and processes and thereby effect a fundamental transformation of the legal system. The Law Reform Commission also took on a number of major projects that flowed from this mission, including explorations of the laws and practices concerning adultery (a criminal offence in PNG since colonial times), customary compensation, sorcery, succession, and even contracts—with an eye to infusing all of them with as much custom as possible.

Beyond the legal realm, Narokobi also initiated a widely discussed weekly column in the leading newspaper, the *Post-Courier*, entitled "The Melanesian Voice." A collection of these columns (and some critical readers' letters in response) was published in 1980 under the title *The Melanesian Way*. Emblematic of Narokobi's passion and approach to the task is this except from a column entitled "Wake Up, PNG, To Your Identity":

> Time is long overdue for Papua New Guineans to wake up out of their Rip Van Winkle sleep, shake off their lethargy and take control of their destiny. It is time they realised their talents and did something with them for all mankind. This is definitely better than imitating the West and coming out second or third rate. Let us use modern techniques if we must, but only to enhance our own uniqueness and identity.[2]

Despite the clear dissatisfaction with the inherited legal system, and the popular belief that customary law should play a central role in the development of new laws and legal institutions, the anticipated legal transformation never eventuated. By 1982, Narokobi was already expressing deep frustration that Parliament simply ignored most of the CPC's vision and the Law Reform Commission's reports and recommendations.

To be sure, some accommodations were made in the lead-up to independence and in the period soon after, whether out of principle or pragmatism. For example, the *Village Courts Act of 1973* rolled out a national system, putting basic dispute resolution in the hands of traditional leaders, elders, and other community leaders, making decisions based on a mixture of common sense and custom, rather than leaving these matters in the Western-style magistrates' courts.

This was unquestionably the most important institutional break with the colonial legal past. With their emphasis on mediation of disputes (arbitration is available as a last resort); procedural and evidentiary informality; the banning of lawyers; the election of village court magistrates by the local community; the reliance on local customs and usages; the blurring of the civil-criminal distinction; and the recognition of group responsibility, the village courts represented a major step away from the substance and procedures of the common law and a critical shift from Western courts run by a professional cadre of judges and lawyers.

By most accounts, the village courts have worked well in the sense that they have been established in large numbers, are very widely used (more than the local, district, and children's courts combined), and serve to increase community spirit and involvement. Despite some practical and structural problems, all of the recent reviews of the PNG legal system regard the village courts as successful overall and recommend an increased role for the courts in future.

The *Inter-Group Fighting Act of 1977* was aimed at combatting the continuing scourge of tribal fighting, by moving away from common law protections for those accused of crimes, recognizing traditional concepts of group responsibility, and requiring compensation as an important part of dispute resolution. The *Business Groups (Incorporation) Act of 1974* and the *Land Groups (Incorporation) Act of 1974* enabled customary groups to organize themselves into something akin to modern business associations, and therefore to conduct business, borrow money, and acquire, hold, dispose of, and manage land; and the *Land Disputes Settlement Act of 1975* established land courts that could mediate disputes over customary land in a relatively informal fashion, relying on customary law.

Almost all of these pluralistic elements were introduced into legislation or have their foundations in inquiries conducted by the colonial administration or the local House of Assembly in the build-up to independence. Few significant innovations have occurred since independence, and it is crucial that Parliament make up for these lost decades by beginning to consider the important question of the basis on which legal development will proceed in PNG. In April 2000, when Narokobi was speaker and as PNG was preparing for its twenty-fifth anniversary celebrations, Parliament at long last enacted the *Underlying Law Act,* which had been called for in Schedule 2 of the constitution and drafted by the Law Reform Commission in 1977 when Narokobi was its commissioner. The act came as a surprise and with little or no fanfare, including none in the media. Indeed, the legislation was not debated at all in Parliament, so there are no ministerial statements about the government's intentions nor any supporting statements or expressions of concern from other members of Parliament. As quickly as the act emerged, it was forgotten. Anecdotal evidence suggests that the act's passage was intended to recognize the imminent independence milestone and to honor Narokobi's vison and leadership, but not to promote any significant change. Other rumors suggest Narokobi himself took advantage of his speakership to push it through quietly.

In any event, it is to be hoped that the courts will at some point start applying the act. It was intended to give the courts a road map for developing the common law in the way best suited to PNG. It is not too late for the judges to make use of it. Nor is it too late for Parliament to begin to legislate on matters of substantive customary law. The development of an

Indigenous jurisprudence could be fostered by the central government introducing broad (if not universal) Melanesian concepts of law and justice that have widespread acceptance. These might include legal recognition of the extended family (the *wantok* system); group responsibility; strict (civil) liability; and compensation as a major aspect of dispute settlement.

This might also spur provincial governments and local government councils into using the powers they already have, but do not utilize enough, to pass ordinances dealing with matters of local custom in greater detail. What is called for is not the mere codification of custom, but rather the progressive development of the law in a way that seeks to suit modern Melanesian circumstances and sensibilities. Much momentum has already been lost from the dynamic years just before and after independence. The longer current court practices go unchecked, the longer Parliament ignores its duty to enact custom, the more likely it becomes that the unadapted common law will become permanently entrenched as the foundation of law in PNG.

No one has suggested in the more than forty years since independence that the CPC's vision of a transformational change in the legal system—from one meekly inherited from PNG's colonial rulers to one based upon customary law, customary social organization, and traditional understandings—has ever been seriously attempted, much less accomplished. Indeed, a leading PNG political scientist recently confirmed that:

> The National Goals and Directive Principles (NGDPs) in the Preamble are prominent aspirational statements in the Papua New Guinean National Constitution. Yet, they are also the most neglected part of the national conversation.[3]

Although the constitution placed an affirmative obligation on the superior courts to ensure that the underlying law "develops as a coherent system in a manner that is appropriate to the circumstances of the country" and to report annually on the progress toward this goal,[4] the courts have seldom if ever done so.

The failure to transform the legal system by making custom a preeminent, or at least a prominent, source of law in PNG, may be attributed to four broad factors. First, there is the well-known global phenomenon that once independence is finally achieved, the vigor of the anticolonial debate makes way for a new set of political realities. The postcolonial period in PNG has seen a de-emphasis on law reform, especially in contrast to the focus on economic development. This is quite apparent from Parliament's failure even to consider major Law Reform Commission reports, from the tone and tenor of parliamentary debates, and from the limited legislative programs of successive governments. Although law and order is a perennially important issue, law reform has not been.

Second, there is an element of technical failure in the provisions of the constitution relating to legal development and the underlying law that makes it difficult for significant change to come about. Or perhaps that was always the intention of the pragmatists? In theory, with custom listed as the initial source of the underlying law, adoption of the common law made subject to consistency with adopted custom, the wide range of subsidiary sources available in formulating a new rule of underlying law, and the affirmative duty placed on the judiciary to develop the underlying law, the constitutional scheme appeared to have made good on the CPC's wish that customary law form the basis of the new legal system and that a uniquely Melanesian jurisprudence be developed. In practice, however, this was far from the case.[5]

In essence, the constitutional scheme failed to propel customary law to the fore because it did not fully take into account the pre-independence experience of the relative lack of impact on the legal system of the *Native Customs (Recognition) Act of 1963*. The act, which provides for the recognition of custom subject to certain qualifications, and the application and enforcement of custom in designated matters of civil and criminal law, was rarely referred to by the superior courts in the dozen years between its passage and independence. Consideration of that experience would have identified several problem areas, including that the written law—particularly in certain areas, such as criminal law—is so extensive that there is often little room for the court to maneuver in incorporating custom, and there is no felt need on the part of the judges to do so.

Further, there are great difficulties in ascertaining customary law on a case-by-case basis, and in separating customary rules of law from customary process, as well as in overcoming conflicts between different customary regimes in a fragmented society, even where the courts and counsel wish to act in the best of faith. Lack of specialized training, time, and resources combine to make it difficult for counsel to adduce evidence of local custom that may be admitted and used properly in court. Courts are generally unfamiliar with ascertainment procedures and tend to prefer the relative certainty and ease of statutory interpretation and the application of common law rules.

For the project to be successful, significant institutional assistance must be provided to the courts, and the wider community needs to be involved in this process through the recognition of chiefly authority in appropriate cases or through the use of assessors or special juries or referees. Similarly, rather than relying on case-by-case ascertainment in the courts, efforts could still be made to promote the recognition of general principles of customary law by referral to national, provincial, or local government authorities.

Given the obstacles and the lack of initiative, it is almost inevitable that where custom may be utilized as a source of law, it will not be. If it were national policy to formulate a distinctively Papua New Guinean legal system, an affirmative and inescapable duty should have been placed on the courts, legal counsel, and others to do the necessary hard work.

In the early years after independence, a number of expatriate judges informally expressed the view that, notwithstanding the constitutional mandate, it would be inappropriate for them as outsiders to effect significant change in legal rules, procedures, or institutions. The judiciary that emerged after 1979 with the appointment of Papua New Guineans to the positions of chief justice (Sir Buri Kidu) and deputy chief justice (Sir Mari Kapi) diminished this concern, but other constraints emerged. For example, both on circuit and at home, the judges are faced with massive caseloads to process. Unlike many English-language jurisdictions, the judges of the appellate court are also judges of the trial court with very heavy trial commitments. This naturally cuts into the time available for pondering and formulating policy decisions on major issues that arise at trial, on appeal, or by special reference to the Supreme Court.

The courts are also severely under-resourced for the important work that must be carried out. The judges operate without court reporters and must themselves take detailed notes of the proceedings—including verbatim transcripts of witness testimony where appropriate. Interpreter services are insufficient and sometimes unreliable. Library resources are inadequate, particularly with respect to journals, comparative materials, texts, and other materials that venture beyond Anglo-Australian cases and statutes—except where internet access is sufficient to find these resources online. All of these problems are magnified on circuit, of course.

The judges have complained that cases before them are often poorly prepared or poorly argued, with submissions inadequate to assist the court in ascertaining custom or formulating a rule of underlying law. In *Constitutional Reference No. 1 of 1977*, Deputy Chief Justice Raine wrote that:

> In some quarters it is fashionable to suggest that the Supreme Court is shirking this duty [under Schedule 2.3 of the constitution, to develop the underlying law]. It is not so. We are not given the tools with which to work.[6]

Similarly, in a 1983 case in which the National Court was asked to consider the effect of a traditional compensation settlement on a criminal sentence, Chief Justice Kidu explained that:

> There are basically two reasons why custom is not recognised by the courts and the underlying law has not been developed. First, in almost every case before the courts lawyers have not made any attempts either to produce evidence or material necessary for the judges to use to recognise custom or to develop the underlying law. Judges have not the time and the resources to undertake their own research in most cases.... Secondly, the Parliament of Papua New Guinea has failed to perform its duties as given to it by the Constitution [to enact legislation promoting development of an underlying law, under section 20]. Until that time... Schedule 2 does not permit the court to ignore the statutory law and the decisions of the Supreme Court and pronounce a new law based on custom.[7]

In his 1981 decision in the "Vanuatu Case," Deputy Chief Justice Mari Kapi remarked in like terms:

> Whether or not custom has any influence in the formulation of principle depends on the evidence that is produced before the court. The court may, in appropriate cases, decline to formulate a law if it considers that not much assistance has been given on these considerations. Formulation of new law depends to a large extent on the evidence of these considerations. It is foreseeable that in appropriate

> cases the formulation of a new law may change from time to time on the subject depending on the evidence that is brought before the court. It is not satisfactory. For these reasons counsel appearing in these cases ought to give these matters the fullest research. This does not mean that the judges should not give the fullest research outside counsel's research. But it must be borne in mind that the judges of the Supreme Court are trial judges in the National Court and have very little time for full research. We do not have the benefit of law clerks as in USA Supreme Court. This undoubtedly puts a heavy burden on counsel who appear in these cases.[8]

These are cogent complaints. However, the judiciary also contributed to this situation by its own actions and omissions. Schedule 2.5 of the constitution provides that in their annual report to Parliament under section 187, the judges shall,

> if in their opinion it is desirable to do so . . . comment on the state, suitability and development of the underlying law, with any recommendations as to improvement that they think is proper to make.

In the first few years after independence, the judges' annual reports did briefly discuss the development of the underlying law, but this central issue received little attention thereafter. The judiciary also failed to provide clear guidelines about how evidence of custom should be formally adduced by counsel in court. In view of this omission, counsel could be forgiven for believing that the courts are not especially interested in receiving submissions on custom.

The CPC had strongly recommended severing the legal link with the law of Australia, requiring that

> all of our present laws . . . be carefully reviewed, and inconsistent laws repealed or amended as is appropriate. We suggest that a period of two years should provide sufficient time for this work to be done.[9]

The CPC further stated:

> We believe that many of the laws that will be in force at independence are more appropriate to the circumstances of colonial rule than to a society seeking to achieve the National Goals and Directive

> Principles. . . . The need for a thorough-going review of our legal system is apparent to all of us.[10]

The CPC suggested that such a review be undertaken by the Law Reform Commission or a specially constituted parliamentary committee, but this did not happen. In its final form, the constitution makes no reference to such a legislative review, instead adopting all pre-independence colonial laws (Schedule 2.4.6), as well as a number of English and Australian laws (Schedule 5). With the extensive colonial statute book covering so much of the field, the role of the underlying law—whether based on local custom, common law, or otherwise—was limited to an interstitial one, filling in gaps in legislative schemes or operating in those increasingly few areas not largely covered by statute law. An enduring irony of the PNG Constitution is that while local custom is enforceable only in limited situations and subject to a number of strict qualifications, colonial era statutes are conclusively presumed to be applicable, appropriate, and dominant, even if they conflict with custom (Schedule 2.7).

Third, there has been a failure on the part of all the institutions charged by the constitution with the development of a uniquely Papua New Guinean legal system to earnestly apply themselves to the task. Parliament has not reviewed the bulk of inherited colonial legislation; has not given draft bills and reports from the Law Reform Commission the required attention or action; and, for decades now has failed to develop its own law reform initiatives aimed at introducing custom into the legal system.

Similarly, the executive branch has rarely thought it necessary to justify or explain policy decisions in terms of the NGDPs, and indeed some politicians and bureaucrats have been openly scornful of them. In 1983, a departmental review of the deteriorating law and order situation recommended that in the future, National Executive Council (NEC, or cabinet) submissions "should be certified by the Principal Adviser to the NEC as to compliance with the Constitution and in particular, with the National Goals and Directive Principles."[11] This recommendation was never taken up, signaling the fact that the CPC's vision of the NGDPs as a "guiding lamp" in national and legal development did not transfer to succeeding governments.

The courts have resisted the clear constitutional invitation to be innovative and activist, and instead have acted largely as successors to the colonial courts in perpetuating the dominance of the imported common law. The CPC envisioned the courts regularly looking to the NGDPs and to the particular customs and conditions of PNG in making policy choices:

> In carrying out their judicial role, judges and magistrates must take full account of the goals of the society in which they live; they must be attuned to the wishes of that society and to that extent must be politically conscious (although not party politically conscious).[12]

In fairness, the CPC did recognize that there were disadvantages in giving the main responsibility for legal development to the judiciary. In particular, it recognized that "courts tend to be formalistic and legalistic"[13] at the best of times, and with a senior judiciary that was at the time predominantly expatriate, it was not the best of times. The CPC also understood that the courts, as final arbiters of the constitution would overshadow "the powers of other institutions which express more directly and clearly the wishes of the people"; the courts have a limited capacity to conciliate and effect compromises;[14] and a built-in tension exists between the court's role as protector of individual rights and liberties and their role as determiners of public policy and facilitators of the programmatic national goals.

Applying the NGDPs in the limited manner provided in the constitution would entail a substantially different judicial technique than the standard common law method of interpretation and decision making, and would require that counsel bring to the proceedings a different range of materials and submissions for the court to work with—a challenge for senior judges trained in the positivist and legalistic Anglo-Australian tradition. In the decades following independence, the NGDPs rarely have been referred to by the judges, even though there were many occasions on which broad policy issues were being determined that would have benefited from the guidance and creative thinking the NDGPs could have provided.

The legal profession in PNG is beset by a range of institutional problems that make organization and action difficult. It is a relatively young profession, with much of its base in the public service—and constrained, therefore, by the ethos of bureaucratic non-activism in matters thought to be broadly political. According to a 1984 study of the PNG legal system, many of these public lawyers are "simply inexperienced, unsupervised and grossly overworked."[15] Most of the more senior national lawyers in the country are already on the bench, in politics, in private practice, or at the top levels of the public service.

The educational background of Papua New Guinean lawyers also may contribute to their lack of professional involvement in law reform and development. Apart from the first few national lawyers admitted in the 1960s after studying in Australia (including Bernard Narokobi and Sir Buri Kidu), virtually all national lawyers have been educated at the Law Faculty of the University of Papua New Guinea. For many years, students were required to complete a unit on customary law and land tenure as part of the LLB program and the Diplomas in Land Administration and Magisterial Service. Unfortunately, the requirement was dropped in 1981, apparently more for staffing reasons than for sound pedagogical, professional or jurisprudential ones.

While it existed, the course served to focus interest and attention on the role of custom in legal development and symbolically asserted the importance and legitimacy of custom as a source of law in PNG. In addition, the course dealt extensively with methods of adducing evidence of, and the ascertainment of, customary law in the courts—a crucial topic which is not now significantly dealt with elsewhere in the curriculum. A number of other courses, in particular Family Law and Land Law, touch on issues of customary law, but in competition with Western law.

In keeping with the spirit of the times leading up to independence, UPNG had attempted to pursue a policy that would have placed a greater focus on customary law and legal development. In 1974, *The Report of the Committee of Enquiry into University Development* (the so-called "Gris Report," after its convener Gabriel Gris) recommended that all university students should, as part of their degree programs, spend time engaged in work experience, preferably in their home areas. In response, the Law Faculty devised a new program that would have divided legal studies into two self-contained modules, split by a year in the field. During that year, students would have been required to do research into the customary law of their home areas, give basic legal advice and information to the community, and possibly assist in development activities.

This approach was approved by the Law Faculty and the university's Academic Board. However, the university's governing council, which has final approval over all academic matters, deferred the proposal indefinitely, effectively killing it. Although a number of leading national lawyers supported the program, the opposition came primarily from expatriate members of the legal profession and the judiciary. One expatriate judge condemned the proposal as a "socialistic experiment."[16]

At the time of this debate in 1976, the faculty's proposal was given a boost when the national Parliament passed by an almost unanimous vote a private member's bill sponsored by Buaki Singeri amending the *Post-graduate Legal Training Act of 1974*. The Singeri Amendment, as it was widely known, provided that all law students had to be certified by the dean of the Faculty of Law as having spent at least one year doing research into customary law and/or doing community legal work before they could be admitted to practice. Unfortunately, and all too typically, the government never brought this legislation into force.

Using the Past to Understand the Present

The forces of modernization and globalization that have provoked so much controversy in the rest of the world have also been the subject of debate in PNG and the Pacific Islands. In recent decades, this debate has focused on efforts aimed at nation-building and on preserving or changing the cultural traditions of the island states. This debate is not new; it stems from the beginning of the colonial period, when modernization was one of the principal justifications for colonialism, and the Pacific Islands were pulled into the global orbit of their distant colonial powers. The ideologies, ways of life, and laws that were introduced in the name of modernity have had a lasting impact on the traditions and identities of PNG and other Pacific Island states.

To this day, from the constitution on down, the fundamental problem remains the unresolved tension between a traditional/communitarian approach and an individual rights approach to the law. The Eight Point Plan and the NGDPs tipped toward the communitarian and the traditional, while the rest of the constitution and the Western legal system tipped strongly toward the individual. When law favors the individual over the community, the formal integration of custom becomes difficult, if not impossible.

The choice between community values and individual rights is not an empty question. It is the basic political and ethical choice for PNG: what sort of society is wanted and needed, and what is the community willing to give up in order to have it? For example, a customary approach would likely foster greater cohesion and social equity, but perhaps at the expense of some individual rights, while engendering the suspicion of the international trade and investment community. Despite the focus of the Eight Aims on economic self-sufficiency, rural development, gender equity, and appropriate technology, the PNG economy at the national level is in fact dependent upon huge natural resource projects, such as gold and copper mining, oil and natural gas extraction, and logging, all of which rely on massive foreign investment and mechanization. Believing that they must knuckle under to the demands of potential foreign investors if they are to obtain the financial benefits of such projects, most developing countries agree to leave majority ownership of the projects in the hands of foreign companies, with limited job opportunities for locals, a constant struggle to ensure that the companies fully pay the meager taxes and royalties they agreed to, and environmental problems—sometimes catastrophic ones—harming local communities and regions.

In the years immediately prior to independence, the PNG government succeeded in negotiating with foreign investors two large-scale mining projects in which PNG had a large equity interest, job opportunities for locals were guaranteed, environmental safeguards were in place, and taxes and royalties were set at levels sufficient to make the project worthwhile to the national economy. Local legislation approving the contracts also provided for a mineral stabilization fund, which would hold most of the profits to even out the flow of income from the mines. Unfortunately, post-independence governments signed deals for later projects that were much less beneficial to the nation, at the same time that they were plundering the fund and failing to police either the labor or the environmental requirements. These early agreements provided for the settlement of contract disputes by arbitration in The Hague, unlike later agreements, which follow the more common practice of allowing the Western proprietors of these enormous natural resource extraction projects to dictate the use of standard commercial contracts and Western law and dispute resolution, as a condition of their investment.

We have chosen to focus on the colonial legal history of PNG for a good reason: that history still resonates very powerfully, and even after a half-century still significantly determines contemporary attitudes, actions, and inaction. The now hoary doctrine of postcolonialism—that the past, especially the colonial past, informs the future of the nation-state that is born from that colony—holds as true for the legal system as it does for the much more studied political and economic systems, and for the same reasons. A colony made thoroughly dependent on the imported legal system cannot by the mere act of declaring itself independent escape from that system, just as a colony made dependent on a foreign economy, as PNG has very much become, cannot easily escape its bonds.

In colonial era PNG, the Indigenous population was subject to the full force of the imported law—particularly the criminal law—but with few of the balancing rights, privileges, and safeguards meant to be part of the liberal tradition of legal systems in Western democracies. So, for example, Papua New Guineans in the colonial era had no role, either directly or through popularly chosen representatives, in the formulation of the law—the foundation of the social contract model upon which Western systems of law and governance are said to rest. There was (and still remains) no right to trial by a jury of one's peers. There was no real separation of powers in a territory in which any officer of the administration could at the same time and in relation to the same case fill the roles of executive, legislature, and judiciary. Fundamental civil liberties—including the right to silence; freedom from unreasonable search, seizure, and arrest; the right to counsel; freedom of speech, association, and assembly; equal protection before the law; the presumption of innocence; and other natural justice requirements—were generally absent from the colonial legal system.

Colonial laws were harsh, intrusive, and overbearing, using the criminal law and punishment to, as the colonizers described it, "educate" Papua New Guineans about what was expected of them, even or especially where those expectations were completely contrary to expectations and obligations under customary law. Beyond that, the colonial administrations used the Native Regulations to control all aspects of Papua New Guineans' lives, including how they should dress, how and to whom they could speak, how their villages should be designed, where and when they had to work, and even whom they could love and marry.

While the legal regime was very extensive, the ultimate power of colonialism lay in its relentless message of relative value:

We are few in number, you are many—and yet we rule.

We give the orders, you must follow them.

We are sophisticated, you are savages (or perhaps just a cut above).

We have guns, you have only spears and arrows.

We have cars and trucks and planes, you have only your legs.

We have riches, you are poor.

We are educated, you are not.

We follow the one true religion, you are still worshipping spirits and sorcerers.

We have the rule of law and formal courts, not to mention police and prisons, you just argue and fight.

We have powerful medicine, you have witchcraft and sorcery.

We are superior, you are inferior.

We are white men, and you primitive natives are our burden.

Despite the manifest evidence of the genius of PNG's traditional societies and cultures that had sustained themselves in sometimes harsh, challenging conditions for many thousands of years, and even the increasing facility of Papua New Guineans to master Western education and religion, it probably should have been clear by 1975 to anyone pessimistic (or realistic) enough to read the signs that the legal system of the independent state of Papua New Guinea would remain for many years to come Papua New Guinean in name only. Everything in 1975—except hope and the brief euphoria of a newly won independence—pointed towards PNG's all but total adoption of the law that had been imported into the territories, leaving little room for custom. That included an Australian court system, staffed by judges and counsel who had been schooled in a conservative and positivist view of the law, applying a common law and statutes inherited almost wholesale from Australia and tested neither for their suitability to the conditions of PNG nor their compliance with custom or traditional Melanesian understandings.

The new nation's increasing dependence on foreign investment, especially from large mining and oil and gas projects, for more and more of its revenue, both in the private sector and to fund governmental programs, led almost inescapably to the retention of a Western legal system that supported the aims and fulfilled the needs of the global corporations and related local businesses. Systemic racism also contributed to the continued maintenance of a Westernized legal system. Most of the actors responsible for determining the role that custom might play were from the classes that benefitted most by keeping things as they had been during the colonial period—and that included keeping the legal system as much as possible like the regime put in place during that time.

The most enduring legacy of colonialism is found not only in a system of imported statutes, and not even only in Western institutions like Parliament and the courts, but in the residual doubt in the efficacy of their own customary laws and legal processes inculcated in Papua New Guineans during ninety years of colonialism. Negative colonial attitudes have persisted to a significant degree, so that the key questions are framed not as how to go about recognizing and implementing customary law, or how to utilize custom in promoting economic, political, and social development in a successful modern society, but as whether custom should be used at all in determining Papua New Guinea's legal future. Those of us who support the integration of customary law are battling against the legacies of colonial history and the associated institutions, power relations, dependencies and attitudes that linger long after independence, continuing to define PNG's economically dependent, postcolonial legal system.

Sources

Books and Articles

Peter Bayne, "Legal Policy-Making," in John A Ballard (ed.), *Policy-Making in a New State: Papua New Guinea 1972–1977* (St. Lucia: University of Queensland Press, 1981) 133–156.

Donald R. C. Chalmers, "A History of the Role of Traditional Dispute Settlement Procedures in the Courts of Papua New Guinea," in David Weisbrot, Abdul Paliwala, and Aki Sawyerr (eds.), *Law and Social Change in Papua New Guinea* (Oxford: Butterworths, 1982) 169–189.

Donald R. C. Chalmers, David Weisbrot, Salamo Injia, and Warwick Andrew, *Criminal Law and Justice of Papua New Guinea* (Sydney: Law Book Co, 3rd ed., 2001).

William Clifford, Louise Morauta, and Barry Stuart, *Law and Order in Papua New Guinea* (Port Moresby: Institute of National Affairs Discussion Paper No. 16, 1984).

Donald Denoon, *A Trial Separation: Australia and the Decolonisation of Papua New Guinea* (Canberra: Australian National University Press, 2005).

Peter Fitzpatrick, *Law and State in Papua New Guinea* (London: Academic Press, 1980).

Peter Fitzpatrick, "The Political Economy of Law in the Post-Colonial Period," in David Weisbrot, Abdul Paliwala, and Aki Sawyer (eds.), *Law and Social Change in Papua New Guinea* (Sydney: Butterworths, 1982) 25–55.

Graham Freudenberg, *A Certain Grandeur: Gough Whitlam in Politics* (Melbourne: Penguin Books, 1987).

Patrick Kaiku, "Make PNG's National Goals Relevant Again," DevPolicyBlog (September 18, 2019) https://www.devpolicy.org/make-pngs-national-goals-relevant-again-20190918/.

John Kaputin, "The Law—A Colonial Fraud?" *New Guinea* 10(1) (1975) 4–15.

John Kaputin, "Ministerial Policy Statement," *Memo* (1973) 1–2.

Bernard Narokobi, "Adaptation of Western Law in Papua New Guinea," *Melanesian Law Journal* 5(1) (1980) 52–69.

Bernard Narokobi, *The Melanesian Way* (Port Moresby: The Institute of Papua New Guinea Studies, 1980).

Nick O'Neill, "The Judges and the Constitution—The First Year," *Melanesian Law Journal* 4(2) (1976) 242–258.

Bruce Ottley, "Reconciling Modernity and Tradition: Papua New Guinea's Underlying Law Act," *Australian Law Reform Commission Reform Journal* 80 (2002) 22–25 and 70–71.

Abdul Paliwala, Jean Zorn, and Peter Bayne, "Economic Development and the Changing Legal System of Papua New Guinea," *African Law Studies* 16 (1978) 21–27.

Abdul Paliwala, "Law and Order in the Village: The Village Courts," in David Weisbrot, Abdul Paliwala, and Aki Sawyer (eds.), *Law and Social Change in Papua New Guinea* (Sydney: Butterworths, 1982) 191–217.

Peter Sack, "'Law' and 'Custom' in Papua New Guinea: Separation, Unification or Co-operation," Paper Presented at the Commission on Folk Law and Legal Pluralism Conference, Sydney, Australia, August 16, 1986.

Michael Somare, "Law and the Needs of Papua New Guinea's People," in Jean Zorn and Peter Bayne (eds.), *Lo Bilong Ol Manmeri* (Port Moresby: University of Papua New Guinea, 1974) 14–18.

Michael Somare, *Sana: An Autobiography of Michael Somare* (Port Moresby: Niugini Press, 1975).

David Weisbrot, "The Law Reform Commission Draft Bill on the Underlying Law," *Melanesian Law Journal* 5(1) (1977) 152–163.

David Weisbrot, "The Law Reform Commission Draft Bill on Criminal Responsibility," *Melanesian Law Journal* 5(1) (1977) 164–169.

David Weisbrot, "Papua New Guinea: Judges and Politicians," *Legal Service Bulletin* 4 (1979) 240–245.

David Weisbrot and Abdul Paliwala, "Lawyers for the People: Reviewing Legal Services in an Independent Papua New Guinea," *Melanesian Law Journal* 4(2) (1976) 184–210.

David Weisbrot, "Integration of Law in Papua New Guinea: Custom and the Criminal Law in Conflict," in David Weisbrot, Abdul Paliwala, and Aki Sawyer (eds.), *Law and Social Change in Papua New Guinea* (Oxford: Butterworths, 1982) 59–103.

E. Gough Whitlam, *The Whitlam Government 1972–1975* (Ringwood: Penguin Books, 1985).

Donald M. Woolford, *Papua New Guinea: Initiation and Independence* (Brisbane: University of Queensland Press, 2013).

Jean Zorn and Jennifer Corrin Care, "Everything Old is New Again: The Underlying Law Act of Papua New Guinea," *LawAsia* [2002] 61–97.

Government Documents

Department of Provincial Affairs, *Report of the Committee to Review Policy and Administration on Crime, Law and Order* (the "Morgan Report") (Port Moresby: Government of Papua New Guinea, 1983).

Papua New Guinea Constitutional Planning Committee, *Final Report* (Port Moresby: Government of Papua New Guinea, 1974) (also accessible at http://www.paclii.org/pg/CPCReport/Cap1.htm).

Papua New Guinea Law Reform Commission, *Declaration & Development of Underlying Law*, Working Paper No. 4 (Port Moresby: Government of Papua New Guinea, 1976).

Papua New Guinea Law Reform Commission, *Taking Customs, Perceptions and Beliefs Into* Account, Working Paper No. 6 (Port Moresby: Government of Papua New Guinea, 1977).

Papua New Guinea Law Reform Commission, *Customary Rules of Succession*, Occasional Paper No. 3 (Port Moresby: Government of Papua New Guinea, 1977).

Papua New Guinea Law Reform Commission, *Adultery*, Report No. 5 (Port Moresby: Government of Papua New Guinea, 1977).

Papua New Guinea Law Reform Commission, *Role of Customary Law in the Legal System*, Report No. 7 (Port Moresby: Government of Papua New Guinea, 1977).

Papua New Guinea Law Reform Commission, *Customary Compensation*, Report No. 11 (Port Moresby: Government of Papua New Guinea, 1980).

Cases

Constitutional Reference No. 1 of 1977 (1978) PNGLR 295

The State v. Paul Pokolou (1983) Unreported National Court Judgment No. 404

Supreme Court Reference No. 4 of 1980 (1981) PNGLR 265

Tabo Sipo v. Mukara Meli (1980) Unreported PNG National Court No. 240

Statutes

Business Groups (Incorporation) Act 1974, No. 59 of 1974 (PNG)

Constitution of the Independent State of Papua New Guinea

Customs Recognition Act 1975 (PNG) (enacted in 1963 as *Native Customs (Recognition) Ordinance 1963, No. 28 of 1963*, amended and renamed 1975)

Inter-Group Fighting Act 1977, No. 43 of 1977 (PNG)

Land Disputes Settlement Act 1975, No. 25 of 1975 (PNG)

Land Groups (Incorporation) Act 1974, No. 64 of 1974 (PNG)

Postgraduate Legal Training Act 1972, No. 7 of 1973 (PNG)

Underlying Law Act 2000, No. 13 of 2000 (PNG)

Village Courts Act 1973 (PNG) (revised restated and redated as the *Village Courts Act 1989, No. 37 of 1989* (PNG))

Notes

1. *Tabo Sipo v. Mukara Meli* (1980) PNG National Court No. 240, per Narokobi J.
2. Bernard Narokobi (Henry Olela, ed.), *The Melanesian Way* (Port Moresby: The Institute of Papua New Guinea Studies, 1980) 53–54.
3. Patrick Kaiku, "Make PNG's National Goals Relevant Again," DevPolicyBlog (September 18, 2019) https://www.devpolicy.org/make-pngs-national-goals-relevant-again-20190918/.
4. PNG Constitution, Schedules 2.4–2.5.
5. Bernard Narokobi, "Adaptation of Western Law in Papua New Guinea," *Melanesian Law Journal* 5(1) (1977) 52.
6. (1978) PNGLR 295, 299.
7. *The State v. Paul Pokolou* (1983) National Court Judgment No. 404, per Kidu C. J.
8. *Supreme Court Reference No. 4 of 1980* (1981) PNGLR 265, 292–293.
9. CPC Report, ch. 15, para 2.
10. CPC Report, ch. 8, para 9.
11. Department of Provincial Affairs, *Report of the Committee to Reviw Policy and Administration on Crime, Law and Order* (the "Morgan Report") (Port Moresby: Department of Provincial Affairs, 1983), 335.
12. CPC Report, ch. 8, paras. 15–16.
13. CPC Report, ch. 8, para.144.
14. CPC Report, ch. 8, paras 15–16.
15. William Clifford, Louise Morauta, and Barry Stuart, *Law and Order in Papua New Guinea* (the "Clifford Report") (Port Moresby: Institute of National Affairs Discussion Paper No. 16, 1984) 152–153.
16. David Weisbrot and Abdul Paliwala, "Lawyers for the People: Reviewing Legal Services in an Independent Papua New Guinea," *Melanesian Law Journal* 4(2) (1976) 197–198.

Index

Q